KU-319-574

DICTIONARY
OF
LIBERAL BIOGRAPHY

NOT TO
BE TAKEN
OUT OF
THE
LIBRARY

UNIVERSITY OF NOTTINGHAM

10 0152245 3

WITHDRAWN
FROM THE LIBRARY

15 Feb

DICTIONARY
OF
LIBERAL BIOGRAPHY

Edited by
DUNCAN BRACK

with
MALCOLM BAINES
KATIE HALL
GRAHAM LIPPIATT
TONY LITTLE
MARK PACK
GEOFFREY SELL
JEN TANKARD

NOTTINGHAM UNIVERSITY LIBRARY

Politico's Publishing

First published in Great Britain 1998
by Politico's Publishing
8 Artillery Row, London, SW1P 1RZ, England

Tel 0171 931 0090
Email politicos@artillery-row.demon.co.uk
Website http://www.politicos.co.uk

© Duncan Brack 1998

The right of Duncan Brack to be identified as author of this work has
been asserted by him in accordance with the Copyright, Designs and
Patents Act, 1988.

A catalogue record for this book is available from the British Library

ISBN 1 90230 109 9

Printed and bound in Great Britain by St Edmundsbury Press.
Cover Design by AdVantage.

All rights reserved. No part of this publication may be reproduced or
transmitted in any form or by any means, electronic or mechanical
including photocopying, recording or any information storage or
retrieval system, without prior permission in writing from the
publishers.

This book is sold subject to the condition that it shall not by way of
trade or otherwise be lent, resold, hired out, or otherwise circulated
without the publisher's prior consent in writing in any form of
binding or cover other than that in which it is published and without
a similar condition including this condition being imposed on the
subsequent purchaser.

1001522453

Picture acknowledgements

All photographs kindly supplied by *Liberal Democrat News*
except for:
Paddy Ashdown MP (cover and p. 15)
  – Campaigns and Elections Department, Liberal Democrats
William Ewart Gladstone (cover and p. 130)
  – taken from Morley's *Life of Gladstone*, published 1903

CONTENTS

FOREWORD
by
Rt Hon Paddy Ashdown MP

This *Dictionary of Liberal Biography* is a comprehensive and very useful aid to anyone with an interest in the many important figures who have helped shape the course of Liberalism and Liberal Democracy over the last two centuries.

From H. H. Asquith, through Bentham, Beveridge and Gladstone, to Lord John Russell, this is a comprehensive guide to the many great ambassadors of Liberalism and some of the most celebrated figures in British history.

The real joy of this book, however, lies in the fact that it does not simply cover Prime Ministers and Parliamentarians, but also party workers, without whom the Liberal Democrats would not be where we are today.

Happy reading,

Paddy Ashdown

FOREWORD
by
Professor Ben Pimlott

There is a continuing debate about the validity of biography, and how it should be categorised. Is it history? Is it politics? Arguably, it is both or neither. Certainly there have been many politicians and historians who have regarded it circumspectly. Social-ists have sometimes been wary of it, on the grounds that it elevates star performers above the classes and movements that really count. Aneurin Bevan once remarked that he preferred his fiction straight: after his death, he got it - in the form of a great, romantic, polemical biography of him, by his Liberal-turned socialist friend Michael Foot, which brilliantly captured the mood and spirit of its subject, while treating inconvenient facts with cheerfully Olympian abandon.

Some regard biography as anecdotage, others as propaganda. It was E. H. Carr - to some extent reflecting a marxian view - who advanced what is still the negative orthodoxy, when he wrote in What Is History? about 'the Bad King John theory of history' - namely 'the view that what matters in history is the character and behaviour of individuals', which he considered out of date. 'The desire to postulate individual genius as the creative force in history' he observed, 'is characteristic of the primitive stages of historical consciousness'.

That biography is primitive can scarcely be denied. It may even be the oldest form of literature - it long predates the novel (the Christian religion, it should be pointed out, is based on four biographies). That individual genius is not a creative force in history, however, is certainly open to challenge, and thirty-seven years after Carr wrote so dismissively on the topic, biographers have gained ground against his posi-tion, rather than lost it. The genre is still very much with us, widely consumed, ever more serious and scholarly, and constantly discussed. Whether or not biography is identical with history (and politics) it is often the best entry route into both - as well as an essential building block. It is not just that, as Thomas Carlyle put it, 'history is the essence of innumerable biographies' (in the end, every movement and idea rests on participation, and frequently the inspiration and leadership, of individuals). It is also that historical understanding becomes arid and two-dimensional, if people are left out of the picture.

It is no accident that one of the finest traditions in British biographical writing should be associated with liberalism and the Liberal Party, for liberals have always placed particular emphasis on the uniqueness and limitless potential of the individual.

If one of the great monuments of the late nineteenth century biographical scholarship (and hagiography) was Morley's life of Gladstone, it was Bloomsbury - playground and cauldron of the liberal spirit - that revolutionised biography in the twentieth. Lytton Strachey's Eminent Victorians and Queen Victoria, in particular, poked disrespectful fun at their subjects, tearing to shreds the notion that biography was the art of glorification, and showing how it could be used to explore the human soul in all its complexity. Biographical essays by Winston Churchill (himself then a Liberal, of sorts) were written in such a spirit. So are the distinguished biographical writings of Roy Jenkins (always a Liberal at heart), which have always used biography as the most sensitive of dialectical tools - from his early biographies of Attlee, Asquith and Dilke through to his most recent collection, The Chancellors.

A dictionary of Liberal biography, therefore, can claim to celebrate many things. On the one hand, it is part of a proud literary heritage. On the other, it is a vital contribution to history and to political thought, and a recognition of the textured nature of a liberal tradition that included Keynes as well as Gladstone, Mill and Lloyd George, and which - out of office even more than in it - had done so much to shape the ideas and policies that exist in turn-of-the-millennium Britain and the wider world. This is a work of reference, of value to politicians, historians and journalists, who want to check up on the facts. But it is also considerably more than that. Taken together, the essays by a range of leading authors provide fascinating jigsaw pieces for a rich and varied history of the - ever developing - liberal ideal.

Ben Pimlott
Goldsmith College, London

Ben Pimlott is Warden of Goldsmith College, London and author of biographies of Hugh Dalton, Harold Wilson and The Queen.

ACKNOWLEDGEMENTS

For some time, the *Journal of Liberal Democrat History* (formerly the Liberal Democrat History Group Newsletter) has been running short biographies of famous and less well-known Liberals, Liberal Democrats and Social Democrats. In 1997 it occurred to us that a dedicated collection of such biographies could be of interest to students of political history and party activists alike. The result is the book you hold in your hands.

Its production would not have been possible, of course, without the effort and hard work of a very wide range of people. One individual above all others deserves our thanks: Mark Egan, for having the idea in the first place, for putting together a group, mostly from within the History Group's executive, to implement it, for laying out the criteria for entries, and for helping us draw up the list of those we wanted included. Mark's employment later prevented him from playing a continuing editorial role, but he also contributed a number of entries.

The editorial team – Malcolm Baines, Katie Hall, Graham Lippiatt, Tony Little, Mark Pack, Geoffrey Sell, and Jen Tankard – drew up lists, identified contributors, processed their entries and tolerated my ever-increasing demands with efficiency and good humour.

Other individuals who provided invaluable help with editing and production include David Cloke, Mike Cooper, Polly Daines, Barry Doyle, Lysianne Egan, Kate Fox, Richard Grayson, Ian Packer, Rachael Reeves and Clare Williamson. Trevor Jones, of Liberal Democrat Publications, and Iain Dale, of Politico's Publishing, never failed to be encouraging and enthusiastic, and Chris Youd and Rachel Morton, of AdVantage, produced an excellent cover design.

Most of all, the contributors – over a hundred and twenty of them drawn from politics, academia, journalism and a wide range of other backgrounds – made everything possible. They are listed towards the back of the *Dictionary;* my sincere thanks go to them all.

August 1998   *Duncan Brack*

GUIDE TO THE *DICTIONARY*

The *Dictionary of Liberal Biography* brings together in one volume the biographies of over two hundred individuals who have made major contributions to the Liberal Party, SDP or Liberal Democrats, or to the development of British Liberalism.

Certain categories have been covered in their entirety, including all Liberal Democrat MPs, MEPs and front-bench peers (as at July 1998), Liberal Party leaders and Liberal Prime Ministers. In other areas we have included the main figures, but considerations of space have forced us to be a little more selective: these include twentieth-century Liberal Cabinet ministers and leading SDP politicians who joined the Liberal Democrats. For politicians of the nineteenth century and before, we have concentrated only on the major individuals. We have also included, however, all the main Liberal thinkers, from Adam Smith onwards.

Each of the entries provides basic biographical information: dates, education, employment, posts held (particularly within the party), seats fought, and main publications and good biographies. In addition, we have aimed to assess the importance of the subject to the Liberal Party/SDP/Liberal Democrats, and to British politics in general both during and after their political career.

Entries are listed according to the name by which the individual is generally known to historians and the media: thus, Paddy Ashdown, L. T. Hobhouse, Viscount Palmerston. Individuals ennobled during their lifetime are given both their name and their title in the contents and the entry's heading, and are positioned according to the name by which they are most commonly known (thus Lord Russell-Johnston, for example, is to be found under 'J'). Full titles are included in the text of the entries.

Also included as appendices are details of all party leaders, leaders in the House of Lords, chief whips, and party chairs and presidents; cabinet ministers since 1859; byelection winners since 1918; MPs defecting to or from the party since 1918; and the location of key collections of manuscripts from some of the figures included here.

Without a doubt, many readers will identify individuals who they think should be represented in the *Dictionary* and are not; there are very many more we could have included, particularly from the period before 1900. Let us know who they are, and we'll put them in the second edition!

August 1998 *Duncan Brack*

LIBERAL
BIOGRAPHIES

Aberdeen is perhaps best known for being Prime Minister at the time of the Crimean War. After his death several copies of a text were found which seemed to indicate he felt a great responsibility for the war. It quoted from 1 Chronicles 22:8: 'Thou hast shed blood abundantly, and hast made great wars: thou shalt not build a house unto my name'. The text may explain why Aberdeen refused to rebuild the parish church of Methlick, which is attached to the family estate at Haddo.

George Hamilton-Gordon was born on 28 January 1784 in Edinburgh. He was the eldest son and first of seven children born to George Gordon, Lord Haddo, and Charlotte Baird. Aberdeen's father died in 1791 and his mother in 1795. Scottish law allowed orphans who had reached the age of fourteen to name their own guardians; Aberdeen appointed Pitt the Younger and Henry Dundas to bring him up. In 1794 he began his formal education at Harrow; in 1800 he went up to St John's College, Oxford. He studied there for only two sessions but still received his MA in 1804 because noblemen were able to graduate without sitting examinations. In 1801 his grandfather died and Aberdeen succeeded to the earldom at the age of seventeen. Towards the end of the year he embarked on his grand tour of Europe, despite the fact that the French wars were being fought.

In 1805 Aberdeen married Catherine Elizabeth Hamilton, daughter of the first Marquis of Abercorn. The couple had three daughters, but Catherine died from tuberculosis in 1812. In 1818, Aberdeen obtained a royal licence to assume the surname Hamilton as a memorial to his late father-in-law. His second wife was Harriet, Dowager Viscountess Hamilton, widow of his first wife's brother. The marriage appears to have been arranged by their father-in-law, the Marquis of Abercorn, who wanted a suitable step-father for his grandson and heir. Aberdeen thought that Harriet was one of the stupidest people he had ever met and the marriage was not a success, although they had four sons and a daughter. Harriet died in 1833.

In 1806 Pitt the Younger died. Aberdeen lost a friend but Pitt's death was also a blow to his own political career. Pitt had promised Aberdeen an English peerage, which would have enabled him to sit in the House of Lords as of right. Instead, he had to canvass heavily to be elected as a Scottish Representative Peer. He took his seat in the Lords in December 1806. In 1807 he refused both the posts of Ambassador to Russia and Minister to Sicily in Portland's ministry. Politically Aberdeen had been aligned with the Whigs, but the latter years of the French wars saw him move towards the Tories. In 1813 he was appointed special ambassador to Austria by Castlereagh, Lord Liverpool's Foreign Secretary. Aberdeen was a central figure in European diplomacy at this time, helping to form the coalition that defeated Napoleon. After signing the Treaty of Paris in 1814, he was created Viscount Gordon of Aberdeen (a United Kingdom peerage) and became a Privy Councillor.

In Wellington's first ministry, Aberdeen served as Chancellor of the Duchy of

Lancaster from January to June 1828, then as Foreign Secretary until November 1830. The most urgent problem with which he had to deal was the Greek revolt. Aberdeen was sympathetic towards the Greeks and wanted to help them as much as possible within the constraints of European diplomacy. The Conference of London in 1830 appeared to have concluded this phase of the Eastern Question but the issue was not resolved. Aberdeen was reluctant to involve Britain in the Portuguese succession question and made only formal protestation to Buenos Aires when the Argentine authorities appointed their own governor of the Falkland Islands. In the uproar in the Lords following Wellington's anti-reform speech, it was Aberdeen who told the Duke that he had just announced the fall of his ministry.

In Peel's 'Hundred Day' ministry (1834–35) Aberdeen was Secretary for War and the Colonies and had to deal with difficulties in Canada, South Africa and the West Indies. As Foreign Secretary in Peel's second ministry, he successfully settled long-standing disputes over the US–Canadian borders in the Webster-Ashburton Treaty (1842) and the Oregon Treaty (1846).

After 1830, Aberdeen was increasingly influenced by Peel and served in both his ministries. They differed in opinion over foreign policy but Aberdeen always supported Peel's economic policies, including the repeal of the Corn Laws. After Peel's death in 1850, Aberdeen took over the leadership of the Peelites, who refused to be absorbed into either of the mainstream parties. These men had voted for Corn Law repeal in 1846 and were convinced that Peel's 'liberal economics' were the way forward. On 28 December 1852 Aberdeen formed a coalition ministry of Peelites, Whigs and one Radical. The new Prime Minister stated that his administration would be 'a Liberal, Conservative government in the sense of that of Sir Robert Peel'. The Liberal Party was not formed officially until 1859, coming to office under Palmerston (*q.v.*). As most of Palmerston's Cabinet had served with Aberdeen, he can therefore be seen as the man who held the Peelites together until they merged as a group into the Liberal Party.

Aberdeen never sat in the Commons and he had difficulty in controlling ministers such as Russell (*q.v.*), Gladstone (*q.v.*) and Palmerston. He also needed the support of the Irish MPs, as his was a minority government. Essentially Aberdeen was a diplomat and conciliator rather than a decisive, dynamic leader. In 1809 his cousin, Lord Byron, criticised Aberdeen and Lord Elgin for removing classical antiquities from their original sites into their private collections, the most famous of these being the Elgin marbles, now in the British Museum. Sir James Graham (1852) and Disraeli (1853) attacked Aberdeen's lack of leadership abilities. As a minister he did have some successes but he is best remembered for his failures in the Crimean War.

In 1853, as his ministry drifted to war with Russia over conflicts of interest in the Middle East, his indecision hampered the peacekeeping efforts of Clarendon, the Foreign Secretary. Britain and France declared war against Russia on 28 March 1854. As Prime Minister, Aberdeen was deemed to be personally responsible for the catalogue of disasters that comprised the Crimean War. John Arthur Roebuck led a parliamentary campaign against Aberdeen, culminating in a vote of no confidence. Aberdeen resigned on 29 January 1855. Although he continued to sit in the Lords he did not hold office again; he died in London on 14 December 1860.

There are three modern biographies of Aberdeen: L. Iremonger, *Lord Aberdeen* (1978); Muriel Chamberlain, *Lord Aberdeen: A Political Biography* (1983); and Sir A. Gordon, *The Earl of Aberdeen* (1983).

Marjie Bloy

SIR RICHARD ACLAND 1906–90

Sir Richard Acland was a radical Liberal who became an evangelical crusader for Christian Socialism during the Second World War. His activities helped to pave the way for the Labour victory at the 1945 general election, which saw the Liberal Party almost destroyed as a political force.

Richard Thomas Dyke Acland was born at Broadclyst, Devon, on 26 November 1906 into an impeccable Liberal pedigree and a privileged background. His father was Sir Francis Dyke Acland Bt, a Liberal MP who had held office under Asquith (*q.v.*); his grandfather and great-grandfather had also been Liberal MPs. Acland's mother Eleanor was an anti-war campaigner. He was educated at Rugby and Balliol College, Oxford, practised as a barrister-at-law of the Inner Temple between 1930 and 1934 and succeeded to the baronetcy in 1939.

Acland unsuccessfully contested Torquay for the Liberals in 1929, and Barnstaple in 1931, winning the latter seat in 1935. However, he began to perceive Liberalism as an ideology unequal to the task of creating a new society. In 1936, he became a zealous convert to an idiosyncratic brand of socialism and, four years later, a devout Christian. From 1939, Acland published a series of booklets and pamphlets advocating the urgent application of a socialism founded on Christianity. The most significant of these was the best-seller *Unser Kampf* (1940), which passionately called for the replacement of the profit motive with the notion of service to the wider community. This, he argued, was essential to win the war and, in any case, ethically correct. Such views were well outside the limits of party opinion and senior Liberals called for the whip to be withdrawn from him.

In 1941, Acland formed the 'Forward March' movement to work for a new socialist millennium. The following year, he merged it with a similar grouping to form Common Wealth and then resigned from the Liberal Party. Standing outside the electoral truce, the new movement contested byelections wherever a 'reactionary' government candidate stood and no 'progressive' alternative was available. By the end of the war, Common Wealth had four Members of Parliament.

With Acland as its leader and prophet, Common Wealth called for the immediate

3

implementation of a libertarian socialist programme. This included: common owner-ship of all essential industries and services and their administration by a non-bureau-cratic civil service; the common ownership of property not essential for personal use; full employment in peacetime; implementation of the Beveridge Report on social security; and 'world unity'. An earnest and moral man, Acland sought to live his life in accordance with the high moral principles he espoused with such passion. In 1943, he donated the Acland family estates to the National Trust.

Common Wealth's doctrine was based on ethics and morality, as opposed to scien-tific socialism. It appealed primarily to the professional middle classes and the young – two groups that Labour had hitherto failed to attract. A skilled propagandist and a tireless campaigner, Acland interested young idealists in socialist ideas and involved them in politics. He provided a focus for the growing progressive mood within the wartime electorate. All this was to Labour's benefit once the electoral truce ended.

The 1945 election saw Common Wealth reduced to irrelevance, with a fraction of one per cent of the vote. Acland was heavily defeated in the Putney constituency but returned to the Commons in 1947 as the Labour member for Gravesend. In 1955, he resigned in protest at the Labour Party's support for developing the hydro-gen bomb. Soon after, he was expelled from the party for announcing an independ-ent candidacy in opposition to the official Labour candidate for the anticipated byelection. An early dissolution intervened and the Conservatives won Gravesend, with Acland coming third.

Although he continued to write and lecture on education, world peace and de-velopment issues, Acland had no political influence after he left Parliament. From 1959 to 1974, he was a senior lecturer at St Luke's College of Education, Exeter. He died on 24 November 1990 and was survived by his wife Anne, whom he married in 1936, and three of his sons. A fourth died in 1945, just five days old.

Sir Richard Acland's main contribution was to the socialist rather than the Liberal cause. Nevertheless, some of his policy planks, most notably class and gender equality, the establishment of works councils and European federation, have been taken up and developed by the Liberal Party, the SDP and the Liberal Democrats. His advocacy of a non-doctrinal, ethical politics that blends libertarian and egalitarian instincts has many echoes in the political debates of the 1990s.

Neil Stockley

LORD ACTON   1834–1902

'Power tends to corrupt, and absolute power corrupts absolutely'. Lord Acton's famous aphorism about the nature of political authority, written in April 1887, may be the most frequently cited of all such references. It is frighteningly simple in its truth and reveals a fundamental theme of liberalism – that power must be dispersed or liberty is in danger.

John Emerich Edward Dalberg Acton was born in Naples on 10 January 1834, the only child of Sir Ferdinand Acton Bt and his German wife, Countess Marie Louise de Dalberg. Acton's father died in 1835 and his mother was soon remarried to Earl Granville the Liberal statesman, later Gladstone's (*q.v.*) Foreign Secretary. The Acton family came originally from Shropshire but later relations settled in France and by the nineteenth century the family possessed a cosmopolitan national and religious background. Acton grew up speaking English, French, German and Italian. He was first educated in Paris, then at the Roman Catholic Oscott College, whose headmaster was Doctor (later Cardinal) Wiseman. Barred from attending Cambridge University in 1848 because of his Catholicism, Acton was sent to Munich University to study under Professor Ignaz von Dollinger, the famous church historian. From Dollinger Acton learnt historical method, criticism of the church and distrust of authoritarianism both civil and ecclesiastical. Acton travelled widely, touring America with Lord Ellesmere in 1855. In 1856 he went to Russia with Granville for the coronation of Tsar Alexander II and the following year he travelled through Italy with Dollinger.

Returning to the family seat at Aldenham, Acton began building up a collection of books for a library which eventually reached nearly 60,000 volumes, and took up a political career. In 1859 he entered Parliament. He represented Carlow, an Irish constituency, as a Whig until 1865. In that year he was elected MP for Bridgnorth by a majority of one but this result was overturned by official scrutiny. He tried again at Bridgnorth as a Liberal in 1868 but lost. His earlier Parliamentary career had not been particularly successful. He did not excel in debates and made only one speech, but he met and became devoted to Gladstone who increasingly came to rely on him. Gladstone personified Acton's vision of the liberal individual, self-controlled, educated and subject to religious and moral influences. In 1869 Gladstone created him first Baron Acton of Aldenham. He was a made a lord-in-waiting at court, 1892–95, when it was reported that Queen Victoria greatly appreciated his ability to speak fluent German.

While his career as a Liberal politician faltered, Acton's reputation as a religious thinker flourished. In 1858, he invested in and subsequently edited a liberal Catholic publication, *The Rambler,* later renamed *The Home and Foreign Review,* which came to exemplify the liberal catholic movement. Acton wrote many articles for the *Review* but his views soon brought him into conflict with the Catholic hierarchy, attracting criticism from Cardinal Wiseman. In 1864 Acton attended the Congress of Munich where his old mentor Dollinger urged the reunion of the Christian churches. Acton reported the proceedings and commented in the *Review,* this time attracting the disapproval of the Pope. Although he tried to compromise, Acton would not be silenced; his article 'Conflicts with Rome' championed individual freedom, scientific and philosophical enquiry. By the end of 1864 Pope Pius IX had had enough. He issued the encyclical *Quanta Cura,* condemning liberal catholic developments. In 1870–71 Acton went to Rome for the Vatican Council to help formulate the opposition to the dogma of papal infallibility. However, when in 1874 Gladstone published *The Vatican Decrees* which reopened the question of possible dangers to England from Catholics holding nominal allegiance to a foreign bishop, Acton wrote to *The Times* objecting to it. It was in trying to reconcile his loyalty to his faith and church – and avoid the danger of excommunication – on one side, and in defending political and religious freedoms on the other, that Acton developed his thinking on the relationship between history, religion and liberty.

From the 1870s Acton pursued seriously the third arm of his famous career, that of historian. He lectured and wrote many books on historical and religious subjects. He received honorary doctorates from Munich, Cambridge and Oxford Universities and in 1891 was made an honorary fellow of All Souls. In 1886 he had helped establish the *English Historical Review*. In 1895, on the recommendation of the Liberal Prime Minister, Lord Rosebery (*q.v.*), he was appointed Regius Professor of Modern History at Cambridge University. From 1899 onwards he began to devote his energies to the launch of the project which became the *Cambridge Modern History*, of which he was the first editor, although he never contributed to it. In 1901 he suffered a paralytic stroke. He retired to Bavaria, where his wife's family lived, and died there on 19 June 1902. After his death his great library was purchased by Andrew Carnegie; he passed it to Lord Morley, who donated it to Cambridge University.

Acton's own writings are today mainly available in three two-volume works edited by J. Rufus Fears: *Essays in the History of Liberty* (1985), *Essays in the Study and Writing of Liberty* (1986) and *Essays in Religion, Politics and Morality* (1988). Papers relating to his historical works are held in Cambridge University Library. A biography by Roland Hill entitled *The Life of Lord Acton, 1834–1902* was published in 1919. Owen Chadwick published the study *Acton and Gladstone* in 1976. The most recent work is Hugh Tulloch's *Acton*, published in 1988 in the series 'Historians on Historians'. Information about Lord Acton can also be obtained from the *Acton Institute for the Study of Religion and Liberty,* a free-market, libertarian American institution, from their internet website at http://www.acton.org.

Graham Lippiatt

LORD ADDINGTON   1963–

Dominic Bryce Hubbard Addington was born on 24 August 1963, the son of the fifth Baron Addington. He was educated at the Hewitt School, Norwich, and Aberdeen University (MA Hons 1988). Upon taking his father's title in 1982, he became the youngest-serving peer. Arriving in the Lords, he found himself in the perplexing situation of sitting across the table from people who were authors of history textbooks he had been reading just a couple of years before.

Three years after succeeding his father, Addington joined the Liberal Party, finding it to be 'the party I least disagreed with'. Since graduating from university he has been an active participant in the House of Lords, and despite his young age he soon found himself taking a leading role in the parliamentary party. During the water privatisation bill he was pushed by the party's Deputy Chief Whip on to the front bench. His youth was used to its advantage during the debates on the student loans bill, when he was able to say, with some confidence, that here was one peer that could talk about being a recent student.

In 1994 Addington took on the role of Liberal Democrat disability spokesman in the Lords, just as the issue of disability rights legislation was climbing the parliamentary agenda.

Addington is an active sportsman. At present he is the captain of the Commons and Lords Rugby Club and has toured South Africa a number of times; he took part in South Africa's Parliamentary World Cup in 1995. He is also a member of the All-Party Rugby League and the All-Party Rugby Union Group. His other sporting activities include being a member of the House of Commons gym, and taking part, since its commencement, in the annual Commons versus Lords tug-of-war.

He believes that the two dominant influences on his life have been his serious dyslexia and his inherited title. The combination of the two has led him to believe that he was perhaps destined to be the party's disability spokesman in the Lords. He currently serves as Vice-President of the UK Sports Association (an organisation for people with learning difficulties) and is Vice-President of the British Dyslexia Association. In addition to his parliamentary activities, he works for the events firm Milton Broadway.

Mark Morris

CHRISTOPHER ADDISON (Lord Addison)   1869–1951

When in November 1918 Lloyd George (*q.v.*) promised to make Britain a fit country for heroes to live in, it fell to Christopher Addison to formulate and carry out the policy through which homes would be provided for the men returning from the Great War. The Housing and Town Planning Act of 1919, under which local authorities were empowered to build unlimited numbers of houses at low, controlled rents, with their losses met by government subsidy, became known as the 'Addison Act'. In the end, it was the political outcry at the costs involved in implementing this policy that caused Lloyd George to sack Addison and began the estrangement between the two men that eventually led Addison into the Labour Party.

Christopher Addison was born in the Lincolnshire village of Hogsthorpe on 19 June 1869, where his family had farmed for generations. There were twelve children of his parent's marriage, of whom seven survived. Addison was the youngest of three boys. He was a clever child and at age thirteen was sent to Trinity College, Harrogate. He attended medical school in Sheffield and went on to St Bartholomew's Hospital where he specialised in anatomy. He then returned north to teach and by 1897 had become Professor of Anatomy at University College, Sheffield. In 1901 he moved back to London to lecture at Charing Cross Hospital and began to publish works on anatomy. As a result of his research he gave his name to a part of the human body, the Addison plane.

In 1902 Addison married Isobel Mackinnon, the daughter of a successful trader. They had three sons, one of whom died in infancy, and two daughters. Isobel died in 1934 and Addison later married Dorothy Low, the daughter of a solicitor. However, his first wife's money had given Addison the opportunity to develop his political ambitions and in 1907 he was adopted as Liberal candidate for Hoxton (Shoreditch). His background gave him a special interest in health and social welfare, chiming in well with the New Liberalism of the government. Addison supported traditional Liberal policies such as Irish Home Rule and land nationalisation but his true political motivation was an idealistic desire to improve the social and working conditions of the poor.

He entered Parliament at the general election of January 1910. His specialist knowledge enabled him to take a role in framing the National Health Insurance Bill of 1911 and he served as a link to the medical profession. In this way he came to the attention of Lloyd George. Addison's political skills were in policy formulation and administration. He envied Lloyd George's oratory and his skills with people, and decided to hitch himself to Lloyd George's wagon as a means of achieving his own social policy agenda. In August 1914, Addison was appointed Parliamentary Secretary to the Board of Education and in May 1915 he joined Lloyd George at the new Ministry of Munitions. Lloyd George was interested in the broad political sweep, while Addison got to work on the detail, organising the 'war socialism' of government controls and regulations to get the economy supplying the war effort, prefiguring later developments in the mixed economy. He was made a Privy Councillor in June 1916.

In December 1916, Lloyd George made his bid for the leadership. Addison was a loyal aide, canvassing Liberal MPs and smoothing the way for the majority of the parliamentary party to support the new Prime Minister's coalition with the Conservatives. As an immediate reward , Lloyd George appointed him Munitions Minister but in June 1917, he was moved to make way for Churchill (*q.v.*) and became Minister for Reconstruction. He was happy with this new work which enabled him to plan the transition to the peacetime economic and social system. But his association with Lloyd George was weakening. The Prime Minister was more interested in post-war high politics, especially international affairs, and had less time and enthusiasm for Addison's domestic schemes.

Despite this, Addison was able to take forward social legislation. In January 1919, as President of the Local Government Board, he introduced a bill to establish a Ministry of Health and he became its first Minister. Then came the housing crisis of 1919–21 which finally ended his political love affair with Lloyd George. In April 1921

Addison was made Minister without Portfolio but, his housing strategy destroyed and the government responsible in his eyes for betraying the homeless and slum dwellers, he resigned in July. Even though his policy had not delivered the results Addison so desperately wished for, he had nevertheless overseen the transformation of the provision of housing from a purely profit-related business activity into an instrument of social policy.

Without government office and with the link to Lloyd George broken, Addison had no power base in the Liberal Party from which to rebuild. After losing his seat at Hoxton in 1922 he turned to the Labour Party as the most suitable vehicle for achieving social reform. He stood unsuccessfully as Labour candidate for Hammersmith South at the 1924 general election and returned to Parliament in 1929 as MP for Swindon. During the intervening years he wrote a number of political works, the most important of which was the tellingly entitled *The Betrayal of the Slums* (1922). In June 1930 he became Minister of Agriculture; his Parliamentary Secretary was Clement Attlee. In the crisis of August 1931, Addison opposed MacDonald. As a result he lost his seat in the National landslide at the general election. He returned to the Commons at a byelection in 1934 but lost again in 1935.

In 1937 he was created a baron. He became leader of the Labour peers in 1940 and Leader of the House of Lords after Labour's victory in 1945. He went on to hold a number of government posts: Secretary of State for Dominion Affairs (1945–47), Lord Privy Seal (1947–51), Paymaster-General (1948–49), Lord President of the Council (1951). In 1945 he was created a Viscount and made a Knight of the Garter in 1946. He died on 11 December 1951 at his home in Radnage, Buckinghamshire.

Addison's papers are in the Bodleian Library, Oxford. He published two sets of memoirs, *Four and A Half Years* (2 volumes, 1934) and *Politics from Within* (2 volumes, 1924). The most recent biography is *Portrait of a Progressive: the Political Career of Christopher, Viscount Addison* by Kenneth and Jane Morgan (1980).

Graham Lippiatt

JOHN ALDERDICE (Lord Alderdice) 1955–

John Alderdice is a rare politician. He pursues wide academic, professional and political interests and has made significant contributions in each.

Born on 28 March 1955, John Thomas Alderdice attended the Ballymena Academy. He studied medicine at Queen's University and qualified in 1978. He married his childhood sweetheart, Joan, in 1977. Joan is a consultant at Antrim Area Hospital; they have three children, two sons and one daughter.

Working his way through a variety of posts, first in Lagan and then in Belfast, Alderdice gained expertise in psychotherapy and psychiatry. He has published articles on a wide range of issues including AIDS, child abuse, substance dependency and anorexia nervosa, as well as insightful analyses of the Northern Irish political situation. In 1988 he was appointed consultant psychotherapist to the Eastern Health and Social Services Board, the first appointment of its kind in Ireland. He was appointed Honorary Lecturer in Psychotherapy at the School of Medicine at the Queen's University of Belfast in 1990, where he helped to establish, and continues to help run, a Master of Medical Science in Psychotherapy degree course. The Human Relations Institute he founded in 1990, and served as Director of until 1994, continues to provide a professional focus for trained psychotherapists. In 1993 he was appointed as the Executive Medical Director of the South and East Belfast Health and Social Services Trust, stepping down from this post in 1997. Alderdice is an active member of numerous medical, psychological and scientific societies.

Northern Irish politics are dominated by sectarianism. The Alliance Party remains the only non-sectarian political party and has provided much-needed leadership for the cause of peace. Alderdice joined the party in 1978 and was elected to its ruling body the following year. During the 1980s he held a range of posts including Chairman of the Policy Committee and Vice Chairman. He was Leader of the Alliance Party from October 1987 to June 1998.

Alderdice was a candidate for Lisburn District Council in 1981, and for the Belfast East constituency in 1987, achieving the best result for an Alliance candidate in parliamentary elections to date. He became a Belfast City councillor in 1989, taking over the seat previously held by Sir Oliver Napier, the former Alliance leader. He was also the Alliance candidate a month later in the European elections.

Standing where it does in Northern Irish politics, the Alliance Party, and its leader, have often been well placed to play a pivotal role in initiatives for peace. Alderdice has played a significant, if often behind-the-scenes, role in the most hopeful of negotiations of the last twenty years. In 1991 he led his party's delegation in the inter-party talks under Peter Brooke, and again in 1992 under Patrick Mayhew and Sir Ninian Stephen.

He was again unsuccessful in East Belfast in the general election of 1992, but successfully defended his local council seat in 1993, achieving the highest vote of any candidate in Northern Ireland. In 1996 he was also elected for East Belfast to the Northern Ireland Forum where he led the Alliance delegation, as he also did during the multi-party talks in Stormont. After the formation of the Northern Ireland Assembly in June 1998, he resigned as leader of the Alliance Party and was elected as the first Presiding Officer (Speaker) of the Assembly at its first meeting on 1 July 1998.

Alderdice has also been active in the international arena. He was elected to the ruling body of the European Liberal and Democratic Reform Party (ELDR) in 1987, as Vice-President of Liberal International (LI) in 1992, Treasurer of ELDR in 1995 and to the Bureau of LI in 1997. He was raised to the peerage in 1996 (the first member of the Royal College of Psychiatrists to be ennobled) as Baron Alderdice of Knock in the City of Belfast, and was one of the youngest-ever life peers.

The Alliance Party is a sister party of the Liberal Democrats. That relationship, sealed in bodies such as ELDR and Liberal International, has deepened and flourished over the last ten years. The leaders of both parties came to their high office around the same time – a time of significant change for both parties. The Alliance Party appreciated the fact that Paddy Ashdown (q.v.) also took on the role of Northern Ireland spokesman, and that his early years in Belfast and his experience there as a soldier gave him a special authority and access for both parties. For their part, the Liberal Democrats have grown to value and respect Alderdice's direct experience at so many levels of Northern Irish life and his special wisdom and insight. Both parties have benefited considerably from this personal and political relationship. Northern Ireland has as well.

Alison Holmes

RICHARD ALLAN MP

1966–

Richard Beecroft Allan was born in Sheffield on 11 February 1966, the youngest of three children. His father, John, is now retired and his mother, Elizabeth, is a receptionist for a local doctor. He was educated at Oundle School, and then went on to Pembroke College, Cambridge, to study Anglo-Saxon, Norse and Celtic studies with archaeology and anthropology. He also worked as a field archaeologist in Wales, York, France, the Netherlands and Ecuador. Returning to the UK in 1989, he studied information technology at Bristol Polytechnic, gaining an MSc in 1990.

He joined the Liberal Democrats in Bath in 1991, and helped in the successful 1992 election campaign which saw Don Foster (q.v.) dislodge the Conservative Party Chairman, Chris Patten. During the campaign Allan ran a ward committee room, organising canvassers and leaflet deliveries. The following year he was elected to Avon County Council for the Bath North West division, and in 1994 to Bath City Council for the Lansdown ward.

He became Deputy Leader of the Liberal Democrat group on the county council, and was spokesman on equal opportunities and finance. Wearing his finance hat, he assisted in negotiating the county budget for balanced councils. From 1991–95, in between his many council and party activities, he was employed by Avon Family Health Services Authority as a computer manager.

In 1995, he was selected as the Liberal Democrat prospective parliamentary candidate for his home constituency of Sheffield Hallam. With the impending abolition of Avon and Bath councils under local government reorganisation, he moved back to Sheffield, where he worked for the Family Health Services Computer Unit, based in Barnsley. The job entailed supplying information systems to health authorities up and down the country, many of which are still being used and supplied to this day.

Allan was elected MP for Hallam in 1997 with the largest swing for any main party candidate in England. He is now Liberal Democrat spokesman in urban affairs and community relations within the home affairs team. In the 1997–98 session, he was the lead Liberal Democrat spokesman on the Crime and Disorder Bill and the Data Protection Bill.

From June 1997 to May 1998 he was a member of the influential Home Affairs Select Committee. In April 1998 he was elected as Chair of the Information Select Committee. He is also a member of the Finance and Services and the Liaison Select Committees. His other parliamentary interests include science and technology, and relations with Latin American countries.

He married Louise in 1991; the couple have one child and live in the heart of his Sheffield Hallam constituency.

Sarah McGrother

DAVID ALTON (Lord Alton) 1951–

The history of the Liberal Party in the 1970s and '80s should record David Alton as one of its leading figures – although whether he really aspired to lead it may never be known. Like many strong characters in politics, his critics would say that he was only capable of operating in his own way, and he certainly had frequent disputes with other Liberals as a result, both in Liverpool and nationally. These became more frequent in the time of the Liberal Democrats, as he grew away from the party and considered establishing his own 'Christian Democrat Party'. He now sits as a crossbencher in the House of Lords.

David Patrick Paul Alton was born on 15 March 1951 and brought up in Brentwood. His father worked at the big Ford factory in nearby Dagenham. By the time he was considering what to do after school, he was already a committed Young Liberal. He noted that the two leading Liverpool Liberal councillors Cyril Carr and Trevor Jones (*q.v.*) 'seemed to be in *Liberal News* every week', so he did his teacher training at Christ College, Liverpool.

Trevor Jones described the 'young lad in the green corduroy jacket who turned up on his doorstep one night offering to help the local Liberals'. Together, they worked to spread the *Focus* deliveries which had begun in the city a few years before Jones joined the party. The result was a series of spectacular council byelection victories and steady progress in the annual city council elections.

In 1972, as he was about to qualify as a teacher, Alton was elected to the city council representing the Low Hill ward. A year later, he was elected to the newly-created Merseyside County Council (which came into office in 1974) and a month after that he was one of the forty-eight Liberal councillors elected to the new ninety-nine-member Liverpool City Council. Much of the achievement in sustaining the success of the Liberal Party in Liverpool was due to Alton and the energetic team of bright and able friends, many of them Oxbridge graduates, whom he knew through the Young Liberals and had persuaded to come to Liverpool. During this time he worked as a peripatetic teacher of children with learning difficulties.

Alton had developed his political skills as an apprentice to 'Jones the vote', who masterminded the Sutton & Cheam byelection victory in 1972. Jones wrote the *Focus* leaflets in his office, a ship chandler's store near Liverpool's docks. Once the artwork was finished, he and Alton would print through the night, alternately sleeping on a camp bed. They would then load the leaflets into the boot of Jones' sports car and speed down the motorways towards Surrey, with Alton looking out for police cars on the motorway bridges.

At twenty-two, Alton fought Liverpool Edge Hill in both the 1974 general elections. He was one of the few Liberal candidates to increase his share of the vote in the October election, when he came second with 26 per cent. His campaign to try and win the constituency thereafter was fanatical. It was a small constituency – 18,000 homes in just four square miles. Almost every home received a *Focus* leaflet at least monthly. Every council seat was won. By 1978, he was Deputy Leader of the Council and Chairman of the Housing Committee.

Edge Hill was one of only a tiny handful of seats which the Liberal Party considered it could gain in a 1978 or '79 election. But a byelection came first, following the death of the sitting MP Sir Arthur Irvine. Jim Callaghan's government had lost a vote of confidence by one vote the night before polling day and nobody was sure what would be the effect in Edge Hill, where it seemed that almost every Liberal activist had been present for the preceding weeks. Alton was elected with a crushing 8,133 majority and the party's national poll rating doubled overnight from five to ten per cent.

In Parliament, Alton undertook a number of different roles within the Liberal team, but often found himself at odds with David Steel (*q.v.*) over his remit. For a while he was a 'special adviser to the leader' as a substitute for a portfolio – but he protested that the leader did not take his advice. His friends admitted he was moody. His critics said that he always sulked when he did not get his way.

Towards the end of his first Parliament, the Boundary Commission effectively abolished the Edge Hill constituency. He opted to fight the new Mossley Hill seat, which had the largest part of his former constituency, but two-thirds of which was new territory to him. His decision to contest the seat became public before the allocation of seats in Liverpool was agreed with the SDP. This did not help the seat negotiation process, which ended in Liberal and SDP candidates both fighting the neighbouring Broadgreen seat.

A very intensive campaign, together with Alton's tremendous personal standing in the city, resulted in a Liberal/Alliance majority of 4,195. Despite a furious row with David Steel after the election, Alton was made Chief Whip in 1985. His drive transformed the Whip's Office into a modern, campaigning effective unit of the party; his changes have long survived his tenure there.

In 1987, he was re-elected in Mossley Hill but with a reduced majority. By the autumn his political role began to change dramatically as he used his place in the ballot for private member's bills to sponsor an anti-abortion bill. He gave up the position of Chief Whip to concentrate on this campaign but failed to overcome parliamentary blocking tactics or to win government time. During this period, he developed cross-party alliances with those who shared his opposition to abortion, alienating some members of the newly created Liberal Democrats. In particular, he had a very poor relationship with the newly elected leader Paddy Ashdown (*q.v.*), who had earlier succeeded Alton as a 'party favourite'. Alton backed Alan Beith (*q.v.*) during the Liberal Democrats' first leadership campaign, strongly attacking Ashdown and threatening to resign from Parliament in protest if Ashdown was elected.

In 1988, he married Lizzie Bell, a former Liberal assembly steward, vicar's daughter and strong supporter of the Society for the Protection of the Unborn Child; they now have three sons and one daughter. He was re-elected as a Liberal Democrat in 1992 but rarely participated in party events. He did, however, make a very significant contribution to the party with his skilful handling of the press conferences for Chris Davies in the Littleborough & Saddleworth byelection in 1995.

In 1995, the Boundary Commission struck again, reducing the number of seats in Liverpool from six to five and splitting Mossley Hill three ways. He fought the proposals vigorously but ineffectively. Dozens of nuns sent in petitions from their convents arguing that the Mossley Hill constituency should not be abolished 'because David Alton was a holy man'. These were not grounds which the Commission could consider.

He did not contest the 1997 general election. He was raised to the peerage that year as Lord Alton of Liverpool.

Chris Rennard

PADDY ASHDOWN MP   1941–

As the first elected leader of the newly-created Liberal Democrats and the party's standard-bearer in the two general election campaigns of 1992 and 1997, Paddy Ashdown's position in the Liberal Democrat pantheon is surely secure. He followed his considerable achievement in leading the party to forty-six parliamentary victories on 1 May 1997 with a promise at that year's conference that 'the best is yet to come'.

Paddy Ashdown's entry into politics, his victory in the Yeovil constituency from third place, and his rapid ascent to the leadership of the Liberal Democrats, have become the stuff of party and journalistic legend. He began his political career in inauspicious circumstances – 1976 – when the Liberal Party was at a low ebb. Ashdown himself faced unemployment, having given up his Foreign Office post in Geneva to return to Somerset. Gradually, and with great energy, he built up his local electoral

base, recruiting a for-
midable local team of
councillors and cam-
paigners. Meanwhile,
he worked as a man-
ager at the local
Westland helicopter
firm and then for a
local firm selling
sheepskin coats. A fur-
ther period of unem-
ployment was ended
by the opportunity to
join Dorset County

Council's Community Programme as a youth worker. By the time he was elected to
Parliament in 1983, Ashdown was already becoming well known within the wider
party for his Yeovil achievements, and had convinced the local electorate that he was
well-placed to win the seat.

For many, it was his glamorous (even exotic) CV that caught the eye. Born in
India on 27 February 1941, John Jeremy Durham Ashdown grew up in Belfast, where
his father took up pig breeding. Following family tradition he attended Bedford
School, where he lost his Irish accent but acquired the 'Paddy' sobriquet. He joined
the navy from school, and saw service with the marines, where he served in the
Special Boat Squadron, in Kuwait, Borneo, Aden and his native Northern Ireland.
Ashdown's service career included a time in Hong Kong, where he studied at the
University and gained a degree in Chinese.

Ashdown had married early, aged twenty, contrary to service regulations; he and
his wife, Jane, lived in the equivalent of military 'sin' for a while. They have two
children, Kate and Simon.

The services were followed by diplomacy, when Ashdown was appointed to the
position of First Secretary to the UK mission in Geneva. Here, he was involved in
international negotiations and brought into contact with leading British politicians.
But he gradually became disillusioned with what he considered the sybaritic lifestyle
of the Foreign Office and Britain's drift towards industrial conflict under the Wilson
and Callaghan Governments. Ashdown had previously been a Labour voter, but had
lost his sympathies at the time of Barbara Castle's abortive attempt to reform industrial relations law in the late 1960s. Now he discovered the Liberal Party in Somerset,
and set about contesting the apparently hopeless constituency of Yeovil.

From his election in 1983, Ashdown was the Liberal Party's spokesman on trade
and industry in the House of Commons. But it was his forays into other policy areas
that received more attention. At the 1981 and 1984 Liberal Assemblies he led the

arguments against Cruise missiles in Europe. The Conservative government's disputes over the Westland helicopter company in 1986 gained him further prominence. His identification with the local government base of the Liberal Party won him many friends and supporters. Shortly before the 1987 election, Ashdown became the Alliance's spokesman on education, a role in which he was able to excel and which was central to the party's electoral appeal.

Ashdown largely stayed clear of the bitter arguments over merger in the winter of 1987–88, publishing, in September 1987, a policy pamphlet, *After the Alliance: setting the new political agenda*, with an eye to the forthcoming leadership contest in the merged party. On 28 July 1988, after a highly professional campaign in which he always seemed ahead, he was elected leader of the newly-merged Liberal Democrats over Alan Beith (*q.v.*), with over seventy per cent of the vote. The party he inherited was demoralised, almost bankrupt and divided over its own name. It was also being challenged by Dr Owen's breakaway SDP, failing to win the Richmond byelection in Yorkshire in 1989 because of the intervention of a popular local Owenite candidate. In June the party came fourth after the Green Party in the European elections, winning only six per cent of the national vote.

It was not until October 1989 that a ballot of members settled on the name 'Liberal Democrats'. Earlier that year, Ashdown published his book, *Citizen's Britain*. At the party's lengthy autumn conference in Brighton, he made a keynote speech almost every day. Slowly but surely, thereafter, the Liberal Democrats recovered their coherence and energy, led from the front by Ashdown.

He drew on his own experience of Hong Kong following the Tiananmen Square massacre to lead calls for UK passports for Hong Kong citizens. In October 1990, the Liberal Democrats won their first parliamentary byelection at Eastbourne. That year, Ashdown was the *Spectator's* 'party leader of the year'. Iraq's invasion of Kuwait, leading to the Gulf War of 1991, brought Ashdown's military and international expertise to the attention of a wider public. By the summer of 1991, he had achieved higher satisfaction ratings in opinion polls than John Major or Neil Kinnock.

The build-up to the 1992 election was nearly thrown off course, however, by the forced revelation of a brief and five-year old relationship between Ashdown and his former secretary. The support of his wife Jane, his own willingness to face a Westminster press conference and some deft public relations saw him through this crisis, though it was to cast a shadow over the coming campaign and was a painful experience.

The 1992 election campaign was a personal success for Ashdown, establishing him as a significant voice in British politics. He followed it by an extensive and largely behind-the-scenes tour of Britain, which led to his second book, *Beyond Westminster* (1994), which addressed the widening gap between Parliament and the people.

He also became a prolific commentator on the break-up of Yugoslavia, visiting the arena of conflict on numerous occasions and campaigning powerfully for proactive UN involvement. Meanwhile, he was beginning to re-position the Liberal Democrats, a process which commenced with a speech at Chard (in Somerset) in May 1992, leading finally to the abandonment of 'equidistance' in May 1995. Despite difficult months following the election of Tony Blair as Labour Party leader and a disastrous party conference in 1994, the Liberal Democrats were, by common consent, better prepared for the 1997 election than a third party had previously ever been.

Since the 1997 election, he has enunciated a strategy of 'constructive opposition', and has led his party into a Cabinet Committee which will oversee the implementation of agreed constitutional reforms. A host of new electoral challenges await in the next few years, many of them using proportional systems of voting. Ashdown is about to discover whether he and his party have a major role to play at the top table of British politics.

Alan Leaman

H. H. ASQUITH (Earl of Oxford and Asquith)   1852–1928

H. H. Asquith, Prime Minister from April 1908 to December 1916, bore the chief part in some of the greatest Liberal achievements of the twentieth century.

Herbert Henry Asquith was born at Morley, West Yorkshire, on 12 September 1852. His father died when he was eight, and in 1863, sent to London to live with relatives, he entered the City of London School. His outstanding abilities were soon recognised and in 1870 he won a classical scholarship to Balliol. At Oxford he gained firsts in classical moderations and Greats and became President of the Union Society. Elected to a fellowship of Balliol in 1874, he was called to the bar two years later. He married Helen Melland in 1877 and started on a struggle to make his way as a barrister. In the 1886 election he won East Fife, where the sitting Liberal had been repudiated for opposing Gladstone (*q.v.*) on Home Rule; he was to hold the seat for thirty-two years. He soon showed his remarkable debating powers, and in 1888 established himself at the bar by a brilliant cross-examination when junior counsel before the Parnell Commission. He took silk in 1890.

In September 1891 Asquith was left as a widower with four sons and a daughter (Violet, *q.v.*) when his wife died during a family holiday. He married the sparkling but eccentric Margaret (Margot) Tennant (*q.v.*) in May 1894 (one son and one daughter of this marriage surviving infancy). He had become Home Secretary in 1892, and was perhaps the only minister who increased his reputation while serving under Gladstone and Rosebery (*q.v.*) during the next three years. In December 1898, being dependent on his income at the bar, he declined the opposition leadership in the Commons. His position in the Boer War, as a leading Liberal Imperialist, was uncomfortable; but in 1903 he was offered his great chance when Joseph Chamberlain (*q.v.*) opened the campaign for tariff reform. He took it superbly, arguing the free trade case in a series of devastatingly effective speeches.

When Balfour resigned in December 1905 Campbell-Bannerman (*q.v.*) defeated an attempt to force him 'upstairs' and make Asquith Leader of the party in the Commons. This was fortunate for Asquith. He might not have led the large but callow Liberal majority produced by the 1906 election as well as Campbell-Bannerman did. Instead he became a very successful Chancellor of the Exchequer, revising the system of grants to local authorities, starting the provision for old age pensions, and reducing the national debt.

By the end of March 1908 Campbell-Bannerman was mortally ill. Asquith's claim to the premiership could not be disputed; he 'kissed hands' on 6 April and formed a strong government. His prospects did not look particularly promising. Trade was depressed and the Conservative peers were wreaking havoc on the government's legislative programme; but in 1909 they made the fatal error of throwing out the budget. In the ensuing constitutional struggle Asquith slipped only once (over the 'guarantee' given by Edward VII to create more peers if necessary to pass government legislation through the Lords). That apart, his conduct of the government's campaign was masterly. The Liberals won both of the 1910 general elections, though with diminished majorities; and the 1911 Parliament Act, under which the Lords' powers were reduced to those of delay, became law without a creation of peers.

Asquith was by now as dominant on the platform as in the House itself. His administration was marked by notable reforms: the 1911 National Insurance Act, for instance, taken with old age pensions, heralded the 'welfare state.' These feats were achieved against a background of strikes, where trade union growth and low unemployment (1911–14) gave syndicalist methods a brief popularity; of suffragette agitation, where Asquith, who then opposed female suffrage, was a prime target; and, above all, of threatened civil war in Ireland, if Home Rule should be enacted and Belfast brought under Dublin's rule. The charge of dangerous procrastination over Ulster brought against Asquith has little substance. He was dependent on the Irish Nationalists for his majority and the Lords were sure to use their Parliament Act powers to delay Home Rule until 1914. By July of that year both he and his opponents were fearful of the outcome. At that point the imminent prospect of a European war brought a suspension of the struggle.

Asquith had a good record on defence: in January 1914, for instance, he prevented a group led by Lloyd George (*q.v.*) from reducing the naval estimates. His conduct during the war crisis (24 July – 6 August 1914) has generally been thought the high point of his premiership. He brought all but two of his Cabinet colleagues round to a policy of intervention until the German government and commander-in-chief completed his work for him by a wholesale invasion of Belgium in defiance of the international treaty establishing its inviolability. Had the decision to send the Expeditionary Force to France been delayed, the war's outcome could well have been different.

Asquith maintained his grip, and his popularity, during the early months of the war; but in May 1915 press revelations about shell shortages, and the quarrel between Churchill (*q.v.*) and Fisher over the Dardanelles, obliged him to reconstruct the government as a coalition.

A coalition cabinet of peacetime dimensions was not an effective instrument for waging war, and the pressure on it was appalling. The failure at the Dardanelles, the long struggle over conscription, the aftermath of the 1916 Easter rising in Dublin; and the huge casualty lists of the Somme (where his son, Raymond, was killed), sapped the government's strength. 'In war,' Bonar Law told the Prime Minister, 'it is necessary not only to be active but to seem active.' Asquith did not take this sound advice, and it was not in him to cultivate those who controlled newspapers for which he had scant regard. In December 1916 he was ousted from the premiership in a 'palace revolution' and succeeded by Lloyd George.

Asquith gave the new government general support, but in May 1918, by pressing a procedural question to a division, he allowed them to brand the 106 Liberals who followed him into the division lobby as traitors to the Allied cause at a critical moment of the war. In the 'coupon election' of December 1918 he lost his seat, his followers were decimated, and the Liberal Party suffered a split from which it did not recover during his lifetime. He was returned for Paisley in a byelection in February 1920 and held the seat until the general election of 1924. Some of his post-war speeches – advocating Dominion Home Rule for Ireland and a reasonable settlement on 'reparations' – were among the best of his career; but a divided party did not impress the new electorate created by the 1918 Reform Act, and Lloyd George was far better funded than the Asquithians.

The two sections united to defend free trade in the 1923 election; but, though the Liberals increased their strength, they remained the third party in the Commons. Asquith rightly refused to deny Labour their chance to form a minority government, but his party gained nothing from this decision, and lost disastrously in the 1924 election. In May 1926 the General Strike occasioned a final rupture between the rival leaders and in October Asquith resigned the party leadership. He had been created Earl of Oxford and Asquith and a Knight of the Garter in 1925. He died at his home, The Wharf, Sutton Courtenay, near Abingdon, on 15 February 1928.

Of the books which Asquith produced in old age to make money, *The Genesis of the War* (1923) is probably the most important. There are biographies by J. A. Spender and Cyril Asquith (2 vols, 1932), R. B. McCallum (1936), Roy Jenkins (1964, third edition, 1986), and Stephen Koss (1976). A number of his personal letters have been published: see especially *H. H. Asquith, Letters to Venetia Stanley*, eds. M. and E. Brock (1982).

Dr Michael Brock

MARGOT ASQUITH (Countess of Oxford and Asquith)   1864–1945

Emma Alice Margaret Tennant later became Mrs Asquith, and eventually the first Countess of Oxford and Asquith, but she was universally known as 'Margot'. Margot was married to an immense personality, yet was also a great personality in her own right, who appears to have exerted significant influence over the career of her husband.

Unlike H. H. Asquith (*q.v.*), Margot started life with a silver spoon firmly in her mouth. She was born in Peeblesshire on 2 February 1864, the sixth daughter and eleventh child of Sir Charles Tennant, a wealthy ironmaster and later a Liberal MP.

Margot was a woman of many parts. Educated privately, then briefly at a finishing school and eventually at Dresden, she became an avid reader of serious literature, for which she had a remarkable memory. In her youth she showed considerable interest in the welfare of people less fortunate than herself, joining with her sister in establishing a crèche at Wapping, in London's East End, and later making frequent visits to a factory in nearby Whitechapel, an area notorious for sweated labour.

Soon she became associated with many of the most remarkable men of her time. Gladstone (*q.v.*) commemorated her with a piece of doggerel. The celebrated classicist Benjamin Jowett, Master of Balliol, was a close friend, and perhaps it was from Jowett that she acquired an enthusiasm for Plato. Soon she became one of the 'souls' – a cross-party group of intellectuals which included A. J. Balfour, the Marquess of Hartington (*q.v.*), Lord Rosebery (*q.v.*), John Morley and Archbishop Randall Davidson.

She had very strong likes, and perhaps even stronger dislikes, for people who came into her circle of acquaintances. As her step-daughter Lady Violet Bonham Carter (*q.v.*) noted, Margot's political concern was with men rather than with measures. When she died, *The Times* would reflect that she was 'not a wholly endearing personality .... but of her scintillating endowment of mind .... there could never be any question'.

In May 1894, she became the second wife of Herbert Henry Asquith, Home Secretary in the Liberal government, and future Prime Minister. She was a mixed blessing to her husband. She was utterly loyal to him, and brought sufficient wealth to make it possible for a man with much talent to attain the highest political office. Both spouses were able to introduce the other into circles with which they had hitherto been unfamiliar. But her tactlessness, and her disposition to see public matters in personal terms, were less helpful.

Perhaps the most important example of her dislikes – or intuitions? – was signalled in July 1916. Lord Kitchener, Secretary for War, had recently died. As Prime Minister of the wartime coalition, Asquith eventually picked on Lloyd George (*q.v.*) as the successor. That night, Margot noted in her diary: 'We are out, it is only a matter of time when we shall have to leave Downing Street.'

Was that a premonition of the inevitable, or a self-serving prophecy? Asquith's position was in some ways a very lonely one, and his wife, who had such pronounced views, was one of the few people in whom he could confide. Later in 1916, a difficult question arose concerning the conduct of the war, with Asquith and Lloyd George inclining to different sides. Until almost the last minute, a compromise appeared likely; but Asquith suddenly backed off. Within a short time, Lloyd George was Prime Minister in his place. Was Margot's influence of crucial importance in bringing about the Asquith-Lloyd George split which would prove so disastrous to both men, and to the Liberal Party?

Margot was capable of astonishing indiscretions. Her scribbled top-of-the-head letters may be found in various political papers. When Bonar Law brought about the destruction of Lloyd George's coalition government in 1922, Margot sent a gushing and congratulatory letter to the new Conservative Prime Minister, assuring him of her husband's 'generosity' in the future, and indicating that the Asquiths would rather be out 'for ever' than encompass a return of the coalition. Whether this correctly represented Asquith's view or not, it is unthinkable that he would have approved the transmission of such a letter, which might easily prove a high political embarrassment.

Margot was the author of several books, including an autobiography (1922) and a novel, *Octavia*, and late in life was an occasional broadcaster. She had five children, only two of whom survived infancy. She died on 28 July 1945, a few weeks before the end of the Second World War.

Roy Douglas

LORD AVEBURY   1928–

Eric Reginald Lubbock, now Lord Avebury, was born on 29 September 1928 and educated at Upper Canada College, Toronto and Balliol College, Oxford. Liberal politics ran deep in the family. His paternal grandfather, Sir John Lubbock, had been the Liberal MP for Maidstone and his maternal grandfather the Liberal MP for Eddisbury 1906–10 and then Governor of the Australian state of Victoria.

He came to national prominence with his victory in the Orpington byelection on 14 March 1962. Although Mark Bonham Carter's (*q.v.*) capture of Torrington from the Tories four years earlier marked the first Liberal byelection gain since 1929, the scale of the victory was much less impressive. At Orpington the Liberals, third-placed in 1959, overtook both main parties. Lubbock won a 7,855 majority and Labour lost their deposit. It was a seismic political event. He held the seat in 1964 and 1966 but lost it in 1970.

Lubbock's first election in Orpington had been in 1961, when he won a seat on the Urban District Council. He stood for the unwinnable seat of Deptford for the Greater London Council in 1973, when he was President of the London Liberal Party. He also stood for Southall in 1977 where his motive was not to win but to recruit more ethnic minority activists into the Liberal Party. He succeeded.

In 1967 Lubbock stood against Jeremy Thorpe (*q.v.*) and Emlyn Hooson (*q.v.*) in the contest to succeed Jo Grimond (*q.v.*) as party leader, the last such contest in which only MPs had votes. Lubbock, who had become Liberal Chief Whip before the 1966 general election, was backed by Richard Wainwright (*q.v.*) and Michael Winstanley. Hooson also had two supporters. Thorpe won with five.

As a London MP Lubbock was always a dedicated attendee of the Commons and threw himself into its activities with great zest. He was the lone Liberal on the Speaker's Conference on Electoral Reform from 1963–65. He moved to reduce the voting age to eighteen, with the support of two other MPs, both Labour. He also moved to introduce the single transferable vote system but there he was on his own. He showed his prescience when, as a member of the Select Committee on Members' Interests (Declaration), he proposed, but without support, a minority report calling for much tougher rules on the declaration of interests.

During the 1960s he was active in the management of the Liberal Party, serving on its National Executive and the Party Council. He was also Chairman of the Candidates Committee.

In 1971 his cousin, the third Baron Avebury, died, leaving a daughter but no sons; Lubbock was faced with the prospect of becoming the fourth baron. He seriously considered renouncing the peerage. He had been a popular and accessible Chief Whip and had wanted to stand again at Orpington. After much reflection, however, he took the guaranteed option of the peerage rather than risk not being re-elected to the Commons. No Liberal or Liberal Democrat has won Orpington since.

At Jeremy Thorpe's request Avebury led the Liberal general election campaign in February 1974. He was Liberal spokesman on immigration and race relations until 1982 but subsequently became more of a semi-detached member of the party. What he did not drop, however, was his commitment to civil rights. A passionate libertarian and egalitarian, he was now free to devote even more time and energy to this issue. As soon as he became an MP he joined the Parliamentary Civil Rights Group. He became Secretary almost immediately and Chairman in 1964. Some time after he left the Commons the group lapsed but in 1976 he founded the Parliamentary Human Rights Group, of which he was Chairman until 1997. He remains Vice-Chairman.

In 1972 Peter Hain, then the best-known Young Liberal in the country (and twenty-five years later a minister in the Blair Labour Government) faced a private prosecution on four charges of criminal conspiracy arising from his leading the opposition to pro-apartheid sportsmen visiting Britain from South Africa. Avebury set up a fund which raised £5,000 towards his defence. In 1973, he established and endowed the Silbury Fund as a charity dedicated to civil liberties and race relations.

Avebury has not limited his fight for human rights to Britain. He has been a scourge of tyrants in Central and South America, Asia and Africa. He has been detained twice – in Sri Lanka and Guyana – and is now banned from entering Turkey. In 1997 he agreed to serve as a member of the Liberal Democrats' foreign affairs team, hoping to raise the party's profile outside Europe.

Apart from his human rights work, Avebury, a Buddhist convert, is a patron of the Buddhist Prison Chaplaincy which involves giving advice on problems which arise when dealing with the Home Office. He believes it wrong that prisons are in the firm and statutory grip of the Church of England and thinks there should be equality there between all faiths.

He was an engineer before entering Parliament and always maintained his interest in science and technology. He was chairman at various times of the Fluoridation Society, of the editorial board of *Design Engineering* and of the Air Safety Group. He also served as a director of C. L. Projects Ltd and of J. G. Franklin Ltd and was a partner, with his agent at Orpington, John Cook, in Cook, Lubbock and Co. He was an adviser to Morgan Grampian Ltd and set up a firm called 20-20, selling computers.

Wonderfully idiosyncratic though impeccably logical, Avebury attracted much media attention when he sought in vain in 1987 to leave his body to Battersea Dogs' Home. In 1983 he was divorced from Kina, with whom he had three children. In 1985 he married Lindsay Stewart, with whom he also has a child.

Mike Steele

NORMAN BAKER MP   1957–

Norman Baker was elected to Parliament in May 1997 after a hard-fought local campaign in the traditional Tory heartland of Lewes, in East Sussex. He first stood for Parliament in 1992, where he reduced the Conservative majority; he eventually saw them off with a majority of 1,300, partly helped by highly publicised support from local Labour Party members.

Baker was a well-known face in East Sussex before being elected to Parliament, having been Leader of Lewes District Council from 1991 to 1997. During this time he championed many respected local causes and some unconventional ones. The towns and villages which make up the constituency are varied and interesting, taking in rural farmland, a fishing community and popular tourist spots. His political style reflects this well and may be due in part to the wide variety of jobs that preceded his election.

Norman John Baker was born on 26 July 1957 in Aberdeen. His family then moved to Essex, and he was educated at Royal Liberty School, Gidea Park. Graduating in German from Royal Holloway College, London University, his early career was in the music business. He soon became a regional executive director of Our Price Records but, becoming disillusioned with the company's approach, left to pursue what he saw as a more worthwhile career. Before becoming the Liberal Democrats' environment researcher in Parliament, he ran Hornsey Railway Station, worked in a wine shop, taught language students and wrote a book of short stories (so far unpublished).

Baker's enthusiasm for the environment and green politics took hold when he moved to Lewes in 1985 and was moved to seek election to the district council. He had been inspired early on by Jo Grimond (*q.v.*) and had been a party member since 1981. In 1987 he unseated the Conservative council leader, taking the Ouse Valley seat, and soon became immersed in the local political scene. He has been active at every level of local government and continues to be a member of his local parish and district councils. He has also served as chair of the Economic Development and Public Transport sub-committees on East Sussex County Council and as chair of the Tourism and Rural Affairs sub-committee of the Assembly of European Regions.

At Westminster he has been no less active, and as well as being a Liberal Democrat spokesman on the environment and a member of the Environmental Audit Select Committee, he also sits on the Select Committee on European Legislation. He quite enjoys ridiculing what he considers the 'antiquated' systems in place at Westminster and, through his time as a researcher, knows better than many other new faces how to use procedure to the full. This, together with his record for speaking forty-eight times in thirty-four sitting days in the chamber, may be why he was dubbed a bore by Matthew Parris in *The Times*. Nonetheless Parris had to concede that 'Hurricane Norman' would go far. In the spring of 1998, *The Observer* reported that he had asked more parliamentary questions in the preceding year than any other MP.

His interests range across the political arena. He is a committed non-meat eater, a campaigner for animal rights and an opponent of fox hunting. He is a member of Greenpeace, Amnesty, Liberty and the Free Tibet Group. In general, he is suspicious of government and trusting of the individual and takes each case on its merits. His request to have 'honourable member' dropped from Westminster formalities and his insistence on being referred to by his first rather than second name are further examples of his enjoyment of challenging sacred cows. He insists on a clear divide between public and private life and is reluctant to name favourites or heroes.

Emma Sanderson-Nash

JACKIE BALLARD MP   1953–

Jacqueline (Jackie) Margaret Mackenzie was born in Dunoon, Scotland on 4 January 1953. (Her Conservative-voting parents did not reveal that a distant Highland cousin had been a Liberal councillor and candidate, and that her aunt had been Russell Johnston's *(q.v.)* constituency secretary until she had established a Liberal pedigree of her own some forty years later.)

When Ballard was ten the family moved to South Wales, where her academic prowess came to the fore thanks to the benefits of the Scottish education system, as well as a fine intellect. At the age of eleven she became the first child from her primary school to sit and win the prestigious annual boarding scholarship to Monmouth School for Girls.

This plunged the daughter of a Scottish woodcutter from a caravan into a world of privilege and wealth. It formed the beginnings of a burning desire to achieve, as well as abiding anger at a system which advantaged the few and ignored the many.

After a rebellious but highly successful school career, Ballard went on to LSE to read social psychology. She threw herself into the political issues of the day: the Arab-Israeli War, anti-apartheid, anti-Vietnam and pro-CND. Her commitment to the rights of others was not a party political stance. Rather, she identified with the hero of Zola's *Germinal* and his fight against injustice. With this in mind she became a social worker, determined to help relieve the social deprivation of London's East End. She soon realised that the power to change people's lives for the good permanently lay with governance of one sort or another.

In 1975, she married Derek Ballard. In 1976 the couple moved to Somerset, to 'settle down', and for the next few years Jackie Ballard became 'Mrs Super House-wife', making jam, pickling onions and being a mother to her baby daughter, Christine. Once Christine was of school age she returned to work as a lecturer and an adult education organiser. Her involvement with the Crewkerne Toy Library Management Committee and the local Youth Club meant that it was inevitable that she would come across Paddy Ashdown (*q.v.*).

It was Ashdown who convinced Ballard that she should put her campaign spirit back into action and it was his definition of Liberalism that made her realise that she had been 'a Liberal all my life'. She joined the party in 1985. As with everything else Ballard does, there are no half measures. By 1990 she was the leader of South Somerset District Council (having been first elected in 1987). In 1992 she was Parliamentary candidate for Taunton, gaining the second biggest swing from the Tories in the country. The following five years saw her serve as a councillor and Deputy Leader on Somerset County Council, as well as working as Council Support Worker for the Association of Liberal Democrat Councillors (ALDC). She was elected as the MP for Taunton in 1997.

Her parliamentary interests reflect her own personal journey; a member of the local government team, she is spokesman on 'women's' issues, a member of the All-Party Parliamentary Social Services Panel, the All-Party Sex Equality Group and the All-Party Parenting Group. She is currently a member of the Federal Executive of the Liberal Democrats, and ALDC, having lost her as a member of staff, has now elected her as its President. She believes that Liberalism is both a philosophy and a movement and that, as a Liberal, she must continue to be a torch-bearer for social justice. Her passions are the causes of her youth: environmental issues, education, health, local government, poverty, civil rights, young people and animal welfare.

Ballard is divorced (since 1989) and lives alone in Taunton most of the time, and with her daughter in London some of the time.

Rachel Oliver

DESMOND BANKS (Lord Banks)   1918–97

Desmond Banks was a leading member of that generation of Liberal candidates in the period following the Second World War which also included Jo Grimond (*q.v.*), Mark Bonham Carter (*q.v.*), Frank Byers (*q.v.*) and Banks' friend and co-founder of the Radical Reform Group, Peter Grafton. Like Banks, many of those candidates in the general elections of 1945, 1950 and 1951 had served in the war. They were instinctively radical. They blamed the Conservatives for failing Britain in the 1920s and 1930s, both in the domestic fight against poverty and unemployment and in the international arena in appeasing fascism. While their experiences made them interventionists, they rejected socialism and class war. They were the inheritors of Keynes (*q.v.*) and Beveridge (*q.v.*) and fought for Liberalism as a cause and a way of life.

Desmond Anderson Harvie Banks was born in Ascot on 23 October 1918. As his names suggest, his family had Scottish roots. He was educated at prep school in Harrow and at University College School in Hampstead, where he joined the Liberals. According to the party organiser for Harrow East in 1945, one of the documents which served to get the Liberals reorganised there after the war was a list of former members in the Kenton area, written in Banks' schoolboy long-hand. When war broke out he volunteered for the King's Royal Rifle Corps, later gaining a commission in the Royal Artillery. He served in the Middle East and finished the war as a prisoner-of-war in Trieste, an experience which toughened him. In 1946 he served as Chief Public Relations Officer to the Allied Military Government in Trieste. On leaving the army, Banks worked with his father's laundry machine company. He later became an independent life insurance broker and pensions consultant. In 1948 he married Barbara Wells, who was herself awarded the OBE for political services to the Women's Liberal Federation in 1987.

Banks renewed his political connection with Harrow East, where he stood in the 1950 general election. The 1945 election had been a disaster and some radical rethinking was required; Banks provided it. His ideas included the delivery of a free newspaper, *The Harrow East Liberal,* to every home in the constituency and the targeting of resources on one local government ward in the run-up to the general election. Commonplace today, these campaigning methods were innovations in the 1940s.

In 1949 Banks joined the staff at Liberal Party headquarters and became editor of *Liberal News* for a time. For six months he edited a monthly journal, *The Middle Road.* He was active within the Home Counties Liberal Federation, the Liberal Candidates Association and the Party Executive, of which he was twice elected Chairman, in 1961–63 and 1969–70. He served as President of the Liberal Party in 1968–69. He was Parliamentary candidate in St Ives in 1955 and Hertfordshire South West in 1959. During this candidacy he helped to produce *Life with the Liberals,* a widely-circulated policy booklet. He regularly attended and spoke at party assemblies, acted as speech writer for Jo Grimond, and was a frequent contributor to *Liberal News*. He wrote many pamphlets and papers on policy issues and co-authored *The Political Insight of Elliott Dodds* with Lord Wade (*q.v.*), published in 1977.

In 1952 Banks co-founded the Radical Reform Group (RRG) to provide a focus for those who feared the Liberal Party was drifting rightwards. He hoped for defectors from a Labour Party engaged in its own left–right struggles, typified by the debates over Clause IV. This foreshadowed the idea, usually associated with Grimond's leadership of the party, of the realignment of the left. Indeed Grimond was sometime President of the RRG, although he never took any organising role. In 1954 the RRG elected to move outside the Liberal Party (as an organisation, although not as individuals) to be more attractive to potential defectors and to provide a half way house to radical Liberals like Lady Megan Lloyd George (*q.v.*) and Dingle Foot (*q.v.*) who were moving towards Labour. However Labour was not ready to split, and at the end of 1955 the RRG voted to return within the Liberal Party, acting as a left-wing ginger group until it was wound up in the late 1960s.

In 1972 Banks was awarded the CBE and was created a life peer in 1974, taking the title Baron Banks of Kenton. He became spokesman on social services between 1975–89 and was Deputy Whip in the Lords from 1977–83. He supported the Alliance, and later the merger with the SDP, although he harboured some reservations about the watering down or loss of Liberal philosophy. He was strongly pro-European, a founder member and one-time Chairman of the Liberal European Action Group, a representative at the Königswinter Conference, a member of the Anglo-German Parliamentary Group, for many years a Vice-President of the European-Atlantic Group and President of the British Council of the European Movement between 1986–94. He was Chairman of the Liberal Summer Schools in the 1970s and 1980s and was President of the National Liberal Club, 1982–93, where his portrait hangs in the Smoking Room.

In his leisure time he had a passion for steamships, publishing a book entitled *Clyde Steamers* in 1947, and he loved the music of Gilbert and Sullivan. He was a committed Christian and was an elder of the United Reformed Church. He died in Amersham on 15 June 1997.

Graham Lippiatt

JOHN BANNERMAN (Lord Bannerman) 1901–69

John MacDonald Bannerman was born in the Shawlands district of Glasgow on 1 September 1901. His father, an employee of the Post Office, was a native of the Hebridean island of South Uist. He helped to found the Gaelic cultural organisation, Ceilidh Nan Gaidheal, and Gaelic was the family language throughout Bannerman's youth. This background shaped his life-long political commitment to Scottish Home Rule and to the Highlands and Islands.

Bannerman was educated at Shawlands Academy and Glasgow High School before entering Glasgow University, from which he graduated in 1926. He gained both academic and sporting distinctions. His postgraduate studies took him to Balliol College, Oxford and Cornell University in the United States, during which time he worked with the famous potato specialist, Donald McKelvie, developing a new potato, the Arran Banner. Throughout his academic career he excelled at shinty, soccer and rugby, particularly the last. He won a rugby blue at Oxford and went on to play for Scotland on thirty-seven occasions between 1921 and 1929. He was regarded as the greatest Scottish forward of the 1920s, and contributed to Scotland's 1925 Grand Slam triumph. Later, in 1954–55, Bannerman served as President of the Scottish Rugby Football Union.

On returning from the US, Bannerman took a post as farm manager on an estate at Loch Lomondside, owned by the Duke of Montrose. In October 1931 he married Ray Mundell and the couple settled in the Old Manse, Balmaha. This was to remain Bannerman's base for the rest of his life and, together with his wife, he maintained a hill sheep farm. Bannerman became involved with a tremendous range of voluntary organisations. He was a Forestry Commissioner 1942–57; a member of the Hill Land Commission; Chairman of the National Forest Parks in Scotland; and President of the Gaelic organisation, An Comunn Gaidhealach. He was also a well-known broadcaster and an expert on Gaelic song.

Bannerman's interest in politics developed during the 1930s. His ambition was to give the ordinary people of Scotland, and in particular of the Highlands and Islands, a fair share in the affluent society. Depopulation and unemployment weighed heavily on his mind. The failure of government to see and to act on the very apparent need to provide the basic transport facilities for the Highland people saddened and annoyed him. Poor ferry services and high freight charges stifled even the most enthusiastic individual endeavour. Bannerman fought to turn the government's spotlight on to the Highlands and to assert Scotland's right to look after her own domestic affairs.

Bannerman attended his first meeting of the Scottish Liberal Federation executive committee in March 1938. His energy and ability soon marked him out as a rising star in a struggling organisation. He unsuccessfully contested Argyll in the 1945 general election and Inverness in 1950. The Inverness Liberals were unable to contest the 1951 election because of financial problems, but Bannerman was again offered as the Liberal candidate in the 1954 byelection. He came within 1,331 votes of victory, the best Liberal byelection result since the war. A year later Bannerman came within 966 votes of winning the seat in the general election and, although he lost by over 4,000 votes in 1959, his efforts prepared the ground for Russell Johnston's (q.v.) successful campaign in 1964.

After the Inverness byelection Bannerman became Chairman of the Scottish Liberal Party, a post he held for ten years until 1965. His tireless effort kept the causes of Liberalism and Home Rule before the public eye during the twenty years after the

Second World War. It was during this time that the party's appeal to Highlands voters was sharpened. Bannerman campaigned for a Highlands and Islands Development Board, a central plank of Liberal policy in the mid-1960s, helping to return four Liberals for Highlands and Islands constituencies in 1964 and three in 1966. Bannerman's appeal was not restricted to the far north. In another sensational byelection performance he lost out to Labour in Paisley by only 1,658 votes in 1961. Again, he was unable to win the seat in the following general election.

Bannerman finally entered Parliament on 6 December 1967, as Lord Bannerman of Kildonan, the title taken from the name of the Sutherland village from which his family were driven by the Highlands clearance after the Napoleonic wars. In his maiden speech he declared that, 'as soon as the equivalent house is set up in Edinburgh I shall gladly take the shorter journey'. Unfortunately, he was never able to enjoy that opportunity, for he died in Tidworth, Hampshire, on 10 May 1969. He left two sons and two daughters, one of whom is Ray Michie MP (*q.v.*). His *Memoirs* were published posthumously, edited by John Fowler (Impulse Books, 1972).

Ray Michie MP

TIM BEAUMONT (Lord Beaumont) 1928–

Tim Beaumont's grandfathers were both Liberal members of the 1906 Parliament, his maternal grandfather being one of Asquith's (*q.v.*) chief whips. On his father's side, there is a straight line of MPs going back six generations, although his father was a right-wing Tory of the squirearchical type.

Timothy Wentworth Beaumont was born (an only child) on 22 November 1928. He was educated at Gordonstoun and (after service in the Royal Army Education Corps) at Christchurch, Oxford. After graduation, he entered Westcott House, Cambridge, one of the Church of England's theological colleges, and was ordained in 1955; he then became Assistant Chaplain at St John's Cathedral, Hong Kong and in 1957 he was appointed vicar of a parish church in the colony.

Although he joined the Liberals at Oxford, his service to the party really began in 1959 on his return from Hong Kong. He met Jeremy Thorpe (*q.v.*) at a dance at Buckingham Palace, and (having inherited some money) offered to help the party financially. The party gratefully made him Party Treasurer (one of three), and after that he became – he likes to think on his own merits – honorary Administrative Head of the Liberal Party Organisation.

During the 1960s and 1970s he filled a number of posts within the Liberal Party, including those of Chairman (1967–68) and, after an election in which he fought against the 'official' candidate, President (1969–70). He was nominated by Thorpe as a life peer in 1968 (being unable, as an Anglican priest, to stand for Parliament) and became the party's spokesman in the upper house on education and the arts. Later (as candidate's friend) he helped Clement Freud win the Isle of Ely, and Bill Pitt win Croydon. He was, for once, not on the winning side as John Pardoe's (*q.v.*) agent when David Steel (*q.v.*) won the leadership election in 1976. He was coordinator of the Green Alliance from 1978–80 and Director of Policy Promotion for the Liberal Party from 1980–83, when he joined the executive of Church Action on Poverty.

It is hard for the biographer to keep track of the many strands of Beaumont's life; he has been devoted to many causes – not only the Liberal Party and its successor and the Anglican church, but also to many charitable and politically radical groups, often as chairman or director. These include, as well as those already mentioned, the Albany Trust, Exit, and 'Make Children Happy'. He resigned his orders in 1973, finding it hard to combine a clerical career with a political one; but resumed them in 1984. In 1986 he was appointed vicar of two churches in Kew.

Beaumont is passionately interested in what might be termed the communication of ideas. He has been proprietor, editor and/or contributor to a large number of journals, including *Prism* and the *New Christian Reader*; he edited *The Selective Ego: the diaries of James Agate* and (in lighter vein) *The Liberal Cookbook*. He combined these literary and publishing interests with his commitment to the Liberal Party when he became, for a short time in the 1960s, Chairman of the Liberal Publications Department, and then editor of *New Outlook*; he has also written many booklets, including *The Yellow Brick Road* (1980) and *The End of the Yellow Brick Road* (1992).

These last-mentioned pamphlets reflect his keen interest in green matters. In 1977 he was a founder-member of the Liberal Ecology Group (LEG), and was rash enough to be guarantor of its first bank account, although the guarantee never had to be invoked! Since then he has had many spells on its and its successors' executive committee, and is now one of the Honorary Vice-Presidents of the Green Liberal Democrats.

From 1992–95 he was a member of the Liberal Democrats' Federal Policy Committee, and is currently the Liberal Democrat spokesman in the House of Lords on conservation and the countryside, successfully piloting the Welfare of Broiler Chickens Bill through the Lords in 1996–97. Now one of the party's elder statesmen (on the radical side), he is always pleased to be consulted or asked to speak, especially on the green, social policy, or arts agendas.

He married Mary Rose Wauchope in 1955, and has one son and two daughters. He lives in London.

Tony Beamish

ALAN BEITH MP   1943–

Alan Beith has consistently been a 'safe pair of hands' and a loyal advocate, initially for the Liberal Party and latterly for the Liberal Democrats. His image is one of reliability and competence rather than of flair, though close party colleagues and personal friends are aware of a capacity for humour and for passion that has been sublimated to the decades of maintaining a Liberal presence in unsympathetic circumstances.

His consistent efforts to support the party line with intellectual substance have enabled him to survive when others have fared badly – he was, for instance, the only speaker on the leadership side of the famous 1986 Eastbourne Liberal assembly defence debate to emerge with any credit. Beith's own policy positions, however, are not always within the mainstream of current party thinking, but they are consistent with his background as a committed Christian and Methodist lay preacher. For instance, he has supported curbs on abortion, opposed the slackening of licensing laws, followed a firmer line on censorship, and demurred from the party's pro-Palestinian stance. He has been a defender of the right of individual MPs to 'free votes' on issues of conscience, in which he includes fox hunting, and, although on the hawkish wing on defence issues, his defence of civil rights and his instinctive opposition to centralisation and to abuses of power, statist and capitalist, places him naturally within the Liberal ranks.

Alan James Beith was born on 20 April 1943, to James and Joan Beith of Poynton, Cheshire. He was educated at King's School, Macclesfield, and Balliol and Nuffield Colleges, Oxford (BLitt and MA). In 1966, he took up the post of lecturer in politics at Newcastle University, where he remained until his election to Parliament. He married Barbara Ward in 1965, and the couple had one son and one daughter; Barbara died of cancer in April 1998.

Beith's commitment to liberalism and his involvement in Liberal politics are of long standing and, though not visible in the radical Young Liberal heyday of the 1960s, he had a greater acceptance with the party's grassroots than many parliamentarians, a consequence of his long service as a councillor in the north east. He served on Hexham Rural District Council (1969–74), Corbridge Parish Council (1970–74), and Tynedale District Council (1973–74).

He was elected to Parliament for Berwick-upon-Tweed in a byelection in 1973, with a majority of fifty-seven, and has held the seat in each of the seven general elections since. He became Liberal spokesman on home affairs 1973–76, education 1977–83, constitutional reform 1983–87, and foreign affairs 1985–87; he was Alliance foreign affairs spokesman during 1987. He was also Chief Whip 1976–85, and Deputy Leader of the Liberal Party 1985–88.

His nine years as Chief Whip encompassed a period of immense strain on party unity, covering both the Lib-Lab Pact and the Alliance. Having in addition to nurse what was, at least initially, a highly marginal seat, he demonstrated his capacity for hard work and his commitment to party solidarity. Although the criticism that he was too embroiled in parliamentary practice and tactics and consequently tended to neglect the linkages with the party outside the House of Commons, failed to take into consideration the virtual impossibility of absenting himself from Westminster, it was true that his métier was and is much more naturally that of parliamentarian, and his milieu that of the House. He has, for instance, always enjoyed his responsibility for the House of Commons Commission – the Commons staffs' employing body – and current reports that he hankers after the Speakership would be in character.

During his period as Chief Whip he successfully hid the mutual antipathy between him and David Steel (q.v.), the party leader, even when Steel attempted to resign as leader after the 1983 election, an event presented, after much pressure and machination on Beith's – and others' – part as Steel's 'sabbatical'. A leadership election at that point would arguably have been more advantageous to Beith's definite ambition to lead the party than his later contest for the leadership of the merged party, and his reticence in the party's then interest should be noted. Though later accused of having prior knowledge of the 'dead parrot' policy document which almost sank the merger negotiations, and of failing for personal reasons to warn Steel of its dangers in order to undermine him, no evidence of this was ever produced.

In the post-Alliance merger negotiations Beith was typically a capable and stalwart defender of the Liberal Party's intellectual and philosophical primacy, right up to the virtual dissolution of the SDP's negotiating team after a number of resignations, whereupon he led the move to offer the SDP more concessions than were arguably required, thus diluting the eventual compromise unnecessarily. In the subsequent leadership election for the Social and Liberal Democrats, the new party decided by a large majority that it preferred Paddy Ashdown's (q.v.) style to Beith's known qualities. Beith has loyally served the Liberal Democrats since then in a number of important portfolios, including Treasury (1988–94) and, since 1994, home affairs; since 1992, he has been Deputy Leader. He was appointed a member of the Privy Council in 1992.

Given Beith's consistent efforts to provide the Liberal Party, and latterly the Liberal Democrats, with more intellectual rigour it is perhaps curious that he has only produced one book in direct support of this task: *The Case for the Liberal Party and the Alliance* (Longman, 1983) published for the 1983 general election; and also one pamphlet, *The Fullness of Freedom* (Hebden Royd Publications, 1987), produced in the run-up to merger and the new party's leadership election. He has also contributed to two books on religion and politics: Alan Beith, John Gummer and Eric Heffer, *Faith in Politics* (1987) and a chapter in John Muir (ed.), *Divided Loyalties – Shared Beliefs* (1994).

Michael Meadowcroft

JEREMY BENTHAM   1748–1832

Jeremy Bentham, the English moral philosopher, jurist, social reformer, political economist and founding father of modern utilitarianism was born in London on 15 February 1748. His ambitious father, also a lawyer, had plans for young Jeremy to become Lord Chancellor of England, not only making his name but also his fortune in the process. Despite showing early promise of fulfilling his father's dream by going up to

Oxford at the age of twelve, and seeking admission to Lincoln's Inn only three years later, Bentham was soon drawn from the path of professional ambition by grander intellectual pursuits shaped by his wide reading of Enlightenment thinkers such as Locke, Montesquieu, Hume, Adam Smith (*q.v.*), Helvetius, D'Alembert and Beccaria. Though called to the bar in 1769, he never practised law but instead turned his attention to cultivating his true genius, one he had acquired through his familiarity with thinkers of the European Enlightenment, namely, 'rearing the fabric of felicity by the hand of reason and law'.

Although Bentham remained in England almost all his life, with the exception of a short trip to Russia in the mid 1780s, his intellectual and political influence was international. He corresponded with most of the notable figures of his day in Europe, the fledgling United States of America and many of the emerging Latin American states, and supported movements for national liberation in Greece and for liberalisation and constitutional reform in Spain and Portugal. From his home at Queen's Square Place in Westminster, Bentham provided philosophical arguments, political pamphlets, reform projects, constitutions, and model prisons, along with a host of other schemes for rational improvement, for an international audience – a word he is credited with introducing to the language. He was also the intellectual force behind a group of early nineteenth-century reformers – the 'Philosophic Radicals' – and inspired the likes of Edwin Chadwick (a one-time secretary) in his work on Poor Law amendment and public health policies.

Through the influence of Chadwick and others, Bentham has often been credited with initiating the Victorian revolution in government. By the end of the nineteenth century, it had become common for writers such as Dicey, Maine, Spencer and Leslie Stephen to characterise the period as an age of Benthamism. This association of Bentham and utilitarianism with a more activist conception of the state has led many to challenge his liberal credentials. Bentham, for many later nineteenth-century liberals, was an advocate of collectivism, rather than the classical liberalism associated with Scottish political economy and laissez-faire. Yet, for reform-minded New Liberals inspired by T. H. Green (*q.v.*), Bentham was still wedded to an outdated individualism.

Distinguishing Bentham's thought from his legacy is a more complex matter. Bentham was first and foremost a utilitarian. He believed that the goal of government and legislation should be 'the greatest happiness of the greatest number'. He began his career as a legislative reformer concerned to turn law into a science of human felicity and to dispense with the obscurities of English common law. In the early part of his career, Bentham was unconcerned about what form of government was best suited to realising such legal reforms. Indeed, in true enlightenment style, he was happy to trust in a benevolent monarch or despot. For Bentham, there was no necessary connection between utilitarianism and traditional liberal commitments to constitutionalism, separation of powers, consent theory or natural rights.

Bentham's conversion to a more liberal policy of radical constitutional reform began in earnest in the years after 1809, following his association with James Mill and as a result of his own experiences of trying to persuade government to adopt utilitarian social reforms. During the last decades of the eighteenth century, Bentham had turned his attention from legal reform to social policy, in particular political economy, penal policy and how to deal with paupers. In 1791, he began a plan to have his model prison, the panopticon, adopted as a response to the growing crisis in penal policy. The government was originally interested, but the implementation of the 1794 Act was frustrated by the Spencer and Grosvenor families, who objected to a prison near their London estates. After more than twelve years and considerable expense Bentham saw the interest of powerful families frustrating both rational reform and the will of Parliament. He experienced a similar frustration with his policy for reform of the Scottish judicial system.

This deliberate frustration of reform by vested interests led Bentham to abandon trust in government and turn his attention to constitutional reform as a way of controlling government, taking it out of the hands of narrow family, group or professional interests and making it accountable to the public. The last decades of Bentham's life were devoted to constitutional reform as part of the construction of a codified legal system for a modern state. Central to this complete code of law was representative democracy and the widest possible franchise as a means of holding government accountable to the public interest. Alongside representative democracy, Bentham also advocated the maximum publicity and transparency of government so that the electorate could serve its essential checking function on government.

Bentham's enduring legacy is a complex one. On the one hand, he is associated with utilitarian projects for social reform which suggested an activist conception of the state and which attracted charges of collectivism. On the other, his constitutional theory, with its suspicion of big government and its democratic commitment to accountability and openness, suggests a liberal. Bentham died in 1832, immediately following the passing of the Great Reform Act. Though modest compared to his radical proposals, this began the process of the slow and painful democratisation of the British polity that Bentham had come to regard as essential in order to govern in the interest of the public.

Bentham has been heavily written about, both in biographies and in studies of his political thought; he has the distinction of attracting numerous works in languages other than English. Two good relatively recent biographies are R. Harrison, *Bentham* (Routledge and Kegan Paul, 1983) and J. Dinwiddy, *Bentham* (OUP, 1989). A perspective from outside Britain is provided by S. Mukherjee and S. Ramaswamy (eds.), *Jeremy Bentham 1748–1832*, (Deep and Deep, New Delhi, 1995).

Paul Kelly

ROBERT BERNAYS   1902–45

Robert Bernays died in January 1945, aged forty-two. He left a young wife and two baby boys. In his short life he achieved a great deal, largely through his own efforts. A Liberal who wore his party colours lightly, he is better defined as a creature of a distinct political regime: the National Government of the 1930s. In this environment he shone, but it is doubtful whether he would have done so under the more rigid terms of party politics in the post-war years

Born on 6 May 1902, the third son of a north London clergyman, Bernays had neither family connections nor money. Leaving Rossall in 1920, he taught for a while at Solihull and went up to Worcester College, Oxford in 1922. There he became a Liberal of the Lloyd George persuasion, was President of the Union in 1925, toured the United States with the University's debating team, and drove a train during the General Strike. Then, having failed to enter the Sudan civil service, he became a journalist with the *Daily News*. Journalism formed the basis of his living until his appointment to junior office in 1937.

Defeated as Liberal candidate for Rugby in 1929, the newspaper merger of 1930 which produced the *News Chronicle* left him out of a job. Luck landed him in India in 1931, where as a freelance he covered Gandhi's release from prison and his talks with the Viceroy, Lord Irwin. From this came his first book, *Naked Fakir*. Later that year he was hurriedly adopted as Liberal candidate for North Bristol in the run-up to the general election. Standing as a 'Samuelite' free-trading Liberal, and helped by his sister Lucy, he benefited from the greatest landslide in British democratic history by winning the seat with a majority of 13,000.

Bernays was proud to represent one of England's great cities and thoroughly enjoyed being an MP. But he realised that he was where he was courtesy of Conservative forbearance and took care not to displease the Bristol Tories. Quickly forgetting attachments to free trade he did not 'cross the floor' into opposition with the Samuelite Liberals in 1933 and accordingly broke many old friendships. Contact with Sir Herbert Samuel (*q.v.*), Dingle Foot (*q.v.*) and 'Crinks' Harcourt Johnstone was severed. However he produced his second book, *Special Correspondent* (1934), in which he wrote with vivid pertinacity on the Nazi regime in Germany. He also kept a diary and wrote weekly letters to his sister Lucy, now married and living in Brazil. These, recently published in edited form, as well as forming a personal and social record of the times also constitute the fullest, least jaundiced eye-witness account of the 1931 Parliament. His zest for politics coupled to a journalist's training ensured that any telling phrase or pithy saying, whether from incidents in the House – where habitually he sat next to Winston Churchill (*q.v.*) – or from smoking-room gossip, were recorded. He worked and played hard. Though unlucky in love, the theatre, the dinner table, or a weekend at Lady Astor's Cliveden were all grist to his diaristic mill. Less doctrinally pure than many Liberals would have liked, most of his political friends were by the mid-1930s Conservatives. But for an agreeable young man making his own way under the National Government regime, there were few other choices left to him. He was a man of his times.

Returned to Parliament in the 1935 general election, Bernays took steps to realise his ambitions. In 1936 he became a Liberal National, that faction of the Liberal Party led by Sir John Simon (*q.v.*), and thus joined the queue for office. He did not have to wait long. When Neville Chamberlain became prime minister in May 1937 he was appointed Parliamentary Secretary to the Minister of Health, Sir Kingsley Wood. Soon he was working under his friend and patron Walter Elliot. Like Elliot, Bernays was much troubled by Eden's resignation in February 1938 and the subsequent course of British foreign policy. A conscience-stricken 'wobbler' over Munich, he remained at his post despite the urgings to resign of his friend Harold Nicolson. His reward for this was to suffer a move to the Ministry of Transport in July 1939, where he served as junior to Euan Wallace until May 1940. Upon the formation of Churchill's coalition government he returned to the back benches, as his office was needed for a Labour minister to fill.

Thus Bernays' political career was brought to an effective end. He came in with Chamberlain and went out with him. The beneficiary of one form of coalitionism was the casualty of a different variant. But Bernays was neither bitter nor downcast. Made deputy regional commissioner for southern civil defence, he was at the nerve centre during the bombing of Portsmouth and Southampton. In 1942 he made three decisions. He married Nancy Britton, the daughter of a constituent, and resigned his deputy commissionership. Joining the army, he took a commission in the Royal Engineers, becoming by the end of 1944 a captain. In January 1945 he participated in a deputation of MPs visiting British forces in the Mediterranean. The plane carrying him and others from Italy to Greece crashed off Brindisi. There were no survivors.

Skin-deep though Bernays' attachment to Liberalism may have been, he was a more successful political operator during the 1930s than most contemporaries bearing the same party label. Intelligent and sensitive, he lived always in eager hope. Public life was the poorer for his early death, as his diaries and letters of the 1930s, edited by Nick Smart (*The Diaries and Letters of Robert Bernays 1932–39: An Insider's Account of the House of Commons* (Edwin Mellen, 1996)) indicate. The record he left might not tell the story of a sound party politician. It nonetheless chronicles a man's passionate engagement with national politics during an exciting period.

Nick Smart

PETER BESSELL   1921–85

Peter Joseph Bessell is chiefly remembered for his rather pathetic performance as the main prosecution witness at the trial of Jeremy Thorpe (*q.v.*) in 1979. Yet the public humiliation that he suffered during the final years of his life was in stark contrast to the period during the 1950s and 1960s when he was regarded as one of the Liberal Party's rising stars. He was an early advocate of community politics and his professional approach to electioneering enabled him to win Bodmin from the Conservatives in 1964, a seat which he held until his retirement from active politics in 1970. In association with Thorpe he also played a crucial role in reviving the party's fortunes in the south west of England. Their success re-established the Liberal Party as the main alternative to the Conservatives in the region, a legacy that remains important to this day.

Bessell was born at Bath on 24 August 1921. He was the only son of Joseph and Olive (née Hawkins) Bessell, and received a private education at Lynwyd School. From 1939 to 1970 he was a Congregational lay preacher. He served as a Ministry of Information lecturer for British and allied forces during the Second World War. In 1942 he married Joyce Thomas; following her death in 1947, he married Pauline Colledge, the mother of his two children. By this time he was establishing his reputation as a successful businessman; by 1955 he was the managing director of a dry-cleaning firm, but he gradually acquired other business interests and by the early 1970s was a property broker with offices in London and New York.

He made his first attempt to enter Parliament in May 1955, when he contested Torquay as a Liberal. Although he came a poor third with just 14 per cent of the vote, the death of the Conservative member, Charles Williams, led to a byelection in which he was able to increase the Liberal poll to 24 per cent. Even at this early stage of his political career, Bessell proved himself adept at exploiting local problems. While his opponents concentrated solely on national issues, he presented himself as the 'local man' who would defend the interests of the community. The rise in the Liberal vote had regional significance since it generated the momentum which led to the victories of Mark Bonham Carter (q.v.) at the Torrington byelection in 1958 and of Jeremy Thorpe at North Devon in 1959. The result also had wider implications since, as Vernon Bogdanor has written, Torquay 'began the first period of Liberal runs of mid-term byelection support which have subsequently become a regular feature of periods of Conservative government'.

In 1956 Bessell was selected as the prospective parliamentary candidate for Bodmin. Although there was a strong Liberal tradition in this Cornish constituency, the party had not won an election there since 1929. Bessell introduced a new professional approach to the party's constituency organisation, while his American-style campaigns in 1959 and 1964 focused on his international reputation and his personal ability to attract new industries to the area. This resulted in a considerable increase in the party's share of the vote (from 28 per cent in 1955 to 49 per cent by 1964), and Bessell was elected to represent the seat in 1964 and 1966. His success also enhanced the party's credibility in neighbouring seats, and contributed to the victories of John Pardoe (q.v.) (North Cornwall, 1966) and David Penhaligon (q.v.) (Truro, October 1974).

As MP for Bodmin he sat on the Estimates Committee from 1964–66 and again from 1966–67. He was also a member of the Parliamentary Commission to South Vietnam in 1967 and served on the Select Committees on Procedure from 1964 to 1965, Agriculture in 1967 and Vehicle Excise Duty in 1969. However, his maverick views ensured that he was isolated from mainstream Liberal politics. During the late 1960s Bessell disagreed with his party colleagues on a number of issues, including Vietnam, Rhodesia and the Common Market, and he admitted that he was 'a very bad party man'. Yet it was this strong sense of independence which, according to *The Times* in 1966, appealed to his constituents. The 1960s witnessed a growing tide of regional discontent in Cornwall. There was a widespread belief that central government was indifferent to the economic problems of the area, while the prospect of Britain's entry into the Common Market was viewed with great foreboding by many small farmers and fishermen. Bessell recognised the political advantages of exploiting these concerns. He even became a member of Mebyon Kernow, an organisation committed to domestic self-government in Cornwall which occasionally stood parliamentary candidates itself.

In 1970 he moved to the United States as an investment consultant. By 1974, however, he was faced with serious financial problems following the collapse of one of his London companies. His British and American debts came to over £250,000, and he 'disappeared' to Mexico in order to avoid his creditors. A few days later, he returned to the United States, accompanied by Diana Kelly, who later became his third wife. Bessell kept a low profile over the next few years, but in February 1978 he was once again attracting public attention when he claimed that he had worked as an agent of the US government while still a MP. Later that year he returned to Britain where, with his allegations about a plot to kill Norman Scott, he figured as the chief prosecution witness at the trial of Jeremy Thorpe. Bessell's testimony was dismissed as 'pure fantasy' by the defence. He admitted that he was a compulsive liar, and his credibility was further undermined by revelations that he would profit financially from the case by publishing his story in a national newspaper. Bessell returned to the United States after Thorpe was acquitted in June 1979 and wrote his own account of the affair, *Cover Up*, which was published in 1981. He died at his home in Los Angeles on 27 November 1985.

Garry Tregidga

WILLIAM BEVERIDGE (Lord Beveridge) 1879–1963

William Henry Beveridge was born in Rangpur, an Indian station in Bengal, on 5 March 1879. He was the second child and first son of Henry Beveridge, a district sessions judge in the Indian Civil Service, by his second wife, Annette Susannah Ackroyd, who had travelled to India, originally in response to a call to bring liberal education to Indian women.

At the age of five, Beveridge was left, with his two sisters and a German governess, at a small Unitarian boarding school in Southport. Annette Beveridge returned after two years to find her children undernourished, unhappy and subdued. Thereafter, private tutors in India took charge of his education until the family's permanent return to England in 1890, when he was sent to Kent House, a preparatory school, as a weekly boarder. In the summer of 1892, he won a scholarship to Charterhouse, where he spent the next five years. He excelled in classics and mathematics, but neither of these subjects captured his imagination, and he was bullied for his lack of sporting ability. Although he acquired the habits of hard work and meticulous accuracy, he was later to complain that his life at Charterhouse had been intellectually and emotionally barren.

Beveridge went up to Balliol College, Oxford, in 1897, initially studying mathematics but switching after a year to classics. He developed a wider social circle, which included Richard Denman, a young historian with ambitions to enter liberal politics, and R. H. Tawney, with whom he shared a growing interest in social reform, fuelled by his belief that the main stumbling block to reform was a lack of precise sociological information.

Upon his graduation, in 1901, with first class honours in *literae humaniores*, Beveridge embarked on a legal career. He studied at the chambers of a London commercial barrister for several terms, and was awarded a prize fellowship from University College, Oxford, in 1902. It was not long, however, before he developed a strong dislike for the work of a barrister, which he saw as having nothing to do with any real problems or difficulties. In the face of fierce parental objection, he accepted, in April 1902, the position of sub-warden at Toynbee Hall.

There, Beveridge fell under the spell of Sidney and Beatrice Webb and was strongly influenced by their theories of administrative reform. He became active in the old age pensions movement, the free school meals campaign and began important work on the problem of unemployment. During the 1904–05 depression, he helped establish the London Unemployed Fund. In 1905, he became a leading member of the Central (Unemployed) Body and began to campaign for a national system of labour exchanges to eliminate casual unemployment.

At the end of the year, he moved from Toynbee Hall to a post as leader writer on 'social problems' with the Conservative daily, the *Morning Post*. In his articles, he argued for a far-reaching programme of 'social organisation' to be implemented by a centralised and interventionist state, and advocated a dual policy of labour exchanges and state insurance to solve the unemployment problem.

At the end of 1907, the Webbs introduced Beveridge to Winston Churchill (*q.v.*), the newly appointed Liberal President of the Board of Trade. In July 1908, Beveridge became a non-established civil servant in the Board of Trade, at a time when the Liberal government was setting out an ambitious plan of social legislation. Over the next three years he assisted the Permanent Secretary, Sir Hubert Llewellyn Smith, in drawing up the Labour Exchanges Act of 1909 and the second part of the 1911 National Insurance Act. In 1909, he became a permanent civil servant, with responsibility for the labour exchanges system, and by 1913, he had reached the rank of Assistant Secretary.

During the First World War, Beveridge fully supported Lloyd George's (q.v.) position that fighting the war required a total commitment of national resources, even if this involved a suspension of civil liberties. With Llewellyn Smith he drafted the Munitions of War Act in 1915, which severely limited wartime collective bargaining and imposed a system of quasi-military discipline upon civilian workers in munitions; and in the summer of 1916, he drafted a new Unemployment Insurance Act, which extended insurance to all workers employed in war production. These actions led to his unpopularity with the labour movement, and he was thus excluded from the new Ministry of Labour, created at the end of 1916, moving instead to the Ministry of Food as Second Secretary, responsible for rationing and price control. Early in 1919, he was appointed KCB and became Permanent Secretary to the Ministry of Food – at the age of thirty-nine, one of the youngest ever to reach that rank.

In June 1919, Beveridge was offered the post of Director of the London School of Economics by his old friend and mentor, Sidney Webb, and duly resigned his civil service position. He spent eighteen years at the LSE, which – despite acrimony and controversy over his despotic and high-handed administrative methods – he succeeded in establishing as a leading centre for the social sciences. As Vice-Chancellor of London University between 1926 and 1928, he also laid the foundations for a new centralised university and was responsible for acquiring and raising funds for the university's Bloomsbury site.

At the same time, in the public arena, Beveridge participated in the Liberal Summer School movement (1922–24), served as a member of the Royal Commission on the Coal Industry (1925–26), campaigned for Eleanor Rathbone's family allowances scheme in the late 1920s, and chaired the Unemployment Insurance Statutory Committee from 1934.

In 1937, Beveridge decided to leave the LSE to accept the mastership of University College, Oxford, and was elected a fellow of the British Academy in the same year. He devoted himself to the study of unemployment, but was increasingly anxious to return to some more central role in public administration. When the Second World War broke out, Beveridge expected to be given the task of controlling and directing civilian manpower and military recruitment, but it was not until a year later that Ernest Bevin invited him to carry out a survey of manpower requirements.

In December 1940, he was appointed Under-Secretary in the Ministry of Labour responsible for listing 'reserved' occupations, and made clear his determination to control the wartime manpower programme. His reputation for bad relations with the unions from the First World War, however, made this undesirable, and he was put in charge instead of an obscure inter-departmental inquiry into the coordination of the social services. Beveridge knew he was being marginalised and accepted the appointment with tears in his eyes. Yet it was the report arising from this inquiry that was to make his name as the father of the welfare state.

Social Insurance and Allied Services was published in December 1942 and outlined a vision of society's battle against 'the five giants', idleness, ignorance, disease, squalor and want. The report proposed a system of cash benefits, financed by equal contributions from the worker, the employer and the state, together with a public assistance safety-net. Underlying this system were three assumptions, all necessary, Beveridge argued, for the abolition of want: a national health service available to all, tax-financed family allowances and a commitment to state action to reduce unemployment (further developed in his book, *Full Employment in a Free Society* (1944)).

The Beveridge Report met with a cool initial response from Whitehall and the Churchill Government, but was immensely popular with the British public. Beveridge became a public figure, addressing large audiences throughout the country to canvass his proposals. After a major parliamentary revolt in early 1943, his plan was adopted as the blueprint for the Attlee Government's legislation of 1944–48, laying the foundations of the British welfare state for the next forty years.

Until 1944, although he had been a participant in the Liberal Summer School movement, Beveridge had had no formal connection with any political party. Almost immediately after the report was published, however, he was invited to stand as a Liberal candidate for the parliamentary seat of Dunfermline by Lady Glen-Coats, an official of the Scottish Liberal Federation. He showed some interest, provided he could have 'sufficient independence of position' and not be tied too closely to official Liberal policies; but by then the Dunfermline opportunity had passed.

In August 1944, he was adopted as the Liberal candidate for the Berwick-upon-Tweed byelection and was forced to resign his mastership of University College. Berwick was a Liberal stronghold, a border constituency of farmers and small tradesmen, which had consistently voted Liberal throughout the inter-war years; Beveridge was elected with six times as many votes as his only opponent, a right-wing Independent (no other parties fought the seat under the wartime electoral truce). He then moved to Tuggal Hall, a manor house in the constituency, and devoted himself to local affairs and the nation-wide revival of Liberalism. He took his seat in the Commons in October and made his maiden speech on the government's Social Security White Paper. He spoke frequently over the next few months, supporting electoral reform, the development of small-scale industry and criticising the powers of the proposed Security Council of the United Nations.

When the 1945 general election was called, Beveridge was regarded by many Liberals as their chief electoral asset. He was placed in charge of the Liberal campaign despite the fact that his formal experience of electioneering had been minimal. The Liberals won only twelve seats in the election, however, and Beveridge lost Berwick to the Conservatives. He was elevated to the peerage as the first Baron

Beveridge by Clement Attlee in 1946, sitting on the Liberal benches. In his old age, he became leader of the Liberals in the Lords, chairman of the Newton Aycliffe New Town Corporation (1947–52) and chairman of the committee that opposed commercial broadcasting (1949–51).

Beveridge retired from public life in 1954 and moved, with his wife, Janet (Jessy) Mair, to Oxford. He died at his home on 16 March 1963 and was buried in Throckington churchyard, on the Northumbrian moors. His barony became extinct upon his death. His last words were: 'I have a thousand things to do'.

Beveridge's autobiography, *Power and Influence,* was published in 1953. The best biographies are Jose Harris, *William Beveridge: A Biography* (1977), and Harris' entry in the *Dictionary of National Biography*; and Janet Beveridge, *Beveridge and his Plan* (1954).

Eugenia Low

AUGUSTINE BIRRELL   1850–1933

Although he ironically bemoaned his mid-Victorian background, Augustine Birrell was in many ways a typical Liberal of the time. Like the Gladstone clan, Birrell's family hailed from Scotland, where the Liberal tradition was strong. Birrell was brought up as a Baptist, in an age when nonconformity and Liberalism were almost synonymous. His early years were spent in and around Liverpool which had strong Gladstonian associations; indeed, the north west as a whole experienced something of a Liberal revival in the late Victorian and Edwardian eras. He was, in addition, one of a group of gifted barristers who entered the House of Commons in the 1880s, and who came to dominate the Edwardian party.

Birrell was born in Wavertree, Cheshire, on 19 January 1850, and was educated at Amersham Hall School, Caversham, and Trinity Hall, Cambridge (BA, law and history, 1872). He served at first in a solicitor's office in Liverpool, but was eventually (in 1875) called to the bar. He developed a chancery practice, and took silk in 1895. But his earnings were always modest, and he was glad to accept an appointment as the Quain Professor of Law at University College London in 1896; he held the chair until 1899.

In some ways this academic foray suited his temperament, for Birrell had scholarly and literary inclinations which political office only served to frustrate. He published two successful legal works during his professorial career. He also built up a reputation in the 1880s and after as an essayist and biographer: his *Obiter Dicta* (1884) and biography of *Charlotte Bronte* (1885) were amongst the numerous volumes which won him contemporary acclaim. There was an inevitable cost to be paid for this multi-faceted achievement: in his autobiography (*Things Past Redress*, 1937) Birrell blithely confessed that he found a Dublin publisher's catalogue more beguiling than his official papers.

After unsuccessful contests at Liverpool, Walton (1885) and Widnes (1886), Birrell entered the House of Commons in 1889 as member for West Fife; H. H. Asquith (*q.v.*), a rising star within the party, represented the neighbouring constituency of East Fife. Birrell earned a reputation as an efficient debater, and in 1900 was prevailed upon – 'far too hastily', he later admitted – by Sir Henry Campbell-Bannerman (*q.v.*) to contest the difficult territory of Manchester North East (where he was roundly beaten). When next he returned to the Commons, in January 1906 (after serving for four years as President of the National Liberal Federation), it was as member for Bristol North, and as a minister in the new Liberal government.

He was briefly President of the Board of Education (December 1905 – January 1907). The key legislative initiative of his tenure, the Education Bill (1906), was eviscerated in the House of Lords. But his agile defence of the measure in the Commons had been noted by Campbell-Bannerman, now Prime Minister; and he was promoted to the Chief Secretaryship for Ireland, in succession to James Bryce. He held this office until May 1916.

In Dublin Birrell substantially modified the strategies of his predecessors, who had often tried to cultivate the centre ground in Irish politics. Instead Birrell looked for a more direct accommodation with the leaders of the Irish Parliamentary Party, and offered a series of legislative concessions. The Irish Universities Act (1908) helped to resolve the sectarian clash over higher education by effectively partitioning off the different traditions into distinct universities; the Catholic and Nationalist interest, hitherto badly served by the higher education system, won a new National University of Ireland. A Land Act (1909) was designed to make government-sponsored land purchase schemes less expensive, as well as to address Nationalist criticisms of an earlier measure, the Wyndham Act (1903). Birrell's law now offered a relatively poor deal to landlords, and created some limited provision for the compulsory purchase of holdings.

But this was perhaps the high point of Birrell's ministerial career. He had successfully maintained a close relationship between the Liberals and the Irish Party through a period when a major grant of devolution seemed unlikely. The constitutional upheavals of 1910–11 restored the centrality of home rule for Liberals; and a third attempt to create a devolved administration in Dublin was launched by the party in April 1912. But Birrell's importance was slipping, as Asquith (now prime minister) took over the political handling of the developing crisis in Ulster, and as able younger colleagues (like Herbert Samuel, *q.v.*) took responsibility for some of the more technical aspects of the Home Rule measure. By 1913 Lloyd George (*q.v.*) was emerging as Asquith's chief lieutenant on major Irish issues. Birrell was sidelined into day-to-day administrative affairs, which held little interest for him. And even here the Irish leaders (who were widely seen as the government of Ireland in waiting) were exercising a growing influence.

The first two years of the Great War saw the rapid spread of a militant separatist conspiracy in Ireland, which culminated in an armed uprising in Dublin in Easter week, 1916. Birrell was held to account (and with some justification): his administration had neglected the machinery for the gathering of political intelligence, and had long tolerated the existence of rival political armies in Ireland. By extension, the Easter Rising reflected a failure of imagination: Birrell could not accept that rebellion remained part of the political armoury of Irish nationalism.

Birrell's reputation has been decided, and damned, by the Rising. His humiliating departure from Dublin in May 1916 has overshadowed his earlier successes. Nor have Birrell's advocates been helped by his discursive and sometimes flippant autobiography. But the substance of his achievement should not be overlooked: he was the longest-serving Chief Secretary for Ireland in the history of the union, and the author of several substantial initiatives in hitherto intractable areas of policy. His essentially Gladstonian analysis of the challenge of Irish government looked, from the perspective of 1912, to be a remarkable success. But he was unfairly neglected by senior party figures in London; his victories during the first five years of his tenure of the Chief Secretaryship went largely unrecognised by Asquith. And exhaustion brought the relaxation of his political grip: his long and arduous years in office took their toll, as did the protracted (and ultimately fatal) illness of his wife. His failure in Ireland reflected a broader and long-standing problem for British Liberalism: it reflected a destructive tension between the party's progressivism and the need, when in power, to sustain a highly centralised and authoritarian administration in Ireland.

After 1916 Birrell retreated into private life and to his extended family; he retired from Parliament in 1918. He had been twice married: his first wife, Margaret Mirrielees, died in childbirth in October 1879 only thirteen months after their wedding. He married Eleanor Tennyson in 1888; this proved to be a long and happy partnership, broken only in 1915 with Eleanor's death from a brain tumour. There were two sons from this second union.

Augustine Birrell died in London on 20 November 1933. Perhaps his greatest personal and political failing was not, as is frequently alleged, that he was indolent; it was rather that he had a dangerous capacity for wishful thinking. Certainly his memoirs suggest a genial if thin-skinned figure who tended to retreat from the buffeting currents of Irish politics. At first this disengagement seemed to be carefully calculated; but the Easter Rising exposed the reality.

Birrell's memoirs, *Things Past Redress*, were published posthumously by Faber in 1937. His career in Ireland is examined by Leon O'Broin in *The Chief Secretary: Augustine Birrell and Ireland, 1907–16* (1969). A sympathetic re-evaluation is offered by Patricia

Jalland in 'A Liberal Chief Secretary and the Irish Question: Augustine Birrell, 1907–14', *Historical Journal* 19:2 (1976). Also of interest are Patricia Jalland, *The Liberals and Ireland: The Ulster Question in British Politics to 1914* (1980) and Eunan O'Halpin, *The Decline of the Union: British Government in Ireland, 1892–1920* (1987).

Alvin Jackson

MARK BONHAM CARTER (Lord Bonham Carter)   1922–94

Mark Raymond Bonham Carter was born on 11 February 1922, the son of Violet Asquith (*q.v.*) (daughter of the Prime Minister H. H. Asquith, *q.v.*), and of Sir Maurice Bonham Carter, who had been Asquith's private secretary from 1908–16. He shared the Liberal beliefs, as well as the intellectual and political gifts, of his Asquithian heritage, but sadly not the Liberal age. He was committed to the cause of liberalism and although not able to exercise this commitment as he wished, in government, he found many other outlets for it.

He was educated at Winchester and won a scholarship to study PPE at Balliol College, Oxford. His university career was interrupted, however, by the onset of war, and in 1941 he joined the Grenadier Guards. In March 1943 he took part in an ill-planned battle on the Mareth Line in Tunisia. There he was captured and sent to a prisoner-of-war camp in Italy, from where he escaped; he was mentioned in despatches. He walked five hundred miles until he reached British lines. Italians daily risked their lives to provide him with refuge, and he retained a life-long love of Italy.

Bonham Carter stood unsuccessfully for Barnstaple in 1945. After the election he returned to finish his studies at Balliol, followed by a year spent as Commonwealth Fund Fellow at the University of Chicago. On his return he joined William Collins and pursued a distinguished career as a publisher, being responsible for the translation into English and publication of *Dr Zhivago*.

In 1958 he returned to active Liberal politics, attracted by the new impetus created by Jo Grimond's (*q.v.*) leadership. Standing in the Torrington byelection, he won a spectacular victory – the first Liberal byelection victory since the 1920s and the harbinger of many to come. He lost the seat in the general election of 1959, and failed to regain it in 1964; had he returned to the House of Commons he would have been a strong future candidate for the party leadership. Nevertheless, throughout Grimond's period of leadership, he was a central figure in Liberal politics, particularly as a member of the influential Organisation Committee.

In 1966 he became the first chairman of the Race Relations Board. Here he found a role and an outlet for his liberal and political gifts. The task was not an easy one; it was the era of a liberalising Labour government but also of Enoch Powell. In 1971, the Race Relations Board and the Community Relations Council were amalgamated and Bonham Carter chaired the new Community Relations Commission until 1977.

His political interests were not confined to domestic issues. A committed European, he was a member of the UK delegation to the Council of Europe 1958–59. He was joint Chairman of the Anglo-Polish Round Table conferences from 1971 until the liberation of Poland from Communist domination made this forum redundant.

Alongside politics he was passionate about the arts; he continued a connection with publishing up until his death; he was a Director of the Royal Opera House, Covent Garden, from 1958–82; Governor of The Royal Ballet 1960–94 (Chairman from 1985); and Vice-Chairman of the BBC from 1975–80 (he was vetoed from becoming Chairman by Margaret Thatcher). He was a regular book reviewer on subjects as various as Marilyn Monroe, cricket, ballet, and the more obvious issues of race relations, broadcasting and politics.

He was an enthusiastic supporter of the Liberal Party's alliance with the SDP and its ultimate merger, and although he did not fight another parliamentary seat after 1964, he was an active campaigner for those who did. In 1986 David Steel (*q.v.*) made Bonham Carter a life peer; he became Baron Bonham-Carter of Yarnbury. Finally back at Westminster, he was at home and, to quote Lord Jenkins of Hillhead (*q.v.*), 'his critical intelligence made him an exceptionally effective critic of government politics'. In 1988 he was made Liberal Democrat foreign affairs spokesman, and his last campaign was to introduce a private member's bill to give British citizenship to members of the non-Chinese ethnic minorities in Hong Kong. This eventually became law just before the handover of the colony to China, sadly after Bonham Carter's death.

He was married in 1955 to Leslie Nast, the daughter of Condé Nast, the American publisher who founded *Vogue, Vanity Fair* and associated magazines. Nast had a daughter by a previous marriage, and together they had three more daughters; he was an immensely fond and dedicated father to all four. He died on 4 September 1994 of a sudden heart attack, in his beloved Italy.

Jane Bonham Carter

VIOLET BONHAM CARTER   1887–1969

Violet Bonham Carter was born in Hampstead on 15 April 1887 as Helen Violet Asquith, the daughter of Herbert Henry Asquith (*q.v.*) and his first wife Helen Melland. In 1891 Violet's mother died of typhoid fever, and in 1894 Asquith married Margot Tennant (*q.v.*). At the time of Violet's birth, Asquith had just entered the House of Commons. His ascent was rapid: in 1892 he became Home Secretary in Gladstone's (*q.v.*) last administration, in 1905 Chancellor of the Exchequer and in 1908 Prime Minister. Violet's lifetime covered the zenith and the nadir of the Liberal Party and she occupied a ringside seat.

Educated at home, and 'finished' in Dresden and Paris, she was, despite this lack of a formal education, a woman of formidable intellect. She was a passionate Liberal, and her father's 'champion redoubtable' (Winston Churchill's (*q.v.*) characterisation): she worshipped him and he depended upon her. After his fall from power she became his standard bearer, discovering her own considerable gifts as an orator as she fought his Paisley campaigns. She continued after Asquith's death to be his most resolute defender, and the voice of Asquithian Liberalism.

She was president of the Women's Liberal Federation twice: 1923–25 and 1939–45. In 1945 she became President of the Liberal Party Organisation, the first woman to do so. She stood for Wells in 1945, and for Colne Valley in 1951; she was unsuccessful in both campaigns. In 1964 she was belatedly made a life peer and entered the House of Lords as Baroness Asquith of Yarnbury. Although by then seventy-seven, she made an immediate impact.

Bonham Carter's interests ranged wide. She was a fervent believer in the League of Nations, and was a member of the League of Nations Union until 1941. Alongside her father, the other dominant political figure in her life was Winston Churchill, whom she first met when she was eighteen. Despite occasional differences of opinion, pursued vigorously on both sides, they remained devoted friends throughout their lives. She was an early and active supporter of Churchill's anti-appeasement campaign, being passionately anti-Nazi. In 1933 she vigorously attacked Franz von Papen for the deal he brokered with Adolf Hitler which led to the Nazi leader's appointment as Chancellor. After the war she embraced the European ideal, and in 1947 became vice-chairman of the United Europe Movement. She was an annual member of the Königswinter Conference, her fluency in German as well as her character ensuring active participation.

She was a governor of the BBC from 1941–46, a role she relished. Subsequently she was a frequent broadcaster on both radio and television. She was also a member of the Royal Commission on the Press (1947–49), a governor of the Old Vic from 1945, and a trustee of the Glyndbourne Arts Trust from 1955. In 1953 she was appointed DBE.

She was a great orator; her first reported speech was in 1909 when she was twenty-two, and she continued until her death sixty years later to speak up for the creed she believed to be the only embodiment of political morality, Liberalism. In 1963 she became the first woman to give the Romanes lecture at

Oxford. She spoke on 'the impact of personality on politics' – a subject of which she had such first-hand knowledge. In 1915 she married Maurice Bonham Carter, her father's principal private secretary, and they had two daughters and two sons. She died in London on 19 February 1969.

During her lifetime Bonham Carter only wrote one book: *Winston Churchill as I Knew Him* chronicled their relationship and shared experiences, and was published in 1965. Since her death two volumes of her letters and diaries have been published: *Lantern Slides, The Diaries and Letters of Violet Bonham Carter 1904–14* (Mark Bonham Carter and Mark Pottle, eds., 1995); *Champion Redoubtable, The Diaries and Letters of Violet Bonham Carter 1914–45* (Mark Pottle, ed., 1998). A third volume, covering the rest of her life, is due for publication in 2000.

Jane Bonham Carter

HORATIO BOTTOMLEY 1860–1933

Most of the individuals represented in this *Dictionary* owe their places to their contribution, philosophical or practical, to Liberalism. Horatio Bottomley was indeed a Liberal MP, in the Edwardian heyday of the party, but owes his place in history to his record as the greatest confidence trickster of his age. As he was to say: 'I hold the unique distinction of having gone through every court in the country – except the divorce court', and he was spared that only by the forebearance of his long-suffering wife.

Horatio William Bottomley was born in Bethnal Green on 23 March 1860, the only son of William King Bottomley, a tailor's foreman, and his wife, Elizabeth, the sister of George Holyoake (*q.v.*) – though Bottomley claimed in later life that he was really the son of Charles Bradlaugh (*q.v.*), a neighbour. He lost both parents before he was five, and was placed by his uncle in an orphanage. He ran away at the age of fourteen, finding employment successively as an errand boy, solicitor's clerk and shorthand court reporter. Bradlaugh introduced him to the world of books, and he worked for a time on the *Secularist* and *Freethinker*, papers produced jointly by Bradlaugh and Holyoake. He married Eliza Norton in 1880.

He entered the printing business and started a string of local papers, all of which failed. In 1893 he was charged with conspiracy to defraud (related to kickbacks from overpriced property transactions), defended himself, and walked away scot-free; the judge was so impressed that he urged Bottomley to read law. Instead he turned to Australian gold-mining, and in ten years floated almost fifty companies, only to liquidate and wind them up after having creamed off much of the shareholders' money. It was estimated that he made a personal fortune of £3 million out of a total capital of about £20 million. The money went on a racing stable, gambling, theatrical adventures, newspapers, lawsuits, mistresses, a country house in Sussex, a flat in Pall Mall and a villa in France.

Between 1901–05, sixty-seven bankruptcy proceedings and writs were filed against him. A brilliant speaker, his skill and wit in defending himself in court drew large crowds and generally baffled leading counsel. He was also a journalist of genuine ability, and founded *John Bull* in 1906. The paper was an early version of today's tabloids, vulgar, cheeky, populist, and appearing under the slogan: 'politics without party – criticism without cant'.

In 1906 Bottomley was elected as Liberal MP for South Hackney, after a previous unsuccessful attempt in Hornsey. He was re-elected in both the 1910 elections. His campaign director, Tommy Cox, organised men to deface rivals' posters and march out of Conservative meetings wearing steel-capped boots, drowning out the speeches. A string of Bottomley's race horses trotted down Hackney High Street wearing saddlecloths reading: 'vote for my owner'. By 1911, however, his financial situation was so desperate that he presented a petition for bankruptcy, with liabilities of almost a quarter of a million pounds; in 1912, he resigned from the Commons. Many of his assets were in his wife's name, however, and he continued to make large sums, this time through organising lotteries and sweepstakes.

When war broke out in 1914, Bottomley assured friends that we would break with his 'sordid past'. His innumerable patriotic speeches (for each of which he charged at least £50) contributed to the recruiting drive and gained him national popularity. This possibly went to his head; he stared to sell government Victory Bonds through *John Bull*, charging £1 against the official price of £5. The subscriptions, of almost a million pounds, were never used to buy the real bonds; Bottomley paid off his creditors and started yet more loss-making ventures. In 1918 he was re-elected for South Hackney, this time as an Independent, with a huge majority.

But his financial affairs were increasingly coming under suspicion, particularly when he made the mistake of suing a former colleague for libel over allegations over the Victory Bonds. The court case revealed embarassing details, and the Director of Public Prosecutions brought an action against him for fraudulent conversion of bonds. In May 1922 he was found guilty on twenty-three counts out of twenty-four, and sentenced to seven years' penal servitude; after his appeal was rejected in August, he was expelled from the House of Commons.

He was released after five years for good behaviour and, supported by his favourite mistress, Peggy Primrose, attempted a comeback as a speaker and journalist. But his attempts failed, and his health was not up to it; he collapsed during a lecture at the Windmill Theatre, London, in 1932, and died on 26 May 1933. His wife had died in 1930; they had one daughter. His *Daily Mail* obituary claimed, reasonably enough, that he could have been a success at anything he wanted: journalism, law, business. He is remembered instead for his reply to a prison visitor who found him one day sewing mail bags. 'Ah, Bottomley,' inquired the visitor, 'sewing?' 'No,' came the reply, 'reaping'.

For biographies, see Alan Hyman, *The Rise and Fall of Horatio Bottomley: the Biography of a Swindler* (Cassell, 1972), and Julian Symons, *Horatio Bottomley: a Biography* (Cresset Press, 1955); and his story is well summarised in Matthew Parris, *Great Parliamentary Scandals* (Robson Books, second edition, 1997).

Duncan Brack

CHARLES BRADLAUGH   1833–91

Charles Bradlaugh was born on 26 September 1833 in Hoxton, London, the eldest of the seven children of a poor solicitor's clerk, and he received only an elementary education. Though brought up in the Church of England, he came to doubt the doctrines of Christianity. Pressure to conform drove him from home in 1850 and he sought lodgings at the Warner Street Temperance Hall with Elizabeth Sharples, widow of Richard Carlile, the free-thinking publisher who had died in 1843. Here he began his career as a free thought lecturer, but soon took the Queen's shilling and was sent with the 7th Dragoon Guards to Ireland, an experience that deeply affected his political outlook.

On return to civilian life in 1852, he worked as a solicitor's clerk and soon became an expert in the law. At the same time, his reputation as a free thought lecturer grew under the pseudonym 'Iconoclast'. His enormous energy and ability as a platform orator were quickly recognised by the secularist movement and he was invited to co-edit a new paper, the *National Reformer*, with which his name was to be associated for the rest of his life, as editor between 1860–64 and 1866–90, and as owner from 1862. In 1866 he formed the National Secular Society with himself as President, a post he was to hold every year, except 1871–74, until 1890.

He was also recognised as a rising star in radical and republican circles and he took a leading part on the executive of the Reform League (1865–67). Though always opposed to violence, he warmly supported the Fenians and helped draft their manifesto in 1867. In the early 1870s he emerged as a leading critic of the monarchy and aristocracy, publishing his two most successful lectures, *The Land, the People and the Coming Struggle* (1871) and *The Impeachment of the House of Brunswick* (1872), and founding the National Republican League in 1873.

Despite this extremism, he thought of himself as a supporter of William Gladstone (*q.v.*) and sought to enter Parliament as a Radical Liberal. In 1868 and twice in 1874, he contested a parliamentary seat at Northampton but without local party support he was unsuccessful. His political reputation was not helped when, in 1877, in association with Mrs Annie Besant, he republished a pamphlet on birth control entitled *The Fruits of Philosophy*, which was prosecuted for obscenity. This trial, which Bradlaugh lost but escaped penalty on a technicality, brought great support to the National Secular Society but determined many good nonconformist Liberals not to accept a man who personified blasphemy, sedition and obscenity.

Nevertheless, disorganisation in the Northampton constituency party and a realisation that, although Bradlaugh could not win, he could split the vote and prevent the Liberals from winning, gained him an official nomination in 1880, and he was returned as the junior of the two members for Northampton. On entering the Commons, he asked to be allowed to make an affirmation instead of the oath on the grounds of unbelief. When a Select Committee ruled against this, Bradlaugh offered to take the oath, but permission was refused. Despite support for Bradlaugh from Gladstone's government, an Affirmations Bill was defeated by three votes in 1883, and the opposition was able to disrupt government business and thwart Bradlaugh's attempts to take his seat for five years, despite four appearances to plead his case at the Bar of the House and successful re-elections for Northampton in 1881, 1882, 1884 and 1885. Attempts to disqualify him by convicting him for blasphemy failed, and prosecutions aimed at bankrupting him were resisted as he defended himself in several cases against the best legal brains in the country. Bradlaugh came to symbolise the people against Parliament and the 'Bradlaugh case' was an acute embarrassment to Gladstone's ministry. Yet when he was finally accepted by the Speaker in 1886 he settled down to become an outstanding backbencher, a master of parliamentary procedure and a champion of individualistic Liberalism against the mounting tide of socialism. He was accorded the honour of becoming recognised as the unofficial backbench spokesman on Indian affairs, and in December 1889 was invited to the Indian National Congress in Bombay.

Bradlaugh was one of the finest popular orators of his generation, and also a great believer in the power of the law. He insisted in all his campaigns that the law must be upheld and he tried to prevent the holding of the rally in Trafalgar Square in November 1887 which led to 'Bloody Sunday' and the deaths of two men. But he had scarcely begun to use his great powers in the service of the House of Commons and the Liberal Party when his health collapsed, and on 30 January 1891 he died at his home in London of Bright's disease. He was buried at the Brookwood Necropolis, Woking.

Bradlaugh married Susannah Lamb Hooper in 1855. She bore him a son and two daughters but later suffered from alcoholism. The marriage broke up in 1870 and Mrs Bradlaugh died in 1877. Of the three children, only one survived her father, the younger daughter, Hypatia, who embodied his spirit and courage, and continued as an active worker and speaker in the Liberal cause for the next forty years.

A good modern biography using Bradlaugh's private papers has been written by David Tribe, *President Charles Bradlaugh, MP* (Elek Books, 1971). This is a useful corrective to the filial record of his life by Hypatia Bradlaugh Bonner, which appears in J. M. Robertson, *Charles Bradlaugh. A record of his life and work by his daughter, with an account of his parliamentary struggle, politics and teachings* (2 vols, T. Fisher Unwin, 1898).

Edward Royle

TOM BRAKE MP   1962–

Tom Brake was elected to Parliament for the Carshalton & Wallington seat, in south west London, at the 1997 general election, on his second attempt to win the seat. He defeated the incumbent Conservative member Nigel Forman, overturning a 10,000 majority for a 2,267 Liberal Democrat majority on a swing of 11.76 per cent.

In Parliament, Brake is part of the environment team with responsibility for natural resources, land use and transport in London. He sits on the Select Committee on Environment, Transport and Regional Affairs and is a member of the All-Party Parliamentary Group on Human Rights.

Thomas Anthony Brake was born on 6 May 1962, in Melton Mowbray, Leicestershire. The son of an information technology manager and teacher, he is the middle of three children. When eight years old, his family moved to France and he was educated at the Lycée International on the outskirts of Paris. Ten years later, he returned to England to study at Imperial College, London for a BSc (Hons) degree in physics. At university, he became actively involved in human rights issues and joined Amnesty International. He was also chair of the Imperial College students' group from 1981–82.

On completion of his degree in 1983, Brake joined Hoskyns (now Cap Gemini) as a trainee computer programmer, where he remained until his election to Parliament, having worked his way up through the ranks to become principal consultant. In the same year, he became actively involved in politics, helping William Goodhart (q.v.), the Alliance candidate, in the London constituency of North Kensington in the 1983 general election campaign. He then joined the Liberal Party and later became a founding member of the merged Social and Liberal Democrats.

In 1988 Brake was elected to Hackney council. In 1990, he moved to Carshalton, Surrey, and in 1994 become one of forty-nine Liberal Democrats on the fifty-six-member Sutton council. He served as a member of the council's Policy and Resources Committee, was vice chair of the Policy sub-committee and became involved in Sutton's Agenda 21 project. Brake's commitment to the Liberal Democrats is based on his support for strong environmental and pro-European policies. He is also a firm believer in pragmatism over dogma.

He is as energetic in his leisure pursuits as he is in his political ones. He cycles and runs and includes in his list of personal achievements spending four months cycling around Europe and completing the Three Peak Race in 1996. He is a member of Greenpeace, Friends of the Earth, Oxfam and Amnesty International, and speaks fluent French and some Portuguese and Russian.

Brake lives with his partner Candida Goulden, whom he met at a parliamentary candidates' training session in Bristol; she was training candidates in the arts of political warfare. They live in Carshalton with their daughter, Julia, born in July 1997.

Jen Tankard

PETER BRAND MP 1947–

In an area like the Isle of Wight, personality plays a large part in politics. To find a politician who is content to rise above the back-biting and squabbling of an insular community is unusual. To find one who is also a leading player in their professional field is very rare indeed. Perhaps because of the local political atmosphere of the Island and its council, on which he spent twelve years, Peter Brand always gives the impression of being laid back and disinterested. The truth is that a certain aloofness is the only defence against being dragged into the mire of scheme and squabble.

Born in Zaandam, Holland, on 16 May 1947, Brand moved to the UK in his early teens. His parents ran a home for people with learning disabilities – a grounding which instilled in Brand a desire to stand up for those less able to stand up for themselves.

Brand attended Thornbury Grammar School in Gloucestershire. He met his future wife Jane (a great-niece of Clement Attlee) while the two were medical students in Birmingham. After qualification and subsequent marriage, the two worked as GPs in Poole before moving to the Isle of Wight in 1975. They have run their practice in the village of Brading ever since, taking on a third partner to cope with the increasing workload when Brand looked like winning the Island seat in late 1996.

Brand has always played a leading role, both on the Island and in the party, in the debate over the structure of the NHS; he was a member of the Liberal Democrat health policy working group in 1994–95. He is a keen proponent of GP fund-holding, introduced by the Conservatives, seeing it as a way of getting more money, and better services, for his patients. Until his election, he was vice-chairman of the Island's Healthcare Consortium.

Brand joined the Liberal Party in 1985, the same year that he first won his Brading seat on the old Island County Council. Over the years he built up his majority without relying over-much on traditional campaigning techniques. He joked that if he went knocking on doors, most of the villagers, being his patients, would assume he had bad news. As well as serving as Deputy Leader of the council, he was also Chairman of Islecare, the arms-length company responsible for running the Island's homes for the elderly. This was Brand's real passion and it caused him much distress when his successor appeared to him to have less concern for the well-being of the residents.

Brand stood for the Island parliamentary seat in 1992 against the incumbent MP, Barry Field. Field himself had succeeded Stephen (later Lord) Ross when he retired in 1987. In the 1992 catalogue of near misses, Brand increased the Liberal Democrat vote and cut Field's majority to just 1,827, or 2.3 per cent, in the largest constituency in the country. Brand was determined to fight again and win next time.

However, being the Isle of Wight, not everything was to run smoothly. In the summer of 1996, Brand was challenged for the candidacy by the Deputy Leader of the council, Steve Cowley. A two-month battle raged, conducted mainly on the front page of the local paper. In the end, the rebels withdrew after admitting that they had the support of just a handful of ordinary members, Brand's popularity on the Island as a whole being something they had not counted on. Then, as election year dawned, Barry Field announced that he would not be seeking re-election because of poor health. His replacement, Andrew Turner, had the twin disadvantages of being from London and having a Conservative machine that was crumbling before his eyes.

Brand won the 1997 election with a swing of 5.5 per cent to a majority of 6,406. He now speaks in Parliament on public health as part of the Liberal Democrat health team led by Simon Hughes MP (*q.v.*). He is also a member of the Health Select Committee.

Peter and Jane Brand have two children, Edmund and Jonathan. They share a joint passion of sailing – not exactly a hindrance for the MP for Cowes Week. The latest in a long line of boats is a Nelson launch which also serves as Brand's London accommodation, moored two miles up-river from the House of Commons when Parliament is in session.

Alex Folkes

COLIN BREED MP   1947–

South East Cornwall had been without a Liberal MP for twenty-three years when Colin Breed was elected to Parliament in May 1997. As the Bodmin seat, it had briefly been represented by Paul Tyler (*q.v.*), now MP for North Cornwall, between the two elections of 1974, with a majority of just nine votes. It had long been considered a Liberal stronghold, however, with the great Methodist Isaac Foot (head of the Foot dynasty, *q.v.*) once representing the area in the 1920s and '30s. The unfortunate Thomas Agar-Robartes had won the seat in the landslide of 1906, only to have it taken away by a successful election petition, and Peter Bessell (*q.v.*) held it from 1964–70.

Born in London on 4 May 1947, Colin Edward Breed moved to the West Country early in life, attending Torquay Grammar School. After school he worked for the Midland Bank for seventeen years, becoming a manager. He moved on investment banking with Dartington & Co. Ltd, a regional merchant bank, and then, with his wife, bought a small regionally based abrasives company, Gemini Abrasives, which they still own today. He married Janet in 1968, and they have two children, Esther (born 1972) and Matthew (1975).

Breed moved to Saltash in the mid 1970s, and steadily became known as 'Mr Saltash', having been a member of the Town Council from 1982–97 and serving as mayor twice, in 1989–90 and 1995–96. He also represented the town on Caradon District Council from 1982–92. Through his work for the Wesleyan Church in Saltash he has become a Methodist lay preacher and is Chair of the Wesley Housing and Benevolent Trust and the Devon Prince's Trust Volunteers.

Breed was selected to contest South East Cornwall after having supported Robin Teverson (now the local MEP, *q.v.*), as his agent, in the 1992 election campaign. Breed had never previously contested a parliamentary constituency, but it was to be first time lucky. In 1997, he seized the seat from the Conservatives with a massive twelve per cent swing, turning a 7,704 Conservative majority into a Liberal Democrat majority of 6,480.

Breed is now one of the party's trade and industry spokesmen in the Commons, with responsibility for competition and consumer affairs.

John Ault

JOHN BRIGHT
1811–89

John Bright has been described as one of the great Victorian moralists, standing at the confluence of the mid-nineteenth century working class movement and of the political wing of nonconformist dissent. By providing leadership to these two movements he made a major contribution to the creed of Liberalism, and a major legacy to William Gladstone (*q.v.*), who reaped the rewards of Bright's work in the form of the alliance between the middle and working classes on which the Liberal Party prospered in the late nineteenth century. But in many ways, Bright was not by origin or predisposition a member of either group; rather, he was more inclined to the Manchester School of the Anti-Corn Law League, and his leadership role was more a product of compromise by both the working class and radical nonconformists.

John Bright was born on 16 November 1811, the son of a Quaker textile manufacturer. He worked for his father in his Rochdale mill after leaving school, and soon became involved in local political causes favoured by nonconformists, notably the opposition to compulsory church rates. Bright first met Richard Cobden (*q.v.*) in 1835, and after the death of his wife, in 1841, he became closely involved with Cobden in the Anti-Corn Law League (he had become treasurer of the Rochdale branch of the League in 1840). Bright was a noted public orator, speaking against the Corn Laws across the country during the years leading up to their repeal in 1846.

Bright had a long career as an MP, although he held ministerial office for only a short period. He was elected MP for Durham in 1843, and then for Manchester in 1847 and 1852. He was defeated in Manchester in 1857, but after a short absence from Parliament he became MP for Birmingham at a byelection later in that year. He held that seat until in the five subsequent elections until 1885 when, following the Third Reform Act, he became MP for Birmingham Central. Bright voted against the second reading of the Home Rule Bill in 1886, and fought the ensuing election as a Liberal Unionist. He retained his seat until his death in 1889.

Bright joined Gladstone's Cabinet in 1868 as President of the Board of Trade (and became a privy councillor), but he resigned in 1870 pleading ill-health (although this was to some extent a cover for his dislike of the realpolitik of government). During 1873–74 and 1880–82 he held the sinecure post of Chancellor of the Duchy of Lancaster, but he resigned in 1882 in opposition to the bombardment of Alexandria in defence of the Suez Canal.

Bright is probably best known for his contribution to the campaign against the Corn Laws, leading up to their repeal in 1846. He was a noted public orator, who spoke across the country against protection for agriculture, and later for other causes that he espoused. He opposed the Crimean War, not only because (like Cobden) he advocated the cause of peace and internationalism, but also for the burden that military expenditure imposed on the taxpayer. It was this stance that cost him his seat in 1857, again like Cobden. Bright's Radical opposition to the European balance-of-power policy was typified by his description of it as 'a gigantic system of outdoor relief for the aristocracy of Great Britain.'

Bright continued to champion the cause of free trade after the repeal of the Corn Laws. He supported Cobden in pushing for a commercial treaty with France; indeed, he, rather than Cobden, is credited with originating the idea. The 1860 Cobden-Chevalier Treaty substantially lowered duties between the two countries and formed a coherent part of his advocacy of internationalism, with free trade and peace as its main planks. But as well as his support for free trade, Bright is perhaps most associated with campaigns for parliamentary reform. He began this campaign after 1858, largely out of his hostility to Palmerston's (*q.v.*) form of aristocratic government, in a parliament that he regarded as a sham dominated by class prejudices and vested interests.

Bright advocated many other causes, including the abolition of newspaper taxes; he challenged the powers of the House of Lords over tax bills, and opposed local government measures such as the Highways Bills of the early 1860s (which created new boards that he regarded as controlled by local magistrates who were in the grip of the aristocracy). He was also prominent in debates over the reforms in Indian cotton cultivation and government and Irish land reform, and he supported the Northern cause in the American Civil War.

In 1880 Bright served as Lord Rector of Glasgow University, and in 1886 Oxford University awarded him an honorary doctorate. He died on 27 March 1889. He had married, in 1839, Elizabeth Priestman, who bore him a daughter and died in 1841; he then married Margaret Elizabeth Leathman in 1847, and had three daughters and four sons, two of which later became MPs.

Volumes of Bright's speeches and addresses were published in 1868 and 1879. The most recent biography is Keith Robbins, *John Bright* (Routledge & Kegan Paul, 1979).

Cheryl Schondhardt-Bailey and Elizabeth Flanagan Prueher

ERNEST BROWN   1881–1962

Alfred Ernest Brown – the first name was seldom used – had a background so typical of a working-class West Country Liberal of his time that few could have guessed that he would eventually attain high office in an overwhelmingly Conservative government.

Born in Torquay on 27 August 1881, Ernest Brown was the eldest son of a Baptist fisherman. He was educated locally, and first appeared on a Liberal platform while still at school. He soon followed his father in his Baptist activities, and also became a dedicated temperance worker. He worked as a clerk, and in 1907 married Isabel Narracott, daughter of a master plumber. In the 1914–18 war, Brown joined the Sportsman's Battalion, for rugby football was another of his abiding interests. He served with considerable distinction, and was one of relatively few men who won the MM as a private, and later the MC and the Italian Silver Cross when he became an officer.

In the 1918 general election, Brown was Liberal candidate in Salisbury, but the coalition's 'coupon' was given to his Conservative opponent and he was defeated. He stood again in Salisbury in 1922, and this time missed election by a very narrow margin. At a byelection in Mitcham in March 1923 Brown ran a poor third, but at the general election later that year he was elected MP for Rugby. A year later, however, he was defeated in the same constituency.

In 1927, the Liberal MP, William Wedgwood Benn – father of Tony Benn – seceded to Labour. Holding that he should not continue to represent a constituency where he had been elected in a different interest, Benn resigned his seat of Leith, causing a byelection. The Liberal Party was undergoing something of a revival at the time, and the byelection was of considerable importance. An apocryphal story tells that senior members of the party were discussing possible candidates in the smoking room of the National Liberal Club, when Brown, an active Liberal speaker, walked in. 'What about him?' said one of them, half-jokingly. Brown became the candidate, and was elected with a slender majority. He held the seat, however, at the 1929 election and for the following sixteen years.

The parliamentary Liberal Party split three ways in the tensions surrounding the formation of the National Government in 1931 and the ensuing election. Brown joined with those MPs most strongly supporting the government, in the Liberal National group headed by Sir John Simon (q.v.). He became Parliamentary Secretary to the Minister of Health in 1931, and Secretary to the Mines Department the following year. In 1935 he became Minister of Labour, and entered the Cabinet. Hearing Brown, who had a very powerful voice, speaking in a telephone booth one day, the Prime Minister, Stanley Baldwin, observed that he never realised that Brown required a telephone to address his Scottish constituents.

Although a Cabinet minister, Brown continued to preach to Baptist congregations. An admirer claimed that 'what he preached on Sundays in Bloomsbury he sought to put into practice on Mondays in Whitehall'.

When war came in 1939, Brown added responsibility for National Service to his duties at the Ministry of Labour. In the following year, Churchill formed his coalition government, and Brown became Secretary of State for Scotland, the first Englishman to hold the post. In subsequent Cabinet reshuffles he became Minister of Health, then Chancellor of the Duchy of Lancaster. In May 1945, the coalition came to an end, and Brown became Minister of Aircraft Production in the brief caretaker government which held office until a general election could be held.

For part of the mid-war period, Brown was Chairman of the Liberal Nationals. In 1943–44, serious discussions took place about possible reunion with the Liberal Party, but eventually foundered, with the Liberals predictably insisting on party independence, and the Liberal Nationals, equally predictably, insisting on continued association with the Conservatives.

In 1945, Brown was defeated at Leith, and never re-entered Parliament. His religious activities continued, and he was President of the Baptist Union of Great Britain and Ireland in 1948–49. In the late 1950s he had a seizure, and for the last two and a half years of his life was a patient in hospital, where he died on 16 February 1962.

Roy Douglas

MALCOLM BRUCE MP   1944–

Malcolm Bruce rose to national prominence in 1983 when he won the Gordon constituency for the Scottish Liberal Party. This was a major influence in the growth of success of the Liberals in north east Scotland in the 1970s and '80s. The seat, previously mainly West Aberdeenshire, had been held by the Liberal James Davidson, a well-known and respected local farmer, from 1966–70, but then lost to the Tories after his resignation in 1970. In taking the seat Bruce displayed the qualities of hard work and a terrier-like pursuit of issues which have been evident in his career ever since.

After being elected in 1983, he held the seat in 1987 with a hugely increased majority, and again in 1992, although his majority slumped along with the depressed fortunes of other Liberal Democrats in north east Scotland. This was attributed to a close identification with Labour in the Scottish Constitutional Convention discussions. In 1997, in a considerably changed seat, his majority was restored, in spite of dire predictions by media commentators.

Malcolm Gray Bruce was born in Birkenhead on 17 November 1944. He attended Wrekin College, Shropshire, and his higher education was at St Andrews University (MA 1966) and Strathclyde University (MSc 1971). One of the honours bestowed on him which he appreciates most was his election as Rector of Dundee University, previously part of St Andrews University, in 1986.

He worked briefly for the *Liverpool Daily Post*, Boots, A. Goldberg & Sons, and then for the North of Scotland Development Authority from 1971–75. Here he started to develop the journalistic, research and debating skills which are now admired. He went on to become marketing director of Noroil, a Norwegian-based publishing house, and then, with a partner, set up Aberdeen Petroleum Publishing in 1981. Thus he gained exceptional knowledge of oil exploration and energy matters. This in turn led to a deep understanding of trade, industry and the problems of the national economy.

With this background it is not surprising that his political career has been dominated by appointments concerning trade, energy and the economy. Thus he was energy spokesman for the Scottish Liberal Party from 1975–83, and from 1983–85 in the Commons for the Liberal Party. From 1985–87 he was Alliance spokesman on trade and industry and, in 1987, employment spokesman. He was Liberal Democrat spokesman on natural resources from 1988–90, trade and industry 1992–94, and on Treasury matters from 1994. National recognition came through his various parliamentary posts, and there was speculation about him as a possible leader of the Social and Liberal Democrats in 1988; in fact, he became Paddy Ashdown's (*q.v.*) campaign chairman.

At the same time he retained an involvement in Scottish affairs and was Deputy Chairman of the Scottish Liberal Party in the 1970s and Leader of the Scottish Liberal Democrats from 1988–92. During the latter time he led the negotiations on behalf of the party with the other groups involved in the Scottish Constitutional Convention. This was one of his most important achievements: the Scottish Liberal Democrat representatives led by him negotiated agreement with the Labour Party on a form of proportional representation for a Scottish Parliament. However, the electoral consequences were nearly disastrous, as his majority almost disappeared in 1992.

Since becoming Treasury spokesman he has gained an increasing respect as an effective debater and a lucid and powerful performer on the media and at Liberal Democrat conferences. Much in demand for radio and television interviews, he played a prominent part as Treasury spokesman in the 1997 general election campaign. His sincerity and cogent exposition of policies undoubtedly helped in the success of that campaign and in party fortunes since.

In his various posts in the Liberal Democrat Parliamentary Party, his attitude is one of 'constructive opposition'. He will advocate cooperation with any government where their proposals are in line with Liberal Democrat policies, but will disagree robustly where they are not. There can be no question that he is not one to tolerate cosy political relationships with any other party, but also will reject opposition for its own sake.

Another example of his energy is that he studied English law and passed the Common Professional Examination over two years by distance learning. He then sat the bar finals at the Inns of Court School of Law, specialising in company law and European competition law, and was called to the bar (Gray's Inn) in 1995.

Bruce married Veronica Jane Wilson in 1969 (marriage dissolved in 1992) and has two children. His daughter Caroline is profoundly deaf, and her problems have stimulated his intense interest in deaf affairs; he has learned sign language to ease his communication with his daughter. He became vice president of the National Deaf Children's Society in 1992, and is president of the Grampian Area Deaf Children's Society.

His other interests are theatre, music, and walking. He married Rosemary Vetterlein in May 1998.

Roy Thomson

JOHN BURNETT MP   1945–

John Patrick Aubone Burnett was born in Oswestry, Shropshire on 19 September 1945, and was educated at Ampleforth College. He held a commission in the Royal Marines from 1964 to 1970, serving as a troop commander in Borneo and the Middle East. On leaving the Marines he studied at the College of Law, London, and became a solicitor with a City law firm. In 1976 he joined a Devon law firm and became a partner. From 1984–96 he served as a member of the Law Society's Revenue Law Committee.

In October 1971 he married Elizabeth (Billie) de la Mare, and the couple have two sons and two daughters. They live at their farm at Petrockstowe (between Hatherleigh and Torrington) and breed Devon cattle; until the 1997 election Burnett was a council member of the Devon Cattle Breeders' Society. They are both active members of the Catholic Church in Torrington.

He joined the Liberal Party in 1985, as the party most closely aligned with his political beliefs. In 1986 he was selected as the Alliance candidate for Torridge & West Devon and in the following year's election he halved the Conservative majority. He remained active within the constituency, but family commitments prevented him standing at the 1992 general election.

In December 1995 the Conservative MP for Torridge & West Devon, Emma Nicholson (*q.v.*), defected to the Liberal Democrats, but announced that she would not contest the seat again. Burnett was selected as the party's candidate in January 1996 and won the constituency with a majority of 1,957 in May 1997. He campaigned in particular on the need for higher expenditure on local village primary schools and for the retention of local community hospitals.

After the election Burnett was appointed as Liberal Democrat legal affairs spokesman, and has also become a member of the Treasury team, with taxation responsibilities.

John Matthew

JOHN BURNS   1858–1943

By the time John Burns died in 1943 he had been retired from active political life for a quarter of a century, but his achievement as the first working man to gain full cabinet rank had long since secured his place in the history of Liberalism.

The son of a Scottish engineer, John Elliot Burns was born in Lambeth on 20

October 1858. His formal education was minimal, since his parents' straitened circumstances made it imperative for him to abandon St Mary's National School in Battersea in favour of paid work. Assiduous attendance at night school and innate determination allowed him to complete an engineering apprenticeship in 1879.

A short spell in Africa confirmed his developing socialist views and, after returning to England to marry Martha Gale in 1882, he threw himself into propaganda work for the Marxist Social Democratic Federation. He contested Nottingham West as a Federation candidate in 1885 but thereafter, despite achieving national notoriety for his part in unemployment riots in 1885 and 1886, he became disillusioned with the Federation's lack of progress. Always a union activist, he secured a sympathetic public response for his leadership in publicising the plight of the London dockers in the great strike of 1889.

In the same year he was elected to represent Battersea as a member of the newly formed London County Council, a position he retained until 1907. As a councillor he played a leading role in establishing a Works Department and in municipalising the capital's transport and water services. Such achievements further strengthened his growing conviction that working class interests were best served by practical action rather than the visionary rhetoric at which he had once excelled. They also served to confirm his view that such action could most effectively be achieved by pragmatic political alliances of the sort he forged with Liberals as part of the Progressive group in the LCC. For this same reason he was deeply suspicious of contemporary moves to establish an independent working-class political party, particularly one led by individuals whose New Testament political vision jarred with his own secularism.

In 1892, Burns was returned to Parliament for Battersea, one of the first three independent Labour member MPs elected. He worked uneasily in the House of Commons, however, with the leading proponent of working class independence, James Keir Hardie, whose electoral defeat in 1895 left Burns as the best-known and most experienced working-class Member of Parliament. So confident was he of his personal standing that he virtually ignored the new Labour Representation Committee set up in 1900, while his opposition to British involvement in the Boer War drew him still closer to the radical wing of the Liberal Party. In 1906 he accepted the Presidency of the Local Government Board in Campbell-Bannerman's (q.v.) new Liberal administration.

History has not judged Burns' eight-year stint at the Local Government Board kindly, generally accepting Beatrice Webb's claim that reactionary civil servants flattered him into incompetence and conservatism. There is no doubting Burns' immense egotism, nor that all the running in social welfare reform was made by his colleagues Churchill (q.v.) and Lloyd George (q.v.). Yet his officials did not shape his views in the way Webb suggested, for Burns had long since evolved into the epitome of nineteenth century working class respectability – a non-smoking, non-gambling advocate of temperance and self-help. His underlying view that individuals were primarily responsible for themselves, and that the state's role should be limited to helping those incapable of helping themselves, fitted neatly with the existing ethos of the Board. What he did fail to do, however, was to overcome the sheer technical incompetence of most of his senior officials. Combined with his own tendency to get bogged down in detail, this generally served to frustrate his policy plans.

By the time he moved to the Board of Trade in January 1914, he had overseen only one significant piece of legislation, the Housing and Town Planning Act (1909) which effectively introduced the notion of municipal home ownership. On the other hand, his administrative interventions helped to humanise the operation of the poor law and to raise public awareness of infant mortality. Had Burns been as totally ineffective as his critics implied, it is difficult to understand how he could have survived the various cabinet reshuffles associated with the premiership of Asquith (*q.v.*) and the two general elections of 1910, or why he was given another post in 1914.

There was, however, little time to make much impact at the Board of Trade before the First World War broke out. Burns' opposition to British involvement was entirely predictable in view of his life-long pacifism, and it was no surprise when he resigned from the government in August 1914, effectively walking out of public life as well. He was dismayed when Asquith was ousted by Lloyd George, a man whom Burns distrusted and once called the 'greatest cad in Europe'. Yet his own previous attitudes, combined with his conservative and parsimonious stewardship of the Local Government Board, had completely alienated the new Labour Party and there was thus no real home left in the political system for his by now rather dated, non-doctrinaire, independence. He toyed briefly with the idea of standing in the 1918 election but any lingering inclination to re-enter politics was dowsed when his only son died from injuries sustained in the war.

Burns spent his declining years pursuing his interests in book collecting and cricket, and frequenting the National Liberal Club. He died in London's Bolingbroke Hospital on 24 January 1943.

For biographies, see: K. D. Brown, *John Burns* (1977); J. Burgess, *John Burns: The Rise and Progress of a Right Honourable* (1911); G. D. H. Cole, *John Burns* (1943); A. P. Grubb, *From Candle Factory to British Cabinet: The Life Story of the Rt Hon John Burns* (1908); W. Kent, *Labour's Lost Leader* (1950).

Kenneth D. Brown

PAUL BURSTOW MP   1962–

Paul Burstow was elected to Parliament for the Sutton & Cheam seat in south west London at the 1997 general election, defeating the incumbent and eccentric Conservative member Lady Olga Maitland, overturning a 10,756 majority for a 2,097 Liberal Democrat majority on a swing of 13 per cent. He had previously fought the seat in 1992, achieving the biggest swing to the Liberal Democrats in Greater London.

In Parliament, Burstow became spokesman for disability issues, before becoming local government team leader in July 1997, with special responsibility for social services and community care. In July 1997 he introduced his Elections (Visually Impaired Voters) Bill and in autumn 1997 ran a national campaign for fairer funding for local public services. He is Vice-Chair of the All-Party Disablement Group and a member of the All-Party Groups on Older People, Charities and the Voluntary Sector, Children, AIDS and Voice (people with learning difficulties).

Paul Kenneth Burstow was born on 13 May 1962 in Carshalton, the only child of a Savile Row tailor, Brian and his wife, Sheila. He was educated at Glastonbury High School, Carshalton, Carshalton College of Further Education and South Bank Polytechnic, where he was awarded a BA (Hons) in business studies. He completed his degree in 1985 and began work in the buying department of Allied Shoes Repairs in Carshalton, then moved to a printing company in Chiswick. In 1988 Burstow joined the Association of Liberal Democrat Councillors and worked his way up to become Political Secretary in 1997.

Burstow joined the SDP in 1982 and was elected to Sutton Council in 1986 with twenty-eight Liberal/SDP Alliance councillors to take control of the council from the Conservatives for the first time, under the leadership of Graham Tope (q.v.). Burstow has continued to represent the same ward, Rosehill, since 1982.

Burstow became chair of Sutton Council's nature conservation and ecology working party in 1986. He introduced many of the environmental policies that are the basis of Sutton's national and international reputation as a centre of environmental excellence. He also served on the Highways and Transportation Sub-Committee, the Environmental Services Committee and the Policy and Resources Committee. In 1991 he became Chair of the council's Disability Forum and has since maintained a strong interest in disability issues. Burstow became Deputy Leader of the council in 1994, standing down shortly before his election to Parliament.

Burstow regularly attends the House of Commons gym, is a keen cook and a Star Trek fanatic. He is actively involved in his local church, St Nicholas, in Sutton. He lives with his wife, Mary (née Kemm), whom he met when she became involved in Sutton Liberal Democrats. In 1994 she was elected as his fellow ward councillor in Rosehill, which she represented until 1998; she now works as Paul's diary secretary. They live in Cheam, with their one-year-old son, Jonathan.

Jen Tankard

FRANK BYERS (Lord Byers) 1915–84

When Frank Byers died from a heart attack on 6 February 1984, the Liberal Party lost a passionate and implacable fighter for their cause. He was one of a small group of people who played the main part in keeping the party alive in its most desolate days.

The Times, in its obituary, described him as 'a dedicated Liberal [who] devoted himself without stint to …. a party whose service brought few rewards'.

Charles Frank Byers was born on 24 April 1915, in Lancing, Sussex. His father was a Lloyd's underwriter. Byers was educated at Westminster School and Christ Church, Oxford, where he was a noted hurdler, and won a blue for athletics. He took an honours degree in philosophy, politics and economics.

He had already marked out the political course which he was to follow throughout his life, and became President of the University Liberal Club. In that capacity he encountered the club's rather inconspicuous Treasurer, Harold Wilson; in 1945, he was to meet Wilson in a different capacity, when they were both new MPs, though for different parties. Byers also met his future wife, Joan Oliver, at Oxford. They married in 1939 and had a son and three daughters. Joan, a keen Liberal herself, was a most loyal and helpful support throughout his career.

When war came in 1939, Frank Byers joined the Royal Artillery, and was commissioned early the following year. His rise was rapid, and by 1943 he held the rank of Lieutenant Colonel. He was on the staff of Field-Marshal Montgomery, but was not one of those staff officers to miss action in the field. He was mentioned in dispatches three times, was created a Chevalier of the Légion of d'Honneur, and awarded the Croix de Guerre, with palm. In 1944 he received the OBE.

In the 1945 general election, Byers recorded one of the few Liberal victories, winning North Dorset from the Conservatives by 1,965 votes, benefiting from the absence of a Labour candidate (the Labour Party correctly believing it had no chance of winning the seat and preferring to see a Liberal elected to a Tory).

Byers' career in the Liberal Party advanced rapidly. In 1946, Tom Horabin retired from the post of Liberal Chief Whip and shortly afterwards joined the Labour Party; Byers was appointed in his place. The effect on the Liberals was immediate; Byers was one of the small group of visionary and indefatigable individuals determined to infuse vigour and determination as well as a sense of organisation into the party. Bad as the Liberal results were in 1950, they would have been a great deal worse without Byers and his associates,

The party's reorganisation was not able, however, to save his own seat of North Dorset at the 1950 general election, when Labour decided to stand as well, helping the Conservative to victory by ninety-seven votes. At the general election of 1951, Byers stood in the same constituency, but again failed by a small margin in a three-cornered contest. He made one more attempt to enter the House of Commons, at a byelection in Bolton East in 1960, and again was unsuccessful.

Only in 1964 did Byers at last despair of re-election to the House of Commons, and accept a life peerage, taking the title Baron Byers, of Lingfield in the County of Surrey. Three years later, when Lord Rea retired, he became leader of the Liberal peers, and in 1972 was created a Privy Councillor. In the following year he became Deputy Lieutenant of Surrey. In modern conditions, a leader in the Lords is necessarily less conspicuous than the principal figures in the House of Commons, and Byers did his own job there competently and well, never attempting to upstage the MPs.

To support his political career, Byers devoted himself to business. In this field too he made his mark, serving as a Director of Rio Tinto Zinc from 1962–73. He became a Fellow of the British Institute of Management, and was Chairman of the Company Pensions Information Committee.

Byers was dedicated not just to his own career, but to Liberalism. In 1950–52, and again in 1965–67, he was Chairman of the party, and served as campaign manager at general elections. He also attracted much attention as a successful broadcaster and as one of the first Liberals to use the new medium of television. Any other party would have been glad to reward his talents and energy with a great political career. But with Frank Byers there could be no compromise over his fundamental Liberal faith, in which he never wavered. It was his bad luck, and that of the country as well, that his time of political activity coincided with the Liberal eclipse.

Roy Douglas

VINCENT CABLE MP   1943–

The current Liberal Democrat MP for Twickenham, John Vincent Cable, had risen to prominence long before entering Parliament, and is heavily tipped as 'one to watch' from the 1997 intake. Historically, he has taken an independent line from firmly within the 'establishment': president of the Cambridge Union in the same period as Norman Lamont and Kenneth Clarke (1964–65); Chief Economist at Shell International, and an author, with Norwegian Prime Minister Gro Harlem Bruntland, of a major environmental report; a Labour councillor on Glasgow City Council (1971); a special adviser to Trade Secretary John Smith (1979); and, finally, a Liberal Democrat MP. It is, perhaps, Cable's academic weight and practical experience which has allowed him to move between institutions and roles whilst retaining respect in such a wide variety of fields.

Cable's personal political career, split between the Liberal Party (until 1964), the Labour Party (1964–82), the SDP, and the Liberal Democrats, has mirrored the chequered history of the social democratic centre-left. From early on, that history has been one with a stress on cooperation rather than implacable opposition. While President of the Liberal Club in Cambridge, he attempted an unsuccessful merger with the social democrats in the Cambridge Labour group. His own experience as a candidate has done much to reinforce his views on the need for cooperation between Labour and the Liberal Democrats. In June 1970, he contested the Glasgow Hillhead seat for Labour, polling half as many votes as Conservative Peter Galbraith. Fighting York in 1983 and 1987 for the SDP/Liberal Alliance, he polled 23 per cent and 16 per cent respectively – though the victor was Conservative Conal Gregory on both occasions. Fighting the

Conservative seat of Twickenham in 1992 and 1997, the need to get the tactical vote out was clear. He wrote openly in the *New Statesman* on the need for tactical voting to keep the Conservatives in 'the political wilderness' for a decade (1996). The message in his 1997 campaign concentrated on squeezing the soft Labour vote. In 1992, he reduced MP Toby Jessel's majority to 6,121. In 1997, he was returned with a majority of 4,281. By his own admission, he is still regarded as 'one of the Liberal Democrat members arguing for the most strongly constructive links with the government'.

Outside politics, Cable's career has combined academia with the type of appointments that have enabled him to be a real-life player in his own right. Born on 9 May 1943 in York, he was educated at Poppleton Road Primary School and Nunthorpe Grammar School. After reading natural sciences and Economics at Fitzwilliam College, Cambridge, he became a Treasury Finance Officer in the Government of Kenya (1966–68). He returned to Glasgow, where he lectured until 1974, also acquiring his PhD. Two years in the diplomatic service followed as Head of Section at the Latin America desk, before taking up the post of Deputy Director of the Overseas Development Institute (1976–83).

There followed seven years as Director of the Economic Division at the Commonwealth Secretariat (1983–90). A further three years were then spent in the Group Planning Department at Shell. In 1993, he returned to academic life, as head of the International Economics Programme at the Royal Institute of International Affairs (1993–95). Cable was then appointed Chief Economist at Shell International (1995–97), a job he combined with the post of Special Professor of Economics at Nottingham University (1996–98).

Three main themes recur in Cable's writing. First, international economics, in particular trade policy, where his anti-protectionist views are evident (*The Case against Import Controls,* Fabian Pamphlet, 1976; *Protectionism and Industrial Decline,* 1983; *Foreign Development and Investment,* with B. Persaud, 1985; the background report for the RIIA 'Britain in the World' Conference, 1995). Secondly, an understanding of the newly industrialising countries (*The New Giants – China and India,* 1995). Thirdly, the need for economics to accommodate environmental factors (*Report of the World Commission for the Environment,* with Gro Harlem Bruntland and Sonny Ramphal; *Report for the Commonwealth Prime Ministers' Conference on the policy implications of the Greenhouse Effect,* 1989).

Cable also wrote the Fabian pamphlet *Kenya Asians* (1968) which focused on the economics of immigration and racial equality. More recently he has turned his attention to the economic impact of the internet and the communications revolution on economics (*Global Superhighways,* 1995). *The World's New Fissures,* a 1994 Demos pamphlet, examined global political trends.

Cable wrote a section of Gordon Brown's *Red Paper for Scotland* (1974). This has not prevented a healthy scepticism about some centre-left economic myths. Notably, he is critical of the Treasury's present claim that the blame for Britain's investment shortfall can be laid entirely at the door of the City; the problem, he argues, is with government policy, rather than the financial markets, which simply provide a range of long- and short-term mechanisms.

Before entering the House of Commons, Cable had been chair of the Liberal Democrat tax policy working group. His membership of the Liberal Democrats' Commons Treasury team has undoubtedly bolstered the party's pro-European stance. Cable is a strong supporter of the single currency, and favours a hard line on inflation, arguing that its main victims are the poor. The Liberal economics of free trade remain a particular concern, especially freedom of the capital markets.

He married Dr Maria Olympia (Rebelo) in 1968, a musician and historian; they have three children, Paul (born 1969), Aida (1972), and Hugo (1979). He enjoys ball-room and Latin dancing, and classical music.

Eduardo Reyes

MENZIES CAMPBELL MP 1941–

Walter Menzies Campbell, better known as 'Ming', has over the last ten years become one of the best-known and most highly respected members of the Parliamentary Party of the Liberal Democrats. Believed to be one of the confidants of the Leader, Paddy Ashdown (*q.v.*), he is an acknowledged expert on foreign and Commonwealth affairs, defence and Europe, for which he is the party spokesman. His views are widely sought and he is a frequent interviewee on radio and television. He is also one of the Liberal Democrat members on the joint Cabinet Committee dealing with constitutional reform.

Born in Greenock on 22 May 1941, Ming Campbell was educated at Hillhead High School, Glasgow, and then took a law degree at Glasgow University. He studied for a further year as a rotary scholar at the University of Stanford, California. During his time at Glasgow University he became well known as an athlete of considerable ability and as a debater of some brilliance. He competed in the 100 metres and 200 metres, as well as the former imperial equivalents 100 yards and 220 yards, for Scotland and the UK on many occasions, culminating in representing Britain at the Tokyo Olympics in 1966. He was a member of the debating society team that won Glasgow University the *Observer* Mace Debating Trophy.

After university he pursued a career in the law as an advocate and became a QC specialising in criminal law. He was equally at home prosecuting, as an advocate depute for the Crown, or defending. It is widely believed that had he not entered Parliament he would long since have been appointed a Scottish High Court judge. Because of his parliamentary career his court appearances are now extremely few and largely confined to planning enquiries.

Campbell became interested in politics at Glasgow University, joining the Liberal

Club and serving for one year as President of the Union, like his fellow Liberal Democrat MP Charles Kennedy (*q.v.*). His prime reason for joining the Scottish Liberal Party was his strong support for home rule for a Scottish Parliament within a federal UK. In both the elections of 1974 he contested the Greenock & Port Glasgow constituency. In 1976, during a two-year term as Chairman of the Scottish Liberal Party, he became prospective Liberal candidate for East Fife, where the Liberal candidate had been fourth with 12.4 per cent of the vote in October 1974. He showed remarkable foresight in judging this to be a seat (part of which had been represented by H. H. Asquith (*q.v.*) as Prime Minister), where the Liberals could progress. In 1979 he secured over 21 per cent of the vote and second place, and in 1983 in the new North East Fife seat, reduced the Conservative majority to just over 2,000. In 1987, at his fifth attempt, he entered Parliament as MP for North East Fife with a majority of 1,447. He held the seat with an increased majority in 1992 and in 1997 secured over fifty per cent of the votes cast.

Campbell has earned a deserved reputation as a conscientious, effective, hardworking constituency MP and is almost revered by his constituents. But he is also regarded as a media personality and a fine debater in the House of Commons, whose views are listened to and respected on all sides. He has won the coveted award of 'back-bencher of the year' in 1996. He has been Liberal Democrat spokesman for arts, broadcasting and sport 1987–88, for defence and disarmament 1988–97, and is now leader of the foreign and Commonwealth affairs, defence and Europe team.

He has served on the House of Commons select committees on defence, trade and industry and members' interests and is a member of many all-party groups. He was a member of the Broadcasting Council for Scotland and the Scottish Sports Council before entering Parliament. Since 1984 he has been a trustee of the Scottish International Education Trust. Again prior to being elected to Westminster he was awarded the CBE for political and public service.

Campbell is married to Elspeth, daughter of the famous General Urquhart of Arnhem (portrayed by Sean Connery in the film *A Bridge Too Far*). Outwith parliament sittings, they divide their time between their home in Edinburgh and a cottage in Gateside in North East Fife.

Political commentators are virtually unanimous in adjudging Campbell an outstanding politician of well above average ability. There is often speculation as to why he has remained a Liberal, then Liberal Democrat, when he would undoubtedly have attained cabinet rank in the Labour or Conservative Parties. Indeed one of his closest friends in politics is the Secretary of State for Scotland, Rt. Hon. Donald Dewar. But anyone who knows the man and has worked with him over the years soon realises that he could never be other than a Liberal Democrat. His Liberalism and Liberal principles and beliefs are evident in everything he says and does.

Dr Derek Andrew Barrie

SIR HENRY CAMPBELL-BANNERMAN 1836–1908

There have been four Liberals at the head of clearly Liberal governments – Gladstone (*q.v.*), Rosebery (*q.v.*), Sir Henry Campbell-Bannerman and Asquith (*q.v.*). Three of them are well-known names. Yet of the four, 'CB' was far and away the best party leader. Only Grimond (*q.v.*), in very different circumstances, can compare with him. Had Campbell-Bannerman not become leader in the post-Gladstonian shambles of the 1890s, it is likely the Liberal Party would not have lasted intact into the Edwardian era, let alone achieved its greatest electoral victory in 1906.

During his life Campbell-Bannerman was thought rather humdrum and unambitious, a solid Liberal and ultimately reliable but a bit lazy and not in the first rank. Now he is largely forgotten.

Henry Campbell was born in 1836 at Kelvinside, near Glasgow, although he spoke with a Perthshire accent. The Bannerman part came in 1871, a condition of a legacy from an uncle; from then on most people called him 'CB'. The 'Sir' came from the GCB, awarded in 1895. Son of a self-made Presbyterian Tory businessman who served as Provost of Glasgow, Campbell-Bannerman had the benefit of comfortable means, but was never very rich. While still quite young he read, talked and thought enough to decide he was an 'advanced' radical Liberal of the mid-nineteenth century kind, and from those views he never strayed.

Formal education at Glasgow High School, Glasgow University and Trinity College, Cambridge (a third in classics) was interrupted at fourteen by a remarkable ten-month trip round Europe with his older cousin, which shaped much of his tolerant and Liberal outlook. He spoke fluent French, stylish German and passable Italian. In modern terms, he was a Europhile, with a particular fondness for France. Every summer the Campbell-Bannermans spent at least six weeks in Europe, much of the time at Marienbad, and he seems to have flitted back and forth to France in a very end-of-the-twentieth-century sort of way.

At thirty-two, Campbell-Bannerman stood in a by-election in Stirling Burghs against a more Whiggish Liberal and lost by a whisker. At the general election later the same year, 1868, on the larger reformed register, he was elected. The Stirling Burghs – Stirling, Dunfermline and the area around the present-day Forth bridges – went on to return him at every election up to 1906.

He married Charlotte Bruce in 1860. She was a rather shy and homely lass, in later life in poor health and overweight, who shared Campbell-Bannerman's tastes and views during a lifetime of mutual devotion. There were no children. They shared everything, including major political decisions; indeed, Charlotte had more ambition for Henry than he had, and her views often seem to have counted when it mattered.

An early parliamentary campaign was for universal elementary education, and for the rest of his career he came to epitomise the description 'radical common sense'. Herbert Samuel (*q.v.*) said he was 'common sense enthroned'. By the 1890s he was in the centre left of the party without having much changed his views. He never had much truck with the more ostentatious radicals such as Labouchere or Dilke.

Most of his career was spent in the 'middle management' of the government and party in parliament. In 1871 he became Financial Secretary at the War Office under the great army reformer Cardwell, serving until 1874. He took the same office from 1880–82, and in 1884 became Chief Secretary for Ireland for seven months. He joined the Cabinet as Secretary of State for War in 1886, and again from 1892, under first Gladstone, and then Rosebery, until 1895 when the fractious Liberals lost office, ironically on the so-called 'cordite motion' to cut the salary of Campbell-Bannerman himself. A quiet record of army reform is one of his enduring achievements.

His brief spell as Irish Secretary was a turning point in gaining Campbell-Bannerman respect and stature amongst MPs. His self-confident and unflappable ability to get on with almost everyone, with a ready Scots wit based much on self-irony and understatement, helped him survive that 'political graveyard' – his own assessment was of the need for a 'light heart and a thick skin'. He never took himself as seriously as he took the things he believed in. He was one of the Queen's favourite Liberals, and got on well with everyone from generals and civil servants to the workers in Dunfermline; and he never lost contact with his real political allies in the parliamentary party. He was at home in the Commons but rarely shined there. He seemed able to get by on a combination of affability and shrewd common sense when others had to work much harder and deploy greater intellectual resources. As a result, he was often underestimated.

The Campbell-Bannermans divided their time between central London, the continent, and a house at Meigle in Perthshire. Gladstone went back to Hawarden and chopped down trees; CB pottered round his estate talking to his. He also talked to the grey African parrot he kept for some forty years, and to his thirty French bulldogs – not to mention his walking sticks! Spender (*q.v.*) reports that 'CB never disguised his opinion that London society was bad for Radical politics'.

In 1895 Campbell-Bannerman thought of applying for the vacant post of Speaker, but the party would not let him. He was one of the few Liberal leaders who was not hopelessly committed to one faction or another, and his party needed him. Then in 1899, after an unsatisfactory cohabitation with Rosebery as leader in the Lords and Harcourt (*q.v.*) in the Commons, he took on the task of leader in the Commons, and thereafter effectively and increasingly, leader of the party and Prime Minister-elect. This was not a job he wanted. But again he was sorely needed to hold things together; and again his inherent loyalty to the party pushed him into it.

The party was deeply divided, particularly over the Boer War. Campbell-Bannerman maintained a stance of never being against the armed forces or their welfare and supplies (with his ministerial career, how could he?); but he criticised the government for starting the war, and later spoke out strongly against the 'methods of barbarism' the British used in the 'ethnic cleansing' of the Transvaal countryside, the burning of the farmsteads and the appalling conditions in the concentration camps. And so in time he was able to create an administration which included Liberal Imperialists such as Grey (*q.v.*) and Asquith, even Haldane (*q.v.*), and 'pro-Boers' such as Morley and Lloyd George – though in the mean time he had to contend with continuing plots from the Lib-Imp right, at first (ludicrously) involving Rosebery and subsequently aimed at shunting him into the Lords so that Asquith could take over in the Commons and effectively lead the party.

But in 1903 the break in the clouds arrived with Joe Chamberlain's (*q.v.*) conversion to protection, an issue which united Liberals and split Unionists as effectively as Chamberlain had split the Liberal Party in the 1880s over home rule. By the end of 1905 Prime Minister Balfour could no longer hold together even his large notional majority and Campbell-Bannerman formed a minority Liberal government. Even at this late stage the Liberal Leaguers (Lib Imps) were still plotting and it took Charlotte, by now terminally ill, to stiffen his resolve to stay in the Commons.

He was determined to achieve a balanced Cabinet, involving all except the most fringe elements of the party. His management of the Cabinet and the government was by all accounts relaxed but efficient, and brilliant. But personally it all came too late for him to go down as a great Prime Minister. Charlotte died within the year, and Campbell-Bannerman, heartbroken, had less than two years left before dying in Number 10 Downing Street on 22 April 1908, a few days after handing over to Asquith. He and Charlotte are buried together at Meigle.

The dissolution early in 1906 brought the Liberals' greatest-ever poll triumph, but much of the Liberal campaign was a crusade against Balfour and the Tories. It took time for the Liberals to construct a programme, and they had the Lords (at their most partisan) to contend with. So the government started slowly and built up over the years into probably the greatest Liberal government of all time. What Campbell-Bannerman bequeathed to Asquith was a party which had held together against all the odds, a huge Commons majority, and truly a 'government of all the talents', on the brink of major Liberal reforms and radical battles, and based on an anti-Tory alliance spanning the Liberal Party, the emergent Labour Party and most of the Irish nationalists.

Campbell-Bannerman was the best and most successful party leader that Liberals have ever had: a man who held his party together and held it to Liberalism, and who briefly went on to reap the rewards. How many times since has the party needed the twinkling wisdom, calm toughness and firm Liberal faith of a CB! And how many leaders have, instead, been led astray by personal vanity and ambition?

Some of Campbell-Bannerman's later speeches can be found in volumes of *The Liberal Magazine* (1892 to his death); there is at least one collected volume (1899–1908) selected and reprinted from *The Times*. *Early Letters of Sir Henry Campbell-Bannerman to his sister Louisa, 1850–51* chosen and edited by Lord Pentland (T. Fisher Unwin, 1925), is a delightful record of his life-shaping trip to Europe as a fourteen year old. There are only two full-length biographies, from different eras: J. A. Spender's

Life of the Rt Hon Sir Henry Campbell-Bannerman, GCB (2 vols, Hodder & Stoughton, 1923), a rather old-fashioned work which benefits from the author having known CB. John Wilson's *CB – A Life of Sir Henry Campbell-Bannerman* (Constable, & St Martin's Press, 1973) is a more solid and definitive modern work which benefits from access to papers of many contemporary politicians, not least Campbell-Bannerman himself, whose papers are in the British Museum.

Tony Greaves

ALEX CARLILE   1949–

Alexander Charles Carlile was born on 12 February 1949 at Rossett in North Wales, the son of Dr Erwin Falik and Sabina Falik, née Lozinska. His father was a doctor, a soldier and a Polish Jewish immigrant, while his mother had fought in the Warsaw uprising. He once recalled that when his father went to study medicine in a very good Polish medical university in 1922, he was only allowed to conduct anatomy on Jewish bodies.

He was educated at Heathfield School, Risworth in Yorkshire, Epsom College, King's College, London, and the Inns of Court. On 19 October 1968 he married Frances, the daughter of Michael and Elizabeth Soley. They have three daughters: Anna (born 1973), Eve (1975) and Ruth (1980).

He was called to the bar in 1970 by Gray's Inn, where he became a Bencher in 1992. He became a QC in 1984 in London and Chester. For many years he earned his living in the London chambers of Emlyn Hooson, the Liberal MP for Montgomeryshire (*q.v.*). He has been Hon. Recorder of the City of Hereford since 1986. He is viewed as an able, sensible, persuasive and eloquent QC, with a vast legal experience on the Wales and Chester circuit.

Carlile's family background was staunchly Liberal, and he himself was a Liberal while still at school. He stood unsuccessfully as the Liberal candidate for the East Flintshire constituency in the general elections of February 1974 and 1979, and served as chairman of the Welsh Liberal Party, 1980–82. In 1983 he succeeded in recapturing highly marginal Montgomeryshire for the Liberals by the slim majority of 668 votes; the seat had been won from Hooson by a Conservative, Delwyn Williams, in 1979. Carlile was re-elected in 1987 and 1992, clearly the beneficiary of large numbers of tactically cast Labour and Plaid Cymru votes in the county.

From 1985 onwards he acted as Liberal (subsequently Liberal Democrat) spokesman on a wide array of subjects, among them home affairs, legal affairs, foreign affairs, trade and industry, Wales, employment, health, justice, and immigration. From 1992 he was a member of the Select Committee on Welsh Affairs. Throughout his period in the House of Commons he displayed a special interest in home affairs, agriculture, legal affairs, the United Nations, and central and eastern Europe. The last-named preoccupation ensured his election as Vice-Chairman of the Great Britain East Europe Centre and Co-Chairman of the Committee for the Return of Britain to UNESCO. He also served as a lay member of the General Medical Council and a Fellow of the Industry and Parliament Trust. His family background made him a strong supporter of war crimes trials. He continued to practice as a QC throughout his period as an MP, remaining devoted to the bar as an institution, and evidently savouring a lucrative income from his legal work.

He was leader of the Welsh Liberal Democrats (as the only Welsh MP in the party) from 1992 until 1997. In 1997 he resolved to retire from the Commons and the marginal Montgomeryshire constituency was retained for the Liberals by Lembit Öpik (*q.v.*). He has consistently advocated a common anti-Tory electoral front, and was originally a strong and sardonic critic of Paddy Ashdown (*q.v.*). He is, first and foremost, a libertarian, who believes that individual liberties are 'the holy grail of Liberalism'.

He has been variously described as 'tall, slim, beaky nose, balding, Middle Eastern look, smooth, slightly aloof, waspish' (*Western Mail*), and 'sharp and sardonically witty, but a negative factor on television' (Robin Oakley in *The Times*). He made efforts to learn the Welsh language, and has continued to champion countryside practices, including hunting. Alex Carlile's family home is Cil y Wennol, Berriew in Powys, a sixteenth-century property which he bought from the Lord Lieutenant of Powys.

J. Graham Jones

JOSEPH CHAMBERLAIN 1836–1914

In a picture postcard (Tuck & Sons Ltd, c. 1905) 'Radical Joseph' was pictured wearing a 'coat of many colours'. Each segment was labelled with different stages in his political career: 'socialist', 'extreme radical', 'Gladstonian', 'Liberal Unionist', 'Conservative' and 'protectionist and food taxer'. 'Inconsistent' was one of the more favourable epithets used of Chamberlain. To the Liberals he was a traitor, to the Conservatives a dangerous radical, and to the people of Birmingham a hero, despite the fact that by birth he was a Londoner.

Joseph Chamberlain, the eldest son of a prosperous shoemaker, was born on 8 July 1836. As a Unitarian, Chamberlain was forbidden entry to a public school, so he was educated at University College School until he was sixteen. He joined the family business for two years and then moved to Birmingham. His uncle, J. S. Nettlefold, had decided to introduce steam-powered lathes to his screw-manufacturing business and approached his brother for financial help. The latter agreed on condition that his son should join the firm. Chamberlain's energy and organisational abilities drove out Nettlefold's competitors and in 1874 he was able to retire with a substantial fortune at age thirty-eight.

Chamberlain married Harriet Kenrick in July 1861 and they had a daughter, Beatrice, and a son, Austen. Harriet died suddenly in 1863 and Chamberlain went on to marry one of her cousins, Florence, in June 1868. The eldest of their four children and only son was the future Prime Minister, Neville. This marriage also ended suddenly, with Florence's death in 1875 after she gave birth to another son, who did not survive. Chamberlain dealt with his grief by throwing himself into public work.

The second Reform Act of 1867 encouraged Chamberlain to become involved in educational provision to 'educate our new masters', and he contributed £1000 to the Birmingham Education League, founded in 1869. He was elected a town councillor in 1869 and a member of the Birmingham School Board. In 1873 he was elected mayor, a post to which he was re-elected in 1874 and 1875. Chamberlain focused on improving the physical condition of the town and its people. He organised the purchase of the two gas companies and the water works; he appointed a Medical Officer of Health, established a Drainage Board, extended the paving and lighting of streets, opened six public parks, saw the start of the public transport service and personally laid the foundation stone of the new Council House. His 'Improvement Scheme' saw the demolition of ninety acres of slums in the town centre. The council bought the freehold of about half the land to build Corporation Street. His pioneering efforts brought him to national prominence and marked social reform as a Liberal platform.

At the general election of 1874 he stood unsuccessfully as a Liberal candidate for Sheffield but was returned unopposed in 1876 as one of Birmingham's MPs, representing the constituency for the rest of his life. In Parliament he was distrusted as a Dissenter and upstart; his genuinely radical speeches frightened the Conservatives. He was a constructive radical, caring more for practical success than party loyalty or ideological commitment. His industrial middle class constituents adored him; his efficient party organisation (the Caucus) resulted in huge Liberal votes in the Midlands. With the Caucus as his pattern, Chamberlain established the National Liberal Federation, launched by Gladstone (q.v.) on 31 May 1877. The Federation was intended to provide Liberals with a political apparatus for fighting elections, publishing posters and pamphlets, enlisting new members, collecting subscriptions and organising meeting and social events.

By 1880 the Liberal Party was increasingly divided over the question of social reform. Chamberlain and Sir Charles Dilke led the radical Liberals in Gladstone's second ministry (1880–85) which was largely occupied by Irish affairs. In 1882 Chamberlain was appointed as President of the Board of Trade and was keen to see further reforms. However Gladstone found the whole issue boring and Hartington (q.v.) was positively hostile. In 1885 the radical wing embarked on the 'Unauthorised Programme', which demanded a graduated income tax, free education, improved housing for the poor, local government reform and 'three acres and a cow' for agricultural labourers. In one of his speeches Chamberlain declared: ' I am told if I pursue this course that I shall break up the party .... but I care little for the party .... except to promote the objects which I publicly avowed when I first entered Parliament'. Although Chamberlain's programme was largely responsible for the Liberal victory of 1885, Gladstone made no concessions to him and ignored the case for social reform, thus setting the party on the road to deeper divisions.

While Chamberlain favoured Irish reform and supported Gladstone in opposing the use of force in quashing Irish agitation, he advocated imperial unity and opposed Gladstone when he committed the party to Irish Home Rule in 1885. In 1886 Chamberlain and the other so-called Liberal Unionists defeated Gladstone's Home Rule Bill and the consequent split in the party proved permanent. The Conservatives, supported by the Liberal Unionists, dominated British politics for most of the next twenty years. Chamberlain used his control of the Liberal Unionists to pressure the Conservatives into adopting a more progressive social policy, but Conservative supremacy marked a new emphasis upon empire and foreign affairs and Chamberlain turned increasingly to these interests.

In 1895 he joined Salisbury's Conservative Cabinet as Secretary of State for the Colonies. He soon became involved in South African affairs and was accused of complicity in the Jameson Raid of December 1895, possibly with foundation, although he claimed not to have known about Jameson's planned invasion of the Transvaal. A select committee of the House of Commons (1897) looked at the evidence and revealed nothing to Chamberlain's discredit – a tactful choice since Chamberlain presided over the committee. However, he was determined to form under British rule a southern African federation incorporating Cape Colony, Natal and the two Boer republics of Transvaal and the Orange Free State. The main result was the Boer War (1899–1902) which Chamberlain supported enthusiastically even though it soon became apparent that Britain was militarily vulnerable and diplomatically isolated in Europe. Consequently Chamberlain looked to the self-governing colonies for international support, announcing a preferential tariff scheme that he hoped would draw Britain and its dependencies together and raise revenue for social reform. When Balfour refused to commit himself to the idea, Chamberlain resigned his Cabinet post and from 1903 to 1906 conducted a campaign to 'think imperially'.

Free trade had been the basis of Britain's economic policy since the repeal of the Corn Laws in 1846, and the Liberals continued to advocate cheap bread. The Conservatives split over tariff reform as irrevocably as the Liberals had over Home Rule; in the general election of 1906 the Conservatives and Liberal Unionists were defeated, largely because of Chamberlain's abandonment of free trade. Chamberlain was himself re-elected in Birmingham, however, by a huge majority. It was his last political victory; in July 1906 he suffered a paralytic stroke that left him a helpless invalid for the rest of his life. He died on 2 July 1914 in London.

Chamberlain's political papers are in Birmingham University library. A six-volume history of his life by J. L. Garvin and J. Amery was published between 1932 and 1969. Other sources include M. Hurst, *Joseph Chamberlain and Liberal Reunion* (1967);

P. Marsh, *Joseph Chamberlain: entrepreneur in politics* (1994), and Robert V. Kubicek, *The Administration of Imperialism: Joseph Chamberlain at the Colonial Office* (1969).

Marjie Bloy

DAVID CHIDGEY MP   1942–

David Chidgey's successful defence of the Eastleigh constituency in 1997 after winning his seat in a June 1994 byelection helped to demonstrate, along with the success of David Rendel (*q.v.*) in Newbury, that byelection victors could still go on to hold their seats in the following general election. His byelection win, the final gain in a string of southern byelections which saw Christchurch and Newbury fall to the Liberal Democrats in the 1992–97 Parliament, helped rebuild confidence in the party in south-central England.

David William George Chidgey was born in Basingstoke, Hampshire, on 9 July 1942, and educated at the Royal Naval College, Portsmouth. He began his career as a civilian student mechanical and aeronautical engineer with the Admiralty in Portsmouth. After qualifying as a mechanical engineer he studied civil engineering at Portsmouth Polytechnic, launching a thirty-year career in civil, structural and building services engineering works.

A five-year period with Hampshire County Council in Winchester developed a speciality in traffic engineering projects. He married April Idris-Jones in 1965, and had three children; a son, David (born 1965) and two daughters, Joanna (1969) and Caitlin (1971). Leaving local government in 1973, he joined consulting engineers Brian Colquhoun & Partners. Traffic management projects took him to West Africa and Oman, as well as developing integrated transport planning systems in Dublin before he set up the firm's regional office in Eastleigh in 1989.

Chidgey's political activities developed, like so many of the era, through local government. First elected to his local town council in New Alresford in 1976, he later served on Winchester City Council from 1987 to 1991. It was his wider European interests which led to his emergence into national politics in the autumn of 1988, soon after the merger of the Liberal Party and SDP. Selected to fight the Hampshire Central European byelection, he contested the same seat in the European Parliamentary elections of the following year, and was selected for his neighbouring Parliamentary constituency of Eastleigh, within Hampshire Central, the same year. He contested the 1992 general election and retained second place for the Liberal Democrats.

The death of Eastleigh Conservative MP Stephen Milligan in the spring of 1994 led to one of the longest drawn-out byelection campaigns of recent years. The Conservative government, not wanting an almost certain byelection loss on local election polling day in May in advance of the European elections in June, held off calling the election in the spring. The local elections became a byelection by proxy; the Liberal

Democrats won thirteen of the fifteen seats contested and all looked set for a traditional byelection with a comfortable win for Chidgey.

John Smith's sudden death in May changed the political landscape. A suspension
of campaigning, sympathy for Labour's position and the early emergence of Tony
Blair as the likely new Labour leader all worked to boost Labour's chances in the
railway town. Chidgey had a fight on his hands. Labour had run the local council
until 1976 and in the early 1970s had come close to winning the parliamentary seat.
What became a three-cornered contest ultimately saw Chidgey win with a 9,000
majority on a twenty-two per cent swing, with the Conservative candidate pushed
into third place.

Chidgey brought his engineering experience to bear in the House of Commons.
As one of a small number of engineers in the House, and with his background in
transport, Chidgey was a natural as the party's transport spokesman at a time when
railway privatisation was being fiercely debated. This gave him a national profile and
helped him in Eastleigh too; railway interests and the decline of a major rail engineering works in the town played heavily on the psyche of his constituency. But could he
reverse the trend of recent parliaments and hold his seat in the following general
election? He is quoted as saying, 'I wanted to be a proper MP, and not just some
byelection blip'. He succeeded, albeit by the finest of margins, with a 754-vote majority. He is now the leader of the Liberal Democrats' trade and industry team

Keith House

PRATAP CHITNIS (Lord Chitnis) 1936–

The Liberal Party has been blessed with much organisational talent, able to marshal
the party's limited resources in such a way as to achieve some remarkable and memorable electoral successes. Amongst the most well-known organisers have been Trevor
Jones (*q.v.*) and Chris Rennard (*q.v.*); the path they have trod was first cleared by
Pratap Chitnis, who in the early 1960s was the Liberal Party's first Local Government
Officer and first Training Officer, and who established his campaigning credentials as
agent at the Orpington byelection of 1962. Chitnis' influence over the party's campaigning and organisational priorities can still be observed within the Liberal Democrats today.

Pratap Chidamber Chitnis was born on 1 May 1936 into an Anglo-Indian family
with a Liberal background – his grandfather had stood unsuccessfully for the Westminster St George's seat in the 1906 general election. Educated at Penryn School,
Stonyhurst, and the Universities of Birmingham and Kansas, becoming a Master of
Arts at the latter, he began work for the National Coal Board (NCB) in 1958, having
previously considered joining the Newman Society. In November 1958 he heard Jo
Grimond (*q.v.*) speak at a rally at the Albert Hall and was inspired to join St Marylebone

Liberal Association as a consequence. Quickly drafted on to the Association's executive committee, Chitnis stood for St Marylebone Borough Council in 1959. He polled ninety-nine votes, finishing fifteenth out of fifteen candidates standing in a five-member ward. It was to be his sole electoral contest.

During 1959, Chitnis left the NCB to work in the library of the National Liberal Club. He quickly caught the eye of senior Liberals and when the Local Government Department of the Liberal Party Organisation (LPO) was established in 1960, on the initiative of Richard Wainwright (*q.v.*), he became its head. There was, at this time, very little contact between the Liberal Party's headquarters and councillors, many of whom were robustly resistant to external interference and embroiled in local political pacts. Chitnis found that his first task was to identify as best he could where Liberal councillors had been elected, often by telephoning round local newspapers. He then toured the country meeting councillors, encouraging more Liberals to contest local elections, at the same time penning the party's local government handbook.

Despite having no previous experience, Chitnis was dispatched to Orpington early in 1962 to mastermind the Liberals' byelection campaign. Eric Lubbock's (Lord Avebury, *q.v.*) victory established Chitnis' reputation as an organisational genius, although the strong local government base developed in the town over the preceding five years is often overlooked. Back at headquarters, Chitnis became the party's first Training Officer, charged with the task of recruiting professional Liberal agents and instilling into them the necessities of careful campaign management and strategic thinking. He served in this capacity from 1962–64, before taking charge of the party's antiquated press office for a further two years. In 1966, Chitnis took over from Tim Beaumont (*q.v.*) as Head of the LPO, resigning in the autumn of 1969 to become Secretary of the Joseph Rowntree Trust.

Chitnis assumed a major role in the Rowntree Trust for twenty years, as Secretary until 1975 and then as Chief Executive until 1988. The Trust funded a range of progressive political organisations and think tanks, including the Liberal Party. At the same time, Chitnis took an active part in a number of organisations involved with race issues. He was a member of the Community Relations Commission from 1970–77; chairman of the BBC Immigrants Programme Advisory Committee 1979–83; Chairman of Refugee Action 1981–86; and Chairman of the British Refugee Council 1986–89. Throughout the 1980s, Chitnis observed elections in trouble spots throughout the world, particularly El Salvador on four separate occasions.

At the nomination of David Steel (*q.v.*), Chitnis was made a life peer in 1977, taking the title Lord Chitnis of Ryedale. Although at first an active member of the Liberal benches, in recent years Chitnis has played little part in politics. He lives in France with his wife Anne, née Brand, whom he married in 1964.

Mark Egan

SIR WINSTON CHURCHILL   1874–1965

Winston Leonard Spencer Churchill was born in Blenheim Palace, Oxfordshire on 30 November 1874, the son of Lord Randolph Churchill and his American wife, Jennie. He was educated at Harrow and Sandhurst, and embarked on a military career which took him to India and Africa. He also began to make a name for himself as a war correspondent.

In 1899 he resigned his commission in the army and returned to England. He fought (unsuccessfully) a byelection as a Conservative at Oldham later in the year, but won the seat in the 1900 general election, thus first losing to and then defeating Walter Runciman (*q.v.*).

Churchill found himself increasingly at odds with the Conservative leadership and crossed the floor of the Commons in 1904. His conversion to Liberalism was controversial: the public reason lay in his continued support for free trade but he may also have suspected that his personal prospects were better as a Liberal, given the Conservative disarray under Balfour. His literary talents were engaged in writing the life of his father. He had, however, shown an interest in social issues and had read Seebohm Rowntree's work on poverty.

When Campbell-Bannerman (*q.v.*) formed his Liberal government in December 1905, Churchill accepted appointment as Under-Secretary for the Colonies. Having been returned as MP for Manchester North West, Churchill remained in this post until April 1908. Asquith (*q.v.*) brought him into the Cabinet, its youngest member, as President of the Board of Trade. He lost his seat in the ensuing byelection which was then obligatory, but found a new parliamentary seat in Dundee. He also found a wife in September 1908 – Clementine Hozier, a woman ten years younger than himself. They eventually had one son and two daughters.

In the Cabinet Churchill by no means confined his interests to trade policy. He retained a keen interest in army matters and in general issues of foreign policy. In the January 1910 general election he was one of the most active Liberal platform speakers; his skill with words on the platform equalled his skill with the pen. At the age of thirty-five he became Home Secretary. It was a controversial period, and he took a firm line in upholding public order at a time of industrial discontent. A certain pugnacity was evident, as was an eye for publicity.

In September 1911, Churchill moved to become First Lord of the Admiralty. In previous years he had had reservations about the scale of naval expenditure, but in his new office he espoused the navy's cause vigorously. He concerned himself contentiously both with broad strategic issues and with the roles of individuals. However, although he concentrated his formidable energy on naval matters, he continued to concern himself with the broad issues of policy confronting the government. He involved himself in the controversies surrounding Irish Home Rule (which he favoured) and dabbled with the possibility of far-reaching devolution within the

British Isles as a whole.

In July 1914 he was not eager for war but nevertheless described himself to his wife as being 'interested, geared up and happy'. He was not among that section of the party which was uncertain about the necessity for intervention. Many supposed that his personal dynamism and strategic vision would make him the outstanding war leader, but it turned out not to be the case. His career became mixed up in the controversies surrounding the disastrous attack on the Dardanelles in 1915. In the new coalition government of 1915 he became Chancellor of the Duchy of Lancaster, but resigned in November and went to serve on the Western Front.

He returned as Minister of Munitions in July 1917. Retaining his Dundee seat as a Coalition Liberal in 1918, he became Secretary of State for War and Air in 1919, and for the Colonies in 1921. After the fall of the Lloyd George (*q.v.*) coalition in 1922, Churchill was defeated at Dundee in the ensuing general election.

The following year, he failed to win Leicester West as a Liberal. His campaign there had become increasingly anti-Labour rather than anti-Conservative, and there was press speculation that he was on his way back to the party he had left. In 1924 he failed to win the Abbey Division of Westminster as an Independent anti-Socialist, but later that year was elected for Epping as a Constitutionalist. His separation from the Liberal Party was complete when he accepted office as Chancellor of the Exchequer in Baldwin's new government.

Churchill's political behaviour thereafter suggested that he was constricted by party politics. The Baldwin government having been defeated in 1929, he took an increasingly independent line, resigning from the Shadow Cabinet in 1931 in protest against proposals for increased Indian self-government. He was out of office, and one of the strongest critics of the government's policy of appeasement, until September 1939, when he again returned to the Admiralty on the outbreak of war.

His great moment came in May 1940, when he became Prime Minister at a time of national crisis as confidence in Chamberlain disappeared. His leadership of the coalition government in wartime became legendary. However, the 'saviour of the nation', as he was frequently held to be, suffered defeat in the 1945 general election, although he himself was safely returned for Woodford as a National Conservative. In opposition, he engaged in writing his own war memoirs, in a role as 'world statesman' at a time of accelerating Cold War.

In 1951, following the Conservative electoral victory, he again became Prime Minister. Before his resignation in April 1955, he strove to be a mediator between East and West. Honours flowed thick and fast in the post-war period, including the Nobel Prize for Literature in 1953. In 1964 Churchill left the House of Commons. He died in London on 24 January 1965 and, after a state funeral, was buried in Bladon churchyard, near Blenheim, in Oxfordshire.

His twenty years as an active Liberal MP had come when he was at the youthful height of his powers. If the Liberal Party had remained as an integrated political force he might in due course have become its leader. In the event, however, his own vision of his country's destiny and his own personal role could not be contained within Liberalism. Yet, for all his subsequent Conservatism, there were strands in his complex outlook which still reflected his Liberal phase.

A selection of his books – *Lord Randolph Churchill* (1906), *The World Crisis* (1923–31) *Marlborough* (1933–38), *The Second World War* (1948–54) – testifies to his powers as an author. Key biographies include Martin Gilbert, *Winston S. Churchill* (1991) – a distillation of the author's massive and meticulous study, the seventh and final volume of which was published in 1988; Keith Robbins, *Churchill* (1992); and H. M. Pelling, *Winston Churchill* (1974).

Keith Robbins

TIM CLEMENT-JONES (Lord Clement-Jones)   1949–

Tim Clement-Jones was born in Neath, South Wales, on 26 October 1949. His political heritage is striking – one grandfather, Sir Clement Jones, had been part of Lloyd George's (*q.v.*) War Cabinet Secretariat and a Liberal candidate in 1910; another was Austen Hudson, the Conservative MP for Hull. He was educated at Haileybury before going up to Trinity College, Cambridge, where he took a degree in economics and law.

At Cambridge he briefly joined the Cambridge Union but soon came to see it as a talking shop for the politically ambitious Young Conservatives. On leaving Cambridge, Clement-Jones settled in to articles in London at the City firm Coward Chance (now Clifford Chance). His responsibilities there were far removed from the work he undertook at the North Kensington Law Centre, where he recognised that action, rather than fine words and grandiose gestures, could change people's lives.

It was not long before Clement-Jones' practical experiences were reflected in his political beliefs. In October 1973, he joined the Streatham Liberal Association, attracted by the Liberals' 'enthusiasm and radicalism'; by 1974 he was ward organiser. In 1976 he became Secretary to the Association of Liberal Lawyers, campaigning for civil liberties, legal aid and, particularly, public order and policing issues. He was a council candidate for the Streatham Hill ward of the London Borough of Lambeth in 1978, 1982 and 1986, losing by just four votes on the last occasion. In 1980 he became the prospective parliamentary candidate for Streatham. Behind the scenes he was elected to the Liberal Policy Committee and then joined the National Executive as Clement Freud's alternate. At Paul Tyler's (*q.v.*) behest he produced the 'warfare paper' and thus firmly established his reputation as a leading strategist within the party.

As Clement-Jones' involvement in politics grew, his career went from strength to strength; moving to Legal Director at Grand Metropolitan Retailing, from Head of Legal Services at London Weekend Television, before becoming Group Company

Secretary and Legal Advisor at Kingfisher plc in 1986.

He had married Vicky Yip, whom he had met at university, in 1973. In 1982 she was diagnosed with cancer; the juggling act of active politics, home and career intensified when Clement-Jones became Chairman of the Liberal Party in 1986. Vicky died on 30 July 1987, seven weeks after the general election. With support from Kingfisher and his political colleagues, the merger process with the Social Democrats which started that autumn gave him a welcome opportunity to look to the future.

It was Paddy Ashdown's (*q.v.*) team-building skills that persuaded Clement-Jones that this was the right person to lead the newly merged party on the platform of the policies that had emerged in 1986 and have sustained the party for the last twelve years. He ran Ashdown's successful leadership campaign in 1988, and was described by the media as 'keen, upbeat and idealistic to a degree that sets the teeth of some MPs on edge'.

He went on to direct the 1994 European election campaign, when the party made its two-seat breakthrough, and was Vice-Chair of the 1997 general election campaign team. He is a member of the Liberal Democrats' Federal Executive and has been Chair of the party's Finance and Administration Committee since 1991.

Clement-Jones was ennobled as a working peer – Lord Clement-Jones of Clapham – in July 1998, and became the party's health spokesman in the House of Lords. His contribution, more than most, will form a bridge between politics and experience. Much of his role will require a return to policy development but it will also be an opportunity to give voice to the cause of Cancer BACUP, founded by Vicky before her death to support patients with cancer and promote their interests.

Clement-Jones' legendary keenness is not diminished by his new responsibilities; he remains a director of Political Context, the public affairs and environmental consultancy, as well as being a founding partner of ICM (Independent Corporate Mentoring), the legal management consultancy. His charitable causes include Crime Concern (formerly as Chairman, now as a director), Lambeth Crime Prevention Trust (trustee) and Opportunity 2000 (steering group member). He lives in Clapham with his second wife, Jean (whom he married in 1994), and baby son, Harry, born on 1 March 1998.

Rachel Oliver

RICHARD COBDEN

1804-1865

Richard Cobden is most famous for his advocacy of free trade and as a leader of the Anti-Corn Law League. He has been described as clothing free trade with a moral cloak. The repeal of the Corn Laws, and the subsequent embedding of the cause of free trade and cheap food in working-class beliefs, were personal triumphs for Cobden above anyone else.

Cobden, the son of a farmer, was born on 3 June 1804 in Heyshott, Sussex. After attending school in Yorkshire, he began a career as a travelling salesman, trading calicoes and muslins. He founded a calico printing firm in 1831, and moved to Manchester a year later, where he found almost immediate success. In 1840, he married Catherine Anne Williams from Wales; they had one son, who died in 1856 of scarlet fever whilst at school in Germany.

Cobden first sought election to Parliament after the succession of Queen Victoria in 1837, but he was defeated at Stockport. In March 1839 Cobden helped to launch the Anti-Corn Law League. His connection with the free trade movement had begun in 1836 when he was elected to the Board of the Manchester Chamber of Commerce. Cobden was in many ways the leader of the League throughout its existence, and it is to him that much of the credit should go for the most successful mass campaign of the nineteenth century, and the creation of the first modern pressure group, culminating in 1846 with the repeal of the Corn Laws. Cobden, like John Bright (q.v.), managed to convince a wider audience that repeal was not just a policy for the benefit of manufacturers, by lowering the cost of cotton goods and opening new export markets, but would also make a major contribution to the standard of living of the working class through cheap bread.

For Cobden the campaign against the Corn Laws was part of a wider concern for free trade and peace. He saw these two goals sitting together. He was convinced that the economic interests of manufacturers and the middle classes were naturally disposed towards peace and free trade, and against high military expenditure and high taxes, in direct contrast to his perception of the aristocracy as naturally bellicose. He continued to advocate these causes after repeal, opposing the Crimean War and negotiating a free trade treaty with France in 1860 (the Cobden-Chevalier Treaty).

Cobden became MP for Stockport in 1841. At the general election of 1847, he was elected as MP for both Stockport and the West Riding of Yorkshire. He chose the latter constituency; it was the largest in the country (and therefore an honour to represent) and his election secured the local victory of town Liberals over the traditional Whig leadership. After the repeal of the Corn Laws Cobden switched his energy to, amongst others things, campaigning for national educational reform. This brought him into conflict with Liberal interests in the West Riding, and his position in the 1857 general election was further weakened by his opposition to the Crimean War. He fought the election in Huddersfield, having decided not to contest the West Riding, but, like Bright and other opponents of the war, he was defeated. At the next general election in 1859, he was returned unopposed in Rochdale, which he represented until his death in 1865.

Cobden never held ministerial office. In 1846, Lord John Russell (q.v.) intimated that he would have a cabinet post in future if first he was prepared to join the government, but Cobden refused. In 1859 he again refused to join the Cabinet, as President of the Board of Trade, following an offer made by Russell to join Palmerston's administration. Cobden was a consistent critic of Palmerston (*q.v.*), arguing that he shifted the basis of his parliamentary position so often that, rather than representing any principles, he had become a despot. Following the Cobden-Chevalier Treaty, Palmerston offered Cobden both a baronetcy and the position of privy councillor, but he declined both. He remarked that his sole satisfaction lay in the furtherance of peaceful commercial relations between neighbouring countries.

Cobden was an accomplished author and orator. Despite little formal education, he taught himself French and composition, and studied education and European history. He began writing early in his career, producing two pamphlets entitled *England, Ireland and America* (1835) and *Russia* (1836), both by a 'Manchester Manufacturer', advocating free trade and non-intervention. In 1853, he wrote *1792 and 1853, in Three Letters,* which spoke of the fear of invasion after the rise of the Second Empire in France, and *How Wars are Got Up in India,* on the second Burmese war. Then in 1856, he published another pamphlet called *What Next? and Next?* After his defeat in 1857, he turned, not for the first time, to travel, and spent three months in the United States, fascinated by its substantial advancements. He wrote a final pamphlet entitled *The Three Panics of 1848, 1853, and 1862.*

Cobden's business career was much less successful, largely because, by his own admission, he neglected it for his public campaigns. Twice, public subscriptions were organised to bail out his finances, but financial stress and his heavy commitments took a severe toll on his health. He died of acute bronchitis, from which he had suffered over a long period, in Suffolk Street House, Pall Mall, on 2 April 1865.

Publications on his life and works include: John Bright and J. E. Thorold Rogers (eds), *Speeches on Questions of Public Policy by Richard Cobden* (1870); *The Political Writings of Richard Cobden* (1867); Morley's *Life of Richard Cobden* (1881); Ashworth's *Recollections of Richard Cobden and the Anti-Corn Law League* (1876); Archibald Prentice, *History of the Anti-Corn Law League* (1968); Norman McCord, *The Anti-Corn Law League, 1838–46* (1958); Nicholas C. Edsall, *Richard Cobden: Independent Radical* (1986); Cheryl Schonhardt-Bailey, *The Rise of Free Trade* (1997) (especially, vols. I & II).

Cheryl Schondhardt-Bailey and Elizabeth Flanagan Prueher

SIR ARTHUR COMYNS CARR 1882–1965

Arthur Strettell Comyns Carr was born on 19 September 1882. His father, J. W. Comyns Carr, was a dramatist and art critic, his mother a novelist. He was educated at Winchester School, then Trinity College, Oxford, and was called to the bar by Gray's Inn. He later became a KC, a Bencher of his Inn, and eventually Treasurer. In 1907 he married Cicely Oriana Raikes, daughter of R. R. Bromage, by whom he had three sons.

In his career, Comyns Carr combined law and politics in more or less equal measure. As a lawyer, he ran a mixed civil and criminal practice, and acquired similar distinction in both fields. He was part-author of *Faraday on Rating* (2 vols, 1934, etc.) and *Recent Mining Legislation* (1932). His forensic activities first attracted public attention during an action brought by the notorious Horatio Bottomley (*q.v.*) against a sometime associate named Bigland in the early 1920s. It was Comyns Carr's cross-examination which broke down Bottomley's case, eventually leading to his prosecution on criminal charges and expulsion from the House of Commons. Much later, Comyns Carr was involved in trials of war criminals, both Japanese and German. The work brought him a knighthood in 1949; but it has been said that the atrocities which these trials revealed so shook him that he never fully recovered.

Comyns Carr's interest in Liberal politics was deep-rooted. In 1912 he became part-author of a major work, *National Insurance*, to which Lloyd George (*q.v.*) wrote the introduction, and during the depression he wrote an influential and controversial booklet, *Escape from the Dole* (1930), which raised the pertinent question of why great sums of money were being spent in supporting unemployed people, instead of providing work for them.

In the general elections of 1918 and 1922, Comyns Carr sought unsuccessfully to enter Parliament for South West St Pancras. In 1923, he was elected for East Islington. Like the large majority of Liberal victors at that election, he fell victim to the party's inept handling of the balance-of-power situation created by the election, and the internecine conflicts which followed, and was heavily defeated in 1924. He stood at a byelection in llford in 1928, and in the same constituency at the general election of 1929, running a fairly close second on both occasions. In 1945 he made another unsuccessful attempt to enter Parliament, this time for Shrewsbury. Later in the same year, he was the candidate at a byelection in the City of London.

His interest in public affairs remained. From 1950–58, Comyns Carr was Chairman of the Foreign Compensation Commission, and he was President of the Liberal Party from 1958–59. The only memorable aspect of his presidency was the Torquay assembly in 1958. His inaudible chairing, caused by reading from notes carefully held between his mouth and the microphone, was a major contribution to what was described as Rasmussen as one of the most farcical post-war Liberal assemblies, though it did help stimulate a series of major reforms. During the debate on foreign affairs, which coincided with a political crisis over the Quemoy and Matsu islands, in the Formosa Strait, he observed from the chair that he hoped nothing anyone said during the debate would exacerbate the situation in Quemoy and the Matsus.

He died on 20 April 1965.

Roy Douglas

BRIAN COTTER MP   1938–

Following his dramatic victory over the Tories in Weston-super-Mare in 1997, Brian Cotter's appointment as the Liberal Democrats' parliamentary spokesman on small business was a fitting culmination to a career spent in commerce and industry. After two year's National Service, Cotter spent twenty years running a small business distributing merchandise to shops. Since then he has been, and remains, the managing director of a small plastics manufacturing company with twenty-five employees. His business experience has made him a staunch believer in the need for a business-like approach to politics – of providing an efficient operation, with a human face, to ensure his constituents are best served.

It was this approach that helped him to win Weston-super-Mare in the 1997 election. After years of returning Tory MPs Weston finally voted Liberal Democrat by electing Cotter with a majority of 1,274 – his second attempt in Weston, and as a parliamentary candidate. In 1992, after moving to the constituency from Woking, where he had been a district councillor, he succeeded in slashing Jerry Wigan's majority to 5,000.

Weston-super-Mare was the town in which Cotter's father had been born and educated before moving to London to work as a doctor in general practice. Cotter's strong family connections and his commitment to campaigning made him the ideal choice for the parliamentary candidate, and after the 1992 campaign he was unanimously reselected by the local party.

Cotter's political career started when he joined the Liberal Party in 1983 and, ever since, he has been an active member of the Liberals and then the Liberal Democrats. During his five years as a district councillor in Woking he was Chair of the council's Youth Committee. Prior to his election to Parliament he was an active member of the party's Parliamentary Candidates' Association (PCA) and continues now as the Parliamentary Party's liaison on the PCA's Executive Committee. On the PCA he had particular responsibility for training prospective parliamentary candidates around the country and his commitment and encouragement of new candidates continues. Despite his own success, he remains a great friend to those whose turns have yet to come!

Cotter's genuine appreciation and respect for people are his great strengths At a gathering he will instinctively seek out and speak to those feeling ill at ease and will be satisfied only if he has helped people to feel worthwhile about themselves, that he cared enough to talk. An extraordinarily sincere, loyal and likeable man with, apparently, limitless energy to pursue his parliamentary responsibilities – perhaps due to his healthy interest in Chinese and other alternative medicines.

Brian Joseph Cotter was born on 24 August 1938 and lived in outer London for most of his childhood, attending St Benedict's School, Ealing and later Downside School, Somerset. He has been married to Eyleen, an occupational therapist, since 1963 and they have two sons and one daughter, all of whom have now grown up. The couple now live in Congresbury, a village in the constituency. He is a member of the Association of Liberal Democrat Councillors, Amnesty International, Green Liberal Democrats and a signatory to Charter 88.

Jane Smithard

EARL OF CREWE   1858–1945

One of the great successes of Edwardian Liberalism was to curtail the power of the House of Lords to veto legislation. But as the Liberals did not abolish the Lords, they still needed the services of the small group of Liberal peers to present and defend the government's legislation in that House. This ensured that Liberal peers remained a significant element in the pre-war Liberal Cabinets, and Crewe was their most prominent representative. Despite being a little-known figure to the public, he was close to the centre of power in the Liberal Party for nearly 40 years.

Robert Offley Ashley Crewe-Milnes was born in London on 12 January 1858. He was the only son and heir of Richard Monckton Milnes, first Lord Houghton, a Yorkshire landowner with a considerable reputation as a man of fashion and literary dilettante. Crewe, like his father, was educated at Harrow and Trinity College, Cambridge. He also shared, though more energetically, his father's interest in Liberal politics and served as Assistant Private Secretary to Lord Granville at the Foreign Office in 1883–85. His father's death in 1885 removed him to the Lords as the second Lord Houghton, as well as giving him command of a substantial income. This was augmented when, on the death of his maternal uncle, Lord Crewe, he inherited Crewe Hall and broad estates in Cheshire and Staffordshire.

Crewe's adherence to the small band of Gladstonian peers in 1886, when the Liberals split over Irish Home Rule, ensured his rapid promotion. The Liberals were desperate for spokesmen in the Lords, and few shared his combination of ability with genuine radicalism. Crewe served as a Lord-in-Waiting in 1886 and then as Lord Lieutenant of Ireland in 1892–95. The latter post was a thankless task, as the office was purely ceremonial but involved the incumbent in huge expense, and he probably felt he fully deserved the Earldom of Crewe he received in the 1895 dissolution honours. In opposition Crewe remained one of the dozen or so active Liberal peers and he was rewarded with the post of Lord President of the Council and Cabinet rank in the next Liberal government of 1905. In April 1908 the octogenarian Lord Ripon retired, and Crewe succeeded him as Liberal leader in the Lords, combining his role with that of Secretary of State for the Colonies in 1908–10. In this office his main task was to steer through the bill giving self-government to the new Union of South Africa.

In 1910 Crewe swapped the Colonies for the India Office, holding this post until 1915 as well as being Lord Privy Seal in 1908–11 and 1912–15. He was promoted to the Marquessate of Crewe in 1911. Crewe's handling of Indian affairs confirmed his reputation as a sound administrator with few original ideas. He helped plan the Delhi Durbar in 1911 and maintained the policies of his predecessor, Lord Morley, in admitting Indians to a share of power in regional councils. Much more troublesome to Crewe was his role as Leader of the House of Lords. He had to deal personally with all government bills before the House, with the help of only one or two other ministers and in the face of a hostile Tory majority. Though ill-health prevented Crewe from playing a central role in persuading the Lords to end their veto by passing the 1911 Parliament Act, his skilful handling of legislation and maintenance of relations with the Tory peers helped prevent government business grinding to a halt in the upper house.

Just as importantly, Crewe became Asquith's (q.v.) most intimate confidant in the Liberal Cabinet. The Prime Minister claimed to value Crewe's advice above all others – probably because the two men seldom differed. Nevertheless, Crewe was always included in the Cabinet's inner councils at crucial moments, including the 1910 constitutional conference and the 1914 Irish Home Rule negotiations. After war was declared, Crewe received several important commissions from Asquith, including chairing the Cabinet committee on manpower in 1915 and serving as joint delegate to the Paris economic summit in 1916. In the 1915 coalition government Crewe moved back to the Lord Presidency of the Council and in August 1916 to the Board of Education. Not surprisingly, he left office with Asquith when the latter fell in December 1916.

However, Crewe continued to lead the Asquithian peers in the Lords until 1922, and took on a number of ceremonial roles, including Chairman of the London County Council in 1917–18 and Chancellor of Sheffield University in 1917–44. Curzon, the Tory Foreign Secretary, retained a high opinion of Crewe's powers and persuaded him to serve as a stylish, if largely ornamental, Ambassador to France in 1922–28. On his return to England Crewe resumed his senior place in the Liberal Party, briefly occupying the War Office in the National Government in August – November 1931, though at the age of seventy-three he was glad to relinquish that post. He served as Liberal leader in the Lords again in 1936–44 and was regularly consulted by Sir Archibald Sinclair (q.v.) on crucial issues such as appeasement.

Crewe died at West Horsley Place, his home in Surrey, on 20 June 1945. He married firstly in 1880 Sibyl Maria, daughter of Sir Frederick Graham, a fellow Yorkshire landowner. She died in 1887, leaving three daughters, and a son who died in 1890. In 1899 Crewe remarried Peggy Primrose, his junior by twenty-three years and daughter of the Earl of Rosebery (q.v.). They had one daughter, and one son who died young. Crewe's interests ranged from horse racing and cattle breeding to literature. He was President of the Royal Literary Fund in 1894–1903 and the author of a volume of *Stray Verses* (1891), the much-anthologised 'A Harrow Grave in Flanders' (1915) and a two-volume biography of Rosebery (1931). There is a slim biography by James Pope-Hennessy, *Lord Crewe, 1858–1945: the Likeness Of a Liberal* (1955).

Ian Packer

RALF DAHRENDORF (Lord Dahrendorf)   1929–

Writing in 1997, Ralf Dahrendorf referred to his favourite countries: 'Britain and Germany, and the Europe – even the Europe – to which they both belong'; his commitment to public service, to academia, to politics and to liberalism has been visible in all of them.

Born in Hamburg, that most anglophile of German cities, on 1 May 1929, Ralf Dahrendorf was brought up in Berlin. His father was the Social Democrat politician, Gustav Dahrendorf. Like his father, Ralf Dahrendorf was an active opponent of the Nazi regime and although still a schoolboy, was arrested and held in a camp in Frankfurt-an-der-Oder during the last year of the Second World War. Dahrendorf was later to comment that he had experienced the feeling of liberation twice in his life: once when the Red Army liberated Berlin and again when he and his father were smuggled out of that city by the British.

After the war Dahrendorf began an illustrious academic career as a philosopher and sociologist. He read classics and philosophy at the University of Hamburg, gaining a doctorate in 1952, before undertaking postgraduate studies in sociology at the London School of Economics between 1952 and 1954, acquiring a second doctorate in 1956. Returning to Germany, he became Professor of Sociology at the University of Hamburg in 1958, and subsequently held chairs at the University of Tübingen (1960–65) and at the University of Konstanz (1966–69), having been Vice-Chairman of the founding committee (1964–66).

Dahrendorf's political career began in Germany in 1968, when he was elected as a Free Democrat member of the Baden-Württemberg Landtag (state parliament). The following year he was elected to the Bundestag, and became a member of Willy Brandt's Social Democrat-Free Democrat coalition government as a junior foreign office minister dealing with European affairs under Foreign Secretary Walter Scheel. In 1970, however, Dahrendorf left domestic politics to become a member of the European Commission. Initially responsible for foreign trade and external relations, he took the research, science and education portfolio in 1973.

After his period as a European Commissioner, Dahrendorf's career was primarily academic and intellectual, and shifted from Germany to Britain. He was Director of the London School of Economics between 1974 and 1984 (and indeed wrote the history of the School to mark its centenary in 1995). After a brief period in Germany, he returned to Britain in 1987, this time as Warden of St. Antony's College, Oxford, a position he held until his retirement in 1997.

Despite his academic commitments, Dahrendorf was highly active in public life in Britain, serving *inter alia* on the Hansard Society's Commission on Electoral Reform (1975–76), the Royal Commission on Legal Services (1976–79) and the Committee to Review the Functioning of Financial Institutions (1977–80). Awarded a knighthood in 1982, Dahrendorf took British citizenship in 1988, and in 1993 was created a life peer, styled Baron Dahrendorf of Clare Market in the City of Westminster. Although he had not previously been active in British party politics the new Lord Dahrendorf opted to take the Liberal Democrat whip in the House of Lords.

Once a member of the House, Dahrendorf was soon playing an active role in British Liberal politics. In 1995 he chaired the Commission on Wealth Creation and Social Cohesion, the independent body set up by Liberal Democrat leader Paddy Ashdown (q.v.). Indeed, one of the things he hoped to do on retiring from St. Antony's was to become more active in the House of Lords, where he became a member of the Select Committee on Delegated Powers and Deregulation and in the same year was coopted on to the Select Committee on the European Communities, Sub-Committee A (economic and financial affairs, trade and external relations), as well as being a member of the All-Party London Group. Dahrendorf succeeded Baroness Seear (q.v.) as President of the Liberal Summer School and was an active participant in the 1998 School, the first under his presidency. He became a Patron of Liberal International (World Liberal Union) in 1987. Alongside his many other directorships and charitable activities – he is a Trustee of the Charities Aid Foundation – in 1997 he became a Director of the Bank Gesellschaft Berlin (UK) plc, while his interest in matters European is amply demonstrated by his place on the Board of Trustees of the Central European University in Budapest.

A Fellow of the British Academy, Honorary Fellow of the LSE, a Foreign Member of the (American) National Academy of Sciences, the American Philosophical Society, the Royal Irish Academy, the Russian Academy of Sciences, and the Polish Academy of Sciences, Dahrendorf had also by 1998 been awarded twenty-five honorary doctorates and had been decorated by seven countries, including the Grosses Bundesverdienstkreuz mit Stern und Schulterband of the German Federal Republic in 1974. Of his numerous writings, many translated into several languages, perhaps the most enduring is his sociological volume, *Class and Class Conflict,* published in 1959 (the original *Soziale Klassen und Klassenkonflikt* was published in 1957).

Dahrendorf has three daughters by his first wife. His second wife, Ellen, whom he married in 1980, is a scholar of Russian history.

Julie Smith

EDWARD DAVEY MP   1965–

Edward Jonathan Davey was born in Nottinghamshire on Christmas Day 1965, the youngest of three sons. His father was a solicitor, and died when he was four. His mother was a teacher and died when he was fifteen. He then lived with either his brothers or his mother's parents.

Davey went to Nottingham High School where he was head boy. After school he took a year off when he worked in a pork pie factory and for Boots plc, hitchhiked around Spain and worked as a holiday courier in France. He took a first class honours degree in politics, philosophy and economics at Jesus College, Oxford, where he was elected president of the Junior Common Room.

Davey was unemployed for several months before being appointed as the economics researcher to the Liberal Democrats in Parliament in 1989. He worked primarily for Alan Beith (*q.v.*) and Paddy Ashdown (*q.v.*), becoming the Liberal Democrats' senior economics advisor. He was closely involved in helping the Treasury team to develop policies such as the penny on income tax for education, and support for an independent central bank, and was in charge of costing the election manifesto in 1992. During his time with the party, Davey attended Birkbeck College, London and gained an MSc in economics.

He left Parliament in 1993 to work for the management consultancy firm, Omega Partners, where he specialised in postal services. During almost four years with the company, Davey visited twenty-eight countries and worked on projects for post offices in countries such as Belgium, South Africa, Sweden and Taiwan. His work ranged from strategic market analysis to business forecasting. Throughout his time at Omega, he remained an active Liberal Democrat, serving on the party's Federal Policy Committee and various policy groups.

Davey was selected to fight the parliamentary constituency of Kingston & Surbiton in March 1995. The Liberal Democrats' success in local council elections plus boundary changes meant that he was strongly placed to challenge the incumbent Conservative at the general election. The seat was won by a majority of fifty-six after three recounts, in an election which saw the Conservatives defeated for the first time in the history of the area.

Davey was appointed to the Liberal Democrat Treasury team following his election, with responsibility for public spending and taxation. He has particularly welcomed the role he has played in exposing the Labour government's 'swingeing cuts to public services' during the first year of its administration. In the long term, Davey would like to see economic strategy with the environment at its heart. He also speaks for the London Liberal Democrats on the economy, employment and tourism.

Davey is a passionate advocate of radical constitutional reform and, although welcoming the initial advances made by the Blair Government, he would like to see reform through which the power of the executive is subjected to real democratic checks and balances. He believes that significant decentralisation of political and economic power and a written constitution are crucial. Within the Liberal Democrats he has been a strong critic of close links with the Labour Party, believing that only by retaining and developing a clear identity can liberal politics succeed.

Davey has a strong commitment to his constituency and secured three adjournment debates on constituency issues in his first year at Westminster. He also represented the Liberal Democrats in the Finance Bill Committee.

Davey received awards from the Royal Humane Society and British Transport in 1994 for rescuing a woman from the path of an oncoming train at Clapham Junction.

Katie Hall

EDWARD CLEMENT DAVIES 1884–1962

Edward Clement Davies was born on 19 February 1884 at Llanfyllin, Montgomeryshire, the youngest of the seven children of Moses Davies, an auctioneer, and Elizabeth Margaret Jones. He was educated at the local primary school, won a scholarship to Llanfyllin County School in 1897 and proceeded to Trinity College, Cambridge, where he became senior foundation scholar and graduated with first class honours in both parts of the law tripos. He won a glittering array of prizes.

He earned his living as a law lecturer at the University College of Wales, Aberystwyth from 1908–09 and was called to the bar by Lincoln's Inn. He joined the North Wales circuit in 1909 and the Northern circuit in 1910. In the same year he migrated to London, soon establishing a successful and lucrative legal practice, displaying a rapid mastery of his briefs and publishing respected works on agricultural law and the law of auctions.

In 1914, at the outbreak of war, he was appointed adviser within the office of the Procurator- General on enemy activities in neutral countries and on the high seas. He was later made responsible for trading with the enemy, a position within the Board of Trade. In 1918–19 he served as Secretary to the President of the Probate, Divorce and Admiralty Division, and subsequently as Secretary to the Master of the Rolls until 1923. He was one of the junior counsel to the Treasury, 1919–25, and took silk in 1926. He served as Chairman of the Montgomeryshire quarter sessions from 1935 until his death in 1962.

From his boyhood Clement Davies had been fascinated by political life. He was approached as a possible Liberal candidate as early as 1910, but did not consent to stand for Parliament until 1927 when he was chosen as the Liberal candidate for his native Montgomeryshire. Seen initially as an avid radical and a stalwart supporter of David Lloyd George (*q.v.*), Davies was returned to Parliament in May 1929 by a majority of just over 2,000 votes. In August 1930 he accepted a lucrative position as legal director to Lever Brothers, which seemed to spell the end of his political career. But, at the eleventh hour, the company resolved to permit Davies to continue in Parliament.

In the general election of October 1931, after some complex political manoeuvres within Montgomeryshire, he was returned unopposed as one of the Liberal National followers of Sir John Simon (*q.v.*), and again in November 1935. As a back-bencher, he served as a tireless member of a number of committees. From 1937–38 he chaired an influential governmental inquiry into the incidence of tuberculosis in Wales, probing the standards of public health care and housing in all the Welsh counties. He consistently argued for the appointment of a Secretary of State for Wales.

At the outbreak of the Second World War he chaired an action committee which pressed for a more effective conduct of the war effort, and he is credited with persuading Lloyd George to speak in the House of Commons in May 1940

in favour of Neville Chamberlain's resignation. Lord Boothby, a first-hand observer of these events, was to describe Davies as 'one of the architects – some may judge the principal architect' of the coalition government led by Churchill.

In 1941 he resigned his position with Unilever, and in August 1942 rejoined the mainstream Liberal Party and spoke extensively throughout Britain. Re-elected with a majority of a little over 3,000 votes in the general election of 1945, Davies was now one of only twelve Liberal MPs. He was made Chairman of the party by his somewhat reluctant fellow members in succession to the defeated Sir Archibald Sinclair (*q.v.*). Throughout his tenure of this position until 1956, he faced an appallingly difficult political task.

At the 1945 Liberal Summer School he warned party members against the 'Tory spider', ever ready to trap Liberal supporters, and he consistently and doggedly distanced himself and his party from doctrinaire socialism. Consequently he faced no Tory opponent in Montgomeryshire in the general elections of 1951 and 1955. Yet his party faced manifold financial and organisational problems, and constantly lost members to both Conservatives and Labour. Even Lady Megan Lloyd George (*q.v.*), whom Davies appointed as his Deputy Leader in January 1949, seemed ever more likely to 'move left'. When Churchill offered him a Cabinet post as Minister of Education in October 1951, Davies refused, thus preserving the integrity of his party as an independent political force.

During subsequent years, until Jo Grimond (*q.v.*) succeeded him in September 1956, he spared no effort to revive and reunite his feud-racked, often ailing party, which he at least kept intact at a most critical time in its history. He was highly popular within Montgomeryshire and earned the respect of members of all parties within the Commons. Rightly described as 'a radical evangelist' by temperament rather than a party boss, he disliked rigid party organisation and conventions. He

93

spoke widely throughout England and Wales, most notably to university audiences, and never wavered in his heartfelt devotion to worthy causes such as social justice and reform, collective security, freedom of the individual, and world government.

He found his role as President of the Parliamentary Association for World Government in his latter years especially gratifying. This work led to his nomination (albeit unsuccessfully) for the Nobel Peace Prize in 1955, a move advanced by over a hundred parliamentarians.

In 1913 Davies married Jano Elizabeth Davies, adopted daughter of Dr Morgan Davies, a London-Welsh surgeon. An accomplished public speaker and astute politician in her own right, Jano gave unstinting support to her husband's public work. Of the four children of the marriage, three died at twenty-four years of age.

Clement Davies died at a London clinic on 23 March 1962, still an MP, shortly after the sensational Liberal victory at Orpington. His seat was held at the ensuing byelection by Emlyn Hooson (q.v.). In 1960 he had announced his intention to retire from the Commons at the next general election, and, had he survived, would probably have accepted a peerage in 1964.

A large group of Davies' personal and political papers have been deposited at the National Library of Wales. His biography remains unwritten, but a scholarly MA thesis by David M. Roberts, *Clement Davies and the Liberal Party, 1929–56,* was accepted by the University of Wales in 1975.

J. Graham Jones

NAVNIT DHOLAKIA (Lord Dholakia)   1937–

In making his maiden speech in the House of Lords on 4 December 1997, Navnit Dholakia quoted one of his former colleagues on the Criminal Justice Consultative Committee, Sylvia Denman, whom he described as a prominent black woman: 'Equality and quality are inseparable. Making sure we treat everyone with respect, dignity and fairness is not something that you do today and forget tomorrow. I wonder if some of the impetus from the disturbances of the early eighties has been lost because there is a tendency to think it has all been taken care of.' With anti-racism, as with liberty, the price is eternal vigilance. It has been one of the guiding tenets of Lord Dholakia's political life and action, as expressed in that maiden speech, that all have the right to live in peace, to receive an education, to get a job, to raise a family free from fear and, above all, the right to be treated fairly without reference to race, colour, national or ethnic origins. The political vehicle he chose to achieve those aims was the Liberal Party of Jo Grimond (q.v.).

Navnit Dholakia was born on 4 March 1937. He received his primary education in Tanzania and secondary and further education at the Home School and the Institute of Science at Bhavnagar, Gujerat, India. He then came to Britain to study at

Brighton Technical College. In 1960 he obtained the post of Medical Laboratory Technician at Southlands Hospital, Shoreham-by-Sea, where he worked until 1966.

He also became active in Liberal politics, joining Brighton Young Liberals and was their Chairman between 1959–62. He quickly made a breakthrough into representative politics, being elected to Brighton Borough Council, serving from 1961–64. From 1962–64 he was Chairman of Brighton Liberal Association, and from 1969–74 Secretary of the Liberal Party's Race and Community Relations Panel. Since the foundation of the Liberal Democrats, Dholakia has been consistently active in the party and in 1996–97 was a member of both the Federal Policy Committee and the Federal Executive. He was nominated as a Liberal Democrat working peer by Paddy Ashdown (q.v.) in the Prime Minister's Honours List on 2 August 1997, taking the title Lord Dholakia of Waltham Brooks.

In 1966, Dholakia entered what those hostile to the cause of anti-racism have often called 'the race relations industry'. In the wake of the events in the Smethwick constituency during the 1964 general election, when the Tory candidate, Peter Griffiths, campaigned on an openly anti-immigration ticket, using directly racist language to win the seat, Harold Wilson's Labour government introduced a Race Relations Act, the first time the state had signalled its intention to end discrimination by the use of legislation. The 1965 Act set up the Race Relations Board (RRB) to investigate and deal with complaints of racial discrimination and the law was later strengthened by a second Race Relations Act in 1968 brought in by Home Secretary Roy Jenkins (q.v.). In 1966 Jenkins had addressed a meeting of voluntary liaison committees, making his famous comment that integration was not a flattening process of assimilation but one of equal opportunity, accompanied by cultural diversity, in an atmosphere of mutual tolerance; Dholakia attended the meeting, and it greatly influenced him. Although both the Race Relations Acts were limited in their objective and impact, they opened up the possibility that discrimination could be eliminated and racist attitudes and beliefs challenged by the weight of the state and the establishment.

In 1966, Dholakia became Development Officer for the National Committee for Commonwealth Immigrants. From 1968 he was Senior Development Officer for the Community Relations Commission (CRC), and from 1974–76 he was its Principal Officer and Secretary. He worked with Mark Bonham Carter (q.v.) who chaired both the RRB and CRC between 1966–77. From 1976, Dholakia worked for the Commission for Racial Equality, the new agency created by Jenkins' 1976 Race Relations Act, which amalgamated the RRB and CRC and strengthened their powers.

However Dholakia's political interests were more widespread than immigration and race relations, with a particular concern for criminal justice and penal affairs. He was made a JP in 1978, the same year he joined the Board of Visitors of Lewes Prison. He was a member of the Sussex Police Authority from 1991–94, a council member of the National Association for the Care and Resettlement of Offenders from 1984 and its Vice Chair in 1995. He has been a council member of the Howard League for

Penal Reform since 1992 and a member of the editorial board of the *Howard Journal of Criminology* since 1993. From 1992–96 he served as a member of the Ethnic Minority Advisory Committee of the Judicial Studies Board, and was a member of Lord Carlisle's Committee on Parole Systems Review. He is the author of a number of articles on criminal justice.

Away from these concerns, Dholakia has been a council member of the Save the Children Fund and since 1992, Chair of its Programme Advisory Committee. Since 1997 he has been a Trustee of the Mental Health Foundation. In 1967 he married Ann McLuskie and they have two daughters. He lists his private interests as photography, travel, gardening and cooking exotic dishes.

Graham Lippiatt

ELLIOTT DODDS   1889–1977

Elliott Dodds lived a life of rich variety and contrast. A southerner by birth, he became indelibly associated with the *laissez-faire* Liberalism of the northern counties. A journalist, whose political beliefs were breathed into every corner of the *Huddersfield Examiner,* he wrote extensively throughout his life on the changing relationship between individual liberty and the role of the state. Although never close to entering Parliament, he was a popular President of the Liberal Party and played a central role in the battle which raged intermittently from 1928 between the right and left flanks of the party over Liberals' relationship with socialism. After the Second World War his name became synonymous with the Liberal Party's policy of co-ownership in industry.

George Elliott Dodds was born in Sydenham, Kent, on 4 March 1889, son of George William and Elizabeth Anne Dodds. His father was a tea merchant, originally from Berwick-upon-Tweed. Dodds was educated at Mill Hill School and New College, Oxford, taking a first in history. At college, he edited *Isis* magazine and was narrowly defeated for President of the Union. His early career was diverse. He worked for a time as private secretary to Herbert Samuel (*q.v.*), including acting as tutor to his sons, before teaching at Calabar College, Jamaica. Returning home he began to read for the bar, but was attracted instead by the post of leader writer and literary assistant at the *Huddersfield Examiner,* in 1914. He remained connected with the *Examiner* for sixty years – as Editor from 1924–59, as Consulting Editor thereafter, and as a Director of the newspaper's proprietors, Joseph Woodhead and Sons Ltd. Nevertheless, during the First World War he returned for a spell in London, editing the *War Pictorial,* a work of propaganda devised by the Department of Information. At the end of the war he married Frances Zita MacDonald, of Cheshire. She shared Dodds' membership of the Congregational Church, and they had two daughters.

Dodds' connections with Samuel, his Oxford pedigree, and his deep commitment to Liberalism would have sufficed before 1914 to carry him into the House of Commons as a Liberal Member. He concluded in his first book, *Is Liberalism Dead?* (1919), however, that 'Liberal principles, as all history proves, suffer eclipse in time of war', and his repeated attempts to enter Parliament – for York in 1922 and 1923, Halifax in 1929, and Rochdale in 1931 and 1935 – were all unsuccessful. His influence within the Liberal Party was to stem from his writing, not from a parliamentary role, though he was continually active in his local Liberal Association and also, throughout the 1920s, in the National League of Young Liberals. Throughout his life he sought to define the boundaries between Liberalism and socialism, the clarification of which would enable the Liberal Party to undertake a radical appeal to non-socialist reformist opinion. He resolutely opposed the Labour Party's 'bureaucratic state collectivism', nationalisation in particular, expressing his views in *Liberalism in Action* (1922) and *The Social Gospel of Liberalism* (1926). Dodds' views, controversial with some left-leaning Liberals, offered a beacon of light to many, illuminating the clouded political situation of the 1920s.

The economic depression of the 1920s and 1930s, and the Liberal Party's answer to it, in the Yellow Book of 1928, posed a formidable challenge to those Liberals who saw no justification for state intervention in the economy. Dodds was at the heart of efforts after 1928 to reconcile the fashionable enthusiasm for central planning and state ownership of industry with older Liberal *laissez-faire* tenets. He chaired the party's 1938 'Ownership for All' Committee, whose report argued that 'property is the pivot' upon which civil and political rights depend. The report, later approved by the party, called for the restoration of free trade, reforms of the rating system and of inheritance taxation, and encouraged the development of co-ownership schemes in industry. While recognising a central economic role for the state 'to create the conditions of liberty', direct intervention in the economy was ruled out in all but the most extreme circumstances.

'Ownership for All' placed Dodds on a collision course with the left of the party, particularly Sir Richard Acland (*q.v.*). Clement Davies (*q.v.*), Megan Lloyd George (*q.v.*) and Tom Horabin, and battle was joined until the end of the Second World War. The left argued that Dodds was unduly pessimistic about the extent to which state intervention could assist the extension of liberty and under-estimated the power of big business to propagate monopolistic conditions. It would be wrong to view Dodds merely as a right-wing reactionary, however. His views were progressive and he was open to argument; he attended conferences of the Liberal Action Group, later Radical Action, and he gave a cautious but generous welcome to the Beveridge Report, helping to ensure for it the almost unanimous backing of the 1944 assembly.

Dodds' views were again modified when a report by a party committee in 1945 advocated compulsory co-ownership for firms with more than fifty employees or more than £50,000 capital, something he had specifically rejected seven years previously. This proposal was bitterly contested at Liberal assemblies in 1948, 1949 and 1956, with Dodds this time firmly in favour. As President of the Party in 1948, and therefore Assembly Chairman, he was accused of breaching the impartiality of the chair by indicating his support for legislation on co-ownership. Dodds' shift reflected further changes in his perception of the boundary between individual liberty and collective need as well as a journalist's eye for the 'big idea' the Liberal Party required to make an impact on the electorate.

Having written a short guide to Liberal policy, *Let's Try Liberalism*, in 1944, Dodds returned to analysing the characteristics of Liberalism in the modern world with *The Defence of Man*, 1947. He was an obvious choice for Chair of the Unservile State Group when it was founded in 1953, primarily to follow up the work of the Yellow Book, and he co-authored, with Erna Reiss, *The Logic of Liberty*, one of the Unservile State papers, in 1966.

Dodds wrote extensively in the *Huddersfield Daily* and *Weekly Examiner* and in the *News Chronicle*. He attached enormous importance to his editorial articles and the tone they set for the newspaper, setting out to educate his readership without patronising them and to ally Liberalism with plain common sense. Arthur Holt (*q.v.*) attributed the post-war strength of the Liberal Party in Huddersfield in part to Dodds' erudite writing. Following his retirement in 1959 Dodds continued to write occasional reviews and articles for a further fifteen years, while devoting considerable time to the golf course. Dodds had a lifelong involvement with Highfield Congregational Church, the Workers' Educational Association, United Nations Association and Union Discussion Society. He was appointed CBE in 1973 and died on 20 February 1977.

His political writing is surveyed by Donald Wade (*q.v.*) and Desmond Banks (*q.v.*) in *The Political Insight of Elliott Dodds* (Elliott Dodds Trust, 1977).

Mark Egan

MASTER OF ELIBANK   1870–1920

The great achievements of the Edwardian Liberal governments are usually ascribed to the party's dynamic combination of social reform with traditional Radicalism. But, just as importantly, the party had, by 1914, developed into a disciplined Parliamentary force and a superb, well-funded electioneering machine. In his role as Chief Whip, Elibank made a vital contribution to this process, though his name is now remembered, if at all, mainly for his involvement in some of the shadier aspects of pre-First World War politics, particularly the Marconi affair.

Alexander William Charles Oliphant Murray was born at Folkestone on 12 April 1870, the eldest son and heir of the tenth Lord Elibank – hence for most of his political life he was known as the Master of Elibank, the traditional style for the heir to a Scottish peerage. His family were modest Borders landowners and, before taking over the family estates, Elibank seemed destined for an army career, proceeding to Sandhurst from Cheltenham College. However, while recuperating from a minor accident, he decided he would be better fitted to public life. Unlike his father, Elibank held Gladstonian Radical views and the Liberals welcomed him as a rare and valuable recruit from the Scottish elite. He served as Assistant Private Secretary at the Colonial Office in 1895 and then unsuccessfully contested a series of elections at Edinburgh West in May 1895, Peebles & Selkirk in the general election of that year and York in February 1900, before being returned for Midlothian at the 1900 general election. He exchanged this seat for Peebles & Selkirk in 1906, returning to Midlothian in January 1910 and holding the constituency until he became a peer in August 1912.

Elibank's talents as an electioneer and organiser won early recognition and he served as Scottish Whip in December 1905–09, with the rank of Comptroller of His Majesty's Household, before briefly becoming Under-Secretary of State for India. In February 1910 he achieved his ambition to be appointed Chief Whip and Patronage Secretary to the Treasury. Elibank faced a critical situation. The Liberals had just won the January 1910 election, but were dependent on Irish Nationalist and Labour votes in the Commons. Moreover, the Cabinet was badly divided and at odds with its allies over how to end the House of Lords' veto. Elibank won grudging admiration from most parts of the political spectrum for his skill in quelling discontent among Liberal MPs, building links with the Irish and inspiring an exhausted party machine. He also correctly advised Asquith (*q.v.*) that the Liberals would not lose ground in a second election in December 1910, despite the stale electoral register. This accurate forecast allowed the Liberals to retain power and go on to defeat the Lords. Elibank naturally received a good deal of credit for this outcome.

However, he also faced increasing criticism for the lengthy honours lists submitted in 1910–12. It was widely, and accurately, alleged that many peerages and baronetcies had been bestowed in return for donations to party funds. Elibank was merely following the practice of all chief whips since the late 1880s, but the expense of two elections in a year and a revamped party machine costing £100,000 a year to run, encouraged him to push the system to its limits. Moreover, his love of intrigue, taste for wealthy and slightly raffish company and smooth manner (he was dubbed 'Oilybanks' by the Tory journalist Leo Maxse) increased the distrust in which he was held by some in all parties. It was ill health, though, that cut short his career. In March 1912 he had to take a complete break from politics and in July he accepted the advice of his doctor and family to retire. On 6 August he resigned as Chief Whip and from the Commons, taking a peerage as Lord Murray of Elibank. He became a director of S. Pearson and Son, a contracting and oil firm headed by the Liberal businessman, Lord Cowdray. Elibank's father had passed the family estates on to him and he was in dire need of money to restore their viability.

However, before he left office, Elibank made the disastrous error of purchasing shares, on his own and the party's behalf, in the American Marconi Company. His friends and fellow ministers, Lloyd George (*q.v.*) and Rufus Isaacs (*q.v.*), also bought shares in this firm. They soon found themselves accused of corruption, as the company was closely linked to the British Marconi Company, which had just been awarded a government contract, and of lying to the Commons about their share dealings. Elibank avoided all comment by going to Bogota on business in January 1913, but in May the bankruptcy of his stockbroker revealed that he had bought £9,000 of Marconi shares for the party and concealed the transaction from his successor as chief whip. This proved the most sensational aspect of the whole affair and Liberal speakers for some time found themselves heckled by Tory cries of 'Bogota'. When Elibank returned to England in 1914, he was censured by a Lords select committee for a 'grave error' and 'most unwise reticence'.

Elibank remained a useful intermediary for Liberal politicians and he played a rather shadowy role in the negotiations for a settlement of the Irish Home Rule crisis in July 1914 and to reconcile Asquith and Lloyd George in 1917 and 1918. His health, though, precluded a more active role and a short stint as Director-General of Recruiting at Munitions in 1915–16 was not a success. For most of the war he flitted between Paris and London on business, though rumours of his financial transactions and relations with the press continued to excite interest in political circles. He died at his Scottish home on 13 September 1920.

Elibank married Hilda Wolfe Murray, the daughter of a neighbouring Peeblesshire landowner, in 1894. They had no children. *Master and Brother: Murray of Elibank* (1945) is an uninformative version of Elibank's life, written by his brother, A. C. Murray, also a Liberal MP.

Ian Packer

DEREK EZRA (Lord Ezra) 1919–

Derek Ezra has spent the past fifteen years as the very model of a working peer. As well as being the party's energy and industry spokesman, and chairing key House of Lords committees, he has remained active in industry where, even at the age of seventy-nine, he still runs a major subsidiary of Compagnie Generale des Eaux.

Born (on 23 February 1919) and schooled in Monmouth, he graduated from Magdalene College, Cambridge. After serving in the army throughout Hitler's war, and being made an MBE at twenty-six, he joined the National Coal Board (NCB) at its creation in 1947. Thirteen years later he was running its marketing division, and by 1965 was on the main board. Between 1971 and 1982 he chaired the NCB, a period during which he was knighted (1974) and became a significant national figure. Even today, fifteen years after he stepped down from the chair, he remains the best-known figure involved with coal management, particularly of the non-confrontational kind.

Ezra ran the coal industry during the miners' strike of 1973 and the 1974 three-day week. Always pursuing a philosophy of working in partnership, rather than confrontation, with the workforce, he formed in the public mind a remarkable rapport with the leader of the then ultra-powerful National Union of Mineworkers, Joe Gormley. Later they were to become colleagues, albeit of different parties, in the Lords. Throughout, the dispute was perceived to be predominantly between the miners and the government, rather than with the management.

During his career with the NCB, he remained uninvolved with party politics. But he had been an active Liberal just before the war when at Cambridge, where he was spotted, after a semi-official visit to Nazi Germany, by Sir Archie Sinclair (*q.v.*) as 'the most promising young Liberal.' Forty-four years later, it was Sinclair's successor-but-three, David Steel (*q.v.*), who made the party political promise come true by recommending him as a peer. Only those who knew him superficially even in his industry role can have been at all surprised at his declared party affiliation.

Subsequently, Baron Ezra of Horsham has been one of the most active of peers. Present in the chamber most days, he is an assiduous user of the 'unstarred question' procedure, thereby stimulating a series of mini-debates on topics within his portfolio. Long a keen European – even back in the 1940s and 1950s he was representing the NCB's interests on the progenitor international committees that eventually evolved into the European Community – he chaired for many years the key Lords European Committee (F), which oversaw energy policy in particular.

For there is no question that it is energy issues that most interest him. Not just coal either, although he is a former President of the Coal Industry Society and of the West European Coal Producers' Association. He has been, at various stages, chairman of Petrolex, of J. H. Sankey, and of Associated Gas Supplies, as well as a member of the advisory board of Petrofina. He has chaired the British Institute of Management, the European committee of the British Overseas Trade Board, and the Keep Britain Tidy campaign, as well as being a governor of the London Business School.

But it is – perhaps surprisingly given his solid fuel background – in the field of energy efficiency that he has recently specialised, and about which he waxes most eloquently, whether at party conferences, in the Lords or on commercial platforms. From 1966, when the NCB set up an energy management subsidiary, Associated Heat Services, he has developed his enthusiasm for fuel saving to become one of its most passionate advocates. Over thirty years on, he chairs a key division of the multinational services giant Compagnie Generale des Eaux, offering energy efficiency services to industry and commerce. Always assiduously declaring his professional interests, he has found an opportunity to speak on energy efficiency issues in the Lords now on approaching one hundred occasions.

He was for many years President of the fuel poverty charity Neighbourhood Energy Action, and was the first legislator to promote the concept of requiring mortgage companies to provide an energy survey for those moving home. He successfully piloted the Energy Conservation (Provision of Information) Bill through the Lords in 1997, to see it picked up the following year in the Commons as the private member's Energy Efficiency Bill by Liberal Democrat MP John Burnett (*q.v.*).

Universally regarded as an utterly honourable and diligent man, Ezra is acknowledged to be an 'expert supreme' by his colleagues, even in a House positively overburdened with great experts. He and his wife of forty-eight years, Julia, live in Eaton Square and in Sussex – whence if he ever retired they would undoubtedly head. But in his eightieth year, he shows neither sign nor inclination of so doing.

Andrew Warren

VISCOUNT FALKLAND 1935–

Lucius Falkland was always an unlikely candidate to be Deputy Chief Whip of the Liberal Democrats in the Lords, not being a party man, having scant regard for officialdom, and possessing a free-wheeling nature not suited to the traditional functions of a Whips' Office, But perhaps for those very reasons he has been a popular and endearing member of the Office since 1988. Dashing, genial, and much given to phone calls about matters such as playing golf or watching films, Lord Falkland adds a touch of glamour to the Whips' Office. He has been Liberal Democrat spokesman on culture, media and sport since 1997.

Lucius Edward William Plantagenet Cary Falkland was born on 8 May 1935 in London and was educated at Wellington College. After National Service in the army, he was for a short time a motoring journalist. He then went into theatrical management, after which he joined the large international company, C. T. Bowrings, where he was involved initially in shipping, rising to become Chief Executive of their trading arm. Later he formed his own marketing company, which took him on frequent trips to Africa on behalf of French industrial companies.

He married Caroline, daughter of late Lt. Cdr. Gerald Butler, DSC, RN, in 1962, by whom he had one son and three daughters (one daughter died in childhood). The marriage was dissolved in 1990. Later that year he married Nicole, daughter of late Milburn Mackey, by whom he had a son.

After inheriting his title in 1984 on his father's death, he immediately joined the SDP and was their nomination to sit on the prestigious Overseas Trade Select Committee with Lord Ezra (*q.v.*) from the Liberal benches. He made his maiden speech in 23 May 1984 on trade with developing countries. In 1988, he joined the merged party.

Falkland made his name in the House when he spearheaded the campaign in 1988 to get rid of the infamous Clause 28 in the Local Government Bill 1988, which prevented local authorities from 'promoting' homosexuality. Although unsuccessful, he was a attractive advocate, and has stayed loyal since then to the gay rights pressure group Stonewall. He was more successful in 1996, piloting the Dangerous Dogs (Amendment) Bill through the Lords in place of Lord Houghton of Sowerby – a Bill which gave the courts discretion in clearly defined circumstances to stop certain dogs being put down. Another of Falkland's concerns is alcohol abuse – he is Vice-Chairman of the All-Party Group on Alcohol Misuse – often making the point that it is at the heart of most domestic violence and other crimes.

Perhaps the two issues dearest to his heart however, are motor bikes – he is Secretary of the All-Party Motorcycling Group – and films, about which he is an undoubted expert. However, if there were any dispute about his suitability for the arts spokesmanship, a debate on the Rose Theatre in May 1989 would have clinched it. As he said: 'I have a family interest in the theatre, since my direct ancestor's brother was the Lord Chamberlain at the time when Shakespeare was working and writing for the Rose Theatre. Indeed my ancestor was his employer and protector, technically speaking, at that time. He used to go over to Somerset House to receive payment for himself and his company. Therefore, I think that in some degree a member of my family has been responsible for William Shakespeare's place as the most important figure in our literary tradition.'

Celia Thomas

RONNIE FEARN MP   1931–

Ronnie Fearn is living proof that if you keep delivering *Focus* leaflets and putting yourself about in your patch – no matter how unpromising your patch may be – you can reach Westminster. There was no convenient byelection, nor a recent Liberal tradition for Southport's Liberals to exploit, although there was always an active Liberal Association in the town. Indeed, both elections which saw Fearn elected to Parliament also saw a national swing *against* the Liberals/Liberal Democrats. Fearn got into Parliament, then got voted out and then got back in again, after forty years of determination and hard work.

Ronald Cyril Fearn was born in Southport, of course, on 6 February 1931, and was educated at Norwood County Primary School and King George V Grammar School. He left school at sixteen and went to work for Williams Deacons Bank – later to become Williams and Glynns Bank and then the Royal Bank of Scotland – until 1987, when he first won his seat in Parliament.

In 1955, Fearn married Joyce, with whom he has had two children, Susan and Martin. Joyce Fearn has worked as his parliamentary secretary and has witnessed every step of his painstaking journey to Westminster. In 1963, Fearn, aged thirty-two, was elected to Southport County Borough Council as the council's sole Liberal. Bit by bit, the local Liberal Association won more votes and more seats on the local council, but progress was slow. Shortly before the reorganisation of local government in the early 1970s, there were still only three Liberal councillors, of whom Fearn was leader.

The reorganisation of local government coincided with the revival in Liberal fortunes after byelection victories in the Isle of Ely, Sutton & Cheam, Berwick-upon-Tweed, Ripon and, most notably, nearby Rochdale. This revival, combined with the tenacity and community involvement of the local Liberals, meant that Fearn was elected to the newly created Sefton Metropolitan Borough Council in 1974 and to Merseyside County Council – also newly created – in the same year. In 1974 he fought and won two council seats and was the Liberal candidate in both the February and October general elections.

Fearn's great strength in Southport has been that he is a genuine local celebrity, famed for his services to amateur dramatics as much as for being an extremely hard-working local representative. Having served as the pantomime dame for many years, he was cast as the 'baddie' after he was first elected to Parliament, public esteem of politicians being such that this probably amounted to typecasting.

Losing his seat in 1992 was a terrible blow to Fearn and the local party. Middle-class fears of Neil Kinnock entering Number 10 'through the back door' led to a late surge in Tory support which saw Southport return to the Conservatives.

In many ways, it was the period between the 1992 and 1997 general elections that saw him at his finest. At sixty-one, he saw no need to return to regular employment and so he 'retired'. Except, of course, he did not retire at all – he had retained his Sefton Council seat all the time he had been in Parliament and used this as his plat-form to remain the town's most notable politician, MP or not. Despite many attempts by the Conservative MP, Matthew Banks, and despite the assurances of Fearn himself, the local telephone directory continued to list Fearn as Southport's MP throughout the period. Whether this error was a result of incompetence or design is unclear, but between 1992 and 1997 Fearn was still regarded by local people as their senior repre-sentative and, effectively, their 'MP'.

His service to his community, outside of conventional politics, had earned him the OBE in 1985. Just because members of that community had knocked him back in 1992, he was not going to stop battling for them. This tenacity was warmly recognised by people on the doorstep during the 1997 election. He was returned to Parliament in 1997 with a 6,000 majority, overturning the 3,500 majority of his opponent.

Throughout some of the lowest periods in the Liberal Party's recent history Fearn has kept knocking on doors, churning out *Focus* leaflets, winning local elections, and inspiring the faithful, however small they were in number. Today he makes a point of speaking at meetings of local Liberal Democrats in unglamorous areas where the party lies third or worse. As a man who successfully slogged his way through the Liberal Party's darkest days, he hopes to inspire a new generation of activists.

Tim Farron

H. A. L. FISHER   1865–1940

Herbert Albert Laurens Fisher was born on 21 March 1865 in South Kensington into a cultivated family with a tradition of ecclesiastical and public service. The Prince of

Wales (later Edward VII) was a godfather, hence his middle name. He married (1899) Lettice, daughter of Sir Courtenay Ilbert, later clerk to the House of Commons; they had one daughter. This comfortable, metropolitan Anglican background did not exactly point towards Liberalism, yet he was to become the architect of the last great landmark of the Social Liberal era, the Education Act of 1918 (the Fisher Act).

He received a traditional classical education at Winchester, where he was fag to Edward Grey (q.v.), and at New College, Oxford, where his first class in 'Greats' in 1888 led to a college fellowship. He then spent twenty-four years as an Oxford don, returning for the final fifteen years of his life on his election as Warden of New College in January 1925, in succession to the legendary Dr Spooner. His public service, and right to a place in this *Dictionary*, was compressed into the thirteen years between. But as student and don, he was an active Gladstonian Liberal supporter and as someone increasingly well-known as an historian and writer, in demand as a Liberal speaker at election meetings. He wrote himself: 'What little I have managed to acquire of the oratorical art was gained from the addresses which I was in the habit of delivering without notes to working-class audiences in Bethnal Green'.

In 1912 he left Oxford to take up the post of Vice-Chancellor of the University of Sheffield, and also to serve on the Royal Commission on the Public Services in India. Both fed his growing wider interest in education. In India he became convinced that the way to expand the numbers of Indians in the civil service (and 'obliterate the race barrier') was more through educational than administrative reforms. In Sheffield the Oxford classicist and historian promoted the application of scientific research to local industry and sought to make the new (1905) university a centre of regional life.

By a stroke of genius Lloyd George (q.v.) invited Fisher to serve as President of the Board of Education when he formed the 1916 coalition Cabinet. On 14 December he took office, and on 23 December was returned unopposed, by arrangement, as a Liberal for the Tory seat of Sheffield Hallam. He set about persuading the Treasury and Cabinet to agree to a substantial increase in national funding of education (his maiden speech, delivered without notes on 19 April 1917 and lasting two hours twelve minutes, was on the education estimates), on bringing the various denominational, local government and professional interests to work together on a programme to enact for the first time a legislative framework for 'A National System of Public Education' and on 'arousing throughout the country an enthusiasm for education', the achievement singled out in his *Times* obituary. This the newcomer to politics brought about through crusading addresses to public meetings in provincial cities during the autumn of 1917, before steering his comprehensive reforms through the Commons in 1918.

Fisher's reforms covered everything from the first legislative provision for nursery schools to the first national government funding of university education. Due to post-war economic problems, much of the Fisher Act remained aspiration, re-enacted in the 1944 Butler Act and only implemented in the conditions of mid-twentieth century affluence. But the architecture was Fisher's. Faced with poorly-paid teachers and local education authorities of enormously varying performance, he insisted on an exchequer contribution to bring all teachers' salaries and pension provision up to a national standard, but resisted calls to turn teaching, as it was in many other European countries, into a national civil service. His autobiography records his passionate belief in 'a wholesome variety of experimentation' through local responsibility for education. England owes its system of partnership between LEAs and central government to Fisher.

The labours of the Fisher Act out of the way, he spent four years both holding the education portfolio and playing a widely ranging role in government. He became chairman of the Home Affairs committee of the Cabinet in November 1918, and at the 1918 general election was returned as one of two members for the newly-formed Combined English Universities constituency. He was re-elected at the three ensuing general elections, each time by the single transferable vote – one of only two Liberal MPs ever to have been elected to the Commons by that system. In the 1918–22 coalition, he was one of the groups of Liberal ministers who resisted both Lloyd George's idea of forming a new centre party and Tory pressures to infringe free trade and to make savage cuts in public expenditure (the 'Geddes Axe'), especially on education.

His interests led naturally into international affairs, and he became one of the three British delegates to the League of Nations Assembly (1920–22). He was nearly moved by Lloyd George to the India Office rather than Edwin Montagu (*q.v.*) but instead took the role of handling Indian affairs in the Commons when Montagu was in India, and duly played a role in combating the Tories' vicious and anti-semitic vendetta against Montagu and in developing Indian self-government. He saw this as a consequence of the principle of self-determination, advocating on the same grounds that the Greek majority in Cyprus should be allowed to join Greece. A keen Home Ruler, during the war he had opposed Lloyd George's plan to extend conscription to Ireland and only accepted Irish partition with regret in recognition of the right of the people of Ulster to decide their own affairs.

Out of government, with a high reputation both as a successful minister and as a firm Liberal, he spent four years as a leading figure in a deeply divided party before resigning his seat in 1926. He was and remained a close personal friend of Lloyd George, but as his sympathies in 1916 had been with the Asquithians, he became a bridge-builder. Had he remained in active politics, he might have played a key role in the 1929 Parliament or the 1931 crisis. How differently might the Liberal Party have played those opportunities if Fisher had been available in the Commons? Instead he became President of the British Academy (1928–32). He received the Order of Merit in 1937, and in 1940 was invited back to perform one final public service as chairman of the Appellate Tribunal for Conscientious Objectors. He was walking on his way to preside at the tribunal when a lorry knocked him unconscious on 11 April 1940; he died a week later, in London.

But his service to liberalism, in the wider and fuller sense, had continued with the writing of his monumental three-volume *A History of Europe* (1935). In this work he displayed his breadth of vision, threading the story of European civilisation from its Greek progenitors through the enriching variety of the peoples of Europe (whom he saw as 'energetic mongrels') to the 'Liberal Experiment' (the title of the final volume). He wrote with a deep sense of morality (e.g. his chapter on slavery) and with a strong perception of a common European cultural heritage. He would have been appalled at the way later, insular, historians have fed the Europhobic prejudices of some modern British politicians and would surely have loved the idea of a Europe of Regions.

His full published output in history is too great to list here. Prior to *History of Europe*, his major works were *The Medieval Empire* (1898) and *Napoleonic Statesmanship, Germany* (1903). He also wrote several more popular works on English and French history, as well as biographies of F.W. Maitland (1910), Napoleon Bonaparte (1911), James Bryce (1927), Paul Vinogradoff (1927) and Mrs Eddy, the inventor of Christian Science (1929). Two more political writings were *Political Unions* (1911), in which he looked at success and failure in uniting, whether in federal or other form, separate countries, and *The Commonweal* (1924), in which he set out his own humanitarian and rationalist philosophy.

H. A. L. Fisher, *An Unfinished Autobiography*, with a foreword by Lettice Fisher (1940), includes his own reflections on his educational reforms but little of his later career. David Ogg, *Herbert Fisher, A Short Biography* (1947), is stronger on Fisher the educationalist and historian than on Fisher the Liberal ('an idealist member of an idealist political party'). Gilbert Murray's (*q.v.*) entry in the *Dictionary of National Biography* provides a good succinct account by one who was a life-long friend, fellow-scholar and fellow-Liberal.

Michael Steed

SIR DINGLE FOOT   1905–78

Throughout Britain, particular constituencies and cities have had a long connection with certain families – for instance, the Chamberlains in Birmingham and the Cecils in south Dorset. In Plymouth, politics has been dominated by the Foot family, principally Isaac Foot (*q.v.*) but also four of his five sons. These include Hugh (later Lord Caradon), John (*q.v.*), and the former Labour Party leader, Michael. The eldest, Dingle, had the unique distinction for the Foots of being elected to the House of Commons for both the Liberal and Labour parties. Yet despite his changing party, he never really embraced socialism; he began his political life as a Liberal, and, to quote Simon Hoggart, 'there his heart remained.'

Dingle Mackintosh Foot was born in Plymouth on 24 August 1905, the son of Isaac Foot and his wife Eva, née Mackintosh. He was educated at Bembridge School,

Isle of Wight; Balliol College, Oxford (where he obtained a second in modern history); and Gray's Inn, where he was called to the bar in 1930. Whilst at Oxford, he was President of both the Liberal Club (1927) and the Union (1928). It did not take him long to transfer his political skills to the House of Commons. Although he lost his first parliamentary contest (to the Conservative candidate in Tiverton in 1929), he was elected in Dundee in 1931, and again in 1935. In 1940, Winston Churchill (*q.v.*) appointed him parliamentary secretary to the Ministry of Economic Warfare, where his role in the furtherance of the blockade of Germany and the Axis powers was vital, being sent on important missions to Washington and Switzerland. In 1945 he was part of the British delegation to the San Francisco conference which framed the United Nations charter. However, his career was cut short in the 1945 general election, when he lost his seat, although in becoming Vice-President of the Liberal Party the following year he remained politically prominent. But he was unable to return to Parliament, coming a close second to the Conservatives in Cornwall North in 1950, and a more distant second in the same seat the following year.

Foot opposed closer links between the Liberals and the Conservatives at a national level, although the two parties cooperated in Dundee to ensure that only one candidate from each party fought Labour for the two-member seat. A 'Samuelite' rather than a 'Simonite' in the 1930s, Foot felt that the both the Conservatives and Labour had put administrative expediency before civil liberties. He perceived a drift to the right by the Liberal Party under Clement Davies' (*q.v.*) leadership, and did not seek re-nomination as a party Vice-President in 1954, claiming to be 'out of sympathy with its present policy'. A close political ally of Lady Megan Lloyd George (*q.v.*), he followed her into the Labour Party in 1956. He felt this was his only way of maintaining political influence, and he (unsuccessfully) urged his brother John to defect too. He soon re-entered Parliament, winning the Ipswich byelection in 1957, and defending the seat successfully in 1959, 1964 and 1966. He lost it by only thirteen votes in 1970.

In 1964 he was appointed Solicitor-General in Harold Wilson's first administration, reluctantly accepting the knighthood which went with it. He resigned in 1967, shortly after becoming a member of the Privy Council, to avoid condoning government policy on Rhodesia; he urged that Britain must not rule out 'police action', if necessary, since the guerrillas could not afford to lose the struggle. His 1970 election address, condemning Labour's manifesto commitments on immigration restrictions, may have contributed to his defeat.

Human rights provided the stimulus for much of Foot's legal work throughout the world. He appeared as counsel in Basutoland, Kenya, Ghana and Nigeria, defending Jomo Kenyatta and Hastings Banda amongst others. His relationship with Nigeria proved problematic – he was expelled from there in 1962 while challenging the validity of the Emergency Powers Act on behalf of the western Nigerian premier, Alhaji D. S. Adegbenro, and as a result was refused entry the following year to defend Chief Enahoro on treason charges. Much of his most distinguished legal work took place when he was out of office, or, indeed, Parliament; he became a bencher of Gray's Inn in 1952 and treasurer in 1968, having become a QC in 1954. He continued to practice after 1970, and he died during a case in Hong Kong on 18 June 1978.

Foot's views were strongly based around his beliefs in social justice, civil liberties and racial equality, underpinned by the scrutiny of Parliament over the executive and the rule of law. In this respect he remained a liberal even when he joined Labour; indeed, in 1974, he wrote that Labour had become the party of human rights in a way which it had not been in the 1930s. Although internationalist in outlook, as his legal career suggests, he opposed British membership of the EEC, and voted down the Labour government's proposals for reform of the House of Lords in 1968 on the grounds that it would enhance the government's powers of patronage. However, he was in favour of electoral reform.

His one book, *British Political Crises* (1976), mostly concerned Liberal Party disunity in the early twentieth century, which he described as 'the principal tragedy of British politics in modern times'.

He married Dorothy Mary Elliston in 1933; her social style contrasted with Foot's Methodist background and she was nicknamed within the family as 'Dingle's Tory wife'. They had a long and happy marriage. There were no children.

Aidan Thomson

ISAAC FOOT

1880–1960

Isaac Foot was born at Plymouth, Devon on 23 February 1880, the fifth child of Isaac and Eliza, née Ryder. His father was a carpenter and undertaker, who, as a young man, had migrated from Horrabridge, Devon, the family home for at least three centuries, to Plymouth, building his own home at 20, Notte Street. Brought up a staunch Methodist, Foot's political and religious beliefs were symbiotic and he first practised oratory in his local chapel. His formal schooling was limited by his family's pecuniary resources; he attended Plymouth Public School, paying tuppence a week for the privilege, and then the Hoe Grammar School, leaving at the age of fourteen.

Not being of practical bent, Foot did not enter his father's carpentry business, instead leaving Plymouth for London to work in the Paymaster-General's department at the Admiralty, preparatory to the civil service examination. The lure of his native city proved too much, however, and he returned to train for five years as a solicitor, qualifying in 1902 and forming the partnership Foot & Bowden in 1903, which still exists today. The partnership provided him with the ability, financial and otherwise, to enter into a political career, of which he was shortly to take advantage. Meanwhile, in 1904, he married a young Scotswoman, Eva Mackintosh, by whom, between 1905 and 1918, he had five sons and two daughters. She was, until her untimely death in 1946, his loving and beloved companion.

Aside from his nonconformity in religious matters, there was another spring to Foot's political beliefs. From his earliest years he was a passionate reader. Later in his life, when his achievements came to merit an entry in *Who's Who*, he listed 'reading and book collecting' as his 'recreations'. It was a description bordering on misrepresentation. His son Michael (who more than any of his progeny shared his reading addiction) wrote of him, more accurately, that it was by reading that 'he taught himself almost everything he ever knew'. He read voraciously, but at an early stage one subject began to emerge as a dominating interest – the history of his native land, and, as Edmund Burke expressed it: 'The achievement of free government [which] is the main glory of the British nation .... this struggle for liberty throughout the world is supremely the effort and accomplishment of the British people'.

To that affirmation of the pre-eminence of British people in the cause of freedom, Foot would have added two riders – that the years of greatest glory had been those in the seventeenth century when an English Parliament had challenged and overthrown a tyrannical king, and that that supreme accomplishment had been achieved under the leadership of a handful of plain English 'esquires', all Members of that Parliament, including John Eliot, John Pym, John Hampden, Oliver Cromwell, Henry Vane and John Selden.

Given these influences and associations, it was not surprising that Foot should have entered politics as a Liberal. He was elected for the Greenbank ward of Plymouth City Council in 1907, serving for twenty years; he was Deputy Mayor in 1920. He stood as Liberal candidate for Totnes, in the general election of January 1910 but lost to the incumbent Liberal Unionist. In the December election of that year he came within forty-two votes of unseating another Liberal Unionist at Bodmin. In normal circumstances, Foot might have hoped to win Bodmin at the next general election, but political events during the First World War were dramatically to alter the course of his career. Foot was a noted supporter of Asquith (*q.v.*) following the formation of the coalition government under Lloyd George (*q.v.*), particularly after the Maurice debate which confirmed and cemented divisions within the Liberal Party. As a consequence, Foot was not in receipt of the notorious 'coupon' granted to supporters of the coalition at the 1918 election and lost at Bodmin by over 3,000 votes.

His fourth electoral contest was in a byelection against Nancy Astor in Plymouth Sutton in 1919, when he was prevailed upon to uphold the Liberal cause in what was from the beginning a hopeless venture. The electors were still in the state of feverish support for Lloyd George's coalition which had characterised the 1918 election; in a three-cornered contest Foot was at the bottom of the poll, only narrowly saving his deposit. Any grief he suffered was more than compensated for by discovering in Lady Astor a life-long friend.

Foot was finally elected to Parliament in 1922. His Tory opponent in Bodmin in 1918 died early in the year and a byelection ensued at which Foot was again Liberal candidate. The coalition government was beset with industrial strife and severe problems in Ireland; the land 'fit for heroes' had not materialised. Fighting on the issue of the government's record, Foot won by over 3,000 votes. His victory, by intensifying Tory dissatisfaction with Lloyd George, played a significant part in the downfall of the coalition at the Carlton Club meeting eight months later.

Foot was re-elected in the general elections of 1922 and 1923, but lost his seat in the Liberal disaster of 1924. Despite fighting eight elections and winning three, he had sat in Parliament for only two years. Nevertheless, he had established a national reputation as a debater and an orator; his son Hugh, later Lord Caradon, was later to describe him as the best speaker he had ever known. Out of Parliament, he was able to concentrate on family affairs, without any relaxation in his work on the party's behalf. In 1927, he moved from Plymouth to Pencrebar, a large manor house in the village of Callington, in the Bodmin constituency, where he remained until his death in 1960.

Campaigning strenuously in favour of the policies contained within the Liberal Yellow Book, Foot could claim some credit for the Liberal victories in all five Cornish seats, including his own, in 1929. Nevertheless, the national result confirmed the Liberals' relegation to the electoral wilderness. In the feverish political atmosphere prior to the election of 1931, Hore-Belisha (*q.v.*), with the concurrence of Simon (*q.v.*), circulated a document among his parliamentary Liberal colleagues which invited them to pledge their unqualified support to the National Government in any measures that it might take after its election. (Over the next eight years those who signed it fulfilled their undertaking to the letter, never dissenting over the emasculation of the League of Nations, the betrayals of Abyssinia and the Spanish Republic, or over Munich or appeasement). Foot rejected the invitation with scorn, reminding Hore-Belisha and Simon that subservient submission of individual MPs to the executive was what the civil war had been all about.

In the negotiations before the election, Foot, like Samuel (*q.v.*), had agreed to join MacDonald's National Government only for the purpose of carrying through the economies necessary to meet the immediate financial crisis, and that on all other matters there should be an 'agreement to differ'. On this limited basis Foot accepted the office of Minister of Mines, and it was on that account that, when the election came, the Conservative Party in Bodmin decided of their own volition not to oppose him; thus, for the first and last time, he was returned unopposed. This, his only experience in office, was short-lived. When Chamberlain, as Chancellor of the Exchequer, sought to implement the protectionist Ottawa Agreements he resigned his post, as did Samuel that of Home Secretary.

If there are any certainties in politics, one is that Foot would have been defeated in the election of 1931 had it not been for the unforeseen 'accident' of his having been given a ministerial appointment shortly before; and as things turned out, defeat was only postponed. In 1935 he lost his seat in Bodmin to a Tory by a majority of nearly 3,000 – a result due, at least in part, to the electors having received letters of advice from Simon, Runciman (*q.v.*) and Hore-Belisha urging them to support his Tory opponent.

He never regained a seat in Parliament, but fought a byelection at St Ives in Cornwall in 1937. Runciman had, with Foot's support, won the seat in 1929 as a Liberal. In 1931 he had joined the Liberal Nationals and been rewarded with the office of President of the Board of Trade; in 1937 he was further rewarded with a peerage and resigned his seat. With the connivance of the local Conservatives, he now sought the right of succession to the constituency for the Liberal Nationals. The local Liberals were not surprisingly outraged and Foot accepted their invitation to fight the election on their behalf. The local Labour Party was scarcely less incensed than the Liberals and agreed to stand aside so that Foot could have a clear run.

Foot fought on two issues. One was a demand for the return of common decency in the conduct of British politics and an end to the deceit of aliases and false identities. More importantly, he warned of the horrors of the Nazi dictatorship, and of the wickedness as well as the futility of seeking an accommodation with dictators by way of surrender. He lost by only 210 votes. He said later, looking back on his career, that, although he had suffered more defeats than won victories, on the whole his eight defeats had been more honourable than his five victories. There can be little doubt that of those honourable defeats he gave first place to those of 1935 and 1937.

Foot was appointed to the Privy Council in 1937 and, although fighting just one more election, at Tavistock in 1945, his career of public service was far from over. He remained a senior figure in the Liberal Party, becoming its President in 1947, and delivering an influential Ramsay Muir (*q.v.*) lecture in the same year; later, he was to offer considerable encouragement to Peter Bessell (*q.v.*) and Jeremy Thorpe (*q.v.*) in their electoral efforts. A Methodist lay preacher, as his father had been before him, he was Vice-President of the Methodist conference (1937–38). He was appointed a Deputy Chairman of Cornwall quarter-sessions in 1945 and Chairman in 1953. Perhaps most impressively, he was unanimously chosen as Lord Mayor of Plymouth in 1945, an honour rarely accorded to a non-member of the council. In 1959 he was given the honorary doctorate of DLitt by Exeter University. He published two books: *Oliver Cromwell and Abraham Lincoln: a comparison* (1944) and *Michael Verran and Thomas Carlyle* (1946). A brief biography, *My Grandfather: Isaac Foot*, has been written by Sarah Foot (Bessiney Books, 1980).

Following the death of his wife he married, in 1951, Catherine Elizabeth Taylor, an old friend of the family. His eightieth birthday was marked by a dinner in his honour, hosted by Plymouth City Council. Months later, on 23 December 1960, he died quietly, survived by his wife and seven children. Four, Dingle (*q.v.*), Michael, Hugh and John (*q.v.*) were or became parliamentarians in their own right, and all recognised their debt to one of the century's most remarkable politicians.

John Foot

JOHN FOOT (Lord Foot) 1909–

Prominent, possibly foremost, amongst the political families of twentieth century Britain stand the Foots. Isaac Foot (*q.v.*) championed Liberalism for over half a century, his Methodist radicalism bolstering the Liberal cause in the West Country from Asquith (*q.v.*) to Grimond (*q.v.*). His household was imbued with the atmosphere of Liberalism, but two of his sons – Michael and Dingle (*q.v.*) – turned to the Labour Party and another, Hugh, later Lord Caradon, pursued a diplomatic rather than a political career. Isaac Foot's third son, John, has combined a long association with the Liberal Party, and latterly the Liberal Democrats, with the pursuit of a successful legal career, building up the solicitor's practice founded by his father.

John Mackintosh Foot was born on 17 February 1909 in Plymouth, shortly before his father was both to establish, with Edgar Bowden, a solicitor's practice in Plymouth, and to fight a parliamentary election for the first time, at Totnes. His mother, Eva, née Mackintosh, was of Cornish and Scottish descent and widely respected for her compassion and generosity. Foot was educated at Forres School, Swanage; Bembridge School, on the Isle of Wight; and Balliol College, Oxford. He presided over both the Oxford Union and the University Liberal Club in 1931 and came down with a second class degree in jurisprudence in the same year.

Foot entered the political fray at the Basingstoke byelection in April 1934, securing over 30 per cent of the vote in a three-cornered contest, a considerable improvement on the Liberal poll at the previous general election. He was unable to make any further impression on the Conservative majority in 1935, however, but was soon to replace his father as Liberal candidate for the highly-winnable seat of Bodmin, when Isaac Foot fought and narrowly lost St. Ives to a Liberal National in a byelection. Foot had high hopes of election to Parliament; Bodmin had returned his father from 1923–24 and 1929–35 and the Liberal Association was as well organised as any other in the country. The political consequences of the Second World War proved crucially adverse. He was discharged early from the army, in which he had served as a major in the Wessex Division, to contest the 1945 general election, but succeeded only in reducing the Conservative majority by a fraction, to 2,048. The Labour vote, never strong in Bodmin, picked up sufficiently to deny Foot victory. The 1950 election was even more disheartening, Foot losing by 7,792 votes. It was to be his last parliamentary contest.

Following the disappointment of his political ambitions, Foot concentrated on his family and his career. He was admitted as a solicitor in 1931 and became a partner in his father's firm three years later. He became the senior partner on the death of his father, in 1960, and remained so for thirty-five years. He married, in 1936, Anne Farr, daughter of a Pennsylvanian doctor, and fathered a son and a daughter. They set up home in Yelverton, Devon, on the outskirts of what became, in 1951, Dartmoor National Park. Foot became a champion of Britain's remaining areas of natural wilderness, being a member of the Dartmoor National Park Committee 1963–74; President of the Dartmoor Preservation Association 1976–94; and President of the Commons, Open Spaces and Footpaths Preservation Society 1976–82.

Although never tempted to abandon the Liberal Party for Labour, Foot was close to neither Clement Davies (q.v.) nor Jo Grimond, and played little part in the party's affairs until Jeremy Thorpe (q.v.) was elected leader. Thorpe, a close friend, persuaded Foot to play a more active political role. He was elevated to the peerage, as Baron Foot of Buckland Monachorum, in 1967, along with John Bannerman (q.v.) and Timothy Beaumont (q.v.), the first life peers to be recommended by the Liberal leader. He served on the Royal Commission on the Constitution 1969–73; was chairman of the United Kingdom Immigrants Advisory Service 1970–78 and President 1978–84; and chairman of the Council of Justice, 1984–89. He has spoken from the Liberal benches on a range of legal issues and has taken a considerable interest in the protection of the environment, speaking most recently on the National Parks Bill 1994. Retiring from legal work in 1995, at the age of eighty-six, he lives in active retirement in his Devon home.

Although Foot has yet to be the subject of biography, the atmosphere of Isaac Foot's family home is well captured by *My Grandather: Isaac Foot* (Bossiney Books, 1980), written by Sarah Foot, daughter of Lord Caradon.

Mark Egan

W. E. FORSTER   1818–86

W. E. Forster was a typical nineteenth century Radical: a successful self-made businessman of nonconformist origins who was driven by conscience to work for the less well off in the community. His great achievement was the successful creation of the framework for a state education system which is still recognisable today. His ill fortune was to take the post of Chief Secretary for Ireland at a time when Irish discontent found its most effective voice in Parnell. A tough policy of coercion earned him the nickname 'Buckshot', but Ireland broke his career and his health.

William Edward Forster was born on 11 July 1818, the only son of William Forster and Anna Buxton, at Bradpole, Dorsetshire. A serious child, who was reputed to have talked politics with his parents before he learnt to play with children of his own age, he was brought up a Quaker at schools in Bristol and Tottenham. After some delay in choosing a career for his son, William Forster Sr. settled on business. Initially employed in the manufacture of hand loom camlets in Norwich, Forster moved to Darlington in 1838 to learn more of the textile trade under the Pease family. In 1841 he entered the woollen business in Bradford, a town with which he was associated for most of his political life. In 1842 he formed an ultimately successful partnership with William Fison.

At about this time, he began to take an active interest in politics, joining the campaign for free trade and making the acquaintance of Robert Owen, the pioneer of cooperatives, and Thomas Cooper, the Chartist. During the Irish famine of 1845 he visited distressed districts such as Connemara as almoner of a Quaker relief fund, together with his father, and published an account of the suffering he encountered. As an 'advanced Liberal' he was willing to compromise with the objectives of the Chartists but cautioned the Bradford Chartists to keep to peaceful campaigning.

In 1850 Forster married Jane Martha, the eldest daughter of Dr Arnold of Rugby, leaving the Quakers and settling in Burley-in-Wharfedale. Over the next few years he appeared regularly on Radical platforms in Yorkshire, speaking in favour of parliamentary reform and on behalf of the working classes. Unsuccessful in the 1859 election in Leeds, he became Liberal MP for Bradford in 1861 and held the seat until his death. Allying with Cobden (*q.v.*) and Bright (*q.v.*), he spoke out on reform and resisted attempts to recognise the South in the American Civil War. In Russell's (*q.v.*) government of 1865 he served as Under-Secretary to the Colonies under Cardwell, dealing with the aftermath of the murderous suppression of the Jamaican riots by Governor Eyre. Russell's government failed to carry a moderate Reform Bill but Forster helped in liberalising Disraeli's 1867 bill which brought household suffrage to the boroughs.

Out of government, Forster was able to visit Greece and parts of the Turkish empire. In Gladstone's (*q.v.*) government of 1868 he rose to cabinet rank. As Vice-President of the Council he held responsibility for education and in 1870 carried the Elementary Education Act for which he is best known today. Until the Forster Act, education was not provided systematically but through a mixture of private enterprise, voluntary organisations, charitable foundations and the churches. Dissenters campaigned for publicly funded secular education, while the Church of England defended one of its key functions. Forster's solution accepted the role of the church schools but provided for the establishment of schools run by directly elected school boards, funded from the rates. Nonconformists were dissatisfied by the compromise, contributing to the defeat of the Liberal government in the 1874 general election, but campaigning for representation on the new school boards inspired the formal organisation of the Liberal Party in many areas.

If the education controversy damaged the Gladstone government, it did no lasting harm to Forster's reputation. When Gladstone resigned the leadership, Forster was the chief rival to the successful Hartington (*q.v.*), though perhaps reflecting the character of his compromise, he drew his support from the Whigs rather than the Radicals. Indeed he had to defy the Caucus in securing the nomination to Bradford for the 1880 election. Drawing on the experience of his 1867 visit, he denounced Turkey for the Bulgarian atrocities but campaigned to keep Britain out of the subsequent Russo-Turkish war.

Under the Gladstone administration of 1880, Forster was Chief Secretary for Ireland, with Lord Cowper as Lord Lieutenant. The timing was unfortunate. Parnell had galvanised the Home Rule Party with disruptive tactics in the Commons and allied himself to the Land League's effective campaign of agrarian agitation. With poor harvests leaving Ireland close to starvation, discontent was not hard to find, but Parnell and his allies were able to substitute 'social ex-communication' (soon known as the boycott) for the more familiar Irish rural violence. Forster's response was to seek a remedy for tenant grievances while cracking down on disturbances in the country-side. In 1880 a commission was established to inquire into the 1870 Land Act, but the temporary Compensation Bill for evicted tenants was resisted by the Lords. The 1881 Land Bill gave greater security to tenant farmers and introduced rent control. It tended to cut the ground from under the rural agitation and was subject to fierce resistance by Irish MPs.

When the ordinary law was insufficient to break the rural crime wave, Coercion Acts of growing severity were introduced, eventually allowing the government to arrest Parnell and other Irish leaders 'on suspicion'. Forster was attacked unceasingly in Parliament by the Irish members, and his life was threatened. Without the restraint of its parliamentary leadership the violence in the Irish countryside grew and Forster increasingly lost the support of his colleagues. The stress and continual travelling between London and Dublin damaged his health. Chamberlain (*q.v.*) opened indirect negotiations with Parnell and in April 1882 a majority of the Cabinet determined to release the 'suspects' under the 'Kilmainham Treaty'. Forster and Lord Cowper resigned.

Out of office, Forster remained a critic of Irish and colonial policy but only voted against the government once, in the censure debate over the death of Gordon. Over-exertion while chairing the committee on the Manchester Ship Canal has been blamed for his final illness and he died on 5 April 1886 at 80 Eccleston Square, London. He had no children of his own, but had adopted the two sons and two daughters of his wife's youngest brother, William Delafield Arnold, who had died on his way back from India in 1859.

The main biography is the *Life of the Rt Hon W. E. Forster* by T. Wemyss Reid, first published in 1888 and reprinted in 1970. A more recent study is Patrick Jackson, *Education Act Forster: A Political Biography of W. E. Forster 1818–1886* (Fairleigh Dickinson University, 1997). A statue of Forster, commemorating his achievements for elementary education, stands in the Embankment Gardens, east of the National Liberal Club.

Tony Little

DON FOSTER MP

1947–

Donald Michael Ellison Foster was born on 31 March 1947 in Penwitham, Lancashire. He was educated at Lancaster Royal Grammar School, Keele University, where he studied physics and psychology, and Bath University, where he gained an MA in education.

Foster was first elected to Parliament in the 1992 general election, when he defeated the then Chairman of the Conservative Party, Chris Patten. He held the seat in 1997, increasing his majority to over 9,000. He was appointed Liberal Democrat education spokesman in 1992 and now heads the Liberal Democrat education and employment team, with specific responsibility for nursery education and schools, and labour market statistics. In his role as education spokesman he has had a high profile in the recent debates over the nature of education funding.

Foster's greatest achievement in Parliament has been the introduction of the Road Traffic Reduction Act 1997. The Act is significant as it represents the first time that the reduction of traffic volumes has been endorsed in legislation as a general policy. It was supported across the political spectrum. The Act started as a private member's bill in November 1996, and, in an effort to achieve consensus and ensure the bill's passage into legislation, Foster had to accept some weakening of the detail. Its critics complained that the Act would have no teeth but, as the first piece of legislation to reduce, rather than increase, road traffic, it is certainly of consequence.

In 1994, Foster stood for election as President of the Liberal Democrats, but was unsuccessful against the well-respected Robert Maclennan MP (q.v.).

Foster was active in local government before entering Parliament. He was first elected to Avon County Council in 1981, was leader of the Liberal/Alliance Group until 1989 and chairman of the Education Committee from 1987–89. In 1987, he was the Alliance candidate for the Bristol East constituency.

Foster is an honorary president of the British Youth Council, vice-chair of the National Campaign for Nursery Education, vice-chair of the British Association for Central and Eastern Europe, treasurer of the All-Party Yugoslav Group. He is a past president of the Liberal Democrat Youth & Students. He is a trustee of both the Open School and Education Extra and a member of the All-Party Parliamentary Science and Technology groups. Prior to his election, he was a science teacher, the director of the Science Project at the Resources for Learning Unit in Bristol, an education lecturer at Bristol University and then a management consultant with Pannell Kerr Forster.

He enjoys listening to Bob Dylan and classical music, watching films, modern ballet and all kinds of sport and reading 'almost anything'. He married Victoria Pettegree in 1968; they have one son and one daughter.

Katie Hall

PHILIP FOTHERGILL 1906–59

In the decade or so which followed the 1945 general election, the Liberal Party might easily have withered out of existence. A small number of people – perhaps around half a dozen – played the leading part in ensuring that this did not happen. One of them was Philip Fothergill.

Charles Philip Fothergill was born in Earlsheaton, Dewsbury, on 23 February 1906, just a few weeks after the Liberal Party had secured its sensational victory at the polls. Like a considerable number of other Liberals of the period, he was a scion of a radical nonconformist family, closely connected with the Yorkshire textile industry. Educated at Wheelwright School, Dewsbury, and then at Bootham School, York, he went into business as a woollen manufacturer, eventually becoming Chairman and Managing Director of C. P. Fothergill & Co. Ltd of Dewsbury. In this work he acquired experience of welfare and labour problems, making a special study of labour economics. He was a life-long bachelor.

Fothergill's interest in Liberal politics developed early, and he became a member of the National Executive of the party while still in his twenties. Three times he sought election to Parliament, on all occasions without success – at Forfarshire in 1945, at Middlesbrough West in 1950 and at Oldham West in 1951. In 1957 he was adopted as prospective candidate for his native Dewsbury, but was forced to retire for reasons of health not long before his death.

Ill-health certainly dogged Fothergill. He was sometimes visibly in pain, yet he never allowed this to deter him from service to the Liberal Party. As party Chairman from 1946–49 he played a major part in developing and putting into effect plans for party reconstruction. This led to the establishment of Liberal organisations in the large majority of constituencies in the country, many of which had known no Liberal activity for years. At the ensuing general election of 1950, Liberal candidates stood in far more constituencies than the party had fought at any time since 1929.

The results of the 1950 election came as a cruel disappointment, and even worse was soon to come. Yet Fothergill's policy of a broad campaign may well have been crucial in keeping the party in existence; awful as election results often were during the 1950s, the party did not disintegrate, as it had done in many places during the 1930s. Fothergill continued to hold office in the Liberal Party, as President from 1950–52, in his old post as Chairman in 1952, and later as Treasurer. Before his untimely death at his Dewsbury home on 31 January 1959, there were real signs of a durable Liberal revival.

Fothergill had other interests as well as Liberalism. An eager temperance reformer, he was President of the United Kingdom Alliance from 1952 until his death. Yet he never sought to impose his deeply-held views on such matters upon others. He cultivated the press carefully, and one of the quality papers playfully described him as the Liberal Party's 'fiery little war-horse'. There was plenty of wit, but no malice, in his frequent attacks on political opponents, particularly the Liberal Nationals.

Philip Fothergill was at all times kind, generous, accessible, completely unassuming, and endowed with a splendid sense of humour. He chuckled at the incident at a reception when he gave his name to a hard-of-hearing announcer, and the life-long Congregationalist found himself proclaimed to the gathering as 'Father Gill'. He was accessible to all Liberals, and most particularly young Liberals. He was always anxious to help, often by stealth. All who knew him retain the very warmest memories of this truly delightful man.

Roy Douglas

CHARLES JAMES FOX   1749–1806

Charles James Fox was born in London on 24 January 1749. His family was firmly placed within the political establishment, with his mother being the great-grand-daughter of Charles II and his father having faithfully served Walpole for many years.

From his early years, Fox mixed both a willingness and aptitude for hard work with periods of dissolute behaviour, marked particularly by drink and heavy gambling. His education at Eton was interrupted by a four-month trip to the continent, which involved much gambling. However, on his return he continued with his studies and at Hertford College, Oxford even found delight in studying mathematics.

He was first elected to Parliament for Midhurst, in Sussex, in March 1768. This was technically a breach of Parliament's rules, as he had not yet reached the qualifying age of twenty-one. This was not the only rule to be bent during his Parliamentary career: it is highly unlikely that he consistently met the property qualifications either. His first years as an MP were marked by a conservative, even reactionary, attitude. He made his name as a Parliamentary orator with a speech in 1769 supporting Colonel Luttrell (Wilkes' opponent in Middlesex), and, after joining the government in 1770 as a Lord of the Admiralty, frequently spoke out in favour of measures to curb the press.

The two events which marked his shift to support of the Whigs and reform of the system of government were, first, the Royal Marriage Bill, and then the American War of Independence. His mother's family had disapproved of his parents' marriage, and consequently Fox opposed restrictions on the rights of people to marry. When the Royal Marriage Bill attempted to restrict, at George III's behest, the rights of the monarch's children to marry, he opposed this and came into conflict with the monarch for the first time. He also resigned from the government. Although he returned to the government afterwards, the King forced him out again in 1774.

Fox's views on the supremacy of Parliament, which had previously led him to oppose Wilkes and the rights of the press, now led him – in the context of the American War of Independence – increasingly to criticise the King's actions and to call for greater powers for Parliament. In this, he increasingly worked with the Whigs who followed Rockingham. By the late 1770s, almost all traces of his earlier views were gone, and he not only regularly attacked the conduct of the war but also opposed measures such as the 1777 suspension of the Habeas Corpus Act.

The force of his speeches, based more on clear arguments and nimble debate rather than great eloquence or rhetoric, made him a significant figure in Parliament.

Attacks on alleged misuse of public money, demands for cuts in the Civil List and support for reforms such as annual parliaments also brought him a popular following outside Parliament. Though his side rarely came close to winning a vote, sporadic attempts were made to bring him and the Rockingham Whigs into government. Such plans foundered on the Whigs' suspicion that they were not being offered a real share of power.

The fall of North's government in 1782 brought Rockingham to power, with Fox as Foreign Secretary. However, Fox was in a minority even in the new Cabinet over the conduct of the American war, the majority being willing to back the King in continuing to oppose independence and not introduce reform in public finances and administration. He was poised to resign from the government when Rockingham died. The same differences of opinion led him to refuse to serve under the next Prime Minister, Shelburne.

This decision split the Rockingham Whigs, with some in the government and some backing Fox. In opposition, he increasingly cooperated with North, who also opposed the new government. Together, they brought it down and forced the King to appoint Portland as Prime Minister, with Fox and North serving under him. This about-turn in relations between Fox and North brought many accusations of cynical manoeuvring, which Fox did little to dispel with his defence: 'If men of honour can meet on points of general national concern, I see no reason for calling such a meeting an unnatural junction. It is neither wise nor noble to keep up such animosities forever.'

He had previously taken a principled stand by spurning overtures to bring him into different governments, despite the financial rewards office would have entailed, useful given his large gambling debts. His apparent cynicism in linking up with North was probably largely motivated by his hostility to the King. As Shelburne was the King's favoured choice for Prime Minister, his coalition with North was the best way of frustrating George. His relations with the King, never good since the Royal Marriages Act, had declined further as he became friendly with the Prince of Wales, and the King saw him as responsible for encouraging dissolute behaviour by his son.

The Fox/North coalition proved to be unpopular, both inside and outside Parliament, and was hindered by the King's constant conspiring against it. The actual cause of its fall was Fox's attempt to reform the government of India. Any proposal ran into two problems — serious reform needed both to take some power away from the private East India Company and to set up some alternative source of power. Given the government's unpopularity, it was easy for opponents to attack the reforms as interfering with the rights of private companies and setting up an unaccountable, potentially corrupt, new form of Indian government.

When Pitt succeeded Portland as Prime Minister, Fox and North still held a great majority in the Commons. However, by assiduously wooing MPs, and by working hard in constituencies, Pitt managed to first whittle the majority down, and then overturn it, in the general election of 1784.

Fox's closeness to the Prince of Wales meant there was a chance of him becoming Prime Minister – if George III went sufficiently mad, the Prince would become Regent and was widely expected to replace Pitt with Fox. However, the combination of Pitt's astute tactics and occasional improvements in George III's health stopped this ever happening.

Fox was greatly excited by the French Revolution, and continued to praise it long after many other people in Britain had – in the face of its growing extremism – began to temper their views. War with France, and fear of revolution at home, led to many of his former supporters shifting to back the government. Fox himself frequently attacked Pitt's conduct of the war and opposed repressive measures at home, but frequently only enjoyed a very small number of supporters. By the later 1790s he rarely turned up in Parliament, but became increasingly associated with popular discontent with the government and calls for radical reform. In 1798 he was removed from the Privy Council for drinking a toast to 'our sovereign, the people'.

He started attending Parliament again in 1803, with a desire to overthrow the then Prime Minister, Addington. His initial alliance, with Grenville (*q.v.*), did not have sufficient strength. As with Shelburne, he met success by cooperating with a previous enemy, Pitt. The fall of Addington led to Pitt becoming Prime Minister once more, though the King blocked Fox from taking any office. On Pitt's death in 1806, Grenville became Prime Minister, with Fox back as Foreign Secretary. He had only a few months in office before his death on 13 September 1806.

Increasingly during his life Fox became associated with views that modern liberals would recognise – belief in power stemming from the people, desire for wide-ranging reform and an optimistic belief in progress through appropriate policies.

Fox married his mistress, Elizabeth Armistead, in 1795, although their marriage was kept secret until 1802. He had one son, who was deaf and dumb and only lived until fifteen.

There have been many biographies and related works, as a result both of his colourful private life and the many political events in which he featured. Some of the more useful biographies are: D. Powell, *Charles James Fox, man of the people* (Hutchinson, 1989); S. Ayling, *Fox* (John Murray, 1991); and L. G. Mitchell, *Charles James Fox* (OUP, 1992). A more colourful biography is I. M. Davies, *The harlot and the statesman, the story of Elizabeth Armistead and Charles James Fox* (Bourne End, 1986). D. Schweitzer, *Charles James Fox, a bibliography* (Greenwood, 1991) is a useful source for further works.

Mark Pack

SIR ROGER FULFORD　　　　　　　　　　　　　　1902–83

In his own life, as in his writing, Sir Roger Fulford stayed close to the historical sweep of liberalism, from Gladstone (*q.v.*) to Grimond (*q.v.*). His was an active and thoughtful contribution to the Liberal Party, from the first meetings of the Liberal Summer School in the early 1920s to the partial success of the Lib-Lab Pact in 1978–79.

Fulford was an inspired choice to write *The Liberal Case* for the 1959 general election, joining Roy Jenkins (*q.v.*) and Viscount Hailsham in the series of Penguin Specials. This wider exposure led to his becoming a popular President of the Liberal Party in 1964–65.

Roger Thomas Baldwin Fulford was born on 24 November 1902, in the vicarage at Flaxley, in Gloucestershire. After Lancing, where he was a contemporary of Evelyn Waugh, he took a modern history degree at Worcester College, Oxford, becoming President of the University Liberal Club, then President of the Oxford Union Society in 1927. In London he joined the editorial staff of *The Times* and was called to the bar in 1931, though he never practiced. When Lytton Strachey died in 1932 his brother James asked Fulford to take on the unfinished task of editing the first unexpurgated edition of the *Greville Memoirs*, helped by Ralph and Frances Partridge. The first volume appeared in 1938, with a short preface by Fulford.

But it was in the writing of royal history that Fulford made his name. *Royal Dukes* (1933) was followed by *George the Fourth* (1935), *The Prince Consort* (1949), *Queen Victoria* (1951) and *Hanover to Windsor* (1960). He also edited five volumes of Queen Victoria's correspondence with her eldest daughter, the Empress Frederick of Germany (1964, 1968, 1971, 1976 and 1981).

Fulford stood as a Liberal candidate for Woodbridge, Suffolk, in 1929, for Holderness, Yorkshire, in 1945 and for Rochdale in 1950, polling more than 10,000 votes on each occasion. In 1939 he joined the civil service, serving from 1942–45 as Assistant Private Secretary to Archibald Sinclair (*q.v.*), the Liberal leader and Secretary of State for Air.

In 1937 Fulford married Sibell, daughter of Charles Adeane of Babraham Hall, Cambridge, and widow of the Hon. Edward James Kay-Shuttleworth (died 1917) and of the Revd. Hon. Charles Frederick Lyttleton (died 1931). Sibell's second husband had been Rector of Hawarden and was descended from George Lyttelton, who shared a marriage ceremony with William Gladstone when both married the Glynne sisters in 1839. Perhaps his additional responsibilities caused him, also in 1937, to take up a part-tine post at King's College, London, where he lectured in English until 1948.

There were no children of the marriage but Sibell had a son and a daughter by her first marriage and two sons by her second, one of whom died in infancy. The survivor, Tom, fourth Lord Shuttleworth, was in 1944 dying of war wounds in the family home at Gawthorpe near Burnley. This dictated the Fulfords' choice of Barbon Manor, Kirkby Lonsdale as their married home for what proved to be the remainder of their lives. A committed Anglican, Fulford became the representative of the Bishop of Carlisle in the court of the new Lancaster University, was a trustee of the Kendal Art Gallery, and supported Geoffrey Acland both as his local Liberal candidate and as Chairman of the Liberal Party Executive.

At Barbon Manor Fulford's writing turned from royalty towards politics. *The Right Honourable Gentleman* (1945) was a satire on a political careerist, illustrated by Osbert Lancaster; *Votes for Women* (1956) an entertaining history of the suffragettes, which won the £5,000 *Evening Standard* Prize. *Samuel Whitbread* (1967) (*q.v.*) portrayed the short but promising parliamentary career of an intimate of Charles James Fox (*q.v.*). In *The Liberal Case* (1959) he looked forward to a world in which existing institutions would be freely challenged; liberties upheld and strengthened; independent thought and action encouraged. Briefed by James Crossley and Frank Ware, then recent ex-presidents of the Oxford and Cambridge Liberal Clubs and both working for the Liberal Research Department, he ended his first Liberal manifesto by revealing that Liberals were already in the majority in those two universities with memberships more than a thousand strong. Sir Julian Critchley has made the same point about his time at Oxford in the mid-fifties, arguing that all the Liberal students lacked were strong leaders.

It is sometimes forgotten that the Liberal revival in the universities began under Clement Davies (*q.v.*). Jo Grimond took it into the constituencies. When discussing House of Lords reform in his *Memoirs,* Grimond says of candidates for the second chamber: 'They should throw into the common pool opinions drawn from a more thoughtful background than the rough and tumble of the House of Commons accommodates. I am thinking of men like Roger Fulford, the historian, whose politics have a perspective, extended in time, building on the past, looking to the future'. Elsewhere he writes: 'I once promised Roger Fulford that if I was ever Prime Minister he should be Master of the Buckhounds – failing Fulford, Hinchinbrooke'. Courteous, serene, but with an impish wit, Fulford was a popular figure in literary and political circles.

He was knighted in June 1980, ten years after being appointed CVO. He died at Barbon Manor on 18 May 1983, predeceased by his wife Sibell in 1980.

David Penwarden

ANDREW GEORGE MP   1958–

Andrew George was born and bred in Mullion on the Lizard peninsula, and was elected MP for the St Ives constituency in 1997, a seat he had first contested in 1992. He is a member of the agriculture, fisheries, food and rural affairs team in Parliament and is the party spokesman on fishing.

Fully imbued with the spirit of his community, George has dedicated his time to the service of Cornwall and her people. Through his co-authorship of *Cornwall at the Crossroads* (1989), which challenged conventional and anglocentric views of Cornwall, George developed powerful arguments in recognition of Cornwall's distinctive identity and characteristics. His twelve years (1985–97) with Cornwall Rural Community Council – as field officer and deputy director – gave him extensive experience of community affairs in fields such as housing, pre-school education, economic development, finance for community projects and the development of Cornwall's voluntary sector.

His deep commitment to Cornwall has led George to challenge metropolitan assumptions about 'peripheral' areas, in which the self-assurance of the centre frequently demonstrates ignorance and misunderstanding of the outside. He believes that current moves towards regionalisation, motivated by bureaucratic convenience, have failed to reflect the strongest justification for devolution, namely the recognition and celebration of local distinctiveness and cultural tradition. It was these beliefs, coupled with a passionate commitment to social justice and a determination 'to correct the imbalance of bigness over smallness', which led him to join the party in 1981 while a student at Oxford.

Andrew Henry George was born on 2 December 1958, one of eight sons and daughters of a smallholding farmer and fisherman and a music teacher. He was schooled at Mullion, Cury, and at Helston Grammar School before winning places at Oxford (University College) and Sussex University College, specialising in agricultural economics. Married at Madron Baptistry in 1987, George and his St Ives-born wife Jill – daughter of the internationally renowned potter William Marshall – now live in Hayle, in West Cornwall. Jill is a nurse at West Cornwall Hospital. They have two young children, daughter Morvah and son Davy. In good local tradition George is an enthusiast for all sports, including football, cricket (as a member of Leedstown Cricket Club), rugby (as a member of the Lords and Commons Rugby Team), tennis (as a member of Hayle Tennis Club), swimming, cycling and many other sports and pastimes.

As Cornwall faces continuing hardship, George stands as one of her four Liberal Democrat Members of Parliament fighting the corner for a unique region of the United Kingdom, celebrating its past, proud of its present, and helping to shape its future.

Oliver Baines

HERBERT GLADSTONE (Viscount Gladstone)   1854–1930

Herbert John, Viscount Gladstone, was the fourth and youngest son of William Ewart Gladstone *(q.v.)* and his wife Catherine. He was born on 7 January 1854 at 12, Downing Street (now No. 11), which his father then occupied as Chancellor of the Exchequer. He was thus born at the heart of politics, and remained there for most of his life. He was educated at Eton, and then at University College, Oxford, where he obtained a first class degree in modern history in 1876. From 1877 to 1880 he was a lecturer in history at the newly founded Keble College, Oxford. But, in keeping with his father's powerful example, he aspired to a political rather than an academic career. In May 1880 he was elected as a Liberal MP for Leeds, a constituency for which his father had just been elected but had left vacant because he chose to sit for Midlothian. Herbert Gladstone sat for Leeds until 1885, and thereafter for West Leeds for twenty-five years until he became a peer in 1910.

After his election, Gladstone acted as a private secretary to his father until 1881, when he was appointed an assistant Liberal Whip and received his first ministerial post as a junior Lord of the Treasury. Probably the most famous incident in his life was his 'flying the Hawarden kite' – his revelation in December 1885 of W. E. Gladstone's conversion to Irish Home Rule. The press immediately broadcast the news and the die was cast, as far as W. E. Gladstone and the Liberal Party were concerned. Gladstone had undoubtedly been indiscreet. But he had acted from good intentions towards his father and his party, believing that the revelation would bring a new unity to the divided and distracted Liberal Party behind a new mission for Home Rule. However, the revelation did the reverse: Home Rule split the Liberals and caused controversy in the truncated Gladstonian party for many years.

Although embarrassed by the results of his action, Gladstone was not disgraced, and he continued to be useful to his party in a ministerial capacity. He was Financial Secretary at the War Office in his father's third ministry in 1886, and Under-Secretary at the Home Office in W. E. Gladstone's fourth ministry in 1892–94. In Lord Rosebery's (q.v.) government (1894–95) he was First Commissioner of Works. In 1899 he became Chief Whip when his party was in opposition and was on the verge of being seriously divided by the Boer War into 'Liberal Imperialists' and 'pro-Boers'. In keeping with the tradition bequeathed by his recently-deceased father, Gladstone was personally a pro-Boer. But he took no decided position on one side or the other, and struggled successfully to maintain official Liberal unity. Through this process he became regarded as a politician of considerable value to his party.

After the Boer War ended in 1902, Gladstone negotiated the Gladstone-MacDonald Pact with the newly founded and rapidly growing Labour Party, of which Ramsay MacDonald was Secretary. Under the agreement, which lasted until 1917, the two parties agreed not to oppose each other in selected constituencies in general elections in England and Wales. In fact the pact proved unnecessary to the Liberals when it was first used, in the general election of 1906. The Liberals obtained a very large overall majority, and did not need the support of the twenty-six Labour MPs (out of a total of twenty-nine) who had been returned through the operation of the pact. The Labour Party proved its ability to exist as a separate organisation, and Gladstone (acting as always from the best of intentions towards his party) had helped to give the new rival its parliamentary foundation. However, the pact was of undoubted value to the Liberal government in the two general elections of 1910, when the majority of 1906 was greatly reduced, and the government left in virtual dependence on alliance with Labour and the Irish Home Rule Party.

For four years from December 1905, Gladstone was Home Secretary in the Campbell-Bannerman (*q.v.*) and Asquith (*q.v.*) ministries. Although he was not among the foremost 'New Liberals' such as Lloyd George (*q.v.*) and Churchill (*q.v.*), Gladstone played a large part in carrying out collectivist policies which represented a substantial departure from his father's much more laissez-faire approach. Among measures which he prepared and piloted through the House of Commons were the Workmen's Compensation Act of 1906, the coal-miners' Eight Hours Act of 1908, and the Trade Boards Act of 1909 which aimed to provide decent wages in the 'sweated' industries. He was also responsible for important criminal legislation, including the Children Act of 1908 which established separate children's courts. He gave complete support to the police in their efforts to control the violence of the suffragettes. But in 1908 he was accused of negligence, and strongly rebuked by King Edward VII, for not taking firmer and more expeditious action to avoid disorder on the occasion of an important Roman Catholic procession through the streets of London.

This embarrassing episode allegedly caused the termination of Gladstone's period as Home Secretary in December 1909, and his appointment as the first Governor-General and High Commissioner of the new Union of South Africa. This appointment reflected his own strong conviction that South Africa should be granted responsible government within a short time after the Boer War. In March 1910 he was created Viscount Gladstone, and he and his wife (Dorothy Paget, whom he had married in 1901) landed at Capetown in May. He called on General Louis Botha to form a constitutional government, and the first Parliament of the Union was opened in November. In 1912 Gladstone had to deal with a political crisis in the Union, and in 1913 he declared and enforced martial law in order to avert the threat of widespread violence. His successful term of office ended in July 1914, and he returned to Britain.

Gladstone did not resume a ministerial career in this country, but did some valuable public work during the First World War. Later he performed occasional important functions, such as visiting Bulgaria in 1924 (where his father's denunciation of the Bulgarian massacres in 1876 was remembered), and working at Liberal headquarters in 1922–23 to re-unify and re-organise the party after the effects of the split of 1916–18. In 1928 he published *After Thirty Years*, a celebration (highly controversial in places) of his father's political and personal life. In the same year he and his brother successfully defended W. E. Gladstone's moral reputation in the law courts. He died without issue on 6 March 1930 at his Hertfordshire home, Dane End.

Gladstone, partly by his own choice, lived to a considerable degree under the shadow of his father. However, without reaching the first rank of politics he was useful to his party and his country in a variety of important spheres. It is unfortunate that the two initiatives for which he is chiefly remembered, the 'Hawarden kite' and the Gladstone-MacDonald pact, had such ambiguous effects on his party's fortunes.

Ian Machin

WILLIAM EWART GLADSTONE 1809–98

As Roy Jenkins (*q.v.*) concluded in his masterly biography, Mr Gladstone was almost as much the epitome of the Victorian age as the great Queen herself. He was the political giant of his lifetime and even at the end of the twentieth century the principles and aspirations he brought to public life are still inherent in the objectives of all the main political parties.

To what personal qualities can the great achievements of his life be attributed? First, he was a man of exceptional physical energy, although he was subject to bouts of serious illness throughout his mature life. He was a keen horseman and, when visiting stately homes, he would often choose to walk the last ten miles; where Lloyd George (*q.v.*) left walking sticks as relics, Gladstone left the axes with which he had hewn down forest trees. After an arduous day of Cabinet meetings and parliamentary work, followed by a formal dinner, it was quite usual for him to venture on to the streets to rescue ladies of the night. The motive for this activity will always be a matter for debate, but there is clear evidence that its origins were genuinely humanitarian and the fact that he was not unmoved by the allures of these women does not contradict his desire to lead them to new lives.

Secondly, his physical prowess was matched by his mental energy and he recorded his life in great detail, not just day by day, but hour by hour. He was a prodigious reader and Jenkins estimates that he read nearly 20,000 works, including light literature, in the course of his life. He enjoyed the theatre, though he is recorded as having slept through Ibsen's *An Enemy of the People*. He was not a great author but he produced a number of serious and controversial works, mostly on religious and classical issues. His lifelong commitment to the Anglican Church and his fascination with Greek civilisation made reconciling the fundamentals of Christianity and the classical world a recurring preoccupation. Even as he waited at Windsor to relinquish his fourth premiership, he was working on his translation of the *Odes* of Horace.

The extent to which religion played the central role in his life may be difficult for later generations fully to envisage. He was an ardent Anglo-Catholic and in earlier years a strong advocate of a close and powerful relationship between church and state to the extent of strengthening the privileges enjoyed by Anglicans and maintaining the disadvantages of Roman Catholics, dissenters and Jews.

William Ewart Gladstone was born in Rodney Street, Liverpool on 29 December 1809, the fourth son of John Gladstone, who had moved south from Leith some years earlier. Gladstone senior was a successful merchant, trading in corn with the United States and cotton with Brazil and owning extensive plantations in the West Indies, which were operated by slaves, although he was not a slave trader himself. John Gladstone's wealth expanded greatly and by 1850 was reckoned to be £750,000, enabling his sons to be active in public life with financial independence. In his old age Sir John was briefly an MP, having previously been several times rejected on petitions of corrupt practice.

Gladstone went to Eton in 1821, having previously been educated in a small school established by his father. In October 1828 he went to Christ Church, Oxford, which was still the dominant college of the University. He took a double first in classics and mathematics and still found time to be President of the Union. His connection with the University proved life-long, although sometimes tempestuous. He was one of the University's MPs from 1847 to 1865, when he moved to South Lancashire.

Gladstone was first elected in 1832 as Tory MP for Newark, which was effectively in the gift of the Duke of Newcastle. His maiden speech was in opposition to the immediate abolition of the slave trade. He remained MP for that seat until 1845 when he lost it on appointment to Peel's Cabinet. In 1839 Gladstone married Catherine Glynn, whose family seat was Hawarden Castle in Flintshire, which Gladstone later acquired. The castle and an associated college has remained in the Gladstone family ever since. The marriage lasted for fifty-nine years and Catherine, a very remarkable woman in her own right, died in 1900. They had four sons and four daughters, including Herbert Gladstone (q.v.), later Liberal Chief Whip.

After a brief spell as junior Lord of the Treasury, Gladstone's first government appointment was in 1835 as Under-Secretary for War and the Colonies. This was a major responsibility, especially as the Secretary of State was in the Lords. Later that year Peel's administration was defeated and Gladstone was then out of office until appointed President of the Board of Trade when Peel returned to power in 1843. The intervening years gave him more opportunity to attend to his personal life and travels abroad. His reputation as a speaker, both inside and outside the Commons, grew year by year, focusing especially on the church and colonial affairs. These years gave him the freedom to speak on a great range of issues and throughout his life he was rarely constrained by holding a particular office from speaking out on any subject about which he felt passionately. For example, he denounced the Anglo-China war in 1840 and the opium trade which was its primary cause.

In the late 1830s the anti-Corn Law League was the major target in his speeches but in the early 1840s, much influenced by a long walk with Richard Cobden (q.v.), he progressively espoused the cause of free trade. This was in tune with Peel's own thinking and Gladstone played a major part in leading the government towards the repeal of the Corn Laws. This policy was bitterly opposed by land-owning interests and led to a lasting split in the Tory party and Gladstone's eventual adherence to what came to be called the Liberal Party.

In 1845, Gladstone's recurrent concern with ecclesiastical matters and especially his desire to defend the Anglican tradition against the resurgent power of Rome, led to his resigning when Peel proposed to treble the annual grant to the Catholic seminary at Maynooth in Ireland. He returned to the Cabinet as Secretary of State for the Colonies later in 1845 but decided not to seek re-election at Newark and was consequently out of Parliament, though still in the Cabinet, at the time the crisis over the repeal of the Corn Laws which led, in turn, to the fall of Peel's government.

The rivalry between Disraeli and Gladstone developed while they were still members of the same party, reaching a high point in Gladstone's famous destruction of Disraeli's budget in 1852. This led to his succeeding as Chancellor of the Exchequer in the Whig/Peelite coalition under Aberdeen (*q.v.*) in 1853. He presented the first of thirteen budgets, notable for the reintroduction of income tax and sweeping reductions and abolitions of customs and excise duties. At the Exchequer Gladstone was renowned for his war on waste and unnecessary extravagance. He preferred raising revenue to increasing public borrowing or public spending, and believed that the public was best served by a prosperous economy and expanding production, stimulated by international free trade.

Gladstone's first term as Chancellor came to an end when the Whig/Peelite coalition dissolved and Palmerston (*q.v.*) replaced Aberdeen as Prime Minister. Such was his reputation on Treasury affairs and as a devastating orator that Gladstone might well have been offered the Treasury by either of the parties contesting the general election of 1859. In the event he returned as Chancellor of the Exchequer in a new coalition led by the Whig Prime Minister, Lord Palmerston, and continued when Lord John Russell (*q.v.*) became Prime Minister in 1865. There was then a brief period of Derby/Disraeli-led Tory government during which time the Liberal Party came into being in its more modern form. The seeds were sown in 1859, and Gladstone became leader of the party in 1867, following the death of Palmerston and the retirement of Russell. The newly formed party inevitably remained a coalition of diverse interests and these differences greatly inhibited the work of all Gladstone's administrations.

In the following year the new Liberal Party won a resounding victory at the polls. Gladstone himself was defeated at South West Lancashire but was elected for Greenwich, a seat which he would then retain until 1880. In December 1868 he became Prime Minister for the first time for what, in terms of its reforming programme, was the greatest as well as the longest of his administrations. In common with his three later periods in office, Gladstone's first government was greatly concerned with the problem of Ireland. Measures to ameliorate the situation included the Irish Church Bill, which shared ancient endowments between the Church of Ireland, the Roman Catholic Church and the Presbyterians. The Irish Land Bill gave peasants some protection against eviction without notice or compensation. Throughout the United Kingdom, the secret ballot was introduced, the purchase of military commissions abolished and steps taken to improve general education. Internationally, Britain was in danger of becoming embroiled in the American Civil War and Gladstone's agreement to allow the *Alabama* case to be resolved by international arbitration was a major step forward in the replacement of military action by diplomacy.

By 1873 the government was in a period of unpopularity made worse by several ministerial embarrassments, one of which led to Gladstone's resuming the Chancellorship of the Exchequer, a double act matched previously only by Pitt and Peel. The Irish University Bill floundered, being attacked as too godless from one side and too favour-

able to Roman Catholics on the other. Meanwhile, Gladstone himself, whose character always aroused bitter personal animosity in some of his acquaintances, was subject to rumours – for example, that he was a crypto-Catholic and practised phrenology.

At the general election of 1874 Disraeli succeeded as Prime Minister and Gladstone retired as leader of the Liberal Party in 1875. The subsequent five years offered him a degree of respite, but he remained active in Parliament, especially on Irish affairs and over his growing concern at the treatment of the Balkan peoples by the Turks (the 'Bulgarian horrors'). By the end of the decade he was ready for his astonishing Midlothian campaign which focused upon these moral issues and culminated in his election for that Edinburgh seat on 5 April 1880. He was greeted by vast crowds on his journey back to London and, having insisted that he was in the hands of the party leaders Granville and Hartington (q.v.) he was prevailed upon to form his second administration. This government was notable for many reforms, including the extension of the franchise. In foreign affairs he was concerned about worsening relations with the Boers following the annexation of the Transvaal. But Egypt and the Sudan were the greatest cause of trouble and the government was much wounded by the death of Gordon at Khartoum.

The general election of 1885 was dominated by the Irish question and led to a brief Salisbury-led government without an effective majority. In 1886 Gladstone formed his third administration in which he introduced the Government of Ireland Home Rule Bill, urging his supporters to '.... think well, think wisely, think not for the moment but for the years that are to come, before you reject this Bill.' However the Bill was defeated with ninety-three Liberals voting against, including Joseph Chamberlain (q.v.).

Gladstone remained fully active in political affairs but there was once more time for a period of reflection. He was able to indulge his delight in European travel and it was from Biarritz that he returned for his final campaign for Midlothian in 1892. The wisdom of his resuming office at the age of eighty-two can be debated, but it was for a single purpose: to pass the Home Rule Bill into law. For Gladstone, Ireland had increasingly become the issue on which he relied to distract the Liberal Party from the growing Radical pressure for state intervention, or 'constructionism', in social policy, an approach which, although it was eventually to underpin the New Liberal achievements of Campbell-Bannerman's (q.v.) and Asquith's (q.v.) governments, was anathema to Gladstonian individualism. Once more he took personal charge of the Bill, but it was blocked in the Lords, and with hearing and eyesight failing, Gladstone resigned for the last time in 1894. He lived for a further four years after his resignation and, until the months of his painful, final illness, remained extraordinarily active for a man in his late eighties.

Amongst the number of outstanding statesmen in Victorian Britain, Gladstone was unquestionably the greatest. He brought to his public life an exceptional physical, mental and spiritual vitality. He was a man of independent but by no means unchanging mind. His combination of moral zeal and the willingness to think on and on, no doubt explains how the opponent of the end to the slave trade became the great champion of liberty for the oppressed peoples of the Austrian and Turkish empires. Likewise, the ardent opponent of the 1832 Reform Bill became responsible for the secret ballot and the great expansion of the franchise. The rather priggish right-wing Tory who won Newark in 1832 became not a Whig but 'The People's William', as leader of the first recognisably Liberal government. Having refused all honours for himself, he died on 19 May 1898 at Hawarden, plain Mr Gladstone.

Gladstone's main political papers are in the British Library, while his family and some minor political documents are at St Deiniol's Library at Hawarden. His diaries are in Lambeth Palace Library but they have also been jointly edited by Professor H. C. G. Matthew and M. R. D. Foot in fourteen volumes. The most accessible recent biography is Roy Jenkins' *Gladstone* (Macmillan Press, 1995). Professor Colin Matthew's *Gladstone 1809–1898* (1997), consolidates his previously published two-volume work. Both these works have extensive bibliographies. A recent collection of essays by leading academics on aspects of Gladstone's career, also entitled *Gladstone,* is edited by Peter Jagger, published by Hambledon Press, 1998.

Roger Pincham

LORD GLADWYN 1900–96

Joining the Liberal Party in his sixty-fifth year, Lord Gladwyn brought to it an unparalleled knowledge and experience of foreign affairs and defence matters, in an era when few Liberals had exercised power or operated within the institutions of government. Among the greatest British diplomats of his generation, he was one of the key architects of the international institutions that shaped the post-war world, and was a passionate advocate of the United Nations and the European Community.

Hubert Miles Gladwyn Jebb was born on 25 April 1900. He was educated at Eton and Magdalen College, Oxford, where he took a first in history. Having entered the Diplomatic Service in 1924, he was sent on his first posting to Tehran. In 1929 he was recalled to the Foreign Office where he was appointed private secretary to the Parliamentary Under-Secretary of State, Hugh Dalton. Three years later he was posted to

Rome to serve as Second Secretary but, following the outbreak of the Abyssinian War in 1935, he returned to London to work in the newly created Economic Section of the Western Department. In 1937 he was appointed private secretary to the Permanent Under-Secretary of State, Sir Alexander Cadogan.

Always more interested in political ideas and policy, Gladwyn was relieved of the burdens of Private Office administration when Hugh Dalton requested that he join him at the newly created Ministry of Economic Warfare. But it was in his next posting in 1942, as head of the reconstruction department within the Foreign Office, that Gladwyn began work on the policies that would define his career. The department was charged with analysing Britain's policy options at the end of the war, and it was here that the initial blueprints for what became the United Nations and other international institutions were first drafted.

Between 1942 and 1945 he concentrated on planning the evolution of the post-war settlement, attending the major Allied conferences in this capacity. Having helped in the initial drafting of the UN constitution, he was appointed secretary of the UN Preparatory Commission and in February 1946 served as Acting Secretary-General of the United Nations, carrying the institution through its fitful early months.

Upon his return to the Foreign Office, he worked until 1949 as Assistant Under-Secretary of State, where he struck up a close working relationship with Foreign Secretary Ernest Bevin. He advised Bevin on UN issues and was sent as the British representative to the Permanent Commission of the Brussels Treaty Organisation. The Commission was charged with considering the proposed creation of the Council of Europe, and it was at Gladwyn's suggestion that the Council, and later the European Parliament, was located in Strasbourg, a city that served as a powerful symbol of Franco-German friendship after years of enmity and war.

It was to the UN that Gladwyn soon returned, when in 1950 he was appointed as the institution's permanent British representative. In these years he found some measure of international fame, for throughout the early 1950s the proceedings of the UN Security Council were transmitted on American television. Elegant and sardonic in demeanour, Gladwyn shone in delivering barbed responses, dripping with irony and ridicule, to the anti-western diatribes of Jacob Malik, the Soviet spokesman. During his tenure in New York Gladwyn also dealt with a number of the early post-war global trouble spots, most prominently the Anglo-Persian oil dispute and the Korean crisis.

In 1954 he was named as Ambassador to France, where he stayed until his retirement six years later. A strong advocate of closer British integration in Europe, in his new position he played a prominent role in the negotiations over the formation of the European Free Trade Area.

It was the relationship between Britain and Europe that occupied much of his time in the years following his retirement. Elevated to the peerage as the first Baron Gladwyn, he initially sat as a cross-bencher in the House of Lords, but in 1965 joined the Liberal Party, in part because, of all the political parties, it had been the most consistent proponent of the European idea. The following year he was a Liberal member of the parliamentary delegation to the Western European Union and the Council of Europe assemblies. In 1966 he was appointed the party's Deputy Leader in the House of Lords and Liberal spokesman on foreign and defence affairs, in which capacity he spoke with great erudition for the next twenty-two years. Between 1973 and 1976, following Britain's decision to join the EEC, Gladwyn served as a member of the UK delegation to the European Assembly. He unsuccessfully stood in the 1979 European election, as the Liberal candidate for Suffolk.

He received a number of honours in recognition of his diplomatic work, among them the GCMG in 1954, and in 1957 the GCVO and the French Grand Croix of the Légion d'Honneur. Throughout his life he wrote extensively on foreign affairs and continued to press the merits of Europe, publishing a number of books, most prominently, *Is Tension Necessary?* (1959), *Peaceful Co-existence* (1962), *The European Idea* (1960), *Half-Way to 1984* (1967), *De Gaulle's Europe* (1969) and *Europe after de Gaulle* (1970). In 1972 he also published the interesting volume, *The Memoirs of Lord Gladwyn*.

In 1929 he married Cynthia Noble, who acquired considerable renown as a hostess during her husband's diplomatic career. Following her death in 1990, her Diaries were published posthumously, to much acclaim. They had two daughters and a son, who succeeded to the peerage when Lord Gladwyn died on 24 October 1996.

Ruth Fox

WILLIAM GOODHART (Lord Goodhart) 1933–

On its formation, the SDP brought into politics a large number of people with a progressive outlook but no previous involvement in partisan activity. One of the most prominent was William ('Willy') Goodhart, who brought the immense skills and expertise acquired during his distinguished legal career to make a superlative contribution to both the SDP and the Liberal Democrats.

William Howard Goodhart was born on 18 January 1933, the son of Arthur Goodhart, an American-born legal academic, and his wife, Cecily. Goodhart was educated at Eton College and graduated with an MA in law from Trinity College, Cambridge in 1959. He won a Harkness Fellowship to study law at Harvard Law School. He was called to the bar in 1957 and began practising at the Chancery Bar three years later. Goodhart was appointed a Queen's Counsel in 1979 and has contributed to legal textbooks and a wide variety of legal periodicals.

In 1966 he married Celia Herbert, who was also to become active in the SDP. They have three adult children.

By his early twenties, Goodhart had developed a broadly liberal political philosophy. In 1972, he joined the board of Justice, the British arm of the International Committee of Jurists. In 1975, he was an active member of 'Lawyers for Europe' during the referendum on Britain's membership of the European Community. Yet he was still not inspired by any of the existing political parties. Margaret Thatcher's economic agenda and personal style held little appeal; Labour was increasingly doctrinaire and trade union-dominated and the Liberal Party appeared too ineffective and disorganised. Then, in November 1979, Roy Jenkins (q.v.) – whom he had long admired – delivered the Dimbleby Lecture, calling for a new political grouping to strengthen the 'radical centre' of British politics. For the Goodharts, this was a call to arms. In January 1981, they both joined the Council for Social Democracy, the core of the putative new party and, two months later, became founder members of the SDP.

Goodhart had an enormous behind-the-scenes role in the birth and progress of the SDP. He drafted the party constitution, acting, according to one account, as 'Gouverneur Morris to Robert Maclennan's (q.v.) James Madison'. Seven years later, undeterred by the difficulties of reconciling the disciplines of a lawyer with the demands of politicians, Goodhart was closely involved in the same exercise for the Liberal Democrats. From 1982 until the merger with the Liberals in 1988, he chaired the SDP conference committee, which was responsible for preparing the conference agenda. He helped to develop the SDP's radical policy proposals on poverty and taxation.

Once the Alliance's disastrous 1987 general election campaign was over, Goodhart became a strong advocate of a merger between the SDP and the Liberal Party. He had long wanted liberals and Jenkinsite social democrats to live under one political roof; such a move now seemed essential. The Goodharts' London home became the headquarters of the pro-merger campaign. In 1989, he was knighted for political and public services.

Goodhart chaired the merged party's Federal Conference Committee until 1991. In this role, he gained respect for his level-headed approach and his success in melding former Liberals and Social Democrats into a united team. He took a more active role in policy formation in the Liberal Democrats, serving on the Federal Policy Committee from 1988–97 (latterly as a Vice Chair) and as an active member of policy working groups covering areas as diverse as the economy, constitutional reform and criminal justice. In 1993, Goodhart chaired the group that developed innovative new proposals on pension policy. The following year, he oversaw a more controversial revision of the party's tax and benefits policies, which abandoned the proposals for a guaranteed 'citizen's income' and strengthened the Liberal Democrats' determination that the tax burden be shared fairly.

Goodhart's contributions to two parties' campaigning efforts have also been considerable. He fought Kensington at the 1983 and 1987 general elections and again in 1988 as the merged party's first byelection candidate. At the 1992 general election, he contested the marginal seat of Oxford West & Abingdon.

In autumn 1997, Goodhart received a peerage, taking the title Baron Goodhart, of Youlbury in the County of Oxfordshire. His elevation was both deserved and appropriate, for his gentlemanly and reasonable style is well suited to the House of Lords. It is also fortunate for the Liberal Democrats; they will continue to benefit from Goodhart's knowledge and abilities, which he intends now to focus on the areas of human rights, the legal system and Home Office matters.

Neil Stockley

DONALD GORRIE MP 1933–

When Donald Gorrie was elected Member of Parliament for Edinburgh West in 1997, it was a triumph of persistence and principle. His achievement came at an age when most people have settled into retirement, and was nearly thirty years afer his first adoption as Liberal candidate in the same constituency.

Donald Cameron Easterbook Gorrie was born in India on 2 April 1933, the youngest child of Duncan Gorrie of the Indian Forestry Service. From 1939, his childhood home was in Edinburgh. He went to Oundle School and graduated from Corpus Christi College, Oxford, in history. He developed his prowess as a runner while at school. He was an athletics blue at Oxford and a victor of national and international championships. Given his subsequent political career, it is perhaps not surprising that he excelled as a long-distance runner rather than a sprinter.

Gorrie spent nine years teaching, first at Gordonstoun and then at Marlborough College. In the rather established conservative tradition of the latter school, he won an early reputation for nonconformity by wearing a brightly coloured shirt in the days when white or discreet stripes were *de rigueur*. It was also at this time that he joined the Liberal Party, like so many of his generation in the renaissance of the Grimond years. He fought his first election two years later, but failed to be elected to Marlborough Town Council. It was an early lesson in the value of targeting. The Liberals put up three candidates and won nothing. The following year they fought and won one, Gorrie being the agent.

He returned to Scotland shortly afterwards. In 1969 he became the Scottish Liberal Party's Director of Research, and wrote pamphlets on Scotland's oil, and tenants' housing cooperatives. He was responsible for the Scottish Liberal manifesto in 1970 and 1974. Latterly, as Director of Administration, he was responsible for virtually everything that the under-resourced Scottish party did centrally, in the days when the skeletal staff had to look as if they were steering a battleship with the engine of a dinghy. This he was combining with his first three attempts at Westminster. Though the West division was the best of the Edinburgh seats, victory was never then a serious prospect.

It was also at this time that, emulating his maternal grandfather, his long and distinguished career in local government began. This would have been impossible but for a change in the law that allowed a candidate to stand for election where he worked, instead of only where he lived; Gorrie lived in Fife at the time. Lacking a candidate in a ward with significant Liberal support, the Corstorphine Liberals persuaded him that his local credentials were sufficient. Unsuccessful the first time, he won a byelection in 1971 on a split right-wing vote and, over the following quarter of a century, turned the area into a Liberal stronghold. He was elected first to Edinburgh Corporation (1971–75), then to its successors, Lothian Regional Council (1974–96) and Edinburgh District Council (1980–95), and then, following a further reorganisation, to the City of Edinburgh Council (1995–97). Whether as Liberal, Alliance or Liberal Democrat, he was group leader for seventeen years (and sole representative for six before that).

His adherence to his Liberalism denied him more than a brief taste of office. He enjoyed a short tenure as a sub-committee convenor in his early days and in a hung council on Lothian Region (1982–86) was chairman of the Performance Review Committee. He was, however, able to offer his talents in less partisan surroundings and served on the boards of the Edinburgh Festival, the Royal Lyceum Theatre and other organisations in Edinburgh, with a particular accent on youth. He was also for time an elder of St Giles High Kirk, but demonstrated his adherence to principle in his private life as much as his public when he resigned out of disapproval of the Kirk session's less-than-Christian attitude in their treatment of Women's Aid, who wanted to lease premises from them.

Gorrie became increasingly frustrated with the emasculation of local councils by central government, especially during the Thatcher years. His long-term commitment to a Scottish Parliament was strengthened by disaffection with a governing establishment which lacked feeling for or understanding of Scottish conditions. When he took up the candidature of Edinburgh West again in 1992, after a gap of eighteen years, he was motivated by a desire to put these wrongs right. Though narrowly beaten then, his moment of triumph came in 1997, though the destination of his ambitions remains the Scottish Parliament. He does, however, take his share of duty as Liberal Democrat spokesman in the Commons for many of the Scottish Office functions.

Gorrie married Astrid Salvesen in 1957; they have two sons. He was awarded the OBE in 1984.

John Lawrie

GEORGE GOSCHEN   1831–1907

Most politicians climb the greasy pole by being remembered when there are appointments to be filled. George Goschen may be unique. He became Chancellor of the Exchequer, the highest office he ever held, by being forgotten. When Lord Randolph Churchill resigned as Chancellor in December 1886 in a bid to strengthen his position in the Conservative-Liberal Unionist government, he never expected the Prime Minister, Lord Salisbury, to accept his resignation. He could not even imagine who Salisbury would appoint in his place. In a discussion about potential replacements, someone suggested Goschen. 'I had forgotten Goschen,' admitted Churchill. Salisbury did not.

George Joachim Goschen was born at his father's house in Stoke Newington on 10 August 1831. His father was a leading financier and merchant in the City and his grandfather, who came from Leipzig, was a publisher and man of letters, a friend of Schiller and Goethe. Goschen attended the Proprietary School in Blackheath before going to boarding school in Germany. In 1845 he went to Rugby, eventually becoming Head of School. He travelled in Europe in 1850 before going to Oriel College, Oxford where he gained a double first in classical honours and made his mark as a debater, becoming President of the Union in his final year. After graduating he joined his father's firm. He married in 1857. At the age of twenty-seven he was appointed a director of the Bank of England and in 1861 he published *Theory of the Foreign Exchanges,* which brought him widespread attention.

He entered the House of Commons unopposed in 1863 as member for the City of London and took up a number of Liberal causes, especially the removal of religious disabilities and Irish disestablishment. His first government post came in 1865 as Paymaster-General, and in January 1866 he entered the Cabinet as Chancellor of the Duchy of Lancaster. Initially, Goschen was a reformer. As President of the Poor Law Board, he introduced systematic local government reforms. As First Lord of the Admiralty he won a reputation as an efficient administrator. However, his refusal to reduce the 1874–75 naval estimates caused Gladstone (*q.v.*) to dissolve Parliament, bringing in six years of Conservative government. In opposition Goschen took an interest in foreign affairs and by invitation of the Viceroy conducted a joint investigation with a representative of France into the financial affairs of Egypt.

Domestically, Goschen was beginning to fall out with the Liberal Party. In 1877 he opposed the equalisation of county and borough franchises. At the general election of 1880 he stood down as Liberal candidate in the City, transferring to Ripon in Yorkshire. Gladstone did not offer him a post in his new government but did propose the Viceroyalty of India, which Goschen declined. Nevertheless in 1880 he did undertake a special ambassadorship to Turkey to oversee compliance with the obligations imposed under the Treaty of Berlin, retaining his seat in the Commons by not accepting a salary. In 1882 he turned down a cabinet post as Secretary for War and in 1883 declined the chance of becoming Speaker. He found himself increasingly disenchanted with the Liberals, believing Dilke and Chamberlain (*q.v.*) to be too radical. In the censure vote which followed the fall of Khartoum in 1885, Goschen voted against the Liberal government. In June 1885, the government faced a vote of no confidence. Goschen supported the party but the vote was lost and Salisbury became Prime Minister.

Ripon had lost separate representation in the 1885 Reform Act and Goschen had to find another seat. He stood in East Edinburgh, where his opponent was described as 'an advanced radical candidate'. Supported by the Conservatives, Goschen won easily. His formal break with the Liberals followed quickly and he became one of the founder members of the Liberal Unionists. Although Gladstone's Irish Bill foundered, Goschen lost Edinburgh at the general election of July 1886 to a supporter of Home Rule.

On 20 December 1886, Lord Randolph Churchill attempted his palace coup against Salisbury, and the Prime Minister invited Goschen to enter Number 11 Downing Street. As he was not an MP, he had to fight a byelection. He lost at Liverpool Exchange in January 1887, but two weeks later he won St George's, Hanover Square, a seat he held 1900. He remained Chancellor of the Exchequer for six years. In opposition after 1892, Goschen formally joined the Conservatives. He later served again as First Lord of the Admiralty but in October 1900, two years after his wife's death, he resigned and went to the Lords, where his main political interest was the defence of free trade.

Goschen was a great supporter of academic life. He was Rector of Aberdeen University in 1887 and of Edinburgh in 1890. In 1903, following the death of Lord Salisbury, he became Chancellor of Oxford University and in the same year published a biography of his grandfather. In 1905 he published a book of essays on economic questions. He died at his home at Seacox Heath in Kent on 7 February 1907.

There are collections of Goschen's papers in the Bodleian Library and the John Dillon Collection at Trinity College, Dublin. Some papers also remain in family hands. All the available documents were consulted by Professor T. J. Spinner for his book, *George Joachim Goschen, the Transformation of a Victorian Liberal* (Cambridge University Press, 1973).

Graham Lippiatt

EDGAR GRANVILLE (Lord Granville) 1898–1998

Edgar Louis Granville was born in Reading on 12 February 1898, the son of Reginald and Margaret Granville. He was subsequently educated in High Wycombe and Melbourne; he joined the Australian Light Horse at the outbreak of the First World War, serving in Gallipoli, where he was wounded, and then in Egypt and France. After the war he set up his own manufacturing business before acquiring directorships in the pharmaceutical and armaments industries.

In 1929, he fought and won the rural constituency of Eye in Suffolk for the Liberals. Eye had been a safe Liberal seat before the First World War, partly because of the strength of nonconformist feeling in the constituency but also due to the relative weakness of the Conservative landed interest. However, Eye had last returned a Liberal in 1922 and at the time of the party's decline, Granville's victory was a notable achievement. He was to remain associated with the seat for the next thirty years, fighting his last election there as a Labour candidate in 1959. Granville's hold on the area was based on assiduous personal contact. He employed two secretaries whose jobs included writing to all those who married in the constituency to offer them their MP's best wishes. The local Liberal organisation was very weak and Granville relied heavily on his personal network of friends and contacts to fight elections.

As an MP he had a relatively undistinguished career. He was Honorary Secretary of the Liberal Agricultural Group from 1929–31. Subsequently he became the Parliamentary Private Secretary to Sir Herbert Samuel (q.v.), then Home Secretary, in 1931 and afterwards Sir John Simon (q.v.), the Foreign Secretary, from 1931–36. However, he never achieved ministerial office.

Of more interest was his shifting allegiance during the period from the 1930s to the 1950s. Originally elected on the coat-tails of Lloyd George's (q.v.) slogan 'We can conquer unemployment', he sided with Sir John Simon when the Liberal Party split over free trade in 1931 and stayed a supporter of Ramsay MacDonald's National Government when the Liberal cabinet ministers resigned the following year. This may have been because of constituency pressure; as a cereal-farming area, Eye was strongly in favour of the agricultural subsidies and tariffs that the government was beginning to introduce.

Granville remained a supporter of the Liberal Nationals, as Simon's group was known, until the Second World War. After briefly serving with the Royal Artillery he resigned his commission in August 1940. By February 1942, along with several other Liberal National MPs, he was disillusioned both with their party and with the conduct of the war. Four of them, including Granville, resigned the whip to sit as Independents. With an election approaching, Granville rejoined the official Liberal Party in April 1945 and was narrowly re-elected in the election in July.

During the 1945–51 Attlee Government, Granville, along with Emrys Roberts and Megan Lloyd George (q.v.) became increasingly at odds with the Liberal leadership, as Clement Davies (q.v.), the party's Leader, steadily moved towards a more anti-socialist position. After the 1950 election, when Labour's majority was reduced to six, he often voted in the government lobbies to avoid defeat by the Conservatives. On one occasion, Granville, Roberts and Lloyd George even voted against a Liberal Party amendment on the cost of living to which all three had actually put their names. Asked to justify his action afterwards, Granville argued that the Liberal motion was simply being used as a cat's paw by the Conservatives to bring down the Labour government.

In the 1951 election, the nadir of Liberal fortunes, Granville was defeated in a three-cornered contest (of the six successful Liberal candidates, only one was elected in a three-way fight). Without a seat in the Commons he quickly moved to join Labour in January 1952, much to the chagrin of Megan Lloyd George, who was not consulted before his defection. He subsequently fought Eye for Labour in 1955 and 1959 without success, although the collapse of the Liberal vote in 1955 showed the extent to which it had been a personal vote for him.

In 1967, he was made a peer by Harold Wilson, and initially sat as a Labour peer before becoming a cross-bencher during the 1970s. Although his recreations included football, cricket and skiing, Granville was also the author of two political thrillers, *The Peking Pigeon* and *The Domino Plan*. He married Elizabeth Hunter in 1943, daughter of the Rev. William Hunter, and they had one daughter. He died on 14 February 1998, two days after his one hundredth birthday.

Malcolm Baines

BERNARD GREAVES   1942–

For thirty years, Bernard Greaves has influenced Liberal, Liberal Democrat and public policy on a range of issues. Generally, he has done so by a willingness rigorously to follow through original ideas based on firm and clear principles and a painstaking application to detail. He has greatly influenced a smaller number by the force of his originality and the example of his courage.

Greaves was the first openly gay man to hold national office in a UK political party. His influence and example were the most important reasons why the Young Liberals and the Liberal Party accepted not just the formal case for law reform but the reality of openly gay lifestyles in a normal social and political setting. Bernard's 'men dancing with men' motion at the Young Liberal Conference in 1972 was a major achievement in its time!

Bernard Greaves was born in Longsdon, near Leek on 29 September 1942 and educated at the Leys School, Cambridge and St John's College, Cambridge (BA Architecture; Diploma in Architecture (Cantab)). He has suffered all his life from multiple allergy syndrome, which was misdiagnosed as depression from 1965–89, since when desensitisation treatment has led to steady improvement. Several serious bouts have prevented Greaves from commitment to full-time work other than with International Voluntary Service from 1979–87, where he was Head of Fundraising and Publicity, Acting and Deputy General Secretary.

His working life has consisted of a large number of commitments, some paid and others unpaid in the fields of liberal politics, gay rights, the voluntary sector and community development and campaigning. These include: Secretary, later Political Vice-Chairman, National League of Young Liberals; Publicity Officer, Gay Rights Campaign; and Director of Policy Promotion, the Liberal Party. He planned the Liberal 1979 general election manifesto, and later acted as policy adviser to Robert Maclennan MP (*q.v.*), Liberal Democrat spokesman on home affairs and later constitutional affairs and as President of the Liberal Democrats.

Greaves was attacked, albeit not uniquely, by Jeremy Thorpe (*q.v.*) as an irresponsible revolutionary and by David Steel (*q.v.*) as a traditional Liberal incapable of adjusting to modern reality. His essential views have not changed! It would be difficult to find someone, other than Nancy Seear (*q.v.*), who has inspired greater affection and respect from those who have worked with him than Bernard Greaves.

Greaves' publications include: editor and essayist, *Scarborough Perspectives* (Young Liberal Movement, 1977); *Communities and Power* in P. Hain (ed.), *Community Politics* (John Calder, 1976); *Liberals and Gay Rights* (Liberal Party Organisation, 1977); *The Theory and Practice of Community Politics* (with Gordon Lishman, *q.v.*, 1980); *Out from the Closet* (with Bruce Galloway, ALC, 1983); *Tackling Crime Together – the Liberal Democrat commitment to Safer Neighbourhoods* (briefing and campaign kit, ALDC, 1993). Over eighty further articles, essays and reports are in the public domain.

Gordon Lishman

TONY GREAVES 1942–

For twenty years from the late 1960s to the late 1980s, Anthony Robert Greaves was an elemental force within the Liberal Party, combining political and ideological clarity with organising drive and ability, occasionally enlivened with flashes of unexpected charm and, more frequently, outbursts of intemperate fury. Tony Greaves is the single most important reason for the success of community politics, which provided the Liberal Party and then the Liberal Democrats with the basis for local government success and the 1997 Parliamentary breakthrough.

Greaves was born in Bradford on 27 July 1942, the son of a policeman (driving instructor) and housewife who were not politically active apart from a small annual subscription to the Bradford Conservative and National Liberal Federation. One great-grandfather, a Bradford schoolmaster, had been a Tory activist and local campaigner for extending the tramway to Eccleshill; he was also an eccentric who went walkabout for weeks on end, reputedly always involving a trip to Lancashire and an ascent of Pendle Hill for 'the best view in the whole of Lancashire' (Bradford *Telegraph & Argus* obituary). Another (Jewish) great-grandfather, who moved to Bradford from London's East End, possibly as a result of anti-semitic loutism, was a blind piano-tuner. They were active Liberals (Tony's grandfather was Laurence Gladstone Greaves) who joined the Independent Labour Party at its founding rally in St George's Hall.

He was accepted for Bradford Grammar School, but went to Q.E.G.S, Wakefield, after a police service move. Nine o levels, four A levels and one S level led to Hertford College, Oxford (BA geography, 1963) and Manchester University (diploma in economic development, 1965). By this time, Greaves' visceral commitment to politics and liberalism was already well founded as the basis for his working life. Chair of the Union of Liberal Students, 1965–67, he was a founding force in the 'Red Guards' revival of the Young Liberals in the 1960s, making a major political and organisational contribution to the debates of the time. He was agent for the Knutsford constituency (candidate: Geoff Tordoff, *q.v.*) from 1965–68.

Greaves married the redoubtable and delightful Heather Baxter (a Lancaster University graduate in English and politics, and later teacher; a councillor on Barrowford

Urban District Council and Pendle Borough Council), and they have two daughters: Victoria (born 1978) and Helen (1982). He moved overnight from political activist who could not understand why people talked about their children to doting father, a position he has retained ever since. From 1969–74 he taught geography at Colne Grammar School (*inter alia,* to sisters of Gordon Lishman, *q.v.*). He ceased to work for Lancashire County Council due to his accidental election to the new county council in 1973. From 1974–77 he was a full-time councillor with various part-time and temporary posts, spending his time on editing, writing, political organisation and training.

Greaves was Chair of the National League of Young Liberals, 1970–71, defeating the incumbent Louis Eaks in a rare electoral outing as the moderate candidate; he argued that, although right, support for the Palestinian cause should not dominate the YL agenda. At the 1970 Liberal assembly in Eastbourne he moved the YL 'community politics' amendment, setting the basis for the party's subsequent local growth.

From 1977–85, Greaves held the new post of Organising Secretary for the Association of Liberal Councillors. He set up a new Liberal local government HQ in Hebden Bridge. By 1985, the staff had grown from one to seven, and the number of Liberal councillors on principal councils from 750 to 2,500. Greaves' materials, training and leadership provided the motivation, drive and techniques for the first and continuing achievement in many authorities. From 1985–90, he was Manager of Hebden Royd Publications Ltd, which ran the party's national publishing and publications operation until it was relocated to the south in 1990. Since 1991, Greaves has moved from non-employed and political organiser in Ribble Valley to self-employed as book-seller, dealing in second-hand and out-of-print books, specialising initially in Liberal Party and political books, moving to related areas and diversifying as the business grows.

Greaves was a member of the Liberal negotiating team in the merger negotiations with the SDP, an experience of physical and nervous exhaustion. He drafted (with Shirley Williams, *q.v.*) the preamble to the Liberal Democrat constitution.

His local authority service includes Colne Borough Council, 1971–74; Pendle Borough Council, 1973–92, 1994–98; and Lancashire County Council, 1974–97. He has been variously Chair of Finance Committee; vice-chair of Policy Committee; Deputy Leader and Chair, Colne & District Committee (his favourite!). Greaves is the direct cause of the Liberal and now Liberal Democrat control of Pendle. He was Parliamentary candidate in Nelson & Colne, 1974 (twice), and Pendle, 1997; agent for Knutsford, 1966; Nuneaton, 1967; Nelson & Colne, 1968 and 1979; Workington, 1976; and Pendle, 1992.

Greaves' hobbies include mountaineering (climbing and walking); botany; election results; train-spotting (anciently, but still occasional stirrings); born-again cyclist; holidays in the Pyrenees.

The bare facts fail to convey the full force and effect of Greaves' leadership in his key period of activism, partly because he has always denied leadership and partly because his firmness and clarity of political and ideological thought has been verbal rather than written. A generation of political activists took their lead from his energy and insight, whether on Vietnam, Czechoslovakia, community politics, local government or the nature of pluralist democracy.

Gordon Lishman

T. H. GREEN   1836–82

Thomas Hill Green was that rare combination, a high-powered philosopher and political theorist who also contributed effectively to practical politics. His friend, the Cambridge philosopher, Henry Sidgwick, said that while he could hold his own with Green in metaphysics and epistemology, when it came to politics, 'I always felt the chances were that before long his superior grasp and insight would force me to retreat'.

Born at Birkin, a village in the West Riding of Yorkshire, on 7 April 1836, Green was the son of a clergyman. His mother died when he was only a year old. Ancestors on his father's side included Oliver Cromwell, to Green's great pride. Temperamentally a republican and opponent of hereditary privilege, Green admired the man who had overturned the monarchy and created the conditions for popular sovereignty, whatever the downside of the Commonwealth experiment.

Green was educated, first at home, then at Rugby School, the late domain of Dr Thomas Arnold. He proceeded to Balliol College, Oxford, in 1855; here he gained a second in classics, a first in Greats (philosophy and ancient history) and a third in modern history. Green was inclined to idleness in early life; even at Oxford, he was at first academically competent rather than intellectually distinguished. But the bracing mix of Balliol's power-house atmosphere and the focused attention of its Master, Benjamin Jowett (the arch Victorian talent-spotter), stimulated his mind and fed his analytical powers.

After graduation he wavered about his vocation between the priesthood, journalism, and academe. Academe won: he had a successful life at Oxford as fellow (1860), tutor (1866) and finally as White's professor of moral philosophy (1878). In the late 1870s the symptoms of heart disorder began to show; he died on 26 March 1882. In 1871 he married Charlotte Symonds, sister of his friend John Addington Symonds, the historian and essayist. There were no children.

Green's two main books were published posthumously: *Prolegomena to Ethics* (1883), to which he was making the final revisions when he died, and *Lectures on the Principles of Political Obligation*, collated from his lecture notes. The *Lectures* were first published by R. L. Nettleship in his edition of Green's *Works* (London, 1885–88) and soon were published separately. There is an excellent modern edition by Paul Harris and John Morrow (Cambridge, 1986). Green's pamphlet, *Liberal Legislation and Freedom of Contract* (Oxford & London, 1881) was a landmark document in recognising that legal freedom of contract can conceal real, unjust inequalities in the powers of the parties and that even voluntary contracts can work against the public interest where such inequalities prevail.

Green was a Christian – of a kind. Brought up in the evangelical tradition, he was nonetheless decisively influenced by German biblical criticism in the late 1850s and early 1860s. From then on, he could no longer accept the Bible as the immediate vehicle of the Word of God. One way of reading his later work is as a reworking in philosophical terms of what he took to be the picture-language of Christianity. This is a very Hegelian approach to both Christianity and philosophy. The German philosopher G. W. F. Hegel (1770–1831) looms, an immense figure, behind Green. But Green was never a disciple of Hegel; he borrowed, but kept his critical distance. He owed much, and no less, to Plato, Aristotle, and Kant. Green was an 'idealist' in the philosophical sense of stressing the role of mind in the construction of knowledge, as opposed to regarding the mind as a mere passive mirror of nature.

Alongside his academic career, Green ran a lively stream of political engagements. He supported pressure groups such as the Reform League (for extending the franchise), the National Education League, and the United Kingdom Alliance (for anti-drink legislation). In 1865–66 he was an assistant commissioner for the Taunton Commission on secondary education. His work was informed by the two principles that education should be diverse, with different types of school serving children of different aptitudes and inclinations; and that no child should be barred from higher education by parental poverty. This last did not automatically mean, though it did not exclude, state provision. Green was active in opening Oxford University scholarships to the needy.

Party politics also claimed him. He was an activist in the Oxford North Ward Liberal Association. In short succession in the mid-1870s he was elected to the Oxford School Board and to the Town Council – the first don to sit on the council by public election rather than university nomination. *Prolegomena to Ethics* was put on hold as he electioneered for the Liberals in the 1880 general election.

Useful books on Green include Melvin Richter's *The Politics of Conscience: T. H. Green and His Age* (London, 1964), which sets the intellectual and cultural background; and *The Philosophy of Thomas Hill Green*, edited by Andrew Vincent (Aldershot, 1986). This explores topics and issues in Green's philosophy. Also on the philosophical side, A. J. M. Milne's chapter on Green in *The Social Philosophy of English Idealism* (London, 1962) contains a clear, informed, and able discussion. A. D. Lindsay's 'T.H. Green and the Idealists', printed as an introduction to *Lectures on the Principles of Political Obligation* (London 1941 *et seq.*) is a minor classic.

Geoffrey Thomas

LORD GRENVILLE   1759–1834

William Wyndham Grenville, later the first Baron Grenville and more commonly known to historians as Lord Grenville, was born on 25 October 1759. Like many Whigs of his generation, he mixed support for repressive domestic measures with modest support for administrative and economic reform. He strongly believed in a limited number of what later became distinctively liberal views. Although a Whig, he spent much of his political career happily working in government with Tories, notably Pitt.

Educated at Eton and Christ Church, Oxford, Grenville went on to study law, although he was never called to the bar. He was elected to Parliament in 1782, in a byelection for one of the seats in the two-member Buckingham constituency. Soon afterwards, he joined the government, as Chief Secretary to his brother, the then Lord Lieutenant of Ireland.

During the rest of the 1780s he progressed through a variety of government posts and became MP for the more prestigious constituency of Buckinghamshire. In 1789, he was appointed Speaker of the House of Commons. At this time being Speaker did not mean holding back from participating in parliamentary debates or withdrawing from normal politics. Indeed, later that same year, he resigned in order to become Home Secretary.

In 1790, he moved on again, becoming a Baron and moving to the House of Lords. This creation of a new peerage to ensure the Prime Minister, Pitt, had the person he wanted in the Lords caused some comment. His closeness to Pitt went back several years; they were cousins, and had spent much time together studying Adam Smith's (q.v.) Wealth of Nations.

The House of Lords better suited Grenville's limited debating skills. Initially responsible for handling government business, he again moved on quickly, becoming in 1791 Foreign Secretary. During the 1790s, he consistently took a hard line on policy towards France, often leading the war party in the Cabinet. He happily supported restrictive domestic measures, designed to head off a supposed threat of revolution. He played an intimate role in some of the most controversial measures, including introducing the Treasonable Practices Bill and the Seditious Meetings Bill to Parliament.

His role at the heart of government was confirmed by work preparing the 1801 Act of Union between England and Ireland, when he cooperated closely with the Prime Minister, Pitt. Both strongly believed that increased rights for Catholics were essential to the enterprise. When the King refused to accept this Pitt, followed by Grenville, resigned.

As someone with a significant band of followers in Parliament, Grenville was naturally involved in the manoeuvrings to bring down Pitt's successor, Addington. Grenville initially combined with Charles Fox (q.v.), also a Whig though in practice much more radical than him, and then later persuaded Pitt to join their opposition. When Addington fell in 1804, Pitt became Prime Minister once more. Grenville did not take up a post in the government, as the King refused to let Fox have a position.

However, on Pitt's death in 1806 Grenville was the natural choice as Prime Minister. Without Pitt, the Tories were seriously short of talent, and George III, finally, had no option but to allow the Whigs to form a ministry. Grenville assembled a broad coalition of different factions in Parliament out of both necessity and his hostility to party politics, preferring grand governing coalitions. The administration was nicknamed the 'ministry of all talents,' but its record was not happy, with internal dissension and a lack of success in negotiations with France. The one significant measure during its office was a resolution attacking the slave trade, which was followed by a bill in 1807. Even the credit for this largely lay elsewhere, with anti-slavery campaigners such as James Stephen. The bill became law on the day the government fell, its demise again being caused by a conflict with the King over rights for Catholics.

Although such a clash was in many ways inevitable – Grenville not only believed in the principle of more rights for Catholics, but also believed they were required to keep Ireland manageable – the actual circumstances of the fall from office were largely self-inflicted. Having failed to persuade the King to allow Catholics and dissenters more rights in the army and navy, Grenville then refused to promise not to bring any similar measures forward in the future. George III took this opportunity to sack the government. Sheridan described the situation aptly, saying he had 'known many men knock their heads against a wall, but he had never before heard of any man who collected the bricks and built the very wall with an intention to knock out his own brains against it'.

In opposition from 1807, Grenville was prominent in support of free trade (and opposition to the Corn Laws), more rights for Catholics and in opposition to slavery. He did, though, continue to take a strong line against France, wanting firm military action until the final conclusion of hostilities in 1815, and being willing to support repressive domestic measures designed to head off any threat of revolution at home.

In 1809 he was elected Chancellor of Oxford University, largely because of a split in the Tory vote between two rival candidates. Both before and after this time there were various attempts to bring him into the government, which foundered because he wanted too much of a change in policy. Only in 1821, when Grenville himself was on the brink of retirement, did his followers join the government, with many envious comments being made about the generous terms they acquired. He finally retired in 1832, following a paralytic attack, and died two years later, on 12 November 1834, at Dropmore Lodge, Buckinghamshire. He had no children to succeed him, his marriage to Anne Pitt in 1792 having left no issue.

As with many other Whigs of the time, Grenville's hostility to France and his willingness to see tough law and order measures at home meant that for many years he worked happily with various Tory politicians. But, during the long period of Tory rule after 1807 he became increasingly identified with reform, and in particular, toleration of different religious beliefs.

For biographies, see P. Jupp, *Lord Grenville, 1759–1834* (Clarendon, 1985), and the brief study, A. D. Harvey, *Lord Grenville, 1759–1834* (Meckler, 1989).

Mark Pack

CHARLES GREY (Earl Grey)   1764–1845

Charles Grey, second Earl Grey, Viscount Howick and Baron Grey, was the Prime Minister who oversaw the Great Reform Act of 1832, which overhauled the country's parliamentary electoral system and was the culmination of two years of intense political crisis.

Born on 13 March 1764, at Falloden in Northumberland, his youth was spent in a manner similar to that of many other members of Whig families: education at Eton, followed by university (King's College, Cambridge) and extensive travels in France, Italy and Germany before finishing off his studies. He became an MP in 1786, for the county seat of Northumberland, and soon made his mark as a supporter of Charles Fox (*q.v.*). His very first speech was an attack on the government for its commercial treaty with France. His faithful support of Fox's increasingly radical views led him to break from the political outlook of the rest of his family.

His marriage in 1794, to Mary Elizabeth, daughter of William Brabazon Ponsonby, brought him into the Irish liberal establishment. This strengthened his opposition to the draconian domestic law and order measures introduced during the 1790s as a result of fears of revolution in Britain. Unlike some colleagues, including Fox, he was ready to criticise leaders of the French Revolution when he saw them as too extreme, but he also gave prominent support to demands for reform such as annual elections and cuts in the monarchy's civil list. As with many later liberals, he saw failures of government – in the 1790s, often military failings in the war with France – as necessitating administrative and economic reforms.

In the late eighteenth and early nineteenth century he faded out from national politics, spending increasing amounts of time in Northumberland and realising that his House of Commons career was limited by his father's acceptance of a peerage. The smallness of the minority that supported his views on measures such as electoral reform probably also encouraged this distance from politics. He willingly spent much of his time on other pursuits, and in 1807 wrote of the forthcoming parliamentary session: 'We shall have the satisfaction of making what are called "good divisions", when the more important business of Fox-hunting, etc., does not prevent'.

In the late 1820s he drifted back into national politics, with increasing talk of him possibly joining the government. He returned to prominence by opposing Wellington's government in 1830, and following the election of that year was the natural leader of the opposition. His track record of radicalism in his younger days, with a relatively quiet more recent past, made him acceptable to a wide spectrum of Whigs and assorted radicals. The fall of Wellington brought him in as Prime Minister.

His first, and main, task was to see some measure of electoral reform introduced. He combined this with a tough line against domestic unrest, organised by Melbourne (*q.v.*). During the parliamentary struggles over reform, he showed a willingness to do what was necessary to get some measure through, including compromising in some areas, but also taking a tough line with opponents when necessary. He saw the middle classes as massing behind demands for some measure of reform and believed that, one way or another, their power would force change, particularly given the economic difficulties then existing and the possible inspiration offered by successful revolutions in France and Belgium. His job was to manage the process in as moderate and safe a way as possible. This meant limited reform – but it did mean forcing some form of reform through, and reform that was radical enough to settle the issue.

When the first Reform Bill fell, he did not resign but instead persuaded the King to call an election, won it by a landslide and then brought in a second bill. Only when this was defeated in the Lords, and the King refused to create sufficient extra peers to see it through, did he resign. Although the King attempted to find an alternative Prime Minister, the widespread support for some measure of reform both inside and outside Parliament, made this impossible. Grey returned to office with the King finally agreeing to create any peers necessary. Faced with this threat, the House of Lords backed down, and electoral reform was achieved. The Great Reform Act, as it came to be known, was a major watershed in the political history of Britain, overhauling much of the Parliamentary electoral system. The electoral franchise was simplified and widened, many old small constituencies abolished and seats granted for the first time to the new industrial areas such as Birmingham.

The next two years, until 1834, showed a rather mixed record as the government suffered from a wide range of splits and personality conflicts, and a lack of a clear programme to drive its actions forward. Grey happily took the opportunity offered by defeats over Irish policy in 1834 to retire from politics. The last eleven years of his life passed quietly; he died at his Northumberland seat, Howick Hall, on 17 July 1845. He had ten sons and seven daughters; his title passed to his fifth son.

Many radicals were disappointed by his time as Prime Minister, particularly as his first Cabinet was largely composed of relatives and peers. Rather than being a radical, he steered a middle course – enough reform to keep the country together and government functioning, but still a long way short of full democracy. The reforms helped to place the country on a much longer road of gradual and largely peaceful change, which did eventually lead to democracy, though he would not have welcomed this culmination of events.

For biographies, see E. A. Smith, *Lord Grey, 1764–1845* (Clarendon, 1990) and J. W. Derry, *Charles, Earl Grey: Aristocratic Reformer* (Blackwell, 1992).

Mark Pack

EDWARD GREY (Viscount Grey) 1862–1933

Sir Edward Grey, third Baronet and first Viscount Grey of Falloden, was the longest serving Foreign Secretary of the twentieth century, guiding Britain's foreign policy in 1905–16. In the 1920s, he was a prominent voice on foreign affairs, and a strong supporter of Asquithian Liberalism. Grey's importance to British politics as Foreign Secretary lay in his maintenance of good relations with France and Russia at a time when Europe was extremely unstable. In later years, his support for the League of Nations left an important intellectual legacy for Liberal internationalists.

Grey was born in London on 25 April 1862, the eldest child of Colonel George Grey and Harriet Grey (née Pearson). His father was an equerry to the Prince of Wales, his grandfather, Sir George Grey, was Home Secretary under Russell (*q.v.*) and Palmerston (*q.v.*), and his great-grandfather was a brother of Charles Grey (*q.v.*), the Prime Minister responsible for the Great Reform Act. Grey was educated at Winchester and Balliol College, Oxford, where he took a third in jurisprudence in 1884, despite being sent down earlier in the year for idleness. Succeeding to his grandfather's baronetcy in 1882, Grey first stood for Parliament in 1885, when he was elected as Liberal MP for Berwick-upon-Tweed. He was created a Knight of the Garter in 1912, and held Berwick until his elevation to the Lords as Viscount Grey of Falloden in July 1916.

As a backbencher, Grey supported Irish Home Rule, and developed an interest in land reform. Having acquired a reputation for good judgment, he became Under-Secretary of State at the Foreign Office in August 1892, serving under two foreign secretaries: Lord Rosebery (*q.v.*) to March 1894, and then the Earl of Kimberley until June 1895. Since both of these foreign secretaries were in the House of Lords, Grey was responsible for speaking on foreign affairs in the Commons. In opposition from 1895 to 1905, he was associated with Liberal Imperialists such as Rosebery, Haldane (*q.v.*), and Asquith (*q.v.*). As a member of this group, Grey was an enthusiast for Britain's effort in the Boer War (1899–1902), which meant that he was not a strong supporter of Campbell-Bannerman's (*q.v.*) leadership of the Liberals. However, concerned to secure balance within the party, Campbell-Bannerman appointed Grey as Foreign Secretary in December 1905.

Grey held this office until December 1916, during which time he dealt with crucial episodes in European diplomacy. Despite criticisms from Radicals who opposed alliances, Grey used the diplomatic system to secure British interests. In 1911, he renewed the 1902 Anglo-Japanese alliance, and one of his major achievements was the negotiation of the Anglo-Russian Entente of August 1907. This resolved differences between Britain and Russia in areas bordering India, which strengthened the British position, and lessened tensions between the two countries. Grey was a strong supporter of continuity in foreign policy, and he built upon the Anglo-French Entente of 1904, negotiated by his Conservative predecessor Lansdowne. Thus Grey backed French diplomacy in the Moroccan crises of 1905–06 and 1911, and allowed the British and French military to hold conversations. Radicals were uneasy over such 'secret diplomacy', believing it involved covert pledges that Britain would intervene in a European war in which France was involved. This was untrue, and Grey was open-minded over the possibility of agreements with Germany; but other than the Baghdad Railway Agreement (1913), no treaty was possible, and his outrage over German violation of Belgian neutrality in August 1914 meant that he was a major influence on the Cabinet's decision to enter the Great War.

After war broke out, diplomacy played a reduced role, and Grey had no significant influence on the direction of the war. When the government was reconstructed under Lloyd George (*q.v.*) in December 1916, he lost office. During the latter part of the war, he became a strong supporter of a 'league of nations', to which all countries would submit their disputes, and which would have the power to make awards and impose sanctions on aggressors. When the League was founded in 1919, Grey became President of the League of Nations Union, a high-profile organisation which supported the League's cause in Britain.

The rest of Grey's career after leaving the Foreign Office has been neglected by historians, but he remained a significant figure in Liberal politics, and his views on foreign affairs were valued by all parties. This meant that he was made a temporary ambassador to the USA in September 1919, when he led an unsuccessful special mission to encourage President Wilson and the Senate to reach a compromise allowing America to enter the League. Some attempted to persuade Grey to re-enter politics in 1920–21, especially Asquith and the moderate Conservative, Robert Cecil, who believed Grey could lead a new centre party. Grey's failing eyesight meant that he was not attracted to the suggestion; but in 1923–24, he was persuaded to lead the Liberal Party in the House of Lords.

He was also President (1927–33) of the Liberal Council, an Asquithian faction within the Liberal Party, formed in response to Lloyd George becoming party leader in 1926. The Council aimed to persuade Liberals that 'true Liberalism' remained alive in the party despite Lloyd George's leadership. Outside politics, Grey was Chancellor of Oxford University from 1928 until his death in 1933. This role at Oxford, like his publication of a book, *The Charm of Birds* (1927), reflected his desire to explore life outside politics in the 1920s.

Grey died on 7 September 1933 at his house, Falloden, in Northumberland. He had married Dorothy Widdrington in 1885, but she died in 1906. Grey married again in 1922, to Pamela, the daughter of Percy Wyndham, and widow of the 1st Lord Glenconner. However, Pamela died in 1928, and there were no children from either marriage.

Grey wrote two volumes of memoirs: *Twenty-Five Years, 1892–1916* (1925). His other publications include: *Fly Fishing* (1899); *The League of Nations* (1918); *The Charm of Birds* (1927). There are two biographies: G. M. Trevelyan, *Grey of Falloden* (1937); and

Keith Robbins, *Sir Edward Grey: A Biography of Lord Grey of Falloden* (1971). A study of his time as Foreign Secretary is: F. H. Hinsley (ed.), *British Foreign Policy under Sir Edward Grey* (1977).

Dr Richard S. Grayson

JO GRIMOND (Lord Grimond) 1913–93

Regarded by many contemporary Liberals as their spiritual leader and mentor, Jo Grimond was a figure of great magnetism and intellectual originality. He was once described as 'a politician on whom the gods smile', and inspired a rare degree of public affection. Within the Liberal Party, neither of his successors, Jeremy Thorpe (*q.v.*) nor David Steel (*q.v.*) enjoyed the same rapport with party members as he did. As former Liberal MP Russell Johnston (*q.v.*) said: 'Liberals are not natural leader-worshippers, but we were captivated and proud'.

Grimond's leadership of the Liberal Party from 1956–67 made a difference not just to the fortunes of his party but to British politics, helping to end the two-party mould into which Britain had seemed to settle. He made the most substantial contribution to Liberal Party politics of any post-war Liberal politician, taking over an ailing party and transforming it into a formidable force. His idealism, his imagination, his ability to communicate, his freshness, made him 'the personification and the hope of post-war Liberalism'; it was quite impossible, from the early 1960s onwards, to think of the Liberal Party without thinking of him.

Joseph Grimond was born on 29 July 1913 in St Andrews, Fife, the son of Joseph Bowman Grimond, a jute manufacturer, and Helen Lydia Grimond (née Richardson). The family could trace their connection with textiles back to the start of the nineteenth century. His father died in 1928, shortly after the family business was absorbed into Jute Industries – a transaction that left Grimond with a lasting bias in favour of small industrial units.

He was sent to a preparatory school near London and then to Eton. This played an important role in shaping the adolescent Grimond, for there he became both an intellectual leader and a social success. He fell under the influence of Robert Birley, an inspiring history teacher with a strong sense of idealism. Grimond was imbued with enthusiasm and curiosity about politics, reflected in his involvement in the school's Political Society, of which in 1932 he became President.

After Eton, Grimond elected to read Modern Greats (philosophy, politics and economics) at Balliol College, Oxford, where he took a first. He made his first political speech in the general election of 1935, in support of Arthur Irvine, the Liberal candidate for Kincardine & West Aberdeenshire. It was largely due to Irvine that his interest in politics flowered and blossomed. Three years later Grimond's marriage to Laura (*q.v.*), youngest daughter of Lady Violet Bonham Carter (*q.v.*) and granddaughter of H. H. Asquith (*q.v.*) helped to underline his potential. Lady Violet was 'the formidable high priestess of Liberalism'. She took a proprietorial interest in the Liberal Party and the political hopes that she had once entertained for herself were transferred to Grimond. Lord Esher, a contemporary and close friend, felt that Grimond took a pretty relaxed view of politics until his marriage: 'Laura not only brought him into the Asquithian inheritance but also confronted him with her (and her mother's) stronger feelings and more concentrated ambitions'.

After Oxford, Grimond studied for a legal career as a barrister, being a pupil in the same chambers of which Quintin Hogg was a member. He was called to the bar (Middle Temple) in 1937. He joined the 2nd Fife and Forfar Yeomanry three days before the outbreak of war and served in Northern Ireland and Europe, rising to the rank of major.

He first stood for Parliament in 1945; undoubtedly the patronage of the Liberal leader, Sir Archibald Sinclair (*q.v.*), helped to secure him the candidacy of Orkney & Shetland. The seat had been Liberal-held until 1935 and was one of the few winnable ones in Scotland. Grimond, however, did not rate his chances of winning highly, and failed to attend the count. Later he was to kick himself when he discovered he was only 329 votes behind the successful Conservative candidate. Nevertheless, a life-long connection with this constituency, the most distant from Westminster, began. Its remoteness and sturdy sense of independence helped to fortify his Liberalism – though these characteristics also made it more difficult for him to understand the realities of life in industrial Britain. It would be impossible to exaggerate the importance of Orkney & Shetland to Grimond. Not only did he relish its inhabitants; he found in their small self-sufficient communities paradigms against which he measured the lunacies of central government and the welfare state.

After the election he was only too happy to be seconded to the United Nations Relief and Rehabilitation Administration (UNRRA) set up by the Allies to help countries devastated by the war and their refugees. Although Grimond was able to do little for them, the experience served to intensify his distrust of bureaucracy and large organisations. He left UNRRA on demobilisation in 1947 and became Secretary of the National Trust for Scotland. He stood again for Orkney & Shetland at the 1950 general election, and captured it with a majority of 2,956. Despite the occasional fluctuation in his vote thereafter, his hold on the seat was never seriously threatened.

Within two days of his election, Grimond became Liberal Chief Whip. His standing was further enhanced in the 1951 election when he doubled his majority even though the Liberal vote in the country collapsed. He realised that the Liberal Party had to change, needing to discard its shibboleths and becoming relevant to modern politics – in other words, it needed modernising. Grimond was able to put this into practice when Clement Davies (*q.v.*) resigned the leadership in 1956. His resignation was not unwelcome; there was a mood for change amongst many leading activists, who had lost faith in Clement Davies' increasingly emotional and rambling oratory.

Grimond became leader of a party close to extinction, commanding the support of little more than two per cent of the electorate and securing the return of only three MPs to Westminster without the benefit of local pacts. In only fifteen constituencies at the 1955 general election did Labour and Conservative candidates not finish first and second. The parliamentary party was rumoured to hold its meetings in a telephone kiosk, and Conservative MP Sir Gerald Nabarro dubbed them 'the shadow of a splinter'.

Grimond, however, rejected any thought that the Liberal Party should be satisfied with a role as a 'brains trust standing on the sidelines of politics shouting advice to Tories and Socialists alike'. He gave it a long-term aim, power, and first halted and then reversed the seemingly remorseless process of electoral decline. At his first assembly as Leader, Grimond proclaimed, 'in the next ten years it is a question of get on or get out'. Under his leadership the first Liberal revival since 1929 occurred, giving early indications that the hegemonic two-party system was showing signs of strain.

Grimond could do what no Liberal had done for many years: appeal to the younger generation of voters, who, as the first products of the Butler Education Act and of post-war universities and polytechnics, were not necessarily committed to the apparently class-dominated major parties. This was his first achievement and it was made possible largely by his enthusiasm and charm. He made the party a respectable political organisation to join, and attracted experts who contributed to a real renaissance in Liberal thinking. In his books, *The Liberal Future* (1959), and *The Liberal Challenge* (1963), and in numerous pamphlets, he gave political liberalism a new direction and purpose, based on a reassertion of the traditional liberal insistence that ideas and principles were more important than interests.

He set about making the party a pacemaker for such ideas as entry into the Common Market and non-socialist planning. It was due to his leadership that the party supported the abolition of Britain's independent nuclear deterrent. He deserves credit for placing on the political agenda issues such as how Britain should handle her relative decline in the world and how government should be brought closer to the people; he was a long-term supporter of Scottish home rule (by which he meant self-government within the confines of a federal system). Celebrating his tenth anniversary as leader of the Liberal Democrats in 1998, Paddy Ashdown (*q.v.*) paid tribute: 'Jo Grimond has always been my guiding star. He established the Liberals as the radicals and thinkers of British politics. The ideas he proposed are now the agenda of government.'

Grimond was a long-term opponent of statism, the view that social advance could only be brought about through the action of the state. He joined fellow Liberals who agreed with his views in the Unservile State Group and contributed a chapter on the reform of Parliament to that body's key publication, *The Unservile State* (1957). His opposition to state action was partly based on the belief that this enhanced the power of bureaucracies, transforming those who received state services into the passive recipients of handouts, devaluing their humanity by depriving them of the ability to

take decisions which affected their everyday lives. His firm belief in the importance of participation and the need for individuals to possess freedom of choice resulted in him viewing communities as the key social unit in which individuals could intellectually develop their full potential by sharing in the pursuit of common goals.

Grimond also gave the Liberal Party a sense of political direction which it had previously lacked. Realignment of the left, the uniting of Britain's progressive forces around the nucleus provided by the Liberal Party, was a central theme of his leadership. In this he was percipient but premature, anticipating the split in the Labour Party which was not to become open for another twenty-five years. Nonetheless, he sowed the seeds of realignment, the fruits of which were reaped at the 1983 general election. Roy Jenkins (*q.v.*) generously paid tribute to Grimond, claiming that he was the father of the Alliance.

The byelection capture of Orpington in 1962 seemed to prove his strategy right. Anticipating the outcome of the next election, he made probably his most famous speech to the 1963 assembly: 'In bygone days, commanders were taught that when in doubt, they should march their troops towards the sound of gunfire. I intend to march my troops towards the sound of gunfire.' The 1964 general election indeed saw the Liberal vote rise above the three million mark for the first time since before the war. The Liberal Party took over eleven per cent of the votes cast and won nine seats; the size of the Liberal support in English county and suburban seats showed that the party had re-established itself as a vital force in British politics.

Paradoxically, however, this election also dashed Grimond's hopes, for the narrow Labour victory rendered the essential element in his strategy inoperative. Instead of the Labour Party splitting to allow the hoped-for realignment of the left, it was to hold office for eleven of the next fifteen years. Moreover, Grimond received little support and much misunderstanding for his overtures to the Wilson government in 1965.

The 1966 general election spelt the end of Grimond's hopes of achieving realignment. It gave, as Liberal MP Emlyn Hooson (*q.v.*) put it, 'Lib/Labbery the axe once and for all'. Labour's substantially increased majority meant that that Grimond's dramatic 1965 assembly speech about the Liberal teeth being in the real meat of power seemed remote. Grimond, believing that he had run out of ideas and exhausted his potential, resigned the leadership in January 1967. A new era dawned, where ideas were subordinated to tactics.

Grimond made a brief come-back as leader in May 1976 for several months after the party was wracked by the Thorpe scandal. In his brief period in charge, he settled the party's nerves and oversaw a clean and confidence-restoring leadership election that culminated in the election of David Steel as leader. When Steel took the Liberals into a formal pact with Labour in 1977, ironically, Grimond was the only dissentient among Liberal MPs, believing on principle, that Labour was undeserving of support, and that in any case the Liberals would not profit from such an agreement.

After thirty-three years' service as MP, Grimond stood down at the 1983 general election. Later that year, in defiance of earlier pronouncements, he was created a life peer as Baron Grimond of Firth in the County of Orkney. He had been made a Privy Councillor in 1961. Throughout his career he was an enthusiastic lecturer abroad and travelled widely. He became a director of the Manchester Guardian and Evening News Ltd. in 1967. He was actively involved in higher education, serving as rector of the Universities of Edinburgh (1960–63) and Aberdeen (1970) and as Chancellor of Kent University (1970–82). He also chaired a committee to look into the constitution and workings of Birmingham University (1971).

Grimond died, aged eighty, on 24 October 1993 in Orkney following a stroke. He left a widow, two sons and a daughter. One son had predeceased him.

He was the author of a number of key works, the most important being *The Liberal Future* (1959), *The Liberal Challenge* (1963), *The Common Welfare* (1978), *Personal Manifesto* (1983) and *The St Andrews of Jo Grimond* (1992). He wrote his own autobiography, *Memoirs* (1979), and collaborated with Brian Neve on *The Referendum* (1976). He wrote a large number of pamphlets; key works include *The New Liberalism* (1957) and *A Roar For the Lion* (1976) (in which he put forward his solution to the then current West Lothian question). A brief assessment of his political career is provided in Peter Joyce, *Giving Politics a Good Name* (1995). There is also a unpublished PhD thesis, *Liberal Revival: Jo Grimond and the Politics of British Liberalism 1956–1967* by Geoffrey Sell (University of London, 1996). The Grimond papers are in the National Library of Scotland.

Peter Joyce and Geoffrey Sell

LAURA GRIMOND   1918–94

Laura Bonham Carter was born in London on 13 October 1918, to a distinguished Liberal family: her father was Maurice Bonham Carter and her mother Lady Violet Bonham Carter (*q.v.*), the daughter of H. H. Asquith (*q.v.*) the former Prime Minister and Liberal leader. She was educated privately in London, France and Austria, and spoke fluent French and German. She married Jo Grimond (*q.v.*) in 1938 and they had four children.

She was an active Liberal on both the national and local political scenes. Her own parliamentary campaigns were confined to one unsuccessful contest in West Aberdeenshire at the 1970 general election, when she failed to hold the constituency captured by James Davidson in 1966. Her main role in post-war general election contests was to serve as *de facto* agent to her husband in Orkney & Shetland, and she formally undertook this role in 1983 to secure the return of Jim Wallace (*q.v.*). She served on the Liberal Party Executive Committee 1963–64 and the Executive Committee of the Women's Liberal Federation 1957–67 (serving as its President 1983–85). She took a keen interest in women's rights, family planning, electoral reform, the independence of African nations and defence issues, serving on the Liberal-SDP Defence Commission, 1984–86.

Grimond was especially involved in local political activity in Orkney, where the family had its home. She was President of the Orkney Women's Liberal Association and served as a local councillor for the parishes of Firth and Harray (1974–80) and as chair of the Orkney Islands housing committee. She was additionally an active member of a large number of local organisations, including the Hoy Trust, the Orkney Heritage Society and the Orkney Mental Health Society. Her other interests included serving as a magistrate in Richmond, where the family had its London home, until 1960.

It would be a mistake to dismiss Laura's political career as being merely supportive of her husband, Jo. While she did perform a wide range of constituency business on his behalf, her personal involvement in local affairs epitomised the importance Liberals have customarily attached to voluntary service and gave practical substance to the emphasis which Jo attached to community as a key social unit.

She suffered a stroke towards the end of 1992 which forced her to retire from public life, and died in London on 14 February 1994.

Peter Joyce

R. B. HALDANE (Viscount Haldane) 1856–1928

The Asquith government of 1908–15 was arguably the most talented ever to rule Britain. Even in its illustrious ranks, Richard Burdon Haldane stood out as a unique figure, whose army reforms of 1907 were one of the administration's most praised achievements. However, after his dismissal by Asquith in 1915 he became one of the Labour Party's most important recruits from Liberalism and a member of the first Labour government of 1924.

Haldane was born in Edinburgh on 30 July 1856. Both his parents' families were closely involved with the legal profession and evangelical religion. He was educated at

Edinburgh Academy and the University of Edinburgh, though in 1874 he spent some time at the University of Gottingen, so confirming a life-long interest in Germany and idealist philosophy. Haldane was called to the bar at Lincoln's Inn in 1879 and became a QC in 1890. He slowly built up a lucrative equity practice, which concentrated on appeals to the House of Lords and the judicial committee of the Privy Council.

Haldane was a committed Liberal from an early age. He won the new seat of Haddingtonshire at his first attempt in 1885 and kept it until his elevation to the Lords in 1911. In the Commons in the late 1880s he formed a close working relationship with H. H. Asquith (*q.v.*) and Sir Edward Grey (*q.v.*) and together they formed the nucleus of the future Liberal Imperialist grouping within Liberalism. All came to look to Rosebery (*q.v.*) as their leader and shared an interest in promoting enthusiasm for an active foreign policy, the Empire and social reform as a way to revive Liberal fortunes. Haldane regarded himself as the group's philosopher and saw much of other collectivist thinkers like the Webbs in the 1890s. He was disappointed not to be invited to serve in the 1892–95 Liberal governments, but he helped Sir William Harcourt (*q.v.*) draft and defend his 1894 budget which introduced death duties. Haldane first became widely known as one of the Liberal Imperialists' leaders in their fight to stop the Liberals opposing the Boer War in 1899–1902 and in 1905 he persuaded Grey and Asquith to join him in the so-called Relugas compact to attempt to dictate a Liberal Imperialist agenda to the party's leader, Campbell-Bannerman (*q.v.*), when he formed a government.

The pact, however, disintegrated in the scramble for office. Haldane wished to be Lord Chancellor, but agreed to accept the War Office, with the right of reversion to the former post. Secretary of State for War in a Liberal government was not an enviable job, as most Liberals were only interested in reducing expenditure on the army. But, to the surprise of many, Haldane proved a great success. His most lasting achievement was the 1907 Territorial and Reserve Forces Act, which merged the existing militia, yeomanry and volunteers into a single home defence force, leaving the regular army free to be sent abroad in wartime. Most Radicals accepted this as preferable to conscription, and few realised the scheme was linked in Haldane's mind with the need to defend France from German attack. He was greatly disappointed not to obtain the Admiralty in 1911 in order to widen the field of his military reforms, and went to the Lords the same year as Viscount Haldane of Cloan to strengthen the Liberal leadership in the upper house. His health was indifferent and the honour brought a welcome break from work in the Commons. Haldane finally achieved the Lord Chancellorship in 1912, though he failed to produce his much-vaunted legal reforms.

In general in the Cabinet, Haldane was an ally of Asquith and he moved close to the centre of power once the latter became Prime Minister in 1908. He provided crucial support both for a robust defence policy and Lloyd George's (*q.v.*) social reforms. But his association with army affairs and an obscure speaking style did not endear him to his party and many of his colleagues distrusted him as an incessant, if clumsy, intriguer.

When a coalition government was formed in 1915 Asquith showed little loyalty to his old friend by sacking him on the insistence of the Tories, who regarded him as suspiciously Germanophile. Not surprisingly, Haldane became disillusioned with Liberalism and, in December 1923 accepted Ramsay MacDonald's offer to head the first Labour government's representation in the Lords. As the only plausible candidate for the job he was able to dictate his own terms, acquiring the Lord Chancellorship and chairmanship of the Committee of Imperial Defence in January – November 1924. He remained Labour leader in the Lords until his death on 19 August 1928 at Cloan, his family home in Scotland. He was useful to Labour in establishing a presence in the Lords, but often pursued an embarrassingly independent line. Significantly, he joined the Fabians in 1924, rather than become an individual member of the party.

Haldane was unmarried, but devoted to his mother, to whom he wrote every day until her death, aged 101, and to his unmarried sister. His interests were mainly in education and philosophy. He chaired many important committees on higher education, especially in London, and served as Chancellor of Bristol University in 1912–28 and was elected Chancellor of St Andrews in 1928. He translated the works of Schopenhauer and published a number of impenetrable works of idealist philosophy, including *The Pathway to Reality* (1903), *The Reign of Relativity* (1921), *The Philosophy of Humanism* (1922) and *Human Experience* (1926). He also published an *Autobiography* (1929) and there are biographies by Sir F. Maurice, *The Life of Viscount Haldane of Cloan* (2 volumes, 1937–39) and D. Sommer, *Haldane of Cloan: His Life and Times, 1856–1928* (1960).

Ian Packer

JOHN HAMMOND   1872–1949

BARBARA HAMMOND   1873–1961

John Lawrence Le Breton Hammond (known as Lawrence) was born in 1872, the son of the Vicar of Drighlington in the West Riding of Yorkshire. Lucy Barbara Bradby (known as Barbara) was born in 1873, the daughter of the headmaster of Haileybury College. Married in 1901, the Hammonds had no children. They became pioneer social historians who are remembered especially for their trilogy: *The Village Labourer* (1911), *The Town Labourer* (1917) and *The Skilled Labourer* (1919). In these texts they gave an account of the condition of the English working class during the period of the Industrial Revolution which became a classic statement of the 'pessimistic' case in a long-running debate over the standard of living. Their historical partnership developed in later years as their increasingly precarious health (hers tubercular, his mainly coronary) led to a steady withdrawal from an active participation in public affairs in London and the establishment of an even-paced life of authorship in the country.

Both the Hammonds received a classical education, Lawrence at Bradford Grammar School and St John's College, Oxford; Barbara at St Leonard's School, St Andrews, and Lady Margaret Hall, Oxford. Their literary work showed them as adept at painting the contrast between ancient Athens and modern Manchester as at elucidating the Homeric references in the discourse of Mr Gladstone. Both came from professional families infused with moral and intellectual earnestness.

The Hammonds gave this heritage a radical twist. Barbara made a striking impression in her youth as an early feminist and became active in social work in London at the turn of the century. Lawrence began a career as a journalist associated with journals on the Liberal left like the *Nation* and, increasingly in later years, the *Manchester Guardian*. He was prominently associated with the 'New Liberalism', which took shape in the social reforms of the Edwardian period, and sought the Liberal nomination at Dover in 1903. His appointment as Secretary of the Civil Service Commission (1907–13) meant that he had to renounce overtly partisan polemics – an initial impetus towards writing history instead.

With their first book, *The Village Labourer* (1911), the Hammonds established their reputation. Technically their work was founded upon Barbara's scrupulous research, especially in the public records, expounded in Lawrence's supple prose. Their account of how agricultural labourers fared under the enclosure measures of the period 1760–1830 opened up a far-reaching debate. They did not deny the economic rationality of the process, but pointed to the way that its costs were borne by the rural poor.

The book culminates in an account of the labourers' revolt of 1830, which they took as the response to an injustice which could only have been perpetrated while the landed interest governed England untrammelled. This was indeed a study of class exploitation; but the Hammonds were neither Marxists nor determinists, but liberals who looked to the advent of representative government for effective remedy. Their work acquired immediate political overtones with the inception of Lloyd George's (*q.v.*) Land Campaign in 1913 which made the land the pivot of Liberal social policy.

In turning their attention next to the urban working class, the Hammonds reinforced the left-wing image of their oeuvre. The *Town Labourer* (1917) did not disparage industrialisation as such but again asked the awkward question: who had paid for it? They regarded the Industrial Revolution as an exercise in exploitation which fitted the ideologies of an age which took social inequality for granted. Published at the end of the First World War, with revolution on the streets abroad and reconstruction in the air at home, their findings once more fed into current political debate.

Their trilogy was completed with *The Skilled Labourer* (1919), which analysed the impact of technological change in making skilled craftsmen redundant in the early nineteenth century. It presented the Luddite movement in an unwontedly sympathetic light, suggesting that it constituted not only an understandable response by the inarticulate in defence of their livelihood but also an excuse for repression by a reactionary government.

Other books followed, notably the study of the Chartist era which Penguin Books later published in an abridged – and bestselling – edition as *The Bleak Age* (1947). But the Hammonds' view of the Industrial Revolution remained their claim to attention – not all of it favourable. In particular, in the 1920s their interpretation was contested by J. H. Clapham, with all his authority as Professor of Economic History at Cambridge.

Lawrence's own historical research in old age was devoted to the great Liberal statesman who had been the hero of his youth. In *Gladstone and the Irish Nation* (1938) he made brilliant use of the privileged access he had been given to Gladstone's diaries to render his Irish policy comprehensible in historical context. Again this is a book in which passion and elegance are counterpoised in giving form to a mass of arcane and rebarbative detail. The resulting portrait of Gladstone succeeds in conveying a sense of the man on which all subsequent scholarship has built. This was his last major contribution to historical scholarship. During the Second World War he returned to his old job of leader writer on the *Manchester Guardian*. But thereafter it was a valetudinarian life for the Hammonds at their home near Hemel Hempstead, where Lawrence died in 1949 and Barbara in 1961.

The Hammonds have often been identified as socialist, and it is true that, in the years 1914–31, they were broadly in sympathy with the Labour Party. Yet their outlook throughout their joint career remained true to Liberal nostrums. Insofar as the Hammonds rested their interpretation of the Industrial Revolution upon a quantitative assessment, it was by no means overturned; and its main thrust, in fact, was qualitative in its concern for the impact of economic change on ordinary people's lives. While they depicted the bleak age of early industrialisation, they also pointed to the civilising process which urban life underwent from the middle of the nineteenth century. Though their work came to serve as a straw man, to be knocked down in a dismissive way by a new generation of professional economic historians, its scholarly credentials have survived with remarkable resilience.

Until the proper biography they deserve has been published, the fullest account of their lives and work is in Peter Clarke, *Liberals and Social Democrats* (1978).

Peter Clarke

SALLY HAMWEE (Lady Hamwee) 1947–

Baroness Hamwee of Richmond-upon-Thames was appointed as a life peer in 1991 – the second working peerage granted by the party in ten years, reflecting the need for a woman peer with local government experience. After making her maiden speech in the House of Lords, Stephen (Lord) Ross, then local government spokesman, took Hamwee for a drink and asked her if she wanted to take over from him to cover local government issues. Hamwee agreed, and remains the Liberal Democrat spokesman on local government, environment, housing and planning.

Sally Rachel Hamwee was born on 12 January 1947 in Manchester, an only child. Her father, Alec, was a solicitor and her mother, Dorothy (née Saunders) a marriage guidance counsellor. Her parents voted Liberal and read the *Manchester Guardian* and *News Chronicle*. Hamwee's father dabbled in local politics, but his enthusiasm was short-lived. He came back from his first Liberal local party meeting in 1947, saying he could never go again. The local party asked him to stand for election, first within the party, then for the council, and then for Parliament. He never joined the Liberals, but continued to support them.

Educated first at Manchester High School for Girls, in 1966 Hamwee went to Girton College, Cambridge to read law and qualified in 1969 with an MA. She then went to work for Clintons, a solicitors' firm specialising in show business. Hamwee worked her way up through the firm, where she remains as a partner.

Hamwee joined the Liberal Party in 1976, during the referendum campaign on UK membership of the European Community, in which she campaigned for the pro-Europeans. She discovered political activity was a good way to meet like-minded people. Later in 1976, when she moved to Richmond, she sought out the local Liberal Party for social reasons and became active in the only ward then held by the party. The Richmond Liberals spotted Hamwee early on as good councillor material and in 1977 asked if she would consider standing in another ward (Palewell). Hamwee threw herself into the campaign and was elected in 1978 with a majority of twenty-two, after a recount. Hamwee's recollection of that first election was sitting in a corner clutching the party's local mascot, Stanley, a white teddy bear, while the recount was going on and realising that it was the extra seat that mattered, not the person representing it. Hamwee held the Palewell seat until she stood down in 1998.

Hamwee developed a close interest in planning issues and chaired Richmond Council's Planning Committee from 1983–87, and the London Planning Advisory Committee (LPAC) from 1986–94. She describes the latter as one of her greatest achievements. It was a balanced committee, with Liberal Democrats holding the balance of power, and could easily have fallen victim to party squabbling. But cooperation between group leaders and officers was established and agreement reached on strategic advice in many areas. Hamwee played an influential part in promoting this cooperation and ensuring that LPAC maintained an influential role in London.

Hamwee's interest in planning also resulted in her becoming a member of the Joseph Rowntree Foundation inquiry on planning for housing in 1991 and President of the Town and Country Planning Association, a position she continues to hold. She enjoyed her time as a councillor, especially chairing meetings and running committees and having contact with constituents. She continues to sit on the governing body of East Sheen Primary School.

Hamwee has also made a significant contribution to the national party. She sat on the Liberal Democrats' Federal Executive from 1988–91, and was a member of the general election team in 1992 and 1997. She is now a member of the Association of

Liberal Democrat Councillors' Standing Committee (and was President 1995–96), and sits on the party's Federal Policy Committee.

Over the last few years Hamwee has increased her efforts to encourage other women to stand for election and get on within the party. In the run-up to the 1997 general election, she chaired the Campaign for Women, and is a trustee of the Nancy Seear Trust, which gives grants to women standing for election.

She also has a strong interest in family issues and is a member of the governing council of the Family Policy Studies Centre. In her spare time, she is a passionate supporter of the arts. As a student, she worked in theatre and she continues to see plays whenever she can; she also enjoys abstract art. She lives in Richmond-upon-Thames.

Jen Tankard

MIKE HANCOCK MP   1946–

During its seven years of existence, the SDP gained five parliamentary seats. Shirley Williams (1981, *q.v.*), Roy Jenkins (1982, *q.v.*) and Rosie Barnes (1987) gave the Alliance byelection victories while Charles Kennedy (1983, *q.v.*) was the sole gain at a general election.

The fifth win, in 1984, came during a depressing year for the Alliance. After a disastrous general election in 1983 in terms of seats won, the two parties of the Alliance were desperately searching for a way back into the headlines; indeed, London-based commentators had already written off the SDP's chances for the Portsmouth South byelection on 15 June. An opinion poll three days before voting showed the party in third place. But journalists visiting Portsmouth were less convinced. They could see the name of Mike Hancock spelt out in giant letters down the side of tower blocks in Portsea, the inner-city area of Portsmouth. And so it came to be that Hancock won the election at the age of thirty-eight and continued his political career which had already covered more than twenty years.

Michael Thomas Hancock was born on 9 April 1946 in Portsmouth, living in the poor, working-class district of Portsea, with a huge extended family. An irregular attender at school – he was once introduced to classmates as a 'new boy' – he preferred to chance his luck on the city's streets. He carried bags for passengers to the Isle of Wight and was a 'mudlark boy', jumping into the mud of Portsmouth harbour to claim pennies thrown by holidaymakers. He left school at fifteen with no qualifications.

Hancock joined an engineering company to earn a living, but his main passion became politics. Seeing the bomb sites of his Portsmouth childhood still undeveloped led him to become active in political life. In the 1960s, despite not being old enough to vote, he acted as election agent for a variety of Labour candidates for local elections across Portsmouth. Elected himself in 1971 for the Fratton & Buckland Ward, Hancock had made a name for himself as a community campaigner, determined to protect the existing terraced housing of Fratton from demolition and replacement with modern flats. It is still possible to see the line where the campaign succeeded and the demolition stopped – a point where Victorian terraced houses now meet 1960s blocks.

This community leadership allowed Hancock to withstand the adverse political tide against Labour. In 1977 he retained his Hampshire County Council seat, won in 1973, and became leader of the mere seven Labour councillors on Hampshire County Council, who formed the opposition during the Conservative landslide. He was reelected as a Labour councillor in 1981, but defected soon after to the newly formed SDP. Disillusioned with the leftward march of the Labour Party in Portsmouth, Hancock felt he could best continue his community-minded political approach with a new party.

A combination of his community-based popularity and the surge to the Alliance enabled him to come second in the 1983 general election in Portsmouth South. This was followed a year later by the byelection. During his three years in Parliament, Hancock maintained his grassroots base. His single-minded efforts saw his vote at the 1987 election rise by 8,000, but he was still defeated by 205 votes and at the subsequent 1992 election, he again came second, this time by a heartbreaking 242 votes.

During this entire period, Hancock retained his council seats on both Portsmouth City Council and Hampshire County Council; at times, he was the sole Alliance councillor in Portsmouth. However, as political prospects improved for the Liberal Democrats, he became Chair of Planning in a joint administration with Labour in Portsmouth in 1991. But his high-profile leadership of that committee and his championing of inward investment and economic development led him into conflict with his Labour partners who still harboured resentment from his defection ten years earlier. As a result, the joint arrangement was terminated in 1994 and Hancock returned to opposition.

In 1993 a new opportunity arose when the Liberal Democrats became the largest party on Hampshire County Council and formed a joint administration with Labour. Hancock became Leader of the County Council. The administration invested heavily in education, and following the line of Hancock's personal interest, in social services. He also led the county council into new relationships with regions across Europe and gained the respect of the Hampshire business community through his strong promotion of the region as a good place for international business. His claim was that despite never having sat an exam and having no qualifications, he had become the most powerful Liberal Democrat in Britain. With local government reorganisation in April 1997, he packed his bags and left the Leader's office in Winchester, confined to a back-bench role with the new Portsmouth Unitary Council. But a few weeks later he was re-elected as MP for Portsmouth South with a majority of more than 4,000.

Returned to Parliament, Hancock is now a member of the foreign affairs, defence and Europe team, with special responsibility for defence. He also continues to play a huge part in the community life in Portsmouth. His commitment to community politics had seen him through some dark days with both the Labour Party and the SDP. His first and abiding concern is to stand up for people in Portsmouth South, to try to get the best for them and their families. Such an approach can generate scorn from political allies as well as opponents. But as Hancock will remind them, 'I am the only MP people in Portsmouth South have got. If they cannot count on me for support, who can they turn to?'

Hancock married Jackie in 1967 and has two children. Following his election defeat in 1987 he worked as a Director of BBC Daytime and then as District Officer for the charity Mencap. He describes his recreations as 'living life to the full'. He was awarded the CBE in the 1992 Birthday Honours.

Matthew Clark

SIR WILLIAM HARCOURT   1827–1904

William George Granville Venables Vernon Harcourt was born at York on 14 October 1827, of a land-owning and clerical family which traced its ancestry to the Plantagenet kings. His elder brother, Edward Harcourt, was a staunch Conservative and for eight years an MP. William Harcourt's views, however, began to take a Liberal turn in the early 1840s, when he opposed protection on account of the dearness and scarcity of bread for the people. He argued in the Liberal cause in the Cambridge University Union when he was an undergraduate at Trinity College from 1847 to 1851. But his political opinions were by no means settled, and until the later 1860s he appeared as an independent, whose outstanding abilities caused him to be wooed as a champion by both parties.

After obtaining a degree in classics and mathematics (with a first class in the former), he studied law in London for three years and was called to the bar in 1854. He soon obtained a large and lucrative practice, first at the common law bar and later at the parliamentary bar. He also became known as an effective writer for newspapers and periodicals (particularly *The Times*), and as an accomplished speaker. He was made a Queen's Counsel in 1866 and was Whewell Professor of International Law at Cambridge from 1869 to 1887.

Harcourt first stood for Parliament as an Independent Liberal candidate for the Kirkcaldy District of Burghs in the general election of 1859, but was narrowly defeated. He was offered a safe Conservative seat in 1866 by Disraeli, but declined it. Soon afterwards he became decisively and permanently Liberal, speaking on platforms with John Bright (*q.v.*), strongly advocating the disestablishment of the Church of Ireland, and being returned for Oxford City as a Liberal in the general election of November 1868.

From 1868 politics increasingly absorbed his attention, and he gradually abandoned his legal work, supposedly sacrificing £10,000 a year (an immense sum at that time) in the process. However, he declined the post of Judge Advocate-General in Gladstone's (q.v.) first government because it carried with it a Privy Councillorship, and at that time the latter would have prevented him from practising law when out of office. He showed striking debating ability in the Commons and became quite radical in approach, arguing especially strongly for religious equality and civil liberty, and criticising some of his own government's measures for timidity. However, he disclaimed any consistent radical tendency at this stage and said he was only 'preaching Whig doctrines'. In November 1873 he accepted the post of Solicitor-General (and a knighthood). He was a constant critic of Conservative policies during Disraeli's ministry of 1874–80, and a firm supporter of Gladstone over the Balkan crisis of 1876–78 and the government's overseas embarrassments of 1878–79.

After the Liberals returned to power in April 1880, Harcourt became Home Secretary. On seeking re-election at Oxford (according to the then convention for ministers) he was defeated, though he had been re-elected the previous month. However, two weeks later, he found a seat at Derby, where Samuel Plimsoll resigned in his favour, and he was returned without a contest. He sat for Derby until 1895.

As Home Secretary, Harcourt carried a measure which was clearly against the privileges of his own land-owning class and in the interests of the tenant farmer – the Ground Game (or Hares and Rabbits) Bill of 1880. This signalled a populist approach to politics which marked him for the rest of his life. He became increasingly known in this period as an effective speaker before vast political audiences running into many thousands. However, he did not go so far as to align himself with Joseph Chamberlain (q.v.) and his 'Radical Programme'. Various reforming measures regarding water supply and juvenile criminality also marked Harcourt's Home Secretaryship, and as serious Irish unrest afflicted the government he had the unenviable but successful job of piloting coercion measures through the Commons.

After the government defeat in June 1885, Harcourt kept his seat in the November general election, and became Chancellor of the Exchequer on the party's return to government in February 1886 – making him, in effect, Gladstone's chief lieutenant and (in the event of accident to the old leader) his expected successor. He strongly supported Gladstone's conversion to Home Rule. As a recent sponsor of Irish coercion measures, he was bitterly attacked by Unionists, but he effectively argued that all policies except Home Rule had failed as a means of settling the Irish question.

Home Rule failed as well; the first bill to establish it was defeated in June 1886, and the ensuing general election returned a large Conservative and Liberal Unionist majority. He was anxious for reunion with the Liberal dissidents, and took part in the unsuccessful Round Table Conference for this purpose in 1887. He was prominent in criticising the new Conservative government, and often triumphed (though sometimes lost) in parliamentary jousts with Chamberlain. He also continued to be a most assiduous speaker in the country, and Gladstone (sometimes suffering from ill health) came increasingly to depend on him. By 1891 Harcourt was urging the wide array of reforms which came to form the Liberals' Newcastle Programme of October that year.

Harcourt was again Chancellor of the Exchequer and 'crown prince' in the last Gladstone Government of 1892–94. This was a time of largely fruitless struggle and, ultimately, of great personal disappointment. The second Home Rule Bill was rejected by the Lords; a local veto bill to restrict the sale of alcohol was abandoned in the Commons. A Parish Councils Bill got through in 1894 only after stringent amendment by the Lords, and Harcourt signalised the rapidly developing antagonism between Liberals and the Upper House by indicting the latter as 'the champion of all abuses and the enemy of all reform'. Gladstone resigned as premier in March 1894. But, despite Harcourt's great prominence and activity as second-in-command since 1886, the Queen (without consulting Gladstone) offered the premiership to the Earl of Rosebery (q.v.), Foreign Secretary and Harcourt's junior by twenty years.

This event virtually robbed Harcourt of the highest political office, to which he had legitimately been able to look forward. While some feelings of antagonism on his part were unavoidable, he bravely continued as Chancellor of the Exchequer and acted as Leader of the Commons in the Rosebery ministry. His 1894 budget included the reform for which he is chiefly remembered – the introduction of graduated death duties on both real and personal property, together with reduction of the liability of lower incomes to tax. Despite the measure's anti-aristocratic tone (and, it was argued, anti-aristocratic retaliation), the Lords did not yet dare to reject a budget. Following a government defeat in June 1895, the general election in July was a Conservative triumph, resulting in a majority of 152 for themselves and their Liberal Unionist allies. Harcourt was defeated at Derby, but once again a Liberal was ready to stand down in his favour, and West Monmouthshire became his new constituency.

As Leader of the Liberal Party in the Commons, Harcourt supported electoral reform and House of Lords reform, defended temperance, and criticised imperialist policies. He was soon able to claim an opposition triumph when the government withdrew its Education Bill of 1896, which had proposed to abolish the school boards introduced by the Liberals' Education Act of 1870. Rosebery resigned as leader of the party in October 1896, after declaring his opposition to both Harcourt and Gladstone over a question relating to Turkish massacres in Armenia. Harcourt was a pall-bearer at Gladstone's funeral in May 1898, but by the end of the year, his increasing difficulties with the Roseberyite Liberal Imperialists caused him to abandon the leadership of the Liberals in the Commons, and in February 1899 Campbell-Bannerman (q.v.) was elected in his place.

Harcourt continued to criticise the Salisbury government over imperial policy and to show his differences from Rosebery. Chamberlain's tariff reform campaign of 1903 provided the ambience of his last great battle, in defence of free trade; public speeches and letters to *The Times* sprang abundantly from him. Before he died on 30 September 1904 at his family estate at Nuneham Courtenay, Oxfordshire (which he had just inherited from his deceased nephew), Harcourt had the satisfaction of seeing the Liberals regain considerable unity over the tariff question.

Harcourt married twice (to Therese Lister in 1859, and to Elizabeth Ives in 1876), and had a surviving son by each marriage. The elder of these, Lewis ('Loulou'), had just become a Liberal MP when his father died, having served as his private secretary, 1881–1904, and took office in the Campbell-Bannerman government in 1905. The younger son, Robert, became a Liberal MP in 1908.

It took Harcourt, like Gladstone, a long time to become a Liberal, but once this affiliation was decided, he became an active and prominent one. He did not completely fulfil his expected potential, being perhaps the classic case of 'the best Prime Minister we never had'. But as a strong contender for another title, that of 'the democratic aristocrat', he achieved notable reforms and, to a very striking degree, worked effectively for his party through thick and thin. The main biography is A. G. Gardiner's *The Life of Sir William Harcourt* (2 vols, 1923).

Ian Machin

EVAN HARRIS MP   1965–

A well-known journalist used to claim that he could tell Liberals and Social Democrats apart according to whether they had memorised *Wisden* or the railway timetable. But if an uncanny memory for minutiae was ever a qualification for either party, Evan Harris at least put his to practical use: he memorised electoral registers. Pick an address in a ward he was targeting, and he could tell you the names of all the occupants, along with past voting behaviour, and quite often a thumbnail sketch of characters and attitudes into the bargain.

Evan Harris was born in Sheffield on 21 October 1965, the second son of South African immigrants disillusioned with the apartheid regime. He won a scholarship to Wadham College, Oxford, to study physiological sciences and medicine, and he qualified as a doctor in 1991.

He became politically active as a student, initially joining the SDP and later supporting merger with the Liberals. He was an obsessive campaigner and election organiser, with a particular aptitude for membership recruitment, leading his Oxford West & Abingdon constituency to the 1994 Penhaligon Award for membership recruitment and retention. When, in 1995, the party headquarters issued a challenge to recruit a hundred members in a hundred days, it was typical of Harris that he left it till the last ten days, but succeeded nonetheless.

Meanwhile, he was pursuing his medical career, holding clinical posts in breast cancer surgery in Oxford and then emergency and internal medicine in Liverpool, before spending two years as Senior House Officer with the Nuffield Department of Medicine at Oxford's John Radcliffe Hospital and Radcliffe Infirmary. In 1994 he took up an honorary registrar post with Oxford & Anglia Regional Health Authority and then Oxfordshire Health Authority's Public Health Department as the medical officer to the Task Force on Junior Doctors' Hours, charged with implementing the 'New Deal' to reduce long and unsafe hours worked by junior doctors, and managing a £4 million budget.

He was local BMA representative and negotiator from 1992–94, and was then elected to represent doctors in the region on the national Council of the BMA. He also served on the executive committee of the BMA Junior Doctor Committee, the Board of Science and Education and the Community Care Committee.

He was selected to fight Oxford West & Abingdon in 1994, gaining the seat at the 1997 general election with a majority of 6,285 on a ten per cent swing from the Conservatives. He became part of the Liberal Democrat health team in Parliament, specialising in NHS structure and staffing issues, and rapidly establishing one of the higher media profiles among the 1997 intake.

Away from health issues, Harris has a long-standing interest in civil liberties, with a record in anti-racism, refugee welfare and gay rights. Roy Jenkins (*q.v.*) was one of his early political heroes.

Harris was married on 21 August 1989 to Louise Goss-Custard (divorced 1997). A member of Oxford's Jewish congregation, he lives in North Hinksey village on the outskirts of Oxford.

Caroline White

JOHN HARRIS (Lord Harris) 1930–

John Henry Harris was born in Harrow on 5 April 1930, the son of Alfred George and May Harris. He was educated at Pinner County Grammar School and became a journalist working on a variety of provincial newspapers. Later in his career, between 1970–74, he wrote for the *Economist*.

He commenced work as Hugh Gaitskell's personal assistant in 1959. During that year's election campaign he urged Gaitskell to make his promise not to increase income tax, which in the end proved counter-productive. He remained with Gaitskell until just before his death, which he subsequently described as 'the worst blow of my life'. From there on in, his career is marked by a remarkable consistency of commitment to what might be seen as Gaitskellism plus a devotion to the European cause.

Harris was the archetypal backroom boy, achieving elective office only as a local councillor in Harlow from 1957–63. He became Director of Publicity of the Labour Party in 1962, a post he held until the election victory of 1964. This was a period of significant achievement and modernisation of the Labour Party's communications strategy; Labour showed themselves to be significantly more adept than the Tories at using the modern media. After the 1964 election victory Harris became assistant to the Foreign Secretary, and from 1965 he was attached to Roy Jenkins (*q.v.*), first at the Home Office and then at the Treasury. Their fortunes became inseparable. Inevitably he attracted criticism, being seen by fellow members of the government as Jenkins' hit-man. Tony Benn opined that 'Roy uses John Harris, his press adviser, quite ruthlessly against anyone who stands in his way'; Barbara Castle noted in her diary (21 November 1966): 'Sunday's papers are full of Roy Jenkins again. There is obviously a campaign to run him as Harold's successor. Ted says it is all due to John Harris.'

For all this, Harris was no mere spin-doctor. He was created a peer in 1974, taking the title Baron Harris of Greenwich, and served in the Wilson and Callaghan Governments as a junior Home Office minister from 1974–79. He was Chairman of the Parole Board from 1979–82.

Harris played a key role in the formation of the SDP, and influenced Jenkins to stand in the Warrington byelection in 1981. His organisational skills were exercised in both the 1983 and 1987 Alliance election campaigns. He led for the SDP in the Lords on home affairs from 1983–88, and performed the same role for the Liberal Democrats from 1988–94. In 1994 he became Chief Whip, a role in which he has been effective and, in so far as it is possible in that function, popular.

He is twice married: first, in 1952, to Patricia Margaret Alstrom (marriage dissolved 1982); and then, in 1983, to Angela Smith. There is one son and one daughter from his first marriage.

Peter Truesdale

SIR PERCY HARRIS 1876–1952

Percy Harris was born on 6 March 1876, the son of a Polish immigrant, Wolf Harris, and his wife, Elizabeth, whose father was a New Zealand businessman. He was educated at Harrow School and then Trinity Hall, Cambridge, where he read history. Afterwards he qualified as a barrister, but never practiced and instead worked for his father's manufacturing business, firstly in London and then in New Zealand. His leisure interests included a boys' club in Camberwell and the Workers' Educational Association; in 1909 he published *New Zealand and its Politics*. In 1901 he married Marguerite Bloxham, herself an artist, and the daughter of John Bloxham, a London surgeon. They had two sons.

Through his interest in New Zealand he came to the attention of Herbert Gladstone (*q.v.*) who placed him as a candidate in Ashford, Kent, for the 1906 election, which he lost narrowly. He joined the Eighty Club, a Liberal campaigning and speaker meeting group formed to commemorate Gladstone's (*q.v.*) victory in 1880 (often used as a venue for key speeches in the period of Liberal splits after 1918). In 1907 he began his association with South West Bethnal Green, when he won one of the two seats on the London County Council. Subsequently, Harris became Chief Whip for the Progressive group in 1912, and then Deputy Chairman of the council from 1915–16. He held the division as a Progressive until 1934. During his time on the council, he specialised in housing, leaving education to the other member for the division, the Rev. Stuart Headlam. He also wrote *London and its Government*, published in 1913 and then updated in 1931.

Harris had not, however, abandoned hopes of a parliamentary career, and fought Harrow unsuccessfully at the general election of January 1910. In 1911, when the resignation of E. H. Pickersgill left a parliamentary vacancy in South West Bethnal Green, Harris stood aside, after some soul searching, so that C. F. G. Masterman could be parachuted in – only to see him lose the seat to the Conservatives a few months later after his resignation on promotion to the Cabinet. At the outbreak of war, Harris was instrumental in forming a volunteer force for the over-aged and the disabled and in 1916 he entered the Commons as MP for Market Harborough at a byelection. He was briefly a member of the Select Committee on National Expenditure, then chaired by Herbert Samuel (*q.v.*), before voting with Asquith (*q.v.*) in the Maurice debate. As a result he did not receive the coupon in 1918 and was defeated by the Conservatives.

In the 1922 election, assisted by Winifred Holtby and Vera Brittain (recorded in the latter's *Testament of Youth*) he finally won South West Bethnal Green, holding it thereafter until 1945, although he came close to defeat in 1924 when his majority over Labour was only 212. He convened the Liberal Education Advisory Committee from 1923, and in 1931 became Chief Whip at Samuel's request, although he took care to ensure that he had Lloyd George's (*q.v.*) approval as well. He was made a baronet in 1932.

A big, extrovert man, Harris played a key role in the party's survival in Parliament from 1931 to 1935. He spoke frequently on every kind of topic in the Commons. After the 1935 election, he was crucial in preventing the Liberal Nationals taking over the Liberal Whips' room. When Sinclair (*q.v.*) entered the government in 1940, he became acting Leader in the Commons (and a Privy Councillor) as well as Chief Whip. At the same time, he took over responsibility for the party's organisation in the country from Harcourt Johnstone. During the war, he helped set up party committees on different policy topics under the umbrella of the Liberal Post-War Enquiry. He also played a role in persuading Beveridge (*q.v.*) to stand for the Liberals. However Bethnal Green was not impervious to the Labour landslide in 1945, and he was defeated by 2,456 votes.

Although Harris then settled down to write his memoirs, *Forty Years in and out of Parliament*, and became President of the Liberal Candidates Association, he was persuaded to stand again for the LCC. This he would do only on the condition that a running mate was found for him, and in 1946, he and Edward Martell (*q.v.*) became the only two Liberals on the council. In the 1949 elections, only Harris was successful and he briefly held the balance of power until the allocation of aldermanic seats. He held the seat until his death in London on 28 June 1952.

Harris was unusual as a radical Liberal who, despite several overtures from Labour, was never inclined to defect to them. He was the quintessential party loyalist whose greatest achievement was to keep the party alive in the Commons during the 1930s. Never a great orator or policy thinker, he nonetheless played a significant role in the party's history and in London government.

Malcolm Baines

MARQUESS OF HARTINGTON (Duke of Devonshire) 1833–1908

The birth of the modern Liberal Party in 1859 brought together three disparate elements, Whigs, Peelites and Radicals. Hartington, as he was known for most of his political life, epitomised the Whig contribution to government – rich, aristocratic but driven by *noblesse oblige* to take public office. When he broke with Gladstone (*q.v.*) in the 1880s it symbolised the end of Whig government and marked the drift of the landed classes into the Tory camp. Hartington is probably the only political leader who was thrice offered the premiership and thrice rejected it. Goschen (*q.v.*) described him as 'a moderate man, a violently moderate man'. His position in the party and the country was built not on brilliance but on his obvious integrity.

Born on 23 July 1833 at Holker Hall, Lancashire, he was the eldest son of William Cavendish and his wife, Blanche Georgiana, daughter of the sixth Earl of Carlisle. She died in April 1840, leaving three sons and a daughter. The children were educated at home, largely by their father. The eldest son, known initially as Lord Cavendish, gained an MA from Trinity College, Cambridge in 1854. During the following three years he led the life of a young man of high social position, hunted a good deal and was an officer in the militia.

In 1857, Cavendish was elected for North Lancashire as a Liberal and supporter of Palmerston (*q.v.*). In January 1858, his father became seventh Duke of Devonshire and he became Marquess of Hartington. After the 1859 general election, Palmerston displaced Lord Derby's government, using Hartington to move the motion of no confidence carried on 10 June. Hartington was appointed junior Lord of the Admiralty and later, Under-Secretary at the War Office. In February 1866 he became Secretary of State for War in Lord John Russell's (*q.v.*) government, entering the Cabinet at thirty-four.

In April 1868 he supported Gladstone's resolutions for the disestablishment of the Irish church. This policy, unpopular in Lancashire, cost Hartington and Gladstone their seats at the December general election. Three months later, however, he obtained a new seat, Radnor Boroughs. Gladstone offered Hartington the post of Lord Lieutenant of Ireland. He declined but accepted a Cabinet seat as Postmaster-General, where he was responsible for the nationalisation of the telegraphs. He also took charge of the 1872 secret ballot act. At the end of 1870 he had unwillingly become Chief Secretary for Ireland, passing a Coercion Bill suspending habeas corpus for areas disturbed by agrarian violence. Hartington was unsympathetic to Gladstone's unsuccessful 1873 Irish University scheme.

The Liberals lost to Disraeli in 1874 and early in 1876 Gladstone resigned the leadership. At the party meeting presided over by John Bright (q.v.) in the Reform Club on 3 February 1876, Hartington reluctantly filled the vacant place. He felt no great objection to Disraeli's chief accomplishments – purchasing the Suez Canal shares and creating Queen Victoria Empress of India – and his speeches were limited to moderate criticism. But the Eastern Question was key to the later 1870s and Gladstone came out of retirement with a series of violent speeches denouncing Turkish atrocities in Bulgaria and Disraeli's fumbling response.

Following Disraeli's defeat in April 1880 the Queen sent for Hartington to form a government, but he stepped aside for Gladstone, who had refused to serve under him. As Secretary of State for India, Hartington resolved the Afghan crisis, reversing Conservative plans to partition the country. Gladstone's second administration was an unhappy affair. Hartington clashed repeatedly with Dilke's and Chamberlain's (q.v.) more radical ideas and disagreed with policy on Ireland, the dominant theme. Then, as now, the argument was between those willing to engage the Irish with offers of reform and those who, like Hartington, felt violence must be suppressed before grievances could be met. Gladstone's fertile mind always reached for new administrative solutions. In 1882 Irish rebels assassinated Hartington's younger brother, Lord Frederick Cavendish, newly appointed Chief Secretary for Ireland, a personal tragedy which reinforced his resistance to Irish demands. Yet it is to Hartington's conciliatory skills and integrity that the 1880–85 government owes its major achievement, negotiating to overcome Conservative resistance to the Third Reform Act of 1884.

In December 1882 Hartington transferred to the War Office, overseeing the occupation of Egypt and sharing responsibility for sending General Gordon to evacuate Sudan. Gordon instead remained at Khartoum and, despite pressure from Hartington, the government delayed sending relief until too late. Gordon's death in January 1885 dealt a heavy blow to Gladstone's faltering government, which fell in June 1885, to be succeeded by that of the high Tory Lord Salisbury.

The resulting general election produced a hung parliament. Failing to persuade the Conservatives to introduce a measure to satisfy the Irish, Gladstone initially held the Liberals together by vague promises of Irish land and constitutional reform. Hartington, sitting for Rossendale in Lancashire, remained outside the government. Gladstone's balancing act faltered when he formalised his Home Rule proposals, losing not just the Whigs but also many of Chamberlain's radicals. Hartington moved the rejection of the second reading of the Home Rule Bill in a strong speech and was supported by over ninety Liberals. In June 1886 the Bill was defeated by a majority of thirty.

Despite their antipathy – Chamberlain once described Hartington as a 'drag on the wheel of progress' – Hartington and Chamberlain combined to form the Liberal Unionist party, agreeing an electoral pact with the Conservatives for the ensuing campaign and winning seventy-eight seats. For the second time Hartington was offered the premiership, in a Conservative/Liberal Unionist coalition. He refused, in the hope of reuniting the Liberal Party, but lent his support to a Salisbury government. Salisbury renewed the proposal in January 1887, after the sudden resignation of Lord Randolph Churchill, Chancellor of the Exchequer, but Hartington again declined. On 21 December 1891 Lord Hartington, aged fifty-eight, became eighth Duke of Devonshire on his father's death, leaving the Commons after thirty-four years.

The 1892 election produced a Liberal/Irish majority of forty. Gladstone's second Home Rule Bill passed its third reading in the Commons on 29 July 1893 but the Duke moved its rejection in the Lords where it was thrown out by 419 to 41, illustrating the scale of aristocratic desertion from the Liberals. Rosebery (*q.v.*) succeeded Gladstone in 1894, but his unsuccessful government fell in June 1895. Salisbury's new administration was formed in coalition with the Liberal Unionists and Devonshire became President of the Council, responsible for state education, but also for the Cabinet's defence committee.

Devonshire remained President of the Council under Balfour and succeeded Salisbury as leader in the Lords, but when Chamberlain adopted protectionism the Duke fought for free trade. Balfour's manoeuvres to conciliate his colleagues led only to a disastrous split. Devonshire resigned from the Cabinet in October 1903, and from the Liberal Unionist leadership in May 1904. The Liberals won the ensuing election overwhelmingly, ending the Duke's public career. He died on 24 March 1908 after illnesses induced by heart weakness.

Outside politics Devonshire's main interest was horse racing, though, unlike Rosebery, he never won the Derby. The family owned extensive estates, including Chatsworth and Devonshire Houses and were responsible for much of the development of Eastbourne and Barrow. In 1892 he married the widowed Duchess of Manchester, a long-time friend, but they had no children and he was succeeded by his nephew Victor Cavendish.

The *Life of the Eighth Duke of Devonshire* by Bernard Holland, published in 1911, remains the main biography of Hartington. *The Last of the Whigs* by Patrick Jackson (1994) focuses almost entirely on politics. The main source of family papers is Chatsworth.

Tony Little

NICK HARVEY MP

If Nick Harvey did not exist, I imagine some particularly English novelist, Evelyn Waugh perhaps, would have invented him. It's that accent, coupled with that wonderfully old-fashioned turn of phrase. He once rather resignedly termed it an affliction, but it is probably the key to one of his outstanding abilities, that of eliciting cooperation and loyalty from a wide range of different people often with disparate, and at times conflicting, concerns.

Nicholas Barton Harvey was born on 3 August 1961 in Chandler's Ford, Hampshire and was educated at Queen's, the Methodist boarding school in Taunton. His first involvement in politics took place at Middlesex Polytechnic in 1981, which, in common with many similar college student unions, was a fiefdom of the far left. Backed by an alliance of everyone to the right of Trotsky, Harvey was elected president of the union. When the Socialist Workers' Party voted to send a donation to the Irish Republican Socialist Party, the political wing of the Irish National Liberation Army, Harvey won a High Court action to stop it. The ensuing death threats added only to the drama of the moment and Harvey, now enjoying the soubriquet 'hammer of the Trots', formalised the alliance into an organisation entitled 'Union for Students'.

Following the completion of a degree in business studies in 1984, a career in communications and marketing with City consultants Drewe Rogerson left time for involvement in local politics. An apprenticeship as Liberal agent for Finchley in 1983, and as a council candidate in Barnet in 1986, led to his selection as Liberal candidate for Enfield Southgate in 1987. Those of us who were still up for Portillo that May night in 1997 were not in the least surprised that the seat did not change hands following the byelection in 1986, but were cheered by the fact that, in a borough where there are to this day no Liberal Democrat councillors, the party's vote remained at the same level and it retained second place.

In the following year Harvey was active in the campaign against merger with the SDP, but like many others of a similar view, he joined the new party immediately and supported Paddy Ashdown (*q.v.*) for the leadership. It was a gloomy and uncomfortable time to be a Liberal Democrat, but the right time to go travelling. Equipped with a lightweight gentleman's jacket for formal occasions, and that accent for a passport, Nick set off, Boot-like, to spend a year going round the world on a trip which included a brief spell of canvassing for Michael Dukakis.

On his return the idea of seriously contesting a seat seemed less fantastic than it had a year before when the party nationally had languished at five per cent in the polls. Concluding, rightly, accent or no, that he was not cut out for a northern constituency, Harvey sought and won the nomination for North Devon. The legacy of the Thorpe (*q.v.*) years had scuppered the chances of the Liberal hopefuls at the two previous elections, but the passage of a generation and the ability of local people to forgive and forget made the seat winnable, but a very long shot. When the scale of the task became apparent, Harvey took the decision to become a full-time candidate, and as the general election was not called in autumn 1991, as had been widely predicted, impecunity, as he would say, was an immediate problem. The gamble paid off in 1992 when the seat was won on a swing of 4.73 per cent, a majority of 794.

Despite being a parliamentary novice Harvey was handed the job of transport spokesman, which meant leading for the Liberal Democrats on the subject of rail privatisation. For a time the leadership favoured supporting the government, although Harvey never did. The matter was decided at the 1992 party conference, when privatisation was overwhelmingly rejected. Harvey played no part in the debate, as he was otherwise occupied opening the Bideford carnival, an event to which one of his predecessors had travelled by helicopter.

From 1994 to 1997 Harvey served as trade and industry spokesman, a brief which at that time covered the work of four government departments including employment and energy. It was during that period that his views on Europe came to the fore and the mythical 'anti-Europe Liberal Democrat' was born. He has always been a fervent supporter of the single market, but regards a single currency as 'dotty in theory and in practice'. Always a decentralist at heart, his criticism of the EU stems not from narrow English-mindedness, but from an affirmedly internationalist perspective. The increasing centralisation of the EU which accompanies closer union might be more acceptable if the EU were not so introspective. Opposition to the 'rich man's club membership which is beyond most states, including many in eastern Europe,' is a view shared by a surprising number of Liberal Democrat members. With characteristic consistency, it is a view Harvey has maintained, despite a great deal of pressure to do otherwise.

Since the last election Harvey has used all those skills, honed whilst defending the honour of a place spared from oblivion only by the perseverance of the Post Office – Middlesex – acting as unofficial party chairman. The innocuous title Chair of the Campaigns and Communications Committee masks the difficulty of managing Liberal Democrats and being responsible for the party's public relations strategy. Perhaps only someone sufficiently determined to win a seat that he risked utter penury would take on such a role. Only someone sufficiently trusted by all sections of the party would manage the role successfully. He is, and he does, and not simply because of that accent.

Liz Barker

DAVID HEATH MP   1954–

David William St John Heath was born in Westbury-sub-Mendip, Somerset, on 16 March 1954, the son of Eric and Pamela Heath. His father was a registered optician. He was educated at Millfield School, Street, St John's College, Oxford (MA in physiological sciences) and the City University, London. He was an exact contemporary of

Tony Blair at St John's and also rowed in the same eight as Conservative Social Security Minister Alistair Burt. He qualified in 1979 as a registered optician and managed
the family practice in Frome, Somerset until 1986. Later he worked as a consultant to
a number of national bodies, including Age Concern, and was appointed parliamentary consultant to the World-Wide Fund for Nature in 1990.

Heath first joined the Liberal Party in 1970, aged sixteen. He was elected to Somerset County Council, for Frome North, at the high watermark of the Liberal/SDP
Alliance in 1985. He immediately became the Leader of the council – at thirty-one,
the youngest ever holder of such a post in England. He retained the post until the
Conservatives regained control in 1989, though he held his own ward. He was awarded
the CBE for political service in 1989.

When the Liberal Democrats returned to power in Somerset in 1993, he became
the Chair of the Avon & Somerset Police Authority, 1993–96, and of Somerset Education Committee (1996–97). He was also the first Liberal Democrat member of the
Audit Commission (1995–97), Vice-Chair of the Association of County Councils,
1993–97, and served on the Service Authority of the National Criminal Intelligence
Service 1993–96. He stood down as a councillor in 1997.

Heath fought the Somerton & Frome seat in 1992, reducing the Conservative
majority to 4,341. He gained the constituency in 1997 with a majority of 130, on a
3.6 per cent swing from the Conservatives.

He is now a member of the Liberal Democrats' foreign affairs, defence and Europe team in the House of Commons, specialising in European affairs. He has taken
a particular interest in the enlargement of the EU into central and eastern Europe,
and in the powers and immunities of Europol. He is the Liberal Democrat member of
the Commons Select Committee on Foreign Affairs, and sits on the Parliamentary
Assembly of the Organisation for Security and Co-operation in Europe. He is also an
elected member of the party's Federal Conference Committee, and, from September
1998, Chairman of the Joint States Candidates Committee.

Heath lives in Witham Friary, near Frome, and lists his recreations as cricket, rugby,
and until recently, pig breeding. He also whiles away the time waiting for late votes in
the Commons by playing bridge with parliamentary colleagues, including Jackie Ballard
(q.v.) and Evan Harris (q.v.). In 1987 he married Caroline Netherton, a self-employed
accountant; the couple have one son (Thomas) and one daughter (Bethany).

Christian Moon

L. T. HOBHOUSE   1864–1929

Leonard Trelawney Hobhouse, born at Liskeard, Cornwall on 8 September 1864,
came from a long line of Anglican clerics. His father, the Venerable Reginald Hobhouse,
was Rector of St Ive, near Liskeard, a position he had obtained through his political

connections with Sir Robert Peel. His mother was a Trelawney from the prominent West Country family.

Although his immediate family were narrow Tories, Hobhouse became a committed radical while a schoolboy at Marlborough College, in the process also becoming a firm agnostic. He was influenced by his uncle, Arthur, Lord Hobhouse, a Gladstonian Liberal. His boyhood heroes included Morley, Dilke, Bradlaugh (*q.v.*) and Bright (*q.v.*), but he despised the conservative wing of the party, especially Rosebery (*q.v.*). He greatly admired John Stuart Mill (*q.v.*) and read Spencer and Mazzini.

At Oxford (Corpus Christi) he came into contact with Marshall and Sidney Ball and was influenced by Green (*q.v.*) and Toynbee. He became increasingly concerned with social questions, especially the plight of agricultural labourers. His radical opinions, in favour of Home Rule, temperance and the abolition of the monarchy, brought him notoriety and the presidency of the Oxford Radical Club. He graduated in 1887 with a first in Greats and immediately won a Prize Fellowship at Merton. He was made a full tutorial fellow in 1894 and until 1897 taught philosophy, specialising in epistemology. He took a close interest in the campaign to unionise local agricultural labourers and became a trustee of the Oxfordshire Agricultural Labourers' Union. At this time Hobhouse was close to the Fabians, although he never joined the society and later became a fierce critic of its elitism, imperialism and opportunism, showing particular hatred for George Bernard Shaw's flippant authoritarianism.

Hobhouse's first major political work, *The Labour Movement* (1893), was strongly collectivist, calling for the profits of industry to be appropriated to consumers in the form of the cooperative movement, trade unions and local and national government, and for a steeply graduated income tax, higher death duties and the taxation of ground rent. Its political doctrine was closer to Green's organicism than to Mill. But Hobhouse soon saw that collectivism in its Fabian form was liable to turn into the glorification of the state and the pursuit of conformity in the name of equality. Hobhouse was also deeply internationalist and was revolted by the Fabian endorsement of the Boer War. His New Liberalism was, above all, the result of his disillusion with Fabian socialism.

Another event in Hobhouse's life drew him back to the Liberal cause. In 1896, C. P. Scott, the editor of the *Manchester Guardian*, persuaded him to write occasional leading articles for the paper. Hobhouse was captivated by political journalism, and in 1897 left academic life and for six years worked full-time for the paper. Hobhouse and Scott revelled in their role as the conscience of the Edwardian Liberal Party, harrying both the Unionists and the Liberal Imperialists and supporting the 'pro-Boers'. Hobhouse's belief in Gladstonian moral rectitude in foreign policy was central to his political development. Both Joseph Chamberlain (*q.v.*) and the Fabians combined collectivism with imperialism. For all his objections to laissez-faire economics, Hobhouse's rejection of imperialism drove him back to the Radical Liberal camp. He subsequently sought to combine Mill's devotion to individuality, his own commitment to social justice and Gladstonian morality in international politics into a theoretical whole.

In 1903 Hobhouse left the *Guardian,* intending to concentrate on academic work, but financial difficulties drew him instead into political activism. He became the paid secretary and organiser of the Free Trade Union, an early Liberal think-tank and campaigning body. The FTU poured out pamphlets and articles attacking Joseph Chamberlain's imperialist protectionism.

In 1905 he left the FTU and became the political editor of a new London-based Liberal-inclined newspaper, *The Tribune.* The paper's first edition came out in 1906, just after the party's landslide election victory, with Hobhouse's editorial warning against reaction in government: 'The work of Liberalism is never done because its essence is the permanent protest of Right against Force, the common good against class interest, of an ideal element in political life against a mere mechanical efficiency.' But like so many new newspapers *The Tribune* could not reconcile the need to gain circulation with its political ideals. To attract new money, the paper moved to a populist line under the direction of a jingoistic managing editor. Hobhouse resigned.

Fortunately, he had managed to maintain his academic interests and had taken an interest in the new study of sociology, publishing in 1901 *The Mind in Evolution* and in 1906 *Morals in Evolution.* In these works, rejecting Spencer and social Darwinism, Hobhouse attempted to establish, both theoretically and empirically, that progress in human thought and conduct was inevitable not as the result of biology or instinct but as the result of self-conscious intelligence. On the basis of this work, in 1907 he was elected to the newly-established Martin White Chair in Sociology in the London School of Economics. Hobhouse thus became the first (and for many years the only) professor of sociology in Britain. (It should be noted that his optimistic view of progress was limited to the moral and mental spheres – he disliked intensely many modern inventions, including motor cars and the games of bridge and golf.)

Hobhouse retained the White Chair until his death and it provided him with an income which freed him from the need to resort too often to journalism. He continued for many years, however, to contribute leaders and other articles to the *Manchester Guardian.* The security of the White Chair also discouraged political adventures. For example, in 1909 he was offered the constituency of Northampton, the seat of his boyhood hero Bradlaugh, but he declined. According to his son, Hobhouse objected to the constraints of party discipline and preferred the freedom of the life of a writer and thinker to the subservience of the life of a Member of Parliament.

It was during this period that Hobhouse's mature political and economic thought emerged, culminating in his extraordinary little book *Liberalism* (1911). He sought to explain the social programme and taxation policies of the Liberal government as an extension, not a reversal, of the economic principles of earlier Liberals such as Mill. His underlying theory, difficult to apply in practice but clear enough in theory, was that wealth was created by a combination of individual effort and social organisation, and that the state was entitled to redistribute for the common good that part which arose from social organisation. He also distinguished between property held 'for use' and property held 'for power', recognising the need for the former but not the latter to be protected by a system of rights. Out of the combination of these ideas, Hobhouse developed Liberal justifications for a guaranteed minimum income funded by income tax.

Hobhouse also developed a distinctive view of liberty and the proper purposes of state power. He maintained, against what we now call libertarianism, that liberty depended on restraint – that 'every liberty depends on a corresponding act of control'. He followed Mill in pointing out the many forms of coercion in social life, including features of existing social and economic conditions. His conclusion was that the proper role of the state was to maximise the availability of liberty by reorganising the existing constraints. But Hobhouse differed from Mill in explaining why paternalism should be opposed. Whereas Mill starts with the harm principle, that no-one should be coerced except to prevent harm to others, Hobhouse says that we should refrain from coercing people for their own good 'not because [their] good is indifferent to us but because it cannot be furthered by coercion'. He believed that the value of liberty lies precisely in its role in human self-development.

In *Liberalism* Hobhouse advanced the view, useful in the political situation of the time, that 'socialism' could be subsumed within Liberalism, though not if 'socialism' were understood in its Marxist or bureaucratic elitist forms. He also advocated a 'Progressive Alliance' between the Liberal Party and the Labour movement, a hope he maintained throughout the 1920s when despair at the divisions in the party separated him from membership of it. Unlike other New Liberal intellectuals, however, Hobhouse did not join the Labour Party. He was hostile to class-based politics, and although a supporter of trade unionism, opposed the idea of a political party based on sectional interest. He participated briefly in the discussions which led to the Liberal Yellow Book. In the last month of his life, following the election of 1929 which had seen a Labour minority government come to power, he wrote that he was 'sorry that the Liberals did not get more seats, as I think (I know it's blasphemy) they carry more brains to the square inch than Labour, most of whose men are merely dull and terribly afraid of their permanent officials'.

Hobhouse died in Alençon, France on 21 June 1929. He had married Nora Hawden 1891, and was the father of three children.

Further references include Stefan Collini, *Liberalism and Sociology: L. T. Hobhouse and Political Argument in England 1880–1914* (Cambridge University Press, 1979); and James Meadowcroft (ed.), *L. T. Hobhouse: Liberalism and Other Writings* (Cambridge University Press, 1994).

David Howarth

J. A. HOBSON   1858–1940

John Atkinson Hobson, the economic writer and radical journalist most associated (along with L.T. Hobhouse, *q.v.*) with Edwardian New Liberalism was born in Derby on 6 July 1858, the second son of William and Josephine (née Atkinson) Hobson. William Hobson was the proprietor of the *Derbyshire Advertiser*, to which his son later contributed, and was twice mayor of Derby during the 1880s. J. A. Hobson was educated at the local grammar school, before winning an open scholarship to Lincoln College, Oxford, where he read classics and Modern Greats, graduating in 1880. Hobson then embarked on a teaching career in classics, English and economics, married an American woman, Florence Edgar, and eventually settled in London in 1887.

In London Hobson became associated with a progressive radical milieu of Fabians and ethical writers, some of whom joined him in founding a discussion group, the Rainbow Circle, and in establishing a journal, the *Progressive Review*. His own work remained focused on the critique of classical economics which he had begun in *The Physiology of Industry* (co-written with A. F. Mummery, 1889), leading to the publication of his *The Evolution of Modern Capitalism* (1894) and other studies of poverty and unemployment. In this work he began to outline his theory of the maldistribution of wealth, brought about by the surplus savings of the wealthy and the underconsumption of the poor.

But what gave Hobson's economic views particular originality and edge was his analysis of British imperialism in southern Africa in the 1890s. In 1899 he went as special correspondent for the *Manchester Guardian* to cover the South African war. Reporting from Johannesburg, Hobson observed that the origins of the war lay in the operations of capitalist financiers, such as Cecil Rhodes, who were using their influence over both the press and the British government. Hobson returned to England with the leading pro-Boer, Cronwright-Schreiner, and the two embarked on a speaking tour of Yorkshire and Scotland. Hobson's journalism was published in a book form as *The War in South Africa* (1900) and he attracted the notice and praise of the pro-Boer element in the Liberal Party. But Hobson himself saw the war and the rough treatment meted out to pro-Boers in Britain as an indictment of the imperialism of the age, and he launched a full-scale assault on it in two works: *The Psychology of Jingoism* (1901) and *Imperialism: A Study* (1902), the latter probably the best-known and most influential of all his works, V. I. Lenin being amongst its devotees. In these studies Hobson not only identified the economic 'tap-root' of imperialism, but also described the atavistic and autocratic political culture by which it was accompanied.

Hobson's solution to the jingoism and illiberalism which loomed so large at the turn of the century was a rejuvenated ethical liberal politics. In time this creed became known as 'New Liberalism', and was to be found not only in Hobson's writings throughout the 1900s – in the *Manchester Guardian*, the *Tribune,* the *Nation* and above all in his book, *The Crisis of Liberalism* (1909) – but also in the work of L.T. Hobhouse and many other academics, journalists, politicians and philanthropists within and on the fringes of the Edwardian Liberal Party. In Hobson's case there was much old radicalism – free trade, parliamentary reform, secular education – to his support for the Liberal Party. But unusually for a progressive thinker Hobson also embraced evolutionist or 'organicist' ideas about the nature of the relationship between the individual and the society, believing that the two could only progress symbiotically, and for this the active intervention of the state in areas such as pensions and poverty was required. The extent to which the Asquithian Cabinet was influenced by all this is debatable, but some measure of Hobson's standing was indicated by the possibility that he was amongst Asquith's (*q.v.*) candidates for new peers during the constitutional crisis of 1910–11.

Hobson's liberalism took a severe blow with the onset of the First World War. Not only did the war shatter the prospects for the internationalism and peaceful arbitration which he had supported for the previous decade, but the wartime cabinet split between Asquith and Lloyd George (*q.v.*) weakened his faith in the Liberal Party. He was one of the driving forces behind the Union of Democratic Control during the war, and he increasingly moved in the direction of the Labour Party. Hobson stood unsuccessfully as an Independent candidate for the Combined Universities seat in the 1918 general election, and joined the Independent Labour Party shortly after. He served on various think-tanks within the ILP during the 1920s, on international relations and on wage reform, and he gave expert evidence to the 1919 Sankey Commission on the coal industry (recommending nationalisation) and to the 1924 Colwyn Committee on the national debt and taxation. As he aged, Hobson's journalism became more infrequent, but conversely his intellectual influence grew. J. M. Keynes' (*q.v.*) *General Theory of Employment, Interest and Money* (1936) acknowledged a debt to Hobson's theory of underconsumption. He died in 1940, aged eighty-one.

For an excellent short overview of Hobson's life and work, see the entry by A. J. Lee in the *Dictionary of Labour Biography*, vol. 1. There are good full-length studies by John Allett (1981) and Jules Townshend (1990). A wide-ranging collection featuring many of the key contributors to Hobson studies in the last two decades is Michael Freeden (ed.), *Reappraising J. A. Hobson: Humanism and Warfare* (1990).

Miles Taylor

RICHARD HOLME (Lord Holme)   1936–

Lord Holme is the great survivor of Liberal and Liberal Democrat politics. One of the most senior and trusted advisers to successive party leaders Steel (*q.v.*) and Ashdown (*q.v.*), he is perhaps the most influential liberal strategist of the past twenty years. A spin doctor and political fixer – who was chair of the massively successful 1997 general election campaign – Holme is credited with having brokered the high profile defection of Emma Nicholson (*q.v.*) from the Conservative Party in 1995. Despite many such remarkable achievements as a backroom politician, perhaps his greatest disappointment is that he has never made it to the House of Commons despite six attempts.

Born in London on 27 May 1936, Richard Gordon Holme is the archetypal English gentleman, who bears the life title Lord Holme of Cheltenham as if he was born to it. Suave, dapper and with military bearing (he served in the 10th Gurkha Rifles in Malaya) his education at the Royal Masonic School, St John's, Oxford, where he studied law, and Harvard Business School comes as no surprise.

His first venture into electoral politics was in the 1964 general election, when he fought East Grinstead on behalf of the Liberals. Fighting the same seat in a byelection the following January, Holme achieved the first of what was to be a string of honourable second places, gaining 32 per cent of the vote.

Having missed a number of elections while working in the United States, Holme returned to England in time to contest Braintree in October 1974. From there, he moved to the Cheltenham seat, which he was to fight and narrowly miss on three separate occasions, in 1979, 1983 and 1987, gaining 41 per cent at his final attempt. The seat, however, stubbornly remained Conservative and eventually, in 1990, Holme accepted a life peerage and the job of Liberal Democrat Northern Ireland spokesman, a brief he still holds in the Lords.

Holme's political career has not, however, been limited to contesting elections. A vice-chair of the Liberal Executive as long ago as 1966, he has held numerous formal and informal positions within the Liberal Party, Alliance and Liberal Democrats, including President of the Liberal Party 1980–81, senior adviser to David Steel during the Alliance, and vice-chair of the Liberal Democrat Federal Policy Committee from 1988–92. In this latter role, Holme was responsible for overseeing the production of the Liberal Democrats' 1992 election manifesto, subsequently described in a *Guardian* editorial as 'easily the most coherent and radical of the manifestos produced by the three main parties'.

His success in this role convinced Ashdown to give Holme – by this time a close personal ally – overall control of the general election campaign in 1997. The appointment was heavily criticised, especially after Holme become a Director of the RTZ Corporation (now Rio Tinto plc) in April 1995. Yet Holme dumbfounded his critics by overseeing the campaign which delivered the Liberal Democrats and its predecessor parties' best result for over sixty years.

Holme has been rewarded for this success with a place on the Labour/Liberal Democrat Cabinet Committee, an institution which is itself a testament to the sort of collaborative and pluralistic politics which he has propounded all his political life, as a founding director of the National Campaign for Electoral Reform (1976–83), a director of the Electoral Reform Centre (1983–89), a founding co-chair of Charter 88, and a vice-chair of the Hansard Society.

Best known for his political achievements, Holme is also an extremely successful businessman, with a career spanning international publishing and strategic communications consultancy in the UK, USA and Europe. He received his original management and marketing training at Unilever before joining Penguin Books as a director in 1965. Currently, he is the Chairman of a group of directory-publishing companies; in spring 1998 he stepped down as a director of Rio Tinto plc, where he had had executive responsibility for external affairs and human resources,

Married (since 1958), with four grown-up children, he lives with his wife, Kay, in Sussex. He swims daily and walks on the Downs at the weekend. He was awarded the CBE in 1983.

Ben Rich

ARTHUR HOLT   1914–95

Arthur Frederick Holt was born in Bolton on 8 August 1914, the son of Frederick Holt JP, a hosiery manufacturer. He was educated at Mill Hill and Manchester University, where he was an active sportsman and President of the Students' Union.

Holt joined the 5th Battalion of the Loyal Regiment (a Bolton Territorial Unit) in 1938. He was promoted to the rank of captain and transferred to the regiment's Reconnaissance Corps. He was captured by the Japanese at the fall of Singapore in 1942 and became a prisoner of war, working on the Burma railway. He was twice mentioned in despatches for his efforts in protecting fellow prisoners against Japanese brutality. Although he very rarely referred to his experiences in the Far East, they scarred him for the rest of his life, and were responsible for later periods of ill health.

Holt's family had a long association with the Liberal Party and, after returning from the war, he was asked to revitalise the Bolton Reform Club and then to perform similar miracles for the town's Liberal Association. As a consequence of this activity he was asked to contest Bolton East at the 1950 general election, finishing third in the poll. The arrangement reached in Huddersfield, whereby Donald Wade (*q.v.*) was elected as Liberal MP for the West of the town without Conservative opposition in return for the withdrawal of the Liberal candidate in the East, quickly influenced the officers of Bolton Liberal Association. An agreement was signed by the Chairmen of the Liberal and Conservative organisations which allowed Holt a free run against Labour in the Bolton West constituency, in return for a straight Tory/Labour scrap in the East. The pact succeeded – both Labour MPs lost their seats at the 1951 election. Holt's victory was repeated at the 1955 and 1959 general elections, but the pact's abandonment by the Liberal Party in 1960 (when Frank Byers (*q.v.*) contested a byelection in Bolton East) resulted in Holt facing Conservative as well as Labour opposition at the 1964 general election. He was defeated, coming third in the poll.

The Huddersfield pact contained a vague statement binding both Liberal and Conservative candidates to oppose further nationalisation, but Holt was careful not to sign any agreement which infringed his activity in Parliament. There were occasional Conservative grumbles that Holt was too left wing for their liking, but none serious enough to undermine his position in his constituency. Liberal outrage at the pact, most vociferously expressed by the National League of Young Liberals, quickly died away after Holt established himself as an effective and sincere Liberal Member. Nevertheless, he was continually careful not to antagonise Conservative opinion and during the Suez crisis of 1956 took the line most supportive of the government of any Liberal MP.

Following his work with Bolton's Liberal organisations, Holt took a particular interest in improving the quality of the party's electoral machinery. He was a member of Jo Grimond's (*q.v.*) Campaign Committee, which organised the 1959 election campaign and continued thereafter as an unofficial Leader's cabinet. He set about persuading Liberal associations that they required a good candidate, adequate financial resources and sufficient organisation to avoid a drubbing before considering fighting parliamentary elections, clashing with headstrong individualists in the constituencies in consequence. Holt served as Chief Whip and Secretary of the Liberal Central Association 1962–63 and was the party's spokesman on health and transport. He also headed the party's Publication Department and acted as a British delegate to the Council of Europe at Strasbourg.

Following his Parliamentary defeat he concentrated on business affairs, becoming first Managing Director and then Chairman of the family business of Holt Hosiery. He returned to active Liberal politics when the firm was sold to a larger commercial organisation, serving as President of the Liberal Party in 1974.

Holt was described as a 'cradle-to-grave Liberal'. His Liberal politics were essentially traditional: he was a staunch nonconformist, free trader and instinctive opponent of all forms of restrictive practices. He was an early convert to the European cause and was a significant voice in persuading the Liberal Party to endorse membership of the EEC.

He married Kathleen Openshaw in 1939, and had one son and one daughter. He lived in retirement near Ambleside and died at Bolton on 23 August 1995.

Peter Joyce and Mark Egan

GEORGE HOLYOAKE   1817–1906

George Jacob Holyoake was born into an artisan family in Birmingham on 13 April 1817. He received little formal education before being apprenticed as a whitesmith, but his intellectual horizons were extended by classes at the Mechanics' Institute.

In 1840 he became a lecturer for the Owenite Universal Community Society, first in Worcester and then Sheffield. Shortly afterwards he was imprisoned in Gloucester gaol for six months (1842–1843) for blasphemous words spoken at a lecture in Chel-tenham. Whilst in gaol his religious views turned to atheism, though in reality he was nearer what would later be called an agnostic. Following the collapse of Owenism in 1845, he became a freelance journalist and lecturer on political and religious subjects and in 1846 began the *Reasoner*, which he edited weekly until 1861. Through this paper he developed the social teachings of Robert Owen into a new movement which in 1851 he called secularism.

In the 1850s he conducted his own publishing business in Fleet Street and began to associate with the Leader group of advanced Liberals, including Thornton Hunt, John Stuart Mill (*q.v.*), George Henry Lewes, Francis Newman and Harriet Martineau. At the same time he took an active part in several political and social campaigns, including the Association for the Repeal of the Taxes on Knowledge, which secured the repeal of the newspaper stamp in 1855. He also collected funds for European republicanism, and in 1860 was secretary of the committee formed to send volunteers to assist Garibaldi in Italy. In the 1860s he worked closely with Joseph Cowen of Newcastle, and joined the Reform League in 1866–67. He had a wide circle of ac-quaintances in the Liberal Party and through his correspondence and journalism he was able to bridge the gap between parliamentary and popular Liberalism in the country. He was also increasingly active in support of the cooperative movement, publishing several histories of local societies, beginning with *Self Help by the People* (1858), which told the story of cooperation in Rochdale since 1844, and largely created the myth of the Rochdale Pioneers. In later life he was regarded as the father of cooperation in Britain, being invited to preside over the Cooperative Congress at Carlisle in 1887, and on several occasions representing the movement abroad.

Holyoake never abandoned his support for free thought, though leadership of secularism passed to Charles Bradlaugh (*q.v.*) in the 1860s. In 1899 he became the first chairman of the Rationalist Press Association. His preference in later life was to work with the grain of Liberal politics and he always regarded himself as a loyal Gladstonian. His moderation alienated some former supporters but his campaigns for freedom of expression and democracy at home and abroad, and for producers' as well as consum-ers' cooperation, placed him on the radical wing of the Liberal Party. He offered himself for election in 1857 (Tower Hamlets), 1868 (Birmingham), and 1884 (Leices-ter), but each time withdrew before the poll took place. His services to Liberalism were recognised with honorary membership of the National Liberal Club in 1893. His last public act before his death at his home in Brighton on 22 January 1906 was to support the Liberals in the general election of that month.

His ashes are buried in Highgate Cemetery. Eleanor Williams, his first wife by whom he had seven children, died in 1884; his second wife, Jenny Pearson, survived him by only a few weeks. His youngest daughter, Emilie, was prominent in the Wom-en's Trade Union League, while one nephew was Horatio Bottomley (*q.v.*), the noto-rious journalist.

Holyoake was a prolific writer, a perceptive journalist, a controversial political campaigner and a witty but unreliable historian. He had a weak, high-pitched voice which made him a poor public speaker. He is best known for his *History of Cooperation* (revised in 2 vols, T. Fisher Unwin, 1905), and his partisan autobiographies, *Sixty Years of an Agitator's Life* (2 vols, T. Fisher Unwin, 1892) and *Bygones Worth Remembering* (2 vols, T. Fisher Unwin, 1905). The only modern biography of Holyoake is L. E. Grugel, *George Jacob Holyoake: A Study in the Evolution of a Victorian Radical* (Porcupine Press, 1976), but see also J. McCabe, *Life and Letters of George Jacob Holyoake* (2 vols, Watts & Co., 1908).

Ted Royle

EMLYN HOOSON (Lord Hooson) 1925–

Hugh Emlyn Hooson was born on 26 March 1925, the son of Hugh and Elsie Hooson of Colomendy, Denbighshire. He was educated at Denbigh Grammar School and the University College of Wales, Aberystwyth, where he graduated in law. In 1950 he married Shirley Margaret Wynne Hamer, the daughter of Sir George Hamer CBE of Llanidloes, a prominent and influential figure in the locality and a powerful Liberal in the politics of Montgomeryshire. There were two daughters of the marriage, Sioned and Lowri. He served in the Royal Navy (Fleet Air Arm) from 1943–46. He is a native Welsh speaker.

Hooson was called to the bar at Gray's Inn in 1949. He subsequently became a Bencher of Gray's Inn in 1968, and served as Vice-Treasurer in 1985 and Treasurer in 1986. He was the Deputy Chairman of the Flintshire Quarter Sessions, 1960–72, Deputy Chairman of the Merionethshire Quarter Sessions, 1960–67, and then Chairman, 1967–72. He was appointed Recorder of Merthyr Tydfil early in 1971 and Recorder of Swansea in July of the same year. He was elected Leader of the Wales and Chester Circuit, 1971–74.

Hooson fought Conway unsuccessfully for the Liberal Party in 1951, and was elected MP for Montgomeryshire at a byelection in May 1962, caused by the death of former party Leader Clement Davies (*q.v.*). At the time, the Liberal Party was experiencing a national revival encapsulated in the sensational victory in the Orpington byelection the previous March.

Although he continued his professional activities as a barrister, a preoccupation which invited sharp criticism in some sections of the party, Hooson was much involved in the revival and re-organisation of the party in Wales in the mid-1960s. He was, in striking contrast to his party leader Jo Grimond (*q.v.*), doggedly determined that the Liberals should reach no formal agreement with the Labour government elected in October 1964, and he imaginatively depicted a distinct future for the Liberal Party as 'a radical, non-socialist party in Britain'.

As a warm admirer of Lyndon Johnson's Appalachian Bill in the USA, Hooson devoted his energies to preparing a Liberal economic plan for Wales. He was also much involved in the negotiations which preceded the establishment, in September 1966, of the independent Welsh Liberal Party, which he served devotedly as Chairman until 1979. On 1 March 1967 he introduced in the Commons a Government of Wales Bill, which proposed a domestic parliament for Wales. Nonetheless, he resolutely refused to countenance any kind of agreement or electoral pact with Plaid Cymru. He meanwhile stood unsuccessfully against Jeremy Thorpe (*q.v.*) and Eric Lubbock (*q.v.*) for the party leadership in January 1967, following Jo Grimond's retirement.

Hooson retained Montgomeryshire in five successive general elections, winning a handsome majority of 4,651 votes in the election of February 1974. From 1966 until February 1974 he had been the only parliamentary representative of Welsh Liberalism. Most of his English colleagues viewed him as a conservative-minded Liberal confined mainly to the Welsh political stage, and consequently somewhat remote from the Westminster vortex. But on occasion Hooson adopted a notably progressive stand on domestic matters, and he was undoubtedly the most fervent assailant within the Parliamentary Liberal Party of the centralising measures of the Heath Government. He encapsulated the progressive Welsh Liberalism of the 1960s and 1970s, looking increasingly to the 'second coming' of the Liberal Party in Wales as a worthy successor to the disintegrating Labour Party. At the same time he remained a warm admirer of Lloyd George (*q.v.*) and the radical Yellow Book proposals of the late 1920s.

Perhaps surprisingly, he was an enthusiastic advocate of the Lib-Lab Pact concluded between Prime Minister Jim Callaghan and the Liberal leader David Steel (*q.v.*) in March 1977. He even played an active role on the Liberal-Government Consultative Committee which, he felt, gave his party a much-needed opportunity to destroy the 'wilderness complex' disadvantage. Many within the ranks of the Liberal Party, including a substantial innately 'conservative' element within Montgomeryshire, were highly critical of their leaders' apparent readiness to keep in office a Labour government so clearly on the brink of ejection.

Hooson did not reap any personal benefit from his warm advocacy of a Welsh Assembly during 1978–79. Powys recorded the highest 'No' vote of all the Welsh counties in the referendum of March 1979, and in the general election in May, when the Liberal vote slumped badly, the seemingly impregnable 'man for Montgomeryshire' unexpectedly lost his seat to the Conservative, Delwyn Williams. A ninety-nine year Liberal tenure of the seat thus dramatically came to an end, though it returned to the party in 1983, with the victory of Alex Carlile (*q.v.*). Shortly afterwards Hooson entered the House of Lords as life peer Baron Hooson of Montgomery.

Emlyn Hooson remains a prominent Liberal Democrat and public figure in Welsh life. He is still the party's spokesman in the Lords on Welsh affairs, legal affairs, agriculture and European affairs. He served as President of the Welsh Liberal Party from 1983–86. Among his numerous business interests were his chairmanship of the Trustees of the Laura Ashley Foundation, 1986–97, and his assiduous membership from 1991 of the Severn River Crossing plc. He continues to farm at Pen-rhiw Farm, Llanidloes, and lives at Summerfield Park, Llanidloes.

J. Graham Jones

LESLIE HORE-BELISHA (Lord Hore-Belisha) 1893–1957

The electoral volatility of the 1920s prevented many younger Liberals from establishing a successful political career at Westminster. A notable exception, however, was Leslie Hore-Belisha. In 1923 he was elected to represent the Plymouth seat of Devonport at a time when Liberalism was enjoying a brief revival. Yet, while many of his party colleagues were swept away by the Conservative landslide of 1924, he continued to represent the seat until defeated by Labour in 1945. During the late 1920s he established a reputation as a clever debater in the House of Commons, but it was not until he sided with the Liberal National group in 1931 that he gained an opportunity for political advancement. Indeed, he emerged as a prominent figure in the National Government of Neville Chamberlain from 1937 to 1940, following a series of promotions in the early 1930s. His contribution to British politics at this time was therefore quite significant, and it is a sad reflection on the condition of inter-war Liberalism that such a talented and ambitious individual had to leave the Liberal Party in order to further his career.

Leslie Isaac Hore-Belisha was born in London on 7 September 1893. He was the only son of Jacob Isaac and Elizabeth Miriam (née Miens) Belisha, and was descended from a Jewish family that had fled from Spain at the time of the Inquisition. Leslie's father died when he was a baby, and following his mother's second marriage in 1912 he added his the name of his stepfather, Sir Adair Hore, to his own. He was educated at Clifton College, the Sorbonne and Heidelberg, and finally at St. John's College, Oxford. During the First World War he served in the army, was mentioned in dispatches, and ended his war service with the rank of major. After leaving Oxford, he studied law and also established a successful career as a journalist with such papers as the *Daily Express* and the *Evening Standard*.

In 1922 he stood as the Liberal candidate for Plymouth Devonport. The Conservatives had easily won the seat in 1918 with 62 per cent of the vote, while the Liberals had come a distant third. Yet Hore-Belisha's populist style appealed to voters. He championed the cause of key groups, including dockyard workers and local traders, while in 1923 he organised a local housing campaign in working-class wards. After substantially reducing the Conservative majority in 1922, Hore-Belisha won the seat a year later with 46 per cent of the vote.

Once he was elected to the House of Commons he quickly established a reputation for himself as a skilful but independent politician. In order to strengthen his personal vote in Devonport he would even vote against his own party, particularly on defence issues, and this emphasis on the needs of his constituency proved successful in 1924 when he was the only Liberal to be returned south of the Thames. He also adopted a pragmatic attitude towards the divisions between the Asquith and Lloyd George factions within the Liberal Party. Although he first stood as an Asquithian Liberal in 1922, he realised that the main priority was to win power at the national level. This explains his decision to become a leading supporter of David Lloyd George (*q.v.*) in the latter part of the 1920s. He believed that the party needed progressive policies on issues such as unemployment, and Lloyd George was the only person who could provide the leadership necessary for a Liberal recovery.

Yet the events leading up to the formation of the first National Government in September 1931 resulted in his defection from the mainstream of the Liberal Party. While he had always been on the radical wing of Liberalism, after the disappointing election of 1929 he emerged a prominent critic of MacDonald's Labour government. During the summer of 1931 he played a key role in organising opposition to Lloyd George's strategy of parliamentary cooperation with Labour, and in October he was appointed chairman of the executive committee of the new Liberal National party. He also received his first government post in 1931, being appointed Parliamentary Secretary to the Board of Trade. A year later he became Financial Secretary to the Treasury, but it was his period in office as Minister of Transport from July 1934 to May 1937 which established his reputation as a reformer. By the early 1930s there was widespread concern over the growing number of road casualties, and Hore-Belisha introduced a package of measures, such as driving tests for motorists, the speed limit in built-up areas and the famous 'Belisha beacon', in order to deal with the problem. Later, as Secretary of State for War from 1937 to 1940 he was responsible for the modernisation of the British army during the vital period prior to the outbreak of the Second World War.

Hore-Belisha's ministerial career was effectively ended, however, by his resignation from the Cabinet in January 1940. Many senior army officers disliked his radical approach to strategy, while he had little support from the political establishment because of his Jewish and Liberal background. Chamberlain decided to remove Hore-Belisha from the War Office and offered him the Board of Trade, which he refused. Although he served briefly as Minister for National Insurance in the caretaker administration of 1945, he lost his seat in the Labour landslide of that year and was defeated when he stood as the Conservative candidate for Coventry South in 1950.

In 1944 he married Cynthia Elliot, a relative of the Earl of Minto, and in 1954 he was raised to the peerage as Lord Hore-Belisha. He died suddenly on 16 February 1957 at Rheims, while leading a British parliamentary delegation on a visit to France. His papers were collected by R. J. Minney and published as *The Private Papers of Hore-Belisha* in 1960.

Garry Tregidga

GERAINT HOWELLS (Lord Geraint)   1925–

Geraint Wyn Howells was born on 15 April 1925 at Ponterwyd in Cardiganshire, the son of David John and Mary Blodwen Howells, farmers. His father also served as secretary of the local eisteddfod. He was educated at Ponterwyd Primary School and Ardwyn Grammar School, Aberystwyth. On 7 September 1957 he married Mary Olwen Hughes, the daughter of M. A. Griffiths. There were two daughters of the marriage: Gaenor, born in 1961, and Mari, born in 1965.

Howells earned his living as a hill farmer at Glennydd, Ponterwyd in Cardiganshire, a substantial holding of some 750 acres where he kept about 3,000 sheep, many of them prize-winning Speckled Faces. He himself was also a champion sheep-shearer. He became the Welsh member of the British Wool Marketing Board in 1966, and served as its Vice-Chairman from 1971 until 1983. He was also Chairman of the Wool Producers of Wales, 1977–87. He served as secretary of the local eisteddfod at Ponterwyd.

The fact that he came from modest farming stock ensured Howells an affectionate place in the hearts of the people of Cardiganshire: 'I remember farming 250 acres on my father's farm when the net takings were only £60 and we were paying farmworkers £5 a year'. He was elected to the Cardiganshire County Council, initially as an Independent, in 1952, and became well known throughout the county. He was selected as the Liberal parliamentary candidate for Brecon & Radnor in 1968, and stood unsuccessfully against Caerwyn Roderick in the general election of June 1970, polling just over 8,000 votes.

In 1972 he was chosen as the prospective Liberal candidate for Cardiganshire, and, perhaps surprisingly, recaptured the seat from Labour's Elystan Morgan in February 1974 with over forty per cent of the vote. He was re-elected there in October 1974 and 1979, and again for the somewhat enlarged constituency of Ceredigion & Pembroke North in 1983 and 1987. He was his party's spokesman on Welsh affairs from 1985–87, and on agriculture from 1987–92.

Throughout his life Howells has been an ardent devolutionist. He consistently pressed for an extensive measure of devolution for Wales throughout Lib-Lab Pact in 1977–78. Like his fellow Liberal MP from Wales, Emlyn Hooson (q.v.), he campaigned strongly for a 'Yes' vote in the referendum of 1 March 1979. He lent his support to David Steel (q.v.) rather than John Pardoe (q.v.) in the party leadership contest of June 1976, and he became the party's agriculture spokesman in the following month. From 1987–92 Howells served as a member of the Speaker's Panel, and early in 1992 he led a deputation to Brussels to discuss the problems of Welsh farmers with the Agriculture Commissioner.

In the general election of April 1992, Howells was, perhaps unexpectedly, defeated by Cynog Dafis who stood on the novel joint platform of Plaid Cymru and the Green Party. Shortly afterwards he entered the House of Lords as Lord Geraint of Ponterwyd. He was appointed Deputy Speaker of the House of Lords in 1994. He remains prominent both at Westminster and in his former constituency, where he is still highly regarded and plays an important role in an array of local activities.

Described by Michael White as 'the Robert Mitchum of the sheep fells', this genial, shrewd Welsh hill farmer has enriched Westminster life for a quarter of a century. Dubbed 'big, shambling [with a] weather-beaten face, tweedy clothes [and] heavy-footed', he will always be remembered for his unwavering commitment and devotion to the interests of farmers and small businesses, his own constituency and Welsh devolution.

J. Graham Jones

SIMON HUGHES MP   1951–

Simon Hughes is perhaps best known for delivering the highest swing between two parties in British political history – 50.9 per cent from Labour to Liberal, in the Bermondsey byelection of February 1983. The byelection also took the then record for the highest number of candidates, sixteen featuring on the ballot paper.

Hughes entered the House as its youngest opposition member, but even at the age of thirty-one, he had already spent nearly half his life as a Liberal. Disappointed by the Wilson Government, in 1966 he sent off for a copy of the Liberal Party manifesto and, agreeing instinctively with its contents, has been a supporter ever since. Although involved in policy-making from a young age, he was never a 'hack', preferring a practical approach to problem-solving.

Simon Henry Ward Hughes was born in Bramhall, Cheshire on 17 May 1951. He moved to Wales when he was eight and to Herefordshire when he was eighteen. Llandaff Cathedral School, Cardiff, and Christ College, Brecon led to a law degree at Selwyn College, Cambridge, where he also became President of the college students' union. He was called to the bar at the Inner Temple in 1974, and received a post-graduate certificate in European studies at the College of Europe in Bruges in 1975, where he was also student union President. He trained at the European Commission in Brussels and the Council of Europe in Strasbourg, returning to London for pupillage and practice as a barrister from 1977. He was junior counsel in the Liberal Party's unsuccessful application to the European Commission on Human Rights against the UK's first-past-the-post electoral system; Anthony Lester QC (*q.v.*) was the silk.

Hughes joined the Liberal Party while at Cambridge. He chaired the party's Home Affairs Panel from 1981–83, and played a major role in the constitutional revision of the party in the late '70s. After settling in south London, he was approached to stand for the party in Beaconsfield. After touring the constituency, he told the local party chairman: 'I don't think Beaconsfield needs representing', and returned to the more urgent needs of the inner city. He fought the GLC and ILEA seat in Bermondsey in 1981, and Riverside ward, Southwark, in 1982.

Since his election, Hughes has become one of the best-known and best-liked of all Liberal/Liberal Democrat MPs in recent years. In every aspect of political life he is prolific. He has been responsible for the parliamentary portfolios of environment (1983–87, 1990–94), health (1987, 1994–97, and since 1997 as leader of the health and social welfare team), education (1988–90), urban affairs and community relations (1994–95) and has also been Deputy Whip. He has held his seat, now renamed North Southwark & Bermondsey, at the four general elections since the byelection, and seen the local council group on Southwark grow from nothing to become the opposition, only two seats behind the Labour group; every councillor in his own constituency but two is a Liberal Democrat.

To say that he focuses most on constituency casework would be to echo many other politicians in this *Dictionary* but would be an understatement. Past awards have included 'most motivated MP', 'member to watch' and 'green MP of the year'. He can usually be spotted with one of his many staff and volunteers in tow, carrying large bags from his 'pending' tray, hurrying from one engagement to another, usually smiling, often late. Even so, he has been quietly contributing up to half of his MP's salary to pay for more helpers in his busy office, keeping material comforts at the bottom of his list. Spare time does not exist for him; even a visit to the Ministry of Sound dance club in his constituency during the small hours can turn into an advice surgery.

As well as generating hundreds of letters on behalf of those he represents, Hughes is also renowned for using the Westminster machine. He has introduced bills on empty property, access to information, disestablishment of the Church of England, and perhaps most famously, to require the monarch to pay income tax and to change the sexist rules of succession to the throne. His appearances in the Chamber are often memorable. In particular he enjoyed introducing the word 'seventeenthly' to Hansard, possibly for the first time, and speaking from the dispatch box when the official opposition were nowhere to be seen – the first Liberal to speak from this position since Asquith (*q.v.*).

Within the Liberal Party, he rapidly gained a reputation as the darling of the radical activists, opposing the leadership on a number of occasions, most notably over the proposal for European cooperation over nuclear weapons in the Alliance defence commission report of 1986. It was his speech more than any other which swung the Eastbourne assembly against the platform. He was instrumental in establishing the Liberal/Liberal Democrat record as the greenest of the main parties. He has jointly authored pamphlets on human rights, the law and defence; *Pathways to Power: Realignment – Bridge or Barrier?* (with others, including Edward Davey (*q.v.*), 1992) foresaw some of the key developments of politics in the 1990s and stressed the need to develop a distinctive Liberal Democrat political identity before attempting any preelection cooperative agreements with other parties.

Hughes is a rare philanthropist whose reasons for becoming a politician have never been diluted or distracted by the trappings of power. Motivated by the case for international justice, he continues to be involved in the All-Party Parliamentary Groups for Bangladesh, Anti-Racist Alliance and South Africa. He is a past President of the British Youth Council, Vice-Chair of the Parliamentary Youth Affairs Lobby, member of the General Synod of the Church of England and President of Liberal Democrat Youth and Students. Closer to home he remains passionate about his home city, being among those tipped to be London's first elected mayor. He helped force the longest sitting of Parliament since the war, in the 1985–86 session, over the Conservative abolition of the GLC and metropolitan county councils.

His commitment to Christianity plays a major part in his dedication to his job, which many view as an alternative calling. He remains a man whose enthusiasm to take on so much is infuriating to many, but whose rare ability to focus and achieve an impact is endearing to all.

Emma Sanderson-Nash

JOSEPH HUME   1777–1855

Joseph Hume was a Scottish radical who devoted his political career to championing the principles of retrenchment. He was born near Montrose, Forfarshire in January 1777, the first son of James Hume. Hume's father, master of a small fishing ship, died when he was nine and the family was forced to fall back on the income provided by his mother's crockery shop. Hume was educated at the Montrose Academy, where he befriended James Mill, four years his senior. At the age of thirteen, he was apprenticed to a local doctor and then in 1793 entered Edinburgh University to study anatomy, midwifery and chemistry. On graduating in 1797, he joined the naval service of the East India Company as a physician.

India was to prove the making of Hume. Having learned Hindustani, he worked his way up through the service of the East India Company during the Mahratta War (1802–03), eventually being put in charge of the supplies in Bengal. From such a position he was able, quite legally, to acquire a fortune and by the time he returned to England in 1808 he had amassed wealth to the tune of £40,000. With some of this in 1812 he 'bought' a seat in Parliament for £10,000, via the influence of the Duke of Cumberland, at Weymouth & Melcombe Regis. Initially Hume pledged his support to Spencer Perceval, the Tory Prime Minister, but within a few weeks of entering the House of Commons he was demonstrating the heterodoxy and independence which became the hallmark of his radicalism. He attacked sinecures and sided with the opposition over the framework knitters' bill. Cumberland withdrew his patronage and in the general election of September 1812 Hume was replaced, although he did receive some financial compensation from the Duke.

Out of Parliament until 1818, Hume became a close ally of Francis Place, the radical tailor and political 'fixer', whom he met through James Mill. Along with Samuel

Whitbread (*q.v.*) they all gave support to the innovative educational system of Joseph Lancaster. Hume also became involved in attempts to break up the trade monopoly of the East India Company and in 1816 gave his backing to the call for decimalisation of weights and measures. In 1815 he married Mary Burnley, the wealthy daughter of a proprietor of East India stock, a marriage which did little to dispel suspicion of Hume's propensity to use private means to augment his public reputation.

At the general election of 1818 Hume was returned as MP for the Borders. Over the next few years he established his reputation as the watchdog of public finance, prolonging parliamentary discussion of the estimates long into the night and remaining on his feet by eating a steady supply of pears. Between 1823 and 1825, with behind-the-scenes prompting from Place, he was involved in attempts to repeal the Combination Acts, chairing a parliamentary select committee on the subject in 1825. Hume's reputation for financial probity took something of a knock in 1826 when he was implicated in the Greek loan scandal. However, he re-emerged at the centre-stage of English radical politics four years later when, with the advent of a new Whig ministry, he was returned, somewhat reluctantly on his part due to the expense, as one of the MPs for the populous constituency of Middlesex.

Hume welcomed the accession of the Whigs to power, believing they were committed to retrenchment. In 1835 Hume was instrumental in bringing about the Lichfield House compact between Whigs, Radicals and the Irish MPs which resulted in the selection of a more sympathetic speaker for the House of Commons. But by the end of the decade his faith in Whig leadership began to expire, as they hesitated over further parliamentary reform and appeared to take an aggressive line in Canada and Jamaica. On the emergence of the Chartist movement Hume declared he was for household suffrage, but, as he had shown twenty years earlier, his preferred palliative for social discontent was fiscal reform and retrenchment. In 1840 he chaired the influential parliamentary select committee on import duties, helping to stack it with free traders, and many of its findings and revelations went on to provide the framework for Peel's reforms in taxation. Hume had lost his Middlesex seat in 1837 and, with Daniel O'Connell's assistance, had been returned instead for Kilkenny. In 1841 he was defeated there, but the following year returned as MP for Montrose, the constituency he represented until his death.

When the Whigs returned to power in 1846 Hume vied with Richard Cobden (*q.v.*) and John Bright (*q.v.*) for the leadership of the large Radical presence in Parliament. He now championed parliamentary reform to a far greater extent than hitherto, introducing motions for household suffrage in three successive years from 1848, and he also joined in the agitation of the National Parliamentary and Financial Reform Association. But, with his typically maverick style, he also managed to offend radical sensibilities, for example by supporting the West India planters in their constitutional struggles of the late 1840s, and by entering an unholy alliance with protectionist MPs over reform of the income tax in 1851. Hume's manoeuvring, however, could still unsettle governments of the day. In 1852 his insistence on the government including the secret ballot in its reform bill was widely perceived to be one of the causes of the fall of Lord John Russell's (*q.v.*) ministry.

Hume's stalwart attendance in the House of Commons diminished as Britain became involved in the Crimean War. Returning from Scotland to his country seat at Burnley Hall, near Great Yarmouth, in the new year of 1855, he fell ill and died on 20 February, aged seventy-eight. Hume was not a popular man. He was considered too dour, pedantic and unpredictable to win many admirers, but his insistence on and knowledge of constitutional propriety, together with his defence of public economy and free trade, long before they became the shibboleths of the Liberal Party, ensured his place in the pantheon of liberalism.

There have been two fairly recent and reliable biographies of Hume: Ronald K. Huch and Paul R. Ziegler, *Joseph Hume: The People's MP* (Philadelphia, 1985); and Valerie Chancellor, *The Political Life of Joseph Hume, 1777–1855* (privately printed, 1986).

Miles Taylor

RUFUS ISAACS (Marquess of Reading)   1860–1935

Rufus Daniel Isaacs was born in London on 10 October 1860, the fourth child (out of nine) of Joseph and Sarah Isaacs. He was an unruly and not particularly hard-working child, though occasionally he showed flashes of brilliance. He was expelled from his first school at the age of six, and attended University College School for a year, before his father withdrew him with a view to a commercial career. He was found a position with the stockbroking firm Keyser and Frederici, and at the age of nineteen lied about his age to gain admission as a member of the Stock Exchange, a mistake that haunted him in later life. A successful career as a jobber in foreign securities came to a sudden end in 1884 when, in the midst of an economic slump, he went spectacularly broke and was 'hammered' for being unable to meet debts of £8,000.

He was prevented at the last moment from emigrating to Panama by his mother, who determined that a legal career was the best way for him to pay off his debts and to restore himself to respectability. In the process of reading for the bar, Isaacs found a new seriousness that displaced his previous rather frivolous character, but without reducing his natural charm. He was called to the bar in 1887; in the same year he married Alice Cohen. Isaacs was an immense success at the bar. He was not a great technical lawyer, nor a great orator, but he was highly organised and persuasive and a pioneer of the modern understated style of advocacy. He specialised in commercial cases and took silk after only ten years at the bar.

His legal career brought him into contact with Liberal politics. By nature, up-bringing and, briefly, schooling he favoured tolerance and social reform, but through his pupil-master, Lawson Walton, a future Liberal Attorney-General, he came into contact with organised Liberalism. Initially his involvement was limited to local debating societies. In 1900, however, he stood unsuccessfully for Parliament in the solid Tory seat of North Kensington.

Isaacs' legal career went from strength to strength. He helped his political career by appearing as counsel for the trade union in the *Taff Vale* case and strengthened his credibility with the 'pro-Boer' wing of the party (Isaacs was by inclination a Liberal Imperialist) by brilliantly defending Dr Krause, an Afrikaner advocate prosecuted for incitement to murder. In 1904, he entered Parliament as a byelection victor, holding the Liberal marginal seat of Reading. He increased his majority in 1906 and hung on successfully in both the elections of 1910.

Isaacs was a backbencher for the entire 1906–10 Parliament. He favoured the moderate Liberal Imperialist position, which made him a natural ally of Asquith (*q.v.*), but he was drawn into Lloyd George's (*q.v.*) circle, having represented him in a libel action against the *People* newspaper. Popular with leading figures on both sides of the party, immensely able though cautious in his work, Isaacs was a natural choice for the post of Solicitor-General, which became free in 1910. His appearance for the Crown in the embarrassing Archer-Shee case, later dramatised by Terence Rattigan as *The Winslow Boy*, did not hinder his further progress to the post of Attorney-General in the same year.

His association with Lloyd George deepened as a result of their working closely together on the National Insurance Bill. Isaacs led for the government on the Trade Union Bill, which reversed the *Osborne* judgement, and on the Coal Mines (Minimum Wages) Bill. A supporter of women's suffrage, he nevertheless played a part in the prosecution of the suffragettes. In 1912, while still Attorney-General, Isaacs entered the Cabinet. Asquith held him in high regard, but his elevation to cabinet rank, highly unusual for a serving law officer, might have had more to do with placating him after Asquith had appointed Haldane (*q.v.*) to the Lord Chancellorship. Asquith probably felt obliged to Haldane as a result of the consequences of the failed 'Relugas Plot' against Campbell-Bannerman (*q.v.*) in 1905, but Isaacs was certainly disappointed not to be offered the Woolsack.

In 1912, Isaacs became embroiled in the Marconi scandal. The original accusation, largely promoted by anti-semites, was that Isaacs had influenced Herbert Samuel (*q.v.*), the Postmaster-General, to grant an over-generous contract to erect a nationwide network of wireless stations to the British Marconi Company, which happened to be managed by Isaacs' own brother, Godfrey. The accusation was false, but Isaacs' reputation was damaged by a subsequent allegation that he, Lloyd George and the Master of Elibank (*q.v.*) had speculated in Marconi shares. Initial denials to Parliament had to be explained away by distinguishing between the British Marconi Company, whose shares the three had not bought, and the American Marconi Company, in whose shares they had speculated. In 1913 Isaacs and Lloyd George offered their resignations to Asquith. Asquith's regard for Isaacs saved both of them, and the resignations were refused. Those digging into Isaacs' past also found out about his youthful indiscretion of lying about his age to the Stock Exchange. Isaacs again offered his resignation to Asquith, who refused it once more.

The Marconi scandal explains Isaacs' next move, to the judicial bench. In 1913, Lord Alverstone, the Lord Chief Justice, retired through ill health. There was a convention that the serving Attorney-General should succeed to the post of Lord Chief Justice if it became vacant. Asquith did not particularly want to lose Isaacs from the Cabinet, and Isaacs did not particularly want to go, but Asquith was persuaded that if he was not elevated, the public, and the opposition, would interpret it as a vote of no confidence because of the Marconi scandal. And so, in October 1913, Rufus Isaacs, the son of a London fruit merchant, became Lord Chief Justice of England and was raised to the peerage, taking the title of Baron Reading, after his erstwhile constituency.

Reading was not a particularly distinguished Lord Chief Justice, largely because during the First World War he was given other work to do. He was, however, a humane, even kindly judge, standing out against the jingoistic sentiments of public opinion to deliver liberal judgements upholding the civil liberties of enemy aliens.

Far more stimulating than his judicial work was Reading's crucial role in making the deals, mainly in the USA, that financed the war. His idea of government guarantees to the accepting houses revolutionised the government's shaky financial position in 1915, although Maynard Keynes (q.v.), who accompanied him in his later missions, thought that he became too cautious in his dealings with the Americans. Indeed Beaverbrook was later to describe him as 'a loveable man with an abundance of personal charm' but 'so cautious that he never gave an opinion until he had to'. For his efforts in arranging the financing of the war, he was created an earl in 1917.

In 1919 he returned full time to his duties as Lord Chief Justice, but the memory of his wartime exertions made the life of a judge even less congenial. In 1921, Lloyd George appointed him Viceroy of India, a post he held, through various governments, until 1926. As Viceroy, Reading exerted himself mainly in the cause of implementing the Montagu-Chelmsford reforms and the 'dyarchy' plan, in which he partly succeeded, despite the initial opposition of many Indian politicians. Later, after leaving office, he came to favour a federal solution for India. His sympathy for the Muslims has been interpreted as motivated by a divide-and-rule strategy, as has his decision, after much hesitation, to have Gandhi arrested for conspiracy. Reading always denied the accusation. He showed considerable distaste for the continuing racism of several aspects of British rule, especially in the criminal justice system, and favoured the admittedly gradual Indianisation both of the civil service and, more controversially, of the officer corps of the Indian Army.

Returning to Britain in 1926, Reading again took an active part in politics as a Liberal peer. He also began a commercial career that led him to the chairmanship of ICI and several other directorships. His main political role was, yet again, as a mediator between Lloyd George and those in the party who distrusted him. Reading, by this time elevated to the rank of Marquess, was one of the few people liked and trusted by both sides.

Reading's career still had one more twist. In 1931, on the fall of the second Labour government and the formation of the National Government, with Lloyd George ill and no other obvious candidate, Reading was offered, and accepted, the office of Foreign Secretary. He remained in the post until the subsequent election, at which point he was replaced, not entirely willingly, by Sir John Simon (*q.v.*).

In the fractious years which followed, in which the Liberal Party split three ways, Reading attempted to lead the party in the House of Lords, an impossible task even for someone of his charm and ability. He died on 30 December 1935, leaving one son. His first wife had died in 1930 and he had married Stella Charnaud in 1931; this union was childless.

Reading's career was one of the most extraordinary of the twentieth century, especially in the light of the anti-semitism to which he was periodically subjected throughout his public life (Kipling, for example, wrote a particularly offensive poem about him in 1913). Though lacking any great personal religious conviction, he re-mained proud of his origins. His abilities spoke for themselves. For further reading, see Denis Judd, *Lord Reading* (Weidenfeld & Nicolson, 1982).

David Howarth

ANTHONY JACOBS (Lord Jacobs)   1931–

David Anthony Jacobs was born in November 1931, and was educated at Clifton College and London University. His highly successful business career spans thirty-three years, during which time he was chairman of three major companies: Nig Securities Group (1957–72); the Tricoville Group (1961–90); and the British School of Motoring (1973–90).

He joined the Liberal Party in 1972, served on both the housing and economic policy panels, and was co-author of *Help for the First-Time Buyer*. He went on to become economics and taxation adviser to the Liberal Party, working closely with John Pardoe MP (*q.v.*) from 1973–78. He fought Watford in both the February and October 1974 general elections, increasing the Liberal share of the vote from six to twenty-four per cent.

He was elected Joint Treasurer of the Liberal Party in 1984 and was returned unop-posed each subsequent year until he stood down in 1987. During his time as Joint Treasurer, he worked tirelessly to put the finances of the party on a sound footing, often using his powers of persuasion to force the Executive to take tough and sometimes unpopular decisions to ensure the solvency of the party. He was a keen supporter of the merger of the Liberal Party and the SDP and served as Chairman of the Party in England and Vice-President of the Federal Party. He received a knighthood in 1988.

Immediately following the 1992 general election, when the party was at a low point, he devised a revitalised approach to campaigning in the best-prospect constituencies. This strategy was based on the campaigning experience of the 1992 election; Jacobs believed that if applied to specific constituencies, it could significantly increase the number of seats the party could win at the next election. This became known as the Target Seats Campaign. The subsequent general election of 1997 saw the election of forty-six Liberal Democrat MPs, the largest number of seats won since the 1920s. Every seat gained had been on the Target Seat list.

He became a life peer in November 1997 and is an active member of the House of Lords. He extensive business experience is enabling him successfully to challenge the government on the disparity between prices paid by British consumers for goods which are available to European and US consumers for a fraction of the price.

His life-long interest in the arts was reflected by his appointment to the Tate Gallery Millennium fund-raising committee for the new Tate Bankside Gallery of Modern Art. He is Trustee of the Jacobs Charitable Trust, and since 1980 has served as a member of the Crown Estate Paving Commissioners. He has been Chairman of the Board of Governors of Haifa University in Israel since 1992, and was instrumental in salvaging a Phoenician ship from 400 BC which is currently being restored for exhibition in the University's Maritime and Marine Faculty.

He lists his hobbies as golf, reading, theatre, opera and travel. He married his wife Evelyn in 1954, and they have two children, Nicola and Simon.

Dee Doocey

ROY JENKINS (Lord Jenkins) 1920–

Roy Jenkins has played a significant role in developing and articulating a new progressive vision of social, political and constitutional change. His reforms at the Home Office helped to transform Britain into a more modern, more civilised society. He was a successful, if orthodox, Chancellor of the Exchequer. He played an important and consistent role in taking Britain into Europe and, in doing so, did enormous damage to his own career. He was instrumental in founding the SDP and became its first leader. Although the SDP did not, in itself, break the mould of British politics, it helped to revitalise and develop the radical centre and to force the Labour Party to change itself. Today, Roy Jenkins stands as a hero of the liberal and social democratic traditions – the great reformist Liberal Prime Minister Britain never had.

Roy Harris Jenkins was born on 11 November 1920, in Abersychan, South Wales. His father, Arthur Jenkins, was an official in the South Wales Miners' Federation who became MP for Pontypool and PPS to Clement Attlee. His mother, Hattie, came from a more well-to-do background. From his parents, Jenkins gained a sense of civic responsibility and a strong commitment to the pursuit of change through peaceful and democratic means.

Jenkins received his formal education at Abersychan School, University College, Cardiff and Balliol College, Oxford. At Oxford, he was Secretary of the Union and Chairman of the Democratic Socialist Club, a group of moderates who had broken with the left-dominated Labour Club. In 1941, he gained a first in PPE, with little apparent effort. He joined the Royal Artillery and was seconded on intelligence work to Bletchley.

In January 1945, Jenkins married Jennifer Morris and they later had two sons and a daughter. After the war, he worked in the City as an economist for the Industrial and Commercial Finance Corporation, a semi-philanthropic body which channelled finance into new businesses. He wrote a brief biography of Clement Attlee, published in 1948. That April, he held Southwark Central for Labour in a byelection and became the youngest MP in the House. In 1950, the seat disappeared in an electoral redistribution and Jenkins became the MP for Birmingham Stechford; his political base for more than a quarter of a century.

In Labour's internal struggles between Bevanites and revisionists, Jenkins enlisted with the latter camp. His book *Pursuit of Progress,* published in 1953, was one of the first attempts to develop a revisionist case. In *The Labour Case* (1959), he described the party's goal in decidedly non-socialist terms: 'a society .... in which everyone will have the opportunity for a full and satisfying life'. Labour, he claimed, was a 'practical party', more concerned with ends than means. His elegantly written and sympathetic portrayal of Asquith, published in 1964, suggested that Jenkins was, at heart, a modern-day Whig rather than a doctrinaire socialist. He was a close friend and strong supporter of Hugh Gaitskell, though differed with him over Europe; in 1960, he quit the front-bench economic team to be free to campaign for Britain's entry.

When Labour returned to office in October 1964, Jenkins flourished. He was a successful Minister of Aviation and, after just fourteen months, became Home Secretary. He embarked on a series of reforms that caught the mood of the 'swinging sixties'. He secured parliamentary time for private member's bills to liberalise the abortion law and legalise homosexual practices between consenting adults. He also set in train a strengthening of race relations legislation and the abolition of theatre censorship.

In November 1967, following the devaluation crisis, Jenkins replaced Jim Callaghan as Chancellor of the Exchequer. His unenviable task was to restore a balance of payments surplus and a stable pound. Jenkins delivered 'two years' hard slog'. He started with swingeing cuts in public spending, with defence bearing the heaviest burden; taxation was increased sharply in successive budgets, bank lending limited and interest rates increased. By the 1970 general election, public finances and the balance of payments were both in surplus, and the economy and exports had grown strongly. Such was the basis of Jenkins' reputation as one of the best post-war Chancellors. Yet his deflationary measures are now seen as too cautious and too late; they delayed the recovery and required him to take harsher measures later. He also failed to control the inflation stemming from wage rises, not helped by the government's climb-down on its proposed trade union reforms (which Jenkins initially supported, then backed away from).

In opposition after 1970, Jenkins gathered around him a coterie of close political supporters, including the sometime Labour MP, David Marquand (*q.v.*), the former Treasury Minister Dick Taverne QC (*q.v.*), the human rights lawyer Anthony Lester QC (*q.v.*) and Jenkins' press aide John Harris (*q.v.*). The Jenkinsites were attracted by, if not in awe of, his achievements as Home Secretary, his success at the Treasury, his steadfast support for the European cause, his stylish performances in the Commons, his mastery of television, his verbal and written eloquence, his broad perspective and clear vision, his grandness and sparkle. Jenkins also had a significant public following and enjoyed the support of such establishment papers as *The Times*. In July 1970, he was elected Deputy Leader of the Labour Party; many saw him as the probable successor to Harold Wilson as leader.

However, over the next six years, Jenkins became more isolated within the party as it moved to the left. The issue of Europe, more than any other, led to his divorce from Labour. When a special party conference voted, in July 1971, to oppose entry on the terms negotiated by the Conservative government, he was appalled. That October, in what many regard as his finest hour, Jenkins led sixty-nine Labour MPs to vote for the terms, in defiance of a three-line whip. In April 1972, he resigned the deputy leadership in protest at the Shadow Cabinet's decision to promise a referendum on Britain's continued membership of the EEC.

In March 1974, he returned to the Home Office in Wilson's new government, though he was unhappy with both Wilson's leadership and the government's overall direction. He soon faced mounting problems over security in Northern Ireland; in particular, new terrorist attacks on the mainland, which led to the introduction, in 1974, of the Prevention of Terrorism Act, which he intended as a temporary measure. Nevertheless, he brought in new legislation to outlaw discrimination on the grounds of gender, and introduced a measure of independence to police complaints procedures. During the 1975 referendum on Britain's membership of the EEC, Jenkins headed up the successful 'Yes' campaign, and thoroughly enjoyed working with pro-European politicians from all three parties.

When Wilson resigned in April 1976, Jenkins came a poor third in the subsequent leadership ballot, won by Callaghan. The vast political differences between Jenkins and most of the party, especially over Europe, were a major cause. Furthermore, many Labour politicians blamed Jenkins' cautious economic management for the 1970 defeat. His personal style was too grand and aloof and he appeared too much of a *bon viveur* to lead the party of the working class.

After Callaghan failed to offer him the Foreign Secretaryship, Jenkins left British politics to take up a four-year term as President of the European Commission. At first,

he found the role difficult and the Commission's machinery cumbersome. There were tensions in his relationships with some European heads of government. Jenkins overcame these obstacles and took a leading role in establishing the European Monetary System.

In November 1979, he presented his Dimbleby lecture, 'Home Thoughts from Abroad', from which the birth of the SDP can be traced. He criticised the false choices, see-saw politics and broken promises of the two-party system and advocated electoral reform. Most crucially, Jenkins called for a new political grouping to strengthen the 'radical centre'. As intended, this caused great excitement amongst those disenchanted with both the Thatcher Government and Labour's capture by the hard left but who did not see the Liberal Party, on its own, as a realistic vehicle for change. During 1980, Jenkins gradually enlisted Labour's 'Gang of Three' – Dr David Owen, Shirley Williams (*q.v.*) and Bill Rodgers (*q.v.*). The following March, they founded the Social Democratic Party, which formed an alliance with the Liberal Party and soon took a commanding lead in the opinion polls.

Jenkins' vision was of a centrist party that would appeal to all sections of society and bring the country together. The party would also take on a radical edge, with policies for devolution and partnership in industry. It would promote equality for women and environmental and third world concerns.

Naturally, Jenkins wanted to lead the new party, but first he had to re-enter the Commons. In July 1981, he came a close second in the byelection at Warrington, a safe Labour seat. Then, the following March, he won the Glasgow Hillhead byelection. On both occasions, Jenkins' sterling performances killed the myth that he was a poor grassroots campaigner. In July 1982, he was elected as the first leader of the SDP. However, his tenure was not a happy one. As a natural man of office, he was ill-suited to leading a third party in opposition; he did not take well to the chaotic demands of party management and the need to maintain a high media profile. He found the House of Commons a far less congenial forum than before and was now a diffident television performer. He did not establish a distinctive image for the SDP.

For the 1983 general election campaign, Jenkins was made the Alliance's 'prime minister-designate', whereas David Steel (*q.v.*) was its 'leader'. This arrangement did not work: Steel was the superior performer and enjoyed better opinion poll ratings. At the Alliance's infamous Ettrick Bridge summit, Jenkins was sidelined. It was agreed that Steel would, in effect, lead the campaign for the final ten days. The election saw only six SDP MPs returned. A weary Jenkins then resigned the leadership, in part due to pressure from Dr Owen, who succeeded him.

The result of the 1987 general election made it clear that the SDP had failed to replace Labour as the main non-conservative party. Jenkins lost Hillhead to a Labour left-winger. He supported the subsequent merger of the SDP and the Liberals, seeing their political differences as being of little import. He accepted a peerage, as Lord Jenkins of Hillhead, and became Leader of the Liberal Democrats in the House of Lords, a position he held until 1998.

In 1986, Jenkins was elected Chancellor of Oxford University. Between 1980 and 1998, he completed seven books. These included a well-received autobiography, *A Life at the Centre* (1991), in which he described himself as a 'perpetual radical' rather than an 'establishment Whig'. His widely acclaimed *Gladstone* (1995) won the Whitbread Prize for Biography.

Jenkins' career has had an intriguing afterlife. He was greatly enthused by Tony Blair's election as leader of the Labour Party in 1994, and soon became one of his key confidants. He called on Labour and the Liberal Democrats to work together so that the progressive forces could establish a long-term ascendancy. Blair appeared to be the sort of Prime Minister that Jenkins would have liked to become. In 1998, he appointed Jenkins to head a commission on the voting system, offering one more chance to break the mould of British politics.

Neil Stockley

RUSSELL JOHNSTON (Lord Russell-Johnston)   1932–

Russell Johnston entered Parliament in 1964, and was joined a year later by David Steel (*q.v.*). Together they were to dominate the Scottish party for just over the next three decades, and today they continue to exert considerable influence. Their careers took very different paths. While Steel became a most effective national leader of the party, Johnston went on to make a significant contribution not just to Scottish and European politics but to the development of Liberalism and Liberal Democracy. In so doing he is acknowledged as the most articulate exponent of Liberalism in the party today.

David Russell Johnston was born on 28 July 1932 in Edinburgh, but was brought up in Skye and educated at Carbost Public School and Portree High School. After graduating MA (Hons) in history from the University of Edinburgh, he did National Service, being commissioned into the Intelligence Corps and rising to become second-in-command of the British Intelligence Unit in Berlin. After National Service, he returned to Edinburgh to take a teaching degree at Moray House College of Education.

In 1961 Johnston succeeded his mentor, John Bannerman (*q.v.*), as the parliamentary candidate for Inverness. He won the seat in 1964 and successfully held it at each of the next eight general elections before retiring from the House of Commons in 1997. He was a front-bench spokesman throughout his parliamentary career, starting, not surprisingly, with education, and moving on to Northern Ireland, foreign affairs, Scottish affairs (1970–73, 1975–83, 1985–88), defence, foreign and Commonwealth affairs and latterly for the Liberal Democrats, European Community affairs. He was a member of the Parliamentary Committee of Privileges from 1988–92.

As a result of his obvious commitment to and understanding of Scottish affairs, he was appointed a member of the Royal Commission on Local Government in Scotland, which sat from 1966 to 1969. Johnston's commitment to the cause of home rule led him to introduce a Scottish Self-Government Bill in 1966 and, in 1979, during the Lib-Lab Pact, he negotiated the Scottish Assembly Bill with the Labour government.

Johnston served continuously on the Executive of the Scottish Liberal Party and then the Scottish Liberal Democrats from 1961 until he stood down in 1994. He became Vice Chairman in 1965, succeeded George Mackie (*q.v.*) to become Chairman in 1970, was elected to the new post of Leader in 1974 and was then elected President in 1988, a post he held until 1994.

Johnston has an analytical mind and brings considerable intellectual rigour to bear on any issue. The result is a deep-rooted philosophical foundation to his adherence to the cause of Liberalism. It was the writings of Elliott Dodds (*q.v.*), the north of England Liberal, which brought him into the party in the early 1950s, and there is no doubt that the speeches and writings of John Bannerman were hugely influential in defining his own approach to Liberalism. Right up to today it is difficult to find a significant speech delivered by Johnston that does not contain a reference to Bannerman.

Johnston's talent for expressing Liberal policy and philosophy clearly and concisely was apparent from his early speeches before he was elected to Parliament. His first publication in 1964 was the pamphlet *Highland Development,* in which the idea of a Highland Development Board was first mooted – a policy platform highly influential in the Liberals winning three Highland seats in the 1964 election.

His next three publications were more reflective of his contribution to the development of Liberal thinking. In 1972 he published *To be a Liberal.* Whilst many before and after have written excellent treatises on Liberalism, *To be a Liberal* is a masterpiece of its kind. Johnston may have been influenced to join the party by the writings of Elliott Dodds, but a significant number of current Scottish Liberal Democrats were inspired to join the party by this piece by Russell Johnston.

As Chairman and then Leader of the Scottish party, Johnston's inspirational speech to the annual conference, in which his well-crafted script was delivered in a classical oratorical style, took on a legendary quality and became as eagerly awaited at Federal assemblies as they were at Scottish conferences. The two volumes of Johnston's speeches (*Conference Speeches 1971–78,* 1979, and *Conference Speeches 1979–86,* 1987), are not only a splendid commentary on contemporary politics from a Scottish perspective, but also are a significant Scottish contribution to Liberal thinking, and they confirm Johnston's constancy of approach in an ever-changing political landscape.

Johnston and the Scottish party gave a lead to negotiations with the newly formed SDP, concluding an Alliance agreement ahead of colleagues in the south. His motion to a special conference in September 1981 was overwhelmingly approved and was, as Johnston put it, 'significant not only in its effect on the subsequent Blackpool conference, but in its own right as a definition of the openness and self-confidence of the Liberal stance in Scotland.' He was appalled, however, by much of the unseemly wrangling which took place over the subsequent allocation of seats. In much the same way as his mentor John Bannerman had observed, ' that he didn't really understand why everyone was not a Liberal', so Johnston had believed that ability should be the sole criterion in candidate selection. This did not detract from his belief in the Alliance, and he went on to promote actively the merger and creation of the Liberal Democrats.

After Britain's accession to the EEC in 1973, Johnston became a member of the UK delegation to the European Parliament and, except for a break of nine months in 1975, remained a member until direct elections in 1979. He lost the Highlands & Islands seat narrowly in that year but fought on, only to lose by an even greater margin in 1984. The guid folk of the Highlands decided that Johnston was their man for Westminster and weren't about to let him go to Europe. He continued to pursue his interests, however, through other means. He was a member of the assemblies of the Western European Union and Council of Europe from 1984–85 and since 1987. He has been Vice-President of Liberal International since 1994. He is currently Leader of the Liberal, Democrat and Reform Group in the Council of Europe (since 1994) and Chairman of the Committee on Culture and Education in the Council of Europe (since 1996).

Johnston married Joan Graham Menzies in 1967 and they have three grown-up sons, Graham David and Andrew. He was knighted in the Birthday Honours List in 1985 and created a life peer on the dissolution of Parliament in 1997, changing his name by deed poll to take the title Lord Russell-Johnston of Minginish. He is an avid reader, a skilled photographer and a compulsive writer of postcards, to the delight of the very many recipients who are kept abreast of his extensive world-wide travels.

Ross Finnie

NIGEL JONES MP

1948–

Nigel Jones is among the ranks of Liberal Democrat MPs who are 'home-grown products', deeply rooted in the life of their own constituency.

Nigel David Jones was born in Cheltenham on 30 March 1948 and was educated at Prince Henry's Grammar School, Evesham. After school he went to work with the

Westminster Bank, but two years later joined ICL Computers as a computer pro-grammer. In the world of computers his career flourished, and he became a systems and design consultant with ICL in 1971, a role which was to take him on a number of assignments in the Middle East, Hong Kong, Scandinavia and the Caribbean.

In the early 1970s Jones married Alexis Rogers, who herself had strong roots in Cheltenham. They set up home in the town and started to get involved in the local political scene. Both were involved in the 'Cheltenham for Europe' campaign which worked for a 'Yes' vote in the 1975 referendum, and both played a role in reviving the Cheltenham Young Liberals between 1975 and 1977. By the time the constituency Liberals came to select a prospective parliamentary candidate in 1977, Jones was well enough established to get the nomination.

The years between the Lib-Lab Pact of 1977 and the general election of 1979 were extremely difficult for the Liberal Party nationally. Jones coped with this situa-tion by robustly defending the Pact and by following a community politics strategy in Cheltenham. By the time the election came, *Focus* newsletters were part of the politi-cal scene in most Cheltenham wards.

In the 1979 general election, against the national trend, Jones improved the Lib-eral share of the vote and comfortably came second to the Conservative. In all the circumstances, this was a remarkable achievement, even though the sitting MP, Charles Irving, was still over 10,000 votes ahead. The Jones strategy was also responsible for a major revival of Liberal fortunes in local government, with the Liberal representation on Cheltenham Borough Council jumping from four to fourteen seats in the local elections which took place on the same day.

After the 1979 general election, Jones withdrew as prospective parliamentary can-didate. His marriage to Alexis, who was by this time a councillor, came to an end. In 1981 he married Katy Grinnell, a local schoolteacher, with whom he had a son and twin daughters.

Continuing the work Jones had done to build up the Cheltenham Liberals, Rich-ard Holme (*q.v.*) fought the 1983 and 1987 general elections in the constituency, narrowing the gap and coming tantalisingly close to ousting the Conservatives. But by the mid-eighties, Jones was back in the thick of local politics. During the Liberal/ SDP merger, he was as staunchly loyal to the leadership as he had been during the Lib-Lab Pact. He and Katy both won impressive victories in the Gloucestershire County Council elections in 1989, so that when Holme accepted a peerage, Jones was well placed to take the nomination once again.

The Conservative choice of John Taylor, a black barrister, to fight the Cheltenham seat was one of the most controversial episodes of the 1992 general election. Un-doubtedly, many local Conservatives disgraced their party by their hostile response to Taylor's selection, and some refused to vote for him. However, the Liberal Democrats also faced a difficult task. It was impossible for Jones to attack Taylor personally, or refer to his own strong local credentials, without risking the charge of pandering to

racism. In the event, Jones fought an honourable campaign, though he was still criticised for emphasising in campaign literature that he was born in Cheltenham. He
won the seat by 1,668 votes. Five years of hard constituency work enabled Jones to
increase his majority to 6,645 in the 1997 general election, this time in a contest
against a well-liked Conservative councillor.

Though not among the obvious stars of the Liberal Democrat parliamentary party,
he has been a loyal and active member of the team, drawing on knowledge and
experience gained in the world beyond Westminster. At various times he has served as
spokesman on local government and housing, science and technology and sport. His
committee assignments have included the Select Committee on Science and Technology, the Standards and Privileges Committee and the Finance Bill Committee. He
has also pursued his own personal causes, such as animal welfare and the equalisation
of duty on beer within the European Union.

John Rawson

SIR TREVOR JONES 1927–

When Sir Trevor Jones came to prominence in the Liberal Party things could hardly
have been at a lower ebb. The 1970 general election had seen the Parliamentary party
reduced to six MPs. The party had only 330 councillors, but in Liverpool there was
actually a council group which was beginning to take seats from both Labour and the
Conservatives. It was also pioneering the new electioneering methods that are now
described as 'the ALDC way'.

At first sight, Jones seemed an unlikely Liberal. Born in Bootle in 1927, of Welsh
parents, he moved from being a seaman to the ownership of Liverpool's (and Europe's) oldest firm of ships' chandlers, Joseph P. Lamb & Sons (prior to 1836, Gladstone,
Nickels & Co., owned by the Gladstone family and run by an uncle of William Ewart
Gladstone, *q.v.*). As a self-made businessman, a more likely avenue for political activity
should have been with the strong municipal Tories of Liverpool. Yet Jones, with his
Welsh roots, was a passive Liberal and when the council promoted grandiose plans
which involved the destruction of large areas of the city centre (including one of his
warehouses), he swung into action.

Promoting his own petitions, posters and publicity which were subsequently to
become the hallmark of Liberal campaigning, he took Liverpool by storm and narrowly failed to get a private bill through Parliament. Realising that campaigning was
not enough, he turned up at the door of the sole Liberal councillor in Liverpool,
Cyril Carr. Elected after the successful Orpington byelection in 1962, Carr ended a
thirty-year Liberal absence from the council. A unique partnership was borne between the intellectual liberalism of Carr and the practical campaigning, instinctive
liberalism of Jones. After two unsuccessful attempts to gain a seat, one councillor

became two in 1968, then two councillors became four and *Liberal News*, always desperate for good news stories, began to home in on the Liverpool experience.

The years 1972–74 were the highlights of Jones' success in the national party. He almost single-handedly turned parliamentary byelections from casual events into a mass involvement 'sport'. The battle emblems gathered on his Triumph Stag and battlebus. The byelection campaigns in Sutton & Cheam, Hove, Chester-le-Street, and Manchester Exchange created a national fervour which led to the gaining of seats such as Berwick-upon-Tweed, Ripon and Isle of Ely. He became President of the Liberal Party in 1973 and laid the grounds for the most successful Liberal general election campaign for more than fifty years. His presidential speech was a barnstorming affair. He lived up to his national press nickname, 'Jones the Vote', and had the assembly on its feet as he declared 'I love those votes'.

The votes came in 1974 but not the seats. Over six million votes translated into just fourteen MPs, but for the first time in living memory the Liberals were actually fighting in more than sixty seats and standing in more than three hundred. Jones helped to guarantee many of those seats being fought as director of the derelict seats campaign. He would bowl into a town and leave them next day with officers, a constitution and a parliamentary candidate.

1973 was, in many ways, the completion of the first phase of the conversion of the party to 'Jonesism'. The 1970 Young Liberal and Liberal assemblies had adopted the 'dual approach' and committed the party not only to getting Liberals elected but also to community politics, which saw the party entering mass and sustained campaigns such as that which had brought Jones into politics a decade before. The council elections of 1973 saw 850 Liberal councillors elected on new large authorities. For the first time Liberals began to be a force in more than the occasional town hall. Liberals discovered that they could win, and they began to campaign to win.

Nowhere was this more evident than in Liverpool. 1973 saw the election of forty-eight Liberal councillors out of ninety-nine, and the Liberals took control of the council. Jones served as Deputy Leader to Carr and became Chair of the Housing Committee. His first act was to declare the bulldozer redundant. The machine he had entered politics to defeat was pensioned off. The wholesale demolition of communities and their removal to the Lancashire towns of Skelmersdale and Runcorn was stopped. Liverpool declared the largest number of housing improvement areas of any council in the country. Communities were rebuilt, owner occupation encouraged, and environments were turned round. Liverpool became the first council in the country to encourage home ownership in the inner areas, with its build-for-sale policies now a cornerstone of every party's inner areas regeneration proposals.

Following the so-called 'Toxteth riots', Jones enjoyed a strong working relationship with a strange ally – Michael Heseltine, then Secretary of State for the Environment. Much of the conversion of Heseltine to the promotion of practical policies to tackle inner-city dereliction can be attributed to Jones' influence.

But despite his obvious success and the adoration with which the party's recruits hailed him, Jones was never fully accepted by the party hierarchy. There was suspicion of someone who did not see success as a seat in the Commons (although he did fight two parliamentary seats). Jones was adamant that the party needed 'coalface politicians', not just 'personalities', and was convinced that building a body of activists would bring the party long-term success. He has no regrets about not entering Parliament, and he did not expect to win either of the contests he fought. He stood in Toxteth in February 1974, to draw fire away from David Alton's (*q.v.*) first serious attempt at the Edgehill constituency. At the October election that year, he accepted an invitation to stand in Gillingham, Kent – a move he later saw as a mistake, believing he should have concentrated on Liverpool.

The award of a scarce knighthood by David Steel (*q.v.*) was scant recognition for his service as the country's first 'spin doctor', and the person who introduced the party to the heady brew of success and votes. Without rancour Jones concentrated on his work in Liverpool running the large council group, and in 1976 became Leader of the group and council. He remained Leader until 1988 and in 1989 left the council determined not to get in the way of his successors. He still works at his ships' chandlers firm.

Sir Trevor Jones inspired an army of devoted followers. Many who are influential throughout the Liberal Democrats served in that army and today use his techniques to win elections. Computers may have replaced letraset, and litho replaced duplicators, but nothing replaces the Jones message: 'If you've got something to say, stick it on a piece of paper and put it through someone's door'.

Richard Kemp

PAUL KEETCH MP   1961–

Paul Keetch had an ambition not just to be a Member of Parliament; he wanted to be the Member of Parliament for Hereford. On 1 May 1997 he achieved it.

Paul Stuart Keetch was born at the family home at 4 Lyndhurst Avenue, Hereford on 21 May 1961, and remained there until moving to London in 1985. He was educated at St Paul's Primary School, Hereford High School for Boys (now Aylestone School) and Hereford Sixth Form College.

Keetch joined the Liberal Party while still at school and began to harbour an ambition to be the successor to Frank Owen (*q.v.*), the last Liberal MP for Hereford, who lost his seat in 1931. He chaired Hereford Young Liberals and the West Midlands Region Young Liberals, which brought him a seat on the National League of Young Liberals' Executive Committee. He worked hard to secure the election of a Liberal MP in Hereford at the 1974, 1979 and 1983 general election campaigns. He was particularly supportive of Chris Green, and served as his election agent in 1983.

Keetch was elected to Hereford City Council in 1983; at twenty-two, he was the city's youngest-ever councillor and the youngest elected in the country at that time. He represented Holmer Ward and chaired the Principal Highways Working Party on the Liberal-controlled council. He resigned after two years, due to work commitments.

After an early grounding in banking and financial services, Keetch developed a career in the water hygiene industry and was transferred to London by his then employer, Franklin Hodge. Latterly, he made good use of his political experience and became a political and corporate affairs consultant, specialising in election procedure and media training, mainly advising non-governmental organisations and charities. He also carried out election monitoring missions in the Baltic states and Albania.

Keetch energetically supported Simon Hughes (*q.v.*) in the 1987 and 1992 Bermondsey general election campaigns, taking on the responsibility of a sub-agent. He was a keen member of the Liberal Party's Defence Panel, chaired by Laura Grimond (*q.v.*), and spent many years as a member of the Development Board of the British Dyslexic Society.

On 21 December 1991 he married his long-standing fiancée, Claire Baker, and their son William was born on 11 February 1995. Claire was born in Hereford and is a native of the county. She is also a committed Liberal Democrat and indispensable to her husband's political success.

When the Liberal Democrats yet again failed to take Hereford in the 1992 general election, Keetch saw his opportunity to secure adoption as the prospective parliamentary candidate, and was selected in 1994. He immediately set about a campaign which culminated in triumph three years later. He overturned a notional majority of 3,154 enjoyed by the Conservative incumbent of twenty-three years, Sir Colin Shepherd, with a Liberal Democrat majority of 6,648.

After entering Parliament, he was appointed Liberal Democrat employment and training spokesman and became a member of the House of Commons Education and Employment Select Committee and the Employment Sub-Committee. He serves on the Council of the Electoral Reform Society and is Secretary of the All-Party Electoral Reform Group.

On a matter more directly associated with Hereford, he is the founding chair of the House of Commons All-Party Cider Group, and has been instrumental in securing the sale of draught cider in the Commons bars – Hereford cider, of course!

Tudor Griffiths

CHARLES KENNEDY MP 1959–

Charles Kennedy was first elected as MP for Ross, Cromarty & Skye (now Ross, Skye & Inverness West) in 1983, a constituency he has held ever since despite boundary changes. Similar to many other areas in the Highlands, his seat had a long Liberal tradition, though it was represented by a Conservative and National Liberal member for most of the post-war period until the Liberals retook the seat in 1964 with the election of Alasdair MacKenzie.

Charles Peter Kennedy was born in Inverness on 25 November 1959, to Ian Kennedy, a crofter, and Mary MacEachen. Brought up in Fort William, he was educated at Lochaber High School and then studied politics and philosophy at Glasgow University, where he was President of Glasgow University Union and won the *Observer* Mace for debating. Following graduation in 1982, he worked briefly as a journalist at BBC Highland before gaining a Fulbright scholarship to study for a PhD at Indiana University in the US. He taught public speaking and carried out research in speech communication, political rhetoric and British politics.

Kennedy's entry into full-time politics was abrupt. At Easter 1983, he gained the SDP nomination for Ross, Cromarty & Skye, the largest constituency in Britain, and faced a quick election in June. As a first-time candidate, Kennedy was able to exploit his political skills, local roots and the popularity of the SDP generally to turn a Liberal vote of 13.9 per cent in 1979 into 38.5 per cent in 1983. He found himself swept into Westminster as the youngest MP, at the age of twenty-three, taking the seat from the Conservative Energy Minister, Hamish Gray.

Since then, Kennedy retained the seat fairly comfortably over the Conservatives in 1987 and 1992, before holding off a strong challenge by Labour's Donnie Munro, of the Gaelic rock group Runrig, in 1997.

At Westminster Kennedy has held a variety of posts. He was SDP spokesman on health, 1983–87; Alliance spokesman on social security, 1987; SDP spokesman on Scotland and social security, 1987–88; and following the merger, Liberal Democrat spokesman on health, 1989–92, and on European affairs, 1992–97. He is currently responsible for agriculture, fisheries, food and rural affairs. He was a member of the Select Committee on Health and Social Security 1985–86 and 1986–87, the Select Committee on Televising the House of Commons 1988–90, and currently serves on the Committee on Standards and Privileges. In 1989 he was accorded the 'Member to Watch' award by the *Spectator*.

However, it has been his media work rather than his parliamentary performances that had brought Kennedy to political prominence in Britain as a frequent contributor to current affairs programmes and commentator on TV and radio, culminating in an inevitable appearance on *Have I Got News For You*. Such activities gave him a continuous public profile which would have been impossible for an ordinary MP from a third party in the 1980s and 1990s, and provided the means for an alternative political career outside Westminster.

Kennedy was the first SDP MP to back merger with the Liberals after the 1987 election, and played an active role in the Liberal Democrats after merger. He was Federal President from 1990–94, and has been frequently tipped as a future leader of the party, but has showed few signs of seeking office despite rumours following Paddy

Ashdown's (*q.v.*) tenth anniversary as leader of the merged party. Similarly, Kennedy has not demonstrated any great desire for involvement in the Scottish Liberal Democrats, preferring the wider stage of Westminster, indicated by his decision to remain a Westminster MP rather than seek nomination to the Holyrood Parliament.

In terms of positioning within the Liberal Democrats, Kennedy is one of the MPs cautious about the party's involvement with the Labour government. Speaking at the spring party conference in 1998, Kennedy stated that 'There is a current of apprehension …. among the members that, while they favour, as I do, cooperation with the Labour Party and the Labour government over constitutional reform, they don't want that process to blunt our distinctive identity. We are an independent political party out to win votes and secure influence and power …. we have to be extremely careful about using words like coalition. It seems to me, in the present Parliament, with a vast Labour majority, that is, frankly, a non-starter.'

Peter Lynch

JOHN MAYNARD KEYNES (Lord Keynes)   1883–1946

Maynard Keynes was an active Liberal as well as one of the most important liberal writers of the twentieth century. He revolutionised economics, creating the case for deficit spending to stimulate employment which became the basis of government economic policy throughout the Western world for almost four decades. He helped to found the international economic institutions which played such a key role in the post-war economic boom.

Many of his views, however, would cause apoplexy in modern Liberal Democrats. For example, at a Liberal Summer School he gave an impassioned defence of privilege in general and inherited wealth in particular (so that there would be a leisured class able both to pursue politics, especially in opposing government, and also patronise the arts). Despite this belief in the necessity of private patronage to ensure cultural freedom, he was the founding father of the Arts Council. This was a development of his work with the Cambridge Arts Theatre (founded in 1936), where he was apparently as concerned that students should enjoy good champagne at low prices as with the more cultural aspects of the theatrical experience. This illustrates both Keynes' ability to be infuriating and apparently paradoxical, and a style that both charmed and irritated. He was also notoriously gay (later bisexual), which probably contributed to the reaction to him. Galbraith and others have told amusing anecdotes about the need to conceal many of Keynes' personality traits when his ideas were introduced to an American audience, and a similar coyness over Keynes' private life marked Harrod's *Life* (1951). Indeed, it is arguable that reactions to Keynes have more often reflected a reaction to his style and image rather than his ideas.

John Maynard Keynes was born into a traditional haute bourgeois Cambridge academic family on 5 June 1883. In a brilliant essay (1978), Harry Johnson argued that this was the key to Keynes' thought. He was an optimist who believed that government could solve all ills in the hands of the right people, preferably Cambridge-educated. By contrast, Milton Friedman was a pessimist as the scion of penniless emigrants from the Habsburg Empire. Certainly, such stylistic differences are probably as important as theoretical matters in understanding why Keynes and Friedman are the totems of rival economic camps. Keynes' review of Hayek's *Road to Serfdom* (1944), and his correspondence with the author, support this view.

Educated initially at Eton, Keynes graduated from Kings' College, Cambridge in 1906 after becoming a devotee of G. E. Moore's philosophy (like so many liberals and Liberals) and a member of what later became known as the Bloomsbury group. He entered the India Office but in 1908 became a Fellow of King's with the responsibility of teaching economics (established as a subject there in 1905). He worked on Indian finance and probability, where his writings are still highly regarded. He joined the Treasury in January 1915 and advised Lloyd George (*q.v.*) on war finance and at the Versailles peace settlement negotiations until his dramatic resignation over the terms of the settlement in 1919. Later that year he published *The Economic Consequences of the Peace.* This became a best seller, and largely contributed to the belief that Germany had been harshly treated at Versailles.

Most of Keynes' formal involvement with the Liberal Party came during this period. He was a pioneer of the Summer School movement and owner, eminence grise and much else of *The Nation*, which was central to Liberal thinking until its absorption into the *New Statesman* in 1931. He was part author of the 1929 Liberal manifesto and of the accompanying *Can Lloyd George Do It?* (which explained the Liberal Party's plans to cure unemployment). He soon after became an official adviser to the Labour government. As the consummate insider he had used his status (unsuccessfully) to try to persuade Churchill (*q.v.*) not to return to the gold standard.

During this period, he became an aggressive speculator. Initially, only a loan of £10,000 from his father saved him from bankruptcy. Thereafter, his success was legendary; on his own behalf and for King's and various insurance companies.

He edited the *Economic Journal* and published a *Tract on Monetary Reform* (1923) and the two-volume treatise *On Money* (1930), which are still regarded as his major works by many monetary economists. Thereafter he worked on what became *The General Theory of Employment, Interest and Money* (1936). This is frequently cited as having demonstrated that governments could and should manage the economy to eliminate unemployment, especially by running budget deficits. Others credit him with having invented macroeconomics. The book reads like a summary of all economics written subsequently. However, its very richness and fecundity has led to literally thousands of articles and books disputing its meaning. Once more, both its totemic significance to liberals and its impact on politicians and academics are undoubted, whatever either Keynes meant or said. Like Marx and the Bible, different interpretations and exegesis are tributes, not criticisms.

Keynes advised various Chancellors from 1940 until his death in 1946. He was largely responsible for both the creation of the International Monetary Fund and the World Bank in the aftermath of the Second World War, and also the decision to accept the American loan in 1946. This decision determined many aspects of policy for thirty years, in that it committed the UK to the American view of liberal international finance rather than policies which sustained autarky, socialism, imperialism or Japanese-style *dirigisme*.

He was created a peer in 1942, taking the title Baron Keynes of Tilton, and devoted his final speech to a denunciation of arrangements such as European monetary union. He died on 21 April 1946 at his home in Tilton, Sussex.

David Gowland

ARCHY KIRKWOOD MP   1946–

Archibald Johnstone Kirkwood, bee-keeper, lawyer and chemist, became the first MP for Roxburgh and Berwickshire in the election of 1983, when my seat of Roxburgh, Sekirk & Peebles was divided in two in the boundary changes.

A Glaswegian, he was born on 22 April 1946 to David and Jessie (née Barclay) Kirkwood. He went to Cranhill School, and then Heriot-Watt University, where he became the first sabbatical student union president. He graduated with a degree in pharmacy; he once claimed that he worked out, during a particularly tiresome House of Commons debate, that if he had stayed in his original chosen profession he would by then have made over two million suppositories.

Kirkwood became the first 'chocolate soldier' (Rowntree Trust fellow) as assistant to the Liberal Chief Whip in 1970, and subsequently resigned his membership of the Labour Party. He married Rosemary Chester in 1972, then Secretary to the Young Liberals; the couple now have one daughter, Holly, and one son, Cameron. They moved to Ettrick Bridge in the Borders, and he began a career as a solicitor, becoming a partner in a firm in Hawick. He assisted me in the two elections of 1974 and returned as the leader's assistant in 1978 during the Lib-Lab Pact. He helped in the May 1979 election, and was adopted as prospective candidate for Berwick & East Lothian in 1980.

He accompanied me on a visit to South Africa and Rhodesia in 1979, when we were memorably arrested on leaving Salisbury airport (having entered by the back door from South Africa). I was declared a prohibited immigrant by Ian Smith's regime. Our bags were searched, some of my documents photocopied, and a Rhodesian telephone directory purloined by Kirkwood from a hotel removed from his luggage as a 'classified document'.

After the boundary changes he fought the 1983 election on the issues of depopulation and the lack of industrial development in the region – the government had removed assisted area status for the region a month before the general election. He defeated the Conservative junior minister, Ian Sproat, who had moved from the marginal Aberdeen South constituency to a 'more winnable' seat (the Conservatives held Aberdeen South). He has held Roxburgh & Berwickshire at each of the three following elections with a steadily increasing percentage of the vote.

After the 1983 election, Kirkwood became Liberal spokesman on social security, adding health and social services in 1985. His impressive command of the technicalities of social security legislation and NHS reform helped the Liberal Party, and the Alliance, to establish a high level of credibility amongst the relevant professions and pressure groups at a time of sweeping government reforms. He was one of the first MPs to raise the issue of AIDS, and its implications for government policy, in Parliament, and is now joint Vice Chair of the All-Party AIDS group.

At the September 1986 Liberal Assembly, he was one of three MPs, along with Michael Meadowcroft (q.v.) and Simon Hughes (q.v.), to vote for the amendment to the Alliance report on defence policy expressing opposition to the development of European cooperation over nuclear weapons.

In 1987, he became the Alliance's spokesman on overseas development, building on a long-standing personal interest in the area; he had visited Ethiopia during the famine of the early '80s. From 1987 to 1988 he was the Scottish Whip; in 1988 he fought and lost the election for the Scottish Liberal Democrats' leadership against Malcolm Bruce (q.v.). In 1989 he moved back to the area of his original portfolio and particular expertise as convenor of the Liberal Democrat welfare team. For the whole of the 1992–97 Parliament Kirkwood was a popular and able Liberal Democrat Chief Whip. After the 1997 election he achieved the notable feat of becoming the first Liberal Democrat chairman of a Select Committee, namely Social Security.

Kirkwood also has two Acts on the Statute Book which he sponsored as a private member. He secured the passage of the Access to Personal Files Act in May 1987, followed by the Access to Medical Reports Act the following year. He has been a trustee of the Joseph Rowntree Reform Trust since 1985. His pastimes include skiing, photography and riding – a useful skill in a Borders MP, given the 'common ridings' which take place in most Borders towns, a relic of the days when the town boundaries needed to be checked for English incursions. He is also an enthusiast for information technology, being one of the earliest MPs to acquire a computer – though it sat largely unused on his desk until a new researcher found the time to read the manual.

David Steel

WALLACE LAWLER   1912–72

Wallace Lawler's key contribution to Liberalism was his active involvement in 'pavement' (later referred to as 'community') politics. Against a background of redevelopment (which resulted in the electorate of his parliamentary constituency of Birmingham Ladywood falling to 20,000 by the late 1960s), Lawler involved himself in the problems which local people faced in the vast social upheavals caused by new housing development, particularly the destruction of local communities. He was a champion of the underprivileged (especially the elderly) and fully supported direct action as a means of ameliorating social disadvantage such as homelessness. His local activity showed that electoral successes could be secured by intense local campaigning at local government level, and helped to popularise such activity throughout the Liberal Party.

Wallace Leslie Lawler was born at Worcester on 15 March 1912, the son of Stephen Lawler and Elizabeth Lawler (née Taylor). He was educated at St Paul's School, Worcester, and privately. He became actively engaged in youth work, establishing the Worcester Boys' Club in 1928. He moved to Birmingham in 1938 to train as an aircraft engineer, but on the outbreak of war joined the 8th Battalion of the Worcestershire Regiment. He was associated with a wide range of organisations, founding the Public Opinion Action Association in 1943. He was additionally Chairman of the Homeless Bureau (1956–72), the Wallace Lawler Friendship Trust (1969) and Citizens' Service Ltd (1970). His business interests were in the plastics industry, and he was chairman of ABCD Plastics.

In 1962 Lawler became the first Liberal elected to Birmingham City Council for twenty-nine years. He was re-elected for the Newtown ward in 1965 and 1968 and became an alderman in 1971. He served as leader of the Liberal Group on Birmingham City Council 1968–72. He served in a number of local Liberal offices, including Chairman of the Birmingham Liberal Organisation, the Birmingham Liberal Federation and President of the Birmingham Liberal Association.

He first stood for Parliament at Dudley in 1955, and then fought Birmingham Perry Barr in 1959, Birmingham Handsworth in 1964 and Birmingham Ladywood in 1966. He was elected to Parliament at a byelection in Ladywood in 1969, becoming the first Liberal returned to Parliament for the city since 1896. He lost the seat in the following year's general election. While a member of the House of Commons he served on the Select Committee on Race Relations and Immigration, and was the party's spokesman on housing and the Home Office.

Lawler was active in national Liberal politics, serving as Vice-Chairman of the Liberal Party Council (1967) and Vice-President of the Liberal Party Executive (1968). He was a controversial figure. His scepticism of the pre-eminence traditionally accorded to parliamentary politics by the Liberal Party was shared by a large number of Young Liberal activists in the late 1960s. However, his views concerning immigration (which ranged from the advocacy of a policy of dispersal to suggesting that most categories of immigrants should be prevented from settling in Birmingham) caused dissension both locally and nationally.

He married Catherine Letitia Duncan in 1943, and had two sons and two daughters. He died in Birmingham on 28 September 1972. His publications included *Pensions for All* (1958) and *The Truth About Cathy* (1968).

Peter Joyce

WALTER LAYTON (Lord Layton) 1884–1966

Walter Layton, like Maynard Keynes (*q.v.*) and William Beveridge (*q.v.*), was one of those great Liberals whose gifts, larger than party, left an enduring mark on the first half of the twentieth century despite their party's eclipse.

Born in Chelsea, on 15 March 1884, into a non-conformist family of musicians, Layton earned his way through a series of schools – St George's Chapel, Windsor, the Temple and Westminster City School – mainly by singing in the choir. After studying at University College, London, and winning an exhibition to Trinity College, Cambridge, he went on to teach in the infant faculty of economics at Cambridge under the wing of Alfred Marshall and alongside Maynard Keynes. While Keynes' intellect soared into the realms of economic theory, Layton lectured on industry, developed useful new statistics and explored practical policies for reform. His first book, *An Introduction to the Study of Prices* (1912), showed the young economist's firm analytical grasp; the philosophy which was to guide his life was summed up in a phrase in a letter to his sister: how can I help?

At Cambridge he met, taught and married Dorothy Osmaston, his life-long partner, and they shared in the intellectual discovery of the times, attending Fabian meetings and walking to London with the suffragettes. Layton also began his life-long practice of doing several jobs at once, lecturing with the Workers' Educational Association and writing each week for the *Economist*, then a specialised city magazine with a circulation of only 4,000.

When war broke out the able young dons, deeply sympathetic to the reforming Liberal government of the time, brought the analytical skills of their new discipline into the heart of government. In 1915, Layton became Director, Requirements and Programmes in the new Ministry of Munitions, first under Lloyd George (*q.v.*) and then Churchill (*q.v.*). He acted, in practice, as both a personal assistant to the minister and as chairman of the committee which planned the nation's economy. One of several life-long partnerships formed then was with a young Frenchman, Jean Monnet, who played a key role in persuading France of the need for systematic wartime planning. Layton also travelled to Washington (with the Balfour mission) to negotiate and finance the Allies' vast arms purchases, and to Moscow (with the Milner mission) on the eve of revolution.

After a brief post-war spell as Director of the Iron and Steel Federation, Layton became editor of the *Economist* from 1921–38, then Chairman and later Vice-Chairman until his death. Under his editorship the magazine's circulation rose to 10,000 and gained greatly in authority and breadth as Layton brought in much new talent and established a new financial structure, and the Trust which continues to guarantee editorial independence.

Layton moved into the mainstream of daily journalism in 1930 when, with the financial backing of the Cadbury family, he negotiated the merger of the *Daily News*, *Westminster Gazette* and *Daily Chronicle* to create the *News Chronicle*, which he led as Chairman. With its circulation of a million and a half and its team of committed journalists, its radical voice became a beacon, not only for British liberals and social democrats, but for all, throughout Europe, who craved a just peace through collective security and the League of Nations.

Widely trusted, Layton undertook several tasks for the government: as an adviser at the Versailles peace conference; as a mediator trying to renegotiate the burdensome reparations placed on Weimar Germany; as financial assessor to the Simon Commission on India in 1928; and as one of the architects of the Bank for International Settlements in 1929. As an economic adviser to the League of Nations he worked continually to bring down the trade barriers created in 1918 which were stifling the economic life of Europe. In 1931, he was entrusted by the British government with abortive but prophetic negotiations to create a European customs union.

Though Layton was not primarily a politician, he stood three times unsuccessfully as a Liberal candidate for Parliament, at Burnley in 1922, Cardiff South in 1923, and for the London University seat in 1929. He polled over a quarter of the vote on each occasion, but was never close to victory. He responded enthusiastically to the idea of the Liberal Summer School and was for several years Chairman of the Executive Committee, Director and later President, bringing to it an indispensable international dimension. At the invitation of Lloyd George, he chaired and guided the star-studded group of committees which produced the Liberal Yellow Book in 1928.

Layton was recalled by Churchill to Whitehall in the Second World War and became Director of Programmes, Ministry of Supply and later Head of the Joint War Planning Staff. He visited the United States (where he worked once more with Monnet) to negotiate arms procurement and lend-lease and brought to bear his skill and experience in strategic transatlantic planning. But he left the public service in 1943 to make time to plan the peace. In his Sidney Ball lectures of that year he spelt out the theme of a united Europe which was to become central to the rest of his life. He was a vigorous participant in the economic debates of the Hague Congress which founded the European Movement in 1948, and, as the only Liberal in the British delegation to the first Assembly of the Council of Europe in 1949, was elected Vice-President of the Assembly.

Layton, who had been made a Companion of Honour in 1918, was made Baron Layton of Dane Hill in 1946 'for public services'. He became Liberal economic spokesman in the Lords and, from 1952–55, served as Deputy Leader of the Liberal peers.

A sensitive and kind man, Layton's integrity and capacity for seeing all points of view made him a deeply respected chairman, mediator and employer. In his heyday of the 1930s his strong mind, practical idealism and appetite for work made him an effective match for his Tory competitors in Fleet Street. He had a natural authority which sprang from his mental powers, determination and commitment to the public good.

His last years were darkened by the financial failure and sale of the *News Chronicle* in 1960 and by the death from cancer of his wife the preceding year. This tragedy inspired him to write *Dorothy*, a book about her death, their love and her life of public service. It revealed the hidden passionate side of this thoughtful man. He and Dorothy had seven childen and many grandchildren. Active to the last, Layton died in Putney in 1966. His abundant life is best described in David Hubback's biography, *No Ordinary Press Baron*.

Christopher Layton

ANTHONY LESTER (Lord Lester) 1936–

Liberalism and liberal democracy emphasise the high value of individual human rights, civil liberties and justice. It is hardly surprising, then, that many of the UK's leading human rights and constitutional lawyers are members of the Liberal Democrats, but few are more active or influential than Lord Lester of Herne Hill QC. Yet Lester, who became a life peer in 1993, started his political career not in the Liberal Party but as the Labour candidate in the Conservative stronghold of Worthing.

Born on 3 July 1936 in South London of a liberal Jewish family, Anthony Paul Lester was educated at the City of London School, before graduating with a BA in history from Trinity College, Cambridge, from whence he went on to Harvard Law School. He was called to the bar in 1963. His attempt to gain elected office at the 1966 general election was unsuccessful, and Lester has not contested a public election since.

Instead, throughout the 1960s and '70s, Lester wrote extensively on public law issues, particularly gender and race equality and human rights. As his legal reputation grew, so he gained political stature and influence. By 1974, at the age of only thirty-eight, he had already taken cases to the House of Lords and the English Court of Appeal, when he was appointed special adviser on human rights to the then Home Secretary, Roy Jenkins (*q.v.*). A year later, he became special adviser to the Standing Advisory Commission on Human Rights for Northern Ireland.

Taking into account Lester's strong political allegiances with Jenkins and with his then rabbi, Julia Neuberger, it is hardly surprising that he was amongst the first to join the newly formed SDP, becoming Area Convenor for Southwark in the heady days of 1981.

Having taken silk in 1975, Lester was, by the 1980s, probably the best-known human rights lawyer in the UK, frequently appearing in the European Courts of Justice and of Human Rights. Many of his cases struck at the heart of the political agenda, including those of the East African Asians expelled from Uganda, the Royal Ulster Constabulary discrimination case, *Spycatcher* and, more recently, Lord Tolstoy's libel action.

His vast experience of the legal system made him a frequent informal adviser to politicians and civil servants of all complexions, although throughout he remained a member of the SDP, and then the Liberal Democrats after merger. Increasingly, he found himself drawn into public policy debates, chairing the Institute for Public Policy Research's judiciary working group on a British Bill of Rights in 1990, as well as the Hansard Society's commission, 'Women at the Top', in the same year.

As a Liberal Democrat peer, he has played an active role in the work of the House of Lords, particularly in its scrutiny of European institutions and legislation. Despite his political allegiances, however, Lester has continued to work closely with a range of progressive political organisations and parties. Currently, he is an honorary professor of Public Law at University College London and president of the United Nations Association. In 1997, he was acclaimed Human Rights Lawyer of the Year.

He lives in Herne Hill with his wife Katya whom he married in 1971; they have two grown-up children.

Ben Rich

GORDON LISHMAN   1947–

The late 1960s were generally a gloomy period for the Liberal Party. However, during this period the Young Liberals, following their triumph at the 'Red Guard' party assembly in 1965, developed into one of the main groups of thinkers and doers within the party. Gordon Lishman emerged as a prime thinker (and activist) within the YLs. It was he who wrote and summed up on the famous community politics resolution at the 1970 Eastbourne assembly. He has been a strong and continuing force ever since.

Arthur Gordon Lishman was born in Bolton on 29 November 1947, the son of a Liberal family. Educated at Colne Grammar School, he took a degree in economics at Manchester University. After graduating, he worked for the Liberal Party until 1972, firstly in the Research Department, focusing on economic and industrial affairs. He then became one of the party's community politics and local government officers, charged with improving party organisation in Tyne & Wear, West Yorkshire, Greater Manchester and Dorset for the 1973 re-organised local government elections. This entailed charging about the country in a little orange mini-van, which, appropriately or not, had the registration letters 'WAR'.

Despite his deep understanding of the concept and practice of community politics, Lishman has amiably led a peripatetic lifestyle ever since. He joined Age Concern England in 1974 as an area field officer, rising to its Operations Director responsible for the successful development of the federal Age Concern movement into the largest charitable operation in the UK. His role has now become increasingly lofty, dealing with government and policy matters.

Lishman first joined the Liberal Party in March 1963, at the tender age of fifteen, and has had a national involvement in it and its successor since 1968. His YL roles included Organising Vice-Chair, National League of Young Liberals and Union of Liberal Students, and Political Vice-Chair, NLYL. Since then he has been at various times Director of Policy Promotion for the party; Returning Officer, President, and Chair of the Association of Liberal Councillors (of which he was a founder member); Chair of the Association of Liberal Democrat Councillors; Vice-Chair, Liberal Democrat constitutional review; joint editor, 1998 policy review, and Chair of the International Relations Committee.

Partly as a consequence of his peripatetic lifestyle, Lishman has only once been successful in real elections. He was elected to Northamptonshire County Council in 1981 and became balance-of-power group leader and Chair of the Policy Review Committee. But this only lasted two years until the pressures of his job and single parenthood forced him to resign. In parliamentary elections he has stood four times – twice in Bradford North (February and October 1974) and twice in Pendle (1983 and 1987), coming third on every occasion.

The main contribution Lishman has made to the Liberal Party and Liberal Democrats has been largely behind the scenes. His service on the various committees of both parties has been important in influencing both the direction and style of liberal politics. Perhaps the most important of his publications to date is *The Theory and Practice of Community Politics* (1980), a relatively short ALC pamphlet written jointly with Bernard Greaves (*q.v.*). Despite its brevity it was, and remains, the best and most effective definition of what community politics is all about.

His other publications include: *Trade Unions after Donovan, The Best of Both Worlds* and *A Redefinition of Retirement* (Liberal Party Organisation); 'Community Politics', an essay in *Scarborough Perspectives* (Bernard Greaves (ed.), 1971); 'Framework for Community Politics', an essay in *Community Politics* (Peter Hain (ed.), 1976); and *Democrats or Drones?* (with Tony Greaves (*q.v.*), 1987). He has also been at various times editor of *Liberator* and *New Outlook* and was a member of the *Radical Bulletin* collective.

Democrats or Drones?, with the sub-title *A party which belongs to its members*, was written for the 1987 Liberal assembly in Harrogate when 'The Future Strategy of the Liberal Party' was debated in the run-up to merger with the SDP. It was written from an unashamedly Liberal standpoint and formed an important contribution to the debate and thereby to the future of Liberalism – at least in terms of which party was to retain and espouse its philosophy.

Lishman's other political (and wider) area of great interest and involvement is internationalism. He has long participated in Liberal International and European Liberal, Democrat and Reform Party activities. Through his work in the field of ageing and older people, he has built up an impressive range of consultancy, policy and conference work throughout the world. In 1993 he was awarded the OBE.

In amongst all this wide-ranging activity Lishan has found time to get married three times – to Beverley Witham, 1968; Stephanie (Steve) Allison-Beer, 1973; and Margaret Brodie-Brown (née Long), 1988. His family, of whom he is immensely fond, Christopher (born 1976), Philippa (1978) and step-daughter Katie Brodie-Brown (1982) continue to play a crucial role in his life. He also claims to have spare time, although his hobbies have changed over the years. In 1980 they were listed as gardening and writing constitutions, but he now suggests they are reading books, eating, drinking and decorating. In truth, his main spare-time occupation is, and nearly always has been, reading books. The length and breadth of his reading and the knowledge and the information he has so acquired is truly impressive.

John Smithson

RICHARD LIVSEY MP   1935–

Richard Arthur Lloyd Livsey was born on 2 May 1935, the son of Arthur Norman Livsey and Lilian Maisie (née James). He was educated at Talgarth County Primary School, Bedales School, Seale-Hayne Agricultural College, and Reading University (MSc in agricultural management). On 3 April 1964 he married Irene, the daughter of Ronald and Margaret Earsman of Castle Douglas, Galloway. They have two sons and one daughter.

Livsey served as an agricultural development officer for ICI from 1961–67, and as farm manager on the Blairdrummond Estate, Perthshire, 1967–71. He was senior lecturer in farm management at the Welsh Agricultural College, Llanbadarn Fawr (near Aberystwyth) from 1971–85. Later, in his temporary absence from Parliament in 1992–97, he became Deputy Director, then Development Manager, of ATB-Landbase Cymru.

Livsey first joined the Liberal Party in 1960. He stood unsuccessfully as the party's candidate for Perth & East Perthshire in 1970, Pembroke in 1979, and Brecon & Radnor in 1983. He entered the Commons as Liberal MP for the highly marginal Brecon & Radnor at a byelection on 4 July 1985 following the death of the Conservative MP Tom Hooson. He was re-elected in the 1987 general election. He served as Liberal spokesman on agriculture 1985–87, as Alliance spokesman on agriculture and the countryside, 1987, and as Liberal Democrat spokesman on Welsh affairs 1988–92. He was the Leader of the Welsh Liberal Democrats from 1988 until 1992.

In the 1992 general election, Livsey was narrowly defeated by Conservative Jonathan Evans, who captured Brecon & Radnor by the tiny majority of 130 votes. Five years later, following a dynamic local campaign based on support for public services, small businesses and farms, Livsey was able to recapture the seat by the impressive margin of more than 5,000 votes to become one of forty-six Liberal Democrat MPs in the new Parliament.

Immediately following his re-election, he was appointed a member of the Welsh Affairs Select Committee and of the Constitutional Reform Strategy Committee. He is the Liberal Democrat spokesman for Wales and, once again, the Leader of the Welsh Liberal Democrats. He was awarded the CBE in 1994. He lives at Llanfiliangel Tal-y-Llyn near Brecon.

J. Graham Jones

DAVID LLOYD GEORGE   1863–1945
(Earl Lloyd-George and Viscount Gwynedd)

Lloyd George, according to Winston Churchill after his death, 'was the greatest Welshman which that unconquerable race has produced since the age of the Tudors'. Yet he was born in England at 5 New York Place, Robert Street, Chorlton-upon-Medlock, Manchester on 17 January 1863.

His parents, William George, a school teacher, and Elizabeth Lloyd, a domestic servant then lady's companion, moved back to Wales when he was four months old. On his father dying of pneumonia on 7 June 1864, his mother returned to Llanystumdwy, her birthplace, and they lived with her mother and brother, Richard, depending on £50 per annum from William George's estate and on the family shoemaking business (which was maintained until 1880). Richard Lloyd, like his father, was the unpaid lay pastor for the Baptist sect, the Disciples of Christ, and was the major early influence on David. He was educated at Llanystumdwy's school.

From July 1878 Lloyd George worked for a solicitor, qualifying as a solicitor himself six years later. In 1885 he set up his own practice, joined by his brother William from mid-1887. His brother's diligence enabled Lloyd George to enter local politics, and he made his name as a solicitor, lay preacher and temperance lecturer. He was active on behalf of many of the pressure groups which formed a part of Welsh Liberalism: the Liberation Society, the Farmers' Union and the Anti-Tithe League (being secretary of its South Carnarvonshire branch). He was selected as candidate for Carnarvon Boroughs in January 1889, winning it by eighteen votes in a byelection in April 1890. He held the constituency at every general election from then until he was elevated to the House of Lords in the New Year Honours List, 1945. From 1889 until his death he was an alderman on Carnarvonshire county council.

Lloyd George was a backbencher until he entered Sir Henry Campbell-Bannerman's (*q.v.*) government on 10 December 1905. During this time he successfully came to prominence as a nonconformist politician, playing a major role in opposing the Conservative Education Bill of 1902, and as a Radical, not least in his opposition to the Boer War. As President of the Board of Trade (1905–08) he brought in legislation which assisted British business, and displayed considerable skills in offering conciliation in industrial disputes, most notably in averting a national rail dispute in 1907.

When Asquith (*q.v.*) became Prime Minister, Lloyd George succeeded him on 12 April 1908 as Chancellor of the Exchequer (1908–15). In this post Lloyd George established himself as a dynamic, radical force in the government. With Asquith, Churchill (*q.v.*) and Masterman, he introduced the major Liberal social reforms: old age pensions (1908) and National Insurance (1911). He also brought in the means to pay for these measures as well as for naval rearmament in his 1909 'People's Budget'. This offered non-socialist, free trade finance. Its rejection by the House of Lords led to a constitutional crisis and two general elections in 1910. These were followed by the substantial curtailment of the Lords' veto, leaving the way open for progress to be made on Home Rule for Ireland. During 1909–14, while some other colleagues became defeatist, Lloyd George remained innovative in policy, pressing ahead not only with National Insurance but launching in 1913 his land campaign, which proved to have some electoral appeal to rural workers.

Before the outbreak of war in 1914 Lloyd George had been a notable opponent of the Boer War and of high levels of military or naval spending, clashing notably with

Winston Churchill over the Admiralty's estimates in December 1913. However, in 1911 over the crisis arising from a German gunboat going to Agadir, Morocco, Lloyd George gave Germany a firm warning that a united Britain would not support 'peace at any price' if her interests were 'vitally affected'. In August 1914, after hesitation, Lloyd George supported the war and as Chancellor of the Exchequer he had to find the financial means to wage it.

He became increasingly concerned at the slowness of expansion of munitions supplies. This led him on 25 May 1915 to become Minister of Munitions (1915–16), a post in which he displayed his dynamism and his negotiating skills in industrial relations. He also became associated with demands for conscription and a more thorough organisation of the country for the war, thereby outraging some of his former supporters but winning admiration, at first reluctant, from many Conservatives. After the Easter Rising in Dublin in 1916 Lloyd George came near to achieving an Irish settlement. On 6 July 1916 he succeeded the deceased Kitchener as Secretary of State for War. In the autumn, Lloyd George's pressure for more effective control of the war by a small committee resulted in a political crisis and Asquith's resignation as Prime Minister. Lloyd George had long struggled to establish himself as crown prince, though while he wished to succeed Asquith eventually, it is unlikely that at this specific time (early December 1916) he intended to oust him.

Lloyd George was Prime Minister from 6 December 1916 until 19 October 1922. Both during the war and after, he was dependent on multi-party support. In 1916–18 his government, like Asquith's 1915–16 coalition, included Liberals, Labour and Conservatives. His post-war government, however, depended on most Conservatives and some Liberals, with Labour the largest party in opposition (even if not formally given the title of H. M. Opposition until 1922). The division of the Liberal Party in 1916 might not have had serious consequences had it reunited before the 1918 general election.

Lloyd George's wartime government built on the changes in organisation under way during Asquith's premiership. He instituted a small War Cabinet of five to seven members, setting up an efficient Cabinet secretariat, creating new ministries and bringing into office businessmen (his 'men of push and go'). Lloyd George was shocked by the continuing scale of the deaths for little advantage on the Western Front, notably at Passchendaele in 1917, and tried to oust Generals Robertson and Haig. He succeeded in replacing Robertson but had not the political support to remove Haig, whose approach eventually succeeded from August 1918. Lloyd George showed courage and resourcefulness during 1916–18, and emerged in the popular press as 'The Man Who Won The War'. In December 1918 he also won a massive victory in the 'coupon election', in which all the leading Liberals associated with Asquith were not endorsed by the coalition leadership and lost their seats.

Lloyd George's post-war coalition government was supported by 335 coalition Conservatives (a further 23 Conservatives giving that party a majority in the House of Commons on its own), 133 coalition Liberals and 10 coalition Labour. As a result he was dependent on Conservative support, and it is all the more surprising that the Conservatives did not dispense with him sooner than October 1922.

The pinnacle of Lloyd George's career was the peace-making at Paris in the first half of 1919, leading to the Treaty of Versailles, signed on 28 June 1919. While rightly criticised in many aspects (such as the 'war guilt' clause, the scale of reparations and many boundaries), Lloyd George tilted the settlement in a more Liberal direction than Clemenceau or much of the Conservative Party wished. The remainder of his premiership was notable for a series of international conferences, but in these he was unsuccessful in overcoming French obduracy over Germany, bringing Soviet Russia back into European trade or on disarmament. His confrontation with Turkey in support of the Greeks in Asia Minor (the Chanak crisis) in the autumn of 1922 damaged his standing in Parliament and contributed to his downfall.

Lloyd George's post-war government was faced with massive demobilisation problems and a desire to decontrol the wartime economy and carry out substantial social reconstruction. During the post-war boom (1919–20) some progress was made with his election promise of 23 November 1918 to make Britain 'a fit country for heroes to live in'. In addition to the important Education Act 1918, passed before the war had ended, substantial numbers of houses were built (albeit at a high cost) under the Housing and Town Planning Act 1919, the Unemployment Insurance Act 1920 extended coverage to a further eight million people, and there were further extensions of pre-war Liberal measures under the Old Age Pensions Act 1919 and the National Health Insurance Act 1920. Two of Lloyd George's long-term causes were tackled with the disestablishment of the Welsh Church in August 1919 and the passage that month of the Land Settlement Facilities Act.

However, in December 1919 the government's adoption of the recommendations of the Cunliffe Committee on Currency and Foreign Exchanges after the War to deflate the economy in order to return sterling to the gold standard at its pre-war parity, combined with middle-class electoral revolts (in favour of 'anti-waste' candidates) in byelections and a severe economic recession from the end of 1920, doomed further reconstruction. The end was marked by the 'Geddes axe' in 1922, severe cuts in public expenditure following the recommendations of a Committee on National Expenditure made up of businessmen which partially undid many of the 1918–20 reforms.

Many policies carried out by the post-war coalition government appalled many of Lloyd George's old radical supporters. They had been affronted during the war by his enthusiasm for conscription, his intolerance of conscientious objectors and his breaking with Asquith in favour of working with Conservatives, not least with figures such as the Ulster Unionist leader Sir Edward Carson, and imperial proconsuls such as Lord Milner. After 1918, they were further outraged by the intervention against the Bolsheviks in Russia, the Black and Tan and other atrocities in Ireland, the support of some coalition supporters for General Dyer after the Amritsar massacre of April 1919 and by much of the tough action against trade unions and the scaremongering of 'red revolution in Britain'. More generally, Lloyd George's undoubted skills at negotiating settlements in industrial relations, or appearing to resolve conflict in Ireland for over forty years, had a down-side, in that his wizardry was increasingly deemed to be close to duplicity. Moreover, the sale of honours – not unknown to the main parties – became a matter of ill-repute under his premiership, partly because the money went to the Premier's own Liberal coalition group, and partly because of the scale of the trade and the fact that wealthy people deemed highly unsuitable were being proposed.

Long before the collapse of the coalition in October 1922, the Conservative Party's rank and file had become increasingly hostile to its continuation. Although most of the leading Conservatives in the coalition remained loyal to Lloyd George, the majority of Conservative MPs did not. Lloyd George left office for good. In the 1922 general election he was left high and dry, unable to attack vigorously his former colleagues. He declared he would 'support any party and any government that pursues a policy of peace, of economy, of steady progress, neither revolution nor reaction, and does it efficiently....' Nevertheless, sixty-two National Liberals were returned to fifty-four independent Liberals (and 142 Labour).

The bid for tariffs by the Conservative Prime Minister Stanley Baldwin in the December 1923 general election reunited the Liberals in defence of free trade. Lloyd George was deputy leader to Asquith until 1926, when there were further divisions over the General Strike. On Asquith's resignation in October, Lloyd George became Liberal leader until 1931.

During the 1920s, he was more alert to new ideas than most other Liberal leaders; as Charles Masterman admitted, 'I've fought him as hard as anyone but I have to confess, when Lloyd George came back to the party, ideas came back to the party'. He used his political funds (derived from the sale of honours) to finance major policy studies, beginning with *The Land and the Nation* and *Towns and the Land* (both 1925) as the basis for his new land campaign. The Liberal Industrial Inquiry (1926–28) involved many of the liveliest Liberal minds, including J. M. Keynes (*q.v.*), Ramsay Muir (*q.v.*), Walter Layton (*q.v.*), E. D. Simon (*q.v.*) and Lloyd George himself, and was published as *Britain's Industrial Future* (1928). A major theme was highlighted in the 1929 pamphlet, *We Can Conquer Unemployment*. In the 1929 general election the Liberal vote increased from the 2.9 million of 1924 to 5.3 million, with the number of MPs rising from forty to fifty-nine. Lloyd George generally supported the second Labour government (1929–31) but chafed at its timidity over unemployment. However, Liberal MPs sympathetic to the Conservatives increasingly went their own way. In July 1931 Lloyd George was taken seriously ill, needing a prostate operation, and was out of circulation during the 1931 political crisis and the formation of the National Government.

Between 1931 and 1935, Lloyd George was an independent Liberal MP, supported only by a small family group of MPs. From 1933 he tried to mobilise the remaining forces of nonconformity and Liberal opinion, pressing for his own 'New Deal' in the 1935 general election. Much of his energy in the 1930s went into foreign affairs. While briefly impressed by Hitler after a 1936 visit to Germany, he became increasingly alarmed by the fascist dictators over Spain, Abyssinia and Munich. In declining health (and possibly morale), the ageing Lloyd George declined Churchill's 1940 offers of being Food Controller or ambassador in Washington. Terminally ill with cancer but still hoping to speak on the peace-making, he accepted an earldom in 1945. He died, as Earl Lloyd-George of Dwyfor and Viscount Gwynedd, on 26 March

1945, and was buried by the river Dwyfor on the edge of Llanystumdwy.

He was married twice, first to Margaret Owen (1866–1941), later Dame Margaret Lloyd George, on 24 January 1888. She became a major figure in her North Wales community, being much involved in various charities, a founder of Criccieth Women's Institute, a member and for three years chair of Criccieth Urban District Council, and president of the Women's Liberal Federation of North and South Wales; but she declined invitations from elsewhere to be a Liberal Parliamentary candidate. They had four children, of whom two, Gwilym (*q.v.*) and Megan (*q.v.*), became MPs. He married his second wife, Frances Stevenson (1888–1972) on 23 October 1943, though they had had a long and steady relationship since early 1913.

Lloyd George published *War Memoirs* (6 vols, 1933–36) and *The Truth About the Peace Treaties* (2 vols, 1938) as well as several volumes of speeches, the most substantial being *Better Times* (1910) and *Through Terror to Triumph* (1915).

At present there are three volumes of John Grigg's excellent biography: *The Young Lloyd George* (1973), *Lloyd George: The People's Champion, 1902–11* (1978) and *Lloyd George: From Peace to War, 1912–1916* (1985). There are so far two volumes of Bentley B. Gilbert's substantial biography, *David Lloyd George: A Political Life* (1987 and 1992). The best single-volume biography is Peter Rowland, *Lloyd George* (1975). For short biographies see Kenneth O. Morgan, *Lloyd George* (1974), Martin Pugh, *Lloyd George* (1988) and Chris Wrigley, *Lloyd George* (1992).

Chris Wrigley

GWILYM LLOYD-GEORGE (Viscount Tenby)   1894–1967

In 1954 Gwilym Lloyd-George commented: 'Politicians are like monkeys. The higher they climb, the more revolting are the parts they expose'. This would seem a surprising remark to come from a Home Secretary; and an even more surprising one from the son of an arch-monkey, David Lloyd George (*q.v.*). However his own career, despite moving from being a radical Liberal to a Conservative, and the addition of a hyphen to his surname, seems to have aroused little hostility in others. This reflected his greater concern with administration and substantive issues than with the game of politics.

Lloyd-George was born, the fourth child of David and Margaret Lloyd George, on 4 December 1894 in Criccieth. Like his sister Megan (*q.v.*) he experienced some hostility at private school (Eastbourne College) for his father's radical rhetoric in 1909–11. Eastbourne was followed by Jesus College, Cambridge, of which, in 1953, he became an honorary fellow.

During the First World War, Lloyd-George rose to be a major on the Western Front in the 38th (Welsh) Division, seeing action at the Somme and Passchendaele. His letters informed his father of the scarcity of ammunition at the front. After the war he joined his father for the Versailles Conference, and he later accompanied his father on the infamous Bertschgaden visit. However neither experience seems to have given rise to a great interest in diplomacy. After his return from Versailles he married Edna Gwenfron (1921), with whom he had two children.

Lloyd-George was first elected to the Commons in 1922, as National Liberal member for Pembrokeshire with a 11,866 majority over Labour. He repeated this victory in 1923, but, like many others, was swept away by the Conservative avalanche of 1924. However, he regained the seat in 1929 – joining Malcolm MacDonald and Oliver Baldwin as a triumvirate of party leaders' sons in the House – and continued to hold Pembrokeshire until 1950. From 1951 until his elevation to the Lords in 1957 he represented Newcastle-upon-Tyne North.

Lloyd-George's first significant political post was as a junior Liberal Whip during the first minority Labour administration in 1923–24. During his five years outside the Commons, his father made him Managing Director of United Newspapers (publisher of *The Daily Chronicle*) and a trustee of the National Liberal Political Fund (formerly the Lloyd George Fund). Lloyd-George's resignation from the newspaper in 1926 coincided with paternal criticism for 'indolence'. However, although their characters were very different – Gwilym a mild (and humorous) breeze to David's tempest – relations with his father were generally congenial.

Their affinity during the 1930s is demonstrated by Lloyd-George's willingness to leave his first government post after one month in 1931, a decision taken before consulting his (approving) father. Lloyd-George joined MacDonald's National Government in September as Parliamentary Secretary to the Board of Trade. He quit on 8 October after the calling of the general election, and subsequently opposed both the Simonite Liberals, for their acceptance of a tariff, and the Samuelites, who opposed a tariff but believed it could best be fought from within the government. During the 1930s Lloyd-George was aligned to the Lloyd George family group of Liberals, along with his father, sister and Goronwy Owen. However, in 1938 David Lloyd George accurately predicted that 'Gwilym will go to the right and Megan to the left', and the start of the war marked the end of Lloyd-George's career as a Liberal in anything but name.

In 1939, Lloyd-George returned to his old post as Parliamentary Secretary to the Board of Trade. From February 1941 until June 1942, he was Parliamentary Secretary at the Ministry of Food. He was then given the newly-created but important position of Minister for Fuel and Power. His key task was to tackle the crisis apparently developing in the coal industry, involving static demand and declining supply, driven by a haemorrhaging of four per cent of the skilled labour force each year. Lloyd-George proposed to tackle this by reinvigorating supply: increasing mechanisation, improving working practices and, most importantly, by moving miners to the most productive seams. These measures required more than limited government planning and encouragement; they needed government ownership and direct employment of managers.

However, in Cabinet, nationalisation was ruled out by Churchill (*q.v.*), and Lloyd-George's ministry was forced to rely on managing demand and increasing the efficiency of coal use. This was done successfully, and the war effort was not inhibited.

In May 1945, in a symbolic reversal of 1931, Lloyd-George did not follow Labour and the other Liberals out of the government in advance of the election. He held Pembrokeshire, by 168 votes, as a 'National Liberal and Conservative' without a Conservative opponent. Although the most experienced Liberal MP, Lloyd-George refused to become either sessional Chairman for the Liberal MPs (Clement Davies (*q.v.*) was selected instead) or Chairman of the Liberal National Party. In 1946, having regularly voted with the Conservatives, the Liberal whip was withdrawn. However, subsequently Lloyd-George continued to use a 'Liberal and Conservative' label, even when, as in 1951, Winston Churchill helped him campaign.

Lloyd-George held two ministerial posts in the Conservative governments of the 1950s. First, as Minister of Food (1951–54), he oversaw the reduction of the rationing he had helped to implement during the war. Second, as Home Secretary and (largely symbolic) Minister for Welsh Affairs (1954–57) he had to deal with the issue of hanging, a cause of major public concern after the Timothy Evans case. In 1938 he had been an abolitionist, but by the 1950s he was ready to argue powerfully for the retention of hanging as a deterrent and as a statement of society's 'moral revulsion for murder'. The number of capital crimes was reduced in the 1957 Homicide Act, but hanging was preserved as the ultimate means of punishment. In 1957 MacMillan replaced Lloyd-George with R. A. Butler, elevating him to the Lords as the first Viscount Tenby. During the last ten years of his life, he filled a number of posts, including President of University College, Swansea, and Chairman of the Council on Tribunals. He died on 14 February 1967, and was succeeded as Viscount Tenby by his son David.

Andrew Sweeting

MEGAN LLOYD GEORGE   1902–66

Megan Lloyd George was born at Criccieth, Caernarfonshire, on 22 April 1902, the third daughter and fifth child of David Lloyd George (*q.v.*) and his wife Margaret. Until the age of four she could speak only Welsh. She was educated privately, in part by Frances Stevenson, who became her father's mistress and in 1943 his second wife, and later at Garratt's Hall, Banstead, and in Paris.

Her natural brilliance was sparked by her unique upbringing; from the age of eight until twenty she spent much of her time at Number 11, and subsequently Number 10, Downing Street. She savoured political life at the hub of events, and, following the death of the eldest daughter Mair in 1907, occupied centre stage in her father's affections. She accompanied him to the Paris Peace Conference in 1919, meeting a glittering array of world statesmen, diplomats and military figures, and to a succession of post-war international conferences. She was at her father's side on his triumphal tour of Canada and the USA in 1923. She spent a whole year (1924–25) as the guest of Lord Reading, Viceroy of India (Rufus Isaacs, *q.v.*).

She was widely regarded by the mid-1920s as her father's natural political heir. In 1928, after some underhand tactics in which both Lloyd George and Dame Margaret were much implicated, Megan secured the Liberal nomination for Anglesey. On 30 May 1929, she was elected to the Commons, the first-ever woman MP from Wales and the only Liberal lady to enjoy a relatively safe seat.

She soon made her own distinctive mark in the House as an independent-minded, highly individualistic MP with strong radical, even Labourite leanings. Her eloquent maiden speech in 1930, witnessed by her adoring father, discussed the problems of rural housing. She subsequently spoke to great effect on agriculture, unemployment and Welsh affairs. In the autumn of 1931 she was one of the tiny group of four Lloyd George family MPs who, unlike the rest of the Liberal Party, opposed the formation of Ramsay MacDonald's National Government.

She secured re-election to the Commons as an Independent Liberal in the general elections of 1931 and 1935. Although flirting ever-more closely with the Labour Party, she remained true to her father's brand of Liberalism. She supported his ambitious 'New Deal' programme in 1935, accompanied him on his visit to Hitler in 1936, and opposed the policy of appeasement, urging him to press for Chamberlain's resignation in May 1940.

During the Second World War Lloyd George served on an array of consultative committees and became a keen advocate of women's issues. She was a member of the 1944 Speaker's Conference on Electoral Reform and a leading light on the Woman Power Committee devoted to women's rights and the employment of women in wartime. She was also an unrelenting champion of Welsh causes, helping to press, unsuccessfully, for the appointment of a Secretary of State for Wales in 1943, and for a 'Welsh Day' debate in the Commons.

In 1945 her majority sharply reduced in Anglesey. She was one of only twelve Liberal MPs re-elected to Parliament and was the only national figure among them. When Clement Davies (*q.v.*) became Chairman of the 'motley group', Lloyd George, who saw herself as 'a minority radical in a minority party', looked increasingly askance at what she perceived as Davies' inclination to veer towards the Tories. 'Small, vital, with unlimited energy', she formed a close bond of friendship with Attlee and Herbert Morrison and, crucially, Labour's General Secretary Morgan Phillips, and was widely considered 'one of us' by Labour MPs.

In January 1949, in an attempt to improve party unity, Clement Davies made her Deputy Leader. But she caused renewed dissension in her party's ranks, culminating in November 1950 with the revolt of four Liberal MPs, including herself, against the party leadership – though this rebellion eventually petered out.

Lloyd George faced Tory opponents on Anglesey in the general elections of 1950 and 1951. In the former contest she was re-elected by a majority of 1,929 votes, but in the latter she was defeated by Cledwyn Hughes (Labour), standing in his third successive general election in the county. A tenure of twenty-two years thus came to an end. In November 1952 she declined to stand again as the Liberal candidate for Anglesey and at about the same time stood down as Vice-President of the Liberal Party.

A number of prominent radicals including Lloyd George and Dingle Foot (*q.v.*) had been considering the possibility of joining the Labour Party en masse, naively hoping to have some restraining influence on the Bevanites within the party. Lloyd George scuppered that plan by announcing her defection in April 1955 and she was subsequently to contribute substantially to the Labour election campaign later the same year. The death of Sir Rhys Hopkin Morris (*q.v.*) caused a fiercely contested byelection in the Carmarthenshire division in February 1957, and Lloyd George returned to the Commons as a Labour MP by a majority of more than 3,000 votes.

During her years in the political wilderness she served as the charismatic and indefatigable President of the tenacious 'Parliament for Wales' campaign of the early 1950s. She appeared on the platform at its inaugural conference at Llandrindod in July 1950, subsequently speaking at meetings and conferences throughout Wales, and serving as one of the deputation which in April 1956 presented a petition of more than 250,000 signatures, ironically to her brother Gwilym (*q.v.*), at the time Conservative Home Secretary and Minister for Welsh Affairs under Anthony Eden.

The personal popularity which Megan Lloyd George had undoubtedly enjoyed in Anglesey soon became evident in Carmarthenshire, where she developed a substantial popular following, gradually increasing her majority to more than 9,000 votes by 1966. Within the Commons she spoke generally on Welsh affairs or on agriculture, but neither Hugh Gaitskell nor Harold Wilson ever invited her to speak from the opposition front bench, and, when Labour returned to power in 1964, she remained a back-bencher.

By this time, she was already suffering from cancer, an illness which prevented her from campaigning at all in the 1966 general election. On 14 May 1966 she died at Brynawelon, her Criccieth home, within days of receiving the CH, ironically from

Harold Wilson, whom she disliked intensely. She was buried at Criccieth in the Lloyd George family vault. She remained unmarried.

Throughout her life, as both a Liberal and a Labour MP, she remained true to the passionate radicalism which was the hallmark of her father's political career. She was addressed in 1949 as 'a true daughter of the Welsh Wizard: she witches friend and foe alike'. Megan was, moreover, a Welsh radical who never failed to advocate policies beneficial to her native Wales, and who served as a member of the Criccieth Urban District Council for several years. An unfailingly eloquent orator, she was equally at home in the Commons, on the hustings, in a packed Royal Albert Hall or on the radio. Whether, had she survived, she would ever have been rewarded with a post in government, however, is debatable.

A brief pictorial review of her life and career by Emyr Price, *Megan Lloyd George*, was published by the Gwynedd Archives Service in 1983. Mervyn Jones, *A Radical Life: the Biography of Megan Lloyd George, 1902–1966* (London, 1991) is a fuller biographical work focusing largely on its subject's relationship with Philip Noel-Baker.

J. Graham Jones

LORD LOTHIAN 1882–1940

Born in London on 18 April 1882 into an aristocratic, Scottish, devoutly Roman Catholic and strongly Tory family, Philip Henry Kerr was the elder son of Major-General Lord Ralph Drury Kerr, the brother of the ninth Marquess of Lothian, and Lady Anne, sixth daughter of the fourteenth Duke of Norfolk. The eldest of four, he was a good-looking child. He had a traditional upbringing, being educated at the Oratory School, Edgbaston, and then at New College, Oxford, where he obtained a first in modern history, but also began to drift away from his parents' Catholicism.

In January 1905, at the age of twenty-two, he left for South Africa, joining the staff of Lord Milner, the governor. Lothian stayed on with Milner's successor, Lord Selborne, for four and a half years, primarily working on the railways and the police. In 1908, he returned to Britain permanently, having started the periodical *The State* a few months earlier to argue for a closer union in South Africa.

Despite receiving several invitations to stand for Parliament as a Conservative, Lothian visited the United States before becoming the first editor of *The Round Table*, which was to become the major periodical dealing with imperial and foreign affairs in inter-war Britain. Lothian remained editor until 1916. *The Round Table* argued for a common imperial policy and system of defence.

Lothian became a Liberal as a result of his role as one of Lloyd George's (*q.v.*) private secretaries during his premiership from 1916–22. Lloyd George recruited him as an expert in foreign and imperial affairs, and he became involved in efforts to reach a separate peace with Austria-Hungary and Turkey, and subsequently in the Versailles negotiations. Unlike many others who worked with Lloyd George, Lothian never quarrelled with him, and indeed Lloyd George gave one of the valedictory speeches (Churchill (*q.v.*) gave the other) in Parliament after his death.

In May 1921, Lothian left Lloyd George's service and until 1925 had no permanent employment, although he wrote frequently for *The Times* and *The Observer* on world order, the development of the British Commonwealth and Anglo-American relations. During this time he became a Christian Scientist. In 1925, he became General Secretary of the Rhodes Trust, which existed to develop scholarships to Oxford University from the English-speaking world outside the UK. He held this post until 1939.

In March 1930, he succeeded his cousin as Marquess of Lothian, having previously declined several Liberal invitations to stand for the Commons. Having told Ramsay MacDonald once that he had an incurably cross-bench mind, Lothian never took a prominent role in the party's internal affairs and in March 1933 declined the chairmanship of the Scottish Liberal Association.

He did, however, accept several duties within the National Government. He was Chancellor of the Duchy of Lancaster, with no clearly defined duties, from August – October 1931, and then after the election, Under-Secretary of State for India, working for Sir Samuel Hoare. He was sufficiently unhappy with the Conservative proposals to introduce tariff treaties, the so-called Ottawa Agreements, that he resigned with the other Samuelite ministers in September 1932, having first consulted Lord Grey (*q.v.*), who reluctantly concurred with Lothian's decision.

Lothian served on a number of government committees both before and after his brief membership of the National Government. From 1929–35, he was involved firstly with the Round Table Conference and then with the Joint Select Committee which began moving the responsibility for Indian government on to Indian shoulders and formed the background to the 1935 Government of India Act.

Despite his involvement in Versailles, Lothian subsequently came to the view that unless Germany received justice a second war could not be avoided. Never convinced that the League of Nations had much to offer, as a result of the absence of the United States, he was also critical of the UK's pro-French foreign policy. He visited Hitler in 1935 and 1937, and although he deplored Germany's methods in the Rhineland and Austria, he accepted the results and did not become finally disillusioned with Hitler until the Sudeten crisis. He never had much influence, however, over British policy; Baldwin distrusted his judgement, Eden disagreed with him on France and the League, and Neville Chamberlain was always determined to pursue his own aims. With no diplomatic training, the Foreign Office saw him as a talented amateur.

This did not prevent his appointment as ambassador to Washington in August 1939, where his informal and unpretentious manner greatly aided efforts to obtain

US support for the Allies. He also proved adept at arguing in favour of US intervention from the standpoint of US national interests. As a result he made it easier for the US to cooperate with the Commonwealth and, when the need arose, as over the destroyers-for-bases deal, he could apply pressure effectively to the US government.

His death in Washington on 8 December 1940 was unexpected and his ashes were scattered, after the war, at Jedburgh Abbey. His significance for Liberals lies more in the causes he espoused, especially world federalism, than in his brief period as a Liberal minister in the National Government – although he spoke fairly frequently for the party in the Lords and at Liberal Summer Schools. He was unusual, too, amongst 1930s Liberals in having some, albeit tangential, involvement at the highest levels. He never married, and was succeeded as twelfth marquess by his cousin, his younger brother having been killed in the First World War.

Lothian published one pamphlet, *Liberalism in the Modern World,* which advocated individual freedom and responsibility as the mainspring of human progress, and numerous articles for *The Round Table* on imperial and foreign affairs. There is no recent biography, but J. R. M Butler's *Lord Lothian*, published in 1960, gives a more detailed summary of his life.

Malcolm Baines

SARAH LUDFORD (Lady Ludford)   1951–

'A one-woman exposition of the principle of subsidiarity' – Sarah Ludford has been peer and pavement politician, a high-powered international businesswoman and an effective local councillor. Currently, this energetic, passionate and challenging woman is poised, as number one on the Liberal Democrat list for London, to return full time to her first love, Europe, this time as an MEP.

Sarah Ann Ludford was born on 14 March 1951, one of a pair of (non-identical) twins, and was educated at Portsmouth High School for Girls. She demonstrated even at an early age a fearless and tenacious intellect and a determination to succeed. She went on to the London School of Economics. where she gained first a BSc and then an MSc in European studies (1977). Subsequently, she broadened her education by reading for the bar.

Ludford's early professional life was spent in Brussels, where she was initially an administration trainee, and subsequently an official, of the European Commission; she gained a not-uncritical insight into the basis of the European Community and its practical workings which, reinforced by fluent French, are gifts she has subsequently placed at the disposal of the party. Whilst working in and commuting to Brussels, she lived with her husband and partner, Steve Hitchins, in Islington. The partnership has been political as well as personal; a shared commitment to Liberal Democracy has been reinforced by their complementary skills and styles.

Once she was contractually free to do so, Ludford was to take up Europe as a political cause and to fight every European election: Hampshire East in 1984, and London North in both 1989 and 1994. She has been from the first, one of the small band of people within the Liberal Democrats who are not merely enthusiasts for Europe and Union, but who has worked tirelessly to influence the party's thinking over the topic.

In the late 1980s, she began to take a much closer interest in domestic politics. In 1990, she was elected Policy Vice-Chair of London Region Liberal Democrats and was in the same year, for the first time, elected to the party's Federal Policy Committee. Policy has been a major preoccupation and area of contribution; she has played a high-profile role, bringing her knowledge and expertise to subjects as diverse as trade relations, financial regulation and human rights and health. She has been Vice-Chair of the committee since 1993 and continues to be a feisty foil to its chair, Paddy Ashdown (*q.v.*).

It was also in the early '90s that Ludford's commitment to social justice found expression in Islington, a mixed part of inner London, smart and expensive Georgian houses bordering large and neglected council estates. Even today, the former home of the Prime Minister lies in a constituency in which there is only 22 per cent owner-occupancy and in which 55 per cent of the voters are council tenants. Ludford first stood for the council in a byelection in Clerkenwell in 1991, and was returned at the subsequent elections (1994 and 1998) with substantial majorities. In her determination to fight for the quality of life of some of the poorest tenants, she has harried the Labour council and generated huge amounts of casework and involvement in many related campaigns. She has been concerned with housing and housing conditions, and has taken the Liberal Democrat lead on social services, exposing the Labour leadership for its incompetence and contempt for their voters.

Typically, local concerns became national campaigns. Ludford took lessons from Islington into the Policy Committee and the Urban Campaigners Network. She was determined to remind the Liberal Democrats that the party could not afford merely to be an antidote to the Tories in the rural south west, but must reach wider and deeper. Her own experience went ever deeper, involving a spell advising the Liberal Democrat group on Tower Hamlets, and a leading role in the 'Save Barts' campaign. It was therefore inevitable that she would be the candidate in the 1992 and 1997 general elections, for her home seat of Islington South & Finsbury. This effort was largely rewarded when, in May 1998, the Liberal Democrats, under the leadership of Sarah's husband Steve, swept within three votes of taking control of Islington council; an astonishing achievement.

Ludford was made a life peer in 1997, being introduced into the House of Lords on 23 October as Baroness Ludford of Clerkenwell. She quickly made her mark in the Upper House, and in May 1998 was re-elected to Islington council. She also campaigned successfully to head the London list in the 1999 European elections, demonstrating in one year a consistent political commitment, finding expression at every level of government.

Helen Bailey

REGINALD MCKENNA   1863–1943

Reginald McKenna was one of the key players in the last Liberal government and, arguably, in the history of Liberal decline, yet he remains a spectral figure, overshadowed by the attention devoted to his colleagues, Lloyd George (*q.v.*), Churchill (*q.v.*) and Asquith (*q.v.*). A government minister for eleven years (1905–16), he controlled education at the height of the religious controversy, the Admiralty during the dreadnought debate, the Home Office in the midst of the militant suffragette campaign and the Exchequer in the early years of the Great War. An efficient and rational administrator, he had little understanding of the passions of politics, and the solutions he implemented in each of these situations helped to weaken the Liberal Party politically and ideologically by undermining fundamental liberal principles and alienating key groups of supporters.

Reginald McKenna was born in London on 6 July 1863. He was educated on the continent, at King's College School, London, and Trinity Hall, Cambridge and was called to the bar by the Inner Temple in 1887, practising until 1895. He contested Clapham unsuccessfully in 1892, but was elected for Monmouth three years later, serving until his defeat in 1918. McKenna came to the attention of the party leadership in the early 1900s through his attacks on tariff reform, and when the Liberals took office in 1905, he was rewarded with the post of Financial Secretary to the Treasury. Within a year he was promoted to the Cabinet as President of the Board of Education. Initially welcomed by nonconformists, he failed to settle the issue of denominational schools, and when Asquith took over the premiership in April 1908, he moved to become First Lord of the Admiralty.

At the Admiralty McKenna became embroiled in two long-standing arguments: naval expansion versus social reform, and a land versus sea strategy On the first he argued for maximising the building programme, whilst the Chancellor of the Exchequer, Lloyd George, urged economies to fund social reform, and though a compromise was achieved, enduring bitterness developed between the two. On strategy, McKenna favoured utilising the fleet to knock out the German navy, whilst the War Office felt it should support any land campaign, but this issue was not resolved before he left the Admiralty in 1911 to become Home Secretary.

McKenna was first and foremost an administrator, and his legislative programme at the Home Office was progressive, if not particularly controversial. He continued the reform of the criminal justice system and the medico-moral control of prostitution and mental health as well as piloting the key 'Old Liberal' Welsh Disestablishment

Bill through Parliament. However, he also found himself embroiled in the policing of violent industrial disputes and the militant suffragette campaign. In the latter case, his solution to the hunger strikers – the discharge and subsequent re-confinement of the women, known as the 'Cat and Mouse Act' – though rational, was politically disastrous and certainly offended many non-militant Liberal suffragists.

The Great War heralded the culmination and collapse of McKenna's political career. Throughout he was closely associated with the Asquithians and often in open conflict with Lloyd George, yet this was a largely personal and political, rather than ideological, stance. On the running of the war, McKenna was much closer to Lloyd George than Asquith and showed little inclination to let principle get in the way of the efficient management of the state. Initially he continued to serve as Home Secretary, but with the formation of the first coalition in May 1915, he became Chancellor of the Exchequer. It was here that he made his most enduring impact on Liberal party politics, for in his first budget, in addition to raising a variety of domestic taxes, he sanctioned an *ad valorem* tax of 33.3 per cent on certain imports. Justified as an emergency measure designed to free up scarce shipping and reduce the outflow of currency, the 'McKenna Duties' were clearly a breach with free trade, and have become a touchstone of the corruption of Liberal principles caused by involvement in the war. Furthermore, though McKenna did tender his resignation over the decision to introduce conscription, his opposition was not ideological but financial and military, and he was persuaded to stay, remaining in office until December 1916, when Lloyd George replaced Asquith as Prime Minister.

McKenna refused to serve under the new Prime Minister, but this decision owed more to personal animosity than any particular loyalty to Asquith (whose abilities he had questioned in April 1916) or even differences about the running of the war. At the 'coupon election' which followed the end of the war he stood as an independent Liberal in the new constituency of Pontypool and was easily defeated by Labour.

In 1917 McKenna joined the board of the London City and Midland Bank, becoming Chairman of the Midland Bank two years later, a position he held until his death in 1943. In 1922 the Conservative Prime Minister, Bonar Law, offered him the Chancellorship of the Exchequer. Initially he refused, claiming that, though not opposed to a Conservative government, his acceptance might have a damaging impact on the remnants of the Liberal Party. However, when offered the post again a few months later he accepted on the condition that he was given a City of London seat and that he was returned unopposed and without a party label, but as this could not be arranged, his chance to return to politics ended.

McKenna's later life was spent working in the City, playing chess and bridge and in a series of country houses designed by his friend Sir Edwin Lutyens. He chaired a committee on the export of German capital in 1924 and in 1928 published a collection of his speeches, *Post-War Banking Policy*. In 1908 he married Pamela (died 1943), daughter of Sir Herbert Jekyll, the couple having two sons. He died in London on 6 September 1943.

For biographies, see Stephen McKenna, *Reginald McKenna, 1863–1943: A Memoir* (1948); and Stephen McKenna's entry on him in the *Dictionary of National Biography*.

Barry Doyle

GEORGE MACKIE (Lord Mackie)   1919–

George Yull Mackie was born on 10 July 1919 in Aberdeenshire, the son of Dr Maitland Mackie OBE, LLD, and his wife Mary (née Yull). The farming family was of a political nature: George's eldest brother, Lord John Mackie, was junior Minister of Agriculture in the Labour Government for six years (1964–70). The other brother, Sir Maitland Mackie, was an active Liberal in local affairs and Convenor of County. Their parents were staunch Conservatives.

George was educated at the local village schools in Tarves and Methlick before attending Aberdeen Grammar School and Aberdeen University, but his main training in farming was as a grieve (foreman) on one of his father's farms and as a stock manager in a big farming company in Norfolk. He later farmed Benshie for forty-odd years, growing soft fruit, mainly strawberries, and Golden Wonder potatoes, which were the biggest part of the farm. He also had ten years of partnership in a large Highland farm.

On the outbreak of war he joined the RAF and flew on Wellingtons in Bomber Command in Europe and the Middle East. He was awarded DSO DFC in 1944 and on finishing his third tour went on the staff of Bomber Ops in London. He voted Liberal in the forces in the 1945 election, and supported the Liberal candidate in South Angus in 1950, contesting South Angus himself in 1959 and coming second.

He became Vice-Chairman of the Scottish Liberal Party in 1959 and was made Chairman of the Organisation Committee, playing a major party in the reorganisation of the Scottish Liberal Party in targeting winnable seats, notably in the Highlands and Islands and the Borders. This bore fruit in 1964 when three extra seats were won in the Highlands, followed by one in the Borders at a byelection, giving the Scottish party the majority of Liberal MPs in the House of Commons. The English Liberals managed to produce only one gain.

His forceful style caused him to have a note of censure passed by the Scottish party executive for his 'interference' in persuading a young David Steel (*q.v.*) to leave the candidature in unwinnable Edinburgh Pentlands and transfer to the Borders, a censure for which he was particularly proud and was the cause of much hilarity at subsequent party dinners where Mackie was a regular speaker.

At Jo Grimond's (*q.v.*) request, he reluctantly moved his candidature to Caithness & Sutherland in 1960, and was one of the winning seats in 1964, becoming spokesman on economic affairs and Scottish Whip. He lost the seat in 1966 by sixty-four votes in spite of raising the total vote; it was won for Labour by Bob Maclennan (*q.v.*), now a Liberal Democrat colleague.

Mackie was made a peer in 1974 as Baron Mackie of Benshie, of Kirriemuir in the County of Angus, and has spoken for the party in the House of Lords on agriculture and Scottish affairs since then. In 1986 he went to the Parliamentary Assembly of the Council of Europe as a Liberal member and spent eleven years there until 1979, being mainly interested in immigration and agriculture. He was President of the Scottish Liberal Party 1983–88.

He retired from farming in 1989. Probably his best work consisted in becoming chairman of Caithness Glass in 1966, when it was bankrupt. It was rescued by a small group and eventually brought to prosperity, employing significant numbers of people in Caithness. He married Lindsay (née Sharp) in 1944 and had three daughters and now has seven grandchildren. Lindsay died in 1985 and he married Jacqueline Lane (née Rauch) in 1988.

Lesley Gill

DUNCAN MCLAREN   1800–86

Duncan McLaren, Liberal MP for Edinburgh from 1865 to 1881, was known as 'the Member for Scotland'. Modern historians have described him as 'the living voice of Scottish middle-class dissenting radicalism', 'a thorn in the flesh of the whips for half a century', and 'the most eminent and individual of the radicals of the period'.

McLaren was born on 12 January 1800 in Renton, Dunbartonshire, the son of John McLaren, a local farmer. He was apprenticed as a draper, moved to Edinburgh in 1818 and, in 1824, opened his own draper's shop in the High Street.

McLaren was elected an Edinburgh councillor in 1834, City Treasurer in 1837 and Lord Provost 1851–54. Edinburgh politics then involved confusing alliances and feuds between the different factions in the dominant Liberal Party – the Whigs and the various church groups. McLaren achieved much, but his manoeuvres antagonised many and led to his defeats in elections for Lord Provost in 1840 and MP in 1852. (See I. G. C. Hutchinson, *A Political History of Scotland 1832–1924* for details.) He himself was a Dissenter and led the formation of the Scottish Central Board of Dissenters in 1834, as a powerful radical force – anti-established church, anti-drink, anti-Corn Laws, and for extending the franchise, and the ballot.

As Treasurer, he negotiated a settlement of the city's debts with its creditors. A leading teetotaller, he was largely responsible for the Public House Bill of 1853, but as Lord Provost he offered drink to his official visitors. He was the originator of the

Heriot Free Schools, using surplus funds in the Trust. He also helped to secure the Meadows as a public park, and other major municipal improvements.

In national politics, McLaren's first great role was as the Scottish leader of the Anti-Corn Law League, as a close ally and then brother-in-law of John Bright (*q.v.*). As an MP he finally ended a long campaign by securing the repeal of the Annuity Tax, a local church rate in Edinburgh and Montrose which had enraged the Dissenters and Free Church members.

McLaren was a leading member of the National Education Association of Scotland, formed in 1850 to campaign for a national, non-sectarian, secular education system. However, he supported the unsuccessful Education Bills of 1854 and 1855, which included state-funded religious teaching in schools, falling out with the mass of Dissenters, whose hostility killed off the bills.

His standing in Edinburgh and closeness to Bright enabled McLaren to organise great rallies on the Corn Laws, a peace conference just before the Crimean War, and an audience of 2,000 for Electoral Reform in 1858. He had considerable influence on the Reform Act of 1867, pressing Scottish claims on Disraeli with some success and supporting some of his tortuous manoeuvres. The increase in the number of Scottish seats and voters was less than the Radicals hoped, but the Act did bring Scotland a great advance towards democracy, continued by Gladstone's (*q.v.*) Ballot Act of 1872 and the Third Reform Act of 1884, which together fulfilled most of the Radicals' constitutional programme.

The National Association for the Vindication of Scottish Rights, from 1853 to 1856, was a widely-based movement devoted to setting out Scottish grievances. McLaren was a prominent member and he pursued its agenda throughout his national political career. This included providing Scotland with its own reformed and separate administration, its fair share of MPs and fair share of UK expenditure, which at that period it definitely did not get. The Association restored the idea of nationhood and advocated responsible nationalism as a basis for internationalism. McLaren continued to set out the ill effects of over-centralisation and parliamentary congestion and parliament's neglect of Scottish issues. The lack of attention paid by Gladstone's first two governments to Scottish issues greatly disappointed the Radicals and must have contributed to McLaren's decision to support Bright in opposing Gladstone over Irish Home Rule. Instead, he advocated 'a measure of home rule which would apply equally to each of the three kingdoms and have a tendency to unite them more and more in one friendly bond of brotherhood'.

The Scottish middle-class radicals never gained power in Victorian Britain but had great influence on many of the reforms adopted. Duncan McLaren was the best example of both their weaknesses – 'probably the greatest exponent of cant in mid-Victorian Scotland' – and their strengths, as in his coup of convening a meeting of 801 dissenting and evangelical ministers to denounce 'the sinfulness and injustice of the Corn Laws'.

McLaren married three times – in 1829, Grant Aitken, who died 1833; in 1836, Christina Renton, who died 1841; and in 1848 Priscilla Bright; there were no children. He died in Edinburgh on 20 April 1886.

Various pamphlets and speeches of his were published on the Annuity Tax, city and borough reform and Contagious Diseases Acts. A two-volume biography by J. B. Mackie, *The Life and Works of Duncan McLaren,* was published in 1888, and a strangely selective article in the *Dictionary of National Biography.* A fine portrait by Sir George Reid hangs in Edinburgh City Chambers.

Donald Gorrie

SIR DONALD MACLEAN   1864–1932

Sir Donald Maclean had greatness thrust upon him. Until 1918, everything in his career suggested that he was living a useful public life which would one day merit an obituary notice in *The Times,* but would hardly bring him into the first rank of politics – yet he was to play a critical and unexpected role in Liberal history.

Maclean was born on 9 January 1864 in Farnworth, Lancashire, the son of John Maclean, a master cordwainer, and Agnes Macmellin, a Highland lady who habitually spoke Gaelic. He was educated at grammar schools in south-west Wales and later qualified as a solicitor. After an unsuccessful attempt to enter Parliament as Liberal candidate for the two-member seat of Bath in 1900, he was elected for that constituency in the Liberal landslide of 1906. In the following year he married Gwendolen Devitt of Oxted, Surrey. They had several children, including his namesake son, who was to achieve notoriety during the cold war, spying for and then in 1951 defecting to, the Soviet Union along with Guy Burgess and Kim Philby.

In the general election of January 1910, Maclean was defeated at Bath, but he was returned for Peebles & Selkirk in December of the same year. His selection for this Scottish constituency may have owed something to the Master of Elibank (*q.v.*), soon to be the Liberal Chief Whip, who had sat there from 1901–10, and was currently occupying the adjoining seat of Midlothian. In any event, Maclean soon became Elibank's Parliamentary Private Secretary.

In 1911, he became Deputy Chairman of Ways and Means. Years later, *The Times* wrote of his 'mastery of Parliamentary procedure' and of his 'combination of gentleness and sweet reasonableness with firmness' in that office. In 1916 he became a Privy Councillor, and in the same year was appointed Chairman of the Treasury Committee on Enemy Debts and also of the London Military Appeal Tribunal. In 1917 he was created KBE, and received another Chairmanship, this time of the Reconstruction Committee on the Poor Law.

When Lloyd George's (*q.v.*) coalition government was formed in December 1916, a serious split in the Liberal Party began to appear. Asquith (*q.v.*), who had been

Prime Minister for the previous eight years, and most of his closest associates continued to control the machinery of the party. In time, Lloyd George's Liberal followers began to establish a separate organisation. When the Armistice came in November 1918, Lloyd George and the Conservative Leader Bonar Law resolved to keep the coalition intact, awarding a 'coupon' to their supporters at the general election in December. Asquith and most of his associates were denied the coupon, and the great majority of them, including all the leading Asquithians, were defeated. Maclean, whose constituency had been redrawn as Peebles & South Midlothian, was one of the few non-couponed Liberals who did not have a couponed candidate against him, and he was elected in a straight fight with Labour.

It was in these circumstances that Maclean suddenly shot to prominence. When the new Parliament met, twenty-three Liberal MPs, most of whom were uncouponed sceptics of the coalition, attended a meeting of their own. It is not clear on what basis they were selected, and their meeting was marked by differences on several important matters. It was by no means a foregone conclusion what general position they would adopt, but they eventually constituted themselves the Liberal Parliamentary Party, and elected Maclean as their Chairman. They also elected their own Whips, and thus effectively required Liberal MPs to choose between taking the Coalition Liberal or the Independent Liberal Whip.

In the months which followed, the Liberal split became increasingly profound. In February 1920, Asquith was returned to Parliament at the Paisley byelection, and inevitably overshadowed Maclean as a public figure. But Maclean remained Chairman of the non-coalitionist Liberal MPs. He played an important part in the selection of candidates and control of party finances until 1921. In the month after Paisley, he pledged support for independent Liberals who decided to organise in opposition to the coalitionists at the constituency level.

In October 1922 the coalition collapsed, and a general election was held shortly afterwards. The independent Liberals made considerable electoral advances, but Maclean, who had to face a three-cornered contest at Peebles & South Midlothian, was defeated. In 1923 he sought election unsuccessfully at Kilmarnock, and in the following year was again unsuccessful at Cardiff East. In 1929, however, he was returned as Liberal MP for North Cornwall, winning the seat from a Conservative. By that time the Liberal split had been – at least in form – repaired: Asquith was dead and Lloyd George leader. Maclean found himself able to cooperate with his former antagonist in the testing period which followed.

When the National Government was formed in August 1931, Maclean was appointed President of the Board of Education, though without a seat in the Cabinet. He strongly opposed Conservative pressure for an early general election with the National Government intact, which he described as 'autumn madness'. When the election was held nonetheless, Maclean, like Sir Herbert Samuel (*q.v.*), found himself opposed by a Conservative, whom he managed to defeat. When the government was reconstituted after the election, Maclean retained his post at the Board of Education and was elevated to the Cabinet. Early in 1932, he was one of the four free-trader ministers who dissented from the decision to introduce tariffs, avoiding resignation by the 'agreement to differ', permitting them to retain their offices and yet oppose government policy on protection.

The last phase of Maclean's career was a tragic paradox. All his life, he had been interested in social causes. He was one of the founders of the National Society for the Prevention of Cruelty to Children, and in his spell out of Parliament in the 1920s he had chaired two important committees on social matters. In other circumstances, the office of President of the Board of Education, with, for the first time in his life, a seat in the Cabinet, would have given him the opportunity to develop new and visionary ideas. As it was, he was forced to defend the National Government's retrenchment policies against growing hostility from the teaching profession. It is not surprising that this undermined his health, and he died suddenly from a heart attack at his London home on 15 June 1932.

Roy Douglas

ROBERT MACLENNAN MP   1936–

When Robert (Bob) Maclennan was first elected President of the Liberal Democrats in the summer of 1994, few realised just how much this seemingly self-effacing politician would come to represent so completely the ethos and values of the Liberal Democrats. Four years later, still fewer have realised quite how hard he has fought for those values. It is characteristic of Robert Maclennan that his career has often been more successful than visible, and that his active and respected participation in the world of the arts and media, which would make him more 'renaissance man' than 'career politician', is not widely known within the party.

Robert Adam Ross Maclennan was born on 26 June 1936 in Glasgow, to Sir Hector Maclennan and his wife Isabel, both doctors. He was educated at Glasgow Academy, proceeding to Balliol College, Oxford and continuing his academic career at Trinity College, Cambridge and Columbia University, New York. He was called to the bar in 1962 and developed an interest in international law, which he was able to pursue in London and New York. After only four years, he took the opportunity to take up full-time politics, able in the future to draw upon his legal experience to become a considerable authority on constitutional law and constitutional change.

At the 1966 general election, Maclennan was elected as Labour MP for the seat of Caithness & Sutherland, defeating the Liberal incumbent George Mackie (*q.v.*), by a majority of just sixty-four votes. He has continued to represent the seat (subject to some boundary changes) with an increasing majority for over thirty years.

His career in Parliament began quickly and in 1967 he was made Parliamentary Private Secretary to the Secretary of State for Commonwealth Affairs. In 1970–74, during Labour's period in opposition, he was a spokesman on defence and Scottish affairs, giving him his first platform from which to speak about the future role of his native country. Labour returned to power for the Wilson and Callaghan Governments of 1974–79 and Maclennan became a minister in the Department of Prices and Consumer Protection, introducing, among other legislation, the Consumer Credit Act.

In the late 1970s and early '80s, Maclennan, like many other long-standing members of the Labour Party, became concerned over Labour's position and future direction. He was one of the first Labour MPs to join the new Council for Social Democracy in 1981. Unlike many of his former colleagues, he held on to his seat at the 1983 election (with a doubled majority) and the 1987 election. He was given many responsibilities in the SDP, from 1983 being spokesman on both agriculture (which he had held since 1981) and home and legal affairs.

When merger was proposed after the 1987 election, Maclennan was a keen exponent. In the wake of David Owen's resignation of the SDP leadership in August after the party voted, against his advice, to open negotiations with the Liberals, Maclennan was elected unopposed as the third, and last, leader of the SDP. He led the SDP team which negotiated the constitution for the new party. It was perhaps at this point that many of his future colleagues realised quite how steely and how principled he was. He tried harder than most to persuade Owen to reconsider and stay with the party he had founded.

In 1988, Maclennan decided not to contest the leadership of the newly merged party, which was won that summer by Paddy Ashdown (*q.v.*) in the first all-member leadership election. He himself won an all-member election when, in 1994, he succeeded his friend and former SDP colleague Charles Kennedy (*q.v.*) as President of the Liberal Democrats. This was a role which gained him wider recognition in the party, and there was no challenger when he became eligible for a second term in 1996.

Within the Liberal Democrats, Maclennan has become an increasingly well-respected figure, holding the home affairs and arts spokesmanships from 1988–94. He has also retained his place on the House of Commons Public Accounts Committee which he has filled since 1970. It is, perhaps however, as constitutional affairs spokesman (from 1994) that he has made the greatest impact. He has been influential in the party's position on home rule for Scotland and Wales. More significantly still, he saw the opportunities latent in the growing rapprochement between Blair's 'New Labour' and the Liberal Democrats in the months running up to the 1997 general election. The eponymous Cook-Maclennan talks led in due course to the participation of a number of key Liberal Democrats, including Maclennan, in a special cabinet committee.

That agreement has been controversial within the Liberal Democrats. While there has been unease about the nature of the discussions and a fear that the larger party may dominate the smaller, Maclennan's presence has been seen by many, including many 'radical Liberals', as a guarantee of integrity of purpose. Some part in the so-called Blair revolution, including devolution for Scotland and Wales, the reform of the House of Lords, and moves toward freedom of information, must have been influenced by his thoughtful understanding of constitutional and legal affairs.

In a life which absorbs many significant political events, Maclennan has maintained an active interest in the arts and media. These are areas of life which, as well as forming part of his political portfolio, reflect his own wide-ranging interests and connections. He also maintains an active involvement in the lives of his wife and children; he has been married to Helen since 1968, and they have two children and a step-daughter.

Helen Bailey

TOM MCNALLY (Lord McNally)   1943–

If anyone wanted a textbook example of how to remain true to one's political beliefs in a changing political world, they could do no better than turn to Tom McNally. In a career that has spanned from student activist to party official, Member of Parliament to the House of Lords, McNally has been a steadfast standard bearer of cooperative politics across the centre-left of British politics. He is proof positive that a fluid political career need not involve the sacrifice of principles.

Son of a chemical process worker, Tom McNally was born on 20 February 1943 to John and Elizabeth. Proud of what he describes as his 'Irish working class' upbringing on the outskirts of Blackpool, he remains fiercely loyal to his roots, becoming Lord McNally of Blackpool in the County of Lancashire when raised to the peerage in 1995. Ever the defender of his home town, he responded to the decision of the Liberal Democrats not to hold any further conferences in Blackpool by saying that they would never be a serious party until they returned. He now regrets this, a similar decision having been taken by the 'New Labour' Party.

A member of the Labour Party from the age of sixteen, McNally was educated at St Joseph's College, Blackpool, and University College, London, where he was President of the Union. Having also been Vice-President of the National Union of Students in 1965–66, his success in student politics was ended by a more 'radical' candidate for the NUS Presidency, one Jack Straw. Nevertheless, McNally remained one of the Labour Party's rising stars, becoming one of its youngest senior officers in 1969 as International Officer, and then special adviser to the Foreign Secretary. His 'tour of duty' included expulsion from the pre-reformed Portugal, being present at the Cyprus peace talks (during which he met a young and dynamic diplomat, one J. J. D. Ashdown, *q.v.*) and being barred entry to Rhodesia by Ian Smith.

McNally became adviser to Prime Minister Callaghan in 1976. As Head of the Number 10 Political Office in 1976–79, he was an avid supporter of the Lib-Lab Pact.

He believed it to have been one of the more successful experiments in relations between the two parties, ultimately destroyed by a combination of lack of imagination among sections of both parties and by trade union bloody-mindedness.

Though 1979 saw Labour defeated by Thatcher's Conservatives, McNally was elected as Labour MP for Stockport South, a seat he held until the 1983 election. The intervening years saw him involved in the establishment of the Social Democratic Party, which gave him an opportunity to set out a positive vision for European interaction, notably at a 1982 Liberal assembly fringe. As an MP he served on the Trade and Industry Select Committee and held the SDP spokesmanship on education and sport (1981–83).

Initially a confidant of Dr David Owen, his happiest experience of the SDP was as 'minder' to Rosie Barnes in the Greenwich byelection in 1987. Though he revealed himself at the 1983 SDP Salford conference to be anti-merger, he was by 1987 a leading light in the 'Yes to Unity' campaign, where he met his second wife Juliet Hutchinson whom he married in 1990 (his 1970 marriage to Eileen Powell ended in divorce in 1990).

McNally is currently the Liberal Democrat home affairs spokesman in the House of Lords. He has characteristically provided the party with one of their most noted procedural triumphs by tabling and pushing through an amendment to the Competition Bill seeking to outlaw the practice of 'predatory pricing' by newspaper companies. Although finally overturned by the government in the House of Commons, McNally proved that coalition across the political divide was once again the Liberal Democrats' greatest tactic.

Outside Parliamentary life, the end of elected politics in 1983 resulted in McNally working briefly as public affairs adviser to GEC Marconi, followed by a stint as Director-General of the British Retail Association (now Consortium) 1985–87. He then moved into agency consulting, first as Head of Public Affairs at Hill and Knowlton (1987–93) and then on to their only serious rival agency, Shandwick Consultants, where he was Head of Public Affairs 1993–96 and is now Vice-Chairman.

Tom and Juliet have three children, John (8), James (5) and Imogen (3), and live in St Albans.

James Gurling

DIANA MADDOCK (Lady Maddock)   1945–

Diana Maddock acquired public renown as the winner of a remarkable byelection victory in Christchurch on 29 July 1993. This long-time activist and political campaigner was catapulted into public prominence. Many byelection winners have been quickly forgotten but Maddock has made an indelible mark, not only on Christchurch, but on the party as a whole. In 1998 she begins her first year as President of the party, giving her an opportunity to put to good effect her disconcerting combination of strongly held values and practical common sense

Diana Margaret Derbyshire was born on 19 May 1945. She was educated at Brockenhurst Grammar School, Shenstone Training College, and what is now Portsmouth University. She became a teacher at Weston Park Girls' School in Southampton in 1966, the same year in which she married Robert Frank (Bob) Maddock.

The late sixties and early seventies were not actively political. Diana and Bob moved to Stockholm in 1969 for three years, in pursuance of Bob's career – a period of considerable importance in generating friends, contacts and an alternative view of the world which have remained with her ever since. Returning to England, she taught English as a foreign language, an occupation which exposed her to new entrants to the UK from all walks of life and many different parts of the world. She gave up formal work in 1976 to bring up her children (two daughters). At this time, partly as a result of her experiences as a mother, she was motivated by her sense of fairness and justice and the need 'to do something' about political campaigning. She returned to teaching briefly in the early 1990s but was soon drawn into full-time politics, becoming the party's organiser for Hampshire and actively involved in the Association of Liberal Democrat Councillors.

The move from local campaigner to local councillor was her first step into public life and public obligations. Maddock was first elected to Southampton City Council in 1984 and remained a member until she was elected to Parliament in 1993. She absorbed herself in local politics and council work. She became particularly interested in housing issues and characteristically concerned from a human, as well as a purely political, point of view. Her understanding quickly grew beyond those aspects which arose in her ward. She was later able to draw upon her experience in Southampton when piloting her 'warmer homes' bill through the House of Commons.

Maddock's great political test arose when Southampton City Council became a hung authority. She was leader of the Liberal Democrats group, steering it through these most difficult of moments. It was a hard way to learn the practical skills of political leadership but they were put to the test again when the Liberal Democrats on Hampshire County Council became the largest group, without overall control. As organiser, Maddock supported and advised the group, sowing the seeds of ongoing success. She became well known locally and the obvious candidate for the seat of Southampton Test in 1992.

In the spring of 1993, she was persuaded to seek selection for the byelection which arose on the death of the popular Conservative member for Christchurch, Robert Adley. Statistically, it appeared unwinnable – Adley had had a majority of over 23,000, but Maddock took it with a remarkable 35 per cent swing and a majority of 16,000.

Maddock entered the House of Commons after the recess in the autumn of 1993. She quickly developed a 'grace', to quote her leader, Paddy Ashdown (q.v.), and an assurance which surprised many. In the Commons, she continued to follow her established interests in housing and homelessness; she was the party's spokesman on housing and Vice Chair of the All-Party Group on Homelessness and Housing Need. Her most lasting achievement was the piloting through, in only her second year in the House, of the Home Energy Conservation Act, or 'warmer homes Act', as it is more popularly known. The legislation required local authorities to assess the energy efficiency of all homes in their area and draw up local energy conservation plans; a practical outcome from those years as a councillor. She was also unstinting in making time available to keep in touch with the party and to work in local campaigns. At the 1997 general election, many commentators were ready to predict an easy Conservative victory in Christchurch; although the seat was lost, the outcome represented one of the strongest swings from Conservative to Liberal Democrat in the country (18.2 per cent).

Ever-practical, Maddock took on a short-term contract for council support work with ALDC and became an elected member of the party's Federal Executive and its Finance Committee. She entered the House of Lords on 12 November 1997 as Baroness Maddock of Christchurch and, in under a year, has already made her presence felt. It was no surprise that when she was persuaded to stand as President of the party in July 1998, she was elected unopposed.

Helen Bailey

EDWARD MARTELL   1909–89

Edward Martell was never elected to Parliament, and his active association with the Liberal Party spanned less than a decade. Yet there is much to be said for the view that he played a major part in keeping the party in existence, when it could easily have disappeared as a serious political force.

Edward Druett Martell was born in Bedfordshire on 2 March 1909. In 1932 he married Ethel Beverley. A journalist by profession, he joined the army in the Second World War, rising to the rank of captain. Like many wartime servicemen, Martell was attracted to the Liberal Party, though in most places in the mid-1940s Liberal organisation was weak or non-existent. His military experience impressed him with the need for a strong organisation to achieve victory in any kind of contest, so he soon became closely associated with people like Frank Byers (*q.v.*) and Philip Fothergill (*q.v.*) who were determined to improve party organisation.

In 1946, Martell achieved his only electoral victory. South West Bethnal Green was perhaps the poorest constituency in London, but it had a strong Liberal tradition. Until 1945, it had been represented in Parliament by the much-loved Sir Percy Harris (*q.v.*) who, long before, had sat on the London County Council (LCC) as well. The constituency returned two members to the LCC, and in March 1946 Harris sought to regain his seat there, with Martell as his running mate. Both men were elected, tipping out the two Labour incumbents. The 1946 victory was the first Liberal victory on the LCC since 1931.

Martell now sought to apply the vigorous tactics which had worked in Bethnal Green on a much wider scale. Along with like-minded colleagues, he aimed to ensure that Liberals in every constituency in the country should be in a condition to fight the next general election effectively. Thus was born the 'G. E. Plan'. It gave careful and detailed instructions, designed to ensure that a small group of enthusiasts in any constituency would be able to build up a local machine which could meet the other parties on conditions of parity or better. The idea caught on, and much enthusiasm was generated.

Soon another Martellian idea appeared: *Liberal News*, which he was to edit for several years. The plan was to sign up subscribers who undertook to pay 3d (1.25p) a week – a perceptible sum in those days. For this they would receive a small periodical, delivered by their newsagent. *Liberal News* was not intended to be value for money, and intending subscribers were firmly advised to that effect. It was designed as a 'painless' and automatic way of collecting money. If a large proportion of existing Liberals could be persuaded to subscribe, this would provide the central machine of the party with broadly-based funds, which would match the finances of the other parties.

In November 1946, Martell stood as Parliamentary candidate at a byelection in Rotherhithe, a London working-class constituency similar to Bethnal Green but with no recent Liberal tradition. A massive campaign was mounted and many organisational innovations introduced. The eventual result fell far short of the victory for which Martell had hoped, but he ran a respectable second, no mean achievement for a Liberal in those days. Many Liberals who helped at Rotherhithe saw a real electoral organisation in operation for the first time.

Martell does not appear to have given great attention to his LCC work. In 1949 there were further LCC elections and he did not stand again. His overwhelming concern was with the impending general election, which took place in February 1950. He wanted the Liberals to fight on the widest possible front, and in particular to ensure that they contested every seat in Greater London. He probably had not intended to be a candidate himself, but eventually stood in Hendon North. He was defeated, of course, but at least had the satisfaction of saving his deposit, which most Liberals failed to do.

Constituency organisations in 1950 were far from perfect, but they were much better than they had been for many years. However, the overall results of the election were deeply disappointing. Nor did Martell's creation, *Liberal News*, go far towards financing the party, and it soon became primarily an information and propaganda weekly.

Martell was one of the architects of the broad-front strategy in 1950, which it could be argued made the Liberal Party a laughing stock, with so many deposits lost.

This strategy was rejected during the rest of the 1950s and '60s – but this does not mean that it was a failure. In many constituencies there remained a substantial group of active Liberals with some idea of what was necessary to achieve victory, even though they lacked the means of delivering it. Bad as Liberal fortunes were in the 1950s, they would probably have been even worse without Martell's initiative.

Martell again played an active part at Liberal headquarters in the general election of 1951, which proved even more disastrous than its predecessor. Thereafter his mind moved in other directions. He proposed to the party's Executive Committee a nationalised membership scheme, primarily intended to tighten discipline within the party, which was badly received. In 1952, he published a booklet, *The Menace of Rationalisation*, in which he argued for coordination of strategy between Liberals and Conservatives. Both parties ignored it, and Martell drifted further from the Liberal fold.

In 1954 he bought an obscure weekly newspaper, the *Recorder*, and relaunched it as an anti-trade union journal, thus beginning his fifteen-year odyssey through the fringes of right-wing politics. Taking advantage of the 1955 printers' dispute both to publish his own newspaper and to assist the publication of *The Listener* and other journals, he gathered the support of other mavericks with Liberal connections, including former Liberal Treasurer Lord Moynihan, former Liberal MP Horace Crauford, and former Independent MP W. J. Brown. Together they founded the People's League for the Defence of Freedom in the spring of 1956, at which point Martell left the Liberal Party. The League's campaign platform advocated the progressive reduction of all rates and taxes, elimination of bureaucratic waste and reform of trade union law. Martell had gained popular acclaim for establishing a fund in commemoration of Winston Churchill's (*q.v.*) eightieth birthday, which he hoped to utilise when the League contested the East Ham North byelection in May 1957. He polled 12.2 per cent of the vote and the League disappeared.

A similar organisation, with similar backers, was established in 1958: the Anti-Socialist Front, heralded by another Martell booklet, *Need the Bell Toll?* This aroused for a short time the hope of Lord Hailsham that it could facilitate a Conservative/Liberal deal at the subsequent general election. Nothing came of the grouping and in 1960 Martell launched another newspaper, 'free of trade union control', the *New Daily*, which ran for six years. Another Martellian front, the Freedom Group, advertised the dangers of socialism during the 1964 election campaign before metamorphosing into the National Party in July 1966. Its aim was to recruit one million members by 1970 and it was allied to Modern Organisers Ltd, which intended to set up mini-markets, or 'superstores for the little man', and to another printing press. Donald Bennett was the party's lone election candidate, polling atrociously at the Nuneaton byelection in 1967. The one million members were never recruited and Martell's corporate empire collapsed in debt in the latter part of 1967.

Martell more or less disappeared from view, and his death in London in 1989 went almost unnoticed. Yet, even though he had played no active part in Liberal affairs for a third of a century, and his judgement was often badly flawed, much of the legacy of his work in the later 1940s remains with Liberal Democrats to this day.

Roy Douglas and Mark Egan

H. W. MASSINGHAM   1860–1924

Henry William Massingham was one of the most influential radical journalists of the later nineteenth and early twentieth centuries. He was born on 25 May 1860 at Old Catton, Norwich, the second son of Joseph Massingham, a private secretary and non-conformist preacher, and his wife Marianne. He attended King Edward VI School, Norwich, to whose headmaster, Dr Augustus Jessopp, he owed much of his lifelong appreciation of literature.

Massingham gained his early experience in journalism on the *Eastern Daily Press* in Norwich, which he joined on leaving school at the age of seventeen. In 1883 he moved to London and became editor of the *National Press Agency*. In 1888 he joined *The Star*, recently founded by T. P. O'Connor (Irish Home Rule MP for the Scotland division of Liverpool). He was editor of this paper for a few months in 1890, and in the following year became editor of the *Labour World*. Soon after this he widened his influence by filling important positions on *The Daily Chronicle*, beginning as literary editor and becoming editor in 1895. He remained editor until 1899, raising the paper to a position of great influence as an organ of radical Liberal viewpoints on home and foreign politics, and maintaining the distinction of its literary section. His strong 'pro-Boer' attitude of opposition to the South African War of 1899, however, won him much criticism from part of his divided readership, and drove him to resign the editorship. For a time he worked for two other Liberal papers, the *Manchester Guardian* (in London) and then the *Daily News*.

Massingham's longest period of attachment to a single paper was from March 1907 to April 1923, when he was editor of *The Nation*, a Liberal weekly periodical. Although his ardent and impatient radical spirit would have preferred a daily to a weekly outlet for his views, he valued the opportunity to express independent radical opinions in this paper. He urged in 1917, for example, that peace should be sought with Germany. He eventually resigned when the paper went into the hands of new proprietors with different political expectations.

Massingham was one of many radical Liberals who, in a period of Liberal disruption after the First World War, contemplated seeking a political home in the Labour Party. He joined this party in November 1923, even though the Liberals became reunited at that time, and began writing for the *New Statesman*, to which he transferred his 'Wayfarer's Diary' from the *Nation*. He died less than a year after.

Massingham was a natural journalist, a writer of bold vigour and immediacy rather than of scholarly subtlety, and his large and wide-ranging contribution covered literature, drama, and the visual arts as well as politics. He was passionately dedicated to the improvement of human welfare, investing his hopes in this respect in a succession of figures or organisations which (including the Labour Party) successively disappointed him. He was constantly meeting the inevitable frustrations of the idealist.

He died suddenly while staying at Tintagel, Cornwall, on 28 August 1924. He was married twice (his wives were sisters), and had a family of five sons and a daughter by his first wife, Emma Snowdon of Norwich. There is one biography, A. F. Havighurst, *Radical Journalist: H. W. Massingham, 1860–1924* (1974).

Ian Machin

CHRISTOPHER MAYHEW (Lord Mayhew)   1915–97

Christopher Mayhew's decision, in July 1974, to leave the Labour Party and join the Liberal benches in the House of Commons was both a measure of the Liberal Party's return to political health and the culmination of his career-long doubts about the Labour movement. As a minister in both the Attlee and Wilson governments, Mayhew was a sizeable catch for Jeremy Thorpe (*q.v.*) and in crossing the floor, he, with Dick Taverne (*q.v.*), presaged the breakaway of Labour MPs which led to the formation of the SDP.

Born on 12 June 1915 into a prosperous family, Christopher Paget Mayhew was educated at Haileybury College and Christ Church College, Oxford. At school he both thrived and rebelled and, in later life, said it was the public school system which made him a socialist. A contemporary of Roy Jenkins (*q.v.*), Edward Heath and Harold Wilson at Oxford, he became president of the Union Society in 1937.

As a protégé of Hugh Dalton and Clement Attlee (a former Haileyburian), Mayhew was selected as the Labour candidate for the apparently unwinnable seat of South Norfolk in 1938. He joined the Surrey Yeomanry in the same year and, when war broke out, accompanied them to France with the British Expeditionary Force. On his return he joined the covert Special Operations Executive, which he served for the remainder of the war. He was present at the German surrender on Lüneburg Heath.

In July 1945 he was elected for South Norfolk with a majority of 5,963. Tipped as the 'golden boy' of an impressive Labour intake, he became PPS to Herbert Morrison, the Deputy Prime Minister, and, in 1946, was promoted to Parliamentary Under-Secretary of State for Foreign Affairs. He married Cecily Ludlam, an official in his department, in 1949.

Mayhew's seat reverted to the Conservatives in the 1950 election, but he was returned for Woolwich East in 1951. He held Woolwich (later Greenwich & Woolwich East) at the next six general elections, paving the way for his Labour successor, John Cartwright, who retained the seat for the SDP from 1981 to 1992.

In opposition, in Parliament at least, Mayhew under-achieved and although he remained on the front bench throughout the 1950s it was in a junior capacity. Outside the Commons, he became a devoted supporter of often unpopular causes. He began a television career, starring in one of the first party political broadcasts, and campaigning doggedly against commercial broadcasting. He adopted the Palestinian cause as his own and continued to support it until his death. His reputation for outspokenness on the issue attracted the attention of Zionists throughout his career, and led to minor difficulties when he joined the Liberal Party. In 1968 he won a High Court libel action against a fellow Labour MP, Maurice Edelman. The *Sunday Times* also apologised for calling him a 'Judaphobe'.

In 1964 Harold Wilson brought Mayhew back into government as Navy Minister in the newly-combined Ministry of Defence, but he soon became openly critical of what he saw as the sterile nature of the Labour movement. It was this, as much as his opposition to Wilson's refusal to renew the carrier fleet, which led Mayhew to resign in 1966.

He remained on the Labour back benches until 1974, becoming active in a group of like-minded MPs who wanted to replace Wilson, the majority of whom later joined the SDP. In a book, *Party Games* (1969), Mayhew bemoaned the state of the Labour Party and the British political scene. He founded the pro-EEC Campaign for Europe in 1967, with the Liberal peer Lord Gladwyn (*q.v.*).

After Labour's defeat in 1970, Mayhew sat in opposition not just to the government, but to much that his own party stood for. He was the only Labour MP to vote for Heath's abortive Industrial Relations Bill, and, behind the scenes, worked to ensure there were enough Labour abstentions to allow legislation admitting Britain to the European Community to pass the Commons. He published *Europe: the Case for Entry* in 1971. In 1972, he joined MIND (the National Association for Mental Health), becoming its Chairman.

Mayhew's July 1974 decision to join the Liberal Party was taken, he recalled, on spec when he passed Jeremy Thorpe, long a friend, in a Commons corridor. It led to scenes of jubilation in the Liberal whips' office. Mayhew sat as a Liberal member until the October 1974 election. He then contested marginal Bath for the party, losing by 2,122 votes.

With his active Parliamentary career apparently at an end, Mayhew threw himself into campaigning for proportional representation, publishing *The Disillusioned Voter's Guide to Electoral Reform* (1976), serving as Vice-Chairman of the Liberal Action Group for Electoral Reform from 1974–80. He also remained a supporter of the Arab cause, writing *Publish it Not …. The Middle East Cover-up* (1975).

In 1981, Mayhew was elevated to the House of Lords at the suggestion of David Steel (*q.v.*), as a working peer, taking the title Baron Mayhew of Wimbledon. He became Liberal spokesman on defence and President of the Parliamentary Association for European-Arab cooperation. In 1987 he published his autobiography, *Time to*

Explain. He lived in Wimbledon, south London, until his death on 7 January 1997, aged eighty-one.

Julian Glover

MICHAEL MEADOWCROFT   1942–

Michael Meadowcroft was Liberal MP for Leeds West from 1983 to 1987, confounding sceptics to win a solidly inner-city seat by using the community politics approach which he had helped to develop over the preceding fifteen years. He was the main, indeed very nearly the only, philosopher of applied Liberalism within the old Liberal Party from the late 1960s onwards. In 1989 he founded the 'continuing' Liberal Party, after opposing the Liberal/SDP merger the previous year.

Michael James Meadowcroft was born on 6 March 1942 and grew up in Southport. He joined the Liberal Party in 1958, around the same time that he left King George V School to become a bank clerk. He became Chairman of the Merseyside Region of the National League of Young Liberals in 1961.

He joined the Liberal Party's full-time staff in 1962, becoming local government officer. In August 1967 he became the party's full-time regional officer in Yorkshire, and the following year began his marathon stint on Leeds City Council, which lasted until his election to Parliament. For most of this period he was group leader. He also served on West Yorkshire County Council 1973–76 and 1981–83.

In 1970 he was appointed assistant secretary of the Joseph Rowntree Social Services Trust, a post which involved contact with African liberation movements and numerous trips to central and southern Africa. He went on secondment to Bradford University in 1975, being awarded an MPhil in 1978 for a thesis on Leeds political history 1903–26. He then became general secretary of the Bradford Metropolitan Council for Voluntary Service until 1983.

Within the party, he served as chairman of the Liberal Assembly Committee from 1976–81. He was the party's President-elect in 1987, but the merger prevented him taking office.

Meadowcroft's track record in urban local government, and in numerous party offices, gave an experience and credibility to his writings on Liberal philosophy which few at the time could match. His pamphlets and speeches established him as an articulate critic of a party leadership which saw radical liberalism as an electoral liability. He provided much of the philosophical underpinning to the party's local campaigning, providing the 'why' when most other party bodies were interested mainly in the 'how' of community politics.

He was profoundly suspicious of the proposed alliance with the Social Democratic Party in 1981, writing a sceptical pamphlet, *Social Democracy – Barrier or Bridge?*, for the radical magazine *Liberator*. As he wrote: 'The SDP is at one and the same time the greatest opportunity and the greatest danger to Liberalism for thirty years. Without careful philosophic analysis and political vigilance the relationship could be that of the spider and the fly.' The growing conviction that David Steel (q.v.) had willingly allowed the Liberal Party to become 'the fly' informed his subsequent attitude to the Alliance and the merger.

Meadowcroft had fought Leeds West in both 1974 general elections, but stood down in 1979. He was readopted for 1983 and won the seat against the expectations both of the national party and of the band of friends and sympathisers who came from around the country to help. Despite good personal relationships with many Social Democrats, his mistrust of that party grew through his spell in Parliament. During this time he served as health spokesman, and was a whip, though his failure to become Chief Whip in 1985 was a source of considerable rancour. He lost his seat in 1987, later publicly blaming David Owen's flirtation with Thatcherism for his voters' disaffection with the Alliance.

He was elected to the Liberal/SDP merger negotiating team, but was among the Liberal negotiators who walked out in January 1988 over what they were convinced were the deal's unacceptable terms. At the Blackpool special assembly later that month he led the last-ditch 'no' campaign. He briefly stayed on to help Alan Beith's (q.v.) unsuccessful campaign to become leader of the merged party.

In the early spring of 1989 he announced the refounding of the Liberal Party. As political and financial disaster engulfed the Social and Liberal Democrats its prospects seemed promising, and many former Liberal members, infuriated by the new party's contempt for its Liberal heritage, seriously considered joining him. But his party needed parliamentary defections to achieve lift-off, and these did not materialise. The SLD's adoption of the title 'Liberal Democrats' in autumn 1989 encouraged most Liberals to remain rather than make the leap into Meadowcroft's party. Since then it has held a few dozen council seats consistently, and fought enough general election seats to secure broadcasting time, but has only very rarely saved a deposit. Its annual assembly seldom exceeds a hundred attendees.

Meadowcroft was appointed a senior visiting fellow of the Policy Studies Institute in 1989, and became Chairman of the Electoral Reform Society. This coincided with the fall of the Iron Curtain and sudden demand for expertise in political campaigning and election organising in eastern Europe and the Third World. He set up ERS' international consultancy and has since been on thirty-three missions in nineteen countries, assisting the transition to democracy, including Malawi, Palestine, Russia, Bosnia, Bulgaria and Cambodia.

Away from politics he is an enthusiastic traditional jazz clarinettist and saxophonist, and for some years led his own 'Granny Lee's All-Stars'. He has also been a director of the Leeds Grand Theatre and Opera House. He married Elizabeth Bee in 1987, and has a son and daughter from his dissolved first marriage.

Meadowcroft is still President of the independent Liberal Party, but, spending most of his time abroad, is little involved in running it. His presence was the single largest factor in giving it credibility in 1989, and were he to leave it would probably destroy what remains. He fought Leeds West for it in 1992, being narrowly beaten into fourth place by the Liberal Democrats. He did not contest the 1997 election. His continuing involvement in such a peripheral party is viewed as an admirable act of principle by its members, as a regrettable waste by his admirers in the Liberal Democrats, and, no doubt, as the best place for him by those who were always uneasy with his uncompromising Liberalism.

Publications include: *Success in Local Government* (1971), *Liberals and a Popular Front* (1974), *Bluffer's Guide to Politics* (1976), *Liberal Values for a New Decade* (1980), *Social Democracy – Barrier or Bridge?* (1981), *Liberalism and the Left* (1982), *Liberalism and the Right* (1983), *Liberalism Today and Tomorrow* (1989), *The Case for the Liberal Party* (1992), and *Focus on Freedom* (1997).

Mark Smulian

VISCOUNT MELBOURNE   1779–1848

Right from his London birth on 15 March 1779, at Melbourne House in Piccadilly, William Lamb, second Viscount Melbourne, was at the centre of Whig social circles. The second son of Peniston Lamb, first Viscount Melbourne, he followed a normal early life for sons of Whig magnates – Eton, Cambridge University, and education for a legal profession. Politics came naturally into his life, but was not his only interest. As Cecil put it in his biography, 'he had learnt to play the political game with practised skill; but like a grown-up person playing hide-and-seek with children, he never entered completely into the spirit of the thing. His thought moved from a different centre and on different lines.'

He married Lady Caroline Ponsonby in 1805, and the following year was elected MP for Leominster. Although an MP for many years, he regularly moved constituency, sitting at various times for Portalington, Northampton, Hertfordshire and Newport (Isle of Wight). His political views also moved around in these early years, from strong opposition to the war with France to keen support of war and a strong interest in the campaigns in Spain and Portugal. A moderate Whig, he supported some repressive domestic measures, such as the Six Acts, but was also willing to argue for Catholic emancipation.

He became increasingly close to Canning and on the latter's ascension to Prime Minister in 1827 became Irish Secretary. Though popular, he made little impact in the post. He, along with the other Canningites, continued in office under Lord Goderich and then Wellington. However, they resigned *en masse* over the East Retford Bill (1828), believing the government was not willing to go far enough in tacking excessive electoral corruption. Although he personally had supported the Bill, he felt that loyalty to his colleagues was sufficiently important to override this, and resigned with them.

Both his wife, from whom he had separated in 1825, and his father, had died earlier that year. His father's death meant he became Lord Melbourne, with a seat in the House of Lords. Although his wife's death ended such public scandals as her relationship with Byron, his private life continued to draw public attention. He twice appeared as the co-respondent in divorce cases (1829 and 1836). In 1829 the case was not continued – there was little evidence against Melbourne other than that he had sent a woman some grapes and pineapples – and in 1836 the verdict exonerated him.

Under Charles Grey's (q.v.) premiership, Melbourne became Home Secretary in 1830. During this time he came under much attack from radicals for his firm line against protesters, even those supporting electoral reform (which the government was pursuing). However, he did not insist on introducing any special measures, preferring to stick to the normal rule of law. His desire to do what was necessary, but no more, was also reflected in his views on electoral reform – willing to support it, as something that was inevitable, but not keen for it to be far-reaching. Likewise, over Ireland, he took the firm line he saw as necessary, but was also willing to try to strike a deal with the Irish radicals led by O'Connell. His success in ensuring that neither Irish issues nor unrest in England spiralled out of control allowed the rest of the government to stick to its main task of passing electoral reform.

On Grey's resignation in 1834, Melbourne succeeded him as Prime Minister. With the government disintegrating over personality conflicts, disagreement over Ireland and tensions between reformers and more conservative supporters, the King took the opportunity later in the year to sack his ministers. The Tories now had a brief chance in power. Starting in a minority, they made some gains in the 1834 general election, but not enough. They were soon defeated, and Melbourne returned as Prime Minister.

His administration limped on for several years, split over many issues, frequently in conflict with the House of Lords and facing a hostile King. Its only consistent policy was a series of moderate reforms to the Church of England, on which a working relationship was struck with Peel. Some other items of major reform were also passed, most notably to local government, with the Municipal Corporations Act, but they were the exception. As with many later Liberal governments, trouble in Ireland consumed much time and passion, and engendered many splits.

William IV's death brought the young Victoria to the throne and Melbourne successfully acted as her political adviser and counsellor, bringing her into her political role. In 1839 she ensured that Melbourne stayed in power when, after defeats over Ireland forced his resignation, she refused to meet Peel's demands and stopped him from forming an administration.

By 1841, however, nothing could save the government and, after a further defeat brought on an election, Peel swept into power. A paralysis attack the following year meant Melbourne spent much of the rest of his life out of politics, though he was surprised at not being offered office when the Tories fell in 1846. He died two years later, on 24 November 1848. He only had one child, a mentally handicapped son, who died in 1836.

As Prime Minister, Melbourne had a thankless task, leading a collection of factions during a period of Tory revival. That his period in office lasted so long, and that he successfully brought Queen Victoria into public life, were redeeming marks of success.

The standard biography for many years has been D. Cecil, *The Young Melbourne* (1939) and *Lord Melbourne* (1954). Also useful is P. Ziegler, *Melbourne* (Collins, 1976). The most recent biography is L. G. Mitchell, *Lord Melbourne 1779–1848* (OUP, 1997); arguably this book, with its comprehensive coverage of many of the aspects of Melbourne's life, is now the standard work.

Mark Pack

RAY MICHIE MP 1934–

Janet Ray Bannerman was born on 4 February 1934 at The Old Manse, Balmaha, Loch Lomond. The daughter of the late Lord (*q.v.*) and Lady Bannerman of Kildonan, she was raised in a political and famously Liberal family. She was educated at Aberdeen High School for Girls and Lansdowne House School, Edinburgh, and qualified as a speech therapist at the Edinburgh College of Speech Therapy.

Michie was active in the party from an early age, canvassing and campaigning in her teens with her father in his unsuccessful bids to become an MP and, with her mother, fundraising for the Scottish Liberal Party. It was the determination to 'right a wrong that has endured for three hundred years' that inspired her to seek political office herself to campaign for a Scottish Parliament.

With the defection of the previous candidate, John MacKay, to the Conservative Party after 1974, the local Argyll & Bute Liberal Party were at a low ebb and although never seeing herself as a career politician, Michie decided to practice what she preached and step in as candidate. She first contested the seat in 1979, coming in fourth but keeping her deposit. Undeterred, she fought it again in 1983 and came second. Loyal support and help from within her local party, and kind words from other influential figures such as David Steel (*q.v.*), kept the momentum going until she eventually won the seat in 1987, resigning from her job as Area Speech Therapist for Argyll & Clyde Health Board.

Faithful to her original intentions, Michie has campaigned single-mindedly for home rule and has earned a reputation as a diligent constituency representative. She is renowned equally for what she does not do at Westminster, refusing to court unnecessary press attention or be drawn into sensationalism, and leaving alone issues which she feels are irrelevant to her constituents.

Her sensible approach to the job makes her a popular figure within the establishment, though she is still willing to criticise when appropriate. Together with other Liberal Democrat colleagues, she has staged a number of demonstrations at Westminster to show her disgust at the lack of proper representation for Scotland, including withdrawing cooperation from select committees and disrupting the Parliamentary timetable. This paid off and Michie represented the party on the Select Committee on Scottish Affairs from 1992–97.

Her first portfolio for the Parliamentary party was transport, but she was most comfortable speaking on Scottish issues and constitutional reform and continues to do so. For a time the lone female voice within the Parliamentary party, Michie thus became responsible for women's issues, bringing her own blend of sensitivity and realism to this sometimes controversial field. She continues to believe firmly in the need for greater equality between the sexes in all walks of life through education, quality childcare and equal pay. She believes that more women will be brought into politics as it becomes more relevant to them, again citing a Scottish Parliament as an empowering solution.

Always interested in language, Michie is a keen promoter of the Gaelic language and is a member of An Comunn Gaidhealach. She has often represented her previous colleagues as Vice-President of the College of Speech and Language Therapists. She is also joint Vice-Chair of the Parliamentary Group on the Whisky Industry, Honorary President of the Clyde Fishermen's Association, Honorary Associate of the National Council of Women in Great Britain and most recently was invited to be a member of the Chairman's Panel at Westminster. She has been Vice Chairman of the Scottish Liberals and chaired the Scottish Liberal Democrats 1991–93.

Her greatest moment to date has been the referendum result of 1997, paving the way for the reestablishment of a Scottish Parliament, and she is optimistic about the current spirit of cooperation in British politics. Michie's consistent and firm set of priorities have meant that at each general election her majority has steadily increased.

In 1957 Michie married a consultant physician, Iain Michie, a fluent Gaelic speaker from the Isle of Skye, and himself a well-known and popular character. They live in Oban and have three daughters. Michie continues to uphold a traditional family life and outside politics enjoys golf, swimming, gardening and watching Scotland play rugby.

Emma Sanderson-Nash

NATHANIEL MICKLEM 1888–1976

Nonconformist church leader and author Nathaniel Micklem was born at Brondesbury on 10 April 1888 into what might be called the Liberal squirearchy. His father, also Nathaniel, was MP for West Hertfordshire in the Parliament of 1906; the young

Micklem was, he said in later life, 'brought up to be concerned with politics, as a citizen of the modern state should be'. He followed the *cursus honorum* of public school (Rugby) and Oxford (New College). After graduating in 1911 with a second in Greats, Micklem moved the three hundred yards or so to Mansfield College, a nonconformist theological institution with which he was destined to be linked for much of his career. His time there studying theology also allowed him to involve himself in the Oxford Union, of which he was President in 1912. In these years, he was approached by the Oxfordshire Liberal Association with a view to his following in his father's footsteps and becoming a parliamentary candidate. He was, however, determined upon the life of ministry; politics was to be his concern, not his career.

He was ordained a Congregational minister in 1914 and served churches in Bristol and Manchester, before working with the YMCA at Dieppe for the last two years of the war, despite being a pacifist. His move across the Channel followed soon after his marriage; he married within the Liberal squirearchy, to Agatha, daughter of T. B. Sillcock. After the war, Micklem returned to Mansfield as chaplain (1918–21); he moved to Selly Oak, Birmingham as Professor of Old Testament (1921–27); and then went further afield, being appointed Professor of New Testament at Queen's Theological College, Kingston, Ontario. In his autobiography, he expressed his contentment in Canada and his regret at having to leave in 1931. Mansfield, however, called him back as Professor of Dogmatic Theology, with an intimation that he would succeed to the Principalship, a promotion which occurred the following year.

Micklem lived in Oxfordshire for the rest of his life; his career was much bound up in the politics of the Free Churches but his spare time was given to Liberal politics. He was President of his local Liberal Association for many years and was closely involved with the famous Oxford byelection of 1938. In 1957–58 he was President of the Liberal Party and, from 1959–71, President of the British Group of Liberal International. He retired from Mansfield in 1953. His wife, by whom he had three sons, died in 1961; he survived until Boxing Day 1976.

Micklem wrote widely and in a variety of genres; he provided autobiographies in prose (*The Box and the Puppets*, 1957) and verse; he wrote a series of theological works and several books which touched on politics. He was convinced that politics needed theology to provide a moral basis, a view most clearly set out in his war-time work, *The Theology of Politics* (1941); this volume, like his notable *The Idea of Liberal Democracy* (1957), bears the mark not only of his reading of both classical and nineteenth-century philosophy but also of his revulsion at the totalitarianisms of his own lifetime. This disgust, based on Micklem's own knowledge of Nazi persecution of Christians and Jews, led him to abandon his earlier pacifism during the Second World War. Throughout his life, however, he stood by his honest liberal belief in the importance of liberty within a framework of morality and civic duty.

David Rundle

JOHN STUART MILL   1806–73

John Stuart Mill, philosopher, economist, journalist, political writer, social reformer, and, briefly, Liberal MP, is one of the most famous figures in the pantheon of Liberal theorists, and the greatest of the Victorian Liberal thinkers. Yet his relevance is not restricted to the nineteenth century; as L. T. Hobhouse (*q.v.*) wrote in 1911, 'in his single person he spans the interval between the old and the new liberalism'.

The eldest son of the Scottish utilitarian philosopher James Mill, John Stuart was educated at home by his father. A precocious pupil, he soon became the rising hope of Philosophical Radicalism. Still a teenager, he wrote for newspapers like the *Morning Chronicle* before becoming editor of the most prestigious radical periodical of the time, the *Westminster Review*. At the age of seventeen he became his father's assistant at India House, and in due course succeeded him as Head of the Examiner's Office of the East India Company, a position roughly equivalent to that of a Secretary of State.

In 1826–27, following an illness, Mill entered into what he described as his 'mental crisis' – a romantic period during which he moved away from Benthamite utilitarianism. Under the influence of Wordsworth, Coleridge, Carlyle and the French Saint-Simonians, Mill came to accept many of the legacies of Kantian and post-Kantian German philosophy. An important aspect of his new political thought was his concern to combine the democratic requirements of government accountability with a role for an elite of cultivated persons – independent intellectuals and 'public moralists' like himself. Thus in his reflections on *M. De Tocqueville on Democracy in America* (1840) Mill discussed the United States as a consumer democracy, and tried to separate the phenomena of a 'mass society', of which he disapproved, from the institutions of political democracy, which he wished to encourage.

In 1843 he published his first major treatise, *A System of Logic* (1843), which combined deduction and induction in a revised approach to empiricist philosophy. In 1848, while Europe was being shaken by democratic and national revolutions, Mill published his *Principles of Political Economy*, which remained the standard university textbook in the English-speaking world for the next thirty years. Mill rejected Ricardo's (*q.v.*) assumption that fixed and rigid 'laws' regulated not only the production of wealth, but also its distribution, arguing that the latter constituted a legitimate sphere for experiments in social reform. In this context he supported the creation of a class of small peasant farmers as a remedy for famine-stricken Ireland. In industrial England he placed his hopes in the development of the cooperative movement and the formation of strong trade unions as means whereby a more equal distribution of wealth could gradually be achieved.

A romantic in political and economic thought, Mill showed even stronger romantic proclivities in his private life. His long love affair with Harriet Taylor (1807–58) became a source of great intellectual stimulus and powerful inspiration for the rest of his life. When the two first met in 1830 she was married to a successful London merchant, John Taylor, but growing bored with the lifestyle of the Victorian middle-class woman. A formidable character, she was a nonconformist by both faith (as a Unitarian) and temperament. After twenty-one years of friendship and intimacy, Mill and Harriet were married in 1851, one year after Taylor's death.

The areas of Mill's thought in which Harriet's personality was most strongly felt were those concerning issues of civil liberty and women's emancipation, which Mill came to see as reciprocally interdependent. His masterpiece *On Liberty* (1859) emphatically vindicated individual moral autonomy, and celebrated the importance of originality and dissent. Though generations of socialist critics have identified Mill's defence of individual freedom against 'the tyranny of the majority' as an expression of bourgeois prejudice against the working classes, the truth of the matter is that Mill was afraid not of some theoretical 'dictatorship of the proletariat' but of middle-class conformism, which he had studied in its contemporary manifestations in the USA, seen at work in Britain in the ostracism of pacifists like Richard Cobden (*q.v.*) and John Bright (*q.v.*) during the Crimean and Opium wars, and was soon to experience personally. Thus his target was, in a sense, the 'political correctness' of his own day, which stultified opposition and a critical cast of mind in the name of an orthodoxy admitting of neither discussion nor criticism. In *Considerations on Representative Government* (1861) Mill expounded his doctrine of democracy. In a systematic attempt to combine participation with competence, Mill emphasised the importance of local government and recommended that intellectuals should be given a plurality of votes within an electoral system based on universal suffrage and proportional representation.

In these years Mill became actively involved in current politics, and in 1865 successfully stood as a parliamentary candidate for the borough of Westminster. As an MP Mill took an active part in the debate on the Second Reform Bill (1866–67), advocating proportional representation as well as the extension of the suffrage to women householders. Taking an active interest in Irish affairs, he strongly opposed the suspension of the Habeas Corpus Act, and maintained that social reform, rather than repression, was the cure for civil unrest in Ireland. Mill was also involved in several civil rights campaigns, defending prostitutes against arbitrary arrest and medical examination under the Contagious Diseases Acts, and opposing the 1867 Extradition Bill, which would have drastically limited the right of foreigners to seek asylum in Britain.

Moreover, he was a leading figure in the campaign for the impeachment of the Governor of Jamaica, Eyre, who had brutally repressed a series of riots by the extensive use of courts martial. This campaign involved issues of civil rights and racial equality in a colony where blacks outnumbered whites by thirty to one. Mill denounced the repression as wholesale murder by crown officials, but was himself violently attacked for 'sentimentalising over a pack of black brutes'. In the face of that very sort of 'tyranny of public opinion' against which he had warned in *On Liberty*, Mill continued to campaign until July 1868, when the case against Eyre was finally dismissed by the Queen's Bench. At the ensuing general election, in November 1868, 'public opinion' took its revenge: Mill lost his seat to the Conservative W. H. Smith, of stationery fame. It was fitting for an age of increasing consumerism that people preferred the man who sold books to the one who wrote them.

A further reason for Mill's defeat at the 1868 parliamentary election was his strong commitment to women's emancipation. In 1867 he had been one of the founders of the first women's suffrage society, which later developed into the National Union of Women's Suffrage Societies. Undeterred by violent criticism and insults, in 1869 Mill published *The Subjection of Women*, a classical statement of the case for women's rights which immediately became influential among politicised women, both in Britain and abroad. After leaving Parliament in 1868 Mill continued to be politically active. His last initiative was the organisation of the Land Tenure Reform Association. The imposition of heavy taxes on the unearned increment of land values and the promotion of cooperative agriculture were the most striking features of his programme, which was to inspire later generations of Liberals until the days of Lloyd George (*q.v.*). This campaign was in full swing when Mill died suddenly at Avignon on 8 May 1873. He had no children.

All of Mill's major works are still in print, as is his *Autobiography* (1873), which gives a persuasive picture of his career and opinions, although in places is primarily a work of propaganda. Other relevant works include: Alexander Bain (a friend of Mill's), *John Stuart Mill* (1882); M. StJ. Packe, *The Life of John Stuart Mill* (Secker & Warburg, 1954); J. M. Robson and M. Laine (eds), *James and John Stuart Mill* (1976); B. L. Kinzer, *A Moralist in and out of Parliament: John Stuart Mill at Westminster 1865–78* (1992); A. Ryan, *The Philosophy of John Stuart Mill* (1998); and J. Skorupski, *The Cambridge Companion to Mill* (1998).

E. F. Biagini

SIR ALFRED MOND (Lord Melchett) 1868–1930

Alfred Moritz Mond was born on 28 October 1868 at Parnworth, Lancashire, the younger son of Dr Ludwig and Freda Mond. His father was a talented German Jew who had left Cassel in 1862 and who, together with John Tomlinson Brunner, set up the great chemical company which developed in 1881 into the public joint-stock company Brunner, Mond & Co. Mond inherited from his father a marked aptitude and flair for science and industry, and from his mother an appreciation of art.

He was educated at Cheltenham College, St John's College, Cambridge, where he studied the natural science tripos, and Edinburgh University. He was called to the bar in 1894 and practiced briefly on the North Wales and Chester Circuit. He viewed the experience as a valuable prelude to the political career to which he was totally committed. But in 1895 he became director, and a little later managing director, of his father's nickel and chemical business. During his subsequent years of business management he formulated a firm industrial philosophy from which he never departed. He became convinced of the need for organisation and research, and was an advocate of industrial rationalisation and amalgamation. He championed close cooperation between employers and the labour force.

Mond's first foray into political life came in the notorious 'khaki' general election of 1900 when, attracted by the social, economic and commercial policies of the Liberal Party, he contested the marginal seat of South Salford. After an exhausting three-cornered contest, he was soundly defeated by the Tory candidate by more than a thousand votes. In 1903 he joined the National League of Young Liberals and became a keen advocate of the New Liberalism. He secured the Liberal nomination for highly marginal Chester where, in the Liberal avalanche of 1906, he was elected by a margin of forty-seven. He subsequently served as Liberal MP for Chester from 1906–10, for Swansea Town from 1910–18, and for Swansea West from 1918–23. He also served for Carmarthen from 1924–28, joining the Conservative Party in January 1926.

Although rightly described as 'blunt, direct, sometimes rather blustering, and occasionally distinctly ill-mannered', Mond made his mark on political life, impressing fellow MPs by his strength of character, business acumen and grasp of detail. At Swansea he was depicted as 'an odd exotic' amongst a predominantly pedestrian group of Welsh Liberal MPs. He was the victim of virulent anti-semitic onslaughts from his Tory opponents, and his spurious patriotism was easily assailed by fiery 'patriots' like Keir Hardie.

Mond first achieved renown as a prominent member of the 'Liberal War Committee' set up in January 1916, the ginger group of Liberals who helped to propel Lloyd George (q.v.) to the premiership. Consequently, the new Prime Minister made Mond First Commissioner of Works, one of the most important posts not of Cabinet rank to be filled by a Liberal. Despite much local resentment, he was narrowly re-elected at Swansea West in the 'coupon' general election of 1918. In the post-war government he emerged as a vocal proponent of constructive social reform. He displayed an avid preoccupation with imperial matters and Welsh affairs and was a diehard opponent of repeated plans to secure the fusion of Lloyd George's Liberal followers and their Tory allies.

In April 1921 Mond succeeded Dr Christopher Addison (q.v.) as Minister of Public Health. In this position, strongly supported by Lloyd George, he was obliged to jettison his predecessor's ambitious house-building programme and far-reaching slum clearance plans. When the coalition government fell in October 1922, Mond stood for re-election at Swansea West as a 'prefixless Liberal' and won by only 802 votes.

In 1923 he became a zealous advocate of Liberal reunion, but, ironically, in the general election which followed in November he was narrowly defeated by socialist barrister Walter Samuel. Within months, however, he was presented with the opportunity to return to the Commons when the ailing Sir Ellis Jones Ellis-Griffith, veteran Liberal MP for Carmarthenshire, resolved to retire from Parliament. This precipitated a byelection in August 1924; Mond secured the Liberal nomination and was easily returned to Parliament by a majority of 4,409.

In the further general election which followed the collapse of Ramsay MacDonald's first Labour government before the end of the year, Mond more than doubled his majority at Carmarthen, but his position within the Liberal Party was growing ever more uncomfortable. As a zealous anti-socialist, he increasingly abhorred Lloyd George's embryonic proposals for a form of quasi-nationalisation of rural land. The publication in October 1925 of the famous Liberal policy document, *The Land and the Nation* (the Green Book), with proposals amounting almost to a nationalisation of rural land, proved the last straw. The following January he resigned from the Liberal Party and joined the Conservatives. He was due to contest the next election in Carmarthenshire as a Tory candidate, but in June 1928 he was elevated to the peerage as the first Baron Melchett of Blandford. This precipitated a byelection in the county on 6 June, during which Mond appeared on Conservative election platforms.

As a peer Lord Melchett played little active part in party politics. He devoted the closing years of his life to the pursuit of Zionism and the achievement of industrial harmony, the rationalisation of British industry and imperial economic unity. His extensive business interests remained of central importance. He was Chairman of the board of Mond Nickel from 1922, a member of the board of Brunner, Mond & Company from 1923, and in 1926 he was one of the leading lights behind the formation of Imperial Chemical Industries Ltd (ICI).

He re-emerged as the instigator of the Mond-Turner industrial peace conferences, first convened in January 1928, an initiative which created a more conciliatory spirit in the aftermath of the General Strike, and won him the respect and trust of some prominent trade union leaders. Mond died at his home in Lowndes Square, London, on 27 December 1930. He had married Violet Florence Mabel, daughter of James Henry Coetze, a coffee merchant of Mincing Street, London in 1894. They had three daughters and one son, the Hon. Henry Ludwig (born 1898), who succeeded him as second baron. He was the author of a number of works including *Industry and Politics* (1927) and *Imperial Economic Unity* (1930). Most of his numerous articles were re-published in *Questions of Today and Tomorrow* (1912).

Mond made an important contribution to British political life. Although 'he had a bad voice, a bad delivery, and a presence unimpressive to all but the caricaturist', he made a number of memorable speeches in the Commons. He displayed a notable common sense and a mastery of industrial and fiscal questions, earning considerable respect and affection in political circles and tackling head-on the housing problem in 1921–22. He emerged as 'the most authoritative critic of the theories of the Socialist Party in the House of Commons .... a man of capability rather than a man of genius'. A biography by Hector Bolitho, *Alfred Mond: first Lord Melchett* was published in 1933. A PhD thesis by G. M. Bayliss, *The Outsider: Aspects of the Political Career of Alfred Mond, first Lord Melchett (1868–1930),* was accepted by the University of Wales in 1969.

J. Graham Jones

EDWIN MONTAGU   1879–1924

Few of the young men swept into Parliament by the Liberal landslide in 1906 endured as meteoric a rise and fall as Montagu. By the age of thirty-eight he was Secretary of State for India, introducing sweeping reforms to the government of the subcontinent. Yet he was forced to resign in 1922 after a bitter Cabinet dispute and he died a disappointed man only two years later.

Edwin Samuel Montagu was born on 6 February 1879 in London, the second son of Samuel Montagu, later the first Lord Swaythling. Swaythling was a prominent financier, a staunchly Orthodox Jew and a Liberal MP for fifteen years. His son was sympathetic only to the last of these activities. Montagu was educated at Clifton College, the City of London School and then Trinity College, Cambridge, where he became President of the Union and developed political ambitions. An allowance from his father enabled Montagu to become a full-time politician and in 1904 he was selected by the local Liberals to fight Cambridgeshire Chesterton. He won the seat in 1906 and held it until 1918, when he became MP for the unified Cambridgeshire constituency.

Montagu was attracted to the Liberal Imperialist strand of thought in the party and had caught the eye of one of its leaders, H. H. Asquith (q.v.), while still at Cambridge. Asquith became his mentor and his friend, making Montagu one of his private secretaries in 1906, and in 1910 promoting him to the post of Under-Secretary of State for India. Unusually, Montagu actually visited India in 1912–13 and soon came to regard himself as an expert on Indian affairs. It was not until February 1914 that Montagu started to move out of Asquith's orbit. In that month he became Financial Secretary to the Treasury, working under David Lloyd George (q.v.), the Cabinet's other commanding figure. In February 1915 he entered the Cabinet as Chancellor of the Duchy of Lancaster.

However, when the coalition government was formed in May 1915, Montagu, as the most recent recruit, was left out of the Cabinet and went back to his post as Financial Secretary. But his work at the Treasury was highly regarded and he returned to the Cabinet in January 1916, succeeding Lloyd George as Minister of Munitions in July of that year. In that post he came to share his predecessor's views about the necessity for the direction of industrial labour and to drift further away from Asquith. He attempted, without success, to mediate between his old chief and Lloyd George during the crisis of December 1916, when he found his loyalties severely torn. He would have liked to have accepted a post under Lloyd George, had he not felt obliged to follow the rest of his Liberal colleagues out of office on Asquith's resignation.

In June 1917, though, Lloyd George offered Montagu the Secretaryship of State for India, after a long mutual courtship. This was too attractive an offer to turn down and Montagu accepted. He had strong views that a further round of reform was inevitable in the government of India. The First World War had produced intense strains in the Raj. Its response to such situations since the late nineteenth century had been to give

Indians a bigger role in local and provincial government, so separating moderates from extremists, while preserving British rule at the centre. Montagu believed this process should be taken a step further and coupled this plan with a declaration that Britain's ultimate goal was Indian 'self-government'. However, this was to be in the far-distant future and Montagu's reforms were meant to swing India behind the war effort and quieten unrest for the next decade or so. His intentions were embodied in the 1919 Government of India Act, planned after a lengthy visit to India in 1917–18.

However, the Act seemed initially to stimulate violent protests, rather than produce calm. Montagu urged the Indian government to moderation in its response and wished for a stronger condemnation of General Dyer for his massacre of demonstrators at Amritsar in 1919. His attitude was fiercely criticised by Tory diehards in a bad-tempered Commons debate in July 1920, but by 1922 the situation in India was quiet and remained so until the late 1920s, seeming to vindicate Montagu's approach. In domestic politics Montagu consistently urged the coalition Cabinet in the direction of social reform. He also took a strong interest in foreign policy – a field in which he claimed an independent voice as the representative of India. In particular, he insisted the government should not provoke Indian Muslim opinion by partitioning Turkey, the only Muslim power and seat of the Caliphate.

The latter issue was Montagu's undoing. In March 1922 he authorised the publication of a message from the Viceroy, setting out India's wish to revise the Treaty of Sèvres that had been imposed on Turkey in 1920. This severely embarrassed the Foreign Secretary in the middle of negotiations on this subject. Montagu had already challenged Cabinet policy in Egypt and Kenya and Lloyd George was finding him an increasingly obstreperous colleague. He took the opportunity to force him to resign. Montagu was devastated and vigorously denounced Lloyd George as a quasi–dictator in a speech to his constituents. But his career was over, and when he lost his seat in the 1922 election he retired from politics, an embittered man. He took a number of jobs in the City and died in London on 15 November 1924.

Montagu married in 1915 Venetia Stanley, daughter of the Liberal landowner and politician, Lord Sheffield. They had one daughter, Judy. Asquith had been in love with Venetia – probably a factor in his estrangement from Montagu. She edited Montagu's *An Indian Diary* (1930). There is a biography by S. D. Waley, *Edwin Montagu: a Memoir* (Bombay, 1964).

Ian Packer

MICHAEL MOORE MP   1965–

Michael Kevin Moore was born on 3 June 1965 in Dundonald, Northern Ireland. His father, the Rev. Haisley Moore, was a Church of Scotland chaplain in the British army, and when he left the forces in 1970 the family moved to Wishaw, in the shadow of the Ravenscraig steelworks. He attended Strathallan School in Perthshire until coming to the Borders in 1981. He joined the SDP in 1983, and worked in the Roxburgh & Berwickshire campaign which saw Archy Kirkwood (q.v.) defeat Ian Sproat.

Moore was first noted as a man of judgement when he summoned the officers of the National League of Young Liberals to Jedburgh in the early '80s, and after a meeting during which they offered to organise demos, direct action and campaigns of civil disobedience, wisely settled for a talk by Sir Alec Douglas-Home to his modern studies group at Jedburgh Academy. Party managers immediately organised a covert surveillance operation on his progress through university and accountancy courses, intent on entrapment before he started to earn unmatchable wealth as a corporate accountant. Known affectionately at school as Basil Fawlty because – he says! – of his height, he was hard to lose.

He graduated in history and politics (2:1) from Edinburgh University in 1987, and then came to Westminster to work for the party as a volunteer for a year before taking up a Coopers & Lybrand trainee place back in Edinburgh. He became a chartered accountant in 1991. While in London, the Kirkwood office set him the task of briefing the newly re-elected member for Roxburgh & Berwickshire on the committee stage of the 1988 Scottish Housing Bill. He was able to produce amendments which tied the Scottish Office housing minister in knots, and won worthwhile concessions from Lord James Douglas Hamilton.

He was duly stalked, then talked, into competing for the vacancy left by David Steel (q.v.) in Tweeddale, Ettrick & Lauderdale and won the seat in May 1997. His solid Presbyterian upbringing reassured the Borders faithful, and the early army family background helped knock the constituency organisation into some semblance of shape. Having a qualified accountant as a candidate reportedly came as a shock to the local party treasurer. Moore's majority of 1,489 in 1997 was a much bigger personal achievement than he is widely credited with, considering the substantial extent to which the seat boundaries had been redrawn, and the scale of the Labour advance.

Since his election, Moore has become a prominent member of the Scottish affairs team, speaking on industry, employment and health. He is also a member of the Scottish Affairs Select Committee. Arguably his biggest challenge will be in his new role as Campaign Chairman for the Scottish Parliamentary elections in 1999. For Jim Wallace (q.v.) to entrust this responsibility to such a relatively new parliamentary colleague is a measure of the extent to which Moore has quickly won the respect of his follow Scottish MPs.

He lives in Innerleithen, in the heart of his constituency, and enjoys jazz and walking.

Archy Kirkwood

SIR RHYS HOPKIN MORRIS   1888–1956

Rhys Hopkin Morris was born at Maesteg, Glamorganshire, on 5 September 1888, the son of the Rev. John Morris, a Congregationalist minister. He received his early education at home from his parents, later secured a position as a pupil-teacher at Glyncorrwg school in 1902, and entered the University College of North Wales, Bangor, in 1910. Here he proved himself an effective debater, served as President of the students' union in 1911, and graduated with honours in philosophy in 1912.

He taught briefly at Bargoed before joining the army at the outbreak of the First World War, soon becoming an officer in the Royal Welch Fusiliers. He was mentioned twice in dispatches and was awarded the MBE. Immediately after the war he studied for a law degree at King's College, London and was called to the bar at the Middle Temple in 1920. He joined the then Oxford and South Wales Circuit.

His first active foray into political life occurred in the famous 1921 byelection in Cardiganshire, where he gave unstinting support to the Independent (Asquithian) Liberal candidate, W. Llewelyn Williams, who was defeated by the Coalition Liberal, Captain Ernest Evans, Lloyd George's private secretary. Then was born a deep-rooted, enduring enmity between Morris and Lloyd George (*q.v.*) which never completely disappeared. In 1922 Morris was narrowly defeated in the county when he stood as an Independent Liberal against Evans. But he easily headed the poll there in a three-cornered contest in 1923, when a Conservative also stood, and was returned unopposed in 1924.

In the mid-1920s he remained virulently opposed to Lloyd George. When Liberal reunion dominated the discussion at the Welsh Liberal Party conference at Llandrindod in June 1924, Morris asserted forthrightly: 'I am not a follower of Mr Lloyd George, and I have no intention of being one'. He voted against Lloyd George's election as Chairman of the parliamentary Liberal Party in 1926 and remained generally hostile, giving at best lukewarm endorsement to his leader's novel policies as the general election of May 1929 approached; even afterwards he sometimes condemned Lloyd George's 'mercenary army' and his 'fancy policies'. After the disappointment of the election, Morris was the only Liberal MP to vote against the re-election of Lloyd George as party Leader – 'I will accept the leadership of Mr Lloyd George in so far as it is a Liberal leadership and no further'.

Morris defeated Cardiganshire's first-ever Labour candidate in October 1931 by a substantial majority. By this time he was considered a future Leader of the Liberal Party in Wales, so widespread disappointment and surprise greeted his decision in 1932 to accept a position as a metropolitan magistrate at London, which required his immediate resignation as an MP. In his new position he soon built up a reputation for professionalism, fairness and courtesy. His career took another turn in October 1936, when he became the first BBC Regional Director for Wales, displaying a notable independence of outlook, especially during the difficult days of the Second World War, when he insisted upon the right to continue broadcasting extensively in the Welsh language. He gave unfailing guidance and support to those responsible for the practical aspects of Welsh-language broadcasting.

Politics remained his first love, however, for in 1945 Morris stood as the Liberal candidate for the highly marginal Carmarthenshire. In the face of the massive Labour landslide, he narrowly captured the seat, the only Labour loss in the whole of Britain. He retained the seat, against the odds, in the general elections of 1950, 1951 and 1955, with tiny majorities on the first two occasions, and relieved of Tory opposition on all three. This record was attributed to his personal popularity and esteem. Jo Grimond (*q.v.*) recalled Morris as 'the most delightful and original man I ever met in Parliament. He had upheld the purest doctrine of traditional Liberalism. Hopkin would neither manoeuvre nor compromise himself, nor had he much tolerance for those who did. He had no ambition for office, nor indeed even to hold his seat on any terms other than his own.'

In 1951 he became Deputy Chairman of Ways and Means, and thus Deputy Speaker of the House of Commons. In this position his innate sense of fair play and keen legal brain made him an absolute guardian of the rights and privileges of back-bench MPs. He probably welcomed the necessity to stand aside from active politics which the position entailed. He also remained generally aloof from Welsh nationalism, conspicuously failing to endorse the 'Parliament for Wales' agitation of the early fifties.

Morris was a member of the parliamentary delegation to East Africa in 1928 and of the Palestine Commission in 1929. In 1946 he met Gandhi as a member of the delegation to India led by Robert Richards. In 1949 he embarked upon a successful lecture tour of the USA. He was made a KC in 1946 and was knighted in 1954.

He married Gwladys Perrie Williams in 1918, and they had one daughter. He died, still an MP, at his home in Sidcup, Kent, on 22 November 1956. All those who came into contact with Sir Rhys were immediately struck by his absolute integrity, inherent tolerance and loathing of humbug; it was these qualities which enabled him to retain Carmarthenshire after the Second World War. As his wife wrote privately after his death, 'the fact that he did not attain the great heights was due to his lack of interest in the heights themselves. He was not interested in office; all he cared for was the furtherance of Liberal beliefs.'

A brief tribute by T. J. Evans, *Rhys Hopkin Morris: the Man and his Character,* was published in 1957, while a fuller biography (in Welsh) by John Emanuel and D. Ben Rees, *Bywyd a Gwaith Syr Rhys Hopkin Morris,* appeared in 1980.

J. Graham Jones

RAMSAY MUIR   1872–1941

Ramsay Muir was a leading figure in the Liberal Summer School movement and the National Liberal Federation in the 1920s and 1930s. He was briefly a Liberal MP, but, more importantly, he was one of the most prominent Liberal thinkers in inter-war Britain, and had a marked influence on party policy. After his death, Muir was described by his Oxford friend Ernest Barker as 'the scholar-prophet of Liberalism', and his writings on liberalism and international policy still have relevance today.

John Ramsay Bryce Muir was born at Otterburn, Northumberland, on 30 September 1872, the son of a Presbyterian minister. He was educated at a small private school in Birkenhead, and won a scholarship to University College, Liverpool, in 1889. He was initially funded by the Presbyterian Church, and was training to be a Presbyterian minister, but after only a year, he switched to a history course, partly due to his own religious doubts. A first at Liverpool was followed by four years at Balliol College, Oxford, where he gained firsts in Greats and modern history. Whilst at Oxford, he became interested in politics, but his strong belief in the Empire meant that he was out of sympathy with many in the Liberal Party of the 1890s.

In 1898, Muir returned to Liverpool as a lecturer, and was later Professor of History in 1906–13. During this time he devoted much of his historical writing to a history of Liverpool, but his political awareness was further awakened by the constitutional crisis of 1910, when he wrote *Peers and Bureaucrats*. The Great War was also important in developing his interest in politics, and he wrote extensively on why Britain was justified in fighting Germany for democracy. Having spent 1913–14 travelling in India, he became Chair of Modern History at Manchester, but he resigned the post in 1921 in order to devote himself to politics.

By 1921, Muir had already become active in the Manchester Liberal Federation, and had made two contributions to Liberal politics. Firstly, he and his colleagues in Manchester had persuaded the party to think seriously about industrial questions. In 1920 he wrote *Liberalism and Industry*, a call to government and industry to work together in setting goals and strategies so that the country could be competitive, but also help remedy social problems. These radical proposals helped to pave the way for Lloyd George's (*q.v.*) industrial enquiry and the Yellow Book of 1928. Secondly, Muir helped to establish the Liberal Summer School in 1921, with Ernest Simon (*q.v.*), Walter Layton (*q.v.*), J. M. Keynes (*q.v.*), and Hubert Henderson. The Summer School was a major source of ideas for the Liberal Party in the 1920s and 1930s, and Muir was active in it throughout.

He was also editor of the *Weekly Westminster*, from November 1923 to January 1926, when the paper merged with the *Westminster Gazette*, for which he continued to write articles. Aside from writing and organising, Muir also stood for Parliament eight times, but was successful only once. His first battle was in Rochdale in 1922, and he took the seat at his second attempt in December 1923. This was an unfortunate time to enter Parliament as MP for a marginal seat; he was defeated in the Liberal catastrophe of October 1924. In March 1926, he then fought the Combined English Universities constituency in a byelection, and again stood in Rochdale in 1929. He fought Scarborough & Whitby at the May 1931 byelection, and at the 1935 general election. In the 1931 general election, he stood in Louth.

Within the Liberal Party, Muir had more electoral success, being Chairman of the National Liberal Federation 1931–33, and its President 1933–36. In 1936–41, he was Vice-President of the Liberal Party Organisation, and Chairman of its education and propaganda committees. Muir also remained prominent as a Liberal thinker in the 1930s. He became a leading publicist for issues which particularly concerned Liberals, such as proportional representation, and wrote a humorous political novel, *Robinson the Great* (1929), on the possibilities open to the Liberals in a balanced parliament. He wrote much of the National Liberal Federation's *The Liberal Way* (1934), which was a powerful statement not just of Liberal policy, but also of the principles underlying modern social liberalism.

Through his historical and political works, especially *The Interdependent World and its Problems* (1932), Muir also popularised the idea of 'interdependency', originally developed through the pages of the *Economist* through its editor, Walter Layton. This argued that due to economic and technological developments, the world was now interdependent in a way it had never been before, which in turn meant that international political and economic issues could not be separated from each other. The idea was in part a restatement of free trade, but its promotion of the concept of a single international system was new, and it challenged the dominant belief that nations could maintain sovereignty independently. This was influential on Liberal international policy in the 1930s and after.

Muir died on 4 May 1941, at Pinner in Middlesex. He never married and had no children. His unfinished autobiography is reproduced in a book containing essays about Muir by his friends and colleagues: Stuart Hodgson (ed.), *Ramsay Muir: An Autobiography and Some Essays* (1943). Muir's historical writings were extensive, but the most important include his historical atlases, used widely in schools, and *A Short History of the British Commonwealth* (1920–22). This latter work used history to show how the British Empire had developed into its contemporary form, and he also used history to illustrate other current issues – in, for example, *Nationalism and Internationalism* (1916); *The Expansion of Europe* (1917); and *The Interdependent World and its Problems* (1932). His most notable political works include: *Liberalism and Industry* (1920); *Politics and Progress* (1923); *The Faith of a Liberal* (1933); *How Britain is Governed* (1930); *The Liberal Way* (1934); *The Record of the National Government* (1936); and *Future for Democracy* (1939).

Dr Richard S. Grayson

SIR ANDREW MURRAY   1903–77

The split in the Liberal Party in 1931 over the issues of protectionism and support for the National Government damaged the party in several ways. One little-documented aspect of this division was the encouragement it gave to the formation of alliances between Liberals and Conservatives in local government, which lasted for as much as three decades, and damaged Liberal prospects in many towns and cities for far longer. Sir Andrew Murray was one Liberal who followed Sir John Simon (*q.v.*) and became prominent in Edinburgh as a progressive Lord Provost. Unlike many, he returned to the Liberal Party during the 1950s, eventually taking high office within it.

Andrew Hunter Arbuthnot Murray was born on 19 December 1903 in Edinburgh, the son of Alfred Alexander Arbuthnot Murray, a solicitor and Fellow of the Royal Society of Edinburgh, and his wife Mary, née Moir. He was educated at Daniel Stewart's College and George Heriot's School, where he was sports champion in 1922.

Murray was elected to Edinburgh Town Council for the North Leith ward in 1928. He served on the council until 1951, latterly being elected for the Liberton ward, albeit with one year's absence in 1934. Leith suffered as much as any other industrial town from the depression of the 1930s, and Murray's record of social work was a distinguishing feature of his career. He quickly rose to prominence on the council, serving as the city's Honorary Treasurer between 1943–46 and as Lord Provost from 1947–51.

Murray was widely respected as Lord Provost, being described by contemporaries as a 'tireless and devoted personality'. His influence over the post-war redevelopment of the city of Edinburgh was central; he also championed the city's artistic scene. Having, during the Second World War, revived the Leith Pageant, he was instrumental in the foundation of the Edinburgh International Festival in 1947. He argued that the Festival could engender a 'better spirit of understanding between men and women, through an appreciation of the arts', and towards that end travelled to Belgrade to bring the Yugoslav National Ballet to Edinburgh. He was awarded the freedom of the City of Athens in 1950, in recognition of his efforts to promote the City of Edinburgh abroad. As Lord Provost he was also in receipt of a number of other honours, including a knighthood in 1949, and an honorary doctorate in laws from Edinburgh University in 1950. After his period of office ended, he was commissioned, in 1953, as a Deputy Lieutenant of the County of Edinburgh.

Leith's Liberal MP in 1931 was Ernest Brown (*q.v.*) who joined the Liberal National grouping, later becoming its leader. Murray supported Brown's stance, but, after his spell on Edinburgh Town Council ended, he was surprisingly adopted as Unionist candidate for the marginal Labour seat of Central Edinburgh, resigning before the 1951 election. Murray was adopted by Leith Liberal Association in 1954 to contest the town's parliamentary seat as an independent, but finished a distant third to Labour in 1955. Seeing no future for the National Liberal cause, he persuaded the

Leith Liberals to rejoin the Scottish Liberal Party, of which he became a Vice-President in 1957. He fought Leith as a Liberal candidate in 1959, but saw his vote drop and he again finished third. It was to be his last parliamentary contest.

Murray was elected President of the Liberal Party in 1960, serving for twelve months, and was a Treasurer of the party for four years from 1962. Murray was not universally popular within the party, given his previous connections with the National Liberals but, nevertheless, the Liberals benefited from association with such a senior figure in lowland Scottish politics as well as from his assistance during a period of considerable financial strain.

Murray was as prominent in Scottish business as in politics, sitting on the boards of several companies and being prominently involved in the defence of small shareholders' rights, in the face of hostile take-over bids. He was awarded an OBE in 1945 in respect of his involvement with the fire service before and during the Second World War. He was closely allied with the Order of St. John of Jerusalem throughout his life, becoming a Companion of the Order in 1949, a Knight of the Order five years later and a Chancellor of the Order in 1963. At his death he was Preceptor of the ancient Knights Templar institution at Torphichen, West Lothian, and held the title of Chancellor of the Priory of Scotland.

In his later years, Murray remained committed to several of the causes he had first espoused in his youth. He was a governor of George Heriot's School and chaired the Governors of Carberry Tower, a Church of Scotland youth centre opened in 1962. He died on 21 March 1977, at 1 Randolph Place, in the New Town of Edinburgh. His obituary in *The Scotsman* recalled the occasion when, as Captain of the Orange Colours, an archaic council post which entitled the holder to the use of a white stallion in an official capacity, Murray had acquired and ridden through Edinburgh such an animal. A subsequent Lord Provost, Sir Herbert Brechin, summed him up as 'a great figure' who 'commanded attention wherever he went'. He was unmarried.

Mark Egan

GILBERT MURRAY 1866–1957

George Gilbert Aimé Murray was born on 2 January 1866 in Sydney, Australia, into the New South Wales landed gentry. His family, of Irish descent and military tradition, had been expropriated after the battle of the Boyne. His first name derived from his mother's cousin, the composer W. S. Gilbert. He was educated in Australia until his father died and his mother returned to England in 1877. He never went back. In England, he attended Merchant Taylor's School and then St John's College, Oxford. Recognised as a talented classicist, Murray spoke frequently at the Oxford Union Society in support of Liberal issues such as Irish home rule; he also made a firm friend in H. A. L. Fisher (*q.v.*).

In July 1889 he became Professor of Greek at Glasgow and shortly afterward married Mary Howard, daughter of Lady Carlisle, then President of the Women's Liberal Federation. Murray turned down a number of invitations from seats in the Oxford area to stand for Parliament and instead concentrated on his academic career, publishing, in 1897, *Ancient Greek Literature*. Murray continued to support radical causes and in summer 1900 contributed an essay to *Liberalism and Empire*, edited by F. W. Hirst. Murray was a 'pro-Boer' and made a handsome donation to the Boer Women and Children's Fund organised by the Women's Liberal Federation.

In 1905 he returned to Oxford and in 1907 published *The Rise of the Greek Epic*; he also helped to launch the Home University Library. By 1914, he had become Asquith's (*q.v.*) favourite intellectual, with close links to Labour through G. D. H. Cole. Impressed by Grey's (*q.v.*) speech to the Commons after war broke out, he became a government apologist, splitting with Bertrand Russell and publishing in 1915 *The Foreign Policy of Sir Edward Grey*. Once Lloyd George (*q.v.*) became Prime Minister, he left government service.

He began instead to campaign actively for the League of Nations and in November 1918 became the first chairman of its Executive Committee, and then South Africa's delegate at Smuts' invitation. In general, Murray overestimated the power of public opinion in influencing foreign policy. He was disappointed by the League's failure over the Manchurian crisis, and it lost its cross-party influence when Austen Chamberlain resigned from its Executive during the Abyssinian crisis. Nevertheless, the UK was the only country in which the League had any influence on government at all.

In party politics, Murray fought the Oxford University seat unsuccessfully in 1918, March 1919 (byelection), 1922, 1923, 1924 (as an Independent) and 1929. He remained loyal to Asquith, even though his wife joined the Labour Party in 1924.

At Oxford he was Regius Professor of Greek from 1908 to 1936, publishing *The Classical Tradition in Poetry* in 1927. A college headship never materialised, but in January 1941 he received the Order of Merit. Murray was also President of Liberal International between 1947 and 1949, but in his final years he seemed to lose his optimism, if not his empirical common sense, voting Conservative in 1950 and supporting the Suez adventure in 1956. Murray died in Oxford on 20 May 1957 and his ashes were placed in Westminster Abbey. He left three sons and two daughters.

Murray was a significant academic figure, and, with Robert Cecil, one of the two major figures in the League of Nations Union. His Liberal role, however, was less prominent. He is most interesting for his transition from pro-Boer radical in 1900 to Conservative supporter in the 1950s, of which he was not the only example. A recent biography was written by Sir Duncan Wilson, *Gilbert Murray OM* (1987).

Malcolm Baines

DADABHAI NAOROJI 1825–1917

When four black Labour MPs were elected to the House of Commons at the 1987 general election, much was made of the political breakthrough this represented for Britain's ethnic minority communities. But the first non-white to win a Parliamentary seat had achieved his victory, as a Liberal, nearly a hundred years earlier.

Dadabhai Naoroji was born at Khadka, near Bombay, on 4 September 1825, the son of a Parsee priest. At the age of eleven he was married to Gulbai, then aged seven, herself the daughter of a priest. Together they had a son, who died in 1893, and two daughters. Naoroji was educated at the Elphinstone School and College in India where he stayed on to teach, becoming the first Indian Professor of mathematics and natural philosophy. He took part in social and political debate as a proponent of reform, opened a newspaper, *Rast Goftar,* in 1851 and was a founder member of the Bombay Association in 1852. He first came to England in 1855 as a partner in the first Indian firm established there, but went on to become Professor of Gujerati and a life governor at University College, London. He developed his interest in reform and was prominent in campaigns to open up the Indian Civil Service to Indians, which he helped achieve in 1870.

On return to India he continued with the political life, serving as Prime Minister of Baroda in 1873–74, but he did not enjoy this role. He went on to become a member of the Corporation and Municipal Council of Bombay between 1875–76 and again from 1881–85 and was a member of the Legislative Council of Bombay from 1885–87. He served as President of the Indian National Congress in 1886, 1893 and 1906.

Naoroji came back to England and was chosen to fight Holborn for the Liberals at the general election of 1886. After he lost, he put himself forward as candidate for Central Finsbury, fighting and winning a divisive selection battle in the constituency. Commenting on the outcome, the Conservative Prime Minister, the Marquess of Salisbury, remarked that he 'doubted that a British constituency would elect a blackman'. Naoroji gained sympathy as a result and at the general election of 1892 defeated the sitting Tory member, F.T. Penton, by 2,961 votes to 2,956 – a majority of just five, but how sweet that victory must have tasted in the aftermath of Salisbury's arrogant, racist, assertion. On a brief return visit to India in 1893, he received an ecstatic welcome and was fêted as the first non-European to be elected to the House of Commons. However, in 1895, he lost the seat by a margin of 805 votes to a new Conservative candidate in the Tory landslide. He never got back into Parliament. Falling out with the Liberal Party, he stood as an Independent Liberal in North Lambeth in 1906, but did not split the vote significantly enough to prevent the official Liberal from winning. He came third, behind the Conservative but ahead of an Independent Tory.

Naoroji espoused many then-unfashionable radical causes, including the equality of women, and was at the heart of many campaigns on behalf of India. He was President of the London Indian Society for many years and moved an enquiry into

Indian affairs in the House of Commons in 1894. He was the first Indian member of a Royal Commission, serving on an inquiry into Indian expenditure between 1895–1900, signing a minority report. In 1894 he was a member of an Inter-Parliamentary conference at the Hague.

In 1907 he retired to India. His wife died in 1910. In 1916 he was awarded an honorary LLD degree by the University of Bombay. He died in Bombay on 2 July 1917.

Naoroji wrote many papers, pamphlets and letters on social, political and economic subjects, mostly about India. A collection of these was published in 1887. He believed that the British Raj was draining away Indian resources, and publicised his arguments most forcefully in his book, *Poverty and un-British Rule in India*, published in 1901. He also wrote *The Rights of Labour* which came out in 1906. A collection of his speeches and writings was published under the title *The Grand Little Man of India: Dadabhai Naoroji*, edited by A. Moin Zaidi. His correspondence was published in 1977 in a book by R. P. Patwardhan. Two biographies of Naoroji have appeared: R. P. Masani, *Dadabhai Naoroji, The Grand Old Man of India* (1939) and, celebrating the hundredth anniversary of his election to Parliament, Zerbanoo Gifford, *Dadabhai Naoroji: Britain's First Asian MP* (1992).

Pash Nandhra

DICK NEWBY (Lord Newby) 1953–

Richard Mark (Dick) Newby was born on St Valentine's Day 1953, the son of Frank and Kathleen Newby. He was educated at Rothwell Grammar School and St Catherine's College, Oxford, where he was a contemporary of Peter Mandelson. He was a strong Labour pro-European, being the General Secretary of Young European Left, a small pro-Europe group of Labour Party members, and a member of the National Labour Committee for Europe.

On leaving Oxford he joined the Customs and Excise and spent a period as Private Secretary to the Permanent Secretary. During this period he was politically active in Lambeth Labour politics on the side of the moderates, at a time when the local party was slipping into the hands of the hard left.

Newby was involved in the SDP from its inception. His principal contribution was organisational, displaying a steady hand, sound judgement and good humour in the execution of his tasks. Initially Secretary to the SDP Parliamentary Committee, he became National Secretary in 1983, and served in that position until the merger in 1988.

Despite his considerable organisational skills, and maybe because of his practical northern common sense, Newby seems to have become an early object of Dr Owen's suspicion. Though a general election unit was set up under Newby and Alec McGivan in 1985, he did not become a member of the planning group for the campaign until March 1987. His direct experience of the difficulties posed by Owen's aversion to too close a cooperation on organisational matters with the Liberals inclined him to believe that the future of the parties lay in closer cooperation rather than the frigid separatism favoured by Owen.

It was supposedly a phone conversation between Newby and David Sainsbury on polling day 1987 that impelled Owen to declare against merger. Newby had advocated merger and scorned the idea of federation between the parties. Certainly he was firmly in the mergerite camp and Owen demanded his resignation. Newby did not oblige. He formed part of the SDP negotiating team for merger, and had the unwelcome experience of handing out copies of the 'dead parrot' statement on the policies of the new party at the abortive press launch on 13 January 1988, only to have them pulled at the last moment as a result of the rebellion of Liberal MPs.

After a period as Corporate Affairs Director of Rosehaugh plc, Newby set up a public affairs consultancy of his own, Matrix Communicatons. A key member of the Liberal Democrat 1997 campaign team, he was created a life peer in the wake of the election.

He married Ailsa Thomson, daughter of Lord Thomson of Monifieth (*q.v.*) in 1978. She set a challenge to the editors of *Debretts* by becoming the first Anglican priest to be both the wife and daughter of a peer. They have two sons.

Peter Truesdale

EMMA NICHOLSON (Lady Nicholson)   1941–

It should not have really come as such a surprise when, on 29 December 1995, Emma Nicholson, the Member of Parliament for the Devon West & Torridge constituency, left the Conservative Party and 'came home' to the Liberal Democrats. Her unashamed internationalism, commitment to the European cause and passionate advocacy of civil rights made her a natural Liberal Democrat. Her defection put the party on the front page of every national newspaper and at the head of every news bulletin. What did come as a surprise, however, was the nature of the vitriolic and personal attack launched by the Conservative Party and the importance which Conservative

279

ministers placed on portraying Nicholson as 'a woman scorned' and a 'frustrated careerist'.

Born on 19 October 1941, in Winterbourne, Berkshire, Emma Harriet Nicholson is by breeding and background the quintessential high Tory. Her father, Sir Godfrey Nicholson, represented the staunchly Conservative seat of Farnham, Surrey, her grandfather was a member of the Commons for many years, and she can count more than a dozen relatives who are members of one of the Houses of Parliament. Yet by inclination and by deed she is anything but a Conservative. In her childhood years she was a constant companion to her father on his Saturday visits to the constituency where she came face to face with stark social problems. She recalls that it was these formative experiences which led her to decide, at the age of four, that she must enter Parliament. She joined her internal vow to 'help the helpless' with one to seek change from within 'the establishment system I honoured'.

Despite a happy childhood, Nicholson's early years were not without pain. A hearing impediment made normal communication difficult and she found her comfort in books. By the age of eight, she had read the Koran; by the age of ten she had mastered the works of Jane Austen and by eleven had tackled Trollope. In the same year, when she became a pupil at St Mary's School, Wantage, deteriorating eyesight was also diagnosed.

Music formed an integral part of her life; she became a Licentiate at the Royal Academy of Music and an Associate at the Royal College of Music. Despite her success, she had to accept that she would never become the concert pianist she dreamed, of and needed to find a job. She found her challenge in the world of computer software, and after a highly successful career as a management consultant, she joined the Save the Children Fund. As Fund-Raising Director (1977–85) she increased the charity's income from £3 million to £33 million a year; one of her major achievements was the Stop Polio campaign.

In 1983, Nicholson followed in her father's footsteps and fought the parliamentary constituency of Blyth Valley ('Papa' Nicholson had been elected as the MP for Morpeth (which included Blyth Valley) in the 1931 general election). Unsuccessful on this occasion, she continued working for Save the Children and accepted an unpaid role as Vice Chairman of the Conservative Party, with special responsibility for women. She served in this role until she was elected to Parliament, for Devon West & Torridge, in 1987. She was re-elected in 1992, and served as Parliamentary Private Secretary to Michael Jack MP at the Treasury, MAFF and the Home Office between 1992–95.

In Parliament, Nicholson focused on children, primary health care and preventive medicine, while working for the handicapped. Despite the best of intentions, the first publication of the Register of Members' Interests saw her with the longest entry, though all of the posts were unpaid. Continuing her interests in international affairs and civil rights, she took up the plight of the Iraqi Kurds, and soon set about seeking finance to build a children's hospital in Baghdad. It was on one of her many visits to the marshlands of Iraq that she met Amar, a nine-year old boy whose face and body had melted in the heat of the flames from aerial bombardment. She brought him back to the UK for surgery; soon afterwards, he became a ward of court, with Nicholson having care and control. He chose to remain in England, and now shares his life with Nicholson and her husband Sir Michael Caine, whom she married in 1987. In 1992, she founded the AMAR Appeal, a charity established to bring relief to the victims of breaches of human rights, war and civil disturbances, and now serves as voluntary Chairman of the Amar International Charitable Foundation, managing over 300 refugee workers in the field, serving 95,000 people.

When Nicholson joined the Liberal Democrats in 1995 she became the party's spokesman on human rights and overseas development. Having made the decision to leave the House of Commons, she became a determined campaigner for Liberal Democrat candidates up and down the country – her home constantly decorated by yellow bouquets presented by welcoming supporters at Liberal Democrat functions. She was elevated to the House of Lords in 1997 and proved her mettle when she led for the Liberal Democrats on the Data Protection Act.

In June 1998, Liberal Democrats in the south east voted to put Nicholson at the top of the party's regional list for the 1999 European elections, virtually guaranteeing her presence in the European Parliament. She has truly come home.

Her publications include *Why Does The West Forget?* (Hodder & Stoughton, 1993) and *Secret Society* (Victor Gollancz, 1996).

Mike Hoban

MARK OATEN MP   1964–

Mark Oaten was born in Watford on 8 March 1964, and educated at Queen's Comprehensive, Watford College, and Hatfield Polytechnic. He was a founder member of the SDP in 1981 and acted as agent in a number of elections. In 1986 he became one of the country's youngest councillors and the first-ever SDP councillor on Watford District Council. He served for eight years until 1994, ending up leading a group of six other SDP councillors. In 1992 he stood for Parliament in Watford, gaining 10,000 votes.

He was selected to fight Winchester in 1995, and elected to Parliament at the 1997 general election. After the longest count in history, he was elected by the majority of two over the Conservative incumbent, Gerry Malone. Malone contested the election in the courts, claiming that a small number of valid ballot papers had not been counted. The election was declared void and a re-run ordered. The ensuing byelection took place in November 1997, and this time the voters of Winchester were rather clearer in their intentions. Oaten held the seat with an majority of nearly 22,000, over sixty-eight per cent of the votes cast. He had received one of the largest swings ever to the Liberal Democrats, nearly twenty per cent.

But Oaten wants to ensure that he makes a more concrete contribution to his constituency and to politics. Driven by a desire to restore the public's trust in politicians, he promised to produce an annual report for his constituents. He published his first such report in May 1998, detailing his work in the constituency, in Parliament and as Liberal Democrat spokesman on disability.

Oaten believes that democracy is in need of overhaul and is eager to make the political system more accountable to the public, so that it engages with individuals rather than disheartening them. To this end, in addition to the annual report, he has made great efforts to get to know his constituents, spending time working in local branches of MacDonald's and Sainsbury's, and with local bin-men, police officers and social workers.

He was asked by Paddy Ashdown (q.v.) to edit the Liberal Democrats' post-election policy review, chairing the editorial board, overseeing the written work of the eight commissions and consolidating the work into a single document. He is determined that the Liberal Democrats should respond to the changing political world and move the party's policy platform by thinking ahead rather than responding to the agendas of others.

Before entering Parliament, Oaten worked as a consultant for Shandwick Public Affairs, part of the large Shandwick public relations consultancy, between 1988–92. He then joined Westminster Communications, where he was made a group director, and set up Westminster Public Relations. He became its managing director in 1996. He resigned from the company after his election to Parliament in 1997. In 1995 he was appointed a director of Oasis Radio, a commercial radio station in Hertfordshire.

Oaten married Belinda in 1992, and they have a daughter, Alice.

Katie Hall

LEMBIT ÖPIK MP   1965–

Lembit Öpik's name – an anagram of 'I like to b MP' – is the most unusual in British politics. So how did a Newcastle City councillor with an Irish accent and Estonian origins come to be the Member of Parliament for the rural Welsh constituency of Montgomeryshire?

Lembit Öpik's roots lie in conflict. His parents, Uno Öpik and Liivi Vedo, met in exile. His paternal grandfather, Ernest Julius Öpik, had been a famous astronomer in Estonia, while his maternal grandparents were businesspeople. Both sides of the family fled, separately, from Estonia in the early 1950s and came to Britain via German refugee camps. Stalin's persecution left deep scars on the family, determining much of Öpik's political outlook.

Öpik's parents settled in Northern Ireland, and he was born in Bangor, County Down, on 2 March 1965, the second of three children. While he was young the family moved to Belfast, where one of his earliest memories is of his mother hanging protective blankets across the window during a bomb scare. From 1976 he attended the Royal Belfast Academical Institution.

In 1983 Öpik came over to mainland Britain, having been offered a place at Bristol University. After brief forays into engineering and economics, he settled on a degree in philosophy and gained an upper second in 1987. While a student at Bristol, he entered the political arena, initially as an independent. In 1985–86 he was president of the University of Bristol Students' Union and the following year won a place on the NUS National Executive.

In 1988 Öpik moved to Newcastle-upon-Tyne to take up a post with Procter & Gamble. His talents as a motivator were soon spotted, and in 1991 he was plucked out of brand management and put to work developing people. From corporate training manager he was promoted to global human resources training manager in 1996, with responsibilities for training in the USA, the Far East and Latin America.

In Newcastle, Öpik joined the newly-merged Social and Liberal Democrats and quickly became active within the party. He stood for the Fawdon ward of Newcastle City Council in 1990 and fought the seat of Newcastle Central in the April 1992 general election. A month later, he was elected as councillor for the South Gosforth ward of Newcastle, with a majority of just fifty. Over the following four years, he succeeded, by dint of hard work, personality, and the best methods of community politics, in facilitating the election of three other Liberal Democrats in what had previously been a Tory stronghold. Öpik himself was re-elected to the council in May 1996, this time with a majority of 1,384.

Meanwhile, he had risen to prominence at a regional and national level within the Liberal Democrats. In the 1994 European elections he stood unsuccessfully in Northumbria. He was a Deputy Chair of the party's Northern Region from 1993 to 1996, with responsibility for membership, and deputy chair of the Party in England in 1995–96. He gave freely of his professional skills, training dozens of Liberal Democrat candidates in presentation and public speaking. He became a member of the party's Federal Executive in 1991, and has been re-elected annually ever since.

In June 1996, Liberal Democrat MP Alex Carlile (*q.v.*) announced that he would not be seeking re-election in the Liberal stronghold of Montgomery, which he had represented since 1983. Öpik, who had been planning to stand for a Newcastle constituency and had just started a small business, submitted his application at the last minute ('I am not Welsh,' it said). He made the short-list only when someone else dropped out, but was selected in September that year. On 1 May 1997, Öpik was elected as the Member of Parliament for Montgomeryshire, with a majority of 6,303.

Since his election, Öpik has achieved a high media profile: in his role as Liberal Democrat spokesman for young people he has been at the forefront of opposition to tuition fees; as the Commons spokesman on Northern Ireland, he has played a necessarily less public but no less important role, liaising between all parties to the peace talks. His passionate debates with fellow Liberal Democrat MP Mike Hancock (*q.v.*) over foxhunting have also attracted interest within the party.

Öpik literally hit the headlines in April 1998 after a sporting accident. He spent seven weeks in hospital after a paragliding crash left him with multiple injuries, including a back broken in six places. He wrote that he had learned three things from the accident: 'First, the NHS is superb in an emergency. It saved my life. Second, it's easy to get stuck into details but breaking your back helps you take the long view. Third …. taking off is optional but landing is mandatory'. He plans to make the most of his 'second chance'.

Fiona Hall

FRANK OWEN 1905–79

At the 1997 general election Paul Keetch (*q.v.*) took Hereford for the Liberal Democrats, thus regaining a seat last won for the Liberals by Frank Owen in 1929. Attracted to the Liberal Party by the fiery radicalism of David Lloyd George (*q.v.*), Owen was elected at the age of twenty-three, and went on to a distinguished career as a journalist, editing both the *Evening Standard* and the *Daily Mail* before returning to contest the Hereford seat again in the 1950s. Owen's brilliant, ambitious mind and independent spirit repeatedly made life uncomfortable for many of those he worked with, whether in politics or journalism.

Humphrey Frank Owen was born on 4 October 1905 at the 'Black Swan' public house, then owned by his parents, on Widemarsh Street in Hereford,. Owen won a scholarship to Monmouth Grammar School and followed this with a further scholarship to study history at Sidney Sussex College, Cambridge. He graduated with a first class degree in 1927, having represented his college at both rowing and rugby.

Returning to Hereford, Owen secured a job on the *South Wales Argus,* a paper with well-established Liberal sympathies. He threw himself into promoting the cause of the party in the Welsh Marches and in 1928 accepted a researcher's job with Lloyd George. Six weeks before the 1929 general election the Liberal candidate in Hereford (a traditionally Tory seat) stood down due to ill health. Owen was persuaded to take his place, and in a barnstorming campaign took the seat with a majority of just over 1,000 to become the youngest MP in the Commons. His time in Parliament was short-lived, however. At the 1931 election he stood as one of a small band of Lloyd George Liberals opposed to the National Government, in contrast to the Liberal factions led by Sir John Simon (*q.v.*) and Herbert Samuel (*q.v.*). The Tories regained Hereford; Owen was later famously to comment: 'In 1929 the wise, far-seeing electors of my native Hereford sent me to Westminster and two years later in 1931 the lousy bastards kicked me out'.

Owen returned to journalism and rapidly came to the attention of Lord Beaverbrook as a leader writer on the *Daily Express*. Indeed, it was Beaverbrook who introduced Owen to Grace McGillvray, a Bostonian, who Owen married in 1939. In 1938 he became editor of the *Evening Standard* (another Beaverbrook paper), although his outspoken criticism of the policy of appeasement sat uneasily with the opinions of his employer. These arguments were most forcefully advanced in the best-selling pamphlet *Guilty Men,* which Owen co-authored with Michael Foot (then assistant editor at the *Standard*) and Peter Howard in 1938.

When Britain entered the war in 1939, Owen's energies were channelled in a less subversive direction as editor of *South East Asia Command,* the official paper of the army in the Far East. Even in this role his direct, uncompromising style occasionally made life difficult for his superiors. Lord Mountbatten was, however, sufficiently impressed to commission Owen to write the official history of the campaign, *The Campaign in Burma* (HMSO, 1946). Owen ended the war as a Lieutenant-Colonel and was awarded the OBE for his efforts at *SEAC*.

After the war Owen went to work for the other great press baron of the period, Lord Rothermere, as editor of the *Daily Mail,* but by 1950 he had returned to Beaverbrook's *Express* as a columnist. In 1954, Owen produced *Tempestuous Journey,* his well-known biography of Lloyd George based on the huge collection of Lloyd George papers recently acquired by Beaverbrook.

Owen returned to active politics at the 1955 general election, finishing second to the Conservatives in Hereford, 1,000 votes ahead of the Labour candidate. In 1956 Owen got another chance to contest the seat when the sitting Tory MP, J. P. L. Thomas, was elevated to the Lords, provoking a byelection. The campaign was closely fought by the Liberal Party on the slogan 'Hereford's Son: Second to None', with visits from senior party figures including Jo Grimond (*q.v.*), Jeremy Thorpe (*q.v.*) and Edwin Mallindine. In spite of a significant increase in the Liberal vote, Owen failed to win the seat by 2,000 votes and in 1958 announced he would not stand again. He was succeeded as candidate by Robin Day.

The 1956 byelection was Owen's last foray on to the political scene. He continued to write (including a biography of Colonel Peron and an account of the fall of Singapore) and worked for a time as a television journalist, interviewing Nasser at the time of the Suez crisis, but he was not to regain the national prominence of his newspaper career. His wife, Grace, died in 1968, and Owen himself died on 23 January 1979 in the Worthing Rest Home where he had been living with his sister; he had no children. Gron Williams published a biography, *Firebrand: The Frank Owen Story,* in 1993.

Richard Kirby

THOMAS PAINE   1737–1809

Thomas Paine was born on 29 January 1737 at Thetford in Norfolk and was educated at the local grammar school. His father was a stay-maker, and this was Paine's first occupation. In 1759, he married Mary Lambert, the daughter of a customs officer, but she died within a few months. This may have determined him to join the customs service, and in 1764 he was appointed to the Grantham round, patrolling the Lincoln-shire coast, but was soon discharged for the common practice of stamping a consign-ment of merchandise without first inspecting it. He was reappointed at Lewes in 1768. Here, in 1771, he married Elizabeth Ollive, his landlady's daughter, and ran their tobacconist shop, but the business failed and was sold up in 1772. Two years later he was discharged a second time from the Excise and his marriage broke up.

During this period of his life Paine learned about oppressive taxation and the heavy hand of government (as an Excise officer); the problems of the poor (as a member of the Lewes Vestry which was responsible for the administration of the poor law); the dangers of credit and the difficulties of the small businessman (from his own failures); and the power of his pen (he led the agitation of the Excise officers for higher pay, and wrote his first pamphlet putting their case).

After his failures in Lewes, Paine emigrated to Philadelphia in 1774 with letters of introduction from Benjamin Franklin. Here, as editor of the *Pennsylvania Magazine*, he showed a strong resentment against Britain and, as the political situation worsened, he was drawn into the propaganda war. In January 1776 he published his first great work, *Common Sense*, in which he caught and expressed the changing tide of public opinion. Demanding independence from Britain, he based his argument on a combi-nation of appeals to first principles and to common sense, uttered in the language not of the classical schools but of modern journalism.

Paine's second literary contribution to the American cause was the *American Crisis*, a series of papers the first of which was written on a drumhead by a camp fire and read out to Washington's demoralised troops before the battle of Trenton. The gran-deur of style of the opening paragraph can only be compared to Shakespeare's Henry V before Agincourt: 'These are the times that try men's souls. The summer soldier and the sunshine patriot will, in this crisis, shrink from the service of their country; but he that stands it now deserves the love and thanks of man and woman.' Paine also served the rebellious colonies as secretary to the Committee for Foreign Affairs until forced to resign in January 1779 after making well-founded allegations of financial miscon-duct against the American agents sent to Versailles to negotiate French military aid.

In 1787 Paine returned to Europe to promote a scheme for building an iron bridge, and was in France when the crisis there broke in May 1789. Returning to Britain he found Edmund Burke denouncing the Revolution. The publication of Burke's *Reflections on the Revolution in France* in November 1790 marked a turning point in public opinion. Paine was one of many to rush into print in defence of the

French against Burke. As his *Rights of Man*, published in February 1791, caught the public mood, opinion began to polarise around Burke and Paine. The latter became the champion of the radicals and Dissenters; he was feared and hated by supporters of Church and King.

The argument was taken further in February 1792 when *Rights of Man, Part 2* was issued in which Paine called for an English Republic – 'an hereditary governor is as inconsistent as an hereditary author.' Moreover, he argued for the abolition of the poor laws, and the provision of work for the unemployed, education for children, pensions for the aged, and gifts of money to individuals on the occasions of births, marriages and deaths, the whole system of welfare to be paid for by progressive taxation on real estate. This theme was taken up again by Paine in 1797 in *Agrarian Justice*, which included a proposal for a ten per cent inheritance tax. Such a challenge to the political establishment could not go unbridled. In May 1792, proceedings for sedition were begun against Paine; having been elected to the French Convention, he was tried in his absence in December, found guilty, and never again returned to his native land.

In Paris, Paine associated with the moderates in the Convention. When Louis XVI was arrested and tried, Paine pleaded for his life as a private citizen, but the king was executed on 21 January 1793, and within a month Britain and France were at war. Paine was subsequently arrested as an enemy alien. During this year of growing extremism, he wrote his great theological work, *The Age of Reason*, to uphold the classical deism of the eighteenth-century enlightenment and to prevent the French people from 'running headlong into atheism'. In Part One, he applied to the churches, the Bible and Christian theology the same scathing reason that he had earlier turned on the British constitution. In Part Two, written while he was in the Luxembourg prison between November 1793 and November 1794, he savagely attacked the Bible on moral grounds. On release from gaol, he remained in France and wrote several further works, of which the most important were *The Decline and Fall of the English System of Finance* (1796) and *Agrarian Justice* (1797), but he became increasingly out of sympathy with the France of Napoleon Bonaparte. He returned to the United States in 1802, where he found public opinion markedly more religious and conservative than it had been in the 1780s. The hero of 1776 was forgotten, and died neglected amid slanders over excessive brandy drinking, on 8 June 1809.

Paine's writings, especially *Rights of Man*, became formative texts for radical politicians. Though progressive in his ideas on welfare, Paine was not a socialist, but always valued the economic, political and intellectual independence of the individual. He spoke the language of the small producer who resented the burdens of taxation, the interference of the state, the inflationary injustices of the credit system and the political monopoly of the titled rich. In the nineteenth century these became the classic doctrines of popular Liberalism.

Paine has been the subject of many biographies. The best of the recent ones include A. O. Aldridge, *Man of Reason: The Life of Thomas Paine* (Cresset Press, 1960), D.

F. Hawke, *Paine* (Norton, 1974) and J. Keane, *Tom Paine: A Political Life* (Bloomsbury Publishing, 1995). For Paine's intellectual biography, see G. Claeys, *Thomas Paine: Social and Political Thought* (Unwin Hyman, 1989) and M. Philp, *Paine* (Oxford University Press, 1989).

Ted Royle

VISCOUNT PALMERSTON   1784–1865

If we date the modern Liberal Party from the 1859 meeting in Willis' Tea Rooms, we must accord Palmerston the honour of being the first Liberal Prime Minister, though he would have thought himself the Queen's minister and the nation's leader rather than a party's. In truth, he was more the last of the old regime rather than the first modern party leader, despite his early recognition of the need to have the media on side.

In his lengthy career of more than forty years in ministerial office, he was premier twice but probably better known for his involvement in foreign affairs and his time at the Foreign Office. His aggressive policy, much misunderstood at the time, was designed to preserve the balance of power in Europe and to reinforce the pre-eminence of Britain; to achieve peace through deterrence rather than provoke war. While he also adopted a forward policy towards British colonial possessions, it would be a mistake to see him as an imperialist in the modern sense of the word. He had less interest in domestic affairs, paying lip service to electoral reform, the major issue of the day, but avoiding practical action. While Palmerston never saw eye to eye with him, Gladstone (*q.v.*) was able to carry out major financial reforms as 'Pam's' Chancellor of the Exchequer, including the 1860 Treaty with France, which cemented free trade as the British commercial system and probably did more than Palmerston's military preparedness to stave off the war with France which was Palmerston's major fear.

Henry John Temple was born in Park Street (now Queen Anne's Gate), Westminster, on 20 October 1784, the son of Henry Temple, second Viscount Palmerston (an MP since 1762) and his second wife Mary Mee, the daughter of a wealthy Dublin merchant. In 1800 he went to Edinburgh University and between 1803 and 1806 attended St. John's, Cambridge. He succeeded to his father's Irish peerage in 1802, though this did not entitle him to a seat in the Lords. His political career began early, fighting the University of Cambridge seat unsuccessfully when he was twenty-one. In 1807 he was offered a junior Lordship of the Admiralty and had to be found a seat in the pocket borough of Newport, Isle of Wight. In 1809 he was moved to Secretary of War, a position he held for more than eighteen years until promised promotion in Canning's short-lived government. As Secretary of War in a series of Tory governments, Pam proved his ability to run a department but until his association with Canning, appeared to take little interest in the wider aspects of government. During this early period of office, Palmerston led an active social life, earning himself the nickname Lord Cupid. He formed an intimate friendship with Lady Cowper (née Emily Lamb) and married her in December 1839, some two years after the death of her first husband.

Following Canning's death in 1827, Palmerston and his fellow Canningites joined Wellington, but only reluctantly in what they saw as an ultra-Tory government. The partnership did not last long and, when Palmerston made one of his first major speeches on foreign affairs attacking Wellington's government, he was bidding for the Foreign Secretary's post that he was granted by Grey (q.v.) in 1830. This first spell at the Foreign Office lasted with a short break until 1841 when Melbourne (q.v.) fell. The great success of the period was securing the existence of a Belgium independent from France and the Netherlands. Palmerston supported constitutionalists in Spain and Portugal, thwarting French territorial ambitions and alienating the autocratic powers, Austria, Russia and Prussia.

The fall of Melbourne brought Palmerston an unwelcome spell in opposition, fretting at the conciliatory approach of his successor, Lord Aberdeen (q.v.). When Peel's party fell apart over the repeal of the Corn Laws, Lord John Russell (q.v.) was forced to take Palmerston back in his former post despite his own and Queen Victoria's reluctance to have such a forthright and independent-minded minister. This second spell at the Foreign Office covered the revolutions of 1848, and Palmerston favoured the liberal/nationalist line against the Queen's support for the *ancien régimes*. His willingness to use the navy to assert British predominance, as in the case of the 1850 dispute between Don Pacifico and the Greek government, infuriated the opposition and the ensuing debate allowed Palmerston the classic statement of his principles in his *'Civis Romanus sum'* speech. Pam finally overstepped the mark when he recognised the new Bonapartist government in France in 1851 without Cabinet authorisation or the approval of the Queen. He was dismissed, but gained his revenge on the Prime Minister, Lord John Russell, a few days later by joining the opposition in defeating the government on a militia bill.

The succeeding, minority Tory government did not last long and was succeeded in turn by the first attempt at a Whig/Peelite/Radical coalition under Lord Aberdeen in December 1852. Palmerston accepted the post of Home Secretary, helping pass legislation controlling factory hours and abating pollution in London. He also ended the transportation of prisoners to Tasmania and arranged for young offenders to be sent to school rather than prison.

As Home Secretary he avoided the blame for the Crimean War when the revelations of military and civilian ineptitude in *The Times* brought about the downfall of Aberdeen at the beginning of 1855. His patriotism and rigour made him the inevitable choice as successor, and despite the desertion of the Peelites he formed his first administration, aged seventy-one – in time to take advantage of an improving military position in the Crimea, enabling him to conclude a successful peace in 1856. It did not take long for the usual pattern to reassert itself, however, and in March 1857 the government was defeated in the Commons on a motion condemning its provocative 'gunboat' policy in China. However, Palmerston increased his support at the ensuing general election. Unusually he then went on to alienate his natural supporters. Firstly, the Indian Mutiny damaged confidence in the competence of the regime, and then Palmerston gave way to French demands for firm action against anti-Bonapartist terrorist groups said to be active in England, alienating the jingoists who supported him in the country and in Parliament. Derby formed another short-lived Tory government which, while gaining seats at the 1859 election, failed to achieve a majority and soon fell.

The era of unstable coalitions was coming to an end. In the course of 1859, the Whigs were able to patch up their quarrels and the Peelites decided which side of the fence to plant their feet. Support for the Italian nationalists in their struggle to cast off Austrian rule provided the key to a unity which, once achieved, sustained Liberal governments for most of the next quarter-century. Outmanoeuvring Russell, Palmerston resumed office in 1859 when the Tory government fell. He retained the premiership until his death, which occurred shortly after his third successive general election victory in 1865 – a rare tribute to his public popularity.

Domestically this was a quiet time; agitation for a second reform bill continued but Palmerston saw no need to bring it to a practical resolution. Gladstone strengthened free trade through the French treaty and continued his rationalisation of the tax system, abolishing the paper tax despite Palmerston's opposition, but retrenchment in government expenditure proved impossible against Palmerstonian pressure to build up the armed forces.

As always, Palmerston's chief preoccupation was with foreign affairs. In retrospect, the chief event of the time may be seen to be the American Civil War. Palmerston hated slavery and had ensured that the navy was used vigorously against the slave trade, but the government entertained some sympathies for the South and resisted the North's attempts to constrain British trade. Despite the distress caused to the textile trade by the blockade on the South's cotton exports, Palmerston kept Britain neutral.

In Europe he maintained his old habits – interfering to restrain the greater states to maintain the balance of power, encouraging the smaller and building British coastal and naval defences against the threat of the French. Although he was not wholly successful in these aims, as in the inability to keep Schleswig-Holstein in Danish hands against Bismarck's Prussia, his policy retained public confidence.

Towards the end of his life Palmerston suffered from gout, but he finally caught a chill and died from the resulting fever at Brocket Hall, Hertfordshire, on 18 October 1865, aged eighty-one.

Palmerston's personal papers are held in the Broadlands Archives Trust; the Hampshire Record Office and the British Library also hold records. Extracts of the correspondence with Queen Victoria have been published in B. Connell (ed.), *Regina v Palmerston: The correspondence between Queen Victoria and her Foreign and Prime Minister,*

1837–1865 (1962), with Gladstone in P. Guedalla (ed.), *The Palmerston Papers: Corre-spondence of Lord Palmerston with Mr. Gladstone 1851–1865* (1928) and with Princess Lieven in Lord Sudley (ed.), *Lieven-Palmerston Correspondence* (1943). There are a wide range of biographies, of which the most accessible modern lives are J. Ridley, *Lord Palmerston* (1970), D. Southgate, *The Most English Minister* (1966), D. Judd, *Palmerston* (1975) and K. Bourne, *Palmerston: The Early Years* (1982). *The Life of Henry John Temple, Viscount Palmerston* (1870–76), Vols I–III by Rt. Hon. Sir H. L. Bulwer and Vols. IV–V by Rt. Hon. A. E. M. Ashley, is the official life.

Tony Little

JOHN PARDOE

1934–

During the 1970s, the Liberal Party was challenged and infuriated by a tough and rambunctious campaigner, a man of grand visions, bright ideas and good intentions. John Pardoe gave the Liberals a new credibility on economic matters, updated and developed its policies and played a controversial role in the Lib-Lab Pact.

John Wentworth Pardoe was born on 27 July 1934, the son of Cuthbert and Marjorie Pardoe. He was raised in Bridgwater, Somerset and educated at Sherborne College and Corpus Christi College, Cambridge. From 1958 to 1960, he worked in market research and then, for a brief period, joined Osborne Peacock, a small adver-tising agency.

Pardoe took no interest in politics until the Suez crisis in 1956, which left him with a deep and profound loathing for the Conservatives. Initially, he became active in the Labour Party, but left following the 1959 general election, disillusioned with Labour's political drift. Within a few months, Jo Grimond (*q.v.*) and his advocacy of Britain in Europe inspired Pardoe to join the Liberal Party. He became business manager for *Liberal News* in 1961 and contested Finchley, where he was an ardent community activist, in 1964. At the 1966 general election, he won North Cornwall for the Liberals.

Between 1966 and 1970, Pardoe was, at various times, Liberal spokesman on edu-cation and social security. It was not until the following Parliament that he became prominent. The disastrous 1970 general election left the Liberal Party with just six MPs, of whom only three – the leader, Jeremy Thorpe (*q.v.*), the Chief Whip, David Steel (*q.v.*), and Pardoe – were consistently active. In the party and the Commons, Pardoe was well known for his vigorous, sometimes combative debating style. He became economic spokesman and chairman of the Standing Committee, which was responsible for making policy between party assemblies.

Pardoe worked with the Liberal Research Department and a range of experts to build up a comprehensive body of party policy. He oversaw the development of a credible economic programme, which included a permanent incomes policy, a tax on inflation and proposals for industrial partnerships that were more substantial than those previously advanced. As a result, the Liberals received favourable coverage from *The Economist* and the *Financial Times*. Pardoe acquitted himself well in the economic policy debates during the two 1974 general elections and was named by the *Daily Telegraph* as a 'shining star' of the October campaign.

In the wake of Thorpe's resignation, Pardoe contested the July 1976 leadership election against David Steel. While the two candidates had no substantive differences over philosophy, policy or strategy, it was generally accepted that Pardoe was the activists' candidate; he offered a more aggressive crusade against the political establishment. When an opinion poll showed that his high media profile during the 1974 campaigns had not translated into superior support – or even wider recognition – from ordinary party members, Pardoe over-compensated. His abrasive style and his quick resort to sharp phrases worried many Liberals and heightened doubts about his political judgement. Steel was elected leader by a margin of nearly two to one. Pardoe promptly relinquished the Chairmanship of the Standing Committee but soon agreed to stay on as economic spokesman, and very quickly became Steel's *de facto* deputy.

These twin roles assumed a new importance in March 1977, with the advent of the Lib–Lab Pact. For eighteen months, Liberal MPs sustained the Callaghan Government in the Commons, in return for being consulted on policy and legislation. Despite misgivings about the lack of policy commitments, Pardoe saw the pact as essential for enhancing the Liberals' credibility and securing a political realignment.

Pardoe and his colleagues achieved little of substance in the economic arena. His working relationship with the Labour Chancellor of the Exchequer, Denis Healey, quickly became impossible. Many believed that the two men's styles were too similar; indeed, Healey later described Pardoe as 'Denis Healey with no redeeming features'. After an explosive confrontation between the two in December 1977, Pardoe negotiated the measures for the spring 1978 budget with the more congenial Financial Secretary to the Treasury, Joel Barnett.

Pardoe was also handicapped by the Liberals' lack of clear policy objectives and strategies. He advocated radical tax reform aimed at providing better incentives and making the system more efficient. This package, controversial within the party, included a massive but phased reduction in the rate of standard income tax, funded by an increase in VAT and employers' National Insurance Contributions. Healey rejected these ideas as excessively inflationary and calculated, correctly, that the Liberals would be forced by political realities into accepting a more cautious package.

Pardoe initially claimed that the pact depended on the continuation of a tough pay ceiling that the trade unions accepted as binding. However, after the TUC refused to be party to a new pay policy, the Liberals had little alternative but to support the government's imposition of a ten per cent pay ceiling in return for tax cuts. While they secured a lower marginal tax for the lowest-paid earners, Pardoe and the Liberals got little credit. Other achievements for which he worked hard, such as tax incentives for employee profit sharing and new measures to help small businesses and farmers, represented core Liberal policies but were of little interest to the wider electorate.

The 1979 general election saw Pardoe defeated in North Cornwall, the victim of a strong swing to the Conservatives across the West Country. He did not try to return to the Commons and rejected Steel's offer of a peerage, believing the House of Lords to be an irrelevant anachronism.

In the 1980s, Pardoe turned to his business activities, as a managing director of Sight & Sound and Sound Education Limited, and as a director of Gerard Medals. From 1979 to 1981, he presented *Look Here*, a television programme about television. Still, Pardoe did not abandon politics altogether. He was a member of the Alliance campaign committee for the 1983 general election and Chairman of the Alliance campaign team in 1987. Pardoe later described the latter role, trying to build an effective campaign in the face of public differences between David Owen and David Steel, as his most disillusioning experience in politics.

Retired since 1989, Pardoe lives in Hampstead with his wife, Joyce, whom he married in 1958. The couple have three adult children, two sons and one daughter. Though a member of the Liberal Democrats, he now plays no part in politics.

Neil Stockley

DAVID PENHALIGON   1944–86

David Charles Penhaligon, born on D-Day, 6 June 1944, narrowly avoided being christened 'Montgomery' by parents caught up in patriotic fervour. So bizarre a combination of names would, surely, have detracted from Penhaligon's demotic charm; yet it was precisely that warmth of personality and humour, the apparent ordinariness of the man, which enabled him to be an exceptional political figure, both for his native Cornwall and for the Liberal Party nation-wide.

Born and brought up in Truro, Penhaligon attended Truro School, leaving at sixteen to become a chartered engineer working for Holman Brothers in Camborne and studying at Camborne Technical College. After his marriage to Annette Lidgey on 6 January 1968, he became the sub-postmaster in Chacewater, west of Truro; the couple later had two childen, a son and a daughter.

Despite Conservative parents, Penhaligon joined the Liberals in 1964. He was moved by the desperation and poverty of the tenants of his father's caravan site, and by his experience as a teenage witness in a murder case which eventually saw two suspects, both tenants of the site, hanged. From this sprang a visceral opposition to Conservatism and to the death penalty; but he also felt that the only prospects of success for small companies like Holman Brothers was by avoiding the Labourite model of state-owned and -directed corporations. Thus Penhaligon brought to his Liberalism a number of themes – concern with the socially marginalised, and a belief in worker participation, without state control, in industry – that lasted throughout his political life.

After six years of intense political activism, Penhaligon was prevented from putting himself forward as candidate for Truro for the 1970 general election because of his youth; undeterred, he was an energetic but unsuccessful candidate in Totnes. A team of activists, led by Penhaligon, then devoted themselves to further intensive local campaigning in Truro, introducing the first overtly partisan candidates in local council elections with considerable success, and practising their campaigning philosophy of keeping in touch with the community all year round through regular leaflets and campaigns. Historically, Truro had not been a bastion of Liberalism; the constituencies to the east were generally more favourable, and the Liberals had not in recent memory moved beyond third place. However, when Penhaligon stood as the Liberal candidate in February 1974, he was not merely in second place but also within 2,561 votes of the elected Conservative.

Despite the temptation to relax after this major advance, the local party worked even harder after February, to make Truro the only Liberal gain of October 1974, when Penhaligon was elected with a majority of 464. Since he was nothing if not a true son of Cornwall, it is, perhaps, appropriate that between February and October the Mebyon Kernow vote was so squeezed that it fell by 466 votes. Subsequently, Penhaligon and his local association made Truro one of the Liberals' safest seats, his majority increasing to 8,708 in 1979 and 10,480 in 1983, despite the electoral disappointments suffered by other Cornish Liberals.

In Parliament, Penhaligon's initial impatience with the irrelevancies of Westminster protocol must sometimes have made him seem naïve. Yet he worked effectively there as a politician during the Lib-Lab Pact – about which he was highly sceptical – and also as Liberal parliamentary spokesman on employment (twice), energy, industry, and finally – with some, though decreasing, difficulty – on economic matters. Among his parliamentary achievements was the, alas temporary, saving of at least part of the Cornish tin mining industry. He also used the Lib-Lab Pact to frustrate Labour plans to centralise electricity supply, much to Tony Benn's annoyance.

But perhaps Penhaligon's greatest achievements lay beyond Parliament. His ability to communicate Liberalism in simple terms meant that he was one of the few nationally recognised Liberal figures of his era. As he somehow combined both being, and appearing, down-to-earth with being somewhat media-savvy, he became popular and well-loved well outside Cornwall and beyond his own party. He was able to use both his popularity and communication skills outside and inside the party, and demonstrated a shrewdness and toughness as a politician which belied his public image. He was a significant supporter of the party leadership's policies on nuclear defence, intervening to help to defeat an anti-nuclear motion at Blackpool in 1980 and bitterly regretting failing to do so during the Eastbourne assembly in 1986. This aside, he was often among the more 'radical' Liberal element within the Parliamentary party, supporting John Pardoe (*q.v.*) for the party leadership in 1976 against David Steel (*q.v.*), and arguing against making Roy Jenkins (*q.v.*) the 'Prime-Minister designate' of the Alliance campaign in 1983.

He was an effective President of the Liberal Party in 1985–86, and was widely seen both as a potential future leader and as a key element in the Liberals' relationship with the SDP in the run-up to the 1987 general election; he had been an early advocate for merger. Yet, almost certainly, he would have regarded his achievements for Cornwall and the Cornish as being of equal importance with his work for Liberalism.

David Penhaligon died early on 22 December 1986, on his way to a regular Christmas meeting with the workers in the Truro postal sorting office, when the car he was driving lost control on ice and collided with another vehicle.

His wife Annette published a biography, *Penhaligon*, in 1989.

Paul Martin

VIVIAN PHILLIPPS

1870–1955

Vivian Phillipps entered Parliament at the age of fifty-two, and almost immediately became Liberal Chief Whip. He was to hold that office during one of the most turbulent periods of the party's history.

Henry Vivian Phillipps was born on 13 April 1870 in Beckenham – now a London suburb, but then a Kentish village – the son of Henry Mitchell Phillipps. He entered Charterhouse School in 1883, but three years later was sent to Heidelberg. He returned in 1889, speaking fluent German, and also proficient in Greek and Latin. In the following year he entered Gonville and Caius College, Cambridge, distinguishing himself in the modern languages tripos in 1893.

Phillipps' first post was as a German teacher at Fettes College, Edinburgh. He annotated Schiller's *Der Neffe als Onkel* (ca. 1895), and wrote *A short sketch of German literature for schools* (1895; 1897). In 1899, he married Agnes, daughter of James Ford, by whom he had a son and two daughters. One of the daughters appears to have prompted his next published work, a children's book entitled *A trip to Santa Claus Land, or Ruth's Christmas Eve* (1905). In 1908, he was called to the bar, and later practiced on the northern circuit.

Phillipps' early attempts to enter Parliament in the Liberal interest were unsuccessful. Tory Blackpool defied his assault in 1906. In both 1910 general elections he came close to victory in Maidstone. In 1912, however, he became private secretary to the Scottish Secretary, McKinnon Wood, and later continued in that post under Wood's successor, H. J. Tennant. It may have been this appointment which drew Phillipps to the attention of Tennant's brother-in-law H. H. Asquith (q.v.).

When Lloyd George (*q.v.*) replaced Asquith as Prime Minister of the wartime coalition government in December 1916, Tennant, like most of Asquith's close associates, left office, and Phillipps then became private secretary to Asquith himself. At the 1918 general election, he stood as Liberal candidate for Rochdale, but the coalition's support – the so-called 'coupon' – went to his Conservative opponent, and he was heavily defeated. The coalition won a huge victory, but more than two-thirds of its MPs were Conservatives. Asquith and the great majority of 'uncouponed' Liberals were defeated. In the years that followed, the split between Lloyd George's coalition Liberals and the independent Liberals (nicknamed the 'wee frees'), led by Donald Maclean (*q.v.*) and then Asquith after the Paisley byelection of 1920, widened.

The coalition came to a sudden end in the autumn of 1922, with Bonar Law replacing Lloyd George as Prime Minister, and Phillipps was candidate for West Edinburgh in the election which followed. A Conservative, equipped with the coupon, had been elected in 1918 in a triangular contest. In 1922, Labour did not stand, and Phillipps was at last successful, though the results of the election nationally saw the Labour Party overtake the Liberals for the first time.

After the 1918 general election, Asquith had selected G. R. Thorne as Chief Whip for the 'wee frees', but the MPs insisted on J. M. Hogge as Thorne's colleague; a third whip, Arthur Marshall, was later added. Early in 1923, Thorne resigned and Asquith promptly invited Phillipps to take the job. With some hesitation, he agreed; Marshall remained Deputy Chief Whip. Hogge, who was *persona non grata* to some leading Asquithians, was at no pains to conceal his fury.

The appointment was remarkable on other counts. Phillipps was a man of high ability, utter probity, and deep loyalty to his chief, who, in different circumstances, would have been an admirable choice for the post. Yet he was a new MP, and he took office at what was certain to be a most difficult time; not least of his problems was the question of whether bridges might now be built between Asquithian and Lloyd Georgeite Liberals – and Phillipps was completely committed to one side.

In the spring of 1923, Bonar Law fell ill, resigned, and was succeeded by Stanley Baldwin. A few months later, Baldwin announced his conversion to protection, and a general election was called. The two Liberal groups reunited in the cause of free trade, the party manifesto was signed jointly by Asquith and Lloyd George, and the 'official' Liberals received a large subvention from the Lloyd George Fund. Phillipps was re-elected in West Edinburgh, this time in a three-cornered contest. When all results were declared, the Conservatives were still the largest single party, but had lost their overall majority. The Liberals, with 159 seats, had improved their position considerably, but were still only the third party.

In January 1924, Labour formed a minority government, with Liberal acquiescence. The Liberals faced difficult questions, not least of which was how to reunify finances and organisation after the earlier disruption. The matter was still not satisfactorily resolved when a new general election took place in October 1924. The Liberals suffered disaster, being reduced to forty seats. Phillipps was one of the casualties, running third in a close contest at West Edinburgh. In the years which followed,

Lloyd George took control of the Liberal Party. Phillipps became one of the secretaries of the new Liberal Council, a 'cave' of intransigent Asquithians. He stood again as candidate for West Edinburgh in the 1929 general election, but finished no better than a respectable third.

For the rest of his life, Phillipps devoted himself to other activities. He had been a Kent JP as far back as 1915; he became Vice-Chairman of the Bench in 1931, and later Chairman of the West Kent Quarter Sessions. Not long before his death, he privately published his autobiography, *My Days and Ways*, a useful record of how matters looked to a devoted Asquithian, which has not been fully quarried by historians. On 16 January 1955, he died at his home in Tonbridge, Kent.

Roy Douglas

TIM RAZZALL (Lord Razzall) 1943–

How do you describe a chameleon? For over twenty years, Tim Razzall has seemingly effortlessly moved between all the different levels of the party and the business world and made a major contribution to them all. He has been Treasurer of both the Liberal Party and the Liberal Democrats, being one of the key people to secure the financial viability of the party after merger and ensuring that it had the resources to fight key national and European elections during the 1980s and '90s. In Richmond-upon-Thames he was one of the two or three key movers and shakers in building up the Liberals as the main opposition, and then Deputy Leader in the long-standing Liberal/Liberal Democrat administration. He spread the secret of their success through the Association of District Counsellors and his Presidency of it.

At the same time, he was pursuing a highly successful career as a commercial lawyer, building up his firm Frere Cholmeley Bischoff from a medium-sized company to one of the major players, before its recent merger, and as a director of a number of public companies.

In his managerial and persuasive skills he has undoubtedly been one of the key influences in the structure and management of the new party since its creation.

Edward Timothy Razzall was born on 12 June 1943, the son of Humphrey Razzall, a taxing master in the High Court and a former solicitor. The Razzalls were a long-standing Yorkshire Liberal family, his father contested the 1945 general election. He was educated at St Paul's, where he was, typically, both captain of cricket and Head of School. He then went to Worcester College, Oxford, where he took a degree in law. He played cricket for the Oxford first team.

In 1967 he joined Frere Cholmeley (as they were then called) as an articled clerk and qualified as a solicitor in 1969. He became a partner in 1973. He married for the first time in 1965, having two children, Katie (who worked for a time for the party at Westminster) and James. He married Deirdre Martineau (née Taylor-Smith) in 1982;

Deirdre was a fellow councillor in Mortlake from 1977 (winning at a byelection the day of the announcement of the Lib–Lab Pact) until 1994.

In 1974, Razzall contested the Mortlake ward in Richmond for the first time, and held it for the next twenty-four years. In 1983, the Liberals under the leadership of David Williams and deputy leadership of Razzall took control of Richmond Borough Council. Razzall proceeded to chair the Policy and Resources Committee for the next thirteen years, always being – in the words of a contemporary – 'adept at pulling financial rabbits out of hats' at a time of increasing central government control over local government expenditure.

In 1986 Razzall became the joint Treasurer of the Liberal Party (with Lord Jacobs, *q.v.*). He then became the Treasurer of the newly merged Liberal Democrats in 1988, a post he has held ever since. He was Vice Chair of the Association of Liberal Democrat Councillors, and then President, from 1990 until 1995.

Razzall became the Chief Executive of Frere Cholmeley in 1990, and put into effect an expansionist strategy for the firm, involving building up its overseas offices – the company moved into the top twenty in the ranks of law firms. He was awarded the title of European Lawyer of the year in 1992. He stepped down as Chief Executive in 1993, and in 1995 left Frere Cholmeley Bischoff to form his own business, Argonaut Associates, which specialises in giving business advice to growth companies.

Razzall played a part in the central organisation of the general election of 1992 and in the 1997 election was one of the key managers of the campaign under Richard Holme (*q.v.*), running the Leader's tours operation and the key 'final week' group. He was awarded the CBE in 1993, and made a life peer in 1997. He is now the party's spokesman on trade and industry in the Lords, steering through the party's response to the Minimum Wage Bill in the last session in particular.

Razzall's outside interests are sport (he is a member of the MCC), food and wine.

Tim Clement-Jones

LORD REDESDALE   1967–

When Rupert Mitford, the sixth Baron Redesdale, first took his seat in the House of Lords, he surprised the House by not following his father and cousins into the Conservative Party, instead choosing to take the Liberal Democrat whip. Only twenty-four at the time, he instantly became the youngest active peer and well known in all quarters of the Lords.

Redesdale was born on 18 July 1967 and educated at Highgate School and Newcastle University, where he read archaeology. The youngest in his family, he inherited his title in 1991, having just returned from two years during which he travelled extensively in southern Africa, including a spell working as a team leader in Zimbabwe for Operation Raleigh.

In 1993 Redesdale became Liberal Democrat spokesman for overseas development, and he doggedly, if sometimes haphazardly, attacked Conservative policies, saw legislation through the Lords and chaired the working group which produced the Liberal Democrat policy paper, *A World of Opportunity* (1996). In 1994 he was given the Liberal Democrat seat on the House of Lords' Science and Technology Committee and since 1994 he has been President of Holborn & St. Pancras Liberal Democrats.

By dint of his relative youth, Redesdale is frequently asked, and always willingly accepts, to do unwelcome but necessary tasks for the Liberal Democrats in the House of Lords and beyond – jobs such as speaking, or just being in the chamber when no-one else wants to, or appearing on late-night television programmes with very small audiences which need an official Liberal Democrat 'name'. He approaches them with the same gusto as he does the parliamentary rugby team and beer club.

Since joining the Lords, Redesdale's interests in development policy and southern Africa have been reinforced by his numerous trips abroad to monitor elections on behalf of the Commonwealth and United Nations. Always open to a challenge, he has monitored in some remote and difficult places, including Mozambique, Malawi, Tanzania, South Africa, Pakistan and Sir Lanka.

Adept at playing the upper-class buffoon, Redesdale hides a caring and more thinking interior which manifests itself in numerous underplayed charitable acts. He is a lieutenant in the Territorial Army, sits on the boards of the Institute of Advanced Motorists and the Know-How Fund, and presides over the Natural Gas Vehicle Association. When not in London, he lives in his adored home in Northumberland, where his many activities in support of the north east include working with SCAN and Kids Cabin. Redesdale is also a member of the Council of the University of Newcastle.

Selena Bevis

DAVID RENDEL MP   1949–

Winner of the May 1993 Newbury byelection, David Rendel follows in a long and proud tradition of Liberal and Liberal Democrat byelection victors. His success, however, set a new high watermark for the party and its predecessors as he piled up a winning majority over the Conservatives of 22,055 – the largest Liberal or Liberal Democrat majority in history.

Rendel went on in the 1997 general election to confound recent trends by holding his seat with ease; his current majority is 8,517. He is now the leader of the Liberal Democrats' social security team, having served as the party's front-bench spokesman on local government and housing from 1994–97. He is widely regarded as one of the party's most reliable performers.

David Digby Rendel was born in Athens, where his father was working in the British Embassy, on 15 April 1949. He returned to the UK when only two months old; his childhood was spent in London but at the age of twelve he won a scholarship to Eton where he first decided to go into politics. 'I was not especially good at anything,' he says, 'and politics seems to be just about the only career in which it is important to be *some* good at everything but not *particularly* good at anything.'

After spending fourteen months as a volunteer teacher in Cameroon and Uganda with the development charity Voluntary Service Overseas (VSO), he went up to Corpus Christi, Oxford, where he studied atmospheric physics, including some of the earliest computer models of the ozone layer 'long before anyone discovered it had a hole in it'. In 1974, he was a member of the Oxford crew which won the Boat Race in what was then the fastest time ever recorded.

Rendel's career after leaving university was in the energy industry, working in computing and finance, first for Shell International and British Gas, and then for Esso Petroleum.

His first love, however, remained politics. In 1973, he joined the Liberal Party and soon become a coopted member of Hammersmith & Fulham Council. In 1979 and 1983, he fought the Fulham seat for the Liberals before being selected as the prospective parliamentary candidate for Newbury in 1984. Ironically, as a result, he missed out on the chance to fight the Fulham byelection in 1986, which was won for Labour by Rendel's close friend Nick Raynsford.

Rendel's own byelection victory was built on the back of Liberal and Liberal Democrat success at local government level. First elected to Newbury District Council in 1987, he was re-elected in 1991 when, for the first time, the Liberal Democrats won control of the council. Rendel took control first of the Finance and Property sub-committee and then the Recreation and Amenities committee.

Despite failing to take the parliamentary seat in 1987 and 1992, Rendel continued to close the gap on his Conservative opponents. Hence, when the Tory incumbent, Judith Chaplin, unexpectedly died only months after her first election, he was perfectly placed to exploit Conservative unpopularity in the wake of Black Wednesday. His election on 6 May 1993 capped what was then the most successful night in the history of the Liberal Democrats, as the party swept to power in local government elections across England, taking over five hundred seats, mainly from the Conservatives.

Rendel is married to Sue, a Newbury GP, and has three teenage sons. He lives in his Newbury constituency.

Ben Rich

CHRIS RENNARD 1960–

The regard with which Chris Rennard is held in the Liberal Democrats can be judged by the rapturous ovation he received at the 1997 party conference – a standing ovation the equal of anything ever accorded to Paddy Ashdown (*q.v.*).

Born on 8 July 1960, he grew up in Liverpool as the Liberal revival of the 1960s got under way. By his early twenties he was at the heart of the party organisation in the city and since then has been responsible for numerous local and parliamentary election successes. The Liberal Democrat run of byelection wins from Eastbourne in 1990 to Winchester in 1997 simply would not have happened without him.

He was delivering some of the earliest *Focus* leaflets in Britain almost as soon as he could walk. His father died when he was three. His mother was very anti-politics but became impressed with the work of the first post-war Liberal councillor in Liverpool, Cyril Carr, when he successfully fought for her widowed mother's allowance. By the time he was fourteen, Rennard was elected as the Liberal candidate in his school's mock election and was Treasurer of his local Church Ward branch. When his mother died, he was only sixteen but he moved into his own flat, finished his A levels (coming first in all his subjects at the very academic Liverpool Blue Coat School) and used his place studying politics and economics at Liverpool University as a base for political campaigning.

The Liberal society at the University won almost all the elections it contested under his leadership. At the same time, he and his university friends played a decisive role in the city council elections, which resulted in a Liberal administration between 1980 and 1983. At twenty-one he was Deputy Chairman of the Liverpool Liberal Party, organising many of the council election campaigns. He learned much from Trevor 'Jones the Vote' (*q.v.*), and worked closely with David Alton (*q.v.*), for whose 1979 byelection campaign he had worked full-time. When the Liverpool constituency boundaries were redrawn in 1982, and Alton opted for the new Mossley Hill constituency, it was considered unwinnable by almost everyone – but not Rennard. He became the full-time agent upon graduating in 1982. Each household received a *Focus* leaflet at almost weekly intervals for six months before the general election, and the Mossley Hill constituency scored a record fourteen per cent swing from Conservative to Liberal/Alliance in 1983.

The head of Liberal Party Organisation at the time, John Spiller, persuaded Rennard to use his campaigning skills across the country. At Spiller's behest he moved to the East Midlands, where he oversaw the election of the first Liberal councillors in Leicester for over twenty years and his work helped to double the number of Liberal councillors in the region. He was a leading member of the Association of Liberal Councillors' Standing Committee and wrote many of their publications, including the 160-page *Winning Local Elections*, which became the bible for Liberal Democrat campaigners in the early years of the new party.

Rennard is probably best known, however, as the man behind many parliamentary byelection successes, including West Derbyshire (1986) and Greenwich (1987). In autumn 1990, as the party's new Director of Campaigns and Elections, he fought off suggestions that the Eastbourne byelection should not be fought or could not be won because of the murder of the Conservative MP by the IRA. All the knowledge which Rennard had acquired over the years in community campaigning was deployed in overturning the 16,000 Conservative majority. When David Bellotti won by 4,550, it was a shock to the party and to the country; Liberal Democrat poll ratings soared from eight to eighteen per cent overnight. For the first time in the new party's troubled first two years of existence, it was clear that it would survive.

In the seven years which followed, the Liberal Democrats won seven more parliamentary byelections. A hugely successful and skilled team was built up for the campaigns, but central to their success was Rennard's campaigning drive, helping to raise the cash, build and nurture the skills of the team, motivate the workers required, and, above all, to oversee the strategy which would secure success.

He was in charge of the general election target seat campaign in 1992, when four gains were made, but four more were to come as a result of byelections, including, in 1993, a record majority in Newbury and the biggest swing against the Tories since 1935 in Christchurch. Eastleigh (1994) was a furious campaign, with Labour trying to get in on the act, but seeing every one of their council seats in the constituency fall to the Liberal Democrats in the local elections preceding the byelection. The Liberal Democrats gained the seat by 9,000 votes. Rennard found himself head to head in competition with Peter Mandelson when the Littleborough & Saddleworth byelection polled in July 1995. New Labour threw everything at the seat and ran what was described as the dirtiest campaign ever but Liberal Democrat Chris Davies gained the seat with a majority of 1,995.

Rennard ran the party's target seat campaign for the 1997 general election, which resulted in the election of forty-six Liberal Democrat MPs. The most dramatic result of the campaign was probably Mark Oaten's (q.v.) win by two votes in Winchester. But by November, Winchester was voting again in a re-run; when the majority of two votes became one of 20,556, the 1997 general election campaign was finally over. Success was crowned with success when Liverpool, Rennard's home town, fell to Liberal Democrat control in May 1998.

John Ricketts

DAVID RICARDO   1772–1823

Less well known than Adam Smith (q.v.), Ricardo nevertheless is his intellectual and philosophical equal. He is credited alongside Smith with founding the 'classical school' of economics.

Inspired by Smith and driven by his friend, James Mill (father of John Stuart Mill, q.v.), Ricardo provides an historical bridge between the economic and political liberals, although his own writings are concerned purely with a narrow, quasi-scientific and fiercely practical capitalist analysis of political economy. His approach was heavily influenced by his practical knowledge of the money and foreign exchange markets, and Ricardo stands apart from his fellow economists as one of the very few not only to theorise, but also to succeed in business.

Born in London on 19 April 1772, into a Dutch orthodox Jewish family, Ricardo did not receive a classical training, instead being sent to his uncle's home in Holland to study Talmud. At the age of fourteen, he returned to England and joined his father at the London stock exchange. He was disowned by his parents, however, when at the age of twenty-one he married a Quaker, Priscilla Wilkinson, and joined the Unitarian Church. As a result, despite his family's wealth, Ricardo was left to make his own way on the exchange. There, his cool head and sound business judgement enabled him to make a considerable fortune (roughly £700,000), at a time of unprecedented financial upheaval caused by the Napoleonic wars.

While still working at the exchange, Ricardo dabbled in mathematics, chemistry and geology, becoming, in 1807, a founding member of the Geological Society. It was political economy, however, which was to become his main interest when, in 1799 – during a stay in Bath for his wife's health – he was introduced to Smith's *Wealth of Nations*. Political economy provided Ricardo with an opportunity to combine his taste for science with his personal and practical knowledge of the money markets.

His first pamphlet, *The High Price of Bullion, a Proof of the Depreciation of Bank Notes*, was published in 1810 and caused significant controversy, leading first to the establishment of the Parliamentary bullion committee and then, eventually, to the resumption of cash payments. In 1815, a second pamphlet on the impact of low corn prices put the case in favour of free trade in grain products, thus prefiguring the liberal position on the abolition of the corn laws three decades later. Ever a realist, however, Ricardo accepted that a moderate duty might be required to counteract special burdens upon agriculture.

In 1817, Ricardo was finally persuaded to publish a comprehensive exposition of his political theories. He achieved this in his magnum opus, *The Principles of Political Economy and Taxation*. Building directly on Smith's work, *Principles* developed Ricardo's theories of 'economical and secure currency', thus laying the basis of the monetary policy of capitalist nations for more than a hundred years. In his thesis, Ricardo set out the argument against protectionist policies and sought to elevate his case against the corn laws to a generally applicable principle. He argued that an increase in wages would always lead to an absolute reduction in profits whether or not employers attempt to protect profits through higher prices. Ricardo believed that such action would simply devalue the money earned.

He is chiefly remembered today for his exposition of the principle of comparative advantage, the idea that nations can maximise their output and wealth by specialising in the production of goods at which they are relatively most efficient, trading with other countries to realise the gains from such specialisation. In the early nineteenth century, this suggested that Britain should concentrate on manufactured goods, selling them abroad to purchase food – which indeed became the basis for the long mid-Victorian economic boom.

In 1819, Ricardo became a Member of Parliament for the pocket Irish borough of Portarlington. He was re-elected in 1820 and held the seat until his death on 11 September 1823, at the age of fifty-one. Although an independent, Ricardo tended to support the Radicals, using his position rigorously to oppose religious persecution, and his appointment to a select committee to advocate reform of the corn laws.

In 1822, Ricardo declared: 'all taxes are bad and, except to avoid a deficit, I will vote for none, considering that a surplus would be an insuperable temptation to increase expenditure.' One can assume that he would not have favoured a penny on income tax to pay for education ....

The influence of Ricardo's *Principles* can clearly be seen in the writings of John Stuart Mill and Karl Marx, and although he was heavily criticised by Keynes (*q.v.*), his attachment to free and international trade has formed a central tenet of Liberalism for the last century and a half.

Ben Rich

D. G. RITCHIE 1853–1903

The New Liberalism of the late nineteenth and early twentieth centuries under-pinned the achievements of the Liberal governments of 1906–14, helping to lay the foundations of the welfare state and ensuring that the British Liberal Party evolved into a social – rather than a classical – liberal party, unlike many of its continental counterparts. The best-known proponents of the New Liberalism are L. T. Hobhouse (*q.v.*) and J. A. Hobson (*q.v.*); but D. G. Ritchie was also of considerable importance in formulating the New Liberal theory of the state.

David George Ritchie was born at Jedburgh on 26 October 1853, the only boy of the three children born to George Ritchie, the minister of the parish, and Elizabeth Dudgeon. He received his early schooling at Jedburgh Academy; not allowed to make friends with other boys of his own age, he never learned to play games, and concentrated his mind on purely intellectual subjects. He studied classics at Edinburgh University (1869–75) and at Balliol College, Oxford (1875–78), winning firsts at both. He became a fellow at Jesus College, and then tutor at both Jesus and Balliol. In 1894 he became Professor of Logic and Metaphysics at St Andrews, remaining there until his death nine years later.

At Oxford, Ritchie was the most brilliant of the pupils of T. H. Green (*q.v.*), and sought to establish the political congruence of the teachings of Green and of John Stuart Mill (*q.v.*). In *The Principles of State Interference* (1891), he argued that Mill's thinking showed 'a process of transition from the extreme doctrines of individualism and *laissez faire*, in which he was brought up, to a more adequate conception of society'. The merely negative work of pruning back mischievous state activities (the traditional concern of Gladstonian liberalism) had now to give way to the positive use of government power, 'because in a vast number of cases the individual does not find himself in a position in which he can act "freely" (i.e. direct his action to objects which reasons assigns as desirable) without the intervention of the State to put him in such a position'. Ritchie went beyond Green, however, in the importance he attributed to the state as reformer of human minds, arguing that laws could help to foster morality even in the absence of appropriate social sentiment.

Ritchie also aimed (in *Darwinism and Politics*, 1889) to counter the arguments of those who, like Herbert Spencer, applied Darwinian evolutionary theory to social and political debates. He insisted that cultural and intellectual improvements were transmitted in the 'social inheritance of the race' and were not dependent on biological heredity. He accepted, however, the validity of the concept of natural selection in the process of competition between ideas and opinions; the social reformer could therefore help to encourage the evolution of mind, and thereby further progress in a self-reinforcing manner.

Ritchie's writing influenced a whole generation of reformers, pioneering the belief in their power to elicit change from society. In this he was at one with the Fabians, who he joined in the 1880s. But he remained politically a Liberal, and did not share Sidney Webb's and other Fabians' faith in manipulation from above. Along with H.W. Massingham (*q.v.*), he resigned from the society in 1893 when it published a manifesto, *To Your Tents, O Israel,* attacking the Liberal government and appealing for an independent labour party. Like all Liberals Ritchie was at base an optimist, resting his faith in humanity and in progress, despite the many set-backs along the way; the foundation of ethics necessarily rested on the ideal end of social well-being.

He died in St Andrews on 3 February 1903, and was buried there. He was married twice: in 1881, to Flora Lindsay (died 1888); and then in 1889, to Ellen Haycraft. He had a daughter by the first marriage and a son by the second. Despite his retiring manner, he had many friends.

In addition to the works mentioned above, his main publications included *Darwin and Hegel* (1893), *Natural Rights* (1895), *Studies in Political and Social Ethics* (1902) and *Plato* (1902). After his death a collection of *Philosophical Studies* was issued in 1905, edited with a memoir by Professor Robert Latta.

Duncan Brack

STINA ROBSON (Lady Robson)   1919–

Baroness Robson of Kiddington is one of the longest-standing Liberal Democrats, with a direct link to the troubled past of the 'dark ages' of the Liberal Party, and a wide variety of experience. As a businesswoman she provided a source of wisdom that was rare in the dark days and which was especially important in revising the reputation of Liberalism as a serious force in British politics.

Born Inga-Stina (known as Stina) Arvidsson in Sweden on 20 August 1919, she was educated in Stockholm, and worked for the Swedish government from 1939 to 1943. It was in the British Embassy at the outbreak of the Second World War that she met Lawrence (later Sir Lawrence) Robson, a noted accountant, farmer and company director. They married in 1940 and settled in Oxfordshire. Lawrence fought Banbury twice for the Liberal Party in the 1950s and became Liberal Party President in 1953–54.

Lawrence Robson introduced Stina to Liberal politics through their London connections. Lawrence was due to be the candidate to restore Liberal fortunes in the Eye division in 1955, after the defection of Sir Edgar Granville (*q.v.*) to Labour. However, he was called upon by a government enquiry and was replaced by 'Mrs Robson'. Unfortunately the era of Liberal success in Eye was over; Stina fought Eye twice (the first time against Granville), narrowly losing her deposit both times; she later fought Gloucester in 1964 and 1966, faring rather better. She was elected to the Chipping Norton Rural District Council for a time.

Robson became President of the Womens' Liberal Federation from 1968–70, although like Nancy Seear (*q.v.*) she had no great passion for bodies representing women. She then became President of the Liberal Party Organisation from 1970–71. She was Chair of the Liberal environment panel from 1971–77, an interest stemming from her experiences in Sweden, and her determination that the UK should follow the example of her homeland. Ennobled in 1974, in the same year she became Chair of the South-West Thames Regional Health Authority, a post which she held until 1982.

After her elevation to the House of Lords Robson was able to use her considerable experience to speak on health matters. As a health authority chair, as governor and trustee of several health bodies, notably as Chair of the National Association of Leagues of Hospital Friends, and with a daughter a practising GP, her contributions were always businesslike, focusing on the need for services to be efficiently run. Never a tribalist, she has made friends with peers of all parties.

One of the major unsung contributions to the reviving fortunes of the party in the 1950s, '60s and '70s was the salvage and then securing of the National Liberal Club. Close to bankruptcy in the mid-1970s, a package was put together which saved, and then began to restore, the fortunes of the Club. The Robsons played a considerable part, and Baroness Robson remains closely involved in the NLC. An adjunct to this was the development of a conference complex at Kiddington Hall, which was used by the party leadership for many summit meetings in the '70s and '80s, and for other party functions to the present day.

Baroness Robson was Liberal Democrat spokesman on health in the House of Lords from 1993–98, and is President of the Charlbury & District Liberal Democrats. Her husband Lawrence died in 1982; she has one son and two daughters.

Gareth Epps

LORD ROCHESTER 1916–

Foster Lamb, the second Lord Rochester, signed up to the Liberal Party in Northwich, Cheshire, in 1962, shortly after the Orpington byelection which saw Eric Lubbock (Lord Avebury, *q.v.*) win a spectacular victory. He had inherited the peerage in 1955 from his father who had been Liberal MP for Rochester from 1906–18 and later Paymaster-General in the National Government from 1931–35.

Foster Charles Lowry Lamb was born on 7 June 1916 and educated at Mill Hill and Jesus College, Cambridge. Following his time as a captain in the 23rd Hussars during the war, he made a career in personnel management in ICI. He was to become the personnel manager of the Mond Division of ICI, where the Liberal founding fathers (Alfred Mond, *q.v.*) had introduced employee share ownership schemes at a very early stage. It was the experience of this participative form of employee involvement in industry which he found attractive in the Liberal Party of Jo Grimond (*q.v.*), although he did not go along completely with the party's more detailed proposals for direct worker involvement in control.

Having not taken much part in the affairs of the House of Lords after he had been signed up as a member of the Liberal Party, by the local candidate Geoff Tordoff (later to be his Chief Whip as Lord Tordoff, *q.v.*) and his agent Dr Jim Bertie (later Bursar of Hertford College, Oxford), Rochester began to play a valuable role in the House as the spokesman on employment matters, and was a regular attender at party assemblies. His rather hesitant manner, combined with his considerable knowledge and common sense, made him a natural House of Lords person and he was always listened to with great respect from all sides of the House.

He remained a firm supporter of the Northwich constituency party and had many local interests in the Cheshire area, as had his wife Mary who was a prime mover in the setting up of the Cheshire Salt Museum. The couple had married in 1942, and had two sons and one daughter. In 1976 he became Pro-Vice Chancellor of the University of Keele, until 1986 when he became Dean, and it was during this period that he was made a Deputy Lieutenant of Cheshire.

His recreational interest is an abiding interest in cricket, no doubt associated with the fact that his second son, Tim Lamb, played for Northants for several years and later became Secretary of the English County Cricket Board.

Geoff Tordoff

BILL RODGERS (Lord Rodgers) 1928–

Bill Rodgers – one of the 'Gang of Four' who founded the SDP, and now (as Lord Rodgers of Quarry Bank) the leader of the Liberal Democrats in the House of Lords – was born in Liverpool on 28 October 1928 and named William Thomas Rodgers.

His father was employed for forty years by the Liverpool Corporation, rising to the responsible position of Clerk to the Health Committee, which ran the city hospitals in the days before the NHS.

The young Bill Rodgers was taken by his father to see the city's hospitals and slums and was deeply influenced by his father's commitment to public service. Rodgers attended Quarry Bank High School (to be made famous a few years later by the Beatles) and was caught up in the excitement of the 1945 election, when he worked for his local Liberal candidate. In 1946 he joined the Labour Party. He went up to Magdalen College, Oxford, in January 1949 and became one of the leading figures in the University Labour Club; he was Treasurer when Shirley Williams *(q.v.)* was Chairman.

On leaving Oxford in 1951, Rodgers almost became a journalist, but accepted an offer of the post of Assistant Secretary to the Fabian Society. In 1953 he became its youngest ever General Secretary, an office which he held until 1960. In 1955 he married a remarkable woman, Silvia Szulman, the daughter of a Communist couple of Polish-Jewish origin who had settled in Berlin and fled from it only months before the outbreak of the Second World War. Rodgers and his wife have three daughters.

Rodgers fought a byelection at Bristol West in 1957 and was a member of the St. Marylebone Borough Council from 1958 until 1962. In 1960 he became the principal organiser and executive chairman of the Campaign for Democratic Socialism, a party group set up to support Hugh Gaitskell in his fight against a party commitment to unilateral nuclear disarmament. The Campaign's founder members included Roy Jenkins *(q.v.)*, Dick Taverne *(q.v.)* and Tony Crosland.

At a byelection in 1962 Rodgers was elected to Parliament as MP for Stockton-on-Tees. Following the Labour victory two years later, he was appointed Parliamentary Under-Secretary at the Department of Economic Affairs. He worked closely with George Brown and moved with him to the Foreign Office in 1967. In 1968 he was promoted to Minister of State at the Board of Trade and moved to the Treasury the following year.

In 1971 Rodgers acted as whip for the pro-European group of Labour MPs, led by Roy Jenkins, who ignored a three-line whip and voted in support of the Heath Government's decision to join the European Community. As a result, Harold Wilson sacked Rodgers from his post as a shadow minister. However, following the election in February 1974 Wilson appointed him Minister of State at the Ministry of Defence. He played a leading part in the 'Yes' Campaign in the 1975 Referendum on Europe. In 1976 Jim Callaghan appointed him to the Cabinet as Secretary of State for Transport.

After the Labour Party's defeat, Rodgers was elected to the Shadow Cabinet in 1979 and 1980. Although he first discussed the formation of a new party with Jenkins at the end of 1979, he was initially sceptical, and is generally thought to have been the most reluctant of the 'Gang' to leave the Labour Party. He did not finally decide to break away until New Year 1981, when, during ten days spent in bed as a result of severe (and probably psychosomatic) back pain, he decided that remaining in the party would be living a lie.

Following the agreement in principle that the SDP and the Liberals would fight the next general election in partnership, Rodgers took charge of the SDP side in negotiations over the allocation of seats. His public criticism of the Liberal Party's approach to the negotiations at the beginning of 1982, by revealing the tensions between the parties, pricked the bubble of euphoria that had followed the spectacular byelection victory at Crosby. During this period he outlined his political views in his book *The Politics of Change*.

Rodgers lost his Stockton seat in the 1983 election, but remained active in the SDP as the party's Vice-President and a member of its National Committee. He worked closely with David Owen, but in 1986 relations between them broke down when Owen publicly attacked the conclusions of the SDP-Liberal Joint Commission on Defence, which Rodgers had been appointed to chair. After the disappointing result of the 1987 election, in which he had unsuccessfully contested Milton Keynes, Rodgers became convinced that the SDP and the Liberals had no future except as a single party, and he became one of the leaders of the merger campaign.

The need to earn a living and to find an outlet for his outstanding administrative skills forced Rodgers to look for a job outside politics. In 1987 he was appointed Director-General of the Royal Institute of British Architects, a post which he held for seven years. His success in that job was recognised by his appointment as an honorary fellow of RIBA on his retirement.

During this period Rodgers' political activity was, inevitably, much reduced. However, in 1992 he was appointed to the House of Lords as Lord Rodgers of Quarry Bank. On his retirement from RIBA he was able to become active as spokesman on home affairs. On the retirement of Lord Jenkins of Hillhead from the leadership of the Liberal Democrat peers at the end of 1997, Rodgers was elected to succeed him. He has also been, since 1995, the Chairman of the Advertising Standards Authority.

Bill Rodgers' career has been dominated by the concept of politics as public service. He was from the start, and remains, a social democrat who tore himself away from his roots in the Labour Party when it abandoned its commitment to social democracy and moderation. Although less in the public eye than the others, he was a crucial member of the Gang of Four.

Willy Goodhart

EARL OF ROSEBERY   1847–1929

Rosebery is perhaps the least well-known of the Liberal Prime Ministers, having the misfortune to serve in the office only as the era of Gladstonian Liberalism was definitively drawing to a close. He had a difficult relationship with the radicals of the parliamentary party, not because of his social policy attitudes (he was a convinced 'constructionist') but because of his forthrightly imperialist views, and, perhaps, his somewhat casual attitude to politics.

Rosebery's declared ambitions were to marry an heiress, own a horse that won the Derby and be Prime Minister. He fulfilled all three. On 20 March 1878 he married Hannah, the only child and heiress of Baron Meyer de Rothschild; his horses won the Derby in 1894, 1895 and 1905; and he headed a Liberal ministry between 5 March 1894 and 22 June 1895. He never sat in the House of Commons and, like others in that situation, found it difficult to lead a government from the Lords. In 1899 he said:'There are two supreme pleasures in life. One is ideal, the other real. The ideal is when a man receives the seals of office from his Sovereign. The real pleasure comes when he hands them back.'

Archibald Philip Primrose was born on 7 May 1847 in London. He was educated at Eton and went up to Christ Church, Oxford in 1866. On 4 March he succeeded his grandfather to become the fifth Earl of Rosebery, taking his seat in the House of Lords on 22 May. He left Oxford in 1869, without taking his degree, when the university authorities gave him the choice between selling his racehorse or departing.

Despite not having completed his degree, Rosebery was considered to be one of the most widely read young men of his day. He was a true bibliophile and kept his collection of rare Scottish books and pamphlets at Barnbougle Castle. In 1927 he presented some three thousand of these items to the National Library of Scotland. Well-educated, wealthy and with all the advantages of social position, Rosebery was able to travel widely and indulge his passions, one of which was writing. In 1862 he published privately a volume of verse; other published works of his include *Pitt* (1891), *Peel* (1899), *Napoleon: the Last Phase* (1900); *Lord Randolph Churchill* (1906) and *Chatham: His Early Life and Connections* (1910). Rosebery's essays and appreciations were published in *Miscellanies* (two volumes, 1921) edited by John Buchan.

Rosebery had a long parliamentary career as a Liberal politician. On 9 February 1871, his maiden speech seconded the Address to Her Majesty following the opening of Parliament. Following his successful return to office in 1880, Gladstone (*q.v.*) twice offered Rosebery the post of Under-Secretary of State at the India Office. Rosebery declined on both occasions, believing that his management of Gladstone's Midlothian campaign would be interpreted as an attempt to further his personal ambition rather than as a commitment to Liberal ideals and the party.

In 1881 Rosebery did take office, as Under-Secretary of State at the Home Office with special responsibilities for Scottish affairs; the following year he complained to Gladstone that Scottish matters were marginalised in Parliament, and in 1883 he resigned, saying that he would not rejoin the government unless he was a Cabinet minister. Shortly afterwards he left the country for a tour of America and Australia.

Perhaps Rosebery's major contribution to the Liberal Party was his attitude towards Britain's overseas possessions. Rosebery held strong beliefs about the British Empire, considering it to be a federation of nations. He promoted this idea whilst abroad and on 18 January 1884 he made a now-famous speech at Adelaide in which he said: '.... There is no need for any nation, however great, leaving the Empire, because the Empire is a Commonwealth of Nations'. Rosebery served as Foreign Secretary in Gladstone's ministries in 1886 and August 1892 – March 1894. In the interim, he was elected as one of the City's representatives to the first London County Council in 1889, and was chosen as its Chairman. He was elected as member for East Finsbury in 1892 and continued in the role of Chairman until he became Foreign Secretary.

He opposed the evacuation of Egypt, insisted on keeping control of Uganda and refused to join the Russians, French and Germans in an anti-Japanese league. In 1893 he intervened in the coal strike and chaired the Conference of Federated Coal-Owners and the Miners Federation, persuading the two sides to reach agreement. When Gladstone resigned in 1894, Rosebery was the Queen's choice as Prime Minister (Gladstone himself probably preferred his Chancellor of the Exchequer, Sir William Harcourt (*q.v.*), but the Queen deliberately avoided consulting him). His first speech in office created an outcry in the Liberal Party when he announced that home rule for Ireland could come only when England, as the senior member of the three kingdoms, agreed. This was unexpected, particularly after all Gladstone's efforts to secure home rule, and Rosebery was criticised in the Commons for his attitude.

Besides being Prime Minister, Rosebery was Leader of the Liberal Party between 1894 and 1896. Increasingly he was at odds with Liberal MPs, especially Harcourt; in February 1895 Rosebery threatened to resign because of lack of support from the parliamentary Liberals. After protests of loyalty from his Cabinet, he withdrew the threat. However he was seriously ill in 1894 and the government was defeated in June 1895; a Conservative House of Lords rejected all legislation but the budget. Campbell-Bannerman (*q.v.*) and the government felt obliged to resign and Rosebery visited Queen Victoria, formally resigning on 22 June 1895. In October 1896 he resigned as leader of the party in the interests of unity. Although he continued to be an active member of the Liberal Party in the Lords, Rosebery refused to accept office again. He ended up a cross-bencher.

In 1901 the Liberal Imperial Council was formed by Rosebery's supporters; in February 1902, the Liberal League was founded with Rosebery as its first President. He consistently advocated a reform of the Upper House, although he spoke against the Parliament Bill of 1910. In November 1918, he suffered a stroke which left him partially disabled; he died at the Durdans, Epsom, on 21 May 1929.

In 1931 the Marquis of Crewe (*q.v.*) published a two-volume biography of Rosebery. The most recent, authoritative study is Robert Rhodes James, *Rosebery: A Biography,* published in 1963 but still available in paperback.

Marjie Bloy

WALTER RUNCIMAN (Viscount Runciman)   1870–1949

Born in South Shields on 19 November 1870, the son of a self-made shipping magnate, Walter Runciman came from a family of Wesleyan Methodists. He was educated at South Shields Grammar School and Trinity, Cambridge (a first in history, 1892), and then became a partner in his father's firm, the Moor Line, a post he retained until 1905; he also became director of various assurance companies, and later in life was a director of the National Westminster Bank, 1925–31.

Having unsuccessfully fought Gravesend in 1898, he won the Oldham byelection in 1899. Within weeks, the country was at war in South Africa, and Runciman's Liberal Imperialist line brought him into conflict with Campbell-Bannerman (*q.v.*). In 1900 he was narrowly defeated by Winston Churchill (*q.v.*). He returned to Tyneside, where he married Hilda Stevenson (later to be Liberal MP for St Ives 1928–29, making the couple the first husband and wife to sit together in the Commons); the couple had five children, including Sir Steven Runciman, the eminent historian.

In 1901 Runciman was selected as candidate for the Dewsbury byelection, against the wishes of Campbell-Bannerman; he held the seat, and retained it until 1918. Once in Parliament he attempted to build bridges with the party leadership, and the result was his appointment as Parliamentary Secretary to the Local Government Board in December 1905. In 1907 he was promoted to Chief Secretary to the Treasury and then in 1908 to the Cabinet as President of the Board of Education. Until November 1908 he concentrated on attempting to settle the problem of voluntary schools. The package negotiated with the Archbishop of Canterbury collapsed, however, when it was sabotaged by Anglican militants. In October 1911 he was transferred to the Board of Agriculture where he was behind many of the proposals for land reform and state-owned rural housing promoted by the Liberal Land Campaign in 1913–14. On the outbreak of war he was moved to the Board of Trade.

In years before the First World War, Runciman had argued that British commitments in Europe should be heavily restricted. He wanted the balance of power maintained on the continent as a way of avoiding a British commitment to other powers, while peace would be kept by appeasement and negotiation. Were Britain to go to war he believed the country's wealth should pay allies to fight, while the Royal Navy would keep open the sea lanes so that trade could continue. The creation of large armies were, in his view, a drain on the economy which diverted manpower from wealth production.

Once war was under way, Runciman fought a rearguard action against the demands for manpower for the army. This strategy collapsed, and the conscription crisis of December 1915 was bypassed only when Runciman, McKenna (*q.v.*) and other leading anti-compulsionists accepted the demands of the army as a last resort. Were the land campaigns of the summer to fail, Runciman could accept no more British involvement in the war; he began to back Lansdowne's doubts about the ability of

Britain to beat Germany. In December 1916, Asquith's (*q.v.*) government collapsed; Runciman, by then a bitter enemy of Lloyd George (*q.v.*), went into opposition. In 1918 he went down to defeat in Dewsbury.

Having fought Edinburgh South in 1920, Berwick-upon-Tweed in 1922 and Brighton in 1923, he finally returned to Parliament in 1924 as MP for Swansea West. He opposed Lloyd George's accession to the Chairmanship of the parliamentary party and led seven MPs to form the 'Radical Group', which adopted a largely traditionalist platform in opposition to Lloyd George. In 1927 the Liberal Council was established, with Runciman as Chairman, and acted as a party within the party throughout the country.

In 1929 Runciman moved to the St Ives constituency. The Labour Prime Minister, Ramsay MacDonald, found him a ready ally in backing the new government against Lloyd George; his reward was the Deputy Chairmanship of the Royal Mail. He was returned unopposed in St Ives in 1931 and a week later was made President of the Board of Trade in the National Government. Until 1937, Runciman was one of the lynchpins of the government, acting as effective second-in-command of the Liberal Nationals (there was no actual 'leader' but Sir John Simon (*q.v.*) was regarded as the leading Liberal National).

Though a free trader, Runciman was pragmatic enough to realise that the huge Conservative majority would force through protection. He therefore worked to reduce the impact of tariffs, which brought him into conflict with the Conservative right wing. For Baldwin, he was a barrier to the extreme protectionists, yet he went too far for the Samuelite Liberals.

In 1937 he retired to the House of Lords, accepting the title Viscount Runciman of Doxford. In July 1938 he was recalled to lead the British mission to Czechoslovakia to mediate an internal settlement between Prague and the Sudeten Germans. This was undermined in September when Neville Chamberlain offered Hitler the transfer of the Sudetenland to Germany. Ironically, Runciman supported the general aim of Chamberlain of turning Germany into a good neighbour by meeting its legitimate grievances. Once the crisis was over, Runciman reluctantly agreed to return to the Cabinet as Lord President of the Council. On the outbreak of war he retired again, this time permanently. He died on 14 November 1949, in Doxford Hall.

Runciman played a leading role in the Liberal divisions of 1916 and after. Holding strongly to the belief that alliances, treaties and commitments should be avoided in peacetime, he opposed Lloyd George's war strategy and led the civil war against the Liberal leader in the 1920s, helping finally to hammer the nails into the coffin of the Liberals as a party of government. In the 1930s, his switch to the National Government helped keep out of power a left-wing Labour Party and the right wing of the Conservatives. He was one of the pillars of appeasement, attempting, with Chamberlain, to create a Europe of peaceful nations in which grievances were settled peacefully, even it had to be at the expense of small countries. It was a policy that ended in ruins.

Only one biography of Runciman has been written, a PhD thesis by Dr Jonathan Wallace. His father, Sir Walter Runciman, produced his own biography in 1924, *Before the Mast.*

Dr Jonathan Wallace

BOB RUSSELL MP   1946–

There are some species of creature that are found only on one island or one small area in the world. Without the habitat, the creature could not exist, and it is difficult to imagine the habitat without that creature to grace it. So it is with Colchester and Bob Russell. Like him or not, no-one can deny his passion for his beloved Colchester, or indeed, within Britain's oldest recorded town, his dedicated work in the ward of New Town, that he has represented continuously since 1971 (longer, as he would no doubt tell you with relish, than anyone in the twentieth century).

Robert Edward Russell was born in Colchester on 31 March 1946, to a family which has lived in the area for at least eight generations, and was educated at Myland Primary, St. Helena Secondary, and North East Essex Technical College (now the Colchester Institute). He became a journalist by profession, working on a number of local papers and in 1968 becoming the country's youngest editor on taking over the *Maldon and Burnham Standard.* He worked in London for four years as a sub-editor on the former *Evening News,* and later the *Evening Standard.* He then spent thirteen years as a press officer for Post Office Telecommunications, later British Telecom, at the regional offices in Colchester. One legacy of this background is his typing speed of seventy-five words per minute, probably the fastest of any MP!

Russell was first elected to Colchester Borough Council in May 1971, serving as a Labour councillor until 1982 when he left to join the SDP, maintaining that it was the Labour Party that had left him rather than the other way round. He quickly became a valued member of the new party and led the Alliance/Liberal Democrat Group in Colchester in 1986–91. He was mayor of Colchester 1986–87, and leader of the council 1987–91.

Russell says he is an unashamed Colchester Nationalist; he would offer himself as a serious contender for Parliament in no other seat (his 1974 debut as candidate for nearby Sudbury represents his only departure from this stance). He stood for Labour in the old Colchester seat in 1979 and after a very hard-fought campaign in 1997 became the first Liberal Democrat MP for the Colchester Town seat. As expected, he at once set about establishing himself as a hard-working constituency member. His decision to continue to serve as New Town councillor was briefly the subject of some local criticism from his opponents, countered by his claim that the public work he undertakes in both spheres is complementary, not mutually exclusive. In Parliament, he is a member of the Liberal Democrat home and legal affairs team.

He is well known in the Scout movement, a Queen's Scout and is a formidable supporter of Colchester United Football Club; his deafening concern for the eyesight of visiting referees is legendary.

He has been married to Audrey since 1967. She supports loyally, but does not hesitate to grumble at, his intense political life, and is a tower of strength. Their three children (twin boys, Andrew and Mark, born in 1968, and Nicola, born 1981) complete a close-knit local family.

John Stevens

EARL RUSSELL   1937–

In 1987, Conrad Russell became the fifth Earl Russell, acquired a seat in the House of Lords, and began his unlikely progress to becoming a radical hero to some in his own party. These inherent contradictions, it can be suspected, add spice and enjoyment to Russell's political activities. The mixture of freedom fighter, modern politician and traditionally schooled intellectual is unusual and potent. He uses the past as a window on the future, and no-one else could use historical allegories as modern political commentary and be so acutely understood.

Conrad Sebastian Robert Russell was born on 15 April 1937, son of the philosopher Bertrand Russell and great-grandson of the Liberal Prime Minister, Lord John Russell (*q.v.*). He was educated at Eton and Merton College, Oxford. In 1962, he married Elizabeth Sanders; they have two children. In 1960 he became Lecturer in History at Bedford College, London and Reader in History from 1974–79, from where he went to Yale University in the United States. He returned to University College, London, in 1984, and in 1990 became Professor of History at King's College, London, where he remains to this day, his career encompassing a number of other honorific lectureships and appointments not mentioned here.

His academic career has been primarily concerned with political and parliamentary history, given rise to many of the insights which pepper his political writings and speeches. His publications include *The Crisis of Parliaments: English History 1509–1660* (1971), *Parliaments and English Politics 1621–1629* (1979), *The Causes of the English Civil War* (1990) and *The Fall of the British Monarchies* (1991). It is notable that Russell's academic life has demonstrated some of the concerns which motivate him in politics. He has written on academic freedom and is a previous Chair (1989–92) of the Campaign for Academic Autonomy. Even now, he is both a Fellow of the Royal Academy and a Trustee of the John Stuart Mill Institute, and has published material on that influential thinker (*q.v.*).

Russell has not merely been an academic; he has been a tutor and teacher. He was, famously, the academic who spoke out publicly about a much-discussed rape case. He debated on TV, in contravention of the advice usually given to politicians, such delicate issues as rape, student life and relationships, managing to talk straight common sense and to maintain the respect of students, colleagues and the public alike. His empathy with a different generation living in different times has led to his practical encouragement of younger people within the Liberal Democrats. He has been a Vice President of the Liberal Democrat Youth & Students (1993–94) and he speaks incisively on the difficulties of young people's lives.

As an active member of the House of Lords, Russell has taken up a number of causes and interests, including, most notably, constitutional affairs, education, social security, refugees and asylum. It is as the party's spokesman on social security in the House of Lords (since 1989) that he has made his most consistent impression. He criticised the policies of the last administration with enthusiasm, but it is suspected that he relishes even more being able to attack a Labour government from the left on such issues as child benefit and the removal of lone-parent benefit. He has sought, in characteristic fashion, to master the topic from all angles, and brings a historian's detailed and factual analysis to every new government (and opposition) policy initiative, whilst displaying a sympathy for lifestyles very far distant from his own. His work in the Lords has not gone unnoticed; he was the Highland Park/ *Spectator* 'Peer of the Year' in 1996, and some commentators have sought to point him out as a one-man demonstration of the value of hereditary peers.

Within the party he has for the last few years been an active member of the Federal Policy Committee, applying himself to all facets of policy-making and debate, and has contributed significantly to party policy-making on tax and benefit issues. He is the Honorary President of the Liberal Democrat History Group. His presence on the platform of conference meetings guarantees a packed house. Attendees know that they can expect a well-honed and highly erudite analysis of developments, spiced with not a few controversial statements about the present.

Russell has been determined and combative in his defence of Liberal Democrat values. He remains cautious about the party's positioning vis-à-vis the Labour government and Tony Blair, whom he has publicly described as a 'Tory'. Currently, he balances a strong commitment to the unity of the Liberal Democrats with the concern that the party should not lose sight of historic values. He has not been afraid to share his views, either privately with Paddy Ashdown (*q.v.*) and others, or publicly through carefully chosen words uttered in print and in the flesh. He seeks not to be a prophet but an influence, and many within the party will listen carefully to him as they consider the challenges ahead.

Helen Bailey

LORD JOHN RUSSELL   1792–1878

Lord John Russell was aptly described (by Sir William Harcourt, *q.v.*) as 'the last Doge of Whiggism', but he could equally be considered the first Liberal Prime Minister, embodying in his own attitudes the mid-Victorian transition from traditional Whiggery to Gladstonian Liberalism. Certainly he was thoroughly imbued with the optimism that was such a hallmark of the Victorian Liberal outlook; as Sydney Smith remarked, he would have been willing to have built St Peter's, commanded the Channel Fleet, or to have operated on a patient for the stone (and would not have been deterred by the collapse of the sacred edifice, the sinking of the fleet, or the patient's death).

'Little Johnny Russell' was only five feet, four and three-quarter inches tall, and weighed eight stones. Explaining this diminutive stature, Smith commented that before the start of the Reform Act crisis, Russell was '…. over six feet high. But, engaged in looking after your interests, fighting the peers, the landlords and the rest of your natural enemies, he has been so constantly kept in hot water that he is boiled down to the proportions in which you now behold him'. One of the main features of Russell's long political career is the number of controversial issues with which he was concerned.

John Russell was born two months prematurely in London on 18 August 1792, the third son of John, sixth Duke of Bedford. For most of his life Russell held the courtesy title of Lord John; he was created first Earl Russell in 1861 on the death of his brother Francis. His family had been involved in the political life of the country for generations and was well known for its radicalism. Because of ill-health as a child, Russell was primarily educated at home although he did attend Westminster School for a short time (1804–05). He went on to study at Edinburgh University (1809–12) but left without taking his degree.

In 1835 he married Lady Adelaide Ribblesdale, a widow, the daughter of Thomas Lister and Mary Grove. Although she was fifteen years his junior, she died in 1838. In 1841 Russell married the twenty-five year old Lady Frances Anna Maria Elliot-Murray-Kynynmound, daughter of the second Earl of Minto. From his two marriages Russell had three daughters and three sons.

In 1813 Russell stood for election for the first time and continued as an MP until his elevation to the peerage. He represented a variety of constituencies: Tavistock (1813–20); Huntingdonshire (1820–26); Bandon (1826–30); Bedford (1830–31); Devonshire (1831–32); South Devon (1832–35); Stroud (1837–41); and City of London (1841–61). In all he participated in twenty-two parliamentary elections. Russell served as Paymaster-General of the Forces (1830–34); Home Secretary (1835–39); Leader of the House of Commons (1835–41, 1846 – February 1852, December 1852 – January 1855); Colonial Secretary (1839–41 and a few months in 1855); First Lord of the Treasury (1846–52); Foreign Secretary (1852–53, 1859–65); Lord President of the Council (1854–55); and Leader of the House of Lords (1865–66).

In 1817 Russell attacked the suspension of habeas corpus and in December 1819 he espoused formally the traditional Whig cause of parliamentary reform when he advocated – unsuccessfully – a Reform Bill to the House of Commons. When the Whigs came to power in 1830 on a platform of 'peace, retrenchment and reform', Russell helped to draft the Reform Bill. On 31 March 1831 he presented it to the

House of Commons; it took eighteen months for the bill, subsequently known as the Great Reform Act, to become law.

As the Paymaster-General in Grey's (*q.v.*) ministry, Russell championed the cause of religious freedom for Dissenters and Catholics alike. He attempted to divert some of the wealth of the Church of Ireland to the Irish Catholics, and, in so doing, frightened such leading Whigs as Lord Stanley into leaving the party. Russell and Daniel O'Connell were the main agents in the Lichfield House Compact that removed Peel from office in 1835 and returned the Whigs to power under Melbourne (*q.v.*).

As Home Secretary in Melbourne's second ministry, Russell was responsible for passing legislation such as the Municipal Corporations Act (1835), the Tithe Commutation Act, the Civil Marriages Act (1836), the Irish Poor Law Amendment Act (1838), and the Rural Constabularies Act (1839); he was reduced stamp duty from fourpence to a penny in 1836 and instituted the penny post in 1840. He began the system of state inspection and support of public education. In 1833 the Whigs allocated £20,000 to be shared between the National Society and the British and Foreign Schools Society for the provision of education in Great Britain. Russell increased the grant to £30,000 in 1839 and made further provision for an annual increase in the subsidy.

In 1845 Russell published the *Edinburgh Letter* supporting free trade. With Whig support, Peel repealed the Corn Laws in 1846, split the Conservative Party and resigned; Russell took office as Prime Minister. His administration passed legislation limiting working hours in factories and was responsible for the passing of the Public Health Act of 1848. It also ended restrictions on colonial trade by repealing the Navigation Acts in 1849. During the Irish famine of 1845–49 the government granted relief for soup kitchens and financed public works to create employment. However, since what was really needed was vast amounts of food, free of all conditions, its efforts to prevent widespread starvation were largely ineffective.

Russell's alternate support for and dissent from Aberdeen's (*q.v.*) policies during the Crimean War caused Aberdeen to lose the leadership of the Liberal Party. In 1855 Russell resigned from the Cabinet, feeling unable to defend the government against a motion criticising its conduct of the war. He retired temporarily from public life and lived on the continent from 1856–57, devoting much of his time to literature. Few English politicians wrote so extensively as Russell, who published a number of books, including *The Life of William, Lord Russell* (1819), *Essays and Sketches of Life* (1820), *An Essay on the History of the English Government and Constitution* (1822), *The Nun of Arrouca* (1822), *The Life and Times of Charles James Fox* (1859–66) and *Recollections and Suggestions 1813–1873* (1875).

After his return home from Europe following the fall of Derby's ministry, Russell served as Foreign Secretary under Palmerston (*q.v.*) between 1859–65. He supported Italian unification and antagonised the United States during the American Civil War by actions that seemed to favour the Confederacy. He retired from political office after briefly heading a second ministry in 1865–66, but continued to sit in the House of Lords where he spoke on a variety of issues. He died at Pembroke Lodge, Richmond Park, Surrey on 28 May 1878.

Russell's papers are in the Public Record Office. A two-volume biography by Spencer Walpole, *The Life of Lord John Russell,* first published in 1889, was reprinted in 1969. John Prest's *Lord John Russell* was published in 1972.

Marjie Bloy

HERBERT SAMUEL (Viscount Samuel) 1870–1963

Herbert Samuel was a leading figure in the Liberal Party for over fifty years from its zenith before the First World War to the nadir of its fortunes in the mid-1950s. With Sinclair (*q.v.*), he was the last independent Liberal to serve in the Cabinet. A respected statesman, formidable mediator and administrator, and notable political thinker, his period as Liberal leader from November 1931 to November 1935 was one of calamitous decline for the party.

Herbert Samuel Samuel was born on 6 November 1870 in Liverpool, youngest son of Edwin and Clara (née Yates) Samuel, whose families – Ashkenazi Jews from what is today western Poland – emigrated to England in the late eighteenth century. The family made its fortune in the international banking boom of the 1850s and 1860s in which his uncle Samuel Montagu, Herbert's guardian from 1877, was one of the most successful figures. Samuel was thus born into the secure Victorian haute bourgeoisie and was able to devote himself to politics, philosophy and travel, untroubled by the need to establish a career and earn a living. Samuel rejected his family's orthodox Judaism at the age of about twenty. He maintained his links with the Jewish community and in later life became one of its respected figures, but his religious ideas were tempered by a rationalist, scientific humanism.

He was educated at the progressive University College School and at Balliol College, Oxford, where he obtained a first. His commitment to Liberal politics and social reform began early, inspired by campaigns in Whitechapel for his uncle Montagu, the local Radical MP and his brother Stuart, a member of London County Council and later an MP. While at Balliol he was selected as candidate for South Oxfordshire, which he contested and narrowly lost at both the 1895 and 1900 general elections. During this period he was also closely involved in building up the Liberal Party organisation in the Home Counties and nationally. In 1897 he married his first cousin, Beatrice Franklin, who became active in Liberal politics and served on the executive of the Women's Liberal Federation. They had three sons and one daughter.

Samuel was firmly on the left of the party, immersing himself in the problems of urban and rural poverty, actively supporting the 1889 dock strike and associating closely with the Fabians, particularly the Webbs and Graham Wallas (*q.v.*). He was prominent, with Ramsay MacDonald, in the Rainbow Circle of Liberals and socialists. Samuel rejected laissez-faire liberalism and took advanced positions on the social issues of the day. However, his thinking remained firmly within the framework of Liberalism and his attachment to the Liberal Party never wavered. The clarity and comprehensiveness of Samuel's ideas can be seen in his *Liberalism: An Attempt to State the Principles and Proposals of Contemporary Liberalism in England* (1902), one of the seminal works of the New Liberalism of the early 1900s.

Samuel became MP for the Cleveland division of Yorkshire at a byelection in November 1902, and became Parliamentary Under-Secretary of State at the Home Office when the Liberals came to power in December 1905. He was in the thick of the social reform programme of the Liberal government, piloting through legislation on working hours, the probation service and child welfare. He entered the Cabinet as Chancellor of the Duchy of Lancaster (from June 1909), serving later as Postmaster-General (from February 1910), and President of the Local Government Board (from February 1914 to May 1915).

As Postmaster-General, the responsible minister, he was mired in the Marconi scandal of 1912–13, though unlike Lloyd George (*q.v.*) and Rufus Isaacs (*q.v.*), his own conduct in the affair had been above reproach. Other unfounded accusations, with an anti-semitic edge, were also made at this time against Samuel and his cousin, Edwin Montagu (*q.v.*), a junior minister at the India Office. At the Local Government Board, his ambitious plans for slum clearance and urban planning, announced in a speech delivered in Sheffield in May 1914, were frustrated by the outbreak of war. He did, however, launch a major expansion of maternity and child welfare centres. His social radicalism did not extend to women's suffrage, on which he took a cautious line, although it was on Samuel's motion that women were given the right to stand for election to Parliament in 1918.

On the peace wing of the party, he nevertheless supported the war when Germany infringed Belgian neutrality. He remained Postmaster-General, outside the Cabinet, when the coalition government was formed in May 1915. He re-entered the Cabinet in November of that year, with the additional post of Chancellor of the Duchy of Lancaster. In January 1916, he replaced Simon (*q.v.*) as Home Secretary when the latter resigned in protest at the introduction of compulsory military service, and was responsible for handling the aftermath of the Easter Uprising in Ireland.

He stood by Asquith (*q.v.*) in the December 1916 crisis despite Lloyd George's efforts to persuade him to stay on at the Home Office. He had little in common temperamentally with Lloyd George and did not expect his government to last. In the Asquithian fiasco at the 1918 election, Samuel lost Cleveland and withdrew from party politics for nearly a decade.

After a few months as Special Commissioner for Belgium, he served from July 1920 to July 1925 as High Commissioner for the Palestine Mandate. Pro-Zionist from before 1914, he supported the establishment of a Jewish national home in a multinational Palestine, but was unable to win Arab agreement for such a constitution. Otherwise his period of office was successful and constructive.

Retiring to Italy to study philosophy, he was persuaded by Baldwin to return to serve as Chairman of the 1925–26 commission of inquiry into the coal industry, part of the deal to head off a miners' strike. During the 1926 General Strike, his unofficial mediation was pivotal in convincing the TUC to abandon the strike. In February 1927, Samuel re-entered party politics as head of the Liberal Party Organisation. As a skilled administrator and mediator, acceptable to all the factions, he played a major part in the Liberal revival culminating in the 1929 general election, in which he gained the traditionally Tory seat of Darwen, Lancashire, by a narrow majority.

Samuel was Lloyd George's deputy in the 1929–31 Parliament and as acting leader during the August 1931 crisis took the Liberal Party into the National Government; he returned to the Home Office. In October he gave way to Conservative pressure for an election. Samuel insisted that the Liberals fight on their own free trade platform, but the election left the government and Commons dominated by an overwhelming Tory protectionist majority. The Liberals were hopelessly split between the Samuelites, Simon's Liberal Nationals, and Lloyd George, who vehemently opposed the election and continued Liberal support for the government, and was loudly critical of Samuel. Only thirty-three Samuelites were elected to fight a rearguard defence of free trade.

In February 1932 the Liberal minority in the Cabinet 'agreed to differ' over the introduction of import duties rather than resign. But when, in September 1932, the Cabinet decided to go ahead with the protectionist Ottawa Agreements, Samuel and his fellow Liberal ministers, under pressure from the party rank and file, resigned from the government while continuing to support it from the backbenches. In November 1933, again under activist pressure, Samuel finally abandoned this strange compromise and took the party into opposition. This lack of political direction was matched by a calamitous decline in Liberal Party organisation, morale and electoral fortunes. Samuel's balanced intellectual approach to politics, sense of duty and rather dry, uncharismatic personality did not inspire the voters. Lacking Lloyd George's funds, the party fielded only 161 candidates in the 1935 general election and won only twenty-one. Samuel lost his own seat at Darwen and resigned the leadership. The Liberals had slid to the status of a minor party in apparently terminal decline.

After his peerage in 1937 (first Viscount Samuel, of Mount Carmel and Toxteth), he acted as Deputy Liberal Leader in the House of Lords, taking increasing responsibility from the (more) elderly Lord Crewe (*q.v.*). Samuel was one of the few leading Liberals to support Chamberlain's appeasement policy and the Munich agreement, and even after the war he continued to believe that this was the correct course. In 1939 Chamberlain offered him a place in the Cabinet, but, having consulted party colleagues, Samuel declined. He was Leader in the Lords from 1944 to June 1955. He remained one of the Liberals' main campaigners, especially in the 1945 and 1950 general elections. When the party was offered the opportunity of Britain's first televised party political broadcast, on 15 October 1951, Samuel was chosen to deliver a scripted address. It was a measure of the party's weakness that an eighty-one year-old peer was deemed the Liberals' greatest televisual asset, primarily because of his popularity as a panellist on the radio show, *The Brains' Trust*. The broadcast was not a conspicuous success, being brought to an accidentally premature conclusion as Samuel continued to read from his notes.

After 1935 Samuel pursued his long-held ambition to write about philosophy and science. He was President of the Royal Institute of Philosophy from 1931–59. Over the next two decades he published a string of books: *Practical Ethics* (1935), *Belief and Action* (1937), his major work of popular philosophy, *An Unknown Land* (1942), *A Book of Quotations* (1947), *Creative Man – A Collection of Essays and Addresses* (1949) and *A Threefold Cord: Philosophy, Science, Religion* (1961). Most remarkably, in his eighties, he produced two critiques of Einstein's ideas in *Essay in Physics* (1951) and *In Search of Reality* (1957). He died on 5 February 1963.

In addition to Samuel's *Memoirs* (Cresset Press, 1945), there are two biographies: *Herbert Samuel – A Political Life* (Bernard Wasserstein, Oxford University Press, 1992) and *Viscount Samuel – A Biography* (John Bowle, Victor Gollancz, 1957). His political papers are in the House of Lords Record Office.

Jaime Reynolds

ADRIAN SANDERS MP 1959–

Adrian Mark Sanders was born in Paignton on 25 April 1959. His parents encouraged him to read widely and take an interest in current affairs. His staple diet was a combination of the *Western Morning News* and the *Daily Mail*: 'a conservative, non-political background'.

He attended Torquay Boys' Grammar School, where he excelled at English and history, but was less enthusiastic about the gap between those who ran the school and the pupils. He demanded and implemented a school council where pupils were elected to make decisions on behalf of their peers. Another great influence was the teaching of the British constitution at O level. The Liberal alternative to Labour and Conservative emerged for Sanders through proportional representation, and throughout his school days his driving force was reform of the constitution rather than any party political motivation.

After leaving school he worked in the insurance industry, where his ability to offer advice and to meet all types of people stood him in good stead for his political career. By 1979, it was clear to him that Labour were jettisoning all their principles in the scramble for economic credibility and that the Tories offered no change. He joined the Liberal Party that year.

In the south west, John Pardoe (*q.v.*) had a huge influence on the way governance was approached, with an awareness of local concerns in local government. This was a defining principle for Sanders; the gap between Torquay's Conservative councillors and the townspeople, and the gap between the Labour government and the nation was the gap that he knew that Liberal community politics could plug. There then followed the 'usual slog': *Focus* deliveries, ward organising, and, at his fourth attempt, in 1984, election to Torbay Borough Council. The following year he was elected as the Vice-President of the Young Liberals

His commitment to and knowledge of local government made him an ideal information and campaigns officer for the Association of Liberal Councillors, followed by a year in the Liberal Democrat Whips Office (1989–90) and then back to the renamed Association of Liberal Democrat Councillors until 1992.

In the general election of 1992 Sanders reduced Rupert Allason's majority in Torbay to an uncomfortable 5,787. After organising Paddy Ashdown's (*q.v.*) 'Beyond Westminster' tour (the first of its kind by a party leader) with Liberal Democracy gaining momentum in the south west, Adrian threw his hat in to the European ring. As Graham Watson (*q.v.*) and Robin Teverson (*q.v.*) won decisive victories in the Euro election of 1994, Sanders, as the candidate for the Devon & East Plymouth constituency, was robbed of victory by a mere 700 votes, as a 'Literal Democrat' rogue candidate took over 10,000 votes.

He returned to full-time work as the policy officer for the National Council for Voluntary Organisations and then the Southern Association of Voluntary Action Groups for Europe, advising voluntary organisations and charities on how to gain access to funds from Europe.

At the 1997 general election, Sanders beat Rupert Allason by twelve votes. After Mark Oaten's (*q.v.*) resounding byelection result in Winchester, he now has the smallest majority in the country (and the second smallest Liberal majority in the constituency this century).

The achievement is not just a political one, it is a human one. There are many people in the the party who have fought and lost, but very few who have been so publicly cheated as Adrian Sanders. As an insulin-dependent diabetic, the physical rigours of campaigning have to be kept in check. He is always quick to point out that behind every good politician there is an even better wife, and that his success is a joint achievement. He is married to Alison, who he met while working in Paddy Ashdown's office, and lives in Torquay.

Rachel Oliver

NANCY SEEAR (Lady Seear)   1913–97

When Lady Violet Bonham Carter (*q.v.*) died, in 1969, the Liberal Party lost its most powerful and indomitable female campaigner. The vacuum she left was filled by Beatrice Nancy Seear, always known by her middle name, a formidable politician possessed of a towering intellect. Seear was an active Liberal and latterly Liberal Democrat for over fifty years, and in the 1990s she remained an enduring link with the bleakest period in the party's history.

Seear was born on 7 August 1913 in Croydon, Surrey. She took a history degree at Newnham College, Cambridge and during the 1930s spent time in Germany. There she observed at close hand the rise of Nazism and her experiences shaped her political convictions. She was a life-long Liberal. For ten years, until 1946, Seear worked as personnel manager at C. & J. Clark, the Somerset shoemakers long connected with the Liberal Party. During that time she was seconded to the Ministry of Aircraft Production, headed at that time by Lord Beaverbrook, where she was an assistant to a member of the Production Efficiency Board. She joined the London School of Economics as Reader in Personnel Management in 1946 and remained there until retirement thirty-two years later.

During the 1945 general election Seear helped Lady Violet Bonham Carter's unsuccessful campaign in Wells. Undaunted by that experience, Seear contested the next seven general elections, fighting Hornchurch in 1950 and 1951, Truro in 1955 and 1959, Epping in 1964, Rochdale in 1966 and finally Wakefield in 1970. She finished third on each occasion but relished every contest. Seear was not a community politician and did not attempt to cultivate deep roots in any one particular constituency. Instead, she relied upon her powers of exposition and debate to win round audiences at public meetings. These talents were to be exploited to the full when she was elevated to the peerage as Baroness Seear of Paddington in 1971.

Jeremy Thorpe (*q.v.*). used his power to nominate life peers to bring into the House of Lords intellectually able Liberals who had little chance of winning election to the Commons, but who were willing to devote their time to the activities of the Upper House. Seear fitted the bill perfectly. She was extremely well respected in the House for her incisive and unscripted comments as Liberal spokesman on economic and employment affairs. In 1981 she chaired a House of Lords Select Committee on the issue of unemployment. She campaigned enthusiastically for equal pay, although she was critical of the feminist movement.

Seear replaced Lord Byers (*q.v.*) as the Liberal leader in the House of Lords on his death in 1984. One year later television was introduced into the House for the first time and in the last decade of her life Seear became a media personality. She was already very well known within the Liberal Party, having been the party's President in 1965. The public met her for the first time through programmes such as *Question Time*. The grandmotherly Baroness, hunched over the famous round table, not only

Nancy Seear with Paddy Ashdown

spoke persuasively across a range of subjects but relished the opportunity to put cabinet ministers forty years her junior firmly in their place. Her sharp-witted good humour was often in evidence on the campaign trail in both general election and byelection campaigns. Sir Robert Rhodes James recalled her remarking, towards the end of the 1987 general election campaign, that :'I never want to meet another bloody pensioner ever again!'

Seear strongly backed the merger of the Liberal Party and the SDP which formed the Liberal Democrats in 1988, and was happy to make way for Lord Jenkins (*q.v.*) as Liberal Democrat leader in the Lords without a contest. She worked as his deputy until her death. Aside from the Liberal Party, Seear participated in a bewildering array of voluntary organisations. At various times she was President of the Institute of Personnel Management, the Fawcett Society, the British Standards Institute and the Liberal Summer School and she was chairman of the National Councils of Carers and Single Women. She never married and divided her time between her flat in Kennington and her cottage near Bergerac, France. She died on 23 April 1997, in London.

Mark Egan

ERNEST SIMON (Lord Simon)   1879–1960

Ernest Simon's career – in business, politics and public service – spanned over sixty years, during which he made valuable contributions to a wide range of national and international social questions. As a Liberal, before the Second World War, he was primarily concerned with the role of local government in the improvement of housing, environmental and other social conditions. After joining the Labour Party, in 1946, his sphere of influence widened, encompassing broadcasting, nuclear disarmament, global overpopulation and, in his last years, higher education; his motion in the House of Lords on 11 May 1960 calling for an inquiry into the provision of further education in the UK led to the establishment of the Robbins Committee later that year (though after his death).

Ernest Darwin Simon was born in Manchester on 9 October 1879, the son of Henry Gustav Simon and his second wife, Emily Stoehr, both German immigrants. His father founded two engineering companies which were later combined to form the Simon Engineering Group. Simon took control of the Group when only twenty years old, on the death of his father in 1899. At that time, he was studying for his engineering first at Pembroke College, Cambridge; he had previously been educated at Rugby School. Simon's business interests, increasingly successful through both world wars, provided him with the financial resources necessary for his long career of public service.

Inspired by the work of Sidney and Beatrice Webb, with whom he was associated in founding the *New Statesman*, Simon was elected to Manchester City Council, as a Liberal member for Withington Ward, in 1911. He chaired the council's Housing Committee from 1919–23 and was Lord Mayor in 1921. Simon was an astute critic of many aspects of local administration, writing in *A City Council from Within* (1926) of the need for more 'vision and imagination' in local government. He also wrote extensively on inner-city housing policies and smoke abatement.

Simon's connections with C. P. Snow and the *Manchester Guardian* brought him into contact with many leading Liberal intellectuals, and he was one of the founders, and chief financiers, of the Liberal Summer School in its early years. He fought the Withington parliamentary seat on four occasions, serving as the district's MP from 1923–24 and 1929–31. He was, for two weeks in 1931, Parliamentary Secretary to the Ministry of Health, but his defeat in the subsequent general election ended his Commons career; he was knighted in 1932. He was not keen to return to Parliament, disliking its protocol, procedure and strict party discipline; he had also, in 1925, lost his seat on Manchester City Council. Simon launched a new project in 1934, the Association for Education in Citizenship, which aimed 'to advance the study of and training in citizenship, by which is meant training in moral qualities necessary for the citizens of democracy; the encouragement of clear thinking in everyday affairs; and the acquisition of that knowledge of the modern world usually given by means of courses in history, geography, economics, citizenship and public affairs'. The Association prospered during the 1930s, but declined and ultimately collapsed during the Second World War.

Simon was a member of the Central Council for Works and Buildings during the war; his experience of the practicalities of central planning led him to write *Rebuilding Britain: a Twenty-Year Plan* (1945) and to his subsequent defection to the Labour Party. He returned to Parliament in 1947 as Baron Simon of Wythenshawe, in Manchester, but he was never a regular attendee of the House of Lords. At the same time he was appointed Chairman of the Governors of the BBC. He served for five years, fighting an unsuccessful rearguard action against the introduction of commercial television and braving press hostility in 1950 for banning a repeat performance of Val Gielgud's *Party Manners* because its plot was based upon politicians' cynical behaviour. He later published *The BBC Within*.

Simon also funded research and publications on demographic and nuclear issues following the war. He cooperated with the Campaign for Nuclear Disarmament to oppose successive governments' nuclear weapons policy in Parliament; funded a study of nuclear policy issues by Wayland Young; and endowed the Simon Population Trust for research on population issues after his death. Associated with Manchester University from 1916, Simon chaired its council from 1941–57 and endowed the Simon Fund for the provision of research fellowships. He was awarded an honorary doctorate by the university in 1944. His interest in education issues, and a belief, long before it was fashionable, in the need for a rapid expansion of the number of university and college places available to prospective students, inspired his last Parliamentary venture.

Simon died on 3 October 1960 in Manchester, the city he had been given the freedom of ten years before. He was succeeded in the peerage by his son Roger, who has never taken his seat in the Lords. Neither of his two sons by his wife Shena (née Potter), whom he married in 1912, continued in the family business. He was also predeceased by a daughter. Mary Stocks published a biography, *Ernest Simon of Manchester*, in 1963.

Mark Egan

JOHN SIMON (Viscount Simon)   1873–1954

Though he never rose to the premiership, John Allsebrook Simon's collection of the highest offices of state – the Home Office (twice), the Treasury, the Foreign Office and the Woolsack – is unique in twentieth-century history. He played a major role in British politics over more than three decades, while also enjoying a distinguished legal career. The leading barrister of his age, it was said that he had an annual income of up to £50,000 in the year immediately before the First World War. He shared with Winston Churchill (*q.v.*) the distinction of being the only man who sat in the British Cabinet at the outbreak of both world wars.

Simon's origins were humble and he owed his political rise above all to his academic distinction. He was born on 28 February 1873 in a terraced house in Moss Side, Manchester, the only son of the Rev. Edwin and Mrs Fanny Simon; his father was a Congregational minister in the Hulme district of the city. Simon was educated at King Edward's School, Bath, before winning a scholarship to Fettes College, Edinburgh. From there he gained an open scholarship to Wadham College, Oxford in 1892, becoming President of the Oxford Union in 1896. After securing a first in Greats, he won a scholarship to All Souls. Coming down from Oxford at the end of 1898, he was called to the bar at the Inner Temple.

In 1899 Simon married Ethel Mary Venables, a student whom he had met at Oxford. Two daughters were born in 1900 and 1901 but, a few days after the birth of a son in September 1902, Mrs Simon died. This tragedy had a profound and perhaps permanent effect upon his personality. He became increasingly reserved as his natural shyness intensified, and he sought solace in ever greater attention to his work. In December 1917 he married Kathleen Manning, the widow of a Dublin doctor. This marriage had its problems. Socially rather gauche, Lady Simon suffered from poor health and excessive drinking.

Simon was elected to Parliament for Walthamstow in the Liberal landslide of 1906 and soon rose from the ruck of newly elected hopefuls as a man marked out for early promotion. In 1910, at the remarkably young age of thirty-seven, he became Solicitor-General, with a knighthood, and was promoted to Attorney-General with, unusually, a seat in the Cabinet, in 1913. But Simon always regarded the law as a vehicle to political promotion and, at the formation of the first wartime coalition in May 1915, he turned down Asquith's (*q.v.*) offer of the Lord Chancellorship, becoming instead Home Secretary. He resigned in January 1916 over the issue of conscription and was not to hold government office again for a further decade and a half. Up to this point he had been regarded by many as Asquith's likely successor as Liberal leader.

Simon lost his seat at the 'coupon' general election of 1918, returning to Parliament as member for Spen Valley in the election of 1922. But the internal dissensions and decline of the Liberal Party seemed to preclude further ministerial appointments. His relations with Lloyd George (*q.v.*) were never easy and his most useful work during the decade was as chairman of the Statutory Commission on India between 1927 and 1930. Simon found his position within the Liberal Party increasingly uncomfortable. On intellectual grounds he was prepared to renounce the Liberal creed of free trade and to consider the possibility of tariffs to ease the country's economic difficulties.

In 1931 he and a number of fellow Liberal MPs broke away from the mainstream party to form the Liberal National group (known as National Liberals after 1947). Simon was rewarded with appointment as Foreign Secretary in November 1931 in Ramsay MacDonald's National Government. By common consent he was not successful in this position. His handling of the Manchurian crisis of 1931–33 was particularly criticised, but it was not an easy time to be in charge of the Foreign Office, as the post-war settlement faced its first serious challenges from the aggressor powers, including Hitler's Germany. Simon seemed unable to make up his mind in relation to key issues. In part this was a tribute to the complexity of his brain, but it was not a strong point in a practising politician.

He was more suited to the Home Office, to which he returned in 1935, and where he played an important backstage part in the management of the abdication crisis. He became Chancellor of the Exchequer in May 1937, where he continued the policy of his predecessor, Neville Chamberlain, in maintaining the strength of the economy as the nation's fourth arm of defence, even if this meant limiting conventional rearmament. A member of Chamberlain's inner circle, and widely regarded as one of the 'guilty men' of the appeasement era, Simon was elevated to the upper house as Viscount Simon of Stackpole Elidor at the formation of Churchill's (*q.v.*)

government in May 1940. There he served with distinction as Lord Chancellor until the end of the war in 1945.

This marked the end of his ministerial career, though he remained hopeful of returning to office as late as 1951. In his final years he became increasingly remote from his fellow Liberal Nationals, whose leadership he had given up in 1940, and he put out feelers to join the Conservative Party. These were firmly rebuffed by Churchill. His uninformative memoirs, *Retrospect*, appeared in 1952. He died in London on 11 January 1954. A modern biography, *Simon*, was published by David Dutton in 1992.

Simon was one of the most intellectually distinguished politicians of the twentieth century. But he lacked warmth and the common touch. The Liberal Party split of 1931, in which he played a leading part, put paid to any last hopes that the party would recover from the internal divisions which had plagued it since the First World War.

David Dutton

SIR ARCHIBALD SINCLAIR (Viscount Thurso)   1890–1970

Archibald Sinclair was the Liberal leader from 1935 to 1945. He was a leading figure in British politics in that period, first as an outspoken critic of appeasement, and then as a minister during the war. For Liberals, his importance lay in his belief in the possibility of a Liberal revival, which was crucial in helping the party to survive the challenges of the 1930s and 1940s.

Archibald Henry Macdonald Sinclair, fourth baronet and first Viscount Thurso of Ulbster, was born in London on 22 October 1890. Educated at Eton, he attended Sandhurst, and became a regular soldier in 1910 with the 2nd Life Guards. Serving with distinction on the Western Front throughout the Great War, he was Winston Churchill's (*q.v.*) second-in-command with the 6th Royal Scots Fusiliers from January to May 1916, and ended the war as a major in the Guards Machine-Gun Regiment. In 1919–21, he was Churchill's personal military secretary at the War Office, and was then his private secretary at the Colonial Office until 1922. At the 1922 general election, Sinclair successfully stood as a pro-Lloyd George 'National Liberal' in Caithness & Sutherland. In each election until 1945 (when he lost the seat), and in 1950, he stood as a Liberal.

Sinclair soon became a prominent figure on the opposition benches, assisting Lloyd George (*q.v.*) with revisions of Liberal policy from the mid-1920s. He was a founder member of the Land Committee, and chaired its Scottish equivalent, which wrote the Liberal 'Tartan Book' proposing Scottish devolution. In November 1930, he became Liberal Chief Whip in the House of Commons, making the maintenance of party discipline and unity his highest priority. In 1931 he took part (with Lloyd George, Samuel (*q.v.*), and Lothian (*q.v.*)) in talks with the Labour leadership over various areas of shared interest. This meant that he was an obvious choice as one of the Liberal ministers in the National Government from August 1931, when he ceased to be Chief Whip.

Sinclair served as Secretary of State for Scotland from August 1931 to September 1932, with Cabinet rank from November 1931. The main battle for the Liberals in the National Government was for free trade, and after agreeing to differ with their Labour and Conservative colleagues over minor tariffs in January 1932, the Liberals eventually resigned from the government in September 1932, when extensive tariffs were introduced under the Ottawa Agreements. Samuel had replaced Lloyd George as Liberal Leader after the 1931 general election and, when Samuel lost his seat in the November 1935 election, Sinclair replaced him.

From then until 1939, Sinclair's leadership was marked by two themes. Firstly, he was a resolute proponent of Liberal independence, vigorously pushing the Liberal viewpoint in Parliament and throughout the country, persistently believing that the Liberal Party was about to make an electoral breakthrough. Secondly, Sinclair opposed appeasement, wanting instead to pursue a policy of 'collective security'. This involved developing the League of Nations' ability to remedy just grievances, while at the same time rearming so that League members could resist aggression. He accepted that Germany and the other expansionist powers had legitimate complaints, but he wanted them dealt with from a position of strength and through international negotiations, rather than by the government's piecemeal concessions to the dictators. Sinclair cooperated with members of all parties in support of the League, including Churchill and Attlee, through the 'Arms and the Covenant' movement. However, their message was often at odds with what most British people wanted to hear, and Sinclair and the other anti-appeasers were constantly denounced as 'warmongers'.

When war broke out in September 1939, Sinclair was invited to join the government by Neville Chamberlain, but he demurred. However, when a broad coalition government was constructed under Churchill in May 1940, Sinclair accepted the post of Secretary of State for Air, holding the post until the coalition broke up in May 1945. Sinclair did not gain a War Cabinet seat, but Churchill agreed to consult him on general issues and principles. Sinclair's influence within the government was questionable and even at the Air Ministry he was weakened by Churchill taking a prominent role in decision-making himself, but Sinclair was important in supporting Arthur 'Bomber' Harris's strategic bombing of Germany. Sinclair believed that it was an effective way of destroying Germany's war effort and morale and maintained that targets were industrial rather than residential.

Party campaigns were effectively suspended on the outbreak of war, and Sinclair strongly believed that military victory was the main priority. This meant, for example, that he did not campaign vigorously for the Beveridge Report, which had provoked much enthusiasm within the Liberal Party and the country, but was put aside until after the war by the coalition government. After pressure from party members he did commit the Party to contest the post-war general election as an independent entity, but he personally favoured the continuation of coalition long after the war. With the war in Europe won, the general election took place in July 1945, and the Liberals did poorly, winning only twelve seats. Sinclair himself lost his seat, and was replaced as leader by Clement Davies (*q.v.*). The change was intended to be temporary following a rash promise by Sinclair's Conservative opponent to resign his seat in Sinclair's favour if he won. Needless to say, the promise went unfulfilled.

Sinclair again stood unsuccessfully for Parliament in 1950 and after the 1951 election there were rumours that Churchill wished to bring him into his Cabinet. When Sinclair became Viscount Thurso in 1952, it was intended that he would lead the Liberals in the House of Lords, but a stroke prevented him from taking an active part there until 1954. Outside Liberal politics, Sinclair was Lord Lieutenant of Caithness (1919–64); Lord Rector of Glasgow University (1938–45); President of the Air League of the British Empire (1956–58); and a member of the Political Honours Scrutiny Committee (1954–61).

A second stroke, in 1959, meant that he was severely debilitated in his last years, and he died on 15 June 1970 at his home in Twickenham. Sinclair had become Fourth Baronet of Ulbster in 1912, a Companion of the Order of St. Michael and St. George in 1922, and a Knight of the Order of the Thistle in 1941. He married Marigold Forbes (died 1975) in 1918; they had two sons (Robin and Angus) and two daughters (Catherine and Elizabeth). Sinclair wrote no books or memoirs, although a number of his speeches were published as pamphlets. There is one short biography: Gerard J. De Groot, *Liberal Crusader: The Life of Sir Archibald Sinclair* (1992).

Dr Richard S. Grayson

ADAM SMITH   1723–90

Adam Smith did for economic liberalism what John Locke had done for political liberalism, namely, to lay the philosophical foundations on which others would build a distinctive liberal tradition. Smith's ideas, however, have permeated the western political tradition to the extent where not only liberals but also other contemporary schools of thought claim to be his disciples. As a consequence, the widespread appeal of Smith's economic theories of free trade, the division of labour and the principle of individual initiative has helped to obscure the rich body of political liberalism to be found in his work. Adam Smith, far from being a laissez-faire doctrinaire, aimed to demonstrate that a liberal polity can enjoy the benefits of individual liberty and a free market economy, but need not – and ought not to – neglect social cohesion and basic human needs.

Smith was born in Kirkcaldy, near Edinburgh. The exact date of his birth is unknown, though it may possibly coincide with the date of his baptism, 5 June 1723. Earlier that year his father, a customs officer, had died and Smith was raised by his mother, Margaret Douglas, and guardians appointed in his father's will. At the age of fourteen, he matriculated at Glasgow University where he was educated in logic, physics and philosophy. After being nominated Snell Exhibitioner in 1740, he went to Balliol College, Oxford. Not surprisingly, given the dismal reputation that Oxford's teachers had in the eighteenth century, Smith spent most of his six years at Balliol studying on his own, reading widely in classics, philosophy, jurisprudence and literature.

On returning to Scotland in 1746, Smith's academic studies soon bore fruit. He began to deliver public lectures in rhetoric, philosophy and jurisprudence in Edinburgh and, in 1751, was appointed Professor of Logic at Glasgow University. Only a year later he became Professor of Moral Philosophy, teaching theology, moral philosophy and jurisprudence for the next twelve years. It was the last of these subjects which allowed him to include in his teaching aspects of politics and economics and, alongside his philosophical studies, to develop a life-long interest in political economy. His academic reputation, however, was initially to be built on the basis of his philosophical work. Smith's first book, *The Theory of Moral Sentiments*, was published in 1759. The treatise critically examined the moral thinking of the time and set out Smith's own theory of moral behaviour and judgement, based on an innate human desire to sympathise with others and arrive at impartial moral judgements. According to Smith, conscience arises from social relationships.

In 1764 Smith decided to leave Glasgow University for good and take up an invitation to travel abroad with the third Duke of Buccleuch. The position as travelling tutor offered Smith not only a higher annual income, including a life-long pension, but also an opportunity to find more time for his economic writings and to meet leading French thinkers of the Enlightenment. In Geneva, Smith was introduced to Voltaire, whose literary and political achievements he greatly admired. During his stay in Paris in 1766, Smith participated in the discussions of a group of liberal economists, the physiocrats; their leading figure, Quesnay, became a close friend of Smith's. Although both Smith and Quesnay criticised the mercantilists' belief in state interference with foreign trade and capital flows as a way of augmenting national wealth, Smith disagreed with the physiocrats' emphasis on agriculture as the solely productive occupation.

SMITH

While Smith used his stay in France in order to broaden his economic understanding, he had already worked out the basic principles of his liberal economic doctrine before embarking on the journey. After his return to Scotland at the end of 1766, he began work on his second book which, eventually, was to gain him worldwide fame as one of the most eminent liberal thinkers of all time. In 1776, *An Inquiry Into the Nature and Causes of the Wealth of Nations* was published to great success and world-wide acclaim. Only five chapters long, the book introduced original concepts such as the division of labour into specialist skills, individual enterprise, a common international currency and what today is known as a market-led economy.

As a result of the success of this economic theory and his reputation as a university administrator, Smith was offered the position of Commissioner of Customs in Edinburgh, which he took up in 1777. During his years in public office, he continued his economic, political and philosophical studies and worked on further editions of his two books. In addition, he embarked on two new projects, to write a history of philosophy and a theory of law and politics; these efforts, however, remained unfinished. At Smith's request, most of his handwritten notes on these subjects were posthumously destroyed. Apart from his two published works, only a small number of philosophical essays, lectures on rhetoric and literature as well as student notes from his lectures on jurisprudence survived. Adam Smith died on 17 July 1790, in Edinburgh. His political and economic liberalism lived on to change the world.

The most recent and authoritative biography of Adam Smith is Ian Simpson Ross' *The Life of Adam Smith* (Clarendon Press, 1995).

Robert Falkner

SIR CYRIL SMITH 1928–

In 1970, the Liberal Party attracted a mere seven per cent of the national vote and secured just six seats in Parliament. For all the promise of the Grimond-led revival in the 1950s and '60s, it seemed to many that the Liberals were only one poor election result away from oblivion; indeed, four thousand votes cast differently in the 1970 election could have wiped out the entire parliamentary Liberal Party.

By the time of the next election in February 1974, the Liberals had secured an additional five parliamentary seats through byelections and had substantially increased their share of popular support. The first of these byelection gains came in Rochdale on 26 October 1972 and the victor was local councillor and businessman Cyril Smith.

Smith was born in Rochdale on 28 June 1928 and educated at a school for delicate children before going to Spotland Primary School and then to Rochdale Municipal High School for Boys (the local grammar school).

He joined the Liberal Party in 1945 and was a member of the National Executive Committee of the Young Liberals in 1948 and 1949. Between 1948 and 1950, he was

333

the Liberal agent in Stockport but the disastrous elections of 1950 and 1951 so disillusioned him that he left the party and joined Labour. The following year, 1952, he was elected as the Labour councillor for Falinge Ward on Rochdale County Borough Council – a seat he held until his resignation as a councillor in 1975 (from 1973–75, he represented Falinge on the newly created Rochdale Metropolitan Borough Council).

Liberal Democrat leaders troubled by Smith's irksome anti-establishment streak may take some comfort from the knowledge that he was just as prone to dissent when he belonged to the Labour Party – in fact it was partly the Liberal Party's tolerance of strongly held personal convictions that persuaded him to return. He was threatened with expulsion for voting against the Rochdale Labour whip on numerous occasions. His position within the Labour Party was not helped in 1963 when he set up his own company – Smith Springs – of which he was managing director.

Things finally came to a head in 1966 when he was mayor. The council found itself in financial crisis and was being forced by the Labour government to balance its books. After a heated meeting of the Labour group, Smith persuaded them to opt for funding the budget shortfall via an equal additional levy on both the rates and council house rents. However, this decision was at odds with the views of the Rochdale Labour leadership, who wanted to raise the whole amount via the rates. At the council's budget meeting, Smith, in the chair, was amazed to witness the Labour group voting to fund the shortfall entirely from an increase in the rates, contrary to the democratic decision of their meeting the previous night. Apparently, the group leader had called another, secret, meeting to which he felt it would be inappropriate to invite Smith. He resigned from the party forthwith, taking four other Labour councillors with him, and set up the Rochdale Independent Party.

He and his colleagues remained independents until January 1968, when he rejoined the Liberal Party. It was as though he had never left; by 1970 he was the Liberal parliamentary candidate for Rochdale. Smith managed to take the Liberals in Rochdale to second place; his was one of only five seats in the UK to see an increase in the Liberal vote in the otherwise miserable general election of 1970.

Then came the byelection. When the parliamentary seat became vacant after the death of the sitting Labour MP, Smith took some persuading to stand. However, once he had agreed to be the Liberal candidate again, he threw himself into the campaign with characteristic zeal and enthusiasm. The ensuing victory – considered impossible by much of the party leadership – was undoubtedly the catalyst that led to the Liberal Party's revival over the next two years.

Following the byelection in 1972, Smith successfully defended Rochdale at five general elections before retiring in 1992. During his time in Parliament, he acted as employment spokesman for fifteen years and was Chief Whip between 1975 and 1977, dealing with the worst of the Thorpe affair. While employment spokesman, he co-wrote the book *Industrial Participation* with Simon Hebditch. In 1977 he wrote his autobiography, *Big Cyril,* and updated his story in *Reflections from Rochdale* in 1997.

After his retirement, he was not appointed to the House of Lords, something that did not disappoint him greatly – he had long referred to the Upper House as the 'chapel of rest'. He was, however, knighted and received a number of other titles and awards including, in 1992, an honorary doctorate from the University of Lancaster where he had served as Deputy Pro-Chancellor between 1981 and 1988.

In 1994, the death of his mother Eva, with whom he had a shared a home for his entire life, left him 'utterly devastated'. Comfort came in the form of a lengthy letter from Princess Alexandra (the Chancellor of the University of Lancaster and a personal friend), which he treasures with great affection. He was able to get on with life again with some enthusiasm following a chance communication from former Tower Hamlets council leader, Eric Flounders. Flounders offered him the chance to host 'Twenty years as an MP: The longest running farce in the West End' as the central cabaret slot on a series of cruises on the *QEII*. He accepted and found that the experience gave him new purpose.

Back on dry land, Sir Cyril Smith has continued to invest his time and effort in the Liberal Democrats. In 1995, he was elected President of the North West Region and he describes himself as having a 'firm but declining role' in the party. There is no doubt that he will continue to remind the party of its need to keep Labour at arm's length and to ensure that it maintains its independence at all costs.

In a party that attracts more than its fair share of colourful characters, eccentrics and individuals worthy of comment, Sir Cyril Smith is unique. His size, belligerence, powers of oratory and humour make him unforgettable. Many people may mistakenly consider him a novelty politician. His impact, however, on the democratisation of the Liberal Party (one member, one vote in party leadership elections came about after a campaign he led) and, most importantly, his role in kickstarting the key Liberal revival of 1972–74, should ensure the recognition of his crucial contribution to the advancement of Liberalism.

Tim Farron

SIR ROBERT SMITH MP   1958–

As a fresher at the University of Aberdeen, Bob Smith became involved in student politics within a few weeks of his arrival, seeking to be elected as a first-year member of the university's Student Representative Council, and succeeding. Letting this success go to his head, he immediately proposed ITN's Sandy Gall as rector, and led that campaign to victory. That was before the end of his first term!

Politics, however, had already been lurking in Smith's blood. The baronetcy which he inherited on his father's death in 1983 was originally awarded to his grandfather, Sir Robert Smith, in 1945, by a grateful Conservative Party leader in recognition of his sterling service as the Tory MP for Aberdeenshire & Kincardineshire since 1924.

Born in London on 15 April 1958, Smith was educated at Merchant Taylors' school, Northwood, progressing to take a BSc(maths) from Aberdeen University in 1983. Although he undoubtedly has the intellect and academic application to have taken an honours degree, the eclectic nature of his course selection, reflecting a mind which is always seeking to know more about more, led him to qualify for an ordinary degree over four years, with many more passes than is usual for such a qualification

Following his father's death, Smith spent some years managing the family's affairs, based on their small estate at Crowmallie, Aberdeenshire. He has recently reacquired his late uncle's half of the house which had been split on his grandfather's death, and supervises the management of a small agricultural tenancy on the estate.

A founder member of the SDP, Smith gave up his hard-won place as Vice-President (Education) of the university SRC, a position generally seen as the springboard to the sabbatical presidency, in order to concentrate on his studies, and thereafter became aware that the real power in university politics lay in the university's court. In 1988, Liberal Democrat educationalist Willis Pickard, the new rector, appointed him as his assessor on the court, a post he held until 1991.

Turning his attention to municipal politics, Smith stood as SDP candidate in the Westburn ward of Aberdeen City in 1984, and Alliance candidate for the Ferryhill ward on Grampian Regional Council in 1986. Following an unsuccessful parliamentary bid in Aberdeen North in 1987 (then Labour's safest Scottish seat), he stood as a paper candidate in the same regional ward in 1990. Having helped at a range of elections in the north east over the years, Bob finally immersed himself totally in the process during the Kincardine & Deeside byelection in 1991, and continued his efforts in support of Nicol Stephen in his bid to retain the seat in 1992. He was then elected to Aberdeenshire Council for the Upper Donside division in 1995. He was appointed Vice-Chair of Grampian's Joint Police Board, a high-profile post, well-handled in difficult circumstances. He left the post only after his election to Parliament.

His personal and political fortunes received a welcome boost on 13 August 1993 when he married Fiona Cormack, a World Service journalist. The addition of two delightful daughters to his family has further expanded his horizons.

When boundary changes forced Stephen to choose only part of Kincardine & Deeside for the 1997 contest, Smith fought a successful selection, and even more successful election battle for the remaining rural part, with some additions from Malcolm Bruce's (q.v.) old Gordon seat, thus recapturing in West Aberdeenshire & Kincardine some of the territory held by his grandfather in the 1920s.

It is difficult to identify the contribution of a Member of Parliament of some eighteen months' standing, but Smith's style is a welcome mixture of the patrician and the community campaigner. The 1991 byelection was caused by the death of Alick Buchanan-Smith, a distant cousin, who shared with Smith his love of the university (his father having been Vice-Chancellor), and Bob's easy 'county' style, mixed with a community politics attention to detail, made him a popular and easily electable candidate. It is likely to make him as easily re-elected.

His intellect is easily engaged and he is unlikely to settle for superficial answers to the questions which present themselves. His attention to the detail of his research can be frustrating for those seeking easy or quick responses, but, when satisfied that his position or understanding is correct, he is as difficult to shake off as a rottweiler with locked jaws. His gravitas gives him stature beyond his experience; when his experience matches his gravitas, he will be a force to be reckoned with.

Sheila Ritchie

J. A. SPENDER

1862–1942

John Alfred (always known as J. A.) Spender was one of a group of Liberal editors who, in the late nineteenth and early twentieth centuries, helped determine the substance and style of debate within the Liberal Party. Spender edited the *Westminster Gazette* from 1896 to 1921. He was the confidant of, among others, Campbell-Bannerman (*q.v.*), Asquith (*q.v.*), Grey (*q.v.*) and McKenna (*q.v.*). The *Westminster Gazette* was to the Liberal side of politics what the *Times* was to the Conservative side – read by men of both parties, and of none. It declined, alongside the party which it represented, in the 1920s.

Spender was born on 23 December 1862 in Bath, the son of prosperous and literary parents. He was the third child (and eldest son) of eight. Two of his younger brothers, Harold and Hugh, also became London journalists. Spender was educated at Bath College and at Balliol College, Oxford, which he entered as a classical exhibitioner in 1882. These were the years (under Jowett's Mastership) from which Balliol was to emerge as the nursery of political and literary life for the next half-century. Among Spender's contemporaries in college were Curzon and Edward Grey and, someone who became a life-long friend, Cosmo Gordon Lang, later Archbishop of Canterbury. Spender's Liberalism was allied, unusually, to devout Anglicanism, and whether Lang influenced Spender's Anglicanism or not, Lang confessed, in old age, that Spender had done much to diminish his youthful Toryism.

After Oxford, Spender freelanced for a year and was then appointed Editor of the *Eastern Morning News* of Hull in 1886. Before 1914, newspapers, even in the provinces, were far more driven by politics than was the case after 1918. Spender took the *Eastern Morning News* in an uncompromisingly Gladstonian direction, especially in its support for Irish home rule. When he took his next post, Assistant Editor of the *Pall Mall* in London in 1892, he lasted only one month. The proprietor sold the paper, it changed its politics to the Conservative cause and the entire staff, including Spender, resigned. It was the 'defection' of the *Pall Mall* which caused the founding of the *Westminster Gazette*. The proprietor was George Newnes, and Spender was appointed Assistant Editor. The *Westminster* was an afternoon paper, circulating mainly in London. The first issue was on 31 January 1893, and from the outset, it sought to be distinctive, Liberal and high-brow. It was printed on green paper and carried its leader columns across its front page. Spender determined its editorial tone, and from the time he became Editor in 1896 until his resignation in 1921, he made the paper the voice of official Liberalism. His own influence ranked alongside C. P. Scott of the *Manchester Guardian*, and ahead of all other Liberal editors. Amongst those who read the *Westminster* were Edward VII, Kaiser Wilhelm II, and Woodrow Wilson. During the great crisis of July – August 1914, Spender was in the Foreign Office every day, and his paper faithfully reflected the views of the Foreign Secretary, Sir Edward Grey.

Yet the *Westminster Gazette* was never a commercial success. When Spender became editor, its circulation was 15,000, and even at the height of the Boer War and the First World War the paper's maximum circulation was 27,000. It was sustained by the largesse of wealthy proprietors, (from 1912 a syndicate of Liberal peers and MPs), several of whom withdrew after 1918 when Spender steered the paper away from Lloyd George's (*q.v.*) coalition, and towards support of Asquith. (Spender's journalist brother Harold became a firm Lloyd Georgeite and the family, like the party, split.) By 1921, the paper was in such serious difficulties that, against Spender's wishes, it became a morning publication, and after only a few months Spender resigned. The *Westminster* was not a success as a morning paper; the constituency to which it had appealed before 1914 had largely perished in the war, and with the dominance of class-based issues and politics after 1918, its high-minded and somewhat lofty approach had become anachronistic.

Although Spender contributed frequently to the press after 1921, he now became a prolific author. He published biographies of Campbell-Bannerman (two volumes, 1923), Viscount Cowdray (1930), Sir Robert Hudson, the former secretary of the National Liberal Federation (1930), and, jointly, of Asquith (two volumes, 1932). He produced a semi-autobiographical work, *Life, Journalism and Politics* (two volumes, 1927) and several volumes of essays, the last two of which were published posthumously. Of all the contemporary partisans involved in the division and decline of the Liberal Party, Spender was the most consistent, and convincing, on the Asquithian side.

Along with other Asquithians, he gradually lost influence in the party. He was elected President of the National Liberal Federation in 1926, but following the final squabble between Asquith and Lloyd George, and the triumph of the latter, over the General Strike, he resigned. Some of the Asquithians then founded a body called the Liberal Council, of which Spender was President from 1936–42, but its influence was minimal.

Spender was a member of two royal commissions, on divorce and matrimonial causes (1909–12), and the private manufacture of armaments (1935–36) – the latter leading him to support the policy of appeasement in the late 1930s. He was also an influential member of the Milner mission to Egypt (1919–20), charged with investigating the causes of civil unrest in the country. He was invested Companion of Honour in 1937 and died in June 1942, still publishing regularly in the *News Chronicle*. He married Mary (May) Rawlinson, eldest daughter of the art collector and writer on Turner, W. G. Rawlinson, in 1891; they had no children.

A biography of Spender was published in 1946 by H. Wilson Harris. There is a portrait of him by Clive Gardiner in the Reform Club (to whose library Spender gave generously), and a pencil drawing of him by Muirhead Bone in the Imperial War Museum.

Michael Hart

MICHAEL STEED   1940–

Manchester was a centre for young Liberal thinkers and campaigners for most of the 1960s, and I first got to know Michael Steed when we were both for a time part of that group. In 1965 he abandoned his D.Phil at Nuffield and took a job lecturing in French politics at Manchester University, where he spent the rest of his academic life, gaining high recognition as a psephologist, before retiring due to the onset of a rare and devastating neurological condition at the end of 1987.

In the later '60s I spent many pleasant evenings at his flat in Owens Park, plotting the Liberal revolution and talking about the world. At that time he had become the first modern collector, improver and writer of political songs for Liberals; many of the classics still sung at Liberal Glee Clubs owe their revival or existence to Steed.

Before moving to Manchester, Steed had been one of those young people who spontaneously took up Liberalism and the Liberal Party in the 1950s. He was born in east Kent on 25 January 1940 to inactively Tory parents – his father was a farmer. But he helped refound the local Liberal Association while still at school. He went up to Cambridge and got hooked into the Liberal Party nationally via a somewhat chance attendance at a seminar run by the World Federation of Liberal and Radical Youth.

This led rapidly to the Chairmanship of the Union of Liberal Students and places on the National Executive Committee and Party Council. Already he was involved in many of the typically liberal causes which made him much more than just a party man: European federalism, anti-hanging, anti-apartheid. Over the years his interests have ranged from gay rights (National Chair of the Campaign for Homosexual Equality in the early 1970s) and other civil liberty issues (he was a leader of the hectic campaign against the Wilson Government's racist 'Kenyan Asians' immigration act), through Northern Ireland and a lifetime's passion for electoral reform, to north of England regionalism, the Channel Tunnel and the saving of a historic Pennine toll-house.

During most of his Manchester-based years Steed lived in the small Pennine textile town of Todmorden on the Lancashire-Yorkshire border. He shared various interesting houses there with Swedish-born Margareta Holmstedt, who he met in European Young Liberal circles and married in 1970.

During those two decades he did more, and gave more to the Liberal Party and Liberalism, than most adherents can cram into a period more than twice as long. Within the party he made huge contributions to policy, particularly constitutional reform as Chairman and Convenor of the machinery of government panel for some fifteen years, and member of the Alliance Commission on Constitutional Reform in the early 1980s – a contribution recently renewed as a member of the 'Cook-Maclennan talks' on constitutional reform before the 1997 general election which led directly to PR for the 1999 European elections. He was instrumental in modernising the Liberal Party constitution, not least in the election of the Leader by the members.

Steed's belief in democracy was a personal imperative as well as a theory. He stood for Parliament six times: in the Brierley Hill byelection of 1967, at Truro in 1970; at the Manchester Exchange byelection in 1973; at reorganised Manchester Central in February 1974; and at Burnley in 1979 and 1983. He fought the Greater Manchester North Euro seat in 1979.

Manchester Exchange was the most serious of these contests and the closest he came to election. The seat was centred round the 'new slums' of Hulme, the ill-fated 'streets in the sky' council estates that were then new but already a social disaster. Liverpool's Trevor Jones (*q.v.*) ran the campaign which came in the middle of a string of Liberal byelection successes involving a rather raw populist exploitation of local issues through the medium of the then quite novel *Focus* leaflets. But it may have been too soon in the life of the new estates, or the campaigning too superficial, or perhaps the Labour Party was still too entrenched in that part of central Manchester; and Steed, the uncompromising honest intellectual, may not have been the ideal candidate for such a contest – though his enthusiasm and commitment were, as always, everything an agent could ask for.

Even more incongruous was Brierley Hill. The Liberal Party had not intended to fight this West Midlands seat, part old industrial towns and part posh suburbs. In 1967, however, the Young Liberals were at the height of their 'Red Guard' boom period, and moved in. Steed was the stand-in Political Vice-Chairman of the National League of Young Liberals for the six months before the byelection. His individualistic Liberal values were not wholly in tune with the somewhat solidly left-wing YL leadership of the day, and he was already seen in YL circles as something of an elder statesman (a few years later he was associated with *Radical Bulletin*, a kind of Liberal Party *Private Eye*, which invariably called him the 'Venerable Steed'). The campaign, slogan 'We Want a Revolution', had an aggressive vigour which attracted YLs in droves from all over the country, but the many leaflets and badges, widespread flyposting and gimmicks such as political sing-songs on buses and pub crawls failed to gain the enthusiasm of the voters. Steed enjoyed himself hugely but was hardly at home.

He did get elected to Todmorden Town Council and served a term from 1987 to 1991 before returning to the drier clime and a slow but real physical recovery in his native Kent.

Everyone's life story is full of 'what-ifs' and Michael Steed's more than most. Academically he became one of an elite few in his chosen field of elections, without ever achieving his potential academic rank. There is little doubt that he held himself back by pursuing his own beliefs through active political engagement. In 1978–79, while still young, Steed gained the highest extra-parliamentary office his party had to offer – the Presidency. He gave over twenty years of intensive service to Liberalism. With his formidable powers of analysis and argument, combined with his determined pursuit of the (invariably clearly liberal) causes in which he believes, Steed would and should have been an outstanding parliamentarian. But he could never have given the kind of attention to a constituency needed to become a Liberal MP under first-past-the-post in modern times. The Liberal Party had no seats such as Ashfield or Tunbridge Wells to offer such a talent. His health problems may prevent his accession to the Upper House which is where he now truly belongs.

Steed has contributed to many voting studies, including acting as author or co-author of 'analysis of results' in Nuffield studies of British general elections from 1964 to 1997. He is a prolific pamphleteer and writer of too many articles to list here, but key ones include: *The Alliance: A Critical History* (*New Outlook*/Prism Pubs, 1983); *Proportionality and Exaggeration in the British Electoral System* (with John Curtice, Butterworth & Co, 1986); and chapters on aspects of the Liberal Party in H. M. Drucker, *Multi-Party Britain* (Macmillan, 1979); Vernon Bogdanor, *Liberal Party Politics* (Clarendon Press, 1983); R. Morgan & S. Silvestri, *Moderates and Conservatives in Europe* (Heinemann, 1982); and Don MacIver, *The Liberal Democrats* (Prentice Hall/Harvester Wheatsheaf, 1996).

Tony Greaves

DAVID STEEL (Lord Steel)   1938–

With the exception of H. H. Asquith (*q.v.*), David (now Lord) Steel has been the longest serving leader of the Liberal Party. During his twelve-year tenure of the leadership, the party enjoyed the highest share of the popular vote cast for a third party in half a century and won more seats in Parliament and in local government than it had held since the Second World War. In taking his party into the Lib-Lab agreement with the minority Callaghan administration in 1977 and in allying the Liberals with the Social Democratic Party during the seven-year life of the latter, he made his party once again a powerful third force in Britain and restored its credibility as a potential party of government.

Yet Steel's leadership was not uncontroversial. His wide popular appeal in the country was never reflected in support from all of the party's activists. He was rarely in sympathy with the growing local government section of the Liberal Party. The distrust, often scorn, was mutual. Active opposition to his belief that it was not necessary for the Liberal Party to fight every parliamentary seat – a central tenet of Steel's strategy of making the Liberal Party a tool for the radical realignment of British politics – was a constant feature of his time at the helm. It reflected what some of his more fundamentalist colleagues saw as a distressing tendency to see allies across party boundaries and to be driven less by partisan politics than by broad issues.

David Martin Scott Steel was born on 31 March 1938 in Kirkcaldy, Scotland, the son of a Church of Scotland minister (and later Moderator). The eldest of five children, he attended Dumbarton Academy; James Gillespie's Boys School, Edinburgh; the Prince of Wales School, Nairobi; and George Watson's College, Edinburgh. He was a reserved pupil, but with a mind of his own and a morality shaped by an upbringing as a son of the manse in Scotland and by four years as the son of a radical minister in Kenya at the time of the Mau Mau uprising, in the dying years of colonial administration.

Steel's failure to shine academically owed more to his energetic pursuit of wider interests than to any lack of intellectual capacity. At Edinburgh University, from which he graduated with an MA in 1960 and a law degree in 1962, Steel joined the Liberal Club and the Scottish Liberal Party, was elected Chairman of the Students' Representative Council and ran a successful campaign to make Liberal Party leader Jo Grimond (q.v.) the university's rector. Some months before leaving university he was adopted as the Liberal PPC for the Edinburgh Pentlands constituency and shortly afterwards took his first job, as the Scottish Liberals' Assistant General Secretary. In October of the same year he married fellow law graduate Judy MacGregor, by whom he now has three children.

In the winter of 1963–64 a vacancy arose for a Liberal candidate in the much more winnable Scottish Border seat of Roxburgh, Selkirk & Peebles, with an elderly and ailing Conservative member. Steel jumped at the chance to move and in January 1964 was adopted as the PPC. He failed to win it from the Conservatives at the general election of that year, but nonetheless moved his home to the Borders and took a short-lived job in television with the BBC. The death of the sitting MP in December 1964 gave him his opportunity. Steel won the byelection in March of the following year with a handsome majority. He held the constituency (subsequently redrawn and re-named Tweeddale, Ettrick & Lauderdale) at the eight general elections from 1966 to 1992 before bequeathing the seat to Michael Moore (q.v.) after more than thirty years in Parliament.

In spite of his championship of Scottish Home Rule and his greater ease in Scottish society, Steel – like his Welsh predecessor Lloyd George (q.v.) – chose to work essentially within the British system and yet managed to remain free of snobbery and side. That his main contribution to political life has been in UK domestic affairs and social policy is the product of a wider ambition and a keen eye for the main chance. Equally, his problems with Liberal Party activists south of the border stemmed partly from his not being 'one of them' or seeking to identify himself with their concerns.

In the House of Commons, Steel was the Party's employment spokesman (1965–67), spokesman on Commonwealth affairs (1967–70), Chief Whip (1970–74) and foreign affairs spokesman (1974–76 and 1989–94). His main legislative achievement of note was the introduction in July 1966 of a controversial private member's bill to permit legal abortion in the UK in defined circumstances. The measure, which passed into law on 26 October 1967, was recognised as a major social reform and earned Parliament's youngest MP a reputation for hard work, affability and an effective grasp of parliamentary tactics.

In July 1976, in the wake of Jeremy Thorpe's (*q.v.*) resignation, Steel was elected Leader of the Liberals in a contest against John Pardoe (*q.v.*) He positioned his party firmly on the progressive wing of British politics on all the major issues of the day. His search for political realignment was to be the constant theme of his leadership and was eventually achieved, though in a rather pyrrhic victory over his rival David Owen, in the merger of the Liberal Party and the SDP in 1988. Having achieved that task and given birth to the successor party – the Social and Liberal Democrats – he re-signed the Liberal leadership in May of that year.

The personal chemistry between David Steel and the so-called Gang of Four – Roy Jenkins (*q.v.*), Shirley Williams (*q.v.*), David Owen and Bill Rodgers (*q.v.*) – was vital to the creation of the SDP (well chronicled in the book *SDP* by Ivor Crewe and Anthony King) and its eventual merger with the Liberal Party. Instrumental in urging

Jenkins to launch a new party, Steel blamed himself for the events of the Ettrick Bridge meeting (at which a Liberal attempt to depose Jenkins from the leadership of the Alliance 1983 election campaign was bungled) and Owen's subsequent assumption of the SDP leadership. He was never to enjoy the friendship and mutually beneficial working relationship with David Owen that he had enjoyed with the other three. His goal became that of 'seeing off' an SDP leader who was hell-bent against Steel's strategy of merger.

A constant feature of Steel's leadership was an ability to keep his eye on the big picture, to an extent that bemused and infuriated those who sought in him a greater interest in the detail of policy. Combined with considerable stamina, it lent him great popular appeal among the electorate. For a number of years he was the UK's most popular politician.

In 1989 Steel became a co-chair of the Scottish Constitutional Convention, which laid the groundwork for the formation of the Scottish Parliament, and returned to play a greater role in Scotland's affairs. He nonetheless maintained wider interests, including his controversial chairmanship of the Countryside Movement (1995–97) and defence of the hunting of wild animals during the fissiparous political debates of the mid 1990s.

Steel has travelled widely and has taken a keen interest in democracy and human rights in developing countries, where he has promoted the monitoring of elections by international observers. His main concern has been for Africa. From 1966–69 Steel served as president of the British Anti-Apartheid Movement. He has been a frequent visitor to Africa and a tireless campaigner against racial injustice, to the extent of jeopardising his own re-election in 1970 through his opposition to the South African rugby tour and in particular the fixture scheduled in his own rugby-loving constituency.

Throughout his career, including during his time as party leader, he has participated eagerly in international political affairs. He was an active campaigner in the European referendum campaign of 1975. He has been a regular attender at (and organiser of) meetings of Liberal leaders from across the world. In the 1989 European election campaign he stood as a candidate in the Liberal-Republican interest in Italy, in protest against the UK's unique failure to hold European elections on the British mainland by proportional representation. From 1994 to 1996 he served as President of Liberal International.

Steel's strategic contribution to UK politics lay in convincing others that cooperation between liberals and social or christian democrats could provide stable government capable of commanding majority support in the country and providing an alternative to the twentieth-century Conservative hegemony. He taught Liberals that the way to power for a small party in a first-past-the-post electoral system was in cooperation with one of the major parties and that the logic of their espousal of a system of proportional representation was support for multi-party government of the kind found in other western European countries. In leading his party into an agreement with the Labour government in March 1977 and in sustaining the agreement in the face of opposition from his own ranks until September 1978 he achieved a goal which had eluded both his immediate predecessors. He also paved the way for the formation of the Social Democratic Party (1981–88), the eventual creation of the Liberal Democrats and their subsequent cooperation with the Labour government of 1997.

Following his elevation to the peerage in June 1997, as Baron Steel of Aikwood, of Ettrick Forest in the Scottish Borders, Steel became Deputy Leader of the Liberal Democrats in the House of Lords. At the time of writing he is a candidate for the first elections to the new Scottish Parliament.

Friend and mentor Ludovic Kennedy once wrote perceptively that although Steel does not possess the commanding Olympian presence of Asquith or Grimond, nor the ego of Lloyd George or Thorpe, his success and longevity are founded in his reasonableness and a cool control of his emotions. Steel's durable telegenic appeal undoubtedly gives rise to the view that his political talent might in other circumstances have been more adequately fulfilled.

Steel has written seven books to date. These are *No Entry* (1968), *A House Divided* (1980), *David Steel's Border Country* (with Judy Steel, 1985), *Partners in One Nation* (1985), *Mary Stuart's Scotland* (with Judy Steel, 1987), *The Time has Come* (with David Owen, 1987) and an autobiography, *Against Goliath* (1989). A biography of David Steel, *David Steel – his life and politics,* was written by Peter Bartram in 1981.

Graham Watson

ANDREW STUNELL MP   1942–

The recent emergence of the Liberal Democrats as the second party of local government follows the dramatic growth of the new party's councillor base from 1,500 in 1988 to over 5,000 in 1997. This reflects the pivotal contribution of the Association of Liberal Democrat Councillors, in which Andrew Stunell was the driving force as Political Secretary from 1989 to 1996. It therefore came as no surprise to his colleagues that on a night of dramatic gains for the Liberal Democrats, Stunell was elected as MP for Hazel Grove on 1 May 1997 with a majority of 11,814, the largest margin of victory in any of the new seats gained, and with the highest percentage of the total poll (54.5 per cent) of any Liberal Democrat constituency.

Robert Andrew Stunell, always known by his middle name, was born on 24 November 1942 in Sutton, Surrey. After Surbiton Grammar School, he studied architecture at Manchester University and Liverpool Polytechnic. He worked in various architectural posts for the Cooperative Wholesale Society, Manchester and Runcorn New Town Development Corporation. While at Runcorn, he was active in his trade union NALGO, including four years developing his negotiating skills as staff side representative on the Whitley Council for New Towns. Following a period of freelance working, when he began to develop a wider advisory role, he entered politics full time from 1985 as Councillors' Officer for the Association of Liberal Councillors.

Stunell joined the Liberal Party in 1968, angered by the Labour Home Secretary's decision to withhold UK passports from Kenyan Asians. As a student, he did voluntary work abroad for UNA and Christian Aid, using his architectural skills to help house homeless refugees. A former Baptist lay preacher and active member of his local Methodist church, he has always displayed a deep commitment to social justice and core Liberal values.

Stunell first came to national prominence in 1981 as Liberal/Alliance group leader on Cheshire County Council, where he developed the 'Cheshire Convention', which has become a widespread model for ensuring the effective operation of authorities where no party has overall control. He served on the county council for ten years from 1981, and on Chester City Council from 1979–90. He was Vice-Chair of the Association of County Councils from 1985 to 1990.

Elected to the Liberal negotiating team for the merger talks with the SDP in 1988, he received some criticism from radical activists for his pragmatic approach to the negotiations. However, he was able to demonstrate negotiating success by ensuring that the federal structure of the new party was coherent and robust, as well as playing a part in devising the youth and students' role in the new constitution.

Stunell fought the Labour-Tory marginal of Chester at three successive general elections in 1979, 1983 and 1987, achieving respectable third places. In 1989, he was persuaded to put himself forward as a contender for the top target seat of Hazel Grove, which had been held by the Conservatives since 1974, when Dr Michael Winstanley briefly held the seat between the February and October elections.

Stunell's dramatic victory in Hazel Grove was the culmination of eight years' highly-planned, consistent and effective community campaigning, strengthening positive support, squeezing the Labour vote and gaining every council seat in the constituency. Following the 1992 election at which he reduced the Conservative majority to just 929, he and his family found a permanent home in the constituency and he continued to strengthen his local roots. In 1994 he defeated a sitting Labour councillor by over 1,000 votes to become an elected member of Stockport Metropolitan Borough Council. As Vice-Chair of Finance, he is part of a Liberal Democrat administration where he is again helping to demonstrate that councils can be run effectively and efficiently where no single party has overall control. He is comfortable with a dual mandate and has been determined to retain his local community links; he was re-elected with a 1,189 majority in May 1998.

In appointing him as Deputy Chief Whip in 1997, Paddy Ashdown (q.v.) was well aware of Stunell's negotiating and strategic skills which are now deployed in helping to manage a parliamentary party which had nearly doubled in size, with over half its members new to Westminster. He has already made his mark on procedural issues as a member of the Select Committee on the modernisation of the House. A keen local campaigner on environmental issues, he has been appointed as spokesman on energy.

He has written several booklets on council practice and procedures; his publications include *Life in the Balance* (1983), *Budgeting for Real* (1984) and *Open, Local and Effective* (1996). A passionate but practical campaigner for the devolution of political and revenue-raising powers to the lowest possible level, including parish and community councils, he helped draw up the party's proposals for democratic regional government and local income taxation. He has been a Vice-President of the Local Government Association since 1997.

Stunell was awarded the OBE for political service in 1995. Married since 1967 to Gillian, a primary music curriculum adviser, they have five children, two of whom are adopted. His interests include camping, outdoor pursuits and theoretical astronomy.

Peter Brook

DICK TAVERNE (Lord Taverne) 1928–

The SDP and the Liberal Democrats had a political prophet. In the 1970s, the Lincoln MP Dick Taverne's support for Europe caused a direct clash with his local Labour Party. Taverne won a personal mandate from his constituents and foreshadowed the Social Democrats' split from Labour and their eventual union with the Liberals.

Dick Taverne was born on 18 October 1928, the son of Dr Nicholas Taverne and his wife Louise, and educated at Charterhouse and Balliol College, Oxford, where he took a first in Greats. Taverne was called to the bar of the Middle Temple in 1954 and took silk in 1965. In 1955, he married Janice Hennessey and they later had two daughters.

Taverne joined the Labour Party at the age of eighteen. He aligned himself firmly with the party's revisionists. They believed that a more equal society could be achieved through successful Keynesian economic management and a modern welfare state; further state ownership, therefore, was not necessary. At the 1959 conference, Taverne publicly supported Hugh Gaitskell in his unsuccessful attempt to abolish Clause IV of the party constitution. Subsequently, he was treasurer of the revisionist organisation, the Campaign for Democratic Socialism (CDS), until 1963.

In 1962, Taverne held Lincoln for Labour in a byelection, having fought Putney in 1959. His political career flourished. When the party returned to power two years later, he became Denis Healey's Parliamentary Private Secretary at the Ministry of Defence. Following the 1966 general election, he was appointed Parliamentary Under-Secretary at the Home Office; in April 1968, he moved up to become Minister of State at the Treasury. From September 1969 until Labour's defeat in June 1970, he was Financial Secretary to the Treasury. In opposition, he was appointed a front-bench spokesman.

However, there was growing tension with the Lincoln Labour Party. The increasingly dominant left faction disliked Taverne's 'social democratic' views and his strong support for Roy Jenkins (*q.v.*). There was also some resentment at his public school and London barrister background. It was Europe that provided the flashpoint. Taverne had long believed that Britain's economic decline would continue if it stayed outside the EEC. The left-wingers in the Lincoln party were staunchly anti-Market. In October 1971, he was one of sixty-nine Labour MPs to vote for joining the EEC on terms negotiated by the Conservative government, in defiance of a three-line whip. The Lincoln Labour Party subsequently voted to 'retire' him as its parliamentary candidate.

Taverne resigned his seat to force a byelection, which he fought under the 'Democratic Labour' banner. He believed that as a Member of Parliament, he was not a party delegate but a representative, with a duty to use his judgement on behalf of the whole constituency. He saw the Labour Party as a lost cause, steadily being taken over by the left, which was not only misguided but would make the party unelectable. Such were the themes of his byelection campaign. On 1 March 1973, Taverne won a huge majority over the Labour candidate. The following year, he became a Member of the European Parliament, taking up one of the seats that the Labour Party had refused.

Early in 1974, Taverne published *The Future of the Left*, recounting his Lincoln experience and setting out core principles for his new Campaign for Social Democracy, which he intended to be a catalyst for breaking the party mould. Social democrats, he explained, stood for 'a society of equal opportunities and equal rights' achieved through the system of representative democracy. His main policy prescriptions were more progressive taxation, high public spending on schools and hospitals, more disclosure, partnership and consultation in industry, British membership of a powerful but more accountable European Community, a statutory prices and incomes policy, and balancing economic development with environmental protection. Taverne argued that, once the Jenkinsite social democrats finally became disillusioned with Labour, a new, progressive party could pursue these goals. It should work with, and eventually subsume, the Liberal Party.

Few outside Lincoln heeded this clarion call. Jenkins and the other pro-Europe social democrats did not bolt. Labour won the largest number of seats at the February 1974 general election, which ended for the time being his hopes for political change. Taverne was returned but his majority was well down and all other Campaign for Social Democracy candidates lost their deposits. Then, at the October election, he lost his seat to a Labour candidate.

The events of the late 1970s and early 1980s vindicated his views on the Labour Party. Taverne played a major role in the formation of the SDP, which embraced the themes he had espoused. He served on the party's National Committee, wrote a radical policy paper on social security, co-founded a think tank, and fought the Peckham byelection in October 1982 and Dulwich in 1983. Still, Taverne did not see the SDP as end in itself. From the start, he advocated a merger with the Liberals, contending that there was room for only one centre party in British politics. In 1987, he enthusiastically backed the successful campaign for merger. He was briefly a member of the Liberal Democrats' Federal Policy Committee and chaired its first economic policy working group.

Outside the Commons, Taverne was the first Director-General and then Chairman of the Institute for Fiscal Studies, which he launched in 1970. He has pursued his business interests with considerable success. These have included directorships of the BOC Group, various investment trusts, and Axa Equity and Law. He founded the public policy consultancy Prima Europe.

In 1996, Taverne was elevated to the Lords as Baron Taverne of Pimlico. There, he pursues his political passions: Britain's entry into economic and monetary union, welfare reform and the reform of corporate governance. He gave up his car in 1974 and continues to cycle to his various activities within London and, for up to three months a year, to sail his boat all over the northern hemisphere.

Neil Stockley

MATTHEW TAYLOR MP   1963–

It is rare for Liberal Democrat MPs, apart from those holding the most senior positions, to take a strong interest in policy development, communications and political strategy at the same time. Despite his youth, Matthew Taylor has broken this mould. In his various roles within the parliamentary party, he has taken all these three elements equally seriously and treated them as an integrated whole. As a result, the party has developed some of its most important policy and campaigning themes.

Matthew Owen John Taylor was born in London on 3 January 1963 and adopted by Ken Taylor, a television author, and his wife, Gillian. He was educated in Truro and London and won a scholarship to Lady Margaret Hall, Oxford University. His involvement in party politics began when he joined both the Liberal and SDP Clubs. After graduating with a BA (Hons) in politics, philosophy and economics in 1985, he was president of the Oxford University Students' Union.

In July 1986, he became economics research assistant to the parliamentary Liberal Party and was seconded to work for David Penhaligon (*q.v.*), the Treasury spokesman and MP for Truro. This appointment lasted just six months until the following December, when Penhaligon was killed in a car crash. Taylor was selected as the Liberal candidate and won the March 1987 byelection. He was, at the age of twenty-four, the youngest member of the House of Commons and retained this distinction for a record ten years. He was the Alliance youth spokesman for the 1987 general election and, following his re-election, was appointed Liberal Party spokesman on energy.

In 1988 he became local government spokesman. In this role, coinciding with the poll tax bill debate, Taylor led the Liberal Democrats' opposition to the poll tax and oversaw the development of a coherent alternative, the local income tax.

Following a somewhat less happy period as trade and industry spokesman from November 1989 to April 1990, he took on the education portfolio and, with the help of a group of informal advisers, brought together a comprehensive and distinctive policy for the Liberal Democrats. This included the pledge to put a penny on income tax, with the revenue earmarked for education – the party's single most attractive policy at the 1992 general election and a focus of its campaigning for the next five years.

Taylor's other key contributions have been in the areas of communications and political strategy. In 1990, he became chair of the Liberal Democrat Communications Committee. This included overall responsibility for party political broadcasts, media relations and party conference presentation. In this role, he oversaw the introduction of the Liberal Democrats' 'bird of liberty' logo.

Following the 1992 general election, his only major parliamentary role was that of Chair of the Campaigns and Communications Committee. Taylor began developing the 'target seats' strategy that proved so successful at the 1997 general election. This built on the team approach used in five Cornish constituencies for the previous campaign. In particular, he played a huge role in the party's coordinated campaign in the vital south west region. However, his attempt to develop a distinctive and simple communications framework – a 'core message' – proved less successful, due to the inherent difficulty of the task and his independent political style. The eventual product of this exercise was the party's adoption of education as its defining issue.

In September 1994, Taylor became environment spokesman, and, in the run-up to the 1997 general election, he oversaw significant developments in the party's programme for environmental sustainability. Most importantly, the Liberal Democrats proposed 'green taxes' that would shift but not increase the overall tax burden. These included the phased introduction of a carbon tax in order to encourage energy saving, using the funds raised to cut VAT and employers' national insurance contributions, and reductions in the annual tax for more fuel-efficient cars, funded by small increases in the duty on fuel. In 1997, he was awarded the 'Green Ribbon' Award as Britain's 'most effective environmental MP'.

At the end of 1997, Taylor could reflect on ten successful years as a Member of Parliament. In addition to his successes as a member of the parliamentary team, he has been a dedicated advocate for his constituency (now Truro & St Austell).

Neil Stockley

ROBIN TEVERSON MEP

1952–

Robin Teverson was one of the only two Liberal Democrat Members of the European Parliament elected in 1994 under the old 'winner-takes-all' system. His constituency of Cornwall & West Plymouth was taken by a majority of 29,498 on a swing of nearly ten per cent from the Conservatives.

His term as MEP has been dominated by constituency interests, notably fisheries, BSE and the peripheral status of Cornwall. Although he lacked the previous European immersion of his colleague Graham Watson (*q.v.*), Teverson quickly became a popular and useful contributor to the work of the Liberal group in the European Parliament. During his term as Chief Whip of the ELDR group from 1997, its voting cohesion and attendance record has been enhanced. His own work has focused on transport and regional affairs.

Teverson was born in Dagenham on 31 March 1952 and went to Chigwell School and Waltham Forest Technical College. He became a member of the Labour Party while a student at Exeter University, but joined the SDP in Weston-super-Mare in

1982. Having graduated in economics in 1973, he went into business. He was managing director of a UK distribution company (SPD Ltd) and director of an international logistics company (Exel Logistics).

But politics pulled. Teverson became active as a campaigner and organiser, and contributed to the growth of the Alliance in local government in Stroud, Gloucestershire from 1984–89. Having failed to win selection to fight the European Parliamentary elections in 1989, Teverson became active in Paul Tyler's (*q.v.*) Euro-campaign. He set up his own consultancy business, and became the Liberal Democrat candidate in South East Cornwall at the general election of 1992, helping to prepare the party for its breakthrough in that constituency five years later. In the 1997 general election campaign, Teverson, now an MEP, chaired the possibly difficult election team in Devon and Cornwall.

Robin Teverson describes his stance as 'constructive opposition' in Europe. His success at the European Parliamentary level should encourage those who see the European dimension as a natural extension of domestic politics and business, rather than as a highly-specialised fad.

Teverson married Rosemary Anne, an ecologist, in 1975; they have two children, Jessica Kate (1987) and Beth Emilie (1991).

Andrew Duff

MARTIN THOMAS (Lord Thomas) 1937–

When we think of fathers of the Liberal Party (or Liberal Democrats) we tend to think back either to the nineteenth century or more recently to the merger of the SDP and Liberal Party. We often forget about the state parties in Scotland and Wales. Martin Thomas was one of the founders of the Welsh Liberal Party in 1966, together with Lord Lloyd of Kilgerran, Lord Ogmore and Emlyn Hooson (*q.v.*). Over the next three decades he became part of the backbone of the Welsh party while at the same time establishing a first-class legal career. In 1996 his ennoblement gave Liberals in North Wales their first real voice in Parliament since Megan Lloyd George's (*q.v.*) departure from Anglesey in 1951.

Donald Martin Thomas was born on 13 March 1937, to Hywel and Olwen Thomas. His father was the Town Inspector and Superintendent and had served at the pithead during the rescue attempts at the Gresford mining disaster of 1935, when some 264 lives were lost and only eight bodies were recovered. Thomas was born on a council estate in Acton, Wrexham, once owned by the famous 'hanging' Judge Jeffreys. Later on he was to become the first QC, judge and peer from Acton since the days of Jeffreys.

His own legal career started because it was either a case of articles or National Service, and Thomas did not feel very military. Over the coming decades he was to become a Deputy High Court Judge, a Recorder and a bencher in Gray's Inn. He became head of one of the most successful chambers in the Temple, 1 Dr Johnson's, which also produced John Mortimer QC, Lord Hooson QC and Helena Kennedy QC. Thomas defended in the Brighton bomb case and prosecuted the charges arising out the killing of a taxi driver during the 1984 miners' strike. He has also been involved in many House of Lords and Privy Council appeals which have clarified or altered the criminal law.

Thomas was educated at Grove Park Grammar School in Wrexham, and Peterhouse, Cambridge, obtaining an LLB. His contemporaries included Tam Dalyell and John Griffith, subsequently president of the National League of Young Liberals and of the Liberal Party, although Thomas himself was not active in politics at Cambridge. He later became an active Young Liberal, and represented the Young Liberal movement as an elected member of the Liberal Party Executive for a number of years. Tony Greaves (q.v.) regarded him as incorrigibly right wing because of his strong and continued attacks on the Labour Party and his tendency to wear suits and shoes at a time when the party was better known for wearing T-shirts and sandals. He was, nevertheless, along with William Wallace (q.v.) a member of Nancy Seear's (q.v.) commission, formed in the 1970s to consider the future of the Liberal Party.

He helped to develop policy for the Welsh party throughout the 1970s and 1980s, especially in the area of constitutional reform. In 1987 he chaired the session of the Liberal assembly when the resolution to merge with the SDP was passed. In 1992 and again in 1994, he was a candidate for the Liberal Democrat Federal Presidency, fighting on the platform that the President of the party ought not always to be an MP. He was beaten by Charles Kennedy (q.v.) and Robert Maclennan (q.v.) respectively. Since then he has served the Federal Party by being a spokesman on the House of Lords home affairs team, helping to defeat substantial parts of former Conservative Home Secretary Michael Howard's legislation on law and order in the dying days of the Major Government. It was a significant victory from someone who had himself re-signed from the Criminal Injuries Compensation Board in response to Howard's alterations to the scheme in December 1993.

After marrying Nan Kerr in 1961 and starting a family, which eventually included three sons and one daughter, Thomas was ready for elected office. In 1964 he contested West Flintshire, pushing the Liberal vote up from 11 to 18.5 per cent. He contested the seat twice more before moving on to Wrexham in 1974; by October he had pushed the Conservatives into third place with 22.1 per cent of the vote. He came second to Labour's Tom Ellis, who ironically was later to defect to the SDP and became the Chair of Wrexham Liberal Democrats, of which Thomas has been President since 1975. He contested the Wrexham seat five times but found it impossible to move away from a core vote of around twenty per cent, although in 1983 he was only some 1,200 votes short of Labour with the Conservatives in between, in what was then the closest three-way tie in Britain.

Thomas proved to be a beacon for Liberals and then Liberal Democrats in North Wales and for the Welsh Liberals as a whole. He moved the Welsh party on through numerous peaks and troughs. Between 1967–69 he was Vice-Chairman of the Welsh Liberal Party, becoming Chairman between 1969–74. He was President of the party between 1977–79 and then President of the Welsh Liberal Democrats between 1993–94. Thomas had an active input into every manifesto from 1970 onwards, and drafted the 1992 and 1997 Welsh general election manifestos. His contribution to both the Welsh and national party resulted in him receiving an OBE in 1982, and being made a life peer in 1996. Ennobled as Lord Thomas of Gresford, his family motto, 'Ar Bwy Mae'r Bae?', or 'Who can we blame?', now adorns his coat of arms. Thomas' maiden speech on Lord Justice Woolf's proposals for the reform of civil procedure and the fast tracking of civil courts became just one of many speeches in the Lords over the coming years. He remains the most active voice of the Welsh Liberals in the House of Lords, battling with the Conservative and Labour Parties over devolution for Wales, just as he had done at the start of his political career, when he drafted the 1967 Parliament for Wales Bill.

Russell Deacon

SUSAN THOMAS (Lady Thomas)   1935–

Susan Thomas became involved in local politics in Richmond in the 1960s when she helped found the successful Kew Association for the Control of Aircraft Noise, one of the first groups protesting against aircraft noise. In 1974 she joined the Richmond-upon-Thames Liberal Association and helped elect the first significant group of Liberals to the borough council. From 1974 to 1977 she was first Chair, and then Treasurer, of the Association and a member of the Liberal Party Council and the London Liberal Party Executive. She served for a total of eight years first on the Liberal Standing Committee and then on the Liberal Democrats' Federal Policy Committee. As joint Chair of the Alliance working group on policy for women she was instrumental in producing *Freedom and Choice for Women*, the first Alliance policy statement adopted by both parties. She stood unsuccessfully for the Presidency of the Liberal Party in September 1987 and, following the merger with the SDP in 1988, was a member of the English Candidates Committee, later becoming its Chair. She was awarded an OBE in 1989. She has been a member of ALDC and its predecessor, the ALC, since 1985.

Thomas contested the Parliamentary seat of Mole Valley in the 1983 and 1987 general elections. She was elected county councillor for Dorking South in 1985, serving on the Education, Highways and Planning Committees. In the 1993 elections Surrey County Council agreed to an all-party administration in which the Liberal Democrats were the second largest party. She became Chair of Surrey's Highways and Transport Committee and from 1993–96 helped lead the successful fight against the government's over-ambitious plans for widening the M25 and the county's opposition to Terminal Five at Heathrow. In 1996 she became the first Liberal Chair of Surrey County Council. She retired as county councillor in 1997. She was Liberal Democrat candidate for Surrey West in the 1994 European elections, gaining a good second place. In 1996 she became a Deputy Lieutenant of Surrey.

Created a life peer in 1994 (Baroness Thomas of Walliswood) she has been Liberal Democrat front bench spokesman on transport since then. In 1997 she was elected joint Chair of the new All-Party Parliamentary Group on Sex Equality.

Susan Petronella Arrow was born in London on 20 December 1935. Her father was a journalist with the *News Chronicle* and during the Second World War worked in the Ministry of Information. Her mother is of Norwegian descent and was a civil servant during and after the war. Thomas' first political act was being pushed in her pram, waving a small red flag, as part of an anti-Franco demonstration in 1937. Educated at Cranbourne Chase School, she took a history degree at Lady Margaret Hall, Oxford, in 1957. In 1958 she married David Churchill Thomas, who had joined the Foreign Office, and accompanied him on overseas postings to Moscow, Lisbon, Lima, Washington and Havana (where he was Ambassador from 1981–84). Her interest in international affairs was most recently shown in being part of the British All-Party Parliamentary Group which helped oversee the elections and referendum on the monarchy in Albania in 1997. She has three children.

Between postings overseas, in 1973–77 and 1984–86 she worked in the National Economic Development Office. From 1977–79 she was Chief Executive of the British Clothing Industries Council for Europe, whose establishment she had recommended in a NEDO report. From 1989–92 she was a member of the East Surrey Community Health Council and from 1992–96 a non-executive Director of East Surrey Hospital and Community Trust. Currently she is a member of the Surrey Probation Committee.

Her interests outside politics, in addition to her six grandchildren, include a life-long fascination with plants, garden design and implementation – having taken a landscape gardening course whilst in Washington DC – which has been developed wherever she has lived and been on holiday.

Peter Knowlson

GEORGE THOMSON (Lord Thomson)   1921–

George Morgan Thomson was born in Dundee on 16 January 1921, the son of James Thomson. Educated at Grove Academy, Dundee, he became a journalist. He served in the RAF during the Second World War, was demobbed in 1946, and joined *Forward,* of which he was editor from 1948–53. He contested the Hillhead division of Glasgow in 1950 for the Labour Party, and was elected for Dundee East at a byelection in July

1952; he held the seat for the following twenty years. While on the back benches he was an adviser to the Educational Institute of Scotland.

Thomson held office through the whole period of the 1964–70 Wilson Governments. He was Minister of State at the Foreign Office 1964–66, Chancellor of the Duchy of Lancaster 1966–67, and Minister of State at the Foreign Office again in 1967. He entered the Cabinet as Secretary of State for Commonwealth Affairs in August 1967. In 1968 he became Minister without Portfolio and in 1969 Chancellor of the Duchy of Lancaster.

This bewildering array of offices, the product of Harold Wilson's somewhat obsessive belief in reshuffling the ministerial pack, masks the fact that throughout the period Thomson was primarily involved in two major issues: the problem of Rhodesia, and Britain's negotiations on entry to the Common Market. In October 1968 he accompanied Wilson to the unsuccessful *Fearless* talks with Ian Smith and subsequently visited Salisbury on a fruitless mission to clinch a settlement. He identified the failure to solve the problem of Rhodesian UDI successfully as extremely damaging to the Wilson Government: 'It did our standing in the world, our programme and, most of all, our self-respect, incalculable damage'. A strong proponent of British entry into the Common Market, it seems likely that Wilson would have appointed him to head a British negotiating team had Labour won the June 1970 election. In the event, in the wake of their defeat he became shadow Defence Secretary.

Although previously identified as a supporter of Callaghan, and having voted for Callaghan in the 1963 leadership election, Thomson was, through the issue of Europe, driven into an ever-closer relationship with Roy Jenkins (*q.v.*). He voted in the shadow cabinet, along with Jenkins, Lever, Crosland, Williams (*q.v.*) and Houghton, against the proposal to commit Labour to a referendum on Britain's membership of the Common Market. He was closely involved in Roy Jenkins' subsequent decision to resign the Deputy Leadership and from the shadow cabinet in April 1972. Thomson and Harold Lever resigned with Jenkins from the shadow cabinet, with Bill Rodgers (*q.v.*), Dick Taverne (*q.v.*), David Owen and Dickson Mabon giving up their frontbench positions – seen by many as a precursor of the SDP split. Thomson was one of the sixty-nine Labour MPs who voted with the Heath Government in favour of the second reading of the bill to join the Common Market. He was one of the hardcore thirteen pro-Europeans who voted for the third reading, which in the event passed by only 301 votes to 284. He chaired the Labour Committee for Europe 1972–73.

Thomson, along with Christopher Soames, became one of the UK's first European Commissioners on accession in 1973 (having resigned his seat in 1972), serving until January 1977. He was created a life peer on his return from Brussels, taking the title Baron Thomson of Monifieth. In 1978 he became involved in a clash with Wilson arising from the Bingham Inquiry, set up to determine whether or not the government had been aware of sanctions-busting by oil companies supplying Rhodesia. He remained active in pro-European politics, becoming Chairman of the European

Movement in Britain, 1977–80. Like so many of the Labour rebels of 1972, he was a founder member of the SDP in 1981.

He joined the merged party in 1989, helping to give it significant credibility in the House of Lords. Since 1990 he has been Liberal Democrat spokesman in the Lords on foreign affairs and on broadcasting.

Thomson was a member of the Advertising Standards Authority, 1977–80, and Chairman of the Independent Broadcasting Authority, 1981–88. He was Chancellor of Heriot-Watt University, 1977–91, and has also been a non-executive director of a number of companies, and trustee of several charities. He married Grace Jenkins in 1948; they have two daughters, one of whom is married to his fellow peer Dick Newby (*q.v.*).

Peter Truesdale

JEREMY THORPE   1929–

The infamy of Jeremy Thorpe's downfall unfairly colours all else in his life. Thorpe was a stylish, progressive and popular politician. Under his leadership the Liberal Party won more votes than ever before or since at a general election and helped drive legislation taking Britain into the European Community through a divided Parliament. But the much-promised breakthrough never came and Thorpe's reluctant resignation left the Liberal Party in a state from which many predicted it would be unable to recover.

John Jeremy Thorpe was born in Surrey on 29 April 1929, the son and grandson of Conservative MPs and part of a political line that can be traced to Mr Speaker Thorpe, beheaded by a mob in 1371. In 1940, as the Blitz began, he was sent to the security of the Rectory School in Connecticut, USA. The contrast between its liberal regime and that at Eton, which he attended from 1943, has been seen as a major influence on his character. At home, he came into contact through his family with the Lloyd Georges; Megan Lloyd George (*q.v.*) was an influential godmother.

Exceptionally, Thorpe served only six weeks of the usual two-year National Service and went up to Trinity College, Oxford, nominally to study law. Cutting an Edwardian dash in period clothes, a Thorpe hallmark, he associated with many at the university who achieved later distinction, as well as notable Liberal figures, including Dingle Foot (*q.v.*), beyond it. Thorpe was noted for his mimicry, speech-making and electioneering. In increasingly acrimonious campaigns he became Chairman of the Liberal Club, the Law Society and, in Hilary term 1951, the Oxford Union.

A third did not stop Thorpe moving to the Inner Temple and looking for a parliamentary seat as a Liberal. Thorpe's persistence with the party, when he could have succeeded as a left-leaning Conservative or as a Labour candidate, points to a commitment to Liberalism greater than critics have claimed. After enquires in North Wales, and the offer of North Cornwall, Thorpe fixed his attention on North Devon, safely Tory but with a Liberal past, and was adopted in 1952. He set about vote-winning with enthusiasm. His electrifying skills at the hustings and on the doorstep won him renown. In speeches he put forward then unusually liberal views on apartheid and neo-colonialism in south east Asia.

Called to the bar in 1954, he combined advocacy on the western circuit with politics and a short-lived career as a television interviewer. He fought the 1955 election with the energy of a congressional campaign, on the slogan 'A Vote for the Liberals is a Vote for Freedom'. The Conservative majority in North Devon halved. Unanimously readopted two months later, he threw himself into the 1959 election campaign, on the back of Mark Bonham Carter's (*q.v.*) 1958 triumph in next-door Torrington. Thorpe played a prominent part in that victory and went on to win North Devon by 362 votes in the 1959 general election. This was the only notable Liberal result in a disappointing election and led to wild celebrations and a torchlit procession in Barnstaple. He was to hold the seat for the following twenty years.

He made his maiden speech early and acquired a name as a backbench wit. 'Greater love hath no man than this, that he lay down his friends for his life', he said after Harold Macmillan's 'night of the long knives'. But there was a more serious side; Thorpe was at the forefront of the burgeoning human rights movement, becoming prominent in the campaign against apartheid and being banned from entering Spain by Franco.

Thorpe's speeches, particularly in 1963, were a highlight of Liberal assemblies. In October 1965, he unexpectedly stood for and won the Liberal Party's Treasurership. He proved a first-rate fund-raiser; the office also provided a platform from which he gained the Leadership and inspired criticism about his personal control of various party funds. His call, at the 1966 Liberal assembly, for V-Bombers to attack Rhodesia was seen as a publicity bid in preparation for the much-predicted resignation of the Liberal Leader, Jo Grimond (*q.v.*). On 18 January 1967 Grimond resigned and the next day, in an election among members of the parliamentary party criticised as unduly hasty, Thorpe emerged as the new Leader. Three of the twelve Liberal MPs stood; Thorpe won six votes to Emlyn Hooson's (*q.v.*) and Eric Lubbock's (*q.v.*) three apiece.

Marking his new role with a dramatic and costly rally at the Albert Hall, linked by television to sites around Britain, Thorpe hoped to strike a note as a modern radical. He became a privy councillor in March 1967 and took delight at attending prestigious official functions; he also adopted a portentous style in Parliament. Many in the party, accustomed to the simpler intellectualism of Grimond, felt uneasy. In June 1968 there was a serious bid to unseat him during his honeymoon (Thorpe had married Caroline Alpass in May). He returned to face the challenge and was overwhelmingly re-endorsed by the party executive.

Victory at the 1969 Birmingham Ladywood byelection raised hopes of a Liberal revival but the Young Liberals proved a persistent sore. Thorpe's political aims and style differed greatly from the outspoken party movement. In the 1970 general election Liberal support crashed. Thorpe only just held his seat and only six MPs were elected. The result was unexpected and Thorpe, who had spent heavily on the campaign, came

under fire. This was suspended two weeks later when Thorpe's wife was killed in a car accident. Deeply upset, he ceased most political activity for the rest of the year, later unveiling a monument in her memory. On his return to active politics, he worked successfully with the Conservative government to achieve British entry to the Common Market, one of his proudest achievements.

Thorpe's return to politics paralleled an upswing in Liberal fortunes. Four notable byelections were won in 1972 and 1973, at the same time as the party's decision to adopt the strategy of community politics was beginning to bear fruit in local government elections. Thorpe's involvement in this was limited but he campaigned to allow Ugandan Asians to settle in Britain (even accommodating a family in his house), calling Idi Amin 'this black Hitler' in a remarkable speech at the Liberal assembly in 1972.

In February 1973 Thorpe married Marion, Countess of Harewood, but his political standing was marred by his directorship of the failed London and County Securities Bank. This event was overshadowed by the economic and political crisis of February 1974, which saw Edward Heath declare a state of emergency and a general election. Thorpe successfully positioned the Liberal Party as a radical alternative; his performance caught the media eye and although he devoted much time to nursing his seat, the party received six million votes, up from two million in 1970. This translated, however, into only fourteen seats.

Heath attempted to form a government with Liberal and Ulster Unionist support. On the Saturday after the election, Thorpe met the Prime Minister, who offered him a seat in Cabinet and other ministerial posts. They discussed electoral reform; after consultation, Heath offered a Speaker's Conference but no pledge to support its recommendations. Thorpe turned this down, to the relief of the Young Liberals, many party members and most Liberal MPs, disquieted by his apparent eagerness to prop up a defeated Prime Minister. Instead, Thorpe announced his backing for a government of national unity bringing together all major parties. The Conservatives showed signs of support, but the general election of October 1974 produced a Labour majority. The result was a disappointment to Thorpe, who had campaigned on the slogan 'One More Heave'.

A deflated Liberal Party spent 1975 campaigning for devolution and for electoral reform, a response to 'The Great Vote Robbery' of the year before. Prior to the Liberal assembly of November 1975, the Young Liberals held a pre-ballot for the party leadership; their distrust of Thorpe was shared by others, but at the assembly he was unanimously backed by Liberal MPs.

This support was short-lived, as the Scott affair emerged to swamp all else. In November 1961, Thorpe had met and become friendly with a groom, Norman Josiffe (later Scott). Scott alleged that a homosexual encounter soon took place, a claim consistently denied by Thorpe. Thorpe certainly helped Scott find work and accommodation, however, and from 1966 his fellow Liberal MP, Peter Bessell (*q.v.*) made payments to him. In 1971 Scott's allegations about Thorpe's behaviour led to a party inquiry under Lord Byers (*q.v.*), which concluded that he had no case. By 1975, however, Scott's mental condition was deteriorating, and he continued to spread ever-more extreme allegations. In response, it was alleged, an assassin, Andrew Newton, was found by senior figures close to Thorpe. In October he drove Scott and his dog Rinka to Exmoor, stopped the car, shot Rinka, threatened Scott and drove off. Either the gun jammed or Newton pretended it had done so.

In January 1976 Scott appeared in court on charges of defrauding the DHSS, and made claims against Thorpe, reported under privilege. Newton was tried and gaoled for the attack on Scott in March, and in May, Bessell sold his story to the press. Thorpe attempted to pre-empt this by publishing his version, including letters to Scott, in the *Sunday Times*. The following day, 9 May 1976, he resigned as Liberal Leader and was temporarily replaced by Jo Grimond.

Newton was released from gaol in April 1977; he immediately claimed he had been hired to kill Scott. Thorpe held a press conference at which he admitted 'a close, even affectionate' relationship. Bessell accepted immunity to act as a prosecution witness; he also signed a contract with *The Daily Telegraph* in which he stood to benefit if Thorpe was convicted. Thorpe was charged with conspiracy to murder. Only one Liberal MP, John Pardoe (*q.v.*), supported his re-election campaign in the general election of the following year, and he was heavily defeated.

Thorpe's trial began on 8 May 1979; he was defended by the rising barrister George Carman QC, who destroyed the credibility of Bessell and Scott and kept Thorpe out of the witness box. The judge famously called Scott a 'crook .... liar .... whiner .... parasite .... fraud'. Initially tied at six all, the jury acquitted Thorpe and his co-defendants on 22 June.

Thorpe's career was ruined and, in the years that followed, he became ill with Parkinson's Disease. He retained a fascination with politics, became President of the North Devon Liberal, later Liberal Democrat, Association, and saw his old seat regained by Nick Harvey (*q.v.*) in 1992. In 1997 he attended the Liberal Democrat conference and received a standing ovation.

Simon Freeman and Barrie Penrose, *Rinkagate: The Rise and Fall of Jeremy Thorpe* (1996) provides a somewhat sensationalist account of the Scott affair and trial; it was inspired by L. Chester, M. Linklater and D. May, *Jeremy Thorpe: A Secret Life* (1979).

Julian Glover

VISCOUNT THURSO   1953–

When a much-loved Liberal Democrat hereditary peer dies, there is always speculation about whether his son will be of the same political persuasion. Any worries that
Lord Thurso might deviate from his family's Liberal tradition were quickly dispelled
when he took his seat on the Liberal Democrat benches in October 1995. With his
immaculate pinstripe suits, dark handlebar moustache, and assured manner, he could
perhaps have been mistaken for a Tory peer, but his speeches both in and out of the
House would soon have shown that he is a true Liberal Democrat.

Born on 10 September 1953, John Archibald Sinclair, third Viscount Thurso and
sixth Baronet of Ulbster, is the eldest son of Robin Sinclair, second Viscount Thurso,
and Margaret Robertson, and grandson of the first Viscount Thurso, better known as
Sir Archibald Sinclair (*q.v.*), the wartime Liberal Leader and Secretary of State for Air.
Educated at Summerfields and Eton he joined the Savoy company as a management
trainee in 1971. In 1978 he was made Reception Manager at Claridges and in 1981
was appointed General Manager of the Hotel Lancaster, Paris. In 1985 he returned to
England as founder General Manager and Operations Director of Cliveden, now
Britain's highest rated hotel. In 1991 he was awarded the prestigious Master Innholder
award by the Worshipful Company of Innholders. From 1993 to 1997 he served on
the Executive of the Master Innholders Association and was Chairman from 1995–97.
In 1998 he was admitted to the Livery of the Worshipful Company.

In 1992 he left Cliveden, having been head-hunted to take on the role of Chief
Executive of Granfel Holdings Ltd., and the prestigious East Sussex National Golf
Course. He is now Managing Director of Fitness & Leisure Holdings, whose principal asset is Champneys, the health resort. The year Lord Thurso spent turning its
fortunes round was captured on television, enhancing his reputation as an astute
businessman. He is now a non-executive director of several quoted companies, chairman of a number of family companies, including Thurso Fisheries Ltd., and Chairman of Scrabster Harbour Trust, Scotland's most northerly deep-water port. He is
Patron of the Hotel Catering and Institutional Management Association and of the
Institute of Management Services, President of the Academy of Food and Wine Service and a Patron of the Keepers of the Quaich.

He married Marion Ticknor, daughter of Louis D. Sage of Connecticut, USA,
and of Mrs Constance Ward, of Kinnaird, Perthshire. They have two sons and one
daughter.

Lord Thurso is a front-bench spokesman in the Lords on tourism and a member
of the trade and industry team. He is a passionate advocate of a national minimum
wage, having an unrivalled knowledge of, and experience in, the catering trade.

Celia Thomas

JENNY TONGE MP

Jennifer Louise Tonge was born in Walsall on 19 February 1941, the youngest of three children, to a family of schoolteachers. She went to Dudley Girls' High School and then University College, London, where she studied medicine. She met her husband, Keith, while dissecting a corpse; they married in the year she qualified, 1964, and now have three grown-up children. After qualification she went into family planning and general practice. In 1983 she was appointed as head of women's services for Ealing Health Authority.

Tonge's family had a history of Liberal attachment from the nineteenth century. She joined the party, inspired by the leadership of Jo Grimond (*q.v.*), at college, but had little time to be particularly active. When the first two of her children were babies she moved to Richmond-upon-Thames, where working part-time meant that she was able to become heavily involved in the local party, then, as now, one of the largest in the country. Starting as Kew Ward secretary, and living in a house just around the corner from Jo and Laura Grimond, she moved on in the local party, becoming Chair of the Richmond & Barnes constituency in 1980.

In 1981 she stood and was elected to the council, and represented Kew until 1990. For five of those years she chaired the Social Services Committee and in 1990 became a member of the Liberal Democrats' health policy working group, which she also ended up chairing. As a full-time doctor, specialising in gynaecology and family planning, Tonge was often in the media spotlight – being based in London did no harm. Several offers to become a parliamentary candidate were made and most rejected.

In 1992 she contested the Richmond & Barnes seat, coming 3,500 votes behind Jeremy Hanley, later to have a unsuccessful period as Chairman of the Conservative Party, followed by other ministerial posts. Convinced she was going to win, Tonge felt badly let down by the result and threw herself back into her medical career, becoming community services manager in Southall.

In 1997, however, 'the old bruiser' as Hanley described her kindly, decided that although she did not think she stood as good a chance, due to boundary changes which hugely increased the Tories' nominal majority, she would have another go. She went on to win the new Richmond Park constituency with a majority of 2,951, a swing from Conservative to Liberal Democrat of 9.69 per cent, with the largest turnout of voters in London.

Being made the Liberal Democrat spokesman on international development felt like coming full circle; Albert Schweitzer was the original reason she went into medicine. Membership of the Select Committee on International Development led to a high-profile involvement in the consequences of the volcanic eruption in Montserrat less than three months into her new role as an MP. She describes the experience as the steepest learning curve of her life. She is an active member of the party's foreign and defence team, while still retaining a keen interest in health matters.

Her time is divided between a tiny flat in Westminster (useful for late-night sittings, and helping her to see more of her husband, a consultant radiologist at St Thomas Hospital, than for most of the last twenty years), their house in Kew and a cottage in France.

Nick Carthew

GRAHAM TOPE (Lord Tope)   1943–

Graham Tope was appointed a life peer in 1994, following a long and energetic career as an activist in the Liberal Party and Liberal Democrats, including a brief spell as an MP following one of the most stunning byelection triumphs of the early 1970s.

Graham Norman Tope was born on 30 November 1943, an only child. His father was a master mariner with the Royal Fleet Auxiliary until he left the sea to join the health service. His mother was born in Bermuda into a colonial background. Tope's paternal grandparents were West Country Liberals from the Portsmouth area; they were nonconformists involved in the temperance movement. Tope's father supported the Liberal Party but was never actively involved, but because of his father's political interest, Tope grew up with a strong awareness of current affairs. He was educated at Whitgift School in South Croydon. In 1961, he went straight from school to employment with various Unilever companies and then in 1968–72, to Air Products Ltd.

Tope joined the Liberal Party in 1967. At the time he was going out with a woman who lived in Epsom, while Tope lived in Coulsdon, so they met regularly at a pub in Cheam, half-way in between. The young woman was a member of the Young Conservatives, but the pub they met in was also the meeting place for the local Young Liberals, and they both joined. Tope had been encouraged by Wilson's 1964 election victory, but became deeply disillusioned by the government's subsequent record. He was impressed by Jo Grimond (*q.v.*) and the activities of the Young Liberals, and so became active in the local Liberal Party, chairing Sutton & Cheam Young Liberals from 1968–69.

Tope was propelled to prominence by his imprisonment in Prague for nineteen days in 1969. Like many other young people in 1968, he was excited by the Prague Spring, the Czech communists' attempt at political liberalisation, later suppressed by Soviet troops. In summer 1969 he went on holiday with a friend, Simon Hebditch, driving and camping in Austria and Czechoslovakia. In Prague they became caught up in demonstrations to mark the first anniversary of the Prague Spring, and Tope was arrested and held without charge. On his release from prison and return to England, he found a national campaign running for his release. Press coverage of his imprisonment included a *Daily Telegraph* leader demanding speedier action by the Foreign Office in securing his freedom. When Tope arrived in England, he went straight to the Liberal assembly in Brighton, to be treated as a returning hero.

In 1970 he fought the GLC seat of Sutton & Cheam, achieving six per cent of the vote. He was Chair of South East England Young Liberals 1970–71, Vice-Chair of the National League of Young Liberals 1971–73, and its President 1973–75.

In 1972 the Conservative MP for Sutton & Cheam, Richard Sharples, was appointed Governor of Bermuda. Tope was invited to stand in the byelection for what was regarded as an unwinnable seat. There was a six-month gap between the announcement of Sharples' appointment and the byelection, however, which allowed the Liberals time to get an effective campaign up and running. It was the first Parliamentary campaign to use the *Focus* newsletter to get the Liberal message across, and people travelled from across the country to help; Trevor 'Jones the Vote' (*q.v.*) masterminded the publishing operation from Liverpool. The Liberal victory, by 7,500 votes on a 33 per cent swing, was a byelection sensation, which again pushed Tope on to the national stage. In Parliament, he became Liberal spokesman on the environment.

Although the Liberal vote held up in the February 1974 general election, the Sutton & Cheam seat suffered from a two-party squeeze and it reverted to the Conservatives. Tope became Deputy General Secretary of Voluntary Action Camden, where he remained until 1990. He then worked as a freelance political consultant until awarded his peerage in 1994.

In 1974, Tope was elected to Sutton council for Sutton Central ward, which he has held continuously ever since. He became leader of the Sutton Liberal Group in 1974 and then leader of the council when the Liberal/Alliance group took control in 1986. He has remained leader of Sutton council and chaired its Policy and Resources Committee since then. He was awarded the CBE in the 1991 Queen's Birthday Honours List, and given a life peerage, taking the title Baron Tope of Sutton, in 1994.

Tope is a highly regarded figure in the local government world, especially within London. He chaired the London Boroughs Association Policy and Finance Committee 1994–95; when the Association of London Government (ALG) was formed in 1995, he became a member of its Leaders' Committee and leader of the ALG Liberal Democrat group in 1997. He was a member of the London Fire and Civil Defence Authority 1995–97, and in 1998 became a Freeman of the City of London, a privilege his father also held.

He has also maintained a national and European profile in local government, acting as a UK representative to the European Union's Committee of the Regions since 1994. He became leader of the Committee's European Liberal Democrat and Reform Group in 1998 and is currently Vice Chair of the UK delegation. Tope has served on the Committee's bureau and on commissions on urban affairs, planning and environment, education and culture and institutional affairs.

Tope has maintained his commitment to the national party and was elected as President of London Liberal Democrats in 1991. He became the party's spokesman in the House of Lords on education and employment issues in 1994, and an assistant whip in 1998. His support for and commitment to the party lies in his belief in the rights of the individual, but not in a selfish society. Grimond's talk of the gap between government and the governed strongly influenced him at the time, and Tope still believes this is as pertinent today as it was then. His greatest political enjoyment is and always was his work with local ward constituents.

Tope lives with his wife, Margaret, a primary school teacher, in Sutton. They met at a Young Liberal conference, became engaged at a Liberal Party assembly, and got married during the 1972 byelection campaign. They have two sons, Andrew (born 1974) and David (born 1976) and a cat. He is a keen cricket-watcher, stamp collector and gardener, and prides himself on the success of his runner beans.

Jen Tankard

GEOFF TORDOFF (Lord Tordoff)   1928–

In the 1979 general election, the Liberal Party was united in running a strong campaign, and won a respectable result. That it was able to do so just months after the end of the Lib-Lab Pact and a lengthy period of electoral disaster was a strong testimony to its Chairman, Geoff Tordoff. Later, his skills as a political manager played a vital part in consummating the party's alliance with the fledging SDP.

Geoffrey Johnson Tordoff was born in Prestwich on 11 October 1928, the son of Stanley Tordoff, a welfare officer. While the family was not overtly political, his up-bringing and education gave him strong liberal and humanist values. Tordoff received his formal education at Manchester Grammar School and Manchester University, where he studied industrial chemistry. After National Service, he worked at Petro-chemicals Limited and from 1955 at Shell Chemicals as a marketing executive. Later, he was Public Affairs Manager (Chemicals) for Shell UK. Tordoff travelled abroad a great deal and developed a deep knowledge of international relations, particularly the affairs of the Middle East. In 1953, he married Mary Patricia Swarbrick and they later had two sons and three daughters.

Tordoff was motivated to join the Liberal Party by a combination of the Suez crisis and Jo Grimond's (*q.v.*) leadership. He played a major role in revitalising the North West regional party after the locust years of the 1940s and 1950s. Tordoff was an office-holder in both the North West Federation and the North West Candidates' Association, which he helped to found. He fought Northwich in 1964 and Knutsford in 1966 (coming second) and again in 1970. He was firmly identified with the pro-gressive Liberalism of the Grimond era and became well respected for his sound grasp of a wide range of issues.

But it was as a 'fixer' that Tordoff made his principal contributions, first as a member of the Assembly Committee and then as its Chairman (1974–76). Through his deep understanding of party opinion and strong links with many groups, he was able to use the party's democratic institutions to absorb and manage conflict.

In 1976, soon after David Steel (*q.v.*) became Leader, he began three years as Chairman of the Liberal Party. In this role, Tordoff successfully guided the party organisation through one of the most difficult episodes in its recent history, the eighteen-month-long formal pact under which Liberal MPs sustained the Callaghan Government in the Commons in return for being consulted on policy and legislation. Tordoff ensured that Steel was kept aware of party members' views about the pact and, in turn, that members knew what their leader was trying to achieve. In so doing, he helped Steel to pass some critical tests with the party, including the formation of the pact in March 1977 and its renewal three months later. In February 1978, a special assembly passed overwhelmingly a compromise motion that Tordoff had played a major part in drafting. The motion made it clear that the party expected the pact to run its course within five months. However, Steel was given a mandate to continue the pact until he decided, after consulting with senior party officers and MPs, that it should end.

Throughout this tense period, Tordoff succeeded in maintaining the integrity of the party organisation. He and his close friend and ally, the party President Gruyff (later Lord) Evans, formed a formidable 'double act' to manage debate and dissent. The sincere and courteous Tordoff adopted the more modest and measured approach. The great majority of party members trusted him as an 'honest insider' who could be relied upon to give both sides an informed perspective. His credibility was greatly helped by the fact that he had earned his political spurs in the unpromising territory of the north west.

As Chairman of the Campaigns and Elections Committee (1980–82) and President of the Liberal Party (1983–84), Tordoff was deeply committed to making a success of the newly formed alliance with the SDP, and built up effective working relationships with many of the SDP's leading figures. During the critical negotiations over the allocation of seats to be fought by each party, he played a key role in managing the inevitable difficulties on the Liberal side – an important contribution, for if those negotiations had failed, the Alliance would surely have collapsed.

Tordoff was elevated to the Lords in 1981, taking the title Baron Tordoff of Knutsford, and took early retirement from Shell in order to play a full part in its work. Three years later, he became Liberal Chief Whip and, following the merger with the SDP in 1988, the new party's Chief Whip. Tordoff used all his bonhomie and experience as a negotiator to make a success of this role. He was extremely well liked by all who dealt with him. He was also a skilful participant in parliamentary manoeuvres, most notably late-night ambushes of the Conservative government. As transport spokesman in the Lords, he was at the forefront of the peers' efforts to mitigate the worst aspects of the legislation to privatise rail.

By 1994, Tordoff needed fresh challenges, and withdrew from party politics to become Principal Deputy Chairman of Committees, and Chairman of the Select Committee on the European Communities. He has been able to forge consensus amongst the committee's diverse range of personalities and viewpoints. Under his leadership, the committee has drawn upon a range of leading authorities to influence the development of 'official' thinking on European integration.

Tordoff was Chairman of the Middle East Committee of the British Refugee Council from 1990–95. He was Honorary President of the British Youth Council from 1986–92 and has been a member of the Press Complaints Commission since 1995. During the 1990s, he has taken part in election monitoring in Bulgaria, Zambia, Kenya, Mozambique and South Africa.

Today, Lord and Lady Tordoff live in Somerset. He continues to enjoy classical music, the theatre, reading and natural history and his garden – 'to sit in, not to work on'.

Neil Stockley

PAUL TYLER MP   1941–

Paul Tyler has laboured under the great problem of having been a Cornishman born and bred in Devon. Claiming to be a direct descendant of Bishop Jonathan Trelawny (on whose behalf '20,000 Cornishmen' threatened to march on London in 1688), in 1969 he complained when he was not allowed to join the Sons of Cornwall.

Paul Archer Tyler was born in south Devon on 29 October 1941, the son of Oliver Tyler and Ursula Tyler, née May. His career has been infused with politics from his days at university in the early 1960s until today. Following schooling at Sherborne School, he went to Exeter College, Oxford, where in 1962 he was elected President of the Oxford University Liberal Club. He then began a long career in the communications field, working in PR, public affairs and journalism. His first job was at the Royal Institute of British Architects from 1966–74, where he eventually became Public Affairs Director. He married Nicky Ingram in 1970, and they have two children, Sophie and Dominick.

In 1964 Tyler was elected Britain's youngest county councillor, in Devon; he was re-elected in 1967. He became Vice Chairman of the Dartmoor National Park Committee and a member of the Devon & Cornwall Police Authority. In 1966, he contested Totnes and in 1968 was selected to fight the Bodmin constituency after the Liberal MP Peter Bessell's (*q.v.*) announcement of his retirement and subsequent move to the US.

He lost Bodmin by 3,920 votes to the Conservative Robert Hicks in 1970, but was elected with a majority of nine in February 1974. He was appointed Liberal spokesman on housing, transport and rate reform. In the October 1974 election he increased the Liberal vote, but not sufficiently to withstand the swing against the party, and lost by 655 votes. After losing the seat, Tyler worked as the Cornwall and Devon organiser for Shelter, the national campaign for the homeless, in 1975–76. He then worked as Managing Director of the *Cornwall Courier* local newspaper group, 1976–81, He was a frequent contributor to a wide range of media, and presenter of BBC South West TV's *Discovery* series in 1978.

Tyler contested Bodmin again in May 1979, when his vote fell to 35 per cent, with Hicks building up a 10,029 majority. He fought the Beaconsfield byelection in 1982 during the outbreak of the Falklands War. The Labour candidate was a young unknown, Tony Blair, who fell to third place. Tyler was joint author of the Liberal report *A New Deal for Rural Britain*, in 1978, and was secretary to the Liberal/SDP joint commission which produced the *Back to Work* report in 1982.

He was David Steel's (*q.v.*) campaign organiser in the 1983 general election, and was elected Chairman of the Liberal Party 1983–86. He was awarded the CBE in the Queen's Birthday Honours List in 1985. He was campaign adviser to David Steel, and a member of the Alliance Planning Group, 1986–87, and a member of the campaign team led by John Pardoe (*q.v.*) in the 1987 general election.

Professionally, he became a senior consultant responsible for political and public issue assignments at Good Relations plc, 1982–92 (acting for, amongst others, the Countryside Commission, Meat & Livestock Commission, European Year of the Environment, Association of County Councils, and Rural Development Commission). After the 1987 election, he set up his own office in Plymouth, advising clients on environmental policy, which he continued until after the 1992 general election.

Tyler was the Liberal Democrat candidate for the Cornwall & Plymouth constituency in the European election of June 1989. He reduced the Conservative majority to 8.7 per cent, cut the Labour share of the poll and gained 68,559 votes to come second – the best result in the country, and, indeed, the only result better than fourth place. He was elected as MP for North Cornwall in April 1992, taking the seat from the Conservative Sir Gerry Neale by 1,927 votes, to hold the record for the longest interval between leaving the Commons and returning. It is interesting to note that Tyler was backed by both his local Green Party and the Cornish nationalists Mebyon Kernow.

He was appointed Liberal Democrat spokesman on rural affairs, agriculture and transport, and was also a member of the Select Committee on Procedure. In 1994–95 he piloted a review of party transport policy, and in 1996 published *Country Lives, Country Landscapes*, a paper on rural policy.

Tyler held his seat at the 1997 general election with the Liberal Democrats' largest majority of 13,933, taking over 53 per cent of the vote. He was elected as Chief Whip and Shadow Leader of the House, and also speaks on food policy for the Parliamentary party. He is a member of the Select Committee on Modernisation, Convenor of the All-Party Group concerned with organophosphates, Chair, All-Party Coastal Group, Joint Secretary, All-Party Water Group and Treasurer, All-Party Tourism Group.

Tyler is an effective parliamentary campaigner who is a first-rate strategist and political tactician. During his time as a PR professional he gained the Institute of Public Relations' Sword of Honour, and has applied his skills in Parliament on a wide range of local and national issues.

Jon Sacker

DONALD WADE (Lord Wade) 1904–88

Donald William Wade was born at Ilkley, Yorkshire, on 16 June 1904, the son of William Mercer and Beatrice Hemington Wade. He was educated at Mill Hill and Trinity Hall, Cambridge where he obtained MA and LLB degrees. He trained for a legal career, and became a solicitor in 1929. In 1932, he married Ellenora Beatrice Bentham, and the couple had two sons and two daughters.

Wade captured the constituency of Huddersfield West at the 1950 general election. His victory was aided by a local arrangement with the Conservative Party in which Wade was given a straight fight against Labour, and the Liberal Party withdrew its candidate in Huddersfield East. No formal pact was signed between the Conservative and Liberal organisations in Huddersfield, although the two parties were close in municipal politics. Wade held his seat at the 1951, 1955 and 1959 general elections, and the arrangement from which he benefited was adopted, although more formally, in Bolton to assist the election of Arthur Holt (*q.v.*) for the West constituency in 1951. The abandonment of the Bolton pact in 1960 resulted in the collapse of the Huddersfield arrangement, and Wade lost his seat, albeit narrowly, in 1964. He was elevated to the peerage the same year, taking the title Baron Wade of Huddersfield.

Wade occupied a number of key offices in the Liberal Party. He served as Chief Whip in the House of Commons between 1956–62 and as Deputy Chairman of the Liberal MPs 1962–64. He subsequently became Deputy Whip in the House of Lords 1965–67 and President of the Liberal Party in 1967.

He was also active in local affairs in Yorkshire. He served as chairman of the Yorkshire Committee for Community Relations prior to the passage of the 1968 Race Relations Act. He was Deputy Lieutenant of the West Riding (1967) and Deputy Lieutenant of North Yorkshire (1974).

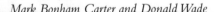

Mark Bonham Carter and Donald Wade

Wade was a passionate advocate of the cause of liberty and his key contribution to Liberalism lay in the evolution of Liberal philosophy. He served as Chairman of the party's commission appointed to examine the Liberal philosophy in 1968. He also made four unsuccessful attempts in the House of Lords to promote a Bill of

Rights incorporating the European Convention of Human Rights into English law. He was a vigorous advocate of co-partnership in industry, and free trade.

He wrote several publications related to Liberal Party politics, including *Liberalism, its Task in the Twentieth Century* (1944), *Way of the West* (1945), *Towards a Nation of Owners* (1958), *Our Aim and Purpose* (first published in 1961), *Yorkshire Service: A Report on Community Relations in Yorkshire* (1972), *The Political Insight of Elliott Dodds* (1977) and *Behind the Speaker's Chair* (1978).

He died on 6 November 1988, in Harrogate.

Peter Joyce

RICHARD WAINWRIGHT 1918–

Throughout his career, Richard Wainwright has been popular with the Liberal Party's grassroots activists who have flown the flag in local and national elections, on councils and within the party structure. He was perceived to be one of them, always approachable, indefatigable not only at byelections but in between, always accompanied on the stump by his wife Joyce, and one of the main pillars of the Yorkshire Liberal Federation. He consolidated his reputation within the party as Chairman of the Research Department from 1968–70, and as Chairman of the Liberal Party between 1970–72. There, and in Parliament, his firm grasp of policy, particularly on the economic front, was appreciated and relied upon by his colleagues.

Richard Scurrah Wainwright was born on 11 April 1918, and educated at Shrewsbury School and Clare College, Cambridge, where he gained a BA (Hons) in history in 1939. During the Second World War, he served with the Friends Ambulance Unit in north west Europe. Methodism has been a strong thread in Wainwright's life, and he was a local preacher.

He was first elected to represent the Colne Valley constituency, which then stretched from the outskirts of Huddersfield across the Pennines to the outskirts of Oldham, at the 1966 general election. He lost his seat in 1970, but was re-elected in February 1974. He then retained the Colne Valley consecutively in October 1974, 1979, and 1983, despite boundary changes. He retired from Parliament in 1987. He had no desire to enter the House of Lords, joking that 'you only visit a cemetery, you don't live there'.

Although the fortunes of the Liberal Party fluctuated widely during his time as an MP, Wainwright played a pivotal part in the two major developments of the seventies, the Thorpe affair and the Lib-Lab Pact.

As the party's spokesman on trade and industry, he shadowed the then Trade and Industry Secretary, Eric Varley, during the Pact, and also had a continuing dialogue with the late Harold Lever, who was Chancellor of the Duchy of Lancaster. These relationships were more productive than some of the prickly partnerships between Labour ministers and Liberal MPs, and he got on particularly well with Lever.

The Thorpe affair was more problematic for Wainwright, and he found himself unexpectedly at odds with the party's grassroots as a result of his call in May 1976 for Jeremy Thorpe (*q.v.*) to stand down temporarily as Leader while he cleared his name. It was a difficult time for everyone in the parliamentary party as they were in possession of much information that was not widely known, and their actions were therefore sometimes misunderstood and misinterpreted. Wainwright suffered antagonism from party workers and consequent media pressure at the Liberal assembly at Southport at which the MPs' attitude to Thorpe's leadership was heavily criticised.

Wainwright was proud to be a member of the Commons Treasury Select Committee from its inception in 1979 until he retired in 1987. During this time he participated wholeheartedly in the Committee's various inquiries, work which he relished. On behalf of the Liberal Parliamentary Party, he was variously the trade and industry spokesman (participating in the marathon committee stage of the Aircraft and Shipbuilding Bill and shadowing Michael Heseltine on the famous occasion when he seized the House of Commons mace), and Treasury spokesman.

Outside Parliament, Wainwright was a partner in the accountants Peat Marwick Mitchell & Co, and was President of the Leeds-Bradford Society of Chartered Accountants from 1965–66. He was Deputy Chairman of the Wider Share Ownership Council, a particularly closely-held and steadfastly promoted belief.

He married Joyce Hollis in 1948. They have always lived in Leeds, and are justifiably well-known for their prize-winning love of gardens and gardening. They celebrated their fiftieth wedding anniversary in January 1998, surrounded by their family. They have one son, Martin, the *Guardian* journalist and broadcaster, and two daughters, Hilary, the editor of the radical *Red Pepper* magazine, and Tessa. Their other son, Andrew, committed suicide during the February 1974 election campaign.

Caroline Cawston

JIM WALLACE MP   1954–

James Robert Wallace was born in Annan, Dumfriesshire, on 25 August 1954. He attended his local secondary school, Annan Academy, where he was soon recognised as an academic high flyer. Lead roles in end of term Gilbert and Sullivan productions showed an early flair for performing in public and a love of these light operettas which he has retained.

His university career brought him a first at Downing College, Cambridge, and a postgraduate law degree at Edinburgh, and helped to hone an almost photographic memory for names, places and dates. It was also the real start of the young Wallace's political ambitions, which had actually begun when he was the Liberal candidate in a school mock election. He joined the party in 1972, having read Russell Johnston's (*q.v.*) *To be a Liberal.*

A member of the Liberal Club at Cambridge, an active Young Liberal on his return to Scotland, and Chairman of the University Liberal Club at Edinburgh, his first foray at the ballot box proper was as the Liberal candidate in Dumfries in 1979, closely followed as the Euro-candidate in the South of Scotland the same year. Respectable votes, membership of the Scottish Party Executive and a growing reputation as a platform speaker, brought him to the attention of senior members in the party. He became an advocate at the Scottish bar in 1979.

Wallace was elected as Vice-Chairman (Policy) of the Scottish Liberal Party in 1982, the year in which politics began to take a new shape with the growth of the SDP. He was much involved in the early negotiations leading to the Liberal/SDP Alliance, and in particular the fraught and difficult seat allocation. Despite this, however, in a local south of Scotland agreement, Dumfries was ceded to the SDP in the run-up to the 1983 general election and he had to turn his sights elsewhere. A brief period as prospective candidate for Perth & Kinross was followed by an invitation to put his name forward for the Orkney & Shetland nomination, vacant following Jo Grimond's (q.v.) decision to retire from the Commons, as assured a passage to Westminster as the Liberal Party could offer. With support from Laura Grimond (q.v.), the candidacy was won. Within a few months he was elected for the seat, the first person since the Second World War to inherit a Liberal-held seat at a general election. In the same summer he married Rosie Fraser from Milngavie, with whom he now has two daughters, Helen and Clare.

Wallace became Parliamentary spokesman on energy, and then on defence during a time when there were many difficult party debates and fall-outs with the SDP over the party's attitude to nuclear weapons. His solid, level-headed handling of this brief and his reputation as 'a safe pair of hands' made him an obvious choice for Chief Whip after the 1987 election (1988–92), and it was in this role that he boosted his reputation among the other parties at Westminster. He was Alliance spokesman on transport from January to June 1987. He was an avid supporter of merger with the SDP and after re-election in 1987, under Paddy Ashdown's (q.v.) leadership, he was given the employment portfolio as well as being Whip. The fisheries spokesmanship, reflecting his own constituency interests, has been an ever-present adjunct to his other jobs at Westminster. In the 1992 general election, Wallace resisted the Conservative come-back in Northern Scotland which led to the loss of byelection victor Nicol Stephen and almost, Sir Russell Johnston and Malcolm Bruce (q.v.).

Bruce stood down as Scottish party leader after the election and Wallace was elected unopposed in his place, in 1993. His passionate advocacy of Scottish home rule was to find an effective channel through the Scottish Constitutional Convention. Here, alongside Donald Dewar and George Robertson, an agreed scheme for the Scottish Parliament, including a measure of proportional representation, was finally agreed just before the 1997 general election. Wallace's first election in charge of the Scottish party led to the election of ten MPs, the largest number in Scotland at a general election for over seventy years. In Orkney & Shetland he was also able to celebrate his own re-election, with the biggest Liberal Democrat percentage majority in the whole of Britain. He also achieved recognition for his assiduous work in many areas of Scottish political life from the retiring Secretary of State for Scotland, Michael Forsyth, by being created a QC.

Alongside Donald Dewar and Alex Salmond, Jim was a prominent leader in the successful Scottish Parliament referendum campaign in autumn 1997, for which he has been recognised with a number of awards, including one from the Saltire Society. With Labour's subsequent implementation of the Convention scheme, a long-held Scottish Liberal cause is finally within its grasp and an historic moment beckons. Wallace's long pondered-over decision to stand for the Orkney half of his Westminster constituency in the Scottish Parliamentary elections in 1999 mean that he stands an excellent chance of becoming part of the first Scottish government in nearly three hundred years – a reward which many Liberal politicians would sell their soul for, and for which he is justly deserving.

Ron Waddell

WILLIAM WALLACE (Lord Wallace) 1941–

Although never elected to Parliament, Westminster was still to play a major role in William Wallace's life, first as a schoolboy and later as a member of the upper chamber.

Born in Leicester on 12 March 1941, William John Lawrence Wallace was a chorister at Westminster Abbey Choir School, becoming Senior Chorister in 1954. He won an exhibition to read history at King's College, Cambridge, in 1959. The son of apolitical parents, Wallace joined all three political clubs in Cambridge, decided that the Liberal Club was the most attractive and in 1961 defeated Michael Steed (*q.v.*) for the Vice-Presidency of the club, going on to become President in 1962. Following three years at Cornell University in the United States, Wallace returned to Britain, this time to Nuffield College, Oxford, to write his PhD on the Liberal revival 1955–66.

While at Oxford Wallace met his future wife, Helen – she was President of the Oxford University Liberal Club at the time. Unlike William, she came from a strong political background: her father, Edward Rushworth, was one of the few who kept the torch of Liberalism alight in the 1950s as a member of the Radical Reform Group.

Wallace served as the Liberal Party's Assistant Press Officer, responsible for Jo Grimond's (*q.v.*) press activities in the 1966 general election. He was appointed lecturer in the Department of Government at the University of Manchester in 1967 and in 1970 fought the first of five parliamentary elections, in Huddersfield West. Wallace fought his local constituency of Manchester Moss Side twice in 1974. In the mid-1970s he was an adviser to then Liberal leader, David Steel (*q.v.*), and served as Vice-Chairman of the Standing (later Policy) Committee from 1977–87. He co-wrote the

1979 election manifesto, a job he also undertook for the Liberal Democrats in 1997, and has served on numerous policy committees.

Wallace fought the Yorkshire seat of Shipley in the 1983 and 1987 general elections and retained strong connections with the constituency, most demonstrably in the title – Lord Wallace of Saltaire, of Shipley in the County of West Yorkshire – he chose when created a working peer in 1995. As a member of the House of Lords, Wallace replaced Christopher Mayhew (q.v.) as Liberal spokesman on defence in 1996 and in 1997 became a member of the Select Committee on the European Communities, and chairman of the Sub-Committee on Justice and Home Affairs. In 1997 he contested the Leadership of the Liberal Democrats in the House of Lords, gaining twenty votes compared to thirty-six for Lord Rodgers of Quarry Bank (q.v.).

Professionally, Wallace was Director of Studies of the Royal Institute of International Affairs (Chatham House) from 1978 until 1990. He was Walter Hallstein Senior Research Fellow at St. Antony's College, Oxford (1990–95) and since 1995 has been a Reader in International Relations at the London School of Economics. He was also Head of the European Studies Department of the Central European University in Prague and later visiting professor when the department moved to Budapest in 1996. Among his publications are *The Foreign Policy Process in Britain* (1976), *The Transformation of Western Europe* (1990), *Regional Integration: the West European Experience* (1994) and *Policy-Making in the European Union* (1996), the last of these co-edited with his wife. His political writing includes the Penguin book, *Why Vote Liberal Democrat?* (1997), the latest in a line of election specials for which former Liberal authors have included Roger Fulford (q.v.) and Alan Beith (q.v.).

He lives in Wandsworth, in south London, and has one son and one daughter.

Julie Smith

GRAHAM WALLAS   1858–1932

Graham Wallas was born in Sunderland on 31 May 1858, the son of an Evangelical clergyman of the Church of England who later became Rector of Shobrooke in Devon, where the young Wallas was brought up. He went to public school at Shrewsbury and thence to Corpus Christi College, Oxford, where he read Greats. Wallas then took a post as a classics teacher at Highgate School in North London. In 1885 came the great crisis in his life: he rejected Christianity on rationalist grounds, resigned accordingly from his teaching post, and threw himself into the study of socialism.

Like his Oxford friend Sydney Olivier, and his new acquaintances Bernard Shaw and Sidney Webb, Wallas now found in the Fabian Society the sort of intellectual milieu where he felt at home. Subsequently overshadowed by the reputation of Shaw and the Webbs, Graham Wallas remains the forgotten man of the early Fabian Society, which he and Olivier joined in May 1885. With them he elaborated the theory of evolutionary collectivism which *Essays in Fabian Socialism* (1889), edited by G. B. Shaw, proclaimed to a wider public. Critical of Marxism, Wallas remained a Liberal in party politics, committed to a strategy of permeation rather than an independent socialist or labour party.

Wallas worked for years on *The Life of Francis Place* (1898), analysing the activities of an early nineteenth-century radical who played a notable part in changing the labour legislation of his day. This readiness to take 'a great deal of trouble to find out how things were really done before we began trying to do them' won high praise from Shaw. It was this practical, well-briefed, dispassionate, empirical aspect of Fabianism which really appealed to Wallas.

In 1895 he was strongly in favour of the scheme for using a bequest to the Fabian Society, not for political propaganda, but for academic research and teaching. This was the origin of the London School of Economics, of which Wallas was appointed the first Director. He declined to serve in this post but remained associated with the LSE, notably as Professor of Political Science 1914–23.

While Wallas' academic career blossomed, his Fabian commitment waned. One influence upon him was his period of service in local government. He was a member of the London School Board, 1894–1904, and chairman of the School Management Committee, 1897–1904. In parallel, he served on the London County Council's Technical Education Board, 1897–1904, and, after the LCC took over responsibility for elementary education, he became a councillor, 1904–07. After the Progressives' defeat in the municipal elections of 1907, Wallas continued as a co-opted member of the LCC Education Committee until 1910. He thus knew local politics from the inside and was thrown into opposition to the Conservatives' Education Act of 1902, which Webb supported on administrative grounds.

Wallas finally resigned from the Fabian Society in 1904 because of Shaw's attempt to associate it with protectionism, another Conservative policy. The root cause was a divergence between the manipulative and authoritarian temper which Shaw and the Webbs increasingly displayed and Wallas' Liberal outlook. In 1898 Wallas had married Ada Radford, a woman of strong literary interests, and a firm Liberal (they had one daughter). The Wallases drifted apart from the Webbs and the Shaws, though remaining on civil terms.

The political thinking of Wallas' mature years was associated with the New Liberalism, as propagated by his friends and colleagues L. T. Hobhouse (*q.v.*) and J. A. Hobson (*q.v.*). Like them, he argued for a democratic collectivism in social policy, to be implemented through a progressive alliance between the Liberal and Labour Parties. Yet in *Human Nature in Politics* (1908) he sought to inject some worldly scepticism into idealistic notions of how a democratic political system actually worked. The critical impact of the book is admittedly more powerful than its constructive suggestions. Wallas sought to remedy this deficiency in later works like *The Great Society* (1914) and *Our Social Heritage* (1921) but they lack the cutting edge of his masterpiece.

For all that his insights into irrationalist trends had made him fearful of war, the events of August 1914 came as a shock to Wallas. He worked with Hobson in organising a British Neutrality Committee, but the German invasion of Belgium doomed their efforts. By 1915 he was telling American readers that 'I intensely desire victory for the Allies' and, like many other Liberals, his hopes were now pinned upon the prospects of post-war international cooperation.

It was the attempt to rethink democratic theory in the light of modern findings in social psychology which became Wallas' lifework. He pointed to the strong irrational – or, at any rate non-rational – forces which influenced political attitudes and to the role of party in mediating electoral opinion. Yet he manifested a strong faith in democracy. Wallas' point was that progressives needed a clear-eyed understanding of the frailties of the democratic process. The influence of his ideas was felt particularly in the United States, which he frequently visited. Retirement from his chair did not diminish his political interests and he remained active until his sudden death in London in August 1932.

There is a useful study of his work by Terence H. Qualter, *Graham Wallas and the Great Society* (1980) and a good intellectual biography by Martin J. Wiener, *Between Two Worlds: the political thought of Graham Wallas* (1971).

Peter Clarke

GRAHAM WATSON MEP   1956–

As head of David Steel's (*q.v.*) private office from June 1983 to September 1987, Graham Watson was at the heart of the Alliance. His suavity and fluency were evident in Steel's polished performance during the final period of his leadership of the Liberal Party. The pair of fellow Scots displayed similar qualities of determination, expediency and self-possession, and with Watson as his right-hand-man, Steel was able to advance the party to unprecedented levels of importance.

Not unambitious in his own right, Watson joined the Young Liberals in 1972 and was very active in student politics at Heriot-Watt University, Edinburgh, from which he graduated in modern languages in 1979. He was also Vice-President and then honorary General Secretary of the International Federation of Liberal and Radical Youth (IFLRY). He was a founding member of the EC Youth Forum and an editor of Young Liberal magazines.

Born in Rothesay, Isle of Bute, on 23 March 1956, Watson had attended thirteen different schools throughout the Empire before his father, a Royal Naval officer, was posted to the Admiralty and his son settled at the City of Bath Boys' School from 1970–74.

After university, Watson spent some months abroad honing his interpretation skills. He was appointed public relations officer at Paisley College of Technology in 1980.

When the national party refused to nominate a candidate, Watson stood as a Young Liberal in a byelection in Glasgow Central in June of that year, followed by a second byelection, this time as the Liberal/SDP Alliance candidate, in Glasgow Queens Park, in December 1982. Membership of the executive of the Scottish Liberal Party led to his employment with David Steel.

After the 1987 general election, Watson worked for the Hong Kong and Shanghai Banking Corporation in Hong Kong and London, and, briefly in 1991, for the European Bank for Reconstruction and Development. By that time he had set his sights on securing the nomination for the Somerset European constituency.

Watson was the first Liberal Democrat prospective candidate in place, and the first to be declared elected, by some hours in front of Robin Teverson (*q.v.*) in Cornwall, in June 1994. His constituency of Somerset & Devon North was taken by a majority of 22,509 on a nine per cent swing from the Conservatives.

Well-equipped as he was for the job, Watson wasted no time before becoming an active Member of the European Parliament, mostly in budgetary, economic and monetary affairs, with a good eye for publicity. He was rapporteur on the functioning of the single market in 1994–95. He has also been noteworthy in promoting human rights issues in Hong Kong. Watson is a true believer in and persuasive advocate of European federalism, while not neglecting the (for a Liberal) essential work in the constituency. In 1998 Watson was elected to head the Liberal Democrat list in the South-West constituency for the 1999 Euro elections.

He married Rita Giannini, an Italian lawyer and Partito Liberale activist, in September 1987; they have two children, Frederica (born 1992) and Gregory (1995).

Andrew Duff

STEVE WEBB MP   1965–

Steven John Webb was first elected to Parliament at the 1997 general election as the MP for Northavon. He speaks on social security and welfare for the Liberal Democrats. Before entering Parliament, he had already established a reputation as an expert in the field of personal tax and benefits and welfare reform.

Webb joined the Liberal Democrats in 1992, following his disappointment at the re-election of the Conservatives at the general election of that year. Since graduating with a first from Oxford in 1986, he had worked as an economist at the Institute for Fiscal Studies (a non-political research institute, founded by Dick Taverne (*q.v.*), which examines the effects of the tax and benefit system on individuals and companies) and then, from 1995, as Professor of Social Policy at Bath University.

During his time at IFS, Webb specialised in the workings of the personal tax and benefit system, and published widely on trends in poverty and inequality in the UK. His major publications include *Inequality in the UK* (with Alissa Goodman and Paul

Johnson, 1997) and *For Richer, For Poorer: The Changing Distribution of Income in the UK 1961–91* (1994). He achieved a number of distinctions, including acting as a specialist advisor to the House of Commons Select Committee on Social Security, then chaired by Frank Field MP, and taking part in an IMF technical assistance mission to the Ukraine to advise on welfare reform.

Webb was a member of the Liberal Democrat policy groups which produced *Retirement with Dignity* (policies for older and retired people, 1993) and *Opportunity and Independence for All* (policies on tax and benefits, 1994). He was a member of the group which costed the 1997 election manifesto. He was a Liberal Democrat representative on Labour's Commission for Social Justice, set up by the late John Smith and continued, after Smith's death in 1994, by Tony Blair. He described his role on the Commission as a 'number-cruncher' and he worked closely with many leading Labour figures.

After his selection in March 1995 as the candidate for Northavon, Webb moved from the strictly non-political IFS to the University of Bath, where he became Professor of Social Policy. He held this post until his election to Parliament in May 1997. Given his background, it was not surprising that the media swiftly nicknamed him 'five brains'. He is member of the editorial board of the Liberal Democrats' 1998 policy review, and a member of the commission reviewing social security policy. He is also a member of the advisory board of the Centre for Reform, a think-tank associated with, but separate from, the Liberal Democrats.

His proudest moment in his first year in Parliament was leading the opposition to the cuts in lone-parent benefits. Although the amendment he moved was lost, it sparked the biggest rebellion by Labour backbenchers since the election. It was acknowledged that he had won the argument, and the government subsequently took on board several of the points he raised as they modified their policy towards benefit cuts. In the long term, Webb would like to see the Liberal Democrats taking a major role in the welfare debate, and to be respected as purveyors of a positive policy of reform rather than noticed only for opposing cuts.

Webb is a committed Christian and takes an active role in his village church, acting from time to time as organist. He has a strong commitment to give marginalised people a voice and is a supporter of the Jubilee 2000 campaign to end Third World debt. Within his constituency, he has made great attempts to stay in touch with all his constituents and to stay aware of their concerns.

Born in Birmingham on 18 July 1965, Webb attended the local comprehensive, Dartmouth High School, from where he won a scholarship to read politics, philosophy and economics at Hertford College, Oxford. In 1993, he married Helen, an Anglican curate working in London. She subsequently became assistant chaplain at Southmead Hospital near Bristol, which prompted the couple's move to the West Country. They have two young children, a daughter and a son, and live in the constituency.

Katie Hall

SAMUEL WHITBREAD   1764–1815

Samuel Whitbread, the leader of the radical Whigs for much of their long spell in opposition during the Napoleonic wars, was born on 17 January 1764 in London, the third child and only son of Harriet (née Hayton) and Samuel Whitbread MP (1720–96), the brewing magnate and Bedfordshire landowner. His mother died shortly after his birth and he was brought up by his maternal grandmother and an aunt. Whitbread went to Eton at the age of eleven and six years later matriculated at Christ Church, Oxford, before transferring to St John's, Cambridge the following year. In January 1788 he married Elizabeth Grey, the sister of Charles Grey, later the second Earl Grey (q.v.), his friend from Eton and university days. They had two sons, one of whom became an MP, and two daughters. On his father's death Whitbread took over the management of the brewing business, proving less successful than his father. He also inherited some 12,000 acres of land, not only in Bedfordshire, but also in Hertford-shire, Wiltshire, Essex and Kent, and like his father before him undertook many of the duties associated with such wealth, serving in Bedfordshire as a Justice of the Peace and as a lieutenant-colonel of the county militia.

However, it was in Whig politics that Whitbread's contribution was to prove most significant. In June 1790 he was returned as MP for the borough of Bedford, a seat he held without a contest until his death. In the House of Commons he joined in with Foxite opposition to the French wars, helping to establish the 'Society of the Friends of the People' in 1792. Whitbread spoke out against Pitt's repressive domestic legislation of the mid-1790s, particularly press censorship and civil disabilities. During the long years of European warfare he also backed a number of schemes for social amelioration. In 1785 and again in 1800 he tried unsuccessfully to make Parliament give JPs the power to determine local agricultural wage rates. In 1807 he introduced a series of bills: to encourage savings amongst the labouring poor, to exempt the very poor from liability for poor rates (which provoked the disapproval of Thomas Malthus), and to provide for free national education. Throughout the period Whitbread also supported parliamentary reform, which he saw in classic Whig terms as a means of reducing the influence of the Crown. Whitbread was also an indefatigable supporter of the peace movement. He was not only convinced of the moral abhorrence of war, but like Richard Cobden (q.v.) and other liberals later in the nineteenth century, he also believed in the principle of non-intervention. In 1808 he presented petitions to Parliament calling for a negotiated peace with Napoleon, but his francophilia alienated many of his Whig colleagues.

Two episodes did most to ensure Whitbread's notoriety as the leader of the radical wing of the Whigs. In 1805 he led calls for the impeachment of Lord Melville, the former Treasurer of the Navy, for his complicity in financial dishonesty. Melville resigned his position as Lord of the Admiralty, but Whitbread persisted and Melville was eventually tried by both Houses of Parliament, much to the government's embarrassment. In a similar manner, during the winter of 1812–13, Whitbread, along with Henry Brougham, masterminded the public relations of Caroline, the Princess of Wales, the estranged wife of the Prince Regent, helping her to secure a parliamentary grant of £35,000 per annum as compensation for her 'injuries'.

Whitbread took his own life on 6 July 1815, following a series of depressive bouts and financial problems which beset him after he became involved in rescuing the Covent Garden theatre from ruin. In retrospect his political liberalism shines through, manifest in his pacifism and desire for retrenchment and in his commitment to parliamentary reform and social welfare. However in his own day he was often at odds with the aristocratic Whiggism to which he aspired. He never achieved office and was considered by his Whig friends to be something of a parvenu, surrounded by flatterers and sycophants.

Samuel Whitbread is well-served by two biographies: Roger Fulford, *Samuel Whitbread, 1764–1815: A Study in Opposition* (1967) and Dean Rapp, *Samuel Whitbread (1764–1815): A Social and Political Study* (1987). There is also an excellent entry on Whitbread by John Dinwiddy in J. O. Baylen and N. J. Gossman (eds), *Biographical Dictionary of Modern Radicals* (1979).

Miles Taylor

BASIL WIGODER (Lord Wigoder) 1921–

The almost continuous decline of the Liberal Party as an electoral force, from the replacement of Asquith (*q.v.*) by Lloyd George (*q.v.*) as Prime Minister in 1916 to the election to the party leadership of Jo Grimond (*q.v.*) forty years later, robbed Parliament of a generation of talent which could not win election under the Liberal banner. Amongst that generation is Basil Wigoder, four times a defeated parliamentary candidate, for whom only the passage of the Life Peerages Act, 1958, offered a realistic opportunity of reaching Parliament.

Basil Thomas Wigoder was born on 12 February 1921, in Manchester; his father was a medical doctor and his mother a JP. After Manchester Grammar School, Wigoder went up to Oriel College, Oxford, in 1939, where he was an open scholar, reading modern history. Like many of his generation, Wigoder's academic career was interrupted by the Second World War. He left Oxford in 1941, serving in the Royal Artillery until 1945, when he returned to university. He served as President of the Oxford Union in his final year; he was later, from 1982–92, a Trustee of the Oxford Union Society.

In joining the Liberal Club at Oxford, Wigoder had been influenced by his father, once a Liberal candidate in Manchester local politics. It was common, at this time, for the Liberal Central Association, effectively the Liberal Chief Whip's secretariat, to trawl the Oxbridge Liberal Clubs for talent. Wigoder soon came to the attention of the LCA's Secretary, Tommy Nudds, who secured his adoption as Liberal candidate for Bournemouth in 1942. Wigoder returned from the war immediately to fight the election, finding Bournemouth Liberal Association to be almost completely devoid of members, activists and resources. The Association's sole asset was its fanatical Chairman, the thriller writer Jack Creasey. Wigoder's election campaign was based so completely on addressing public meetings rather then canvassing that he spent polling day at the cinema, but still achieved one of the biggest Liberal votes in the south of England, finishing second, and pushing the Labour candidate, a conscientious objector, into third place.

Shortly after the election, a vacancy was caused at Bournemouth by the elevation to the peerage of Charles Lyle (to enable Brendan Bracken, defeated at Paddington North in the general election, to return to Parliament). The byelection generated considerable interest, attracting major politicians from all three parties. Wigoder, back at Oxford by this time, was again adopted and this time received help from Liberal members throughout the country who flooded into the constituency. Prior to nomination day Wigoder approached Harold Laski, an acquaintance of his father's, to explore the possibility of an electoral pact whereby Labour would stand down in Bournemouth and the Liberal candidate withdraw from the contemporaneous Bromley byelection. Nothing came of this approach and Wigoder lost ground in the election to the Labour candidate, Edward (later Lord) Shackleton.

Wigoder was called to the bar in 1946 and decided, in the light of the Liberals' continuing reverses, to concentrate on his legal career. He was one of the team of Liberal lawyers to defend Harry Willcock in the Willcock v. Muckle case in 1951 which sounded the death knell for wartime identity cards. He returned to active politics in the mid 1950s, becoming primarily involved with the Liberal Party's Executive Committee, which he chaired from 1963–65, and serving as Chairman of the Assembly Committee following the disastrous 1958 assembly. He contested Westbury in both the 1959 and 1964 general elections, polling respectably on both occasions, but nevertheless finishing third. He was Chairman of the Organisation Committee, which effectively handled the day-to-day running of the Liberal Party, from 1965–66, but again bowed out of active politics on taking silk in 1966.

Wigoder's legal career continued to advance. He became a member of the council of Justice in 1960; served as a member of the General Council of the Bar 1970–74 and of the Crown Court Rules Committee 1971–77; was a Recorder of the Crown Court from 1972–84; and was made a Master of the Bench in 1972. Despite these extra commitments, Wigoder was keen again to commit himself to the Liberal Party; upon the recommendation of Jeremy Thorpe (q.v.) he was made Baron Wigoder of Cheetham in 1974. From 1977–84 Wigoder was the Liberals' Chief Whip in the House of Lords, serving during a difficult period which included the Lib-Lab Pact and the formation of the Alliance with the SDP.

Wigoder has spoken regularly for the Liberal Party and, more recently, the Liberal Democrats, on legal issues, while at the same time accepting a wide range of prominent public and other appointments. During the 1990s, he has gradually retired from public life, speaking less frequently in the Lords after 1995, although he remains a member of the Lords' Committee for Privileges, President of the British United Provident Association and continues his membership of the Home Office Advisory Committee on Service Candidates and of the council of Justice. He also continues in active membership of the National Liberal Club and the Marylebone Cricket Club.

In 1948, Wigoder married Yoland Levinson, and has four children, one of whom was a Liberal Democrat candidate in the 1992 general election.

Mark Egan

SHIRLEY WILLIAMS (Lady Williams) 1930–

As the byelection car cavalcade drove slowly through a council estate in Warrington, Shirley Williams, microphone in hand, was drumming up support for SDP candidate Roy Jenkins. Standing precariously on the front seat, her head and shoulders poking through the sun-roof, Williams was in her element. As she passed a broken-down car, its grease-stained owner raised his head from beneath the bonnet and found himself within a few feet of Williams. 'Hello, Shirley' he said, grinning broadly as if greeting a long-lost friend. No other contemporary politician could have evoked such a warm, familiar response from a complete stranger. For me, it captured, in an instant, the Williams magic.

Shirley Vivien Teresa Brittain Catlin was born on 27 July 1930. Her parents, the political scientist George Catlin and the feminist writer Vera Brittain, were left-wing intellectuals. She had a peripatetic education in the UK and USA before taking a degree at Somerville College, Oxford. She began her career as a journalist with the *Daily Mirror* and *Financial Times* before becoming General Secretary of the Fabian Society in 1960, a post which she held until being elected as Labour MP for Hitchin in 1964. Williams held the seat (albeit with revised boundaries and renamed as Stevenage from 1974) until 1979. By this stage she had already stood three times unsuccessfully, twice in Harwich (1954 and '55) and once in Southampton Test (1959). Her rise up the ministerial appointments ladder was smooth, with junior ministerial appointments in the 1964–70 government at the Ministries of Labour, Education and Science and Home Office. With the return of the Labour government in 1974 she joined the Cabinet as Secretary of State for Consumer Protection and two years later moved on to Education and Science, where she is best remembered for her efforts to extend the comprehensive school system.

She lost her Parliamentary seat in 1979, but remained on the Labour Party National Executive, to which she was first elected in 1970. Increasingly in a small minority on policy issues on which she felt particularly strongly – Europe, defence, internal party democracy – she resigned in January 1981 to become one of the Gang of Four (with Roy Jenkins (*q.v.*), David Owen and Bill Rodgers (*q.v.*)) who formed the SDP.

381

In the heady days of 1981, she scored one of the SDP's most sensational byelection wins, at Crosby, turning a Conservative majority of 19,272 into a SDP majority of 5,289. Major boundary changes, however, played a key role in her losing the seat at the 1983 general election and she then remained outside Parliament for a decade. In 1982 she became SDP President, a position she held throughout the party's independent existence. An early supporter of the Alliance with the Liberal Party, she was increasingly at odds with the style and substance of David Owen's leadership and their relationship became one of open hostility after the 1987 general election and the moves towards merger of the SDP and Liberals, which she enthusiastically supported .

1987 also saw her second marriage to US political scientist Professor Richard Neustadt (her first marriage to Bernard Williams was dissolved in 1974; they had one daughter) and a move across the Atlantic to become Professor of Elective Politics at the John F. Kennedy School of Government, Harvard University. She became a Liberal Democrat peer in 1993, taking the title Baroness Williams of Crosby, and the party's spokesman on foreign affairs in the Lords in 1997.

During her period outside Parliament in the mid 1980s, she was based at the Policy Studies Institiute, where she concentrated on employment policy issues. This interest in employment policy, particularly youth unemployment, is reflected in her publications: *Politics is for People* (1981); *Jobs for the 1980s: Youth Without Work* (1981); *Unemployment and Growth in the Western Economies* (1984); *A Job to Live* (1985); and *Snakes and Ladders, a diary of political life* (1996). She chaired the Liberal Democrat working group on employment policy in 1993–94.

Williams is a remarkable politician not just for her achievements, but just as importantly for her approach to politics. One of the most charismatic politicians of her generation, she brings a passion and commitment to the causes for which she fights which make her a formidable performer in Parliament, at party conferences – she notably defeated Paddy Ashdown (*q.v.*) in 1994 to swing the Liberal Democrats behind a commitment to the minimum wage – and on the stump. She combines an amazing ability to empathise with her audience – whether a full hall or an individual – with a steely determination and a shrewd understanding of the low arts of political cunning. As a friend she is generous, thoughtful and kind.

In an age of soundbites, cynicism and ideology-free politics, Williams remains an idealist in supporting democracy, equality and freedom, and has promoted these virtues in the new democracies of Eastern Europe and southern Africa. She has a phenomenal energy and a huge enthusiasm for discussing the big issues of politics. This love of politics and the warmth of her personality communicates itself to everyone Williams meets. It explains the tremendous affection in which she is held – and that smile in Warrington.

Dick Newby

PHIL WILLIS MP   1941–

George Philip Willis was born in Burnley, Lancashire on 30 November 1941. His father, George Willism was a postman and his mother, Hannah (née Gillespie) a nurse, who also had one other (older) child. His mother's family comes from Ireland, where the family still has several small farms. He was educated at Burnley Grammar School (1953–60), where he had particular success at sport. At one time he was a trialist for Burnley FC, and later spent several years as coach to Leeds City Boys' soccer team. First studying history and music at the City of Leeds and Carnegie College, he then qualified as a teacher at the University of Leeds, in 1963.

Willis began a successful teaching career, working mainly in Leeds and quickly rising to become Deputy Head at West Leeds Boys Grammar School in 1974. In 1978 he gained a BPhil degree from Birmingham University and became a head teacher for the first time, at Ormesby School in Middlesbrough. Five years later he returned to Leeds as Head Teacher at the large John Smeaton Community High School. His teaching career was marked by a strong belief in integrating children with learning difficulties and physical impairments into mainstream education; his success with this approach earned him national attention.

Politics came relatively late in life; it was only in 1985, in his mid-forties, that he joined the Liberal Party. He was particularly attracted by the Liberals' record on defending the local environment. As with his teaching career, he swiftly rose through the ranks, becoming a councillor on Harrogate Borough Council in 1988, council Leader in 1990 and Deputy Group Leader on North Yorkshire County Council in 1993. Just two years later he was selected as prospective parliamentary candidate for Harrogate.

Although he made only a muted impact during his time on the county council, under his leadership Harrogate Borough Council has achieved some striking successes, including turning the famous Harrogate Conference Centre (a popular venue for Liberal Democrat conferences) from a loss-making white elephant into a financially viable operation.

Aided by favourable boundary changes, and a highly effective determination to campaign to win, he turned the Harrogate parliamentary seat from a frequent good second into a highly winnable constituency. When the election came in May 1997, his opponent was the controversial ex-Chancellor Norman Lamont, the Tory incumbent having been effectively deselected by the local party for not working hard enough. For many journalists, the highlight of the campaign was car chases around Harrogate as they attempted to locate Lamont, who repeatedly refused to be interviewed. The swing from Tory to Liberal Democrat was, at 15.7 per cent, one of the largest in the country. During the count, strains of 'je ne regrette rien', which Lamont had famously quoted during the recession he presided over as Chancellor, briefly floated through the hall.

Once in Parliament he was a natural spokesman on further and higher education, and benefited from the high profile his portfolio gained as a result of the Labour government's plans to introduce tuition fees. His natural political instincts, based on heartfelt concern for the less well-off, have fitted in well with a national political scene where the modernisation of the Labour Party has often left only the Liberal Democrats defending those he feels deeply about.

In addition to high politics, he has also revelled in the idiosyncracies of parliamentary behaviour. He was one of the Liberal Democrat MPs who, during 1997, regularly went to the Commons at very early hours in order to claim seats, during an ongoing struggle with the Tories over who could sit where.

He is married to Heather, also a teacher. They have two children, Michael and Rachel.

Mark Pack

DES WILSON   1941–

Des Wilson is Britain's best known campaigner. From journalism at a young age to campaigning and latterly public affairs, his reputation for changing the law is breathtaking. Known for his tenacity and energy, Wilson has been responsible for highlighting issues such as homelessness, the environment, freedom of information, and lead-free petrol. Wilson had an active role in the Liberals and then the Liberal Democrats for over twenty years.

Wilson was born on 5 March 1941 in Oamaru, New Zealand. He left school at fifteen to become a newspaper reporter. In 1960, aged nineteen, he left New Zealand for journalism in the United Kingdom. Six years later he began his campaigning career as the first Director of Shelter, the National Campaign for Homeless People, and built it into one of the country's most effective campaigning charities. He was Head of Public Affairs at the Royal Shakespeare Company from 1974–76, Editor of *Social Work Today* 1976–79 and Deputy Editor of *Illustrated London News* from 1979–81.

In the 1980s Wilson became a major figure in the environmental movement. He led the campaign that won lead-free petrol for the whole of Europe while at CLEAR

(Campaign for Lead-Free Air). He became Chairman of Friends of the Earth and Campaign Director for FoE International. He was named by ITN as environmentalist of the decade. Other campaigns included the Campaign for Freedom of Information and Parents against Tobacco.

Journalism has also played a large part in Wilson's career. He was a columnist for the *Guardian* from 1968–70, the *Observer* from 1971–75 and the *Illustrated London News* from 1972–85. Following the 1992 general election he became the UK Director of Public Affairs with Burson-Marsteller, the world's largest public relations consultancy. In 1994 he became Director of Corporate and Public Affairs for British Airport Authorities plc.

Wilson stood as a parliamentary candidate for the Liberals in Hove in 1973 (byelection) and 1974. He was a member of the Liberal Party Council from 1973–74, and 1984–85, a member of the National Executive from 1984–85 and President of the National League of Young Liberals from 1984–85. He was President of the Liberal Party from 1986–87. He was also a member of the Federal Executive of the Social and Liberal Democrats in 1988, though was beaten for the first Presidency of the party by Ian Wrigglesworth (*q.v.*)

Wilson was General Election Campaign Director from 1990 up to the 1992 election (he had been a member of the Alliance campaign team in 1987). The party's election priorities were to hold on to its existing seats, to enhance Paddy Ashdown's (*q.v.*) reputation and to run a professional campaign. For the campaign he was given *PR Week's* award for an outstanding individual contribution to the communications industry.

Des Wilson ceased his involvement in the party after the 1992 general election. For some time he had viewed the campaign as his 'last throw' before changing direction and building a career in business. In 1994 he resigned his membership. He made little attempt to hide his disenchantment with the leadership of the Liberal Democrats, particularly in a series of articles in the *New Statesman* during the 1997 general election campaign. He was critical of the decision to enter into a closer relationship with Tony Blair and the Labour leadership, arguing that the democratic process required two alternative parties on the centre left.

Married to Jane Dunmore in 1985, he has one son and one daughter from a previous marriage. His publications include: *I Know it Was the Place's Fault* (1971), *Des Wilson's Minority Report (a diary of protest)* (1973), *So you want to be Prime Minister: a personal view of British politics* (1979), *The Lead Scandal* (1982), *Pressure: the A to Z of Campaigning in Britain* (1984), *The Environmental Crisis* (1984), *The Secrets File* (1984), *The Citizen Action Handbook* (1986), *Battle for Power – Inside the Alliance General Election Campaign* (1987), *Costa Del Sol* (a novel, 1990), *Campaign* (a novel, 1992), and *Campaigning* (1993).

Olly Grender

SIR IAN WRIGGLESWORTH 1939–

Sir Ian Wrigglesworth has on more than one occasion played a major role in the development of the Liberal Democrats: in 1980–81, as an integral member of the team which rocked the political establishment with the formation of the SDP, and, again, between 1988 and 1990, when as President of the newly formed Social and Liberal Democrats, he instigated the structural changes that saved the party from organisational chaos and financial disaster.

Ian William Wrigglesworth was born on 8 December 1939 in Stockton-on-Tees and educated in Stockton and at the College of St Mark & St John in Chelsea where he read music and English. He was President of the University of London Institute of Education Students Association and Vice-President of the National Union of Students (1964–68). He worked for the General Secretary of the National Union of Teachers; as Head of Research for the Cooperative Party; and as Press and Public Affairs Manager of National Girobank (1970–74).

He returned to Teesside in 1974 as the Labour and Cooperative Party candidate to fight the Conservative seat of Teeside Thornaby, a mixed seat comprising Thornaby and the western suburbs of Middlesborough. He was first elected in February of that year and went on to represent the area for thirteen years. From 1983, boundary changes incorporated part of his town of birth, creating the Stockton South seat.

He moved quickly into a junior role within the new Labour government as PPS to the Home Secretary Roy Jenkins (*q.v.*) and served on many committees dealing with issues relating to, amongst others, banking, finance and the European Community. He travelled extensively, partly in his role as Vice-Chairman of the Anglo-Hong Kong Parliamentary Group.

When the Labour Party lost the 1979 general election Wrigglesworth was appointed to the position of shadow minister for the civil service but he became increasingly dismayed with events within the party during the next eighteen months, including its adoption of an anti-European Community stance and more dogmatic left-wing policies in general. He became one of the small group of MPs to be involved from the very beginning in the planning and launch of the new Social Democratic Party.

He became the SDP trade and industry spokesman in 1981 and for the next two years worked energetically in Parliament and in the country, particularly within the north east. He had already established himself as a very popular local MP and was able to build a strong constituency organisation.

The 1983 general election saw the SDP reduced to a team of six MPs. His own victory was very slim – 103 votes after several recounts. His popularity, hard work and strong local team contributed to his victory, though the revelation during the campaign that the Conservative candidate, Tom Finnegan, had previously been a member of the National Front undoubtedly helped his cause.

From 1984 he served as Alliance trade and industry spokesman and worked closely with the SDP leader, David Owen. Despite his strong local reputation, the slippage in national vote share for the Alliance in the 1987 general election, together with the resilience of support for the Conservatives, resulted in the loss of his seat to the Conservative by less than 800 votes.

Wrigglesworth believed that the best course of action for the SDP was a period of reflection, and although he had felt for some time that a merger would be inevitable, he was dismayed at the speed with which events were forced, a haste which he believed was responsible for much of the subsequent conflict within the SDP. He could not, like many senior members of the SDP, be pigeonholed into either of the party's conflicting camps, having worked closely with both Jenkins and Owen, but was firmly convinced that the membership's support for merger must be respected and that the establishment by Owen of the 'continuing SDP' was an act of dishonesty.

He put his energy into the launch of the new party whilst professionally joining industry as part-time Director of CIT (Research), a London-based communications research company, and as Deputy Chairman of John Livingston & Sons, a Middlesborough-based engineering and industrial property group. In 1988 he also became Director of Fairfield Industries, an Anglo-Dutch associate company of Livingston's.

The Social and Liberal Democrats were launched in 1988 and Wrigglesworth stood for the key role of President that year. In a hard-fought campaign he defeated the former Liberal Des Wilson (q.v.). The organisation that he took over had major problems. Membership was disappointingly low and the new party was very near bankruptcy. Drastic action was required: party headquarters was slimmed down and finances made sound with the help of a small number of personal guarantors. The changes attracted criticism, but without these reforms the renaissance of the party from 1990 could not have been possible. He was awarded a knighthood in 1991 for political and public service.

He has since remained active within the Liberal Democrats, including as Chairman of the Liberal Democrat Business Forum, while pursuing a successful business career in industry, as Chairman, from 1996, of an industrial property company, UK Land Estates, and in public affairs as European Chairman of a worldwide public policy consultancy GPC Market Access. He was appointed deputy Chair of the Board of Governors of the University of Teesside in 1993 and has held a number of senior positions within the CBI.

He married Patricia Truscott in 1968 and they have three adult children.

Peter Dunphy

INDEX
TO
CONTRIBUTORS

John Ault (*Colin Breed*)
was Colin Breed's constituency agent from February 1995 – August 1997. He is now the Liberal Democrats' Campaigns and Target SeatS Officer for the North West.

Helen Bailey (*Sarah Ludford, Robert Maclennan, Diana Maddock, Conrad Russell*)
is currently Deputy Chair of the Liberal Democrats' Federal Executive and of the Joint States Candidates Committee. She works as a management consultant with public sector organisations.

Malcolm Baines (*Edgar Granville, Percy Harris, Lothian, Gilbert Murray*)
read History at Cambridge, followed by a DPhil at Oxford on *The Survival of the British Liberal Party, 1932–1959*. He has written a number of articles on Liberal Party history and works in corporate tax for a large accountancy firm.

Oliver Baines (*Andrew George*)
is Director of the Cornwall Rural Community Council, Chairman of the Cornwall Voluntary Sector Forum, and holds a number of directorships.

Liz Barker (*Nick Harvey*)
was Chair of the Union of Liberal Students in 1982–83. and is now Chair of the Liberal Democrats' Federal Conference Committee.

Dr Derek Andrew Barrie (*Menzies Campbell*)
is Campaigns Officer of the Scottish Liberal Democrats. Liberal candidate himself for East Fife in 1966, he was election agent for Menzies Campbell in 1979 and 1983 and Campaign Manager when he won North East Fife in 1987.

Tony Beamish (*Tim Beaumont*)
co-founded the Liberal Ecology Group (now Green Liberal Democrats). He has written several short papers on ecological economics, and the booklet *No Free Lunch*.

Selena Bevis (*Redesdale*)
has worked throughout her career for Liberal Democrat politicians – in the Commons, Lords,

and currently the European Parliament.

E. F. Biagini (*John Stuart Mill*)
is a Fellow of Robinson College, Cambridge, and lecturer in modern British history. An alumnus of the Scuola Normale Superiore of Pisa, he has taught at Newcastle-upon-Tyne and Princeton.

Marjie Bloy (*Aberdeen, Joseph Chamberlain, Rosebery, Lord John Russell*)
is a history teacher. She graduated from London University in 1981 and was awarded a PhD by the University of Sheffield in 1986.

Jane Bonham Carter (*Mark Bonham Carter, Violet Bonham Carter*)
is a daughter of Mark Bonham Carter, and works in television.

Duncan Brack (*Horatio Bottomley, D. G. Ritchie*)
is Editor of this *Dictionary*, a former Policy Director of the Liberal Democrats and now Head of the Energy and Environmental Programme at the Royal Institute of International Affairs. He edited *Why I am a Liberal Democrat* (1996).

Dr Michael Brock (*H. H. Asquith*)
is an 'Oxford historian' who served three colleges (Fellow and Tutor, Corpus Christi, Vice-President and Bursar, Wolfson, Warden, Nuffield). Author: *The Great Reform Act* (1973), editor (with Mark Curthoys) *Nineteenth-Century Oxford, Part 1* (1997). CBE, Hon. DLitt, FR, Hist, S, FRSL. Foundation member, SDP.

Peter Brook (*Andrew Stunell*)
helped achieve Andrew Stunell's election victory, as Hazel Grove constituency chairman. He has been a key contributor to Liberal Democrat policy on employment and regional economic development.

Kenneth D. Brown (*John Burns*)
is Professor of Economic and Social History at The Queen's University of Belfast and Dean of the Faculty of Legal, Social and Educational Sciences. He has written extensively on the early

history of the labour movement, including a prize-winning biography of John Burns.

Nick Carthew (*Jenny Tonge*)
works as assistant to Jenny Tonge MP, has been a councillor in the London Borough of Richmond-upon-Thames since 1990, and is now called the 'Prince of Darkness' by the opposition groups!

Caroline Cawston (*Richard Wainwright*)
worked as Richard Wainwright's secretary from February 1974 until August 1982. She now owns and runs a public affairs consultancy, Harcourt, based in Whitehall.

Matthew Clark (*Mike Hancock*)
is chef de cabinet for Mike Hancock's office. He was elected to Hampshire County Council in 1989 and is group leader for the Southampton Unitary Authority and Chairman of the Hampshire Police Authority.

Peter Clarke (*Hammonds, Graham Wallas*)
is Professor of Modern British History and a Fellow of St John's College, Cambridge. His books include *Lancashire and the New Liberalism* (1971), *Liberals and Social Democrats* (1978), *The Keynesian Revolution in the Making 1924–1936* (1988), and *A Question of Leadership: from Gladstone to Thatcher* (1991).

Tim Clement-Jones (*Tim Razzall*)
– see entry.

Russell Deacon (*Martin Thomas*)
is a Senior Lecturer in Government and Politics in the University of Wales Institute, Cardiff's Business School. He is the author of a number of studies on Welsh political life, including *Hidden Federal Party*.

Dee Doocey (*Anthony Jacobs*)
is a management consultant and Chairman of Women Liberal Democrats. She was formerly Finance Director, Liberal Party and Liberal Democrats and a councillor, London Borough of Richmond-upon-Thames.

Roy Douglas (*Margot Asquith, Ernest Brown, Frank Byers, Arthur Comyns Carr, Philip Fothergill, Donald MacLean, Edward Martell, Vivian Phillipps*)
is Emeritus Reader, University of Surrey. Author, *History of the Liberal Party 1895–1970; Land, People and Politics*; several books on international relations, and four books on international cartoons.

Barry Doyle (*Reginald McKenna*)
lectures in modern British history at the University of Teesside. He is an Associate Editor of *Urban History* and is currently writing a social history of twentieth-century Britain for Longman.

Andrew Duff (*Robin Teverson, Graham Watson*)
is Director of the Federal Trust and has written widely on EU affairs. He has been Vice-President (England) of the Liberal Democrats 1994–97, a Cambridge councillor, and four times a parliamentary candidate.

Peter Dunphy (*Ian Wrigglesworth*)
worked full-time for Ian Wrigglesworth 1984–85 in Stockton as assistant agent. He is the Director of a city recruitment firm, Darwin Rhodes.

David Dutton (*John Simon*)
is Senior Lecturer in History at the University of Liverpool and Visiting Professor in the School of Arts and Science at Bolton Institute. He is the author of biographies of Austen Chamberlain, John Simon and Anthony Eden.

Mark Egan (*Pratap Chitnis, Elliott Dodds, John Foot, Arthur Holt, Edward Martell, Andrew Murray, Nancy Seear, Ernest Simon, Basil Wigoder*)
is a House of Commons clerk. He is currently completing a DPhil thesis on the Liberal Party's constituency associations between 1945–64.

Gareth Epps (*Stina Robson*)
is a Parliamentary researcher and a former sabbatical officer of the Liberal Democrat Youth & Students. He is active in West Oxfordshire Liberal Democrats.

Robert Falkner (*Adam Smith*)
is Lecturer in Politics at New College, Oxford.
He is the author of *A Conservative Economist?
The Political Liberalism of Adam Smith Revisited*
(John Stuart Mill Institute, 1997).

Tim Farron (*Ronnie Fearn, Cyril Smith*)
is a university administrator at the University of
Lancaster. He is a councillor on Lancashire
County Council South Ribble Borough Coun-
cil, and Deputy Leader of Lancashire Liberal
Democrats.

Ross Finnie (*Russell Johnston*)
is Leader of the Opposition on Inverclyde
Council. He has held a number of senior positions in the Scottish Liberal Party including
Chairman 1982–86, and Chair, 1987 general
election campaign.

Elizabeth Flanagan Prueher (*John Bright,
Richard Cobden*)
is a candidate for the Public Administration and
Public Policy MSc at the LSE. She completed a
BA in Comparative Politics at the University of
California, Los Angeles.

Alex Folkes (*Peter Brand*)
was agent for Peter Brand at the 1997 general
election, and now works for the Electoral Reform Society.

John Foot (*Isaac Foot*)
– see entry.

Ruth Fox (*Gladwyn*)
is a postgraduate in the School of History at the
University of Leeds, currently writing a PhD
thesis on 'The philosophy and political strategy
of the Liberal Party 1970–83'.

Lesley Gill (*George Mackie*)
is George Mackie's niece.

Julian Glover (*Christopher Mayhew, Jeremy
Thorpe*)
was Deputy Editor of the *Economist's World in
1996* and currently works for the *Times* as an

assistant to Matthew Parris, the paper's parliamentary sketch-writer and columnist.

Willy Goodhart (*Bill Rodgers*)
– see entry.

Donald Gorrie (*Duncan McLaren*)
– see entry.

David Gowland (*J. M. Keynes*)
is Professor of Economics at the University of
Derby. His previous jobs included working at
the Bank of England in the 1980s, where he
advised the government on monetary policy.

Dr Richard S. Grayson (*Edward Grey, Ramsay
Muir, Archibald Sinclair*)
is Director of the Centre for Reform, the Liberal Democrat think-tank. He was previously a
university lecturer, and is the author of *Austen
Chamberlain and the Commitment to Europe: British Foreign Policy, 1924–29* (1997).

Tony Greaves (*Henry Campbell-Bannerman,
Michael Steed*)
– see entry.

Olly Grender (*Des Wilson*)
has been Director Of Communications at Shelter since June 1995. Prior to that she was the
Director of Communications for the Liberal
Democrats, and has worked for Paddy Ashdown.

Tudor Griffiths (*Paul Keetch*)
is a former full-time election agent for
Leominster and former chair of Lewisham Borough Liberal Democrats. He is an independent
financial adviser working for a firm of Lloyd's
Brokers in the City.

James Gurling (*Tom McNally*)
is a local councillor in the London Borough of
Southwark, Editor of *The Reformer*, and currently
Head of Parliamentary Affairs at the British
Retail Consortium.

Fiona Hall (*Lembit Öpik*)
first worked with Lembit Öpik in the 1994 Eu-

ropean election campaign. Formerly a teacher, writer and environmental campaigner, she now works full-time as Press Officer to the Welsh Liberal Democrat MPs.

Katie Hall *(Edward Davey, Don Foster, Mark Oaten, Steve Webb)*
worked for Matthew Taylor MP and Paddy Ashdown MP in Parliament 1989–92. She then worked in public affairs for four years, mainly in consultancy, and now lives and works in Brussels.

Michael Hart *(J. A. Spender)*
is a History Fellow at Exeter College, Oxford; his doctoral thesis was concerned with the decline of the Liberal Party until 1924. He served during the 1980s as a Liberal member of Oxfordshire County Council.

Mike Hoban *(Emma Nicholson)*
is a friend of Emma Nicholson's and was the Liberal Democrats' Parliamentary candidate for the Bridgwater constituency in the 1997 general election.

Alison Holmes *(John Alderdice)*
worked as Irish Affairs advisor to Paddy Ashdown, and for the Liberal Democrat general election campaigns in 1992 and '97. She is now Project Manager for the Communications Strategy Unit at the BBC.

Keith House *(David Chidgey)*
became Leader of Eastleigh Council when the Liberal Democrats gained majority control in 1994. He is Director of Membership Services for the Liberal Democrats nationally.

David Howarth *(L. T. Hobhouse, Rufus Isaacs)*
Is a Fellow in Law at Clare College, Cambridge and University Lecturer in Land Economy; specialist in tort law, comparative law and jurisprudence; Cambridge City Councillor; member of Liberal Democrats' Federal Policy Committee.

Alvin Jackson *(Augustine Birrell)*
is Reader in Modern History at the Queen's University of Belfast. Among his books are *The Ulster Party* (1989), *Sir Edward Carson* (1993), *Colonel Edward Saunderson* (1995) and *The Blackwell History of Modern Ireland* (1999).

J. Graham Jones *(Alex Carlile, Edward Clement Davies, Emlyn Hooson, Geraint Howells, Rhys Hopkin Morris, Richard Livsey, Megan Lloyd George, Alfred Mond)*
is an Assistant Archivist at the National Library of Wales, Aberystwyth, currently responsible for the Welsh Political Archive. He is the author of *A Pocket Guide: the History of Wales* (1990) and several articles on late nineteenth and twentieth century Welsh politics.

Peter Joyce *(Jo Grimond, Laura Grimond, Arthur Holt, Wallace Lawler, Donald Wade)*
teaches in the Politics and Philosophy Department of Manchester Metropolitan University. He has made a number of contributions to Liberal Democrat History Group publications.

Dr Paul Kelly *(Jeremy Bentham)*
is Lecturer in Politics at the London School of Economics. He is author of *Utilitarianism and Distributive Justice: Jeremy Bentham and the Civil Law* (1990), and co-editor, with D. Boucher, of *The Social Contract: From Hobbes to Rawls* (1995).

Richard Kemp *(Trevor Jones)*
served on Liverpool Council as Chair of Housing, Education and Finance between 1975–84, returned to the council in 1992, and currently leads the Liberal Democrat groups on the Merseyside Fire Authority and the Urban Commission of the Local Government Association.

Richard Kirby *(Frank Owen)*
works for Birmingham Health Authority. During the 1997 general election, he was the Liberal Democrat candidate for Cannock Chase as well as part of the campaign team which regained Owen's Hereford seat.

Archy Kirkwood *(Michael Moore)*
– see entry.

Peter Knowlson (*Susan Thomas*)
was Head of Policy/Director of Policy of the Liberal Party from 1974–87, and a member of the 1987 Liberal/SDP merger negotiating team which created the Liberal Democrats. He is currently Chair of Mole Valley Liberal Democrats.

John Lawrie (*Donald Gorrie*)
is Executive Chairman of Aberdeen Asset Management Ireland. A former Treasurer and Chairman of the Scottish Liberal Party, he was also a member of the Scottish negotiating team for merger in 1988.

Christopher Layton (*Walter Layton*)
is Walter Layton's youngest son and was personal assistant to Jo Grimond and Economic Adviser to the Liberal Party in the 1960s. He was a chef de cabinet and Director in the European Commission from 1971–81.

Alan Leaman (*Paddy Ashdown*)
is a public affairs consultant with a major international firm. He was on Paddy Ashdown's staff 1988–93 and was Director of Strategy and Planning for the Liberal Democrats 1995–97.

Graham Lippiatt (*Acton, Christopher Addison, Desmond Banks, Navnit Dholakia, George Goschen*)
is a civil servant, former Liberal councillor and member of the Liberal Democrat History Group executive. He holds masters degrees in international history and race and ethnic relations from London University.

Gordon Lishman (*Bernard Greaves, Tony Greaves*)
– see entry.

Tony Little (*W. E. Forster, Hartington, Palmerston*)
is a pension fund manager and has been student of Victorian politics for more than thirty years. He is Secretary of the Liberal Democrat History Group and former leader of the Liberal group on Hillingdon Council.

Eugenia Low (*William Beveridge*)
is a postgraduate student at St John's College, Oxford.

Dr Peter Lynch (*Charles Kennedy*)
is a lecturer in politics at the University of Stirling and author of 'Third Party Politics in a Four-Party System: The Liberal Democrats in Scotland', *Scottish Affairs* 22, Winter 1998.

Ian Machin (*Herbert Gladstone, William Harcourt, H. W. Massingham*)
has taught at various universities at home and overseas since 1958. Since 1989 he has been Professor of British History at the University of Dundee. He is the author of several books and many articles on the political, religious, and social history of Great Britain in the nineteenth and twentieth centuries.

Paul Martin (*David Penhaligon*)
is researching the process of decision-making on constitutional and supreme courts at Nuffield College, Oxford, and is a lecturer in politics at St Anne's College, Oxford.

John Matthew (*John Burnett*)
was a Liberal candidate in the 1960s and '70s in Basingstoke, Winchester and Hampshire West (European election). He served on Winchester City Council and Hampshire County Council.

Sarah McGrother (*Richard Allan*)
is Campaigns Assistant in the Campaigns and Elections Department at Liberal Democrat HQ. Before moving to London she worked as Casework Officer for Richard Allan in Sheffield.

Michael Meadowcroft (*Alan Beith*)
– see entry.

Ray Michie (*John Bannerman*)
– see entry.

Christian Moon (*David Heath*)
is the Deputy Head of Policy and Research for the Liberal Democrats. He was previously David

Heath's Office Manager and Researcher in the Commons.

Mark Morris (*Dominic Addington*)
is the Campaigns Research Officer for the RNID. For over three years he was a parliamentary researcher working for David Chidgey, Liz Lynne and Paul Burstow.

Pash Nandhra (*Dadabhai Naoroji*)
is a teacher and businesswoman. She was first elected a councillor in Harrow in 1986 and has been a parliamentary candidate. She is currently Chair of the Ethnic Minority Liberal Democrats.

Dick Newby (*Shirley Williams*)
– see entry.

Rachel Oliver (*Jackie Ballard, Tim Clement-Jones, Adrian Sanders*)
is Head of Campaigns and Parliamentary, RNID. She worked for Nick Harvey MP 1993–95, and was a Mid Devon District Councillor in 1995.

Dr Mark Pack (*Charles Fox, Charles Grey, Grenville, Melbourne, Phil Willis*)
works in the computer industry in the City of London. In 1995 he completed a PhD at the University of York on the nineteenth-century English electoral system.

Ian Packer (*Crewe, Elibank, R. B. Haldane, Edwin Montagu*)
has taught at the Universities of Oxford, Exeter and Teesside and is currently Visiting Fellow at Queen's University, Belfast. He has published a number of articles on the Edwardian Liberal Party, and a biography of Lloyd George.

David Penwarden (*Roger Fulford*)
chaired the Liberal Party's Candidates Committee 1978–80 and was a councillor in West Ham and Reading. He has held board appointments with the Guardian Media Group, Trusthouse Forte, Associated British Foods and the E. A. P. European School of Management.

Roger Pincham (*W. E. Gladstone*)
was Chairman of the National Executive of the Liberal Party 1979–82. He founded the Gladstone Club in 1974, and remains its Chairman. He is a trustee of the John Stuart Mill Institute and President of the Lloyd George Society.

John Rawson (*Nigel Jones*)
was a Cheltenham borough councillor 1980–87 and has been a Gloucestershire county councillor since 1981. He was elected Chair of Gloucestershire County Council in May 1998.

Chris Rennard (*David Alton*)
– see entry.

Eduardo Reyes (*Vincent Cable*)
was Deputy President, Cambridge University Students Union (1994–95), researcher, Emma Nicholson MP (1996–97), and legal affairs researcher, John Burnett MP (1997–98).

Dr Jaime Reynolds (*Herbert Samuel*)
was awarded a PhD for research on the political history of Poland. He is a civil servant at the Department of Environment, Transport and the Regions, working on international environmental policy.

Ben Rich (*Richard Holme, Anthony Lester, David Rendel, David Ricardo*)
is Vice Chair of the Liberal Democrats' Federal Policy Committee. He was previously Deputy Policy Director for the party, 1991–95, and Chair of the Student Liberal Democrats in 1989.

John Ricketts (*Chris Rennard*)
worked in the Liberal Democrat Whip's Office 1987–91, and is currently a Director at Parliamentary Communications Limited, publishers of *The House Magazine, The Parliamentary Monitor* and *The Parliament Magazine*.

Sheila Ritchie (*Robert Smith*)
has been a Liberal and Liberal Democrat since 1980, friend of Robert Smith's since 1978, councillor, Gordon District 1988–96, party hack.

Keith Robbins (*Winston Churchill*)
is Vice-Chancellor of the University of Wales, Lampeter, having previously been Professor of Modern History in the University of Glasgow. His many books include *The Eclipse of a Great Power: Modern Britain 1870–1992* (1993), *The Blackwell Biographical Dictionary of British Political Life in the Twentieth Century* (1990), *Great Britain: Identities, Institutions and the Idea of Britishness* (1998), and *World History since 1945: A Concise History* (1998).

Edward Royle (*Charles Bradlaugh, George Holyoake, Thomas Paine*)
is a Reader in History at the University of York, where he has taught since 1972. He has published several books on aspects of religion, free thought and radical politics in nineteenth-century Britain, as well as a general survey, *Modern Britain: A Social History 1750–1997* (second ed., 1997).

David Rundle (*Nathaniel Micklem*)
is a history fellow at Mansfield College, Oxford; he studied previously at Christ Church, Oxford, where he gained his undergraduate and doctoral degrees.

Jon Sacker (*Paul Tyler*)
is Director of Public and International Affairs for a national representative organisation. A former member of staff for the Liberal Democrats, he worked for Paul Tyler after the 1992 general election.

Emma Sanderson-Nash (*Norman Baker, Simon Hughes, Ray Michie*)
left postgraduate studies at the LSE to work for Simon Hughes MP and has since worked for the party (several MPs and peers). She runs her own small marketing business and is a member of the party's Equal Opportunities Audit Group.

Cheryl Schonhardt-Bailey (*John Bright, Richard Cobden*)
is Lecturer in Government at the LSE. She completed a PhD thesis on *A Model of Trade Policy Liberalization: Looking Inside the British 'Hegemon'*

of the Nineteenth Century, and has recently completed a four-volume work documenting the rise of free trade in nineteenth-century Britain.

Geoffrey Sell (*Jo Grimond*)
is a college lecturer and member of the Liberal Democrat History Group executive. He completed a PhD thesis on *Liberal Revival: British Liberalism and Jo Grimond 1956–67*.

Nick Smart (*Robert Bernays*)
is senior lecturer in History at the University of Plymouth. He has edited the Bernays diaries, has produced a number of articles on inter-war British politics and has just completed a book on the National Government.

Dr Julie Smith (*Ralf Dahrendorf, William Wallace*)
is a Teaching Fellow at the Centre of International Studies, Cambridge, and Fellow of Robinson College, Cambridge. Her publications include *A Sense of Liberty: The History of the Liberal International 1947–1997* (1997) and *Voice of the People: The European Parliament in the 1990s* (1995).

Jane Smithard (*Brian Cotter*)
is a lawyer and an executive member of the Liberal Democrats' Parliamentary Candidates' Association.

John Smithson (*Gordon Lishman*)
edited *Radical Bulletin* from its inception in 1970 until 1976. A former Treasurer of the Association of Liberal Councillors, his career as a councillor on various authorities stretches back over more than thirty years.

Mark Smulian (*Michael Meadowcroft*)
is a journalist. Since the mid-1980s, he has been involved with the production of *Liberator* magazine and with writing for the Liberal Revue's satirical shows at conferences.

Michael Steed (*H. A. L. Fisher*)
– see entry.

David Steel (*Archy Kirkwood*)
– see entry.

John Stevens (*Bob Russell*)
was a founder member of the SDP, and has been a Colchester councillor since 1984.

Neil Stockley (*Richard Acland, Willy Goodhart, Roy Jenkins, John Pardoe, Dick Taverne, Matthew Taylor, Geoff Tordoff*)
was the Liberal Democrats' Director of Policy 1995 –97. He was executive assistant to New Zealand Prime Minister, David Lange and, subsequently, Director of the New Zealand Parliamentary Labour Research Unit.

Mike Steele (*Avebury*)
has worked at the House of Commons as a journalist since 1962, and was Liberal Party press officer 1966–72. He has been Treasurer of the Silbury Fund, of which Eric Avebury is Secretary and Peter Hain Chairman, since 1973.

Andrew Sweeting (*Gwilym Lloyd-George*)
is a former President of the Oxford University Liberal Democrats. He is a professional economist specialising in the economics of competition law and regulation in London and Brussels.

Jen Tankard (*Tom Brake, Paul Burstow, Sally Hamwee, Graham Tope*)
is an executive member of the Liberal Democrat History Group, and lives in Kingston-upon-Thames.

Miles Taylor (*J. A. Hobson, Joseph Hume, Samuel Whitbread*)
is a Lecturer in Modern History at King's College, London. He is the author of *The Decline of British Radicalism, 1847–60* (Oxford, 1995), editor of *The European Diaries of Richard Cobden, 1846–49* (1994) and co-editor of *Party, State and Society: Electoral Behaviour in Britain since 1820* (1997).

Celia Thomas (*Falkland, Thurso*)
had a varied career, working mainly in choir schools in Winchester and Oxford, then worked for Jeremy Thorpe 1975–76. Since 1977, she has worked in the Liberal Whip's Office in the House of Lords.

Geoffrey Thomas (*T. H. Green*)
is a Departmental Fellow in Philosophy, Birkbeck College, London. His main books are *The Moral Philosophy of T .H. Green* (1987) and *An Introduction to Ethics* (1993). He is shortly to publish *An Introduction to Political Philosophy*. His party publications include *A Philosophy for Liberal Democracy* (1993) and *Liberal Democracy: The Radical Tradition* (1994).

Aidan Thomson (*Dingle Foot*)
was President of the Oxford University Liberal Democrats in 1993. A former leader of the National Youth Orchestra of Scotland, he is currently working on his doctorate, a study on the reception of British music in Germany before the First World War.

Roy Thomson (*Malcolm Bruce*)
has been President of the Scottish Liberal Democrats since 1990. He was the leader of Aberdeen City Council Liberal group 1974–88, and Malcolm Bruce's agent in the general elections of 1983, 1987 and 1992. He is the president of Mental Health, Aberdeen and a past president of the Scottish Ballet.

Geoff Tordoff (*Rochester*)
– see entry.

Dr Garry Tregidga (*Peter Bessell, Leslie Hore-Belisha*)
is the Assistant Director of the Institute of Cornish Studies. His PhD thesis was based on the history of the Liberal Party in south west England 1929–59, while he is currently preparing an edited collection of the political correspondence of Sir Francis and Lady Eleanor Acland.

Peter Truesdale (*John Harris, Dick Newby, George Thomson*)
represents Bishop's Ward on Lambeth Council and is Leader of the Liberal Democrat Group. He is a regular contributor to the *Reformer*.

Ron Waddell (*Jim Wallace*)
is currently Senior Teacher of Geography at Firrhill High School, Edinburgh. He was Vice

Chair, Scottish Liberals 1980–81 and 1982–85, Political Director, Scottish Liberals 1985–88, and Director, Scottish Liberal Democrats 1988–92.

Dr Jonathan Wallace (*Walter Runciman*)
was awarded a PhD from Newcastle University for a thesis on *The Political Career of Walter (Viscount) Runciman*. Currently deputy leader of the opposition in Gateshead and Liberal Democrat councillor for eleven years.

Andrew Warren (*Derek Ezra*)
is Director of the Association for the Conservation of Energy. A former adviser to the Commons Environment Select Committee, he is currently the Energy Efficiency Adviser to Commissioner Christos Papoutsis.

Graham Watson (*David Steel*)
– see entry.

Caroline White (*Evan Harris*)
worked for the Liberal Democrats as Constituency Organiser in Truro & St Austell and as Communications Officer at the party's headquarters. She now works as a producer at BBC's *On The Record*.

Chris Wrigley (*David Lloyd George*)
is Professor of Modern British History at Nottingham University. He is President of the Historical Association (1996–99). As well as a biography of Lloyd George, his many books include *David Lloyd George and the British Labour Movement* (1976) and *Lloyd George and the Challenge of Labour* (1990).

APPENDICES

LEADERS

Feb 55	Viscount Palmerston
Oct 65	W. E. Gladstone
Feb 75	Marquess of Hartington
Apr 80	W. E. Gladstone
Mar 94	Earl of Rosebery
Oct 96	Sir William Harcourt
Feb 99	Sir Henry Campbell-Bannerman
30 Apr 08	H. H. Asquith★
14 Oct 26	David Lloyd George
4 Nov 31	Sir Herbert Samuel
26 Nov 35	Sir Archibald Sinclair
2 Aug 45	Clement Davies
5 Nov 56	Jo Grimond
18 Jan 67	Jeremy Thorpe
7 Jul 76	David Steel
28 Jul 88	Paddy Ashdown

★ *Asquith was out of Parliament from the general election of 1918 until January 1920, when he won the Paisley by-election. The Rt. Hon Sir Donald Maclean MP was the acting party leader in the House of Commons from February 1919.*

LEADERS IN THE HOUSE OF LORDS

1855	Earl Granville
1865	Earl Russell
1868	Earl Granville
1891	Earl of Kimberley
1894	Earl Rosebery
1897	Earl of Kimberley
1902	Earl Spencer
1905	Marquess of Ripon
1908	Earl (Marquess) of Crewe
1923	Viscount Grey
1924	Earl Beauchamp
1931	Marquess of Reading
1936	Marquess of Crewe
1944	Viscount Samuel
1955	Lord Rea
1967	Lord Byers
1984	Lady Seear
1987	Lord Jenkins of Hillhead
1997	Lord Rodgers of Quarry Bank

CHIEF WHIPS IN THE HOUSE OF COMMONS

1859	H. B. V. Brand
1866	G. G. Glyn
1873	W. P. Adam
1880	Lord R. Grosvenor
1885	A. Morley
1892	E. Marjoribanks
1894	T. E. Ellis
1899	H. Gladstone
1905	G. Whitely
1908	J. Pease
1910	Master of Elibank
1912	P. Illingworth
1915	J. Gulland
1919	vacant★
1923	V. Phillipps
1924	Sir G. Collins
1926	Sir R. Hutchinson
1930	Sir A. Sinclair
1931	G. Owen
1932	W. Rea
1935	Sir P. Harris
1945	T. Horabin
1946	F. Byers
1950	J. Grimond
1956	D. Wade
1962	A. Holt
1963	E. Lubbock
1970	D. Steel
1976	C. Smith
1977	A. Beith
1985	D. Alton
1987	J. Wallace
1992	A. Kirkwood
1997	P. Tyler

★ *J. Hogge and G. Thorne were elected joint whips, not chief whip, in Feb 1919.*

CHIEF WHIPS IN THE HOUSE OF LORDS

1896	Lord Ribblesdale
1907	Lord Denman
1911–22	Lord Colebrooke

1919	Lord Denman (Ind Lib)
1924	Lord Stanmore
1944	Viscount Mersey
1949	Marquess of Willingdon
1950	Lord Moynihan
1950	Lord Rea
1955	Lord Amulree
1977	Lord Wigoder
1984	Lord Tordoff
1994	Lord Harris of Greenwich

LIBERAL CABINET MINISTERS

The Palmerston Administration formed June 1859

Prime Minister	Viscount Palmerston
Lord President of the Council	Earl Granville
Lord Privy Seal	Duke of Argyll
Home Secretary	Sir G. Cornewall Lewis Bt.
Foreign Secretary	Lord John Russell
Colonial Secretary	Duke of Newcastle
War Secretary	Sidney Herbert
India Secretary	Sir C. Wood Bt.
Chancellor of the Exchequer	W. E. Gladstone
First Lord of the Admiralty	Duke of Somerset
President Board of Trade	Thomas Milner Gibson
Irish Secretary	Edward Cardwell
Postmaster General	Earl of Elgin
Lord Chancellor	Lord Campbell
Chancellor Duchy of Lancaster	Sir G. Grey Bt

The Russell Administration formed November 1865

Prime Minister	Earl Russell
Lord President of the Council	Earl Granville
Lord Privy Seal	Duke of Argyll
Home Secretary	Sir G. Grey Bt
Foreign Secretary	Earl of Clarendon
Colonial Secretary	Edward Cardwell
War Secretary	Earl De Grey & Ripon
India Secretary	Sir C. Wood Bt
Chancellor of the Exchequer	W. E. Gladstone
First Lord of the Admiralty	Duke of Somerset
President Board of Trade	Thomas Milner Gibson

President Poor Law Board	Charles Pelham Villiers
Lord Chancellor	Lord Cranworth
Postmaster General	Lord Stanley of Alderley
Chancellor Duchy of Lancaster	George Goschen

The first Gladstone Administration formed December 1868

Prime Minister	W. E. Gladstone
Lord President of the Council	Earl De Grey & Ripon
Lord Privy Seal	Earl of Kimberley
Home Secretary	Henry Bruce
Foreign Secretary	Earl of Clarendon
Colonial Secretary	Earl Granville
War Secretary	Edward Cardwell
India Secretary	Duke of Argyll
Chancellor of the Exchequer	Robert Lowe
First Lord of the Admiralty	Hugh Erskine Childers
President Board of Trade	J. Bright
Irish Secretary	Chichester S. Fortescue
Postmaster General	Marquess of Hartington
President of Poor Law Board	George Goschen
Lord Chancellor	Lord Hatherley

The second Gladstone Administration formed April 1880

Prime Minister & Chancellor of the Exchequer	W. E. Gladstone
Lord President of the Council	Earl Spencer
Lord Privy Seal	Duke of Argyll
Home Secretary	William Harcourt
Foreign Secretary	Earl Granville
Colonial Secretary	Earl of Kimberley
War Secretary	Hugh Childers
India Secretary	Marquess of Hartington
First Lord of the Admiralty	Earl of Northbrook
President Board of Trade	Joseph Chamberlain
President Local Government Board	John Dodson
Irish Secretary	William Forster
Lord Chancellor	Lord Selborne
Chancellor of the Duchy of Lancaster	J. Bright

The third Gladstone Administration formed February 1886

Prime Minister	W. E. Gladstone
Lord President of the Council	Earl Spencer
Home Secretary	Hugh Childers
Foreign Secretary	Earl of Rosebery
Colonial Secretary	Earl Granville
War Secretary	Henry Campbell-Bannerman
India Secretary	Earl of Kimberley
Scotland Secretary	George Trevelyan
Chancellor of the Exchequer	Sir William Harcourt
First Lord of the Admiralty	Marquess of Ripon
President Board of Trade	Anthony Mundella
President Local Government Board	Joseph Chamberlain*
Irish Secretary	John Morley
Lord Chancellor	Lord Herschell

* *Resigned in April 1886 and was replaced by James Stansfield.*

The fourth Gladstone Administration formed August 1892

Prime Minister	W. E. Gladstone
Lord Chancellor	Lord Herschell
Lord President of the Council & Secretary of State Indian Department	Earl of Kimberley
Chancellor of the Exchequer	Sir William Vernon Harcourt
Home Secretary	H. H. Asquith
Foreign Secretary	Earl of Rosebery
Colonial Secretary	Marquess of Ripon
War Secretary	Henry Campbell-Bannerman
Scottish Secretary	Sir George Trevelyan Bt
First Lord of the Admiralty	Earl Spencer
Chief Secretary for Ireland	John Morley
Postmaster General	Arnold Morley
President Board of Trade	Anthony Mundella
President Local Government Board	Henry Fowler
Chancellor of the Duchy of Lancaster	James Bryce
First Commissioner of Works	George Shaw-Lefevre
Vice President of the Council	Arthur Acland

The Rosebery Administration formed March 1894

Prime Minister	Earl of Rosebery
Lord Chancellor	Lord Herschell
Lord President of the Council & Chancellor of the Duchy of Lancaster	Lord Tweedmouth
Chancellor of the Exchequer	Sir William Vernon Harcourt
Home Secretary	H. H. Asquith
Foreign Secretary	Earl of Kimberley
Colonial Secretary	Marquess of Ripon
War Secretary	Henry Campbell-Bannerman
Secretary of State Indian Department	Henry Fowler
Secretary of State Scotland	Sir George Trevelyan Bt
First Lord of the Admiralty	Earl Spencer
Chief Secretary of Ireland	John Morley
Postmaster General	Arnold Morley
President Board of Trade	James Bryce
First Commissioner of Works	George Shaw-Lefevre
Vice President of the Council	Arthur Acland

The Campbell-Bannerman Administration formed December 1905

Prime Minister	Sir Henry Campbell-Bannerman
Lord President of the Council	Earl of Crewe
Lord Chancellor	Lord Loreburn
Lord Privy Seal	Marquess of Ripon
Chancellor of the Exchequer	H. H. Asquith
Foreign Secretary	Sir Edward Grey
Home Secretary	Herbert Gladstone
First Lord of the Admiralty	Lord Tweedmouth
President Board of Agriculture & Fisheries	Earl Carrington
Colonial Secretary	Earl of Elgin
President Board of Education	Augustine Birrell Reginald McKenna 23 Jan 07
India Office	John Morley
Chief Secretary of Ireland	James Bryce Augustine Birrell 23 Jan 07
Chancellor of the Duchy of Lancaster	Sir Henry Fowler

President Local Government Board
Samuel Buxton
Secretary of State Scotland   James Sinclair
President Board of Trade David Lloyd George
Secretary of State for War   Richard Haldane
First Commissioner of Works   Lewis Harcourt
27 Mar 07

The Asquith Administration formed April 1908

Prime Minister   H. H. Asquith
Lord President of the Council
Lord Tweedmouth
Viscount Wolverhampton 13 Oct 08
Earl Beauchamp 16 Jun 10
Viscount Morley 3 Nov 10
Earl Beauchamp 5 Aug 14
Lord Chancellor   Lord Loreburn
Viscount Haldane 10 Jun 12
Lord Privy Seal   Marquess of Ripon
Earl of Crewe 9 Oct 08
Earl Carrington 23 Oct 11
Marquess of Crewe 13 Feb 12
Chancellor of the Exchequer
David Lloyd George
Home Secretary   Herbert Gladstone
Winston Churchill 14 Feb 10
Reginald McKenna 23 Oct 11
President Board of Admiralty
Reginald McKenna
Winston Churchill 23 Oct 11
President Board of Agriculture & Fisheries
Earl Carrington
Walter Runciman 23 Oct 11
Lord Lucas 6 Aug 14
Attorney General   Sir Rufus Isaacs 4 Jun 12
Sir John Simon 19 Oct 13
Colonial Secretary   Earl of Crewe
Lewis Harcourt 3 Nov 10
President Board of Education
Walter Runciman
Joseph Pease 23 Oct 11
India Office   J. Morley (Vt)
Earl of Crewe 3 Nov 10
Viscount Morley 7 Mar 11
Chief Secretary of Ireland   Augustine Birrell

Chancellor of the Duchy of Lancaster
Vt Wolverhampton
Lord Fitzmaurice 13 Oct 08
Herbert Samuel 25 Jun 09
Joseph Pease 14 Feb 10
Charles Hobhouse 23 Oct 11
Charles Masterman 11 Feb 14
Edwin Montagu 3 Feb 15
President of the Local Government Board
John Burns
Herbert Samuel 11 Feb 14
Postmaster General   Sydney Buxton
Herbert Samuel 14 Feb 10
Charles Hobhouse 11 Feb 14
Secretary of State Scotland   Lord Pentland
T. McKinnon Wood 13 Feb 12
President Board of Trade   Winston Churchill
Sydney Buxton 14 Feb 10
John Burns 11 Feb 14
Walter Runciman 5 Aug 14
Secretary of State for War   Viscount Haldane
John Seely 12 Jun 12
H. H. Asquith (PM) 30 Mar 14
Earl Kitchener 5 Aug 14
First Commissioner of Works   Lewis Harcourt
Earl Beauchamp 3 Nov 10
Lord Emmott 6 Aug 14

Liberal Cabinet Ministers in the Asquith Coalition Government formed May 1915

Prime Minister   H. H. Asquith
Lord President of the Council
Marquess of Crewe
Lord Chancellor   Lord Buckmaster
Chancellor of the Exchequer
Reginald McKenna
Foreign Secretary   Sir Edward Grey
Home Secretary   Sir John Simon
Sir Herbert Samuel 10 Jan 16
President Board of Education
Marquess of Crewe 18 Aug 16
Chief Secretary of Ireland   Augustine Birrell
Chancellor of the Duchy of Lancaster
Winston Churchill
Herbert Samuel 25 Nov 15
Edwin Montagu 11 Jan 16
T. McKinnon Wood 9 Jul 16

Munitions Secretary   David Lloyd George
                    Edwin Montagu 9 Jul 16
Secretary of State for Scotland
                       T. McKinnon Wood
                      H. Tennant 9 Jul 16
President Board of Trade   Walter Runciman
Secretary of State for War   Earl Kitchener
                    David Lloyd George 6 Jul 16
First Commissioner of Works
                      Lewis Harcourt (Vt)

Liberal Cabinet Ministers in the Lloyd George Coalition Government formed December 1916

Prime MinisterDavid Lloyd George 10 Dec 16
Home Secretary   Edward Shortt 10 Jan 19
Attorney General
                   Sir Gordon Hewart 7 Nov 21
Colonial SecretaryWinston Churchill 13 Feb 21
President Board of Education
                        H. Fisher 10 Dec 16
Secretary of State for Health
                 Christopher Addison 24 Jun 19
                       Sir A. Mond 1 Apr 21
Secretary of State for India
                    Edwin Montagu 17 Jul 17
Chief Secretary of Ireland
                    Edward Shortt 5 May 18
                   Ian Macpherson 10 Jan 19
                  Sir H. Greenwood 2 Apr 20
Minister of Labour
                Thomas Macnamara 19 Mar 20
Chancellor of the Duchy of Lancaster
               Sir Frederick Cawley 10 Dec 16
President of the Local Government Board
                    Lord Rhondda 10 Dec 16
                 Christopher Addison 10 Jan 19
Minister of Munitions
              Christopher Addison 10 Dec 16
                Winston Churchill 17 Jul 17
Minister without Portfolio
                Christopher Addison 1 Apr 21
Secretary of State for Scotland
                    Robert Munro 10 Dec 16
President Board of Trade
                  Sir A. Stanley 10 Dec 16
Secretary of State for War
                Winston Churchill 10 Jan 19

Liberal Cabinet Ministers in the MacDonald National Government formed August 1931*

Home Secretary   Sir Herbert Samuel
Foreign Secretary   Marquess of Reading
President Board of Education
                      + Sir Donald Maclean
Scottish Office Secretary
                   + Sir Archibald Sinclair Bt.

+ *Maclean and Sinclair had Cabinet rank as from November 1931, but were not members of the Cabinet. Maclean died in May 1932.*

* *They resigned from the Government on the 28th September 1932.*

PRESIDENTS OF THE PARTY

Liberal Presidents normally held office from Annual Assembly to Annual Assembly. Until 1970 they were instituted at the beginning of the Assembly which marked the start of their term, and performed the President's duties during that Assembly. From 1970 they were instituted at the end of an Assembly and no longer actually presided over debates.

National Liberal Federation: Annual Conferences, 1877–1935

31 May 1877	J. Chamberlain
22 Jan 1879	"
3 Feb 1880	"
26–27 Jan 1881	J. Collings
25 Oct. 1881	H. Fell Pease
19 Dec. 1882	"
26 Nov 1883	J. Kitson Jr
7 Oct 1884	"
1 Oct. 1885	"
3 Nov 1886	Sir J. Kitson
18–19 Oct. 1887	"
6–7 Nov 1888	"
3–4 Dec 1889	"
20–21 Nov 1890	R. Spence Watson
1–2 Oct 1891	"
1892	No meeting
19–20 Jan 1893	R. Spence Watson
12–14 Feb 1894	"

16–18 Jan 1895	"
26–27 Mar 1896	"
17–18 Mar 1897	"
22–23 Mar 1898	"
7–8 Mar 1899	"
27–28 Mar 00	"
14–15 May 01	"
13–14 May 02	A. Birrell
14–15 May 03	"
12–13 May 04	"
18–19 May 05	"
23–24 May 06	A. Acland
6–7 Jun 07	"
18–19 Jun 08	Sir W. Angus
1–2 Jul 09	"
25 Nov 10	"
23–24 Nov 11	Sir J. Brunner
21–22 Nov 12	"
26–27 Nov 13	"
1914–1918	No conference held
27–28 Nov 19	Sir G. Lunn
25–26 Nov 20	J. Robertson
24–25 Nov 21	"
17–18 May 22	"
30 May–1 Jun 23	Sir D. Maclean
22–23 May 24	"
14–15 May 25	"
7–18 Jun 26	J. Spender
26–27 May 27	Sir C. Hobhouse
11–12 Oct 28	"
3–4 Oct 29	"
16–17 Oct 30	A. Brampton
14–15 May 31	"
28–29 Apr 32	"
18–19 May 33	R. Muir
2–5 May 34	"
23–25 May 35	"

Liberal Party Assemblies 1936–88

18–19 Jun 36	Lord Meston
27–31 May 37	"
19–20 May 38	"
11–12 May 39	"
1940	No assembly held
18–19 Jul 41	Lord Meston
4–5 Sep 42	"
15–17 Jul 43	"

1944	No assembly held
1–3 Feb 45	Lady V. Bonham Carter
9–11 May 46	"
24–26 Apr 47	I. Foot
22–24 Apr 48	E. Dodds
24–26 Mar 49	Sir A. MacFadyean
27–28 Jan 50	"
29–30 Sep 50	P. Fothergill
1951	No assembly held
15–17 May 52	R. Walker
9–11 Apr 53	L. Robson
22–24 Apr 54	H. Graham White
14–16 Apr 55	Lord Rea
27–29 Sep 56	L. Behrens
19–21 Sep 57	N. Micklem
19–21 Sep 58	Sir A. Comyns Carr
1959	No assembly held but H. Glanville became President
29 Sep–1 Oct 60	Sir A. Murray
21–23 Sep 61	E. Malindine
19–22 Sep 62	Sir F. Brunner
10–14 Sep 63	Lord Ogmore
4–5 Sep 64	R. Fulford
22–25 Sep 65	Miss N. Seear
21–24 Sep 66	Lord Henley
20–23 Sep 67	Lord Wade
18–21 Sep 68	D. Banks
17–20 Sep 69	Lord Beaumont of Whitley
23–26 Sep 70	"
15–18 Sep 71	Mrs. S. Robson
19–23 Sep 72	S. Terrell
18–22 Sep 73	T. Jones
17–21 Sep 74	Lord Lloyd of Kilgerran
16–20 Sep 75	A. Holt
14–18 Sep 76	Mrs. M. Wingfield
26 Sep–1 Oct 77	B. Goldstone
12–16 Sep 78	Lord Evans of Claughton
28–29 Sep 79	M. Steed
8–13 Sep 80	Mrs. J. Rose
14–19 Sep 81	R. Holme
20–25 Sep 82	V. Bingham
19–24 Sep 83	J. Griffiths
17–22 Sep 84	Lord Tordoff
16–21 Sep 85	A. Watson
21–26 Sep 86	D. Penhaligon
13–18 Sep 87	D. Wilson
22–23 Jan 88	A. Slade (Special Assembly)

Liberal Democrats

1988–90	I. Wrigglesworth
1990–94	C. Kennedy MP
1994–98	R. Maclennan MP
1998–	Baroness Maddock

CHAIRS OF THE EXECUTIVE

In 1969 the post of Chairman of the Executive Committee was combined with the Chairmanship of the Party.

1936	M. Gray
1946	P. Fothergill
1949	Ld Moynihan
1950	F. Byers
1952	P. Fothergill
1954	G. Acland
1957	D. Abel
1959	L. Behrens
1961	D. Banks
1963	B. Wigoder
1965	G. Evans
1968–69	J. Baker
1969	D. Banks
1970	R. Wainwright
1972	C. Carr
1973	K. Vaus
1976	G. Tordoff
1980	R. Pincham
1983	Mrs. J. Rose
1984	P. Tyler
1986	T. Clement-Jones

BYELECTION WINNERS AFTER 1918

General Election of 1918 to General Election of 1922

1/3/1919	Alfred Newbould	Leyton West
29/3/1919	Hon. J. M. Kenworthy	Kingston upon Hull Central
16/4/1919	Murdoch Wood	Aberdeenshire & Kincardineshire Central
10/7/1919	David Matthews	Swansea East
6/9/1919	Walter Forrest	Pontefract
12/1/1920	Rt. Hon. H. Asquith	Paisley
27/3/20	Henry Fildes	Stockport
31/3/1920	Rt. Hon. T. J. Macnamara	Camberwell North West
1/4/1920	Rt. Hon. C. A. McCurdy	Northampton
24/4/1920	Sir Harmar Greenwood	Sunderland
3/6/1920	T. Wintringham	Louth
22/11/1920	Sir William Adkins	Middleton & Prestwich
18/2/1921	Ernest Evans	Cardiganshire
16/4/1921	Rt. Hon. F. E. Guest	Dorset East
23/4/1921	Rt. Hon. F. G. Kellaway	Bedford
17/5/1921	Sir Malcolm Smith	Orkney & Shetland
22/9/1921	Mrs. Margaret Wintringham	Louth
24/2/1922	Isaac Foot	Bodmin
16/3/1922	Sir M. Macdonald	Inverness
21/6/1922	Thomas Guthrie	Moray & Nairnshire
22/6/1922	Sir R. Rhys Williams Bt	Banbury

General Election of 1922 to General Election of 1923

3/3/1923	Harcourt Johnstone	Willesden East
7/4/1923	Sir Robert Thomas Bt	Anglesey
21/6/1923	Rt. Hon. F. D. Acland	Tiverton

General Election of 1923 to General Election of 1924

| 14/8/1924 | Rt Hon Sir A. Mond Bt | Carmarthen |

General Election of 1924 to General Election of 1929

24/61925	William Wiggins	Oldham
23/3/1927	Ernest Brown	Leith
28/3/1927	Edward Strauss	Southwark North
31/3/1927	Sir William Edge	Bosworth
9/2/1928	Robert Tomlinson	Lancaster
6/3/1928	Mrs. Hilda Runciman	St. Ives

7/3/1928	Kingsley Griffith
	Middlesbrough West
28/6/1928	William Jones Carmarthen
20/3/1929	Richard Russell Eddisbury
21/3/1929	James Blindell
	Holland with Boston

General Election of 1929 to General Election of 1931

None

General Election of 1931 to General Election of 1935

22/7/1932	Rt. Hon. Sir Francis Acland
	Cornwall North
22/9/1932	David Evans Cardiganshire
7-12/3/1934	Dr. George Morrison
	Combined Scottish Universities

General Election of 1935 to General Election of 1945

13/7/1939	T. L. Horabin Cornwall North
7/8/1940	Harcourt Johnstone
	Middlesbrough West
18/8/1941	George Grey
	Berwick upon Tweed
25-29/1/1943	Prof W. J. Gruffydd
	University of Wales
17/10/1944	Sir William Beveridge
	Berwick upon Tweed
26/4/1945	David Davies
	Caernarvon Boroughs.

There were no Liberal byelection victors during the 1945, 1950 and 1951 Parliaments.

General Election of 1955 to General Election of 1959

27/3/1958	Mark Bonham Carter Torrington

General Election of 1959 to General Election of 1964

14/3/1962	Eric Lubbock Orpington
15/5/1962	Emlyn Hooson
	Montgomeryshire

General Election of 1964 to General Election of 1966

24/3/1965	David Steel
	Roxburghshire, Selkirkshire & Peebleshire

General Election of 1966 to General Election of 1970

26/6/1969	Wallace Lawler
	Birmingham Ladywood

General Election of 1970 to General Election of February 1974

26/10/1972	Cyril Smith Rochdale
7/12/1972	Graham Tope Sutton & Cheam
26/7/1973	Clement Freud Isle of Ely
26/7/1973	David Austick Ripon
8/11/1973	Alan Beith
	Berwick-upon-Tweed

General Election of Ocober 1974 to General Election of 1979

29/3/1979	David Alton
	Liverpool Edge Hill

General Election of 1979 to General Election of 1983

22/10/1981	Bill Pitt Croydon North West
26/11/1981	Shirley Williams Crosby★
25/3/1982	Roy Jenkins Glasgow Hillhead★
24/2/1983	Simon Hughes
	Southwark, Bermondsey

General Election of 1983 to General Election of 1987

14/6/1984	Mike Hancock
	Portsmouth South★
4/7/1985	Richard Livsey Brecon & Radnor
8/5/1986	Elizabeth Shields Ryedale
26/2/1987	Rosie Barnes Greenwich★
12/3/1987	Matthew Taylor Truro

★ *Byelection gain by SDP.*

General Election of 1987 to General Election of 1992

18/10/1990	David Bellotti	Eastbourne
7/3/1991	Mike Carr	Ribble Valley
7/11/1991	Nicol Stephen	
		Kincardine & Deeside

General Election of 1992 to General Election of 1997

6/5/1993	David Rendel	Newbury
29/7/1993	Diana Maddock	Christchurch
9/6/1994	David Chidgey	Eastleigh
27/7/1995	Chris Davies	
		Littleborough & Saddleworth

General Election of 1997 to present

20/11/1997	Mark Oaten	Winchester

DEFECTIONS AFTER 1918

Parliament of 1919–22

Apr 1919	Labour	J. Wedgwood
		Newcastle-under-Lyme
Nov 1919	Independent	C. Malone
		Leyton East
Feb 1922	Independent	A. Hopkinson
		Mossley

Parliament of 1922–23

Jul 1923	Conservative	A. Evans
		Leicester East

Parliament of 1924–29

Jan 1926	Conservative	Sir A. Mond
		Carmarthen
Feb 1926	Independent	E. Hilton Young
		Norwich
Oct 1926	Labour	J. Kenworthy
		Hull Central
Feb 1927	Independent	W. Benn Leith

Parliament of 1929–31

Jun 1929	Labour	Sir W. Jowitt
		Preston
Feb 1931	National Party	C. R. Dudgeon
		Galloway
Jun 1931	Independent★	E. Brown Leith
Jun 1931	Independent★	Sir R. Hutchison
		Montrose
Jun 1931	Independent★	Sir J. Simon
		Spen Valley

★ They became Liberal Nationals in October 1931. At the same time, twenty-three Liberal Members broke with the party to form the Liberal National Group (see below). A further four Liberals, David, Megan and Gwilym Lloyd George, and Goronwy Owen became Independent Liberals.

Liberal Nationals

Formed in 1931 by twenty-three Liberal MPs who split from the official party to join the ranks of the National Government. In the 1931 general election they won thirty-five of the forty-one seats they contested. In 1932 the 'Samuelite' Liberals left the National Government in protest at its protectionist policies. The 'Simonite' Liberals under their leader Sir John Simon remained. The Woolton-Teviot agreement of May 1947 urged the constituency parties of the Conservative and Liberal Nationals to combine and in 1948 the party adopted the name National Liberal Party. In the 1966 Parliament the four remaining members of the group became fully integrated into the Conservative Party.

Liberal National MPs during the 1931 Parliament

W. Allen ★	Stoke on Trent, Burslem
Sir R. W. Aske Bt	Newcastle upon Tyne, East
Sir C. Barrie	Southampton
J. Blindell	Holland with Boston
A. E. Brown	Leith
E. L. Burgin	Luton
G. Campbell ★	Burnley
Sir G. Collins	Greenock
A. C. Curry +	Bishop Auckland

E. C. Davies +   Montgomeryshire
J. P. Dickie   Consett
Sir W. Edge   Bosworth
Viscount Elmley   Norfolk, Eastern
E. L. Granville +   Eye
A. Harbord   Great Yarmouth
L. Hore-Belisha   Plymouth Devonport
Sir R. Hutchison Montrose District of Burghs
Dr. J. Hunter   Dumfriesshire
Rt. Hon. G. Lambert   South Molton
J. A. Leckie ★   Walsall
F. Llewellyn-Jones   Flintshire
W. McKeag   Durham
W. Mabane   Huddersfield
Sir M. Macdonald   Inverness
Rt. Hon. J. I. Macpherson Ross & Cromarty
J. D. Millar   East Fife
J. H. Morris-Jones   Denbigh
L. Jones   Swansea West
S. J. Peters   Huntingdonshire
P. J. Pybus   Harwich
T. B. W. Ramsay   Western Isles
Rt. Hon. W. Runciman   St. Ives
R. J. Russell   Eddisbury
G. H. Shakespeare   Norwich
Rt. Hon. Sir J. Simon   Spen Valley
E. A. Strauss   Southwark, North
C. H. Summersby   Shoreditch
J. Wallace   Dunfermline District of Burghs

★ *Allen, Campbell & Leckie were elected as National supporters of the Government and joined the National Liberals during this Parliament.*

+ *Curry, Davies & Granville subsequently rejoined the Liberal Party.*

Parliament of 1931–35

Nov 1932   Liberal National   J. Leckie
                                     Walsall
Jun 1934   Liberal National   W. McKeag
                                     Durham
Jun 1934   Liberal National   J. Hunter
                                    Dumfries
Early 1935 Liberal National   G. Morrison
                        Scottish Universities

Parliament of 1935–45

Oct 1936   Liberal National   R. Bernays
                               Bristol North
Oct 1938   Liberal National   H. Holdsworth
                               Bradford South
Sep 1942   Commonwealth   Sir R. Acland
                                   Barnstaple

Parliament of 1945–50

Oct 1946   Independent★   T. Horabin
                             North Cornwall

★ *He took the Labour Whip in November 1947.*

Labour MPs defecting to the SDP in the 1979 Parliament

Tom Bradley   Leicester East
Ron Brown   Hackney South & Shoreditch
John Cartwright   Woolwich
Richard Crawshaw   Liverpool Toxteth
George Cunningham   Islington South &
                                     Finsbury
Ednyfed Hudson Davies   Caerphilly
Bruce Douglas-Mann   Mitcham & Morden
James Dunn   Liverpool Kirkdale
Tom Ellis   Wrexham
David Ginsburg   Dewsbury
John Grant   Islington Central
John Horam   Gateshead, West ★
Edward Lyons   Bradford West
Tom McNally   Stockport South
Dickson Mabon   Greenock
Robert Maclennan   Caithness & Sutherland
Bryan Magee   Leyton
Richard Mitchell   Southampton Itchen
Eric Ogden   Liverpool West Derby
Michael O'Halloran   Islington North
David Owen   Plymouth Devonport
John Roper   Farnworth
William Rodgers   Stockton North
Norman Sandelson   Hayes & Harlington
Jeffrey Thomas   Abertillery
Mike Thomas   Newcastle upon Tyne East
James Wellbeloved   Erith and Crayford
Ian Wrigglesworth   Thornaby

* *After his defeat in the 1983 general election, Mr. Horam subsequently joined the Conservative Party and became MP for Orpington in 1992.*

The only Conservative MP to defect to the SDP was Christopher Brocklebank-Fowler, Norfolk North West.

Christopher Mayhew, the Labour MP for Woolwich East in the February 1974 Parliament was the only post-war defector to the Liberal Party. Mr. Mayhew fought Bath in the October 1974 general election as a Liberal candidate but was unsuccessful.

Defections to the Liberal Democrats

During the 1992 Parliament, Emma Nicholson, Conservative MP for Devon West & Torridge, and Peter Thurnham, Conservative MP for Bolton North East, joined the Liberal Democrats. Neither contested the 1997 general election.

MANUSCRIPTS

Addison, C	Bodleian Library, Oxford
Asquith, H. H.	Bodleian Library, Oxford
Avebury	Brynmor Jones Library, University of Hull
Beveridge, W.	British Library of Political and Economic Science
Bright, J.	British Library
Burns, J.	British Library
Campbell-Bannerman, H.	British Library
Chamberlain, J.	University of Birmingham
Crewe	Cambridge University Library
Davies, Clement	National Library of Wales, Aberystwyth
Elibank	National Library of Scotland, Edinburgh
Foot, D.	Churchill College, Cambridge
Gladstone, H.	British Library
Gladstone, W. E.	British Library
Goschen, G.	Bodleian Library, Oxford
Green, T. H.	Balliol College, Oxford
Grey, E.	Public Record Office
Haldane, R. B.	National Library of Scotland, Edinburgh
Hammonds	Bodleian Library, Oxford
Harcourt, W.	Bodleian Library, Oxford
Harris, P.	House of Lords Record Office
Holyoake, G. J.	Library of the Cooperative Union, Manchester
Hooson, E.	National Library of Wales, Aberystwyth
Isaacs, R.	India Office Library and Records, London
Keynes, J. M.	Marshall Library of Economics, Cambridge; Public Record Office; King's College, Cambridge
Layton, W.	Trinity College, Cambridge
Lloyd George, D.	House of Lords Record Office
Lloyd George, M.	National Library of Wales, Aberystwyth
Lothian	Scottish Record Office, Edinburgh
Maclean, D.	Bodleian Library, Oxford
McKenna, R.	Churchill College, Cambridge
Melbourne	Royal Archives, Windsor
Mill, J. S.	British Library of Political and Economic Science
Montagu, E.	Trinity College, Cambridge
Murray, G.	Bodleian Library, Oxford
Runciman, W.	University of Newcastle-upon-Tyne Library
Russell, J.	Public Records Office
Samuel, H.	House of Lords Record Office
Simon, J.	Bodleian Library, Oxford; Public Record Office; India Office Library
Sinclair, A.	Churchill College, Cambridge
Steel, D.	British Library of Political and Economic Science
Wallas, G.	Newnham College, Cambridge

LIBERAL DEMOCRAT HISTORY GROUP

The only organisation for the study of Liberal, SDP and Liberal Democrat history ...

Meetings • Publications • Research advice • The *Journal of Liberal Democrat History*

Contributors include:
Michael Brock
John Curtice
John Grigg
Roy Jenkins
Colin Matthew
Bill Rodgers
Michael Steed
David Steel
and many more

The Liberal Democrat History Group promotes the discussion and research of historical topics, particularly those relating to the histories of the Liberal Democrats, Liberal Party and the SDP. See our web site at
www.dbrack.dircon.co.uk/ldhg/

Annual membership of the History Group, including four issues of the ***Journal of Liberal Democrat History***, costs £10.00 (£5.00 unwaged); from:

Liberal Democrat History Group
6 Palfrey Place, London SW8 1PA.